Between Poland and the Ukraine

Frank E. Sysyn

Between Poland
and the Ukraine

THE DILEMMA OF
ADAM KYSIL, 1600–1653

Distributed by Harvard University Press
for the
Harvard Ukrainian Research Institute

Publication of this volume was made
possible by donations from:
The Jarema S. Kurdydyk Publication Fund
Wasyl Lahoshniak
Orysia Lagoshniak

ISBN 0-916458-08-3
Library of Congress Catalog Number 84-80052
Printed in the United States of America

The Harvard Ukrainian Research Institute was established in 1973 as
an integral part of Harvard University. It supports research associates
and visiting scholars who are engaged in projects concerned with all
aspects of Ukrainian studies. The Institute also works in close cooperation with the Committee on Ukrainian Studies, which supervises and
coordinates the teaching of Ukrainian history, language, and literature
at Harvard University.

I dedicate this book to my grandmother, whose tales of her native land first awakened my interest in its history.

Присвячую цю книжку моїй бабуні, якої розповіді про її батьківщину розбудили в мене зацікавлення історією України.

Rossia Te patrem canit atque Polonia Patrem,
  Rossia Te Civem Sarmata Teque suum
Lis de Te.

Theodosius Wasilewicz Baiewski, *Tentoria
Venienti Kioviam cum novi Honoris
fuscibus Illustrissimo Domino, I. Adamo
de Brusiłow Sventoldicio Kisiel Castellano:
Nosov: & Capitaneo a Collegio Mohil:
Kiou: (Kiev, 1646), fol. 7.*

Contents

Acknowledgments   ix
Note on Nomenclature and Terminology   xi
Geographic Names   xv

Introduction   1

1. The Commonwealth and the Ukrainian Lands in the Early
   Seventeenth Century: The State and Society of the Nobles   5
   The Commonwealth of the Nobility in the Silver Age   9
   The Ukrainian Lands   20
   Religious, National, and Cultural Relations in the Ukraine   26
   The Ruthenian Nobility: Acculturation and Assimilation   32

2. The Formative Years (1600–1632)   37
   Volhynia at the Time of Kysil's Birth   38
   The Kysil Family   43
   Education   46
   The Launching of a Career   50
   The Synod of 1629   54

3. The Beginning of the New Reign (1632–1635)   64
   The Interregnum and the Election   64
   The Smolensk War   71

4. The Ukrainian Lands in the 1630s   78
   The Zaporozhian Cossacks   78
   The Defense of Orthodoxy in the Diet (1633–1641)   89
   The Regionalism of the Incorporation Lands   104

5. The Senatorial Chair   115
   The Attempt at a New Church Union   117
   The Commonwealth's Foreign Policy   128

6. The Khmel'nyts'kyi Uprising   141
   The Convocation Diet and the Second Peace Mission   152
   The Election of Jan Kazimierz   159
   From Pereiaslav to Zboriv   164

7. Mediator between the Commonwealth and the Cossack
   Hetmanate   175
   The Ratification of the Zboriv Agreement   175
   From Zboriv to Bila Tserkva   180

The Last Years   194

8. The Unresolved Dilemma   202

Appendixes   215
  A. Kysil's Estates and Offices   215
  B. Biographies and Secondary Literature   222
  C. Sources   230

Notes   239
Bibliography   349
Index   391

Maps

Administrative borders of the Polish-Lithuanian
Commonwealth, first half of the seventeenth century.   xviii

Places of importance in the life of Adam Kysil.   xix

Prevailing religious allegiances in Eastern Europe, end of the
sixteenth century.   xx

Illustrations (following page 268)

The Coat of Arms of the Kysils and the dedication page from
Molitvy povsednevnyi.

Abraham van Westerveldt, *Janusz Radziwiłł Receiving the
Envoys of Bohdan Khmel'nyts'kyi in Kiev, 1651* (18th-century
copy). The castle of the palatine of Kiev on the hill called
Kisilivka is pictured on the right.

Church of the Protectress, Nyzkynychi.

Bust of Kysil in the Church of the Protectress in Nyzkynychi.

Sarcophagus of Mykola Kysil in the crypt of the Church of the
Protectress, Nyzkynychi. It contains the remains of Adam
Kysil.

Acknowledgments

From the conception of a plan for a doctoral thesis to the completion of a monograph, many people have assisted me in many ways.

The original impulse for my work on the seventeenth century came from Viacheslav Lypyns'kyi (1882–1931), who argued so brilliantly that the role and political culture of the old Ruthenian nobility should be reassessed. My thesis adviser Edward L. Keenan encouraged me to pursue my interest in the old Ruthenian nobility through an in-depth analysis of Adam Kysil. The directors of the Ukrainian Research Institute, Omeljan Pritsak and Ihor Ševčenko, have shared their rich knowledge of many fields in challenging me to consider diverse aspects of Kysil and his world. As my teacher and, later on, reader of my work, Wiktor Weintraub guided me to a broader understanding of old Polish culture and society. During my research visits to Poland, numerous Polish scholars offered their expertise and advice. In particular, I must thank Zbigniew Wójcik, Józef Gierowski, and the recently deceased Adam Kersten, who assisted in my research and read and discussed my work. Among my colleagues and friends who have offered support and criticism have been Olga Andriewsky, Gregory Freeze, George Gajecky, Lubomyr Hajda, Zenon Kohut, Nancy Shields-Kollmann, András Riedlmayer and Peter Shaw. For assistance in revisions, translations, and proofreading, I am most grateful to Paulina Lewin. I also wish to thank Bohdan Strumins'kyi for his advice on Slavic texts and Nina Pritsak for her help with German palaeography.

Research for this work was carried out in 1972–73 in Poland and in 1980 in Poland and the Soviet Union under the auspices of the International Research and Exchanges Board (IREX) in New York. Thanks to the support, not only financial, but also moral, of the IREX program and staff, I have been able not only to use the archives and libraries of Eastern Europe but also to come to know many of the fine scholars there. Ultimately even the IREX staff could not open the doors of Soviet archives and Soviet Russian libraries, but their persistence eventually gained access to Soviet Ukrainian libraries and contributed considerably to my work.

In both Poland and the Ukraine, I have met with informed and efficient assistance by librarians and archivists. Each of the institutions mentioned in the bibliography provided enthusiastic support for this American scholar, as did the universities in Warsaw and Cracow, with which I was affiliated. I should also like to thank the scholars at Kiev University and the Institute of History of the Ukrainian Academy of Sciences who assisted me during my stay in the Ukraine.

The form and style of this work has been greatly improved by Margaret Ševčenko. I also wish to thank Uliana Pasicznyk for her editorial advice. My gratitude to Brenda Sens, who typed accurately and cheerfully, is immense. I thank the managing editors of the Harvard Series in Ukrainian Studies, Donald Ostrowski and Maxim Tarnawsky, for bringing the manuscript to print. I am also grateful to the Ukrainian Studies Fund and its generous benefactors, the late Jarema Kurdydyk, Wasyl Lahoshniak, and Orysia Lagoshniak, for their financial assistance. Finally, I thank my family and friends for their encouragement.

Frank E. Sysyn
Cambridge, Mass.
March 22, 1984

Note on Nomenclature and Terminology

The Polish-Lithuanian Commonwealth of the seventeenth century was a complex multilingual, multinational political entity. Consequently, the problem of creating a suitable nomenclature is considerable.

Except for cities with accepted English forms, e.g., Moscow, Warsaw, Kiev, Cracow, I use current geographic names, based on the official language of the state or, in the case of the Soviet Union, of the republic which holds the territory. As desirable as using names of the period would be, the free and easy linguistic environments of the past make "official" languages and names difficult to define. Current names appear to be the best solution. Therefore, I use Lviv, not Lwów, Lemberg, or L'vov, and Przemyśl, not Peremyshl'. It must be remembered, though, that the inhabitants of the seventeenth-century Baltic port probably called their home city Danzig, and not Gdańsk, and that the inhabitants of Vilnius were more likely to use Belorussian and Polish designations for their city rather than Lithuanian. A chart of frequently used place names, with variants in relevant languages, follows this note.

For personal names, there is no satisfactory system. Ideally, names should be rendered in the original legal form or in the person's native language. However, men who wrote in Latin, Polish, Ukrainian, and Slavonic, or who were descended from Lithuanian families, Ukrainianized in the fourteenth century, and Polonized in the seventeenth, are not so easy to categorize. Also, seventeenth-century spelling had not been standardized. I have therefore used the form I believe most sensible, and I have provided alternative forms in parentheses. As a rule of thumb, I render the names of Orthodox and Uniate Ruthenians in Ukrainian and the names of Latin-rite Catholics (including Jeremi Wiśniowiecki, a descendant of the Orthodox Vyshnevets'kyi princes) in Polish. Therefore, I use Kysil, not Kisiel. I modernize the spelling in conformity with present practices. For the kings of the period, I use the Polish forms Zygmunt III, Władysław IV and Jan Kazimierz.

I have kept the text as free as possible of foreign names of institutions and offices. Wherever accepted English equivalents exist, I employ them: "Diet" for *Sejm,* "dietine" for *sejmik,* "palatinate" for *województwo,* "palatine" for *wojewoda,* and "castellan" for *kasztelan.* In some cases, such as *starosta,* a royal official who, in the Middle Ages, was appointed to defend a castle, but who, by the seventeenth century, was a royal appointee with rights to the revenue from the royal lands around a castle, I find no acceptable English term. Therefore, I use the Polish word *starosta* to describe the royal official and *starostwo* to describe his benefice. I have consistently translated the Polish word *szlachta* as nobility and avoided the word gentry. The *szlachta,* like the European nobilities, was a legally defined estate which transmitted noble status to all its heirs. Confusion is often introduced by using both "nobility" and "gentry" to describe the *szlachta,* translating *Rzeczpospolita szlachecka* as "Gentry Republic," and then using gentry as a term to designate the lower levels of the *szlachta,* that is, those who were not magnates.

The Zaporozhian Cossacks are called either "army" or "host." The differences between the numerous "hetmans" mentioned in the book should be remembered. The armies of the Kingdom and Grand Duchy were both led by a great and a field hetman. The leader of the Zaporozhian Host was called "hetman" by the Cossacks, but *starszy* by the Commonwealth's authorities. In order to retain this distinction, I, at times, use *starszy.* For the Polish word *konstytucja,* a law passed by the Diet, I use the English cognate "constitution."

Terms that appear rarely and for which equivalents cannot be found are written in the original, with an explanation of their meaning. Translations are always dangerous because they may be a literal rendering, may not really describe the functions of the office or institution, or may have connotations in English totally lacking in the original. For example, a *voevoda* in Muscovy and a *wojewoda* in the Commonwealth were two very different officials in the seventeenth century, despite the common origin of their titles. The Muscovite official was a short-term military commander, while the senatorial rank of *wojewoda* in the Commonwealth was conferred for life, usually to a noble of the area, and gave the holder recognition as the leader of the area's nobility. Also, a *województwo* in the Commonwealth was a large, historical territorial unit, not, as in Muscovy, the lands around a border outpost. Therefore, I retain the term *voevoda* for the Muscovite office.

One of the major difficulties of this work has been to describe the states and peoples of Eastern Europe with precision. Loss of precision is often caused by the desire for brevity. We lack a word to describe the inhabitants of the Polish-Lithuanian Commonwealth, and so they become "Poles." The inhabitants of the Grand Duchy of Lithuania are "Lithuanians." The specialist may at times keep in mind that among the "Poles" were a Polish minority and a Lithuanian-Belorussian-Ukrainian majority, while ethnic Lithuanians were a minority in the Grand Duchy. But often even specialists use the same words for ethnic-cultural and political designations, and their readers understandably become confused. In order to avoid these problems, I am forced at times to use phrases such as "inhabitants of the Kingdom of Poland," even though such terms are at times cumbersome. At times, the word "Crown" is used to designate officials and institutions of the Kingdom of Poland, in contrast to the Grand Duchy of Lithuania. To designate the state as a whole, I use the word "Commonwealth." The term "Muscovites" refers to the inhabitants of the Muscovite state, but it must be remembered that in Polish and Ukrainian, the designation refers to Russians.

In using the words "nation" and "nationality" to translate the terms *natio, gens, naród, narod*—that is, the peoples and states of Eastern Europe, I do not wish to convey the impression that I am speaking of modern nations. I use these terms to translate seventeenth-century statements about community and group identities.

In the seventeenth century, *the Ukraine* as a geographic term described the lands of the Dnieper Region. *Rus'* often described the territories inhabited by Ukrainians, although it sometimes included a larger territory, the Belorussian lands and, at times, a smaller territory, the Volhynian, Bratslav, Kievan, and Chernihiv palatinates. To avoid ambiguity, I have not used *the Ukraine* in its seventeenth-century meaning, and I have replaced it by names of the palatinates or phrases such as "the Dnieper region." *Rus'* is used in translating quotations, but when an approximation of the present-day Ukraine is being discussed, the term *the Ukraine* will be used. For the land which the Kingdom of Poland incorporated from the Grand Duchy of Lithuania in 1569 (the palatinates of Bratslav, Kiev, and Volhynia) and the Chernihiv palatinate, which was granted the privileges of the palatinate of Kiev, I use the term *incorporation lands.* Although the Chernihiv lands were not incorporated during the Union of Lublin, the term is useful to describe an important regional entity.

Occasionally, I use *Ukrainian* to designate the ancestors of present-day Ukrainians, even though they did not use this term. Use of the names *Ukrainian* and *Belorussian* is not totally satisfactory, since the division of Ukrainian and Belorussian national identities was only in the process of developing in the seventeenth century. When I refer to both peoples collectively, I use the term *Ruthenians,* although in order to emphasize cultural-historical factors I, at times, use *Ruthenians* to designate Ukrainians.

Finally, I use *Rus'* as both a geographic designation and an adjective to describe institutions and characteristics of the Ruthenian populace of the Commonwealth, for example, the Rus' faith, Rus' privileges. I do this in order to avoid distorting seventeenth-century texts and thought. I treat the problem of seventeenth-century uses of the term *Rus'* in the text.

I am aware of the various uses of *Rus'* and its derivatives among seventeenth-century Russians, but in the confines of the Commonwealth, *Rus'* usually meant the Ukraine and Belorussia, their inhabitants, or a particular region of these territories. This problem will be dealt with at greater length in the first chapter.

Throughout this work, a modified Library of Congress system is used to transliterate Ukrainian and Russian. Names and titles have been modernized. In order to avoid the unfortunate form "Kysil''s," I have dropped the apostrophe indicating a soft sign after the "l" in Kysil. Unless otherwise indicated, dates are given according to the Gregorian Calendar.

Geographic Names

I. The Ukrainian Soviet Socialist Republic

Ukrainian	Polish	Russian	German/English
Belz	Bełz	Belz	
Berestechko	Beresteczko	Berestechko	
Bila Tserkva	Biała Cerkiew	Belaia Tserkov'	
Bratslav	Bracław	Bratslav	
Busha	Busza	Busha	
Chernihiv	Czernichów	Chernigov	
Chornobyl'	Czarnobyl	Chernobyl'	
Chyhyryn	Czehryn	Chigirin	
Dorohynychi	Dorohinicze		
Hadiach	Hadziacz	Gadiach	
Hlyniany	Gliniany		
Hoshcha	Hoszcza		
Kam"ianets' Podil's'kyi	Kamieniec Podolski	Kamianets Podol'skii	
Khotyn	Chocim	Khotin	
Korsun'	Korsuń	Korsun'	
Kumeiky	Kumejki	Kumeiki	
Kyïv	Kijów	Kiev	Kiev
Lubny	Łubny		
Luts'k	Łuck	Lutsk	
L'viv	Lwów	L'vov	Lemberg/Lviv
Nizhyn	Nieżyn	Nezhin	
Nosivka	Nosówka	Nosovka	
Novhorod Sivers'kyi	Nowogród Siewierski	Novogrod Severskii	
Nyzkynychi	Nieskinicze		
Okhmativ	Ochmatów	Okhmatov	
Orynyn	Orynin	Orinyn	
Ostroh	Ostróg	Ostrog	
Ovruch	Owrucz	Ovruch	
Pereiaslav	Perejasław	Pereiaslavl'	
Podillia	Podole	Podol'e	
Polissia	Polesie	Poles'e	
Putyvl'	Putywl	Putivl'	
Pyliavtsi	Piławce	Piliavtsi	

Staryi Konstantyniv	Stary Kontantynów	Starii Konstantinov	
Tovmach (Tlumach)	Tłumacz		
Volodymyr	Włodzimierz	Vladimir (Volynskii)	
Volyn'	Wołyń	Volyn'	Volhynia
Zbarazh	Zbaraż	Zbarazh	
Zboriv	Zborów	Zborov	
Zhovti Vody	Żółte Wody	Zholtye Vody	
Zhytomyr	Żytomierz	Zhitomir	
Zolochiv	Złoczów	Zolochev	

II. Belorussian Soviet Socialist Republic

Belorussian	*Ukrainian*	*Polish*	*Russian*
Brest	Berestia	Brześć	Brest
Dzisna	Disna	Dzisna	Disna
Hrodna	Hrodno	Grodno	Grodno
Mahilioŭ	Mohyliv	Mohylew	Mogilev
Minsk (Mensk)	Mins'k	Minsk	Minsk
Mstsislaŭ	Mstyslav	Mścisław	Mstislav
Navahrudak	Novohrodok	Nowogródek	Novogrudok
Orsha	Orsha	Orsza	Orsha
Pinsk	Pyns'k	Pińsk	Pinsk
Polatsk	Polots'k	Połock	Polotsk
Vitsebsk	Vytebs'k	Witebsk	Vitebsk

III. Polish People's Republic

Polish	*Ukrainian*	*Russian*	*German/English*
Chełm	Kholm	Kholm	
Gdańsk	Gdans'k	Gdansk	Danzig
Kraków	Krakiv	Krakov	Krakau/Cracow
Krasnystaw	Krasnastav		
Lublin	Liublyn	Liublin	
Podlasie	Pidliashshia	Podliash'e	
Przemyśl	Peremyshl'	Peremyshl'	
Warszawa	Varshava	Varshava	Warschau/ Warsaw
Zamość	Zamostia	Zamost'	

IV. Russian Soviet Socialist Republic

Russian	*Ukrainian*	*Polish*
Belgorod	Bil'horod	Biełgorod
Sevsk	Sevs'k	Siewsk

Smolensk	Smolens'k	Smoleńsk
Trubchevsk	Trubchevs'k	Trubczewsk

V. Rivers

Form used in book	*Ukrainian*	*Polish*	*Russian*
Boh	Boh (Pivdennyi Boh)	Boh	Iuzhnyi Bug
Buh	Buh	Bug	Zapadnyi Bug
Dnieper	Dnipro	Dniepr	Dnepr
Dniester	Dnister	Dniestr	Dnestr
Prypet	Pryp''iat'	Prypeć	Pripiat'
San	Sian	San	Sian
Vistula	Vysla (Visla)	Wisła	Visla

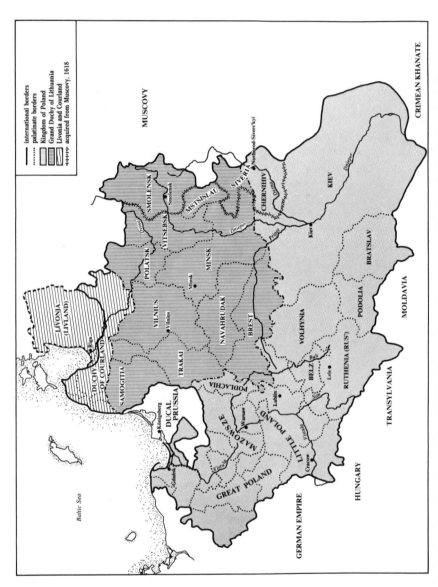

Administrative borders of the Polish-Lithuanian Commonwealth, first half of the seventeenth century.

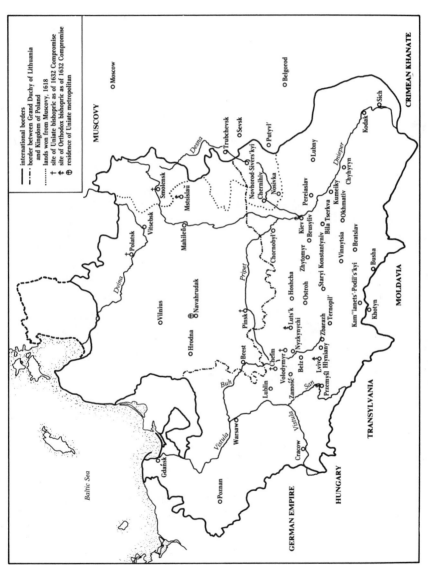

Places of importance in the life of Adam Kysil.

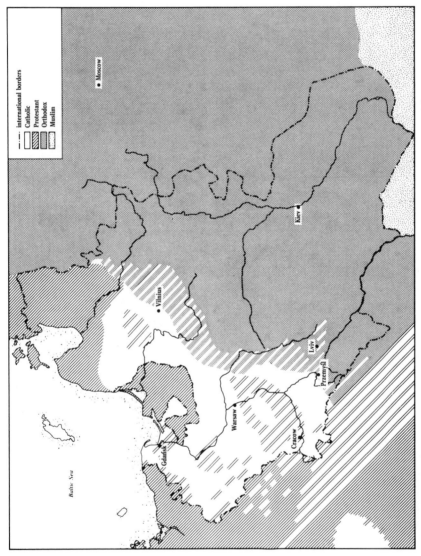

Prevailing religious allegiances in Eastern Europe, end of the sixteenth century.

Introduction

In discussing the events of 1653 in his voluminous synthesis of the Khmel'nyts'kyi uprising, the greatest modern Ukrainian historian, Mykhailo Hrushevs'kyi, digressed from his analysis of diplomatic intrigue and plans for renewed conflict to evaluate the career of Adam Kysil, palatine of Kiev. He informed his readers:

> Almost unnoticed came the death of our old acquaintance, one of the pillars of the politics of peace, the palatine Kysil. . . . To the end he remained an advocate of compromise, and as the voice of the disappearing stratum of nobles "of the Ruthenian people and of the Polish nation" (Gente Ruthenus, Natione Polonus) his word retained some significance. There left the stage the last participant of the great parliamentary struggle by which the Ukrainian-Belorussian nobles sought to solve the national problem before they drowned in a "plebeian sea." Kysil outlived the parliamentary struggle, but he could not find a place for himself in the new revolutionary conditions.[1]

Hrushevs'kyi, the populist critic of history's rulers and oppressors, displayed unusual compassion toward a magnate and exploiter of the peasantry when he discussed Kysil's plight. That he did so may be explained by his difficulty in reconciling Kysil's "negative" class background with his "positive" policies. Unlike many other Ukrainian nobles of the first half of the seventeenth century, Kysil had shown deep loyalty to his ancestral faith and national tradition. Thus, he had not "deserted" the Ukrainian people, and therefore did not fit neatly into Hrushevs'kyi's category of leaders and elites who so often betrayed the Ukrainian people. Also, though Kysil did not join the Khmel'nyts'kyi uprising, which Hrushevs'kyi saw as a struggle encompassing strivings for both national and social justice, he did seek a compromise with the rebels. Hence Hrushevs'kyi viewed Kysil as a figure tragically trapped by divided loyalties in conflicts between Poles and Ukrainians, and between exploiting and exploited classes. He regretted that historians had not given this complex figure the attention that his importance warranted.

Hrushevs'kyi had become convinced of Kysil's importance while undertaking groundbreaking research for the over one thousand pages of the *Istoriia Ukraïny-Rusy* (History of Ukraine-Rus') on the second quarter of the seventeenth century. He had frequent occasion to discuss

Kysil's activities and to quote his statements because Kysil emerged in the 1620s as a leader of the Orthodox nobility, played an active role in the government's relations with the Cossacks in the 1630s, participated in Władysław IV's plans for a war against the Ottomans in the 1640s, and shaped Warsaw's policies toward the Khmel'nyts'kyi uprising after 1648. Hrushevskyi's call for study of Kysil, however, has had meager results.

Other than a few superficial sketches, most written over a hundred years ago, no biography of Kysil has been undertaken.[2] Kysil's importance in the events of the period has ensured that scholars have devoted considerable attention to him while writing works on the Khmel'nyts'kyi uprising, the Orthodox-Uniate struggle, and the history of the Zaporozhian Cossacks. These works, however, discuss only aspects of his activities without examining them as a part of his total career.

On the whole, the superficial biographical sketches and the general monographs about the period share one characteristic, the tendency to evaluate Kysil by the standards of the dominant Eastern European ideologies of the nineteenth and twentieth centuries—nationalism, religious belief, and Marxism. The judgments vary from the measured, careful opinions of Hrushevskyi and Ludwik Kubala to the partisan, inflammatory statements of Franciszek Rawita-Gawroński and Oleksandr Kasymenko, but they all reflect the tendency to put Kysil before the court of their own day's morality and to use the criteria of national good, religious truth, and class interest to make their decisions. The passions that these issues have aroused in modern Eastern Europe have allowed for candid as well as strident formulations of opinion. Although the three ideologies have often been intermixed, it has been nationalism, most directly Polish and Ukrainian, that has dominated historians' evaluations of Kysil. Seldom far from the surface has been the question of Kysil's loyalty and treason to national interest. Kysil has served as a useful symbol for those who wish to influence and form national relations between Poles and Ukrainians. To understand how ardent these views remain to this day, one need only look at the present Soviet view, keeping in mind that Soviet scholars dominate all research on the history of seventeenth-century Ukraine:

> Kysil was a Ukrainian magnate, a sympathizer with Poland. . . . Kysil played a particularly shameful role when the Cossack-peasant rebellion of 1637 broke out in the Ukraine. . . . For his treason Kysil received large estates in the Ukraine and became a magnate. . . . Ukrainian and Polish bourgeois nationalist historiographies, falsifying historical facts, characterize Kysil as a defender of Orthodoxy and remain silent on his treasonous activities.[3]

While present-day Polish scholars take less strident and anachronistic national and class positions, they very seldom deal with seventeenth-century Ukrainian problems or the figure of Kysil.

In undertaking a biography of Kysil, I do not dismiss the questions and opinions posed by prior historians, but I do not share their certainties about correct attitudes and proper goals for a work of this type. I differ from them in writing my work at a remove from the cultural and intellectual environment of Eastern Europe.

Through this study of Kysil, I hope to contribute to a number of fundamental questions on the history of the Polish-Lithuanian Commonwealth and the Ukraine. To what degree did the Ukrainian problem hasten the malfunctioning in government and ultimately the decline of the Polish-Lithuanian Commonwealth? How much continuity in political culture was there between the Ukrainian lands of the Commonwealth of the first half of the seventeenth century and Cossack Ukraine after the great revolt of 1648? What were the mechanisms, contemporary perceptions, and consequences of the acculturation and assimilation of the Ruthenian nobility in the sixteenth and seventeenth centuries in the Commonwealth? Is it possible to discuss Polish-Ukrainian relations and conflict in the period prior to and during the Khmel'nyts'kyi uprising in national terms?

These questions fall within the parameters that many specialists on Western and Central Europe in the early modern period have dealt with so exhaustively since World War II. Regrettably their discussions of the "Crisis of the Seventeenth Century," and of the preconditions and nature of revolts, the formation and transformation of elites, and the manifestations of national consciousness and regionalism have largely excluded the Polish-Lithuanian Commonwealth and the revolt in the Ukraine. Eastern European historians have done little to bring these cases into scholarly discussions, with the exception of Polish historians' studies and discussions on the general economic crisis. I have broached a number of these questions in preliminary studies and I plan to turn to them again.[4] While my present book does not treat them directly, it does examine the life of an official who tried to rectify the inadequacies of a central government, of an administrator who had to deal with a revolt, of a nobleman who saw the need to compromise with an ascending new elite group, and of a leader of a religious and cultural minority faced with problems of adjustment, acculturation and assimilation to a dominant faith and culture.

That this study has been undertaken is not only testimony to the stature of Kysil, but also to relatively good fortune in the preservation of his documentary legacy. The historian of the Commonwealth, and of the Ukraine in particular, must all too often make do with what fires, wars, and revolution have not destroyed. To this consideration must be added, for this Western scholar, the denial of access to significant materials in the Soviet Union. Hence I use "relatively," for colleagues in Western European history may find the materials on which this work is based rather scanty in comparison to what they have available for seventeenth-century figures. Above all, the extant sources do not include family records and personal archives. The steps by which Kysil built his fortune as a magnate and his managing of his far-flung estates remain largely unknown to us. (An appendix lists the limited information gleaned from fragmentary sources.) Too little material is included on Kysil's cultural patronage and esthetics, which might have been found in private archives. Material evidence is lacking since his manor houses were long ago destroyed and the few extant churches he built are barbarized, closed and inaccessible to Western scholars. There are no memoirs or diaries that record Kysil's life and there is all too little information on his personal relations with his family, neighbors and acquaintances.[5]

It is Kysil's public career that is the focus of this biography, and here the documentation is quite abundant. His influential posts and his reputation for eloquence ensured that his contemporaries preserved and copied his correspondence. From it emerge not only Kysil's actions but also his views on the affairs of the day and his opinions on state and society. The purpose of this biography is therefore twofold. First, it reconstructs the public career of Kysil, almost all of which dealt with issues of seventeenth-century Ukraine and its relation to the Polish-Lithuanian Commonwealth. Through a discussion of Kysil's successes and failures, it explores these issues and that relationship. Second, it examines Kysil's attitudes about his state and society. Through this study of an influential man's views, it aims to deepen perception of the world view of his contemporaries who have not left behind such a rich legacy of their opinions. Kysil the individual was, of course, unique, as his prominence demonstrates. Nevertheless, by studying the man who most poignantly faced the dilemma posed by the relationship of Poland and the Ukraine, we should better understand the range of actions and views of his contemporaries, many of whom saw no dilemma at all.

Chapter 1

The Commonwealth and the Ukrainian Lands in the Early Seventeenth Century: The State and Society of the Nobles

The sixteenth century has been called the "Golden Age" of Polish civilization, the first half of the seventeenth, the "Silver Age."[1] The designations derive largely from the two periods' relation to the precipitous decline of that civilization after the mid-seventeenth century. Therefore, they are based on subsequent generations' evaluation rather than on contemporaries' perceptions. Yet however unaware men of the Silver Age may have been of the essential differences between their civilization and that of their forefathers, the processes changing an innovative and dynamic civilization into a conservative and rigid one were indeed at work.

In almost all aspects of life, the sixteenth century was a period of prosperity, creativity in political life, peace amidst several military victories, and cultural achievements.[2] The demand for grain in Western Europe spurred a prosperity manifested in demographic growth and expanding cities. The nobles who turned their lands into demesne saw a rise of their standard of living, while their new demands for peasant labor services did not impoverish their subjects in an expanding economy. The century began with the final formation of a powerful national Diet in the Kingdom of Poland, a well-functioning institution that brought about a remarkably uniform administrative system in contrast to the particularism and divisions characteristic of most contemporary European kingdoms. The nobles were the dominant order of the Kingdom, but vigorous burgher groups were still considered part of the body politic and contributed much to cultural and intellectual achievements. In the reign of Zygmunt August (1548–1572), an increasingly assertive middle nobility, in an alliance with the monarch, curbed the power of the great nobles. Yet while the monarch remained a powerful figure, the powers of the Diet were so broad that the polity was able to survive the extinction of the traditional dynasty and to create a fully elective monarchy. The Kingdom expanded through the incorporation of Masovia early in the century, and it was transformed into Europe's largest state, except for Muscovy, by the real union negotiated with the Grand Duchy of Lithuania in 1569. At a time when religious wars raged in Western Europe and the Ottoman onslaught troubled Hungary and the Habsburg lands, the Kingdom of Poland enjoyed a period of peace. The victory in the Thirteen Years' War (1454–1466) had ensured an outlet to the sea, and the Baltic littoral remained peaceful throughout the first half of the sixteenth century. Peace with the Ottomans and payment of tribute to the Crimea gave even the southern flank of both the Kingdom and the dynastically allied Grand Duchy of Lithuania some respite from Tatar raids.

In general, the Grand Duchy of Lithuania was not as fortunate as the Kingdom. Muscovy successfully pressed that state's possession of East Slavic lands in the first decades of the century. However, just as the pressure of the Teutonic Knights had spurred the formation of a personal dynastic union between Poland and Lithuania in the fourteenth century, so pressure from Muscovy was partly instrumental in bringing about the real union of 1569. The dissolution of the Livonian Order had encouraged Ivan IV to seek a Baltic outlet for his realm, but Sweden and the newly formed Polish-Lithuanian Commonwealth thwarted Ivan's goals, and the great military leader, King Stefan Batory (1576–1586), recouped some of the losses that Lithuania had sustained earlier in the century. The wars even prompted military reforms, including the formation of peasant infantry units and the establishment of a fisc to support a small standing army. For most of the Commonwealth's inhabitants, the victorious war brought no hardships to their lives.

The sixteenth century, in particular, was the Golden Age of Polish culture. Humanism, the Renaissance and the Reformation reached the Kingdom in quick succession and brought about a flowering of literature, learning, and the arts. Not only did Polish become a literary language, but also within a generation, it found a figure of genius in Jan Kochanowski. Education and literacy spread dramatically, and new institutions of higher learning were founded. The age produced men of great calibre, scientists like Copernicus, political theorists like Andrzej Frycz Modrzewski, and churchmen like Jan Łaski, each of whom questioned basic assumptions about the world around him. Within a few decades, the level of culture and learning seemed to be approaching that of the old centers of civilization in Southern and Western Europe. In one way, indeed, Polish culture seemed to be in the forefront of developments. While the successes of the Reformation were great, they were not total in the Kingdom and the Grand Duchy. Therefore, in lands that had long tolerated an Orthodox minority and had invited the settlement of Jews cast out of Western Europe, voices were raised for a general religious toleration, finally enacted by the Confederation of Warsaw in 1573.

Like all golden ages, that of the Polish sixteenth century had its dark sides. It was a time when the nobles reduced the peasantry to serfdom and infringed on the rights of the cities. Yet if the second serfdom and the political emasculation of the cities were general phenomena in Eastern Europe, the success of the nobles and their Diet in curbing the powers of the monarch was not. This success caused republican virtues and individual liberties to flourish in the land among the nobles, but it was eventually to weaken the state. Still more crippling for succeeding generations, the Golden Age created a state and society that tried to maintain every aspect of their perfection long after the conditions that created them had changed.

If the Golden Age was one of creativity, the Silver Age was one of preservation and, at times, ossification. As with many such derivative historical periods, the limits and content of the Silver Age are less clearly marked than those of its predecessor. Still, if historians have debated exactly when significant changes occurred in various areas of life, they have generally agreed that the period of change in the Commonwealth began about the 1580s.[3] For historians who emphasize the indicators of economic downturn and the rise of the magnates, the Silver Age is seen as quite tarnished; for those who underline the continued prosperity, the artistic achievements, and the adequate functioning of government and institutions, it glitters. No historian questions, however, that in contrast to the first eighty years of the sixteenth century, the sixty years that followed were ones of conservatism rather than creativity, of hardening rather than openness, and of a declining dynamism in state, society, and economy.

The political structure of the Diet, royal election procedures, and military practices had all been established. Modifications were made after 1580, but the institutional basis of the state changed little. Monarchs schemed to increase their power, but the Diet and nobility were determined to preserve their liberties. Wars engendered numerous expedients, but no sweeping and lasting military reforms. While the Commonwealth remained a regional power and even intervened in Muscovite affairs in the early 1600s, in general the nobles were little interested in expansion. The Commonwealth became more and more committed to the status quo, but unlike the situation in the sixteenth century, it was beginning to face changing and reforming neighbors intent on altering that status quo.

The most marked difference between the Golden and Silver Ages was the hardening of divisions between corporate orders and the increasing identification of state and fatherland with the nobility. This trend appeared in the legislation enacted against new ennoblements and in the restrictions of burghers' commercial privileges. It was even more manifest in thinking and ideology. The age when Modrzewski criticized the nobles for ignoring the role of burghers and peasants in the state was no more, and the nobility thrived on the assertion that it alone collectively constituted the fatherland and the Commonwealth. Convinced of the perfection of the Commonwealth, the nobility became increasingly resistant to new ideas and models.

In religion, the rising tide of the Reformation ended in the 1580s, and a devoutly Catholic monarch and a revitalized church began to recoup the losses to Protestantism and even to make new gains from the Orthodox church. Commitment to religious toleration eroded as religious disputes came to the fore throughout the first half of the century. The success of the new Jesuit schools speeded the spread of the Catholic Counter-Reformation and the break from the tolerant traditions of the Golden Age.

In culture and the arts, the 1580s mark a clear break, although it was not perceived as such by contemporaries. While the figures of the Polish Renaissance saw themselves as the exponents of a new learning and of new forms, albeit in the guise of a revival of Classical culture, their successors of the late sixteenth and early seventeenth century saw themselves as merely carrying on from their predecessors. However, the cultural trends that modern scholars call Baroque differed substantially from those of the Renaissance, and in the Commonwealth became integrated with new developments in the culture of the nobility. Taking firm hold at the end of the sixteenth and in the early seventeenth century, a Polish Baroque culture identified with the nobility prevailed in the Commonwealth long after the Baroque gave way to other trends in Western Europe.

To be sure, the transformation from the Golden to the Silver Age was not abrupt. The ossification in different facets of life took place at different rates, and the early seventeenth century still displayed some of the creativity and dynamism of the earlier age. If the dominant trends in the entire Commonwealth changed significantly between 1580 and 1600, the size of this state, with so many differences in social structure, economy and culture, meant that its various regions were affected by these changes in varying degrees. Thus the lands of Royal Prussia, with their great cities, prosperous peasants, vibrant Lutheranism and strong German influences were affected differently than were Masovian territories, with their numerous petty nobility and their devout Catholicism, or than were the Volhynian lands with their dominant princely magnate families and ancient Orthodox traditions.

In many ways, a time lag existed between developments in the western lands of the Commonwealth and in the territories of the east. Demesne farming and increased peasant labor services, for instance, only slowly reached the eastern lands; the Reformation took root in the eastern territories only after it had peaked in the West; and the middle nobles of the East were drawn into the world of Polish nobiliary prosperity and assertiveness only belatedly. In some ways the situation in the eastern lands prefigured such developments in the whole state as the increase of magnates' powers, the preponderance of rural life over urban, and the Orientalization of culture. Indeed, the Silver Age witnessed the increasing importance of the eastern lands, and of the Ukrainian lands, in particular, in a Polish civilization and state that had been transformed through the creation of the multinational Commonwealth. Ultimately, the difficulties of integrating the Ukrainian lands into the structure of the Commonwealth were to bring the state and civilization of the Silver Age to a crisis that hastened their decline.

The Commonwealth of the Nobility in the Silver Age

"The Commonwealth of Two Nations" (*Rzeczpospolita obojga narodów*) was created by the Union of Lublin (1569), when the Kingdom of Poland and the Grand Duchy of Lithuania were amalgamated into a single state through a real union and the Ukrainian lands of Lithuania were ceded to Poland.[4] Although the union called for a joint Diet, a common foreign policy, and standard administrative practices, the two realms continued to have separate armies, administrations, and judicial codes, and the Lithuanian government retained special privileges in formulating foreign policy toward Muscovy.[5]

Insofar as the new Commonwealth's inhabitants were concerned, loyalty to the fatherland did not preclude strong attachment to their native realms. They took their status as residents of the Kingdom of Poland or Grand Duchy of Lithuania seriously not only because they possessed patriotic sentiments, but also because the two separate administrations provided two separate systems for career and economic advancement, even though the Union of Lublin had removed restrictions on rights to hold land in the other realm, thus diminishing the separateness of the two populations. In its success as a federal state, the Commonwealth provided a model for a political contractual union of elites.[6]

The most important political and social distinction among the Commonwealth's inhabitants was that between noble and commoner.[7] In the seventeenth century, the nobility comprised five to eight percent of the population, and controlled the Commonwealth's political, economic, and cultural life. The nobility enjoyed such preponderance in rights and power that the Commonwealth was in fact a republic of the nobility. In the fourteenth and fifteenth centuries, the nobles had successfully curbed the powers of the king, deprived the burghers and peasants of influence, and thwarted attempts to introduce gradations among their own ranks.[8] The success of the "execution of the laws" movement in the mid-sixteenth century had limited the power of the magnates. The Kingdom's code of nobiliary rights and freedom proved attractive to the Lithuanian elite, so that when the two were united, the Lithuanian elite was happy to assume the rights and privileges of Polish nobles. As a result, though the Commonwealth's nobility was not homogeneous in language, nationality, or religion, it was firmly united by its bond as the ruling corporate order of the country.[9]

The nobles treasured their rights of liberty and equality. They extolled the liberty they enjoyed both as an order and as individuals, and they contrasted the Commonwealth with other states in which noble privileges were circumscribed by royal power or by the influence of other orders, or in which individual rights were limited.[10] They viewed their government and society as perfect, and were determined to keep it that way. Liberty was seen as the prerogative of the "Sarmatians"; and by the early seventeenth century, the favored Sarmatian genealogical myth of sixteenth-century Polish historians developed into an ideology for the nobility of the Commonwealth. One variant of Sarmatism contended that only the nobles of the Commonwealth descended from the ancient Sarmatians and that the non-noble orders of the Commonwealth had had a different origin.[11] Therefore, only the brotherhood of the nobility could have liberty because only they were the real sons of the Fatherland.

Within the noble order, the principle of equality formed the bond. Through determined struggle, culminating in the "execution of the laws movement" of the mid-sixteenth century, the Polish nobility had won the assurance that the masses of the nobility would remain legally equal to the wealthy and powerful, and that neither provincial offices nor titles would become hereditary. Equality and brotherhood among the nobility were therefore enshrined as unquestioned tenets of the Commonwealth's laws and ideology.[12] Of course, "equality" had nothing to do with wealth or power. The thousands of nobles in the Commonwealth included landless paupers along with owners of hundreds of towns and villages. In the seventeenth century, the power and wealth of the upper stratum of the nobility—the magnates—increased tremendously, but unlike the concept "noble," which was a legally defined category, the term "magnate" merely referred to a noble who had attained great wealth and influence. Although the magnates might, by virtue of their wealth, dominate political institutions and wield power that put them above the laws, they did not seek to separate themselves legally from the nobility or to alter the Commonwealth's institutional structure. They operated as individuals, often contending among one another, securing their goals by manipulating the existing institutions and by posing as the defenders of the Commonwealth's tradition of equality. Since the magnates were not a closed caste, all nobles could rise to magnate status.[13]

The nobility controlled the Commonwealth through the Diet or, more strictly speaking, the House of Delegates, which constituted, along with the Senate and king, the three component "estates" of the realm. Every noble owning land in a region had full rights to participate in the numerous provincial dietines, whose duties were to send delegates to the national Diet, hear reports from it, send delegates to judicial bodies, and decide tax matters. The king was required to call a Diet at least every two years. At these Warsaw Diets, lasting from two to six weeks, the delegates could lobby for the instructions they had received, speak out on the issues of state that were introduced by the royal spokesmen, and make decisions by unanimous assent. While the sixteenth century witnessed the increasing power of an active, effective House of Delegates that embodied the unity of the state, the early seventeenth century was a period of decline in parliamentary practices, reflecting the waning fortunes of the middle nobles, the increasing influence of magnates on local dietines, the greater reluctance of dietines to entrust delegates with discretionary powers or to surrender power to the central Diet, and stalemates over controversial issues such as religious tolerance. Though the lower house continued to function relatively well, the number of deadlocks that prevented the house from passing legislation increased. In the early seventeenth century, parliamentary skill was as sure a road to success as military or royal service, since the ability to control dietines and to influence the House of Delegates meant political power, which could be converted into gain, especially from a monarch interested in securing support.[14]

The upper house of the Diet, the Senate, consisted of the Roman Catholic ordinaries, the palatines and castellans, and the major functionaries of the central government. Appointed by the king, the senators were drawn from the wealthiest and most powerful nobles in the realm; although, except for the bishops, they obtained little income from their offices, they could use the powers of their senatorial office to accrue additional wealth and influence. Not every noble of magnate status was a senator, since enmity with the monarch or incompetence could keep a rich and powerful noble out of the Senate. By the same token, not every senator came from, or attained, magnate status, since the king would at times distribute posts to lesser nobles or a senator might fail to make use of his office well. But while to a non-magnate from a family that had never sat in the Senate, a senatorial chair was a goal for which to strive avidly through persistence and hard work, to men who came from families of magnate ranking and senatorial position, the post came more easily and earlier.

Although posts in the Senate were distributed by the king, and most of its members were magnates, the body became neither an organ for royal authority nor an institution of magnate rule. The king might favor his supporters with senatorial posts, but once appointed for life a senator could change his opinion at will; furthermore, the king frequently was obliged to appoint political opponents to mollify them. The Senate was populated largely by magnates, yet the senators did not combine to convert the institution into a formalized magnate order. Magnates also sat in the House, and the magnates of the Senate were after all first and foremost nobles, linked by family and loyalty to family and to regional groupings of other nobles. Within the Senate, magnates clashed, and all senators tried to find support in the dietines and the House of Delegates for their personal affairs and for public policies. The status of each senator depended on his position within the brotherhood of nobles, and though he might privately sneer at his impoverished noble brothers, he would manipulate them, rather than combine with his senatorial magnate rivals against them. While the Senate did not become synonymous with the magnate stratum, its increasing influence in the early seventeenth century reflected, in part, the growth of magnate influence. In addition, the decline in the effectiveness of the House of Delegates gave the Senate a greater place in affairs of state. The House of Delegates, however, frequently challenged the growth of the Senate's powers, and the two houses were often in conflict.[15]

The Diet was an extremely cumbersome institution by which to rule a state. Decisions based on unanimous consent could be reached only very slowly by gathering a consensus. Minor issues could take up entire sessions, and, since a Diet was limited in length to six weeks, decisions had then to be postponed until the complicated process of calling a new Diet could be completed. For any problem (foreign embassies, demarcation of borders, payment of troops), the Diet appointed members as "commissioners" to act in their place, but they had to be guided by the Diet's instructions, even if the situation for which the instructions were issued should change. The system depended on a patriotic, well-educated, and responsible nobility. It functioned surprisingly well for a time, partly because of the limited range of governmental functions in the period, the decentralization of authority to the dietines, and the *de facto* recognition that the king, military leaders, and senators appointed as the king's advisers would have to make essential decisions, subject to the Diet's subsequent review. The Diet, however, jealously guarded its privileges, especially over taxation and the right to declare war.[16]

The Diet's procedural rules contained one clause that eventually proved fatal. The concept of each noble's freedom was carried to such great lengths that the veto of one delegate, or refusal to prolong the Diet, could invalidate all the measures enacted. The first Diet broken by a single member was that of the famous *liberum veto* of 1652, but malfunctioning began earlier in the century.[17]

The Commonwealth's system left the king with much less power than he would have possessed in other states, yet he was by no means an insignificant force. After the extinction of the Jagiellonian dynasty in 1572, the monarchy became a fully elective office, with each election accompanied by considerable disorder as numerous candidates vied for the throne. The election process was lengthy, involving the entire nobility and necessitating three Diets—Convocation, Election, and Coronation—each of which had to be preceded and followed by dietines. The successful contender was required to sign a *pacta conventa,* or agreement, with the nobility, but after the election, an energetic monarch could secure a party of loyal noble supporters and through them exert considerable control and influence. Still, the nobility's dedication to the constitution and abhorrence of a strong monarchy thwarted the king's attempts to institutionalize any power he might acquire in that way. The monarchs of the first half of the seventeenth century, Zygmunt III Vasa (1586–1632) and his sons Władysław (1632–1648) and Jan Kazimierz (1648–1668), had particular grounds for discontent: the revolt of Zygmunt's Swedish subjects had deprived them of a hereditary throne in which they would have wielded much greater power, while the Zebrzydowski revolt of 1606–1609 had decisively thwarted attempts to change the Commonwealth's political structure. The nobles' distrust of their "foreign" kings was increased by their fear that foreign consorts (often Habsburg princesses) and advisers would convince the king to subvert the Commonwealth's constitution.[18]

The mainstay of the king's power was his right to distribute offices and royal lands. He appointed all the officials who sat in the Senate (bishops, palatines, and castellans) as well as court and government functionaries (chancellors, marshals) and military leaders (hetmans).

Although some of these posts brought revenue in addition to power and authority, it was the king's right to appoint *starostas* (or stewards of royal castles and lands) that allowed the monarch to distribute wealth. Once granted, the position was for life, and considerable pressure was brought to bear by heirs to succeed to a *starostwo*. During a long reign, as Zygmunt III's was, the king could assemble a strong following in the Senate and could punish his enemies by overlooking them when making appointments. Even the wealthiest magnates could gain considerable advantage by currying royal favor; for lesser nobles, royal favor was crucial in amassing wealth.[19]

The success of the nobility in retaining control over the state effectively disenfranchised the other orders. In contrast to many European estates or parliamentary systems, in the Commonwealth burghers and cities sent no representatives to the Diet. Major cities were self-governing under Magdeburg or Chełmno (Kulm) law, but outside of West Prussia, their burghers had no role in making extra-urban decisions. Burgher patriciates existed in Cracow, Lviv, Warsaw and in other major cities, yet the wealthiest burgher had fewer rights than the most impoverished noble. Although the burghers had extremely limited possibilities of entering the noble order, they increasingly imitated the culture and life style of the nobility, rather than developing their separate urban burgher culture.[20] Nobiliary influence was more direct in small towns, which were frequently owned entirely by a local magnate. Even in the large cities, the nobles were able to exploit religious and communal divisions to undermine the cities' autonomy. The nobles undercut the burghers' position by securing a right to sell the produce of their own estates. Therefore, Dutch merchants and the almost autonomous city of Gdańsk could deal directly with producers, excluding the burghers in the hinterland from dealing in the major exports of the Commonwealth. At the same time, a favorable balance of trade allowed the nobles of the Commonwealth to import manufactured goods from the West. Although some regions, such as the Baltic littoral and the Ukraine, continued to maintain a rapid expansion of cities in the first half of the seventeenth century, in most of the Commonwealth urban growth slackened and the relative economic position of the cities declined.[21]

The power of the noble order was based on its virtual monopoly of land ownership. The overwhelming majority of the peasantry lived on land owned by nobles and rendered dues and services, while the minority lived on royal or church lands, which were usually administered by nobles. In the fifteenth and sixteenth centuries, the rural economy of major areas of the Commonwealth was revolutionized by the growing demand for grain in the Low Countries and in other

Western European states. This demand inflated the price, and thus in order to increase their revenue, many nobles, especially along the great water artery, the Vistula, began to convert their estates into demesne farms. They increased the exactions of labor services from the peasantry and decreased the extent of the land that the peasants farmed for themselves. The nobles succeeded in reducing the status of village officials and in abolishing the jurisdiction of the king over the peasants. The peasants' fate varied in different regions, with the best conditions occurring in the prosperous Vistula delta, where the so-called "Dutch village" enjoyed considerable autonomy, and in the eastern lands, where the system was not fully established. Initially, the general prosperity cushioned the peasants from some of the shocks of the increasing second serfdom; but when the economy later took a downturn, the peasants found themselves at the mercy of their landlords. Profits were greatest among nobles who had enough land to operate numerous manors and thus produce a large enough quantity to warrant Baltic merchants' trading with them directly. This, in turn, hastened the differentiation in wealth in the noble estate and increased the competition for land.

At the beginning of the seventeenth century, grain prices peaked when cheap Muscovite grain began to compete on the European markets. The nobles could only maintain their revenues by increasing their land holdings still further. Inferior lands were brought into cultivation and yields began to drop. As agricultural production on the estates or demesne farms approached its limits the nobles expanded into sparsely settled regions where exploitation was less intense. But these lands could only be productive if labor were secured, and the nobles had to ensure that the old inhabitants and new settlers of territories would be subjected as quickly as possible to serfdom, even though these populations were likely to be most resistant to this process. The nobles had succeeded in reducing the peasantry to serfdom and in excluding them from participation in the Commonwealth, but in so doing they had created a wall of mistrust and enmity between themselves and their peasants that prevented them from relying on peasants. With noble exactions increasing in the early seventeenth century, the peasants in many regions were being cruelly oppressed, and in some regions, resistance was mounting.[22]

Maintaining noble privileges depended on the Commonwealth's maintaining a strong position among the states of Central and Eastern Europe, and its foreign policy was generally cautious. The nobles were not only reluctant to spend money on wars, but also were wary of the strength that war could bring to the monarch's position.[23] On the other hand, the magnates' private armies, over which the king had little control, could as easily embroil the Commonwealth in wars as could the monarch's goals, claims, and disputes.[24] The majority of the nobles, however, remained overwhelmingly pacifist, and could only with difficulty be cajoled into an expansionist policy. All nobles were adamantly opposed to ceding territory to any foreign state.[25]

On the whole, the Commonwealth fared well in conflicts with its neighbors in the first half of the seventeenth century. The Union of Lublin had been undertaken as a move against Muscovy. The Commonwealth embarked on a number of successful campaigns to resist Muscovite attacks in Stefan Batory's reign (1576–1586) and intervened in the Muscovite Time of Troubles (1606–1613). Władysław's expedition to claim the Muscovite throne was repulsed (1617–1618), but he annexed the Smolensk and the Chernihiv lands (1619), and defeated a Muscovite attempt to recoup those losses (Smolensk War, 1632–34). The Commonwealth was less successful in dealing with the rising Swedish power in the Baltic, but managed to score some major victories (most notably Kirchholm, 1605) and to keep territorial losses to a minimum. Although the Vasas were pro-Habsburg throughout most of the first half of the seventeenth century, the Commonwealth played only a minor role in the Thirty Years' War. Confrontation with the Ottoman Empire, brought about in the second decade of the seventeenth century by magnate incursions into Moldavia, met with defeat at the debacle at Tsetsora (1620), and with victory at Khotyn (1621). But, despite the raids of the Ottoman Empire's vassals, the Crimean Tatars, and of the Commonwealth's subjects, the Zaporozhian Cossacks, which were a constant source of friction, no other Turkish conflicts broke out. Tatar incursions continued to devastate the southern frontier, and the Commonwealth responded by payment of tribute and occasional shows of force.[26]

Despite the Commonwealth's successes, its military organization was far from imposing. The armies of both the Kingdom and the Grand Duchy had originally consisted of levies of the nobility—the mandatory participation of the martial class. By the first half of the seventeenth century, the levy was outdated and inefficient. It was brought into action only during major emergencies such as the Turkish War (1621). The cavalry had become the backbone of the army. It constituted a small standing force paid by revenue from the royal lands and composed of professional soldiers, many of whom were drawn from the petty nobility. The Kingdom and the Grand Duchy had two separate armies led by two sets of great and field hetmans who were an extremely powerful influence on the Commonwealth's foreign policy. In wartime, additional troops were paid by taxes voted by the Diet, and each palatinate raised detachments to join the two standing armies. The private armies in the service of the magnates, particularly from the Grand Duchy of Lithuania and the Ukraine, also fought with the regular army.[27]

The Commonwealth's military performed well in the first half of the seventeenth century, but a chronic shortage of funds to pay the troops made an extended military undertaking difficult. Unpaid soldiers often formed "confederations," that is, unions of armed resistance, and demanded their pay and other rights from the king and the Diet. Those episodes could turn the most brilliant of the Commonwealth's military victories into a lost war. Although insubordinate, unpaid troops were endemic to seventeenth-century Europe, particularly during the Thirty Years' War, the Commonwealth's lack of strong central authority made confederations an especially difficult problem. The virtual certainty that no punishment would follow increased the frequency of confederations, and unpaid armies often pillaged the countryside in which they were stationed.[28]

The commanding position of the nobles both ensured their rights to profess the faith of their choice and gave them a privileged place in the various denominations. Although Roman Catholicism was the established faith and the monarchs of the Commonwealth were Catholic, the Commonwealth was notable among the states in Europe for the latitude of its religious tolerance.[29] Polish kings and Lithuanian grand dukes were in fact virtually forced to accept religious pluralism among their Christian subjects. In the fourteenth century, the Kingdom of Poland had annexed a considerable Orthodox population whose nobles enjoyed the same rights and privileges as their Catholic counterparts and never suffered the discrimination endured by the Orthodox burghers in cities governed by Magdeburg law. After the conversion of the Lithuanian grand dukes to Catholicism, in the late fourteenth century, and the Union of Horodlo (1413), Orthodox nobles were barred from higher offices. The pressure of the Orthodox majority later overcame these restrictions in practice and secured full equality in the sixteenth century.[30] In addition, the Reformation made such rapid gains among the nobility of the two states in the sixteenth century that Protestants rivaled Catholics in dominating parliamentary and cultural life.[31] Four years after the Union of Lublin, in 1573 at the Confederation of Warsaw, the non-Catholic "dissenting" nobility combined to secure a *pacta conventa* guaranteeing religious freedom.[32] As for non-Christians, Muslim subjects enjoyed considerable religious rights, and Poland had long served as a haven for Jews who were persecuted in Western Europe, and were granted communal autonomy in the sixteenth-century Commonwealth.[33]

The nobility's right to religious freedom became so ingrained that
Catholic attacks on religious antagonists in the seventeenth century
acclaimed the nobility's liberty of religion and contrasted the Commonwealth favorably with those states of Europe whose intolerance had
resulted in the bloodletting of the Thirty Years' War.[34] Even the
Antitrinitarians or Socinians, a group persecuted by Catholics and
Protestants alike throughout Europe, were able to operate relatively
freely for a time, partly because their ranks included numerous prominent nobles.[35] The tolerance the nobility enjoyed was less pronounced
among other estates. Both Protestant and Catholic urban patriciates
persecuted religious minorities, and the Lutheran cities of the Baltic
persecuted other Protestants. Orthodox burghers faced numerous political and economic restrictions. Freedom of conscience for the peasantry was not even discussed; the nobles' patronage rights allowed those
who took an interest in their subjects' faith to "convert" them simply by
replacing the local clergyman.

One of the major reasons for the rapid success of the Reformation
was the resentment of nobles over the Catholic church's power and
economic prerogatives, above all against the tithe. Frequently, Catholic
nobles equaled their Protestant and Orthodox brothers in insisting that
the juridical privileges of the clergy and of Rome be abolished and that a
prohibition be enacted against the acquisition of nobles' lands by the
church. Protestantism, and particularly Calvinism, appealed to the
nobility because of the elevated position that lay dignitaries were given
in the administration of the church.

Despite this handicap, however, the Catholic church retained considerable powers and advantages and exerted influence through its superior
organization and wealth. Catholic bishops—unlike their Orthodox
counterparts—sat in the Senate so that Catholics were guaranteed the
support of senators. Outside the cities, the Protestant sects were totally
dependent on the religious preferences of the local noble. The Protestants lacked a base among the peasantry, whose conservatism was an
important factor in the ultimate preservation of Orthodoxy. Finally, the
papacy and the Habsburgs exerted influence on both the Commonwealth's monarchs and its political leaders in support of the Catholic
camp.[36]

Religious tolerance and the influence of the Protestant nobility
reached their high point in the Articles of Confederation of 1573. The
regrouping of Catholic forces, which took place throughout Europe
after the Council of Trent, became particularly pronounced in the long
reign of Zygmunt III (1587–1632). Although the nobility was sufficiently united in its support of liberty to prevent major infringements of

the Toleration Act of 1573, Zygmunt's consistent policy of advancing Catholics to high posts, the increasing effectiveness of Jesuit schools, and the influence of Rome and the Tridentine reforms on the hierarchy and state altered the Commonwealth's religious balance. Not only did conversions to Catholicism increase among the nobles, but also more effective religious education made Catholic nobles more willing to espouse militant Catholic policies. The king's stubborn support of the recognition by part of the Orthodox hierarchy of Rome's primacy in the Union of Brest (1596) and the refusal of the militant Catholic faction to allow major concessions to the Orthodox even when they were in the interest of the state were further indications of the decline of religious tolerance. By the early seventeenth century, the Protestants and Orthodox nobles were a beleaguered, albeit powerful minority, adamantly fending off the incursions of a vigorous Catholic church.[37]

"The Commonwealth of the Two Nations" contained great ethnic diversity. The Kingdom of Poland included among its inhabitants not only Poles, but also large numbers of Germans, along the Baltic and in the cities, and of Jews, in most of the cities outside of Masovia. Ukrainians predominated in the southeast, along with large Armenian communities in the cities. The Grand Duchy's titular nationality, the Lithuanians, formed only a minority of the state's population, with Belorussians and Ukrainians, often collectively referred to as Ruthenians, occupying large areas, and Poles, Germans, and Jews numerous in the cities and towns.[38]

Divisions in literary language often did not coincide with those in nationality or vernacular tongue. Latin retained an important place in bureaucratic and literary Poland, although the use of Polish made considerable advances in the literature of the sixteenth century, as it did against German in the cities. The official written language of the Grand Duchy of Lithuania and the Ukrainian lands ceded to Poland in 1569 was Ruthenian (or Middle Belorussian-Ukrainian), and it was used even by the Lithuanians well into the sixteenth century. Although Ruthenian remained the official written language of the Grand Duchy until 1696, Polish and Latin made inroads there as well. Latin was used for foreign correspondence, except with Muscovy, where "Chancery Ruthenian" (referred to in Muscovy as "Belorussian writing") was obligatory. Latin was the sacral language of Catholicism; vernaculars (predominantly German and Polish) were used by the Protestant groups; Church Slavonic was the language of Orthodoxy; and Hebrew of Judaism.[39]

The Commonwealth was, then, a heterogeneous state and society held together mainly by a patriotic nobility that was able to manage the rest of the population. Despite the "brotherhood" of all nobles, however, a small group of magnates derived a disproportionate share of the power and benefits from the order's political and economic privileges. Nobles earned their income almost entirely from rents and sales of produce and raw materials from estates and royal lands. Accumulation of land and exactions from the peasantry were the basis of wealth, and few controls existed to supervise a nobleman's treatment of his subjects. In fact, emphasis on the liberty of the nobility resulted in a system that was ill-equipped to punish a noble even for direct violence against a fellow noble. The constitutional and military structures of the state had inherent weaknesses that became all too visible after the middle of the century. Ultimately, religious and ethnic diversity proved to be divisive factors. It was in the government of the Ukrainian lands that the Commonwealth's social and political order met difficulties that could not be resolved.

The Ukrainian Lands

The Ukraine did not compose a unified administrative division in the Commonwealth, and the name "Ukraine" was restricted, in the seventeenth century, to the Dnieper Region.[40] Those territories inhabited by Ukrainians, which until the thirteenth century had been part, and indeed the core, of Kievan Rus', had been annexed at different times by the Kingdom of Poland and the Grand Duchy of Lithuania and had thereby become different administrative units, each with its own social structure, traditions, and linguistic and ethnic composition.[41] Since the Lublin Union (1569), almost all the lands of the Commonwealth that were inhabited by Ukrainians except Polissia had been part of the Kingdom of Poland.

The Galician half of the independent Galician-Volhynian Principality had been annexed to Poland in the fourteenth century. Reconstituted as the Ruthenian palatinate in the mid-fifteenth century, the last vestiges of its different legal structure were abolished. In the sixteenth century, the Ruthenian palatinate included a large number of wealthy noble families originating in ethnic Poland, as well as converts from the local elite. Even the petty nobility had been strongly influenced by Polish society and culture. Orthodoxy, however, still remained strong among the numerous petty nobility and peasantry, and among a minority of the burghers. The relatively thickly settled area contained the large city of Lviv, the Orthodox bishoprics of Lviv and Przemyśl, and numerous Orthodox monasteries and shrines. The Roman Catholic archbishopric of Lviv and the bishopric of Przemyśl dated from the fourteenth century. They surpassed their Orthodox counterparts in wealth, and in the prestige, if not in the numbers of their faithful. Latin and Polish were the languages of administration, and, despite its name, the Ruthenian palatinate was well integrated into the political and social structures of the Polish Kingdom.[42]

The Belz palatinate also showed strong Polish and Roman Catholic influence, but retained a predominantly Ruthenian population and a well-developed network of Orthodox institutions. It had been detached from the Ruthenian palatinate in the fifteenth century. This was also true of the Chełm land, separated from the Grand Duchy's Volhynian land and attached to the Kingdom in the fifteenth century. The last of the Kingdom's old Ukrainian territories, the Podillian palatinate, however, was different. Exposed as it was to raids from the steppe, it was thinly settled until the sixteenth century and lacked the strong indigenous Orthodox church structure of the other lands. Although both nobles and commoners of the Ruthenian, Belz, and Podillian palatinates and the Chełm land played a major role in Orthodox and Ukrainian cultural and religious life, by the seventeenth century the assimilation of their nobility into the Kingdom of Poland had progressed so far that they had little awareness of a past predating their annexation to the Kingdom of Poland, or of distinct rights and privileges that might differentiate their lands from the ethnically Polish palatinates.[43]

The eastern palatinates of Kiev, Bratslav, Volhynia and Chernihiv differed markedly from the western Ukrainian lands. The first three had been annexed by the Kingdom of Poland in 1569 at the Union of Lublin; the fourth had been won from Muscovy in 1619.[44] Before that, the first three, along with the Belorussian territories, had been part of the Grand Duchy of Lithuania since the Volhynian and Kievan principalities had been abolished and absorbed into the Lithuanian state in the fourteenth and fifteenth centuries. They had retained many of their own legal, social, and cultural traditions, although they were affected by the administrative and legal reforms of the Grand Duchy in the sixteenth century—many of which stemmed from Polish influence in Lithuania.[45] When the Kingdom negotiated to annex these lands as part of the Union of Lublin, part of the local elite was more than willing to join the Kingdom, and the opposition of the Grand Duchy's magnates proved futile.[46]

In return, the nobility of these lands were granted special privileges assuring the rights of the Orthodox church and its adherents, declaring Chancery Ruthenian the legal language, confirming the Second Lithuanian Statute as the legal code, and providing for special chancery books.[47] Although the privileges were granted separately to the Kievan and Volhynian palatinates (the Bratslav palatinate was created from the Volhynian in 1569), the formulation of the annexations as a joint program and the similarity of the privileges gave the area unity and common interests. In 1635, the Kievan palatinate's privileges and customs were extended to the newly created Chernihiv palatinate, in effect making it part of the territory incorporated at the Lublin Union (1569).[48] The nobility in these lands remained aware that its allegiance to the Kingdom of Poland was recent and had taken effect only after negotiations and the assurance of local privileges. A sense of separateness and unity was reinforced by the relatively homogeneous nature of the populace, Ukrainian and Orthodox.[49]

The social structures of the palatinates incorporated at Lublin differed from those of the other palatinates of the Kingdom in two major ways. First, unlike the rest of the Kingdom, these lands had not gone through the gradual process by which the nobles' republic was built. Just prior to the Union of Lublin, the various orders of the Grand Duchy's elite had been recast into a Polish *szlachta*-nobility.[50] Most of the lower serving orders (boiars and *zemiany*) had thus been raised to the level of citizen-nobles, and princely families had implicitly been lowered in status. However, the importation of the social structure of the Commonwealth threatened to reduce those segments of the lower serving orders that were not included in the noble category to the status of peasants.[51] The retention of princely titles was the only ostensible difference between the nobility in the incorporation lands and the rest of the Kingdom's nobility, but the weaker tradition of equality and the predominance of large-scale holdings gave the area a different social make-up.[52] Moreover, the nobility of the incorporation lands, particularly the Kievan, Bratslav and Chernihiv palatinates, represented a much smaller proportion of the population than they did in the western Ukrainian palatinates or in the Polish lands.[53] A much higher proportion of the populace was therefore "non-citizens," and the equation of the nobility with the entire citizenry was even further from reality.

Second, the incorporation lands, or more precisely the Bratslav and Kievan palatinates, also were home to the Zaporozhian Cossacks, a group that existed nowhere else in the populations of the Commonwealth. Considerable controversy surrounds the origins of Cossack formations in Eastern Europe. The Zaporozhian Cossacks evolved in the sparsely populated Dnieper basin, under conditions of border warfare between the Tatars and the Grand Duchy of Lithuania. By the sixteenth century, they had set up military communities that lived by a combination of hunting, fishing, farming and looting. The loose control exerted by the Grand Duchy in this area and the need for military assistance against the Tatars reinforced the Cossacks' *de facto* position as a free class in the Dnieper region. Most Cossacks settled areas on the Right Bank, south of Kiev, but their military camp was in the lower Dnieper—the Sich, a stronghold beyond the reach of both the Commonwealth's armies and the Turkish fleet. It was from the Sich that the Cossacks raided the coasts of Asia Minor and carried on border warfare with the Crimean Tatars.[54] Recruits from numerous nationalities joined the Zaporozhian Cossacks, although they remained predominantly Ukrainian and Orthodox.[55] Even some nobles joined, although following the Cossack way of life put a man's nobility in question.

In the reign of Stefan Batory, the Commonwealth's urgent need for military forces convinced the king to grant the Zaporozhians *de jure* privileges by enrolling a part of them in official registers.[56] At first these registered Cossacks numbered in the hundreds; by the seventeenth century, there were six to eight thousand government-paid soldiers divided into regiments. Their numbers swelled in time of war to tens of thousands of men who followed the Cossack way of life, but who were not fortunate enough to attain the status that the official register conferred. Although the government urgently needed the large armies the Zaporozhians fielded in wartime, it resisted Cossack demands that the quota for the register be increased. During peacetime, government insistence on limiting the register created a division between the favored, recognized Cossacks and those who considered themselves Cossacks but had no government sanction. Those who were excluded from the register realized that war was the only way to gain recognition, and the Sich provided a rallying point for these elements.[57]

The Zaporozhian army posed a number of problems for the government. Although the registered Cossacks called themselves the Zaporozhian Army of His Royal Majesty, they often followed their own policies toward neighboring states, and elected their own officers, or *starshyna,* and commander, or hetman.[58] The king only had the power of confirmation, and the Commonwealth was hampered in dealing with them by the turbulent nature of Cossack politics. The hetman and officers had almost complete authority over the Zaporozhian army during campaigns, but in peacetime a General Assembly, or *Viis'kova Rada,* could depose them at will. Hetmans' administrations were therefore usually short-lived and often ended in bloodshed. The Commonwealth's authorities could manipulate and influence Cossack politics, but the Cossack leadership's dependence on the rank-and-file made for instability in Cossack affairs.[59]

The Commonwealth's difficulties with the Cossacks were exacerbated by the intensive colonization of the Dnieper basin lands and the accumulation of large estates by nobles and magnates there. The Western European demand for Commonwealth grain in the sixteenth century had led to the rapid growth of large-scale farming in the Vistula basin, including the Ruthenian palatinate and parts of Volhynia. Toward the end of the century, pressure for land, the opening up of the area to nobles from the Kingdom, and better security on the frontier made possible the rapid colonization of the Dnieper basin. The established nobles of these territories, the predominantly Ruthenian nobles of Volhynia, and the nobles of the other palatinates of the Kingdom all took part in a scramble for land and subjects. By the seventeenth century, grain, oxen and potash from Dnieper Ukraine had become marketable commodities and nobles who could secure major land grants from the king and appointments to administer royal castles and lands acquired great wealth. In the unsettled conditions of the new frontier, might often prevailed over right, especially since land claims in this area were often poorly documented and violent conflicts between claimants were common. A noble with enough influence at court to obtain land grants and the power to retain control of lands that he claimed could rapidly acquire vast territories. Large landowning thus became possible on a scale unknown in Poland proper or in the western Ukrainian lands. Soon, an oligarchy of magnates arose from the fortunes made in the east.[60]

Profits stemmed largely from payment in kind, millers' fees, alcohol monopolies, and tax farming. The large landholders would often put their estates and rights in the hands of an agent, or tax farmer, who would return a certain percentage of the revenues to them. The increasing Jewish population in the Kingdom provided settlers for landlords who wished to take advantage of Jewish expertise as estate managers or urban dwellers. The economic growth led to growth in population of older royal cities throughout the area, and landlords formed numerous new private cities, most of which were a combination of agricultural, commercial and artisan centers. Prosperity also made this area attractive to peasants from the Ruthenian palatinate, Volhynia, Belorussia, and the Polish palatinates, so the rural population grew rapidly. Although some came as a result of colonization sponsored by the landlords, more were enticed there by promises of freedom from taxes and labor dues for substantial periods of time; thus subsequent attempts to impose obligations that would have been considered light in the Ruthenian palatinate and Volhynia were strongly resented.[61]

The Cossack way of life was both threatened and threatening in this new environment. The nobles, in particular the magnates, whether Ukrainian and Orthodox or Polish and Catholic, viewed the Cossacks as a hindrance to the new order. They desired to curb their privileges and reduce their numbers. The Cossack alternative to peasant life prevented the nobility from increasing the peasant corvée to a level equal to that in the western palatinates. The nobility wished to acquire a monopoly over land ownership and other privileges, such as the distilling and sale of alcohol, comparable to those enjoyed in the other palatinates of the Kingdom, and thus to deprive the Cossacks of these rights. Cossack and peasant discontent against the administration, nobility, and royal troops resulted in a series of rebellions in the 1590s, and in 1625, 1630, and 1637–38, which only confirmed the nobles' fear that the Cossacks encouraged rebellion.[62]

Disorder and violence were more pronounced in the eastern palatinates, not only because of the struggle for lands and the Cossack presence, but also because these territories were most exposed to the threat of foreign intervention. Crimean Tatar raids were frequent. Even when the Commonwealth was at peace with the Crimea, the khan was unable to control his subjects and the Crimean economy required both loot and prisoners to sell or ransom. The Commonwealth's authorities often spared the Ukraine by diverting Crimean raids to Muscovy, but the Tatars remained a major threat. Just as the Commonwealth could not control Cossack raids in the Black Sea area, but could occasionally utilize the Zaporozhians for attacks on Crimea and Turkey, so the Ottoman Porte could not fully control the Tatar raids, but could redirect these attacks to suit its foreign policy.[63]

The Tatar and Turkish threat most directly affected the Bratslav palatinate and southern areas of the Kiev palatinate, and the neighboring Podillian and Ruthenian palatinates. Although areas such as the Left Bank of the Kiev palatinate and the Chernihiv lands were relatively safe, they were exposed to danger from Muscovy. In the competition for the thinly settled lands from the Dnieper to Putyvl' and Sevsk, possession and settlement were important factors in shifting the vaguely defined border. Aside from the constant irritants of border incursions and disputes, the Commonwealth's conquest of the Chernihiv and the Smolensk lands, in the early part of the century, provided a constant point of contention between the states. Although Muscovy was on the defensive in the first half of the century, the tsars' claims to the entire inheritance of Kievan Rus' posed a major, if dormant, challenge to the Commonwealth's possession of Kiev and the rest of the Ukraine.[64] A third source of danger was the southeastern, or Moldavian, border. The Bratslav, Podillian, and Ruthenian palatinates were exposed to attacks from the Ottomans, the suzerains of the Moldavian rulers. The competition between the Commonwealth and the Porte for influence in Moldavia was a constant source of tension.[65]

To provide for the defense of the Ukraine, the Kingdom's small standing army was permanently stationed in the Podillian and Bratslav palatinates. The Crown hetmans of the seventeenth century were all major landowners in the Ukraine and were interested in the area's security. Its inhabitants were intensely concerned with military affairs as well, not only because they sought protection from external foes, but also because the Diet's failure to provide adequate payment and quartering often left them at the mercy of lawless troops. The employment of the standing army against the Zaporozhians during the Cossack rebellions made for particular enmity between those two forces.[66]

In sum, the political and social order of the Polish-Lithuanian Commonwealth faced considerable problems in the Ukrainian lands. The frequent foreign attacks produced a high degree of internal strife. In most of the Ukrainian lands, moreover, the social structure that had evolved over centuries in Poland proper was a recent importation, and one that provided no place for an important group of the Ukrainian populace, the Zaporozhian Cossacks. The political and social conflicts might have been resolved had it not been for overlapping tensions involving religious, cultural, and national issues.

Religious, National, and Cultural Relations in the Ukraine

For the inhabitants of the Commonwealth, and their descendants up to the twentieth century, religion, culture and nationality were frequently intertwined. The association of the Polish nationality and historical tradition with Western Christianity and the Ruthenian-Ukrainian nationality and historical tradition with Eastern Christianity made religion and nationality appear interchangeable; indeed, religion was often a more important factor than language or descent in distinguishing Poles from Ukrainians. Still, it can be demonstrated that distinctions between religion and nationality were drawn even in the seventeenth century. Of course, evidence about attitudes toward religion, nationality, and culture in the early modern period is almost exclusively available from the elite groups, making it almost impossible to discuss the attitudes of the masses. The discussion of "national" factors is particularly problematic since national consciousness and national designations were so amorphous and inchoate. They also occupied such a different position in the world view of early modern men. All too often they have been seen as more well defined and important than they really were by Eastern European historians.[67]

The association of Polish nationality and Western Christianity was the simpler of the two problems, because it was of importance only in the context of Polish-East Slavic relations. So far as most of the other nations of Europe were concerned, Polish adherence to Western Christianity and the Latin rite was not a distinguishing characteristic. In the sixteenth century, Polish Christianity included Protestant groups; only in the course of the seventeenth century did Roman Catholicism become an almost necessary part of Polish identity.[68]

The Ukrainian-Eastern Christian association was stronger and the Rus' church served more fully to define Ruthenian culture and nationality than the Roman Catholic church did for Polish culture and nationality. Christianity came to the Ukraine in its Byzantine form during the Kieven Rus' period; in the seventeenth century, "Greek religion" or "Greek faith" still defined the Ukrainian church and its faith as Eastern Orthodox.[69] However, since Eastern Christianity had been established in the Slavonic rite and identified with the Kievan Rus' ecclesiastic province, in the Ukraine it had a local cultural, historical, and ecclesiastical tradition that defined it as Ruthenian. The term "Rus' faith" was an accepted local variant of the "Greek faith," and even when groups of Eastern Christians united with Rome, their churches continued to be identified as Ruthenian.[70]

The beginnings of the Polish national community and the origins of Polish national consciousness go back to the Middle Ages, but the transformation of a relatively homogeneous medieval Polish state into the multinational "Commonwealth of the Nobility" made for a particularly complex evolution of these phenomena. The terms "nation," "Polish nation," and "Pole" were ambiguous in the seventeenth century. "Pole" could refer to any inhabitant of the Commonwealth, to an inhabitant of the Kingdom of Poland as opposed to the Grand Duchy of Lithuania, or to a member of the nationality which spoke Polish and identified itself with a cultural-historical Polish community. Equally, the word "nation" could refer to the Commonwealth as a whole, to Poland or to Lithuania, to a given nationality or to a region ("the Volhynian nation"). Because the nobility was the Commonwealth's only recognized citizenry, the designations often referred solely to the nobility; "We Poles" frequently meant the noble Polish nation.[71]

For seventeenth-century Ukrainians, the situation was quite different, for there was no Ukrainian-Ruthenian state or political entity to which a national designation was applied. In fact, the East Slavic population of the Ukraine, the Ruthenians, or "Rusyny," were not viewed as entirely distinct from other East Slavs. Seventeenth-century ancestors of the modern Ukrainians, Belorussians and Russians all used variants of the term "Rus'" when referring to themselves. On the other hand, although Ukrainian elite groups were aware of religious, cultural, historical, and even ethnic affinities with Russians, they were also aware that allegiance to different states and to different church jurisdictions, reinforced by cultural, linguistic, and historical differences, made for clear distinctions between them. In significant ways, the Ukrainian-Ruthenians regarded the inhabitants of Muscovy as alien, and they referred to them as "Muscovites."[72]

Both Ukrainians and Belorussians called themselves "Ruthenians" (Rusyny), and referred to themselves collectively as "Rus'." Both employed the same literary languages—Chancery Ruthenian and Church Slavonic. Since the vernacular was rarely used in writing, sharp distinctions between Ukrainian and Belorussian speakers are difficult to make on the basis of written texts. In short, Vilnius, Lviv and Kiev were three centers of one cultural sphere, and churchmen passed freely from Ukrainian to Belorussian ethnic territory, since both were regarded as one cultural-historical-religious entity called Rus'. After the political division in 1569 of Ukrainians and Belorussians between the Grand Duchy and the Kingdom, this sitution began to change, and the process of cultural and political differentiation was intensified. Hence, we can refer to the "Rusyny" of the Kingdom of Poland as Ukrainians and to those of the Grand Duchy of Lithuania as Belorussians. However, it is important to keep in mind the numerous ways in which they still constituted one Ruthenian people.[73]

In the sixteenth century, the word "Rus'" could mean the Orthodox faithful in the Commonwealth, as well as ethnic Ukrainians and Belorussians sharing a common cultural-linguistic-historical heritage. The people called Ruthenians ("Rusyny," "Rusnacy"), or the "Ruthenian nation" wrote in the "Rus' language" and were listed in sixteenth- and seventeenth-century accounts as one of the peoples of the world, alongside Italians, Poles, French, and Muscovites. But "Rus'" was also a geographic term, referring to the Rus' palatinate, to all the Ukrainian lands, or to the Belorussian and Ukrainian lands. The Ruthenian-Ukrainian nobility of the seventeenth century was often viewed as constituting the nation, so that references to "Rus'" and its rights often simply referred to the ethnically Ukrainian (or Belorussian and Ukrainian) nobility professing adherence to the Eastern church, or to the nobles of a geographic Rus'—such as of the Ruthenian palatinate.[74]

Differences in religion and nationality came to have a destabilizing influence in the Ukrainian territories in general, and in the incorporation lands in particular, because of the rapidly weakening position of the Ruthenian Eastern Christian tradition in the late sixteenth century. Although the process had begun before the Union of Lublin, the incorporation hastened it by opening up the Ukrainian lands to inhabitants of the Kingdom of Poland and their cultural and religious institutions. The balance of cultural vitality thus shifted away from the Byzantine-based Orthodox Slavonic culture of the Ukraine, which in the medieval Kievan federation had produced a literature and art that compared favorably with those of the Latin-based Poles, but which now had become sterile through want of state patronage, economic decline, the danger from steppe marauders, the fall of Byzantium itself, and the inherent limitations of Byzantine Slavic culture. Whatever the causes of this decline, and whatever the causes of the rise of the Latin West, the Ukrainians of the sixteenth century had fallen behind culturally. So had their fellow East Slavs, the Muscovites, but unlike the Muscovites, the Ukrainians had to face the new Latin culture without the protecting wall of a state determined to preserve the position of Orthodoxy, the traditional languages, and older cultural forms.[75]

Religious affiliation separated the Ukraine from the Italian and German centers of European culture, just as it united the Poles to Europe. The renewed interest in the Classical world, the foundation of universities and other educational insitutions, Humanism, and the use of the vernacular in literature were transferred to Poland by a Latin West that was also making considerable advances in technology and science, especially military. Taking part more and more in the political and cultural life of the Polish Kingdom, the Ukrainian elite found that their traditional Slavonic-Ruthenian Orthodox culture could not compete and was not of great utility in the Commonwealth.[76]

The Ruthenian Orthodox church found itself unable to deal with the intellectual and institutional challenges of the Protestant and Catholic churches.[77] Even more alarming, it could not find ready sources of support to meet these challenges. Byzantium had transmitted to its East Slavic converts the ideal of a church protected by a true-believing Christian monarch, but for over two centuries Ukrainians and Belorussians had lived under a Catholic monarch.[78] The metropolitan see of Kiev received limited intellectual and financial assistance from other Orthodox churches or states. Its superior, the patriarch of Constantinople, did at times intervene in Kievan affairs (the deposition of Metropolitan Onisyfor Divovych) to preserve Orthodox practices, as did the other Eastern patriarchs.[79] However, the internal problems and corruption of the church of Constantinople and its role as a tool of Ottoman policy made close ties with the patriarch difficult. Contacts with Muscovy and the Russian Orthodox church were impeded by political enmities, and the newly created Muscovite patriarchate (1589) lacked the legitimacy that history lent to the Constantinople patriarchate. The Russian church, isolated from European cultural life, was little prepared to understand the problem of the Commonwealth's Orthodox.[80] The Orthodox rulers of Moldavia provided some financial assistance, but Moldavia was a vassal state of the Ottomans and lacked the power and the resources to shore up the whole Kievan church.[81]

Traditionally, the Ruthenian Orthodox church had depended on its lay patrons. When many of these protectors began to convert, a crisis ensued in the Ruthenian church. By 1596, the internal weakness of the church and pressure from a militant Counter-Reformation Catholicism led most of the Orthodox hierarchy of the Ukraine and Belorussia to accept a local version of the Union of Florence (1439). This Union of Brest provided for the retention of Church Slavonic services, married clergy, communion in two kinds, the Julian calendar, and a separate, autonomous administrative structure. The Kievan metropolitan was required to submit to the Roman pope, rather than to the patriarch of Constantinople, in securing confirmation of office and to accept Catholic teaching on the traditional points of theological difference. The Polish-Lithuanian government declared the Union of Brest binding on all Eastern Christians in the Commonwealth. However, the hope that the Uniate solution would resolve the crisis in the Ruthenian church proved ill-founded.[82]

The reaction to the Union by some members of the Orthodox hierarchy and by segments of the nobility, the Zaporozhian Cossacks, the burghers, and the peasantry resulted in a bitter struggle in the first decades of the seventeenth century that partially restored the position of the Orthodox church. In 1620, an "illegal" Orthodox hierarchy was consecrated; in 1632 official recognition was granted by the government to the church. Despite the ability of the Orthodox faction to hold its own in the struggle with the Uniates, it never managed to abolish the union.[83]

The challenges of the Reformation and Counter-Reformation and the polemics over the Union of Brest sparked a revival among Ruthenians that centered on church affairs, but also penetrated other cultural and intellectual spheres. It originated among those strata longest exposed to the Latin challenge—the burghers of Lviv, Vilnius and other towns. The formation of Orthodox brotherhoods, schools and printing presses, starting in the 1580s, provided the bases for an Orthodox response.[84] At the same time, a number of Orthodox nobles followed the example of their Protestant and Catholic peers and founded schools and printing presses. The new centers of learning, which increased rapidly in number in the early seventeenth century, combined study of traditional aspects of Ukrainian culture, such as Slavonic and Greek, with Polish and Latin studies.[85] Although naturally drawn to Greek intellectuals and traditions, which were in any case part of the pan-European currents of Humanism and the Renaissance, the Orthodox found that Greek could not substitute for Europe's preeminent scholarly tongue, Latin; thus they had to overcome their distaste for the Latin West to find models for their schools.[86]

The most imposing of these new Orthodox schools was the collegium founded in Kiev in 1632, which was modeled on Jesuit institutions. The collegium drew on the revival of Orthodox and Slavonic learning and publishing that dated to the 1570s, and on the educational work of the Kiev Caves monastery and of the Brotherhood of the Epiphany in the 1610s and 1620s. Its founding and program was chiefly due to Peter Mohyla (Movila) archimandrite of the Caves monastery (from 1627) and metropolitan of Kiev (from 1633). Son of a hospodar of Moldavia, Mohyla combined loyalty to the Orthodox tradition, close contacts with the magnates of the Commonwealth, and a knowledge of Latin learning and culture. He made Kiev the major center of Orthodox learning and publication in the 1630s and 1640s, largely by adapting Latin cultural models.[87]

Orthodox efforts were paralleled by a Uniate response, which, if less vigorous, could at least depend on the intellectual and financial support of Rome. But even more important, Roman Catholic and later Uniate attacks on the Orthodox church provoked an intellectual polemic. While its level could not compare with that raging between Catholics and Protestants, it did incite church leaders to codify and explain their faith and to provide proofs from the histories of the Eastern church and of the Ruthenians to support their positions.[88]

The Orthodox revival and the Uniate-Orthodox polemic reformed the Eastern church, promoted philological studies, and increased awareness of the Ruthenians' history and traditions. However, both its goals and successes were relatively limited. Unlike the Reformation in the Western church, the Orthodox revival gave little impetus for the growth of secular learning or for the development of national cultures and vernacular languages. Orthodox intellectuals were more interested in securing a guaranteed place for the Orthodox church in the new cultural and political climate of the Commonwealth than in reversing the trend toward the use of Latin and Polish. They wanted to encourage the production of liturgical works, grammars, primers, and dictionaries of Slavonic as a way of raising the church's prestige. Although their efforts improved considerably the quality of the Slavonic used by both the Orthodox and the Uniates, the extent of the use of Slavonic remained relatively circumscribed. Moreover, if a number of scholarly, poetic, and polemical works appeared in "Ruthenian"—a vernacular adaptation of the chancery language—its use was never considered truly legitimate; the use of the vernacular was, in fact, discouraged. By the 1630s, when one wanted to reach large audiences, Polish was the language to use, even for Orthodox polemical works.[89]

The reforming of the Ruthenian church had only limited success in preserving its own integrity and that of the Ruthenian people. The religious-cultural-historical community of Rus' had been gravely weakened. Its language had fallen into disuse, replaced by Polish. Throughout its territory, newly arrived nobles from ethnic Poland held positions of power and influence, while its numbers had been diminished by conversions to Catholicism. The most striking failure had been the inability to win back to their ancestral faith Ruthenian nobles who had converted to Protestantism or Catholicism or to put an end to new conversions. In the Commonwealth of the Nobility, neither the Ruthenian church nor the Ruthenian "nation" could be secure without an active noble component.

The Ruthenian Nobility: Acculturation and Assimilation

The Ruthenian people and the Ukrainian territories had several weaknesses that militated against their separate identity in the Commonwealth. The Ruthenians were not, like the Armenians or Jews of the Commonwealth, a virtually autonomous estate governed by internal community laws and administration. The Ukrainian lands did not constitute a unified separate political entity like the Grand Duchy of Lithuania. The major distinguishing characteristics of the Ruthenians, their language, culture, and church, faced grave difficulties in competition with Polish culture and the Western churches. The preservation of Ruthenians in the Commonwealth as anything more than a plebeian linguistic community was in question, and the outcome depended on the actions and attitudes of their nobility.

Why did the Ukrainian nobility experience such a rapid abandonment of its historical-cultural-religious community in the last decades of the sixteenth and first half of the seventeenth centuries?[90] Other early modern elites under the political-cultural hegemony of a state or sovereign with a different religion and culture resisted assimilation for decades, even centuries. Many Hungarian nobles of the seventeenth and eighteenth centuries tenaciously clung to their political traditions, and, in substantial numbers, to the Reformed faith, in the face of Habsburg and Catholic assimilatory pressures. Many Bohemian nobles showed a loyalty to the Czech culture and language, the Protestant faith, and

Bohemian political traditions which only the defeat at White Mountain and the destruction of the old nobility could root out. The gradual French and Catholic penetration of Alsace in the seventeenth and eighteenth centuries stands in marked contrast to the events which occurred in the Ukraine in the sixteenth and seventeenth centuries. In analyzing the causes of assimilation, one must turn to three factors—the policy of the Commonwealth's government and institutions, the pressure of Polish society, and the internal composition and strength of the Ukrainian Eastern Christian cultural entity.

First, to what degree was pressure exerted by the government of the Commonwealth on the Ukrainian upper classes? Although religion and national culture are almost inextricable in defining Ruthenian-Ukrainian identity in relation to Poland and Polish identity, it seems clear that the Ruthenians had experienced discrimination chiefly on religious grounds. On issues such as language, the government readily complied with the request of the Ukrainian nobility of the incorporation lands that royal decrees be issued in "Ruthenian." Thus, infractions appear largely due to bureaucratic difficulties in using an unknown script, not to a policy of Polonization.[91] In the early centuries of Polish rule in the Ruthenian palatinate, there had been sporadic religious intolerance and persecution, and after the official conversion of the Lithuanian royal family to Roman Catholicism in the late fourteenth century, examples of marked discrimination against the Orthodox in the distribution of high offices had occurred in the Grand Duchy. By the sixteenth century, however, discrimination was rare in either realm, and full religious freedom seemed assured by the time of the Union of Lublin. The major disability of the Orthodox church, and of the nobles who aspired to its sees, was that Orthodox bishops, unlike their Catholic counterparts, did not sit in the Senate. In contrast to the nobles, who suffered little discrimination, Ruthenian burghers were denied their rights by urban governments controlled by Roman Catholics.[92]

Discrimination against Orthodox nobles did increase with the accession to the throne of the Counter-Reformation Catholic Zygmunt III in 1587, since the king favored Catholic nobles in granting posts. Open persecution came only with the Union of Brest, after which the king and the Diet viewed the Orthodox church as illegal. The struggles accompanying the restoration of Orthodox rights led the Orthodox nobles to protest that they suffered more religious discrimination in the Commonwealth than did the Orthodox Greeks in the Ottoman Empire. Even after the compromise of 1632 and the legalization of the Orthodox hierarchy, the Commonwealth's government was unable, or unwilling, to stop entirely discrimination against the Orthodox. Those Ruthenians who accepted the union also faced some discrimination, since the Uniate church was never granted the full privileges of the Roman Catholic, and its bishops did not sit in the Senate.[93]

It would be a mistake to overemphasize the role of governmental or official persecution or discrimination, however. Nobiliary liberty and governmental decentralization ensured that the Orthodox nobles were able to practice their faith, to retain many church buildings, and to protect Orthodox commoners even after the proclamation of the union. It must be remembered that conversions of Ukrainian nobles from Orthodoxy to either Roman Catholicism or to the various Protestant denominations were already common before the Union of Brest. Indeed, the major impetus for the union came not from the government, but from the Orthodox hierarchy itself, from Rome and from members of Catholic religious orders, notably the great Jesuit Piotr Skarga.

The assimilation of the Ruthenian nobles also resulted from their closer integration into the Commonwealth. Polonization was stimulated by the growing numbers of Polish nobles from the Kingdom who immigrated to the Ruthenian lands. Especially in the incorporation lands, the Ukrainian nobles' desire to participate fully in the wider political life of the Kingdom and to associate with Polish nobles hastened assimilation. In addition to these pressures for assimilation that were inherent in any integration of one elite into another, more overt pressures began to appear as a result of the Counter-Reformation and the decline of religious tolerance. Beginning in the 1570s, largely as a part of the attempt to convert Rus' to Catholicism, attacks against various aspects of the traditional culture of the Ukraine became common. Not only were the Orthodox church's dogmatic differences with Catholicism held up as errors, but also the Ruthenian Orthodox clergy were described as "barbarous" and the Ruthenian and Slavonic languages as incapable of conveying learning. The charge of Ruthenian cultural inferiority permeated the Catholic polemical literature. Those Polish nobles who were influenced by this thinking came to look down on Ruthenians in general, and became particularly intolerant of those Ruthenian Orthodox nobles who insisted on adhering to their "inferior" faith and by so doing involving the Commonwealth in endless controversy.[94]

The pressure of the government and of Polish society would have hardly been sufficient to effect the rapid assimilation had it not been for the weaknesses of the Ukrainian Eastern Christian tradition. The deficiencies in religious and cultural affairs have already been discussed. Just as important for the nobility were the political and institutional weaknesses of the Ukrainian legacy. Before Polish and Lithuanian rule was introduced, the Ukrainian elites did not constitute a political nation in the sense that the Polish, Bohemian or Hungarian nobilities did. Therefore, the political traditions of Kievan Rus' and Galicia-Volhynia did not live on in a Ukrainian political nation that saw itself as an embodiment of an abstract polity like the "Crown of St. Stephen" or the "Crown of St. Wenceslaus." The attractiveness of the Polish political system to the Ukrainian nobility, especially the privileges it granted, explains the lack of opposition to the Union of Lublin's incorporation of the Volhynian, Bratslav, and Kievan palatinates. Although further privileges were sought with respect to the use of language, law, and customs, demands for a separate Rus' polity were not made. On the contrary, the Ukrainian elite was interested in full participation in the nobility's Commonwealth.[95]

In the seventeenth century, numerous Ruthenian nobles in the Ukraine went through the process of assimilation in stages. Generally, they first became members of the Polish political nation; then, they adopted the language, culture, and life style of the Polish nobility; later, they converted to Catholicism or Protestantism; finally, they lost all feelings of separateness from the nobles of the Polish territories or perception that they had once belonged to a different Ruthenian tradition. In the first half of the century, however, total assimilation was rare. Rather, Ruthenian nobles were in a process of acculturation, and in the course of that process new patterns in Ruthenian culture, political thought, and consciousness emerged.[96]

Each generation produced Ruthenian nobles who sought to preserve and develop elements of their traditional culture. Above all, the loyalty of many nobles to the Orthodox church ensured that they would pay attention to the "Ruthenian question." The increasing number of defections among the great princes and wealthy nobles only strengthened the feeling of crisis among those who remained. Church leaders lamented the losses and reminded those who remained of their Ruthenian roots. In this way the Orthodox revival brought new awareness of Ruthenian historical and cultural traditions to nobles who were called upon to defend the church.[97]

Considerable Ruthenian intellectual ferment resulted from the revival of Slavonic, the founding of Orthodox schools, and the adaptation of new art and literary forms, but by that time defections from the ranks of the Ukrainian elite had already taken place. The deprecatory charges made in Polish Catholic polemical literature about the Eastern church were thus affirmed in the action of the converts. Yet attributing the elite's rapid assimilation to the inherent vulnerability of the Rus' cultural tradition and describing the response as limited do not imply that the Rus' nobles did not see what was happening. Many endured a crisis made all the worse by their inability to cope with it. Loyalty and treason were potent concepts even then, and converts were labeled renegades and traitors.[98]

As many of their number converted to the new faith and adopted the new identity, other nobles stoutly defended the old: the Rus' church, the Ruthenian language with its cultural and educational institutions, and their own rights to royal appointments. Yet, as the century wore on, the defenders of Rus' also adopted Polish cultural, linguistic, and social norms, even as they continued in their self-appointed role as the representatives of, indeed as the entirety of, the Ruthenian "nation." Their inability to respond effectively allowed other groups, such as Cossacks and burghers, to play a part in the defense of Rus'. In a society strictly stratified according to social order, the Orthodox brotherhoods were a rare form of social organization, linking nobles, clergymen, Cossacks, and burghers in a common cause. The prominent role of the Cossacks and burghers in the Ruthenian community challenged the nobles' concept of themselves as the sole representatives of the Rus' faith and nation.[99]

A widespread perception of cultural crisis and persecution was a crucial factor governing relations between the Ukrainian lands and the Commonwealth. Between 1569 and 1648, conflicting class, religious, national, and state loyalties made the position of the Ruthenian nobles particularly difficult. On the one hand, the opportunity to participate in the Commonwealth's politics and institutions and to make suitable marriages for their children argued strongly for assimilation, while the increasing influence of the Counter-Reformation and the Jesuit order on the Catholic nobility and educational system made loyalty to Orthodoxy and maintenance of a separate identity more and more difficult. On the other hand, the Orthodox church worked hard to retain the nobles' loyalty, and consequently developed a new Ruthenian culture and a new Ruthenian identity. Since in the end neither the government nor the Catholic church could convert all the Ruthenian nobles, much less the Cossacks and burghers, a program of religious compromise became necessary. A brilliant career might be made by a Ruthenian noble who could marshal the forces of dissent behind him and offer the government a solution to its predicaments in the Ukraine.

Chapter 2

The Formative Years (1600–1632)

Only in exceptional cases do we have detailed information on the early lives of the sons of the most prominent magnate houses of the Commonwealth. The formative years of men of more modest descent were even less likely to be mentioned by their contemporaries or to leave traces in the fragmentary records that have come down to our time. True to this pattern, the sources offer only sparse facts about Adam Kysil's first three decades. Frequently we are provided these facts only by panegyrists who included them in their praises to him after he had risen to prominence in the 1630s and 1640s.

In general, the limited documentary evidence and the few personal statements by Kysil do not provide us with evidence that can substantially increase our understanding of his environment and of the patterns of life of his stratum of the nobility. Instead, we must turn to what is known about nobiliary lives and careers in the early seventeenth century in order to provide a framework for the scanty information about his early life.

In the decentralized Commonwealth, it was the palatinate, or more specifically, the nobiliary society of the palatinate, that constituted the political, cultural, and social milieu of a young noble. A noble's status was determined by the prominence of his paternal family, the network of marital connections in the few preceding generations, his father's career, and the share of family possessions that he inherited. In a multireligious society, his career patterns and social circles were also influenced by his ancestral faith and his decision on whether or not he should convert to another faith. In the parliamentary and litigious society of the Commonwealth, a noble's success often depended on his native intellectual abilities and his educational preparation. Benevolent patrons among the magnates and middle nobles were necessary for rapid advancement. Military exploits were sure ways to gain both fame and fortune as well as royal favor. Finally, a good marriage brought economic benefits and defined a new geographic and social sphere of activity for a young noble. The ideal formula for a young noble's rise to magnate status was for him to become a leader among fellow-nobles while, at the same time, a favored servitor of the monarch. Although we cannot penetrate the mind of Kysil and the intricacies of his activities during his formative years, we can follow the steps and decisions by which he emerged to prominence by the 1630s.

Volhynia at the Time of Kysil's Birth

Volhynia was the land of Kysil's family seat, birth, childhood and early career. In later years he obtained offices and estates in other palatinates, but Volhynia and the Volhynian nobility continued to occupy a position of importance in his activities. Although he later made his fortune in the newly colonized Chernihiv palatinate, he used his resources to expand his estates in his native Volhynia. Volhynian nobles elected him to Diets in the 1620s and 1630s and provided him with political allies and clients in the 1640s and 1650s. At the end of his career, with his great estates in the east lost to the Cossack rebels, Volhynia provided him with sustenance and a final resting place.

Around 1600, the nobility of the Volhynian palatinate differed significantly from that of the other Ukrainian lands. The palatinate's historical traditions, social structure and institutions allowed it to exert a tremendous influence on Ruthenian culture, the Orthodox church, and the political life of the lands incorporated at the Union of Lublin. The great Volhynian families also played a major role in the Commonwealth's government and hastened the process of the rise of the magnate stratum to a position of dominance in the Kingdom of Poland.

Volhynia's critical role among Ruthenian territories derived from its position as a land that had undergone no major disruptions since the thirteenth century.[1] It had been spared the ravages of the more eastern and southern Ukrainian lands. Unlike the Ruthenian, Belz, and Podillian palatinates, it had not been assimilated into the Polish body politic and cultural sphere. Unlike the amalgamation of the Belorussian lands, the integration of the Volhynian principality and Volhynian society into the Grand Duchy of Lithuania had been to a considerable degree superficial. Although the Volhynian princes had been defeated in their support of the Lithuanian Prince Švitrigaila against King-Grand Duke Władysław-Jogaila in the 1430s and the principality had been transformed into a Lithuanian province in the middle of the century, local administrative and legal traditions remained strong.[2] The protracted rivalry between Lithuania and Poland over Volhynia in the fourteenth and fifteenth centuries, the influence on Volhynia of neighboring Polish Ukrainian lands, and the need to defend the palatinate from Tatar incursions, resulted in its society evolving differently from those of the other lands of the Grand Duchy. Vilnius was distant, and the Orthodox Volhynian great lords were deprived of the major offices and hence not well integrated into the state's elite, which was primarily Lithuanian and Roman Catholic.

The small influence of the grand ducal court and the structure of Volhynian society were evident in Volhynia's landholding patterns.[3] The palatinate contained numerous large, compact estates held by princes descended from the Rus' Rurik or Lithuanian Gedimin dynasties. The Ostroz'kyi, Korets'kyi, and Zbarazhs'kyi holdings amounted to separate principalities, and the great princely families had their own feudal tenants and servitors. Beneath the level of the wealthy princes were the poorer princely families and the wealthier descendants of old boiar families. The privileged class's lower orders included the boiars who had remained small landholders and various categories of feudal servitors, but these groups were a smaller part of the population than in the Belorussian or Lithuanian lands. The grand duke had only small landholdings. Those of the Orthodox church were substantial, but not equal in extent to even one of the major princely domains.[4]

Despite the grand duke's official espousal of Catholicism in the fourteenth century and the restriction of certain privileges to Catholic nobles, the Volhynian elite was almost entirely Orthodox until the middle of the sixteenth century. Orthodox bishoprics existed in Volodymyr and Luts'k, and Volhynia contained such important monasteries as Zhydychyn, Dubno, Pochaïv, and Derman.[5] The great monasteries of Volhynia were centers of Orthodox religious and manuscript culture. Throughout the sixteenth and early seventeenth centuries, the princely and noble families of Volhynia established numerous monastic foundations, and their patronage gave them considerable influence in church affairs. High church positions were the preserve of the nobility, and initiation of a layman into monastic orders before a high office was conferred upon him became a common practice.[6]

Although some Polish and Roman Catholic influence had penetrated Volhynia before the Union of Lublin, when it was incorporated into the Kingdom of Poland, Volhynia was a stable land of ethnically homogeneous population and social norms. Just before the union, the middle and lower orders of the elite were granted szlachta status which gave them legal equality with the princes. The stability of Volhynian ways seemed to be ensured by privileges that guaranteed the status of the Ruthenian language, promised full rights to Orthodox believers, and provided for separate chancery books. The princely families were also allowed to retain their titles.[7]

Landholding patterns changed little after 1569, and large princely holdings continued to be the rule. The integration of the Volhynian palatinate into the Baltic grain trade increased the value of land and brought new prosperity to the landowning classes. After the restraints against ownership by inhabitants of the Kingdom were abolished, intermarriage, the extinction of princely families, and purchase placed some estates in the hands of families from Great and Little Poland.[8] In addition, Polish petty nobles leased properties from the estates of the great magnates, or were granted use of them for services rendered.[9] The process was gradual, however, partly because in contrast to the Kiev and Bratslav palatinates, the Crown held few lands for distribution in Volhynia, and partly because the great princely families retained their position simply by dint of the power that accrues to great wealth.[10] Their status as magnates guaranteed them influence far beyond Volhynia. Although the building of massive estate-empires in the Kievan and Bratslav palatinates brought forth new magnates whose wealth rivaled that of the richest Volhynian princes, a number of Volhynian princes, such as the Vyshnevets'kyi family, also managed to extend their influence and estates into those territories. By the early seventeenth century, the wealthiest of these princely families were well integrated into a magnate group of the wealthiest Little Polish, Great Polish, and Lithuanian families, but their landholdings and offices were still predominantly in Volhynia or in the Kiev and Bratslav palatinates.

The other Volhynian privileged orders—princely, boiar, and former servitors—took on the ethos and customs of the Polish nobility. The great prince-magnates stood at the head of the order, yet princely titles did not grant special status. The titles were still prized, but, in practice, princely families with little money melded into the szlachta together with the old boiar families and the lower serving orders. The Volhynian nobility that was formed in 1569 comprised an articulate political class, with strong regional loyalty.[11] Deference to the ways of the past ensured that the princes and noble families long resident in the palatinate would retain a dominant position. It is this deference that also explains the dietine's defense of Orthodoxy even after the major princely families had converted to Catholicism, a number of other Volhynian noble families had become Catholic, Calvinist, or Antitrinitarian, and numerous Polish Roman Catholic nobles had arrived in the area.[12]

The increase in Catholic and Polish influence from the outside was at first gradual, but it quickened after 1569. Members of the Sangushko (Sanguszko), Chartorys'kyi (Czartoryski), Korets'kyi (Korecki), Zbaraz'kyi (Zbarazki), and Zaslavs'kyi (Zasławski) families had all converted to Catholicism by the 1620s or 1630s.[13] These defections represented not only the loss of a patron to the Orthodox Church, but a corresponding gain to the Roman Catholic Church. Consequently the network of Roman Catholic parishes and lands increased rapidly.[14] Although no conversions of great lords to Protestantism can be compared in importance to that of the Radziwiłłs of Lithuania, noble families as notable as the Chaplych-Shpanivs'kyi, Ivanyts'kyi, Seniuta, and Hois'kyi were sympathizers or converts to Reformed sects, particularly Antitrinitarianism.[15] The religious conversions occurred at a time when use of Ruthenian letters was on the wane, while Polish and Latin were increasing in usage.[16]

Volhynia played a crucial role in the initial stages of the revival of Orthodox learning and the controversy over the Union of Brest. Although Roman Catholic and Protestant institutions and education did not begin to expand in Volhynia until after 1600, the impact of Volhynian youths' education in institutions in other areas of the Commonwealth and abroad was already apparent at the time of the Union of Lublin in 1569.[17] These outside influences encouraged conversions to the Catholic and Protestant faiths and increased the use of Latin and Polish, but they also called forth a reaction that renewed Orthodox Slavonic culture. The most important of the Volhynian princes, Konstantyn Konstantynovych Ostroz'kyi, supported a program of Orthodox Slavonic printing, which produced such major achievements as the Ostroh Bible of 1581. He also founded a Greco-Slavonic-Latin academy in Ostroh.[18] Substantial activity was initiated by the brotherhoods of Vilnius and Lviv, great urban intellectual centers the likes of which were unknown in Volhynia, but neither Lviv's Ruthenian palatinate nor the Belorussian lands around Vilnius could boast patrons who could rival the Ostroz'kyis' wealth.[19] Backed by the phenomenal Ostroz'kyi resources, the Ostroh academy and press became the nucleus of a cultural center that drew talent from throughout the Ukraine and Belorussia and the wider Orthodox world. It laid the groundwork for the work of the next generation of Orthodox cultural leaders in Lviv, Kiev, and Vilnius.

It was in Volhynia that the first struggles over the Union of Brest were fought. Prince Ostroz'kyi's power was also crucial in defeating the terms of the Union of Brest. Ostroz'kyi was far from being an Orthodox fanatic. He had even been favorably disposed to the idea of a church union, but when the two Volhynian bishops, Ipatii Potii and Kyrylo Terlets'kyi, in conjunction with the Metropolitan Mykhailo Rohoza and other members of the hierarchy, negotiated a union of the Kievan ecclesiastical province with Rome, Ostroz'kyi objected to any union in which the patriarchate of Constantinople did not take part. It is indicative of the position of the laity in the Orthodox church of Volhynia and of the power of the Volhynian magnate that the church hierarchy was ineffective in imposing its will, even though it was supported by the monarch. Ostroz'kyi's campaign against the union rallied the bishops of Lviv and Przemyśl, the urban brotherhoods, and segments of the nobility against it.[20]

By 1600, controversy between Orthodox and Uniates raged throughout Volhynia, but when Ostroz'kyi died in 1608, it was clear that the Orthodox church had survived.[21] It retained a substantial following, a significant number of churches and monasteries, and powerful backing among the nobles and burghers. However, the adherence of the majority of the hierarchy, led by the able Bishop Ipatii Potii, to the union, and the determined support of Zygmunt III, the papacy, and staunch Catholics assured that the division of the eastern church into Orthodox and Uniate faithful would continue.[22]

The death of Ostroz'kyi signified the beginning of a new phase. The Ostroh academy and the press had already declined; and after the prince's death, Ostroh ceased to be an Orthodox cultural center. His children, following their mother's faith, were Roman Catholics, so his death brought an end to magnate support of Orthodoxy in Volhynia.[23] The Orthodox church there instead had to depend on the less wealthy princes, such as the Chetvertyns'kyi and Puzyna families, on substantial landholders, such as the Hulevych and Drevyns'kyi families, and on the Luts'k brotherhood.[24] Although conversions to both Catholicism and Protestantism continued, the Orthodox nobles retained the support of the Volhynian dietine, and their activities in the Diet were crucial to restoring the position of the Orthodox church.[25]

In the thirty years that followed the Union of Lublin, the religious homogeneity of the palatinate disintegrated. Many Polish families settled in the area. Institutions of higher education had been established and printing had been introduced. Although the Orthodox pioneered these innovations, they acted in response to Polish, Catholic, and Protestant stimuli. Western Christian educational institutions as well as Latin and Polish printing soon spread into Volhynia. Polish had come to replace Ruthenian in public life; and the Eastern church faithful had embarked on a bitter internecine struggle. Compared to the Volhynia of 1550, the Volhynia of 1600 was a complex and divided society, fraught with numerous controversies and tensions.

The privileges of the Polish nobility had long since taken hold and by 1600, middle and lesser nobles viewed the rights of the Polish nobility to be their birthright as citizens of the Commonwealth. In fact, the power of the entire Volhynian nobility in some ways was more pervasive than that of the nobility in Polish palatinates and other Ukrainian lands. No major urban center competed for commercial rights or intellectual leadership, and royal landholdings were limited. The Orthodox nobility controlled their church and selected its leadership, a practice unknown to Roman Catholicism. Still, real power remained in the hands of the stratum of great landholders and magnates.

The Kysil Family

In the Commonwealth, extended families served as political factions, economic units, and barometers of social status.[26] Loyalty to family members and the duty to further a family's interests could supersede the most intense disagreements over religion and politics.[27] The inheritance system, which discouraged alienation of lands, favored male descendants of male lines, but provided for inheritance by all offspring, thus ensuring that descendants of a common ancestor had long-term financial dealings and frequently lived in close proximity with one another.[28] Each family emphasized the antiquity of its line, the high status of the families with which it had intermarried, and the glorious deeds of its ancestors. The cult of family honor united nobles who bore the same family name even when they were only distantly related or did not live nearby. Feelings of solidarity even existed among members of heraldic groupings. It was customary for numerous families to use the same coat of arms, thus creating heraldic clans and bonds.[29] The heraldic tradition had even encouraged unity between the Polish and Lithuanian elites, when at the Union of Horodlo in 1413, Polish families had conferred their coats of arms on Catholic counterparts in the Grand Duchy. Heraldic and genealogical studies flourished among nobles dedicated to the glorification of their lineage. In the seventeenth century, the mania for ancient lineages reached its height, and the creation of myths of descent of nobles families from classical heroes, or Roman and medieval grandees, was widespread.[30]

The Kysils were a family of Ruthenian boiars whose residence in the Volhynian land can be documented from the end of the fifteenth century and whose reliable family tradition extends to its beginning.[31] Their family seats were the villages of Dorohynychi and Nyzkynychi in the northwest corner of Volodymyr county near the Buh River. This area had the largest percentage of small- and middle-ranking landholders, descendants of ancient boiar families, in the palatinate.[32] Like many Orthodox families in the incorporation lands, the Kysils did not belong to one of the major heraldic families and had their own device, a tent surmounted by a cross and three towers.[33]

In the early sixteenth century, Adam's great-grandfather Tymofei, or

Tykhno, played a prominent role in Volhynian society. In a long career, he served as a deputy for the Ostroz'kyi family and an arbitrator on numerous commissions to resolve local disputes. Finally, he was elected judge of the local nobility.[34] Tykhno appears to have been a man of considerable means, and in addition to the villages of Nyzkynychi and Dorohynychi, he gained title, or reaffirmed prior claims to a large tract of land known as the "Kysilivshchyna" in the Ovruch area of the Kiev palatinate, an area that may well have been the ancient seat of the family. Maryna Kysilivna, who married Prince Ivan Fedorovych Chartorys'kyi, was probably Tykhno's daughter.[35] Seventeenth-century genealogies claimed that the Kysils had intermarried in the fifteenth century with the Chetvertyns'kyi and Nemyrych families, but the Chartorys'kyi link is positive proof of the influential position of the Kysil family in Volhynian society.

The Kysil family appears to have undergone a decline in relative wealth at the end of the sixteenth century. The proliferation of the family and consequent pressure on the family estates resulted in one of Tykhno's sons migrating to the Grand Duchy of Lithuania soon after the Lublin Union and in the division of Nyzkynychi and Dorohynychi.[36] Kysil's father, Hryhorii (dc. 1616–21), inherited the village of Nyzkynychi from his father Hnevosh, but only the leasing of the nearby villages of Tyshkovychi and Polupanshchyna, owned by the Orthodox bishopric, could have possibly provided sufficient land and peasants to allow his estate to function as a small manor.[37] The family's economic position took a definite turn for the worse in 1604, when the Kysils lost a court case to the Butovych and Lozka families over claims to the Kysilivshchyna tract.[38]

Despite the relative decline of the family fortunes, Hryhorii was prominent in Volodymyr county, where he served as the associate county judge.[39] His wife and Adam's mother (d.c. 1650) was from the relatively well-off Ivanyts'kyi family, who were later to provide substantial support for Antitrinitarianism in Volhynia.[40] Despite Hryhorii's signature on documents about the Union of Brest, and despite Teodora Ivanyts'ka Kysil's intriguing connection with the Antitrinitarian movement, information on the religious attitudes of Kysil's parents is scanty. Adam Kysil's frequent comments that he was born into the Orthodox faith of his forefathers indicate that both parents were Orthodox; furthermore, his mother ended her life in an Orthodox convent.[41] After 1596, however, Hryhorii Kysil, whose tenancy to Tyshkovychi depended on the bishop of Volodymyr, might well have supported the union, at least for a time.

Hryhorii and Teodora had three sons: Adam, the eldest (born in

1600), Mykola, and Ianush; only the first two reached adulthood.[42] Hryhorii also had a daughter, Teodora, who may have been the issue of an earlier marriage, since she reached maturity considerably before the beginning of the century and Hryhorii is known to have entered into a marriage contract in 1570. Teodora married a member of the Orans'kyi family and was the mother of Pakhomii Orans'kyi, a Uniate bishop and polemicist.[43]

Thus, Adam Kysil came from a family that, while not wealthy, had long been influential in the palatinate. The Kysils were intermarried with numerous indigenous Volhynian noble families such as the Ivanyts'kyi, Svishchivs'kyi, and Orans'kyi. A generation before they had married into the Chartorys'kyis and the Belorussian Tryznas and they claimed to descend from alliances with the Chetvertyns'kyis and Nemyryches.[44] Their circle was exclusively Ukrainian-Belorussian and Eastern Christian, and their tenancy of Tyshkovychi was another indication of their connections with the Orthodox church. At the time of Kysil's birth, Hryhorii was a judicial functionary who kept official records in Ruthenian, even though the documents he registered were often in Polish. The conservative nature of the Kysil family's milieu is evident even in the choice of alphabet for its signatures. At a time when most Volhynian nobles used the Latin alphabet, Hryhorii's cousins in nearby Dorohynychi signed documents in Cyrillic.[45] The Kysil family did not belong among those Volhynian nobles who had assimilated by intermarriage, religious conversion or schooling.

Although Adam was born at a time when the Kysil family was reduced from its earlier prominence, he later claimed a genealogy for the Kysils that was both illustrious and distinctive. Beginning in the late 1630s, he added the appellation "Swiętoldycz" or "Sviatoldych" to his name and claimed descent from a leader of the Rus' armies who had saved Kiev from the Pechenegs in the reign of Volodimer the Great. The first account of this genealogy, which his peers universally accepted, albeit in various versions, appeared in Syl'vestr Kosiv's dedication to Kysil in the 1635 *Paterikon,* a Polish translation of the lives of the Kievan saints.[46] Kosiv's adaptation of an account from the Primary Chronicle can be explained by his desire to encourage Kysil's patronage of the Orthodox church by flattering a rising political figure and emphasizing his connection with Kievan Rus'. Kosiv's genealogy is based on an incident in the Kievan Rus' chronicles in which a ruse employing *kysil'*, a sour pudding, saved the city of Bil'horod from the Pechenegs in 997. It is, of course, possible that the genealogy had some basis in family lore. However, it is certain that the adoption of this official genealogy emphasized the Ruthenian origins of the family and affirmed an illustrious descent approaching that of the Ruthenian princes.

A second part of Adam Kysil's official genealogy included an ancestor who had defended Kiev during Bolesław Chroby's eleventh-century capture of the city, but whose progeny accepted Polish rule and were rewarded by the Polish kings. Since Bolesław's Kievan adventure was one of the major justifications for Poland's annexation of the Kievan land during the Union of Lublin, Kysil's ancestor served as evidence of the family's early transfer of loyalty to the Polish Kingdom.[47]

Both elements of the Kysil genealogy date from the 1630s, the period of Kysil's prominence and evident involvement in religious affairs and politics in the incorporation lands. As such, they belong more to the history of the 1630s and 1640s when Adam had attained power and influence than they do to the position of the Kysil family in Volhynian society in the first decades of the century.

Education

In the early seventeenth century, the education of sons of the nobility frequently combined lessons at home with a tutor, study at the pre-scribed courses of one of the academies within the Commonwealth, and, for the sons of the wealthy, foreign travel and matriculation at Western European centers of learning. What constituted the proper upbringing for a nobleman was much debated, but all discussants agreed that it should make him conscious of his high station as a noble citizen of the Commonwealth.[48] They all advocated that he should acquire skills in military service, love for the family estate, and the learning appropriate for a man of public affairs in a free republic. Although nobles appreci-ated the high quality of foreign education, particularly in disciplines useful for military subjects, and sent their sons abroad in large numbers, they feared the demoralizing influence of foreign climes. For many, xenophobia combined with a fear of pro-absolutist leanings in foreign institutions to put the value of study abroad in question.[49] Universally, nobles acknowledged the worth of religious education and saw religious bodies as the appropriate organizers of educational institutions. In the multiconfessional Commonwealth, this resulted in a profusion of Catho-lic and Protestant academies, and competition for students served as a stimulus to maintain a high level of studies. Even in this matter, the nobles displayed their reservations toward foreign models, however superior they might be. Voices were raised maintaining that Jesuit curricula appropriate to educating the noble sons of Spain were not entirely beneficial for sons of the free nobility of the Commonwealth.[50] Still, the Jesuit schools, like the more lay-influenced schools of the Protestants, provided the young nobles with the basic skills necessary for life in the Commonwealth: Latin, rhetorics, knowledge about the republics of antiquity, and mathematics. In addition, they usually instilled the moral values and confessional allegiances approved by the young nobles' families.

The Orthodox nobles upheld the general views on education of their peers, but they faced great problems in raising their sons in their threatened traditional religion and culture. Their quandaries were voiced as early as 1577, by a neighbor of the Kysils, Vasyl' Zahorovs'kyi.[51] In his will, he ordered that at seven his sons were to begin study of Ruthenian letters and the Bible, either at home with a deacon or at the Church of St.Illiia in Volodymyr. Later a teacher of Latin was to be found for them, and when they were sufficiently prepared they were to be sent to the Jesuits in Vilnius for seven years, "because the teaching there is much praised." Then they were to serve in a great house to learn proper manners and then be given in service to the king, but "also they should not disregard Ruthenian writing and speech with Ruthenian words and honorable and obedient Ruthenian customs, and above all their faith, to which God called them and in which He created them for this world." Already Zahorovs'kyi realized that by giving his sons the proper education for a nobiliary career, he was undermining their attachment to the Ruthenian culture and faith. The Orthodox Ostroh academy, founded at this time, did not develop into a successful alternative to the Catholics' schools for young nobles, and appears to have been in decline even before its patron's death in 1608.[52] Therefore, when the Kysil family planned their son's education, they, like Zahorovs'kyi before them, saw the need to send their son to a "Latin" school.

Before reaching his tenth year, Adam Kysil left his family estate to study at the Zamość academy, in the Chełm land on the Ukrainian-Polish ethnographic border, about fifty miles from Nyzkynychi.[53] Jan Zamoyski, hetman and chancellor of the Kingdom of Poland, had founded the academy in 1593 in the seat of his vast domains.[54] An outstanding representative of both the Polish Renaissance and nobiliary culture, Zamoyski had risen from a middle noble to an influential magnate and statesman. He had founded his academy as a training ground for responsible citizen-nobles for the Commonwealth. He carefully planned a humanistic program of studies for it and gathered an eminent group of scholars as professors.[55] He also secured a papal privilege that granted the institution rights to a full university program, including theology. He conceived its detailed curriculum and endowed seven chairs—civil law, Polish law, moral philosophy, physics and medicine, logic and metaphysics, mathematics, and rhetoric—and three lesser posts for elementary lessons in rhetoric, philosophy and classical authors, in syntax, and in grammar and orthography.[56] The readings he prescribed were intended to give the classical and contemporary education necessary for a governing elite. He required the study of Latin, Greek, and Polish (according to the orthography of Kochanowski). He required that the speeches of Cicero and Demosthenes be memorized, and Herodotus, Livy, and Thucydides be read "so that the nobility might familiarize itself with major military events from these readings." He prescribed the study not only of Justinian's code, but also of feudal and Magdeburg law, Polish statutes, Diet resolutions, chancery forms, and court procedures. Examinations at his school consisted of disputes and declamations based on Greek and Roman treatises of judicial and governmental institutions. In short, Zamoyski planned to train young nobles to take an active role in the parliamentary life of the Commonwealth.

Zamoyski's project to gear the course of studies to the needs of the Commonwealth contrasted with the Jesuit programs, which were relatively uniform throughout Europe.[57] Although Zamoyski required the reading of Cardinal Hosius's *Confessio Catholicae Fidei Christiana* and the participation of students in Catholic religious services, the program of the Zamość academy was secular and patriotic in comparison to that which the regular Jesuit schools offered. In the long run, the academy did not fulfill Zamoyski's expectations. After the founder's death in 1605, the academy declined and took on a more clerical complexion. The proportion of nobles in the academy decreased, and the Jesuit schools proved more effective in influencing the Commonwealth's nobility.[58] But in the first years of its existence, the academy represented the finest education available in the Commonwealth, and it attracted sons of prominent families, many of whom later played an important role in the political life of the Commonwealth. Among them were Jakub Sobieski, Jan Żółkiewski, Mikołaj Ostroróg, and Mikołaj Potocki.[59]

The only specific reference Kysil made to his education at Zamość concerned the doctrine of the nobility's equality, taught there. Kysil's expertise in oratory, his reputation for erudition, and his interest in public service can be assumed, in part, to be derived from that education, and to this extent he, at least, fulfilled Zamoyski's intentions.[60] He and his family showed considerable loyalty to the institution; he sent both of his brothers there, his cousins Havrylo and Pavlo and his nephew Volodymyr.[61] Paweł Radoszycki, a scholar at the academy, dedicated a book he published in 1620 to Kysil, praising Kysil's devotion to the academy and learning, and, of course, requesting Kysil to be his benefactor.[62]

The founder divided the academy into five "nations"—Poles, Lithuanians, Prussian-Livonians, Ruthenians, and "foreigners."[63] The "Ruthenians," who came to the academy in considerable numbers, included not only Roman Catholics, inhabitants of the Ruthenian palatinates, but also Orthodox and Uniates. In 1631, Metropolitan Mohyla, dedicating a book to Tomasz Zamoyski, the son of the academy's founder, maintained: "The Zamość Academy has brought benefit and comfort to so many of our nation, and from it have come scholarly, wise, and serious people, so necessary to our Orthodox church."[64] The list of the academy's alumni includes such important churchmen, cultural leaders, and writers as Sylvestr Kosiv, Isai Trofimovych-Kozlovs'kyi, and Kasiian Sakovych.[65] It is probable that the devout Orthodox found the academy's environment more congenial than they found the Jesuit schools. The selection of the academy by Lavrentii Drevyns'kyi (a most energetic defender of Orthodoxy in the early seventeenth century) for his son's studies is an indication of Orthodox preference for the institution.[66]

Kysil's enrollment in the Zamość academy did not place him in an environment wholly removed from his religious and cultural upbringing. Zamość had an Orthodox church and an active Orthodox brotherhood within the city limits, and other Orthodox Ukrainian and Belorussian nobles had already had the benefit of the academy's education without converting or becoming alienated from their culture.[67] It is possible that Kysil's contacts with men such as Trofimovych-Kozlovs'kyi or Kosiv, with whom he closely worked in the 1640s and 1650s, had originated at the Zamość academy.[68]

But like the elder Zahorovs'kyi, Hryhorii and Teodora Kysil did not leave their son's training in the Ruthenian culture and faith to chance. They hired Kasiian Sakovych, an Orthodox clergyman, as a tutor, and his duties included accompanying the young Kysil home on his vacations.[69] The son of an Orthodox priest, Sakovych was one of the most controversial figures of the time. After tutoring Kysil, he served as rector of the Kiev brotherhood school, chaplain of the Lublin brotherhood, and (after accepting the Union of Brest) as abbot of Dubno monastery. He made his mark in Ukrainian literature with his elegy to Hetman Petro Konashevych-Sahaidachnyi, in which he depicted the Cossacks as knights defending the Orthodox faith.[70] His forte, however, was scathing religious polemic, a genre that he used with particular effectiveness after he abandoned the Uniate church for Roman Catholicism in 1641. His attacks concentrated on the Byzantine rite, and Ruthenian customs, history, and traditions. Displaying the fervor of a new convert, he scandalized both Orthodox and Uniates with his *Overview and Explanation of the Errors, Heresies and Prejudices of the Greco-Ruthenian Church,* a work that elicited the famous Orthodox response by "Euzebii Pimin" (usually thought to be Mohyla and his associates), as well as a Uniate response by Kysil's nephew, Pakhomii Orans'kyi.[71]

Sakovych's ultimate rejection of the Ruthenian faith and, implicitly, of its culture were results of doubts that were to arise long after his tutorship of Kysil. At the time he educated his young charge, he stood out as one of the prominent Ruthenian Orthodox intellectuals who understood the learning of the "Latins" and were seeking to provide a response to its challenge. Sakovych's influence on Kysil during his tutorship probably resulted in the young nobleman's increasing attachment to Ruthenian religious and cultural traditions.

The Zamość years also provided Kysil with a powerful patron in the person of Jan Zamoyski's son Tomasz, who later proved of invaluable aid in furthering Kysil's career.[72] Zamoyski, born about 1594, was a few years Kysil's senior and had studied under the tutorial direction of Szymon Szymonowicz at the academy until 1614.[73] In later years, Kysil did not hesitate to remind Tomasz of their common bond to advance his family's interests, and Zamoyski entrusted Kysil with economic and political missions.[74] Zamoyski, with his vast holdings and prominent offices in the Ukraine, constituted a powerful patron for Kysil until his death in 1638.

Precisely when Kysil finished his studies at the academy is not known, but the latest possible date is 1617, when he appears in military service. A royal charter of 1646 mentions his having studied abroad—the usual completion of education for wealthy noble sons—but until more concrete evidence is discovered, it can only be considered likely. The decree may reflect the kind of education a magnate, as Kysil was by that time, should have had, and not what he actually did.[75]

The Launching of a Career

Kysil spent a number of years in the army, a common source of employment and even advancement for sons of the middle nobility. In some cases, notably that of Stefan Czarniecki, they could even follow that route to magnate status.[76] Kysil's military exploits in the 1610s and 1620s were no doubt a major factor in advancing his career.

The years 1617–1621, when Kysil began his military service, saw many armed conflicts with Muscovy and the Ottoman Empire. They were the last years of activity of some of the Commonwealth's greatest military leaders—the Crown Hetman Stanisław Żółkiewski, the Lithuanian Hetman Jan Karol Chodkiewicz, and the Zaporozhian Hetman Petro Konashevych-Sahaidachnyi.[77] Kysil took part in the Muscovite expedition to rescue the throne for Zygmunt's son Władysław[78] and in the major battles with the Tatars and Turks on the southern front—Busha (Iaruha), 1617; Orynin, 1618; Tsetsora, 1620; and Khotyn, 1621.[79] Like most middle-ranking nobles, he had signed up in a regiment with a small detachment of followers (*poczet*).[80] At the Khotyn battle, he led a five-man contingent, which included his nephew Ivan Orans'kyi, under the hussar banner of a fellow Volhynian, Prince Jerzy Zasławski.[81] He lost one of his men at Orynyn, but his contingent, unlike most of the Commonwealth's army, apparently escaped being taken prisoner at Tsetsora.[82] His service at Khotyn prompted a laudatory letter from Hetman Jan Karol Chodkiewicz.[83] After the battle, he was elected representative from Zasławski's hussars to a "confederation" of soldiers,[84] and was later praised for his part in finding a resolution to the soldiers' grievances and thereby avoiding rebellion.[85]

Aside from the bare facts that Kysil participated in these events, Chodkiewicz's commendation of Kysil for his participation at Khotyn, and Kysil's comment that he spent his *tirocinium,* or first military service, under Żółkiewski, we have little information about this period in Kysil's life; but, rich as it was in dramatic events, it must have been important in Kysil's development.[86] He first came into contact with Muscovy and Russians, and he took part in the military ventures which resulted in an end to the Commonwealth's decade of intervention in Muscovite affairs. The events of 1617–1618 led to a stalemate and *de facto* recognition of the Romanov dynasty, but they also garnered a great deal of Muscovite territory (the Smolensk and the Chernihiv lands) which remained in the Commonwealth's hands throughout Kysil's career. He witnessed Tatar raids, the humiliation of the Commonwealth by the Ottomans at Tsetsora, and the fortunate reprieve at Khotyn. Finally, in all the events of 1617–21, he saw a powerful Zaporozhian army, led by Konashevych-Sahaidachnyi, loyally and effectively serve the Commonwealth against both Muscovy and the Ottoman Empire. There is no concrete evidence that Kysil's later policies of forming an alliance with Muscovy, launching an anti-Turkish war, or utilizing the Zaporozhians as an essential component of the Commonwealth's power derive from this period, and, admittedly, other participants later came to quite different conclusions, but it does seem at least possible.

Kysil's election to the soldiers' confederation testified not only to his influence among his fellow soldiers, but also to his political acumen. Not only did he avoid arousing the ire of the monarch; he also attracted royal interest in his considerable talent for persuasion and negotiation. In 1622, King Zygmunt named him royal emissary to the Volhynian dietine, a post reserved for nobles with abilities to win over dietines to a king's program.[87] Zygmunt's selection indicates that Kysil had won a favorable opinion at court and that the king viewed him as a man of importance in Volhynian affairs. Kysil's political influence was on the rise. As early as 1624 he was elected a delegate from Volhynia to the national Diet; and there is evidence that he may have served as early as 1621.[88]

Kysil represented a dietine adamant in its support of the Orthodox church and the newly restored (1620), but still illegal, Orthodox hierarchy.[89] The 1620s were a particularly tense period in Eastern church affairs. The restoration of the hierarchy under Iov Borets'kyi provided a rallying point for Orthodox faithful, while the murder of the Bishop of Polatsk, Iosafat Kuntsevych, in 1623, gave the Uniates both a martyr and a propaganda weapon.[90] Volhynian leaders, such as Lavrentii Drevyns'kyi, vociferously demanded a reversal of the court's religious policy, and the Orthodox nobility protested at every Diet.[91] The turbulence of the period was increased by the dissatisfaction of the Zaporozhian Host, which, combining religious grievances with its own issues, revolted in 1625 and 1630. The 1630 insurrection was a moderate success for the Cossacks; the register was expanded from the 6,000 allowed in 1625 to 8,000.[92]

Kysil advanced quickly, partly because of the patronage of Tomasz Zamoyski,[93] who had by then become palatine of Kiev, a post he held from 1618 to 1629; he was subsequently crown vice-chancellor, from 1629 to 1635, and chancellor to his death in 1638.[94] Zamoyski's support extended to securing royal grants for Kysil and proposing him for the post of royal delegate.[95] In return Kysil made himself useful by assisting in economic dealings, by supporting Zamoyski's policies at the dietine, and by serving under his standard during the Swedish war of 1626–1629.[96] In 1626, after the Swedish invasion of Prussia, Zygmunt called on Zamoyski to organize a regiment,[97] and Zamoyski designated Kysil as a detachment leader, or *rotmistrz,* requesting him to recruit a 150-horse unit.[98] Kysil energetically recruited the necessary troops.[99] At the battle of Gniew (November 1626), in which two of his cousins died and his brother Mykola was wounded, Kysil, at the head of his detachment, made a particularly brave showing before the king's son Władysław.[100] Although Kysil's military career from Gniew to the Smolensk War is unmentioned in the sources, subsequent royal decrees continue to refer to him as "our rotmistrz."[101]

At the same time Kysil advanced in his military and political career, he assumed leadership of his family and inherited their ancestral seat. Sometime between 1616 and 1621 his father Hryhorii had died, leaving Adam to care for his mother and two younger brothers, and giving him effective control over Nyzkynychi. In a will that Adam wrote before the Khotyn campaign, he mentions only the village of Nyzkynychi as the family's property, but the former judge's family appears to have been considerably better off than most owners of a single village would have been.[102] Adam arranged to settle 5,000 zł. on his mother should he or his brothers die, to repay his father's debts of 600 zł., to bequeath 200 zł. to the family church, and to provide for his brothers' continued studies at the Zamość academy, and later at the Cracow academy. These provisions, combined with Adam's five-man detachment at Khotyn, suggest considerable resources beyond the confines of Nyzkynychi.

The will also provides information about Kysil's religious beliefs and social milieu. He avowed his allegiance to the "Holy Eastern Church" of his ancestors and gave the bequest mentioned above to his family church. The executors of his will were all neighboring Volhynian nobles, among them Prince Hryhorii Chetvertyns'kyi, whose inclusion demonstrates that Kysil had highly-placed connections even at the beginning of his career.[103] The other executors were small landholders of Volodymyr county—Kysil's peers in the Commonwealth's social structure.[104]

In the mid-1620s Kysil chose a wife from beyond the confines of his native land in the person of Anastaziia Bohushevychivna Hulkevych-Hlibovs'ka, who came from an Orthodox family in the Kievan palatinate.[105] Her grandfather Bohush Hulkevych-Hlibovs'kyi was from the village of Hlebiv on the Irpen River.[106] He served as castle secretary of the Kievan palatinate and administrator of the St. Sophia cathedral and the Orthodox metropolitan's estates. He is reported to have spent considerable sums on restoring the cathedral church. In 1585, Bohush secured tenure of the church estates of Novosilky in the Kievan palatinate, and these properties were inherited by his son Filon, Anastaziia's father.[107] The success of the Bohushevych-Hulkevych family in utilizing their connection with the church to aggrandize their wealth is demonstrated by Filon's transfer of estates formerly belonging to the Orthodox metropolitanate, the castle and village of Zorenychi, on the Irpen' River, to Kysil in 1628.[108] Later Novosilky also came into Kysil's hands.

Adam's marriage linked him to a family with substantial wealth and interests in the Kievan palatinate. Anastaziia's role in his life must remain in the realm of conjecture, but the fact of their marriage is in itself a matter of considerable significance. Because Kysil chose his wife from the Kievan middle nobility and from a family who owned lands in the Kievan palatinate, his marriage marked a renewal of Kysil family interest in that area.[109] It also seems to have reaffirmed his claims to the "Kysilivshchyna" tract that his family had lost in a court case of 1604–1605. There is some indication that Anastaziia was the widow of Mykhailo Butovych, whose family, together with the Lozka family, had won the court case. Soon after his marriage, Adam added the appellation "of Brusyliv" to his signature. Brusyliv was part of the tract won by the Butovych family. Although he never gained possession of Brusyliv, Kysil demonstrated his tenacious memory of his family's lost lands by naming a settlement in the Chernihiv region "New Brusyliv."[110] The marriage also reinforced Kysil's commitment to Orthodoxy through a wife whose family had particularly close historical and material connections with his ancestral faith.

Kysil's marriage was but one sign of the eastward drift of his interests and his growing involvement in the political and religious life of the Dnieper Ukraine. Other than Vytkiv in the Belz palatinate, which he and his wife were granted by the king in 1632 through Tomasz Zamoyski's intercession, Kysil's major acquisitions were in the newly conquered Chernihiv lands.[111] Zygmunt made the first grants to him there between 1618 and 1632 when Władysław was its administrator,[112] but Kysil continued to add to those holdings and to obtain offices there throughout the 1630s.[113]

The Synod of 1629

Kysil's increasing stature in the Ukraine and his allegiance to the Eastern church inevitably drew him into the intractable problem over the Union of Brest. His involvement in this issue provides the only detailed view of his diplomatic skills and his religious attitudes in the formative years of his career. Unlike Kysil's other missions of mediation in the 1620s, his service as royal delegate to the Orthodox synod at Kiev in July 1629 is well documented. His appointment by Zygmunt to that mission is not only indicative of the favor he enjoyed at court, but also of the king's awareness of his contacts with the Orthodox and Uniate hierarchies.[114]

Kysil emerged as a major figure in the Eastern church question just at the time when a number of the principals involved in the struggle were willing to consider a new compromise. The Uniate metropolitan, Iosyf

Ruts'kyi (1613–1637), a man of dedication and piety, had come to realize that in spite of his tireless efforts to secure acceptance of the union, the majority of the Orthodox clergy and nobility continued to find the Uniate church unacceptable. After 1620, Ruts'kyi had to compete with an Orthodox rival, Iov Borets'kyi, and Ruts'kyi's protests to the authorities were of no avail against Orthodox power in the Dnieper basin. He sought to buttress the position of his church by securing a papal edict against transferring rites, by establishing a Ruthenian seminary, and by requesting the elevation of the Kievan see to a patriarchate. He was particularly disturbed by the Latin-rite clergy's contempt for the Uniates and their success in convincing the Eastern clergy and nobility to join the Roman Catholic church directly. Ruts'kyi obtained the papal edict and had some success in his efforts to raise the educational level of his clergy, but he continued to be hard pressed by a vigorous Orthodox resurgence and the contempt and indifference of his Latin-rite coreligionists.[115]

Ruts'kyi's competitor, Iov Borets'kyi, also had considerable cause for dissatisfaction. Although the Orthodox faithful had succeeded in restoring an Orthodox hierarchy in 1620, had retained control over a considerable segment of Eastern church properties, and had pressured the government into making concessions at many Diets, the Orthodox hierarchy had not been granted official recognition.[116] In areas of western Ukraine and Belorussia where Cossack power and Orthodox noble support were less effective, the bishops who had been consecrated in 1620 were not able to assume their offices.[117] Depending on force to secure Orthodox rights was a dangerous practice. The murder of the Uniate bishop of Polatsk, Iosafat Kuntsevych, by the Orthodox burghers of Vitsebsk in 1623 had unleashed a persecution of Orthodoxy and had provided the Uniates with the powerful symbol of a martyr.[118] Borets'kyi had sought foreign support for Orthodoxy and had made approaches to Muscovy, but that, too, was a dangerous game, since it made his church liable to charges of treason. In any case, substantial Muscovite support was not forthcoming.[119]

The stronghold of the Orthodox metropolitan's power was the city of Kiev, where the Orthodox controlled almost all the churches and monasteries, and the Kievan brotherhood and its school had developed its Orthodox intellectual life. In the early 1620s, the Caves monastery had become a major publishing center, and Peter Mohyla's ordination and election to the position of archimandrite of the Caves monastery in 1627 further strengthened it as an Orthodox center.[120] Mohyla, the son of a Moldavian hospodar, and a relative of the Vyshnevets'kyis (Wiśniowieckis) and of other powerful Commonwealth families, brought the wealth, respectability, and connections of a grand seigneur to the Orthodox church.[121] His loyalty to the Commonwealth and the favorable opinion he enjoyed in government and Catholic circles increased the likelihood of discussions about Orthodoxy's position. Mohyla, unlike Borets'kyi, was not compromised by having accepted an unauthorized episcopal consecration or by having openly struggled against the Uniates.

Despite its successes in the 1620s, the Orthodox church vitally needed government recognition. Royal approval was necessary even for convening a synod to discuss essential problems of the church's organization.[122] Semi-legal synods had been convened in 1627, after the election of Mohyla to the position of archimandrite, and in 1628, after the Diet had passed tax provisions concerning the Orthodox church.[123] But if Orthodoxy wished to shed its image as a faith of rebels, it had to secure official approbation. The conversion, in 1628, of Meletii Smotryts'kyi, archbishop of Polatsk, a major intellectual and cultural leader, to the Uniate church demonstrated the weaknesses of a non-recognized Orthodox church.[124] Despite Orthodoxy's successes in controlling church properties and in retaining the loyalty of the nobility and peasantry, the leadership of an illegal institution could be won away by the substantial rewards the Uniate church and Commonwealth government could offer. Without formal recognition, the Orthodox church would have to rely solely on popular pressure to ensure its existence.

The king and the Diet formed the third factor in negotiations. Thirty years after the Union of Brest, dissension in the Eastern church continued to hinder Diet after Diet's proceedings.[125] One segment of the Catholic nobility viewed the union as a total failure: Metropolitan Ruts'kyi complained to Rome that many Latin-rite Catholics preferred the Orthodox church to the Uniate.[126] Even Latin-rite Catholics favorably disposed to the union, including King Zygmunt himself, were concerned about the rising wave of Orthodox discontent and the disruption of the Commonwealth's parliamentary life. While not abandoning support of the union, the king was willing to allow new discussions between the Orthodox and Uniates.

The most consistent voice in the religious controversy came from the Holy See. Through its nuncio in Warsaw, it supported the Union of Brest and the Uniate church, and protested any concession to the Orthodox.[127] Papal policy discouraged innovations that would weaken the Holy See's control over the Uniate metropolitan see, opposed conferences with the Orthodox as dangerous to Catholic interests, and demanded submission to the pope as a precondition to any discussion.[128] Even in the powerful Roman circles of the Society for the

Propagation of the Faith, however, a faction willing to discuss changes in the Eastern church's status quo existed.[129]

In the 1620s the various principals cautiously worked their way toward a reconsideration of their positions. In 1624, Ruts'kyi proposed plans for creating a patriarchate that would be both loyal to Rome and accepted by the Orthodox.[130] Rome equivocated over the various plans for the project before demanding (in 1627) Orthodox submission to the Holy See as a precondition. Ruts'kyi's probes on renewing that dialogue found an audience in Orthodox Kiev, but Smotryts'kyi's discussions of differences between Orthodoxy and Catholicism at the Kiev synod of 1628 aroused the Orthodox masses' wrath and forced Borets'kyi and Mohyla to condemn him.[131] Although the reaction to Smotryts'kyi's discussions gave Mohyla and Borets'kyi considerable reason for caution, they were at least willing to entertain the possibility of discussion. Finally, the king and the Diet had allowed Orthodox synods in 1627 and 1628, and they were interested in resolving the Eastern church issue. All sides were, of course, extremely reluctant to admit that they were ready to make any concessions. Each had to convey different impressions to different audiences in order to justify discussion, and the likelihood of recrimination was always great.

The proposal calling for separate Orthodox and Uniate synods, followed by a joint synod in Lviv, appears to have originated with Metropolitan Ruts'kyi, who acted without prior papal approval.[132] The metropolitan was anxious that the king back the project, but that it appear the Orthodox had initiated the discussions.[133] In January and February 1629, the Diet provided Ruts'kyi with the forum he needed to carry out his plan.

When Ruts'kyi first contacted Kysil about his project is not clear, but Ruts'kyi's suggestion to the king that Kysil be named royal delegate to the Orthodox synod, and his subsequent laudatory remarks about Kysil's service indicate that the two men worked closely together from the first.[134] In 1629, Kysil was elected to the Diet from the Volhynian dietine. At the Diet, he took part in discussions with Ruts'kyi's emissary, the Uniate abbot of Zhydychyn monastery, Iosyf Bakovets'kyi, Iosyf Bobrykovych of the Vilnius brotherhood monastery, and the Orthodox lay leaders Fedir Sushchans'kyi-Proskura, delegate of the Kievan palatinate, Mykhailo Kropyvnyts'kyi, delegate from the Bratslav palatinate, and Lavrentii Drevyns'kyi, delegate from the Volhynian palatinate.[135] Kysil drew up a draft constitution calling for a series of synods. The Orthodox discussants signed, but the Diet did not act on the proposal.[136] Nevertheless, the discussants continued to meet after the Diet had formally closed, and Bakovets'kyi attempted to convince the Orthodox leaders that the synods could be called by the king.[137]

The subsequent web of recriminations and justifications makes it difficult to establish either side's positions during the negotiations, but it appears that before Kropyvnyts'kyi, Drevyns'kyi, and Bobrykovych departed, they agreed to the proposal that the king call the synods. In any event, they later fully supported the synod convened by the king's decrees. In February and March, Zygmunt issued decrees convening an Orthodox synod in Kiev, a Uniate synod in Volodymyr on July 9, and a joint synod in Lviv on October 28.[138] It is likely that the planners of the synods avoided introducing a Diet constitution because they feared the papal nuncio might have protested any constitution calling for synods before papal approval had been secured. The Orthodox delegates had also not been empowered by the dietines to negotiate a synod, and an attempt to pass a constitution on the Greek faith might have encountered resistance in the Diet.[139] Moreover, the decrees issued by the king differed substantially from the proposed Diet constitution Kysil had drawn up. Instead of the "pacification of the Greek Faith" they called for discussion about a church union.[140]

Since Kysil not only drew up the original constitution, but served as royal delegate to the Orthodox synod in Kiev as well, the nature of his own religious convictions is of considerable importance.[141] The question of Kysil's formal religious affiliation in 1629 has troubled historians for some time.[142] On the basis of Albrycht Stanisław Radziwiłł's assertion that Kysil renounced the union on Easter day (April 11) 1632, it has been supposed that sometime between 1621, when he wrote his will, and 1632, Kysil accepted the union.[143] Older views of Kysil as an ardent proponent of Orthodoxy were disproved by the publication of material about the synods of 1629 and Kysil's part in framing the synodal project and serving as the king's delegate.[144] On the basis of these materials, Kysil was described as a Uniate during the synod of 1629, though a Uniate with strong ties to Orthodoxy and one who was ready to describe himself as an Orthodox to that camp.[145] The assertion that Kysil was an openly professed Uniate, as opposed to a Uniate sympathizer, is disproved by a letter of July 27, 1629, from Metropolitan Ruts'kyi to the Papal Nuncio Santa Croce describing Kysil in the following terms: "In the future he could be of great use to us; he has great influence among them [the Orthodox]; and they take him as theirs, and because of this they believe everything, while for all that he is inwardly united with us, although not yet externally."[146] Thus, Kysil was officially Orthodox in 1629, though considered by the Uniate camp as one of their own.

Kysil's religious affiliation has not only been a problem for subsequent historians; it represented a major quandary for his contemporaries. In 1629, and throughout his career, he was formally Orthodox, and his Orthodox contemporaries accepted his allegiance at face value. But in 1629, as in numerous other instances in his career, he was also able to convince highly placed Uniates and Latin-rite Catholics that he was really a Uniate, and that he held back from conversion only in order to retain his influence in the Orthodox church. Unlike Smotryts'kyi, he never appears to have made a formal profession of faith, but the example of Smotryts'kyi's secret adherence to the union must have led Ruts'kyi into giving credence to Kysil's assurances.[147] Ruts'kyi was, of course, well aware of the pressures exerted by the Orthodox nobles and Cossacks, pressures that made Borets'kyi, Mohyla, and other Orthodox leaders so hesitant to enter discussions about church union. Kysil's ability to convince Ruts'kyi and the king of the sincerity of his Catholicism, while not sacrificing his position with the Orthodox, was undoubtedly a major factor in his successes during Zygmunt's reign.

After receiving his confirmation as royal delegate to the Orthodox synod, Kysil traveled to Kiev to work out a program of procedure with Metropolitan Borets'kyi two weeks before the synod opened.[148] Borets'kyi cooperated with Kysil throughout, though his actual position on the advisability of religious union is difficult to determine. Kysil's major supporter among the Orthodox clergy, Peter Mohyla, arrived the day before the synod began. His role was crucial because Metropolitan Ruts'kyi looked to him as the probable candidate for a Uniate patriarchal post in a reunited Ruthenian church.[149]

Kysil's report to Metropolitan Ruts'kyi is one major source for the synod.[150] In this detailed account he maintained that, while the clergy were favorably disposed toward a projected union, the Cossacks and the majority of the nobles were ardently opposed and refused to take part in discussions. The nobility maintained that the delegates to the Diet of 1629 had no right to arrange a synod, because a synod could be called only by a Diet constitution. Cossacks were present in Kiev during the entire synod to demand that no concessions be made to the Uniates and that the very discussions be terminated.

The synod that convened on July 9, 1629, was thus far from a broadly based gathering of Rus' society. Borets'kyi was the only hierarch present. Izaak Boryskovych, bishop of Luts'k and exarch of the patriarch of Constantinople, questioned the very legitimacy of the synod. On the first day, Lavrentii Drevyns'kyi was elected head of its lay members, but since most Orthodox nobles stayed away, the lay assembly's authority was questionable. The monk Teodor, the emissary of Iarema Tysarivs'kyi, bishop of Lviv, was elected head of the clerical assembly. When

Kysil presented his proposals on the first day, he requested that all points of conflict in the dogmas and administration of the Orthodox and Catholic churches be defined, suggestions for resolving conflicts be made, and delegates to the Lviv joint synod be selected.[151]

On the second day, after the Cossacks intervened and tried to eject Kysil from the proceedings, the synod debated whether or not to send delegates to the joint synod. Peter Mohyla and delegates from the Vilnius brotherhood were in favor; delegates of the Lviv brotherhood and Teodor, the emissary of the bishop of Lviv, were opposed, arguing that because the synod was convened by order of the king alone, and not the Diet, any Orthodox participation might simply jeopardize their rights and privileges. Kysil tried to convince them that, while the Orthodox had nothing to lose by participation, they had much to gain.[152]

According to Kysil, on the third day, two Orthodox lay leaders spoke in favor of participation, but since the nobility still had not appeared, and the Cossacks continued to cause trouble, the synod reached an impasse. Kysil's attempts to calm the Cossacks met with sharp rebuffs and threats of physical violence. He was forced to admit to the proceedings a delegation that had been sent from the Zaporozhian Host to the Diet, and the synod was held behind barred doors, with armed Cossack agitators outside. Borets'kyi was under particular pressure, and for his personal safety, spent the night at the more secure Caves monastery.[153]

Unable to control the Cossacks or to secure the election of delegates to the general synod, Kysil tried a new tactic. At a secret meeting with Drevyns'kyi, Kropyvnyts'kyi, Proskura, Borets'kyi, and Mohyla, he proposed that a selected inner synod elect delegates. Kropyvnyts'kyi and Drevyns'kyi refused to do so without authorization from the absent nobles. The clergy refused as well, insisting that they were authorized to make decisions only in spiritual matters and that, since the points now under consideration affected the liberty of noblemen, they could only be decided with the nobility's participation. Over the objection of Mohyla and the Vilnius brotherhood's delegate Bobrykovych, the synod was closed on its fourth day, July 12.[154]

The various parties now had to justify their actions before both the king and Rus' society. On the day the synod closed, Kysil, as the king's delegate, filed a short report in the local court books on the reasons for its failure.[155] The Orthodox clergymen registered a protest against the synod, justifying their indecision by claiming that the synod had not adhered to the original project formulated at the Diet, that it lacked approval from either the patriarch of Constantinople or his exarch, Izaak Boryskovych, and that it had been boycotted by the nobility.[156]

Kropyvnyts'kyi and Drevyns'kyi denounced the contradictions between the plan as it had been worked out at the Diet and the king's decrees.[157] Kysil later analyzed the obstacles to union as they appeared from his discussions with Borets'kyi and Mohyla.[158] The Orthodox prelates had been willing to concede most points of dogma, but not their insistence on the Constantinople patriarch's agreement to any synod and on the retention of his authority over the Kievan see. Kysil, though aware of the magnitude of the difficulties their insistence entailed, was nevertheless encouraged by their willingness and that of at least some nobles to discuss union at all. He felt that the hostility of the common people was an obstacle that could be overcome. Although he apologized for his failure to control the synod in a letter to Metropolitan Ruts'kyi (written two days after closing and maintaining that shame kept him from writing to the king or the chancellor, Jakub Zadzik), he was in reality optimistic about the progress made at the synod and pleased with his accomplishments.[159]

Kysil's tactics as delegate to the synod reflect the flexibility of his own allegiance. He had informed both the Orthodox Mohyla and the Uniate Ruts'kyi privately that he was of each prelate's respective faith.[160] In practice, his religious views appear to have consisted of a tolerant adherence to Christianity in the Rus' rite and a desire to end the conflict in the church. His primary concern was for the unity of the Rus' church. On the first day of the synod's deliberations, he had said:

> Gentlemen, you are not the only ones to weep. We all weep at the sight of the rent coat and precious robe of our dear Mother the Holy Eastern Church. You, Gentlemen, bemoan, as do we all, that we are divided from our brethren, we who were in one font of the Holy Spirit six hundred years ago in the Dnieper waters of this metropolis of the Rus' Principality. It wounds you, Gentlemen, and it wounds us all. Behold! There flourish organisms of commonwealths composed of various nations, while we of one nation, of one people, of one religion, of one worship, of one rite, are not as one. We are torn asunder, and thus we decline.[161]

Here Kysil did not urge unity by considering the relative merits of Catholicism or Orthodoxy. Instead, he simply expressed the conviction that the fratricidal struggle among the Ruthenians must stop.

Kysil's program to the synod had been one that called for a resolution of the division of the Ruthenian church and for an amelioration of the problems of the Orthodox church. But although he had a receptive audience and the king's support, his mission was bound to fail. The obstinate opposition of the Cossack Host intimidated the pro-union elements among the clergy. In vain did Kysil try to curb their influence by ridiculing them as "rabble."[162] Despite his insistence that church problems were the responsibility of the higher clergy and the nobility, the synod of 1629 demonstrated that the Cossacks could enforce their position as self-proclaimed protectors of the Orthodox church. Although Kysil and Bakovets'kyi also managed to win over Drevyns'kyi and Kropyvnyts'kyi, the leaders of the Orthodox nobility, to the idea of compromise as the price for royal concessions to the Orthodox, the majority of nobles were unwilling to involve themselves in a compromise that might ultimately weaken the Orthodox position. In fact, they correctly assessed that the king really wanted to find a formula that would guarantee Orthodox agreement to the Union of Brest. Even the higher clergymen in whom Kysil placed such confidence had set conditions about the participation of the patriarch of Constantinople that could hardly be fulfilled. They may have merely wished to placate the king. Indeed, Kysil himself may not have been as optimistic about the potential for union as he seemed in his reports. We only know his views as he conveyed them to the king and the Uniate metropolitan, and the clever politician undoubtedly recorded his opinions with his audience in mind.

A whole array of external influences worked against any possibility of achieving union and of healing the rift in Ruthenian society. The Protestant reluctance to see the Rus' church's problem solved through Orthodox consent to a union, whether Brest or a new one, caused the great Calvinist magnate, Krzysztof Radziwiłł, to intervene to shore up Orthodox opposition during the synod. Most important of all, the papacy was hostile to real compromise, so Ruts'kyi, Kysil and Zygmunt had had to initiate the program of separate and joint synods without the consent of Rome. Although Ruts'kyi pleaded the case for such a step to the Holy See, Rome eventually forbade the calling of a joint Catholic-Orthodox synod, because Rome felt such discussion would lead to questioning the degree of its papal control over the Uniate church.[163] For the same reason, it opposed the creation of a Uniate Rus' patriarchate. The papacy therefore continued to insist on Orthodox acceptance of the Union of Brest, and to demand that resistance be put down with a firm hand. The Orthodox refusal to appoint delegates to the Lviv joint synod in fact saved face for the Uniate hierarchy, since the congregation for the Propagation of the Faith had already ordered Ruts'kyi to prevent its convening.[164]

Although Kysil ostensibly failed in his mission to the Kiev synod, he did not regard the incident as a disaster. In many ways, it was in fact a success. He had advanced agreements on dogmatic problems and worked out terms by which the Orthodox leadership would consent to a new synod. His relations with Borets'kyi, Mohyla, Drevyns'kyi and

Kropyvnyts'kyi remained cordial, for he had skillfully assisted them in a potentially dangerous situation, and they were grateful for his favorable reports to the authorities on their attitudes and activities.[165] Kysil's relations with the Uniate hierarchy were equally amicable. The Volodymyr Uniate bishop, Illiia Morokhovs'kyi, with whom he worked throughout the synod, named him an executor of his will (it endowed the Uniate school in Volodymyr).[166] Metropolitan Ruts'kyi wrote to Santa Croce praising Kysil for his dedication, industry, and courage during the synod and suggesting that he be commended to the king.[167] Kysil had proven his worth as a negotiator in religious affairs at the synod of 1629. The ambitious noble did face one major obstacle to further advancement. As long as he remained Orthodox, he could not expect appointment to high office from the devout Counter-Reformation Catholic Zygmunt.

Chapter 3

The Beginning of the New Reign (1632–1635)

At the beginning of the 1630s, the Commonwealth anxiously awaited the new era sure to follow the death of the aged Zygmunt. His reign of over forty years had seen major transformations in the Commonwealth favoring increasing power of the magnates and the triumph of Counter-Reformation Catholicism. In his early years, the wily and determined monarch had encountered violent opposition from the nobility against his schemes to increase royal powers and to involve the Commonwealth in his attempts to regain the Swedish throne. Stymied in achieving these goals, Zygmunt nevertheless learned to manipulate the political institutions of the Commonwealth in order to aggrandize the power of the king. Although many of his subjects resented his machinations, all had learned what they might expect from the old king. His death would create a new political situation, replete with both danger and opportunities. The most immediate uncertainty would be the functioning of the Commonwealth's institutions during the interregnum. Few alive had witnessed the last royal election of 1587. That election had been only the third after the extinction of the Jagiellonian dynasty and the creation of a fully elective monarchy. The turbulence accompanying those elections did not presage well for the period following Zygmunt's death on April 30, 1632.

The Interregnum and the Election

The interregnum allowed factions in the Commonwealth to express their discontent and provided foreign powers with an opportunity to intervene. While few doubted that Władysław, Zygmunt's eldest son, would be elected, the drawn-out election process in itself presented a number of dangers.[1] The enmity between the Polish and the Swedish Vasas made it certain that King Gustavus Adolphus of Sweden would use the interregnum to compromise Władysław, for he had considerable cause to intervene.[2] Władysław claimed the Swedish throne and could be expected to continue Zygmunt's pro-Habsburg foreign policy. Although Gustavus Adolphus was not likely to overextend himself by attacking the Commonwealth while he was fighting in Germany, he could be expected to weaken his potential enemy by intervening in the politicking of the election. He was fully aware of the problems the Commonwealth had on its eastern frontier. In 1631, he tried, albeit unsuccessfully, to exploit the dissatisfaction of the Zaporozhian Cossacks to recruit them for the Protestant side in the Thirty Years' War.[3]

The major threat to the Commonwealth was posed by Gustavus's negotiations with Muscovy.[4] The Truce of Altmark, concluded after the Prussian War (1626–1629), had guaranteed peace between Sweden and the Commonwealth until 1635, and it was assumed that Sweden would not renew hostilities, at least directly, until then. But conflict with Muscovy was nearer, for the truce of 1619 was to run out in 1633 and Muscovy had long been preparing for war. The death of Zygmunt in the spring of 1632 provided Muscovy with an opportunity to strike even before the end of the truce period, and Sweden might well provide assistance, if not join in the attack.[5]

Protestant Sweden and Orthodox Muscovy could exploit the discontent of the Commonwealth's Protestant and Orthodox minorities while it remained without a king. The Counter-Reformation policies of Zygmunt, particularly his discrimination against Protestants in distributing offices, had antagonized the Protestant nobles.[6] Led by magnates such as Krzysztof Radziwiłł and Rafał Leszczyński, they now determined to secure reconfirmation and practical application of the Toleration Act of 1573,[7] threatening to support Gustavus Adolphus in order to exact concessions.[8] Both Radziwiłł and Leszczyński were on good terms with Władysław, however, and were convinced that his election would moderate the Counter-Reformation's influence in the Commonwealth.[9]

Maintaining the loyalty of the Orthodox population was a prerequisite to repelling a Muscovite attack. Even before Zygmunt's death, the Commonwealth counted on the Zaporozhian Cossacks to defend Smolensk and the Chernihiv lands.[10] Already in the 1620s Metropolitan Borets'kyi had initiated a program of seeking material assistance from Muscovy.[11] After Borets'kyi's death in 1631, Isai Kopyns'kyi, a representative of the militant Orthodox faction which was popular among the monks of the Left-Bank monasteries, was chosen as metropolitan.[12] Kopyns'kyi continued Borets'kyi's policy of seeking support from Muscovy.[13] The government had to fear that the metropolitan might dissuade the Cossacks, who were already smarting under the harsh conditions imposed on them after their 1630 revolt, from fighting against their Muscovite Orthodox co-religionists.

At the last Diet of Zygmunt's reign, the Orthodox nobles and emissaries from the Zaporozhian army once again complained about the restrictions against Orthodoxy, but the Diet put off discussion of the problem.[14] Although the new Cossack leadership under Kulaha-Petrazhyts'kyi was loyal to the government, the situation remained explosive.[15]

Władysław was almost assured of election, but during the election process he needed to ease domestic tensions in order to create internal stability and unity in the face of foreign enemies.[16] Unlike his sternly Catholic father, he was both moderate in his religious devotion and willing to compromise with non-Catholic groups.[17] He had to figure out a way to win over the dissidents without alienating ultra-Catholic elements, the Uniates, or the Pope. To deal successfully with Orthodox discontent, he had to negotiate an agreement with the Orthodox church that would ensure the nobility's support in the election and also secure the loyalty of the church to the Commonwealth, thereby making it impervious to intrigues by Orthodox Moscow. He had to eliminate the religious issue as a factor alienating the Zaporozhian Host and to secure the Zaporozhian army's support in war with Muscovy, without granting the Cossacks rights that would antagonize the Commonwealth's nobility. Finally, he had to save as much as possible of the Uniate church's position and convince the papacy to accept the compromise.[18] To carry out this program, Władysław needed moderate Orthodox allies.

In all these complex negotiations, Kysil became a major spokesman. His status as a bona fide Orthodox believer had been established by his public renunciation of the Union of Brest in the spring of 1632,[19] which had won him both the trust of Orthodox leaders and the opprobrium of zealous Catholics.[20] He had done this immediately after the last Diet of Zygmunt's reign, and his decision may have been prompted by the strength and determination of Orthodox forces at that Diet, combined with pressure from his Volhynian Orthodox electors.[21] The renunciation took place around the time of Zygmunt's death on April 30, and Kysil was undoubtedly aware that in the election and the new reign to follow, his allegiance to Orthodoxy would not be a hindrance.[22]

The Orthodox camp that Kysil joined was well prepared to demand concessions. As early as the rejection of Orthodox demands for recognition of their church at the Diet of 1623, Lavrentii Drevyns'kyi had recognized that no changes could be expected during the king's lifetime, but that the interregnum would supply the opportunity.[23] Orthodox delegates from the Kingdom of Poland and the Grand Duchy of Lithuania supported by emissaries from the brotherhoods of Lviv and Vilnius and an Orthodox church delegation led by Mohyla quickly coalesced into an Orthodox lobby at the Convocation and Election Diets of 1632 and the Coronation Diet of 1633. Throughout 1632, Protestants and

Orthodox cooperated, although not always without friction, and even prior to the Convocation Diet, Mohyla contacted Krzysztof Radziwiłł, the Lithuanian Calvinist, to form a united front with the Protestants.[24]

Kysil's political involvement began with the dietines that were convened to elect delegates to the Convocation Diet. On May 15, Władysław had written to Kysil, thanking him for the affection shown him during Zygmunt's lifetime, and asking for his support and help in the election.[25] He promised in return to demonstrate his gratitude to Kysil and his family. Although Kysil was only a middle-ranking nobleman with influence in the politics of Volhynia, it was apparently clear from the beginning that Władysław would need his services. Kysil could also provide essential assistance in obtaining support from Orthodox nobles and in strengthening the Commonwealth's position in the Ukraine should Muscovy attack.

Kysil's Volhynian dietine met in early June, but he was not among those elected to the Convocation Diet.[26] Those who were chosen were instructed to demand recognition of the Orthodox church. Kysil may or may not have attended the Convocation Diet as a delegate of another dietine, but he certainly played no major role in its discussions.[27] Lavrentii Drevyns'kyi, Mykhailo Kropyvnyts'kyi, and Iurii Puzyna, representatives from the palatinates of Volhynia and Bratslav, coordinated their efforts with Mohyla's against the Uniate delegates from the Grand Duchy of Lithuania, the Uniate metropolitan, Ruts'kyi, and the ultra-Catholic faction.[28] The Diet rejected the Zaporozhian Cossacks' request that as "knights" they should be allowed to take part in the election, but the Cossack emissaries at least were able to reiterate Orthodox demands that their church be granted recognition.[29] A commission to resolve Uniate-Orthodox disputes presented a series of proposals and counter-proposals that were to be brought back to the local dietines for consideration, and the Orthodox agreed on condition that privileges would be granted at the Election Diet.[30]

The Convocation Diet delayed, but did not ultimately avoid, confrontation. Both the Vilnius Uniate and Orthodox brotherhoods published pamphlets arguing their respective cases and attacking the opposing side.[31] When in August dietines met to elect delegates to the Election Diet and to decide on programs for the *pacta conventa,* or contract with the new king, Orthodox and Catholic factions fought bitterly over the religious issue at the Luts'k dietine that Kysil attended.[32] The Orthodox faction triumphed; Kysil and five other delegates were elected on a platform that called for withholding election until far-reaching concessions were made to the Orthodox church.[33] The Catholic faction immediately filed protests against the Orthodox faction, demanding that this decision be overturned.[34] The Orthodox victory was, of course, not at all inimical to the policy or election of Władysław. When Kysil informed Władysław of the decisions of the dietine, he received a letter on August 29 thanking him for his loyalty.[35]

Because all nobles had a right to elect the king, an Election Diet was more subject than others to pressure from the entire nobility. The status of the Orthodox church was a major issue at the Diet, and Kysil spoke more frequently on its behalf than any other delegate. He argued that the Orthodox church was the legitimate descendant of the first Christian church of Rus' and was entitled to all privileges granted to that church before 1596. He maintained that the majority of the nobles were Eastern Christians who favored the Orthodox church, and that it would be foolhardy for the Commonwealth to ignore their wishes and accede to the demands of a few Uniate bishops. Finally, he urged that the issue be settled internally and not involve papal consent.[36]

That compromise would be difficult was evident from the beginning. The Roman Catholic bishop of Luts'k, A. Grochowski, protested that the concessions to the Orthodox negotiated at the Convocation Diet were illegal.[37] Tempers flared frequently and on one occasion Kysil threatened to resort to the sword if the demands of the Orthodox nobles were not met.[38] The Orthodox delegates also took care to remind the Catholics of the great number of Orthodox nobles who inhabited the lands between the rivers San and Dnieper.[39] Since a large number of Orthodox nobles had assembled in Warsaw to take part in the election, the pressure of great numbers was easy to argue. If they were to walk out in protest, as Kysil threatened, any election would be invalid.[40]

Kysil's militancy was needed to convince the ultra-Catholic faction that concessions were inevitable, making it possible for Władysław and other Catholic moderates to suggest a compromise. They proposed a commission composed of Roman Catholic senators and delegates to represent the Uniates, and Protestant senators and delegates to represent the Orthodox. The idea was accepted, and the commission met on October 19.[41] Under the supervision of Władysław himself, it worked out a division of bishoprics and church properties, and provided for the creation of two metropolitan sees and for the legal recognition of an Orthodox hierarchy.[42] To avoid forcing the ultra-Catholics publicly to accede to these concessions, only a general article calling for the "pacification of the Greek faith" was inserted in the *pacta conventa*; the Orthodox, however, were sent the terms of agreement in royal charters.[43] A major role in negotiating the compromise was played by Krzysztof Radziwiłł, who had also secured satisfaction of some Protestant demands.[44]

By mid-November, Władysław had placated numerous factions and had reduced the possibility of intrigue. On November 17, the assembled nobility elected him King of Poland and Grand Duke of Lithuania. He could be well pleased over the compromise he had worked out with the Orthodox. The Orthodox church was legally recognized, but only at the price of installing new leaders the king and Diet could trust, for although Władysław's charter granted the church the right to an Orthodox metropolitan in Kiev and four diocesan bishops, it did not confirm the illegally consecrated hierarchy already in place. New elections were to be held and the candidates submitted to the king for final approval. Recognition of Metropolitan Kopyns'kyi, who had been elected in 1631, was undesirable for a number of reasons. First, he had defied the government by accepting his unauthorized election. More important, he represented a militantly Orthodox wing that ruling circles regarded as politically unreliable. His support came from the Left-Bank monasteries, the very ones who had sympathized with Cossack rebellions and backed Borets'kyi's appeals to Muscovy for assistance.[45] Archimandrite Mohyla's ambition was also a factor in deciding to make new appointments.[46] He had forged the alliance with the Protestants and had brought about a compromise with the regime. A new election would allow him to take control of the church. He had considerable support; the Orthodox nobles could take pride in having their church headed by the son of a Moldavian ruler, and Władysław and the governing circles approved of him because his father had favored the Commonwealth and because he was related to some of the Commonwealth's leading families. He would be a loyal and trustworthy head of the church.

For Kysil, the successful establishment of a new church hierarchy would have a decisive impact on his career. The king had immediately appointed him a royal secretary and more royal favor could be expected if the new policies on the Orthodox question succeeded.[47] Kysil had directed the nobility's struggle for church recognition and could therefore be held responsible if the church misbehaved. He could only gain if it performed well as a patriotic and stabilizing force in the Ukraine. Kysil had worked closely with Mohyla during the synod of 1629. By securing Mohyla's succession to the metropolitan see, he could be sure that the church would be led by a hierarch with cultural and political views similar to his own. On November 13, immediately after the Diet, he attended a conference of Orthodox nobles and clerics; controlled by the nobility, it selected Mohyla as one of two candidates for metropolitan.[48] Władysław's rapid confirmation of Mohyla presented a *fait accompli* both to the Catholic faction, which had hoped to undo the legalization, and to Kopyns'kyi's supporters.

After Mohyla's election, Kysil departed for the Ukraine to report on the new compromise, to assure Orthodox nobles that the terms were acceptable, and to investigate the military situation, since the Muscovites had, as expected, attacked the Chernihiv lands in August. On December 30, Władysław wrote to Kysil, lauding him for his services at the dietine of the Kievan palatinate, thanking him for his advice, urging immediate action against the Muscovite offensive, and informing him that a campaign would be launched in the spring.[49]

The religious problem was far from over, however. Many Catholic nobles had signed the *pacta conventa* only after adding the reservation *"salvis iuribus Ecclesiae Catholicae,"* thereby providing themselves with the option of protesting the king's charters.[50] As directed by the papal nuncio, the Catholic party maintained that Catholic rights, particularly the title to churches and properties, could not be abridged without the pope's consent.[51] The Coronation Diet, which met on February 8, 1633, witnessed a renewal of Catholic-Orthodox debate. Władysław, mindful of the power of the Roman Catholic faction, appeared to be disposed toward reneging on the concessions. Kysil, leading the Orthodox delegates, demanded that the compromise agreement be maintained and claimed that the king had full authority to make decisions without papal approval.[52] Władysław's determination to solve the issue and his realization that war with Orthodox Muscovy was imminent worked to the Orthodox advantage. A delegation of Zaporozhian Cossacks made clear that should the privileges to the Orthodox church be tampered with, they would refuse to serve in an expedition against Muscovy.[53] Władysław dispatched an embassy to the Pope to explain the concessions, but held firm in backing the compromise solution.[54] He even had to threaten the Lithuanian chancellor, Albrycht Stanisław Radziwiłł, with appointing a Protestant as the chancellor's successor in order to force this pious Catholic to affix his seal to the charter granting privileges to the Orthodox.[55]

In the course of the election, Kysil had demonstrated his abilities as a parliamentarian. He had won the king's favor not only for his support, but also for his part in working out a solution to the difficult problem of granting the Orthodox church legal recognition. Władysław began his reign confident that a settlement of the troublesome controversy had been reached. Kysil had assisted in bringing about a compromise by his intransigent demands that the Diet adopt a constitution authorizing the division of church properties and the government's recognition of an Orthodox hierarchy. His determined and skillful pressure in the Diet had allowed Władysław to serve as a mediator. His talented leadership had also won him recognition as one of the most influential protectors of the Orthodox church.

After the Coronation Diet, Kysil traveled to Lviv, where the grateful Orthodox brotherhood gave a reception in his honor.[56] A year later, Kysil joined the brotherhood, thereby publicly committing himself to protecting Orthodox rights.[57] Until then, unlike Drevyns'kyi and Kropyvnyts'kyi, he had not even joined the Luts'k brotherhood in his native Volhynia.[58] Now, together with Mohyla's elevation to Kievan metropolitan, Kysil's emergence as a major lay patron provided a new type of leadership for the area. Even his signature symbolized this change. He was the first member of the Lviv brotherhood to abandon Cyrillic and to use the Latin alphabet and the Polish form of his name.

The Smolensk War

Much of the Coronation Diet was taken up by preparations for war against Muscovy. The Diet designated Kysil as one of its deputies in conducting the war.[59] Since his influence in the eastern lands of the Commonwealth would be useful, the king also appointed him to a number of important posts there. On February 12, 1633, he was made starosta of Nosivka in the Chernihiv region, which Muscovy had already invaded.[60] He was also appointed podkomorzy of Chernihiv, the highest provincial honor below the senatorial rank of castellan.[61] Kysil's continued influence and position depended on the outcome of the war, however, for only a determined and successful defense of the Ukrainian lands by the Orthodox nobility and Zaporozhian Cossacks would demonstrate that the policy of concessions to Orthodoxy had been successful. Should the Commonwealth lose the war and Muscovy regain the Chernihiv area, Kysil's new offices would be worthless and his lands would be lost.

Although Muscovite expectations that Sweden would launch war on a second front were dashed by the unexpected death of Gustavus Adolphus, the Commonwealth was still in dire straits.[62] The tsar's father, Patriarch Filaret, had built up a formidable army, which included numerous mercenaries and Russian units organized on Western models.[63] The rapid Muscovite advances of 1632 had recaptured most of the lands that Muscovy had lost in 1618 and had trapped a relatively small defense force in Smolensk. Muscovite negotiations with the Ottoman Empire endangered the southern flank of the Commonwealth, and Hetman Stanisław Koniecpolski had to retain the Kingdom's standing army in Podillia for the defense of the area against Tatar raids. As always, the Commonwealth was desperately short of the funds necessary to raise extra troops.[64]

Władysław initially ordered Kysil to appear at Smolensk by the end of June, but the king soon reversed this order and commanded him to proceed instead to the Ukraine to organize the defense of the Chernihiv lands.[65] The situation in the Ukraine was grave. At the Election Diet, Aleksander Piaseczyński, the castellan of Kam"ianets', had been placed in charge of the Chernihiv and Siverian front. He was given 20,000 złotys to raise a force among the Zaporozhians, who were then to drive the Muscovite armies from the Chernihiv and Siverian lands and then go to the defense of Smolensk.[66] Although the Muscovites retired northward, the siege of the Muscovite town of Putyvl' had been unsuccessful, and the Zaporozhians had refused to fight until they received full payment for their services.[67] Instead, they planned to raid Ottoman settlements on the Black Sea, a move that threatened to provoke an Ottoman offensive against the Commonwealth. In an effort to convince the Cossacks to remain neutral in the struggle, in early 1633, the Muscovite government forbade its military commanders to attack Cossack settlements.[68] It was essential for the Commonwealth that the Zaporozhians return to obedience and go to the aid of Smolensk. It was equally essential that those who remained in the Chernihiv lands support the local nobility in defending the Left Bank.

Thus, when Kysil arrived in Lviv in the spring of 1633, he faced an already difficult task, made even more difficult by the tense situation in the Orthodox church. In late April, Mohyla was consecrated as metropolitan at Saint George's cathedral in Lviv, but before he could take up residence in Kiev, he had to be accepted by the Kievan clergy and the Zaporozhians.[69] Kopyns'kyi had refused to renounce his claims to the office, and this refusal both endangered the new course in Orthodox policy and impeded the war effort.

Mohyla remained in Lviv until June, and it is likely that he and Kysil met to discuss church policy and to draw up a plan of action.[70] Mohyla then went to Kiev in July and initiated a vigorous campaign to regain St. Sophia cathedral from the Uniates and to force Kopyns'kyi to resign from the Kievan see. Although he finally succeeded, he was still not recognized by the powerful Zaporozhian army.[71]

The king, in the meantime, had left it to Kysil to secure the Zaporozhians' loyalty and to dispatch them to Smolensk.[72] The remnants of the Cossack army that had retreated from Putyvl' were encamped at Pereiaslav, where Kysil arrived in early August, along with an emissary from Hetman Koniecpolski, Pawłowski, who was also ordered to bring the Cossacks back into battle.[73]

They faced a formidable task.[74] The Zaporozhians were adamant about payment. They also refused Koniecpolski's proposal that they march to Smolensk along the Muscovite border lands. That route would have saved the Commonwealth's territories from the devastation of an army in transit, but would have greatly increased the hardships on the Zaporozhians by exposing them to Muscovite attacks. They were also unwilling to allow regular Commonwealth troops to be stationed in the Left-Bank lands in their absence, claiming that, while they were fighting the Muscovites, their wives would be violated by Commonwealth regulars.

When Kysil and Pawłowski read the king's instructions to the Zaporozhians and argued for their return to royal service, the Cossack officers were won over, and the troops eventually accepted the emissaries' promises that they would soon be paid. The Zaporozhians' demand that regulars not be quartered on the Left-Bank lands in their absence was settled by a compromise—a Cossack regiment would remain behind to defend the Left Bank and secure Cossack interests. It would operate in conjunction with Kysil's detachment. The Cossacks agreed to await a messenger carrying orders from the Lithuanian hetman, Krzysztof Radziwiłł, who was in charge of the Smolensk front.[75]

Having succeeded in this critical diplomatic mission, Kysil sought and gained approval of these terms from Hetman Koniecpolski.[76] His services were praised by the king, who on August 9, wrote to thank him for providing the forces so essential to the war effort.[77] The Zaporozhians arrived at Smolensk on September 18.[78]

In the course of these negotiations, Kysil finally secured Metropolitan Mohyla's acceptance by the Host, even though Kopyns'kyi had fled Kiev and had taken up residence at the Cossack camp, where he withdrew his registration and agitated against Mohyla as a usurper.[79] Mohyla and a large number of clergy and nobles had encamped near the Zaporozhians and were conducting an equally energetic propaganda war against Kopyns'kyi. Mohyla accused him of being a traitor and a supporter of Muscovy. Kysil pleaded Mohyla's case before the Host and convinced the Zaporozhians to acquiesce. In a compromise, Kopyns'kyi was to resign the metropolitan see, but would retain his position as abbot of the monastery of St. Michael in Kiev; in return, the Cossacks reluctantly agreed to abandon him. Mohyla had triumphed. The new metropolitan of Kiev and a great number of clergy entered the Cossack camp where the Zaporozhian Host received him with the respect due their spiritual leader. Mohyla blessed the cannons that were to be used in the Muscovite war, and thereby gave Orthodox approval to Zaporozhian participation in a war against Orthodox Muscovy.[80]

Kysil had succeeded brilliantly in his mission. The Zaporozhians, blessed by the new metropolitan of Kiev, returned to do battle against Muscovy and played a major role in relieving the pressure on Smolensk. Władysław's eastern policy was a success, and Kysil could expect further rewards for his role in that triumph.

By autumn, Kysil's major concern was the defense of the Chernihiv lands. He had at his disposal the regiment left behind by the Zaporozhians and his own small personal detachment. The king had promised that Hetman Koniecpolski would send reinforcements. Even though Koniecpolski successfully resisted the Tatar raid, he was unwilling to weaken his position on the southern front and never sent Kysil significant help, suggesting instead that Kysil rally the local nobility.[81] Lack of allocations by the Diet forced the king to deny Kysil's requests to increase the size of his detachment[82] so Kysil raised troops at his own expense while continuing to press for royal recognition and reimbursement.[83] Yet, as late as November, the king's only response was to promise Kysil that Koniecpolski would be sent to his aid as soon as possible and to authorize use of the local military units of the city of Kiev.[84] To these forces, Kysil added units drawn from the local nobility, primarily those belonging to the magnate Jeremi Wiśniowiecki.

In the meantime Kysil had to face the considerably more numerous units assembled by the Muscovite military commanders during the defense of Putyvl'. A Muscovite force led by Grigorii Aliab"ev had begun the siege of Chernihiv in September.[85] According to Kysil's account, they broadcast circulars among the local nobles maintaining that the Muscovite soldiers were not "simple people," but "boiar sons" and that they were there because Chernihiv belonged to the tsar by right of inheritance. They asserted that the tsar did not wish to shed blood; when he had regained the city, he would allow the Poles to depart freely with all their possessions, while "those who are of Rus'" would remain and live in liberty.[86] If Kysil's account is accurate, the Muscovites showed considerable perspicacity when it came to judging the local mentality. The tactic of impressing local nobles with the army's high birth and promising liberty, the most cherished of noble rights, was carefully calculated to convince the Ruthenian nobles that Muscovite rule would be acceptable. None of the circulars has survived, so it is impossible to check on Kysil's version of it, but in any event, it did not achieve its goal. The besieged forces held firm. Kysil's troops, augmented by some men sent by the starosta of Chernihiv, Marcin Kazanowski, came to Chernihiv's defense. Prior intelligence deprived the Muscovite forces of the element of surprise, and that, combined with the stubborn defense, forced Aliab"ev to raise the siege and withdraw.[87]

The Muscovites soon returned with a larger army, but this time bypassed Chernihiv and turned toward Myrhorod.[88] Again they met with no success and started to withdraw; this time Kysil's force, Wiśniowiecki's men, and Colonel Lavrynenko's Cossacks tried to cut off their return. They were not successful, however, and the army withdrew in good order. Kysil later maintained that his meagre forces prevented him from attacking and that throughout the campaign, he spent most of his energies keeping up morale and convincing the nobles and burghers of the Left Bank not to flee.[89] He did at least defend the territory; Władysław again wrote to praise him for his service on December 3, 1633, and rewarded the local nobles with grants of land.[90]

The new year saw a shift from defense to offense. Łukasz Żółkiewski and Jeremi Wiśniowiecki led attacks against Putyvl', Sevsk, Kursk, and Briansk.[91] Kysil recruited a large number of Cossacks (reputedly 20,000) to join the campaign.[92] Most of these were non-registered Cossacks, a customary, but potentially dangerous, method of raising an army. The siege of Sevsk in March failed, and the campaign scored no victories until the capitulation of Shein at Smolensk and the Peace of Polianovka.[93] The Zaporozhians were much more interested in embarking on a more lucrative expedition on the Black Sea, and the Cossacks had not yet been paid. But although the Commonwealth's forces achieved no major victories in the spring of 1634 on the Ukrainian front, they at least served to keep a substantial number of Muscovite troops occupied elsewhere while the main Muscovite army was forced to capitulate on the Smolensk front.

The Smolensk campaign and the peace treaty that followed were regarded as a victory by king and Commonwealth alike. Despite the interregnum and an ill-prepared army, the Commonwealth defeated the Muscovite offensive. In return for Władysław's renunciation of his unrealistic claim to the Muscovite throne, the two states agreed to accept the pre-war territorial status quo, made plans for a commission to adjust border disputes, and established new title protocols for both sovereigns.[94] The Treaty of Polianovka was conceived not as a truce, but as an "eternal peace." Its recognition that the Romanovs legitimately sat on the Muscovite throne and that the Commonwealth rightfully possessed the lands it had won finally solved the problems that had grown out of the Commonwealth's intervention in the Time of Troubles.

Kysil also emerged victorious from the Smolensk War. During the war he had not been remiss in pushing his claims for land, offices, and authority in the Chernihiv region.[95] After it he retained all those land grants and offices in territories no longer disputed. In his native Volhynia, he would always have been regarded as an upstart, but in Chernihiv the social mobility of a new society prevailed. Kysil helped to transplant the Commonwealth's institutions to the area.

Negotiating the borders turned out to be more difficult; it remained a point of contention throughout most of Władysław's reign.[96] In spite of the treaty, the Muscovite delegates struggled to retain, or to regain, every piece of land they could in this vaguely defined border area. The Commonwealth's nobles struggled equally to resist any concessions of territory over which they had even the most tenuous claim. According to the Polianovka Treaty, with minor exceptions, the border was to run along the line determined at Deulino, and joint boundary commissions were to set the line exactly by checking deeds of ownership and adjusting holdings so that no private lands belonging to citizens of one state remained on the other side of the border.[97] On November 1, 1634, the first of these commissions met. For the troublesome district around Novhorod-Sivers'kyi, Kysil was named head; the other members were Szczęsny Wizeły and Łukasz Witowski, from the Commonwealth, and Grigorii Pushkin and Grigorii Aliab"ev, Kysil's antagonist during the war, from the Muscovite side.[98] The Commonwealth's delegates had to negotiate with a stubborn opposition, but at the same time had been ordered by their government not to reach final agreements until a truce with the Ottomans would place them in a more favorable bargaining position. They were also subject to pressures from the border magnates who owned lands in the area.[99] In fact an attempt had been made to influence Kysil soon after his appointment, when on August 30, 1634, his benefactor Tomasz Zamoyski wrote, asking him to intercede on behalf of Jeremi Wiśniowiecki.[100] Wiśniowiecki's refusal to allow the cession to Muscovy of any of the lands he claimed was to remain a major stumbling block to a border settlement for over a decade.

On October 3, Hetman Stanisław Koniecpolski provided Kysil with documents and materials to begin his work.[101] Soon after, the king wrote to advise him "not [to] be surprised at Muscovite stubbornness or their claims. As we found out in past years, this is their standard procedure, but when they see their demands are in vain and that you, my faithful friend, and your colleagues stand up courageously. . . . they will abandon their customary determination."[102] The king also warned him that the "lawlessness" of the border landlords could play into Moscow's hands.

Kysil complied with the king's request to avoid making any final decisions; his commission reached no major agreements. When a new commission was appointed after the first Diet of 1635, Kysil, though still a member,[103] was outranked by two eastern magnates: Łukasz Żółkiewski, starosta of Kalush, and Marcin Kalinowski, the first palatine of the Chernihiv palatinate that the Diet of 1635 had established.[104] The Muscovites protested those appointments on the grounds that having two new members on the commission who claimed title to some of the disputed territories would hinder negotiations.[105]

In the decades that followed, Kysil often dealt with the same Muscovite officials whom he had first encountered in 1634.[106] His experience made him an expert on diplomacy with Muscovy. Unlike the magnates of the borderlands, notably Wiśniowiecki, who had claims to some of the disputed lands, Kysil acquired most of his estates after 1634, and therefore had no conflict of interest when it came time for territorial concessions to Muscovy.[107] The Muscovites therefore had no objections to Kysil, and he was later able to convert their good opinion into economic concessions in the very lands the Commonwealth had surrendered.[108] The Commonwealth's new policy of rapprochement with Muscovy was in need of such men. Although Kysil was not active in high-level negotiations until the 1640s, he had here managed to establish himself as a useful contact. His attitudes also accorded with those of the new king.

By 1635, Kysil, a minor but influential official, had neither the wealth nor the connections of the magnates; nevertheless, his ambition was already apparent. When Marcin Kalinowski received the royal appointment as Chernihiv palatine, Kysil was furious at having been overlooked.[109] His anger was temporary, however, and he did not allow it to damage his career. He continued to serve the king and Commonwealth, in the process becoming a major figure at the Diets as a leader of the Orthodox nobility and increasing his landholdings throughout the Ukraine.

Chapter 4

The Ukrainian Lands in the 1630s

After the conclusion of the Smolensk War, Kysil continued to take an active part in the political life of the Commonwealth, attending all the Diets of the 1630s and serving on numerous commissions.[1] As a delegate to the Diets, he was elected to numerous posts and honors: as the Chernihiv palatinate's representative to the taxation tribunal at Radom,[2] as the census taker and surveyor for royal lands in the palatinates of Kiev, Bratslav, and Podillia (in 1635);[3] as a commission member for the payment and quartering of the standing army (in 1633, 1638, 1640, 1641),[4] for the demarcation of the Chernihiv palatinate from the palatinates of Kiev and Smolensk (in 1638),[5] and for the demarcation commission for the palatinate of Kiev (in 1641);[6] and as negotiator of a settlement with the city of Gdańsk, which had refused to comply with the king's attempts to collect new tariffs (in 1638).[7] He also spoke frequently at the Diet. Although his interests were broad, the issues over which he had influence and for which his opinions were recorded in reports of Diets and contemporary correspondence all concerned the Ukraine.

The Zaporozhian Cossacks

The ordinances adopted after the Cossack uprising of 1630 were satisfactory to neither the government nor the Zaporozhians.[8] During the Smolensk War, Kysil and other Commonwealth officials had recruited far more Zaporozhians than the 8,000 provided for in the Ordinance of 1630, and most of them were discontented. They wanted to campaign on the Black Sea, to revenge offenses committed by the starostas of the eastern lands, and to receive their back pay. When peace came, the Commonwealth authorities feared that they would embark on a campaign in the south, thus giving the Turks a pretext to attack and provoke Tatar raids. That fear proved to be unfounded.[9] The Turks did not attack, and Koniecpolski was easily able to fend off Tatar raids, but the Commonwealth's position still needed strengthening. The Diet of 1634 had appointed Kysil commissioner to aid Hetman Koniecpolski's preparations to defeat a Turkish or Tatar attack,[10] and, as we have seen, he had delayed any decisions on the Muscovite boundary line until the Turkish threat had passed.[11] Kysil's major service was to dissuade the Cossacks from making their raid; later encomia lauded both Kysil and Łukasz Żółkiewski for having dealt with the Cossacks' discontent.[12]

In 1635, Cossack dissatisfaction was given a new outlet for expression when the truce with Sweden ran out and Władysław decided to press his claims to the Swedish throne.[13] The death of Gustavus Adolphus had weakened Sweden's position, and Władysław actively embarked on a program to build a navy, so essential for any war with Sweden. Władysław sought to use Cossack boats, which had proved so effective on the Black Sea, to attack Sweden on the Baltic. Because of the nobility's opposition, however, Władysław's Swedish war plan came to nothing, and the truce was converted into a treaty. But the preliminary preparations had whetted Cossack ambitions and provided the opportunity to frustrate Hetman Koniecpolski's intentions to place them under closer supervision.[14]

The first Diet of 1635 set the Cossack register at 7,000 and provided for commissioners to supervise its compilation, called for a fort to be built on the Dnieper to keep the Cossacks from rallying in Zaporizhzhia and ordered starostas in the borderlands to prevent them from gathering the wood and supplies necessary for a sea campaign.[15] Unlike most previous Cossack ordinances, the 1635 decision was actually implemented—a fort was built by forced Cossack labor at Kodak and two hundred dragoons were stationed there.[16]

The Swedish war plan, however, weakened the government in the southeast, because the Cossack administration loyal to the government left for the Baltic, and this allowed discontented Cossacks to take action. Ivan Sulyma led a rebellion that destroyed the fortress at Kodak, and was in the midst of preparing a campaign to the Black Sea, when Koniecpolski returned unexpectedly after the failure of the Swedish war plan. He put down Sulyma's revolt, but the advantage he had won from enforcing the Ordinance of 1635 had been swept away. Negotiations to bring the Cossacks back to obedience were placed in the hands of Łukasz Żółkiewski, who had influence among the Cossack elite, and of Kysil, who bought loyalty with bribes.[17] The second Diet of 1635 ordered Sulyma's execution and called for a new commission to resolve the Cossack problem, although until money was made available to pay them it was in fact insoluble.

The prevailing mood was one of apprehension; and the political situation was unstable as various factions in Crimea sought to enlist Cossack support for a civil war and the border disputes with Moscow

remained unresolved.[18] Hetman Koniecpolski, afraid that the Muscovites would exploit the instability in the Ukraine and seize the border
areas that they claimed, requested Kysil to return early from the
sessions of the Tribunal in Lublin in the spring of 1636 and to investigate
Muscovite intentions.[19] Kysil did so, and reported that the Muscovites
had no plans to press their claims by force, because, in contrast to the
situation in 1635, no Turkish threat weakened the Commonwealth's
position. He maintained, however, that the Ukraine would not be
secure until the border disputes with Muscovy were completely settled
and that, in order to fulfill his obligations as a citizen and a servant of the
king, and in response to Koniecpolski's orders, he always had "one eye
on Moscow, the other on the Cossacks."[20] He passed on information to
the king and court from his informants in Muscovy and the Crimea.

In the summer of 1636, Kysil and Żółkiewski went empty-handed to
Pereiaslav to meet the Cossacks, who had been promised two years'
back pay.[21] Nevertheless, they did manage to resolve complaints against
Stanisław Daniłowicz (a borderland magnate and starosta who had
persecuted the Cossacks and had seized property belonging to the
monks of St. Nicholas monastery in Kiev), to enforce the ordinances,
and to postpone an outright confrontation.[22]

Because Żółkiewski fell ill, when August came, Kysil had to undertake a mission to a second Cossack council alone.[23] Once there, it was
only with great difficulty that he was able to convince the Host to wait
another four weeks before launching a campaign to the sea and to
refrain from plundering the lands in the possession of the border
starostas.[24] After the council, Kysil wrote a detailed account of his
methods of dealing with the Cossacks in the form of a "Discourse" to
Hetman Koniecpolski, and probably to the king as well. He pointed out
that the Cossacks were not a monolithic unit but a tripartite group: the
officers who could be won over with bribes and favors; the "honorable"
men with homes and families "to whom one should call to mind the
unity of the Fatherland, and the freedoms guaranteed to their descendants"; and the "wild rebels" who must be dealt with by the sword, since
"reason, piety, religion, liberty, wives, and children mean nothing to
them."[25] He had won over the first by buying them off, thereby
obtaining their services to set aside the decisions of the council. He had
won over the second by having Metropolitan Mohyla send two monks to
appeal to them with a letter actually drafted by Kysil himself, which he
described as having moved those "who among them have God in their
hearts, who are to some degree pious in religion, to whom freedom,
wife, and children are dear." He had silenced the third by deception and
by having the officers help in controlling them. The deception, "even

greater than that at Sevsk" (during the 1633 siege), to which he resorted was to pretend that he had received a letter from the king threatening the disloyal with punishment and promising payment.[26] It was this fictitious letter that enabled Kysil to reverse the council's decision to begin a campaign on the Black Sea. He concluded his discourse by maintaining that the problem could best be solved by "the glitter of thalers," that is by paying them the back wages owed.[27]

Kysil expanded on the ideas of his discourse in a letter to Koniecpolski written in late August.[28] He noted three factors that had to be taken into account in dealing with the Cossacks: first, they had a great love for their clergy of the Greek faith and rite—though he judged them in many ways closer to Tatars than to Christians; second, among them fear was a more important instrument than benevolence; and, third, they could easily be bought off. Kysil mentioned once more the service Mohyla had provided in convincing the Cossacks not to revolt by sending on the letters Kysil had written: "I have used the services of His Grace, the Father Metropolitan. He sent two clergymen to the Zaporozhian Host to appeal to the depths of their mercy that if they call themselves sons of that Church, for whose integrity they have so often offered [to shed] their blood, they should not wish to be guilty of their own destruction and that of their liberties and those of their Mother Church because of their rebelliousness, ugly impatience for money, and insults to the Commonwealth."[29] The letters threatened the Cossacks with the metropolitan's malediction if they did not comply with the requests of the king's emissaries.

In addition to bribery, threats, and clerical influence, Kysil encouraged the Cossacks to place their trust in him because they had in common both religion and nationality. In a letter of August 27, 1636, to the Zaporozhians, for example, he maintained that he expected their cooperation because they were both of the same faith and of the same Ruthenian people, and because he had always had their good will.[30] These various ploys averted a confrontation in the autumn and winter of 1636, even though Kysil himself spent most of the winter confined by illness to the Caves monastery in Kiev, suffering from what was probably an attack of gout in his hands and feet, which was later so often to plague him.[31]

The Cossacks still sought both concessions and back pay, and now set their hopes on the Diet that convened in January 1637.[32] By then, wages were owed them for four years, and they complained as well of persecutions by borderland starostas and the failure of the royal commissioners to fulfill their promises. They maintained that they had proved their loyalty by not taking advantage of the Commonwealth's weakened position during the illness, death, and funeral of Łukasz Żółkiewski.[33] They believed that any limitation on the number of Cossacks who could be registered would only be temporary, because they knew that Hetman Koniecpolski wished to intervene in the Tatar civil war and would therefore need additional Cossack forces.[34]

The Diet appropriated funds sufficient to pay at least some of their back wages and appointed Kysil and Stanisław Potocki commissioners to the Zaporozhians, with Kysil taking Żółkiewski's place as senior member.[35] When Kysil reached the Cossack camp, he reported the Cossacks were much less interested in money than in a war against the Ottomans.[36] Anticipating the lenient policies of wartime, the Cossacks were unwilling to participate in forming a new register, and this made the commissioners' task even more difficult than expected. The commissioners and the officers were nevertheless able to begin compiling a register by threatening the intervention of the regular army and by promising that vacancies would be filled at Kaniv and Pereiaslav at a later date. As usual, Kysil's method was to divide and conquer by appealing to the more trustworthy men who had long been registered Cossacks over those who were seeking admission to the Cossack ranks for the first time. The latter saw through this maneuver, however. They began to complain that the commissioners had no money to distribute, and attempted to convince the Host to embark on a Turkish campaign. Kysil countered by showing the actual bullion and won over the registered Cossacks.[37]

When the commissioners required that the registered Cossacks swear loyalty on the basis of the Cossack Ordinance of 1625, however, disturbances finally did break out, since the Cossacks had expected that the Ordinance of 1630—which was more favorable to them—would remain in force. The commissioners then told the Cossacks that if they continued to be obstinate the Commonwealth would destroy "the very name of Cossack, since it would rather look at a desert and wild beasts, than rebellious masses."[38] Although the Cossacks might flee to the lower Dnieper, their wives and children would have to remain behind abandoned, and they could not settle any place else because "the Dnieper is their Fatherland, and there is no place like it anywhere. The Don cannot be compared to the Dnieper, or the slavery of those parts to the freedom here: as a fish cannot live out of water, so a Cossack cannot live away from the Dnieper, and whoever owns the Dnieper also owns the Cossacks."[39] When the commissioners then began to leave and the Cossack hetman threatened to resign his office, the Cossacks yielded and swore the required oath. Kysil and Potocki did complete the register at Kaniv and Pereiaslav, as they had promised.[40]

After the council, Kysil wrote a second discourse on the Cossack problem.[41] Unlike the first, which was simply an account of his dealings with the Cossacks, this second one was a practical program for the reform of the Cossack administration. Also addressed to Stanisław Koniecpolski, it began by describing the Cossacks rather too graphically as "a boil perennially on the verge of bursting." He blamed the situation on the starostas who derived income from the royal lands and castles entrusted to them but often did not reside in the area, and were therefore oblivious to the dangers that could arise from Cossack dissatisfaction. In fact, they often merely aggravated the problem by their excessive exactions. He described the Cossacks as a "flock without a shepherd," and he maintained that only when a "manager" would be permanently stationed in the Ukraine could each spark of rebellion be put out, "since when there is no one to put it out, it becomes a great and uncontrollable conflagration."

Kysil proposed to create a new office, a sort of ombudsman who would be stationed in the Ukraine and adjudicate any disputes that arose between the Cossacks and starostas or other local administrators. This new official would disburse funds to the Cossacks, expel rebellious Cossacks from the register, and serve as the intermediary between the hetmans of the Kingdom and the Cossack hetman. Kysil emphasized that the official must be supplied with ample funds so that he would be able to buy supporters. He mentioned Łukasz Żółkiewski's activities during the 1635 Sulyma rebellion as a type of administration he favored and maintained that, although he had been able to contain the Cossacks all by himself in 1636, such a feat would no longer be possible. To prove his objectivity, he ended by remarking that he himself was determined never to serve as an intermediary to them again, because although he had considerable experience and an extensive system of informants, he was unqualified for the proposed post.[42] Obviously, that protestation was merely pro forma. He would have been happy to be the one to elevate the position of Cossack commissioner, to which he had been appointed after the death of Żółkiewski, into a higher and more powerful one. Since he had already complained of the drain on his resources that his service as commissioner had entailed, he probably wrote the discourse to ensure that when appointed he would be provided with sufficient funds.[43]

Some of Kysil's proposals were incorporated into the Cossack Ordinance of 1638, but it was passed only after the suppression of the Cossack rebellion of 1637–38, and, instead of creating an ombudsman and intermediary, it abolished the office of Cossack hetman and designated the new official as administrator of the registered Cossacks.[44]

Kysil's failure to head off that rebellion was probably the major reason why he was not appointed to the new post.

The spark that Kysil foresaw ignited a conflagration in the summer of 1637, when the Diet expressed its willingness to pay part of the wages due the Cossacks, but turned down their request that the artillery, seized from them after the 1635 rebellion, be returned.[45] Hetman Koniecpolski had allowed the Cossacks to intervene in the civil war in Crimea and this, too, had both raised Cossack expectations and introduced dissension over which Crimean faction should be supported.[46]

A Cossack contingent led by Pavlo But, or Pavliuk, was dissatisfied with the officers' policies in the Crimean struggle. In the spring of 1637, Pavliuk began to plot against the Host leaders; in May, he seized the Cossack artillery and transported it to the Lower Dnieper, whereupon the Cossack Hetman Tomylenko avoided conflict by immediately resigning his office. Pavliuk then circulated charges that the Cossack officers were guilty of malfeasance in office because they had not secured the return of the artillery, and he rallied the nonregistered Cossacks around him by claiming that all Cossacks were equal and that therefore the distinction between registered and nonregistered Cossacks should be abolished.[47]

Pavliuk's agitation came at an especially dangerous time, because in the summer of 1637 the authorities of the Commonwealth were on the verge of war with the Ottoman Empire.[48] In August, Koniecpolski drew his troops up to the Moldavian border and called upon the Cossacks to join him. This placed loyal Cossacks in a difficult position. In July, the government had recognized Sava Kononovych, the colonel of Pereiaslav, as Tomylenko's successor, but Pavliuk charged the whole leadership with incompetence and failure to act in the interest of the Cossack rank-and-file. He attacked them for their close relationship with the deceased Łukasz Żółkiewski. Frightened by the attacks, many of the compromised officers fled to Koniecpolski's camp.[49] While Koniecpolski tried accommodation, Pavliuk, playing for time, continued to affirm his loyalty and to blame the former officers—especially the newly appointed hetman, Sava Kononovych—for all difficulties. He cleverly condemned the new hetman as an "unworthy, foreign, Muscovite"—an accusation the authorities of the Commonwealth, who had often warned the Cossacks against contacts with Muscovy, found hard to refute—and promised to cooperate with Koniecpolski, if Koniecpolski would recognize him as hetman.[50] Then, Pavliuk captured Sava Kononovych and ignored Koniecpolski's demands to release both him and the Cossack officers already in Pavliuk's hands. Since a large part of the standing army was scheduled to be mustered out on December 1, no funds were available to pay them beyond that date. The king could not provide additional troops, so Hetman Koniecpolski ended negotiations in early November and ordered his forces, under the command of Field Hetman Mikołaj Potocki, to march against the rebels.[51]

Kysil had from the first attempted to head off the revolt. In the summer of 1637, two of his subjects had joined the rebellious Cossacks and had driven him from his estates in the Chernihiv palatinate.[52] In September, he contacted Pavliuk in search of compromise,[53] and Pavliuk demanded recognition as Cossack hetman, the punishment of starostas against whom the Cossacks had grievances, and a permanent return of the artillery to the Cossacks.[54] If these demands were met, he promised to assist Koniecpolski on the Turkish front, but Kysil did not obtain acceptance of them from Koniecpolski.[55]

The Cossack rebels then attempted to win over other segments of the populace to their cause. In November, Pavliuk's field hetman, Pavlo Skydan, circulated rumors along the Left Bank to the effect that "certain and indisputable information has come to us that the enemies of our Christian Ruthenian people and our ancient Greek faith—that is, the Poles [*Lachowie*]—having conceived an evil plan, forgetting the fear of God, are coming into the Ukraine in order to shed Christian blood, defile our wives, and enslave our children."[56] The Cossacks were as aware as Kysil that appeals to religion and nationality could be effective; they even used the same tactics on him as he had directed toward them, addressing him as "friend, long well disposed to the Host" and "Patron of Our Holy Mother, the Eastern Church."[57]

The troops led by Potocki had entered the Right-Bank Ukraine in late November,[58] and in early December, Kysil joined the army with his private detachment.[59] The Right Bank had been left with only a few Cossack troops led by Skydan to defend it, but the initial advantage that the government troops had was nevertheless short-lived.[60] Potocki's lack of funds pushed the standing army to near rebellion, and Pavliuk soon came up from Zaporizhzhia to join his troops to Skydan's forces.[61]

The confrontation that Kysil had worked so hard to avoid finally took place at Kumeiky, near Moshny on the Right Bank. Szymon Okolski, who was there, reported that "looking upon their faces, the ardent adherent of the Greek Faith, the Lord Podkomorzy [Kysil] cried and said: 'Beautiful is that band of men, and the spirit among them is not bad—if only they [fought] against the enemy of the Holy Cross and not against the King and the Commonwealth and their Fatherland there would be something to praise them for, while this way they must be condemned."[62] The Cossacks were routed, although some of the officers, including Pavliuk and Skydan, escaped capture.[63] Kysil was later commended by Mikołaj Potocki for his heroic role in the battle.[64]

On December 19, Potocki caught up with the main body of the Cossack forces at Borovytsia, and the next day the Cossacks began to sue for terms, with Kysil serving as negotiator.[65] Potocki demanded that the leaders of the rebellion be handed over, but promised amnesty to the rest, so they surrendered Pavliuk the following day.[66] The terms of submission were complicated by Koniecpolski's insistence that they include a permanent solution to the Cossack problem and keep the Cossack artillery in the government's control. He refused to appoint a new hetman, calling instead for a royal commissioner and government appointees to replace the Cossack colonels.[67]

A Cossack council met on December 24 to hear the conditions brought by Kysil and Stanisław Potocki; they amounted in effect to a total capitulation. The Cossacks were forced to acquiesce to Koniec-polski's decision not to appoint a hetman before the king and Diet reached a decision; until then Iliiash Karaimovych, the colonel of Pereiaslav, was to lead the Host. They promised to campaign only when—and as soon as—they were ordered by the king and Crown hetman, and they pledged full compliance with the register compiled by the commissioners.[68] The oath to uphold these conditions was adminis-tered by Adam Kysil and signed, among others, by the scribe of the Host, Bohdan Khmel'nyts'kyi.[69]

Many of the rebel leaders had fled across the Dnieper, however, so this did not end the rebellion.[70] To destroy Cossack opposition to the new regime, Mikołaj Potocki continued the campaign of subjugation, while Kysil returned to his estates where he entertained Potocki at Divytsia.[71] Potocki finally ended his campaign with a series of public executions in Kiev,[72] a procedure that Kysil did not appear to have approved, since ten years later he referred to these executions as "cruel examples" that the Cossacks would undoubtedly seek to avenge.[73]

Potocki now entrusted his brother Stanisław and Kysil with the task of compiling the Cossack register. On February 15, they began their new series of registrations in Trekhtymiriv, while crown troops settled into winter quarters throughout the Ukraine.[74] The commissioners ex-plained the terms of registration in detail, and, contrary to earlier practice, had each Cossack give his oath of allegiance individually. Awareness that the rebellion was still continuing in Zaporizhzhia made the commissioners' task difficult, but eventually the entire Host swore loyalty to the Commonwealth. From them the commissioners drew a punitive force that was ordered to apprehend additional rebels whom

Koniecpolski had ordered to be executed. The commissioners ended a report on their registration activities by noting that a march to Zaporizhzhia was necessary, but would be dangerous without a larger force. In spite of this, a campaign was undertaken in February of 1638, and was—as they had anticipated—unsuccessful.[75]

In March, Kysil attended the Diet called to deal with the rebels and solve the Cossack question.[76] Koniecpolski presented to a special Diet commission that he headed his project for reform, which incorporated Kysil's proposal for a permanent commissioner who would be equipped with the necessary forces to keep the Cossacks in bounds.[77] He did not suggest, as Kysil had done, that this commissioner be an intermediary official between the Kingdom's hetmans and the Cossack hetman, but rather that the commissioner should replace the latter altogether. He also proposed that the colonels be selected by the king, that only the lower officials be elected by the Host, that the government's appointees should all receive both salary and a personal guard paid for from the Kingdom's treasury, and that sums be set aside for the Host's pay. The rebuilding and staffing of Kodak was outlined in a secret document.[78]

Kysil's reaction to Koniecpolski's program is not really known. It is known, however, that when Koniecpolski's proposal was brought up for discussion, Kysil made a motion to postpone debate until the demands of the Orthodox church were satisfied. Thus, it would appear that Kysil had fallen out with the policy makers, including Koniecpolski.[79] This became even more apparent in the debate over sentencing Pavliuk and the other Cossack leaders: Kysil was the only delegate to oppose the death sentence, arguing that the honor of the Commonwealth would suffer if "promises" were not kept.[80] He did so in vain; Pavliuk was executed.[81]

To what "promises" did he refer? None are mentioned either in Okolski's diary or in the reports of Koniecpolski and Potocki. But ten years later, Kysil, when asked to intercede between the government and the Cossacks, lamented: "Although I have always desired their confidence for such an occasion, I am afraid they will remember Kumeiky, where they surrendered on the strength of my word of honor that their leaders' lives would be spared, and that [oath] was later broken."[82] While it is not clear whether Kysil had any authority, either from the king or from hetmans Koniecpolski or Potocki to promise to spare Pavliuk's life, Pavliuk's execution during the 1638 Diet was a disaster for Kysil personally and marked the temporary end to his role in Cossack affairs. Whether the king and Koniecpolski were displeased with Kysil's pledge at Borovytsia or with his actions thereafter and who or what lay behind the decision are questions difficult to answer. Kysil could not have been totally out of favor, since the Diet still appointed him to the commission to see to the payment of the army and to a boundary commission for the Chernihiv palatinate. If Władysław was displeased, his displeasure was temporary; a year later he offered Kysil the post of castellan of Chernihiv. Still, there is no doubt that the March Diet of 1638 marked the end of Kysil's role as Cossack commissioner. He did not participate in putting down the renewed Cossack rebellion under Iats'ko Ostrianyn in the spring and summer of 1638. Whether or not he had refused to cooperate after the execution of Pavliuk, his broken pledge would in any case undoubtedly have ended his usefulness as a negotiator with the Cossacks. It hardly mattered, however, since the harsh regime of 1638 had temporarily removed Cossack discontent as a major problem.

On balance, Kysil had been a successful Cossack commissioner. His adroit handling of the Zaporozhians in 1632–1634 had proved him worthy of the new posts the king had bestowed upon him, and his manipulative skills between 1634 and 1636 had at least put off the inevitable confrontation for a considerable time. At Borovytsia, his tactics were clearly less successful, but whether Kysil was misled or overstepped his authority will probably never be known. He could not have been entirely successful, whatever the case; the Diet was unwilling to pay the registered Cossacks, and neither the hetmans nor the Diet were anxious to punish the starostas and magnates who had seized Cossack lands and attempted to enforce the corvée. Yet, though the Commonwealth would not conciliate the Cossacks, neither could it do without them, since it could not raise funds sufficient to maintain a standing army large enough to guard the southeastern frontier. Hetman Koniecpolski knew full well that if the Ottomans and Tatars invaded in full force, Cossack assistance would be as essential as it had been at Khotyn. In fact, Koniecpolski was partially responsible for the turmoil among the Cossacks, in that his plans for an offensive war against the Crimea gave the Cossacks not included in the register hope that their status would soon be changed. To avoid a repetition of the numerous rebellions of the 1630s, Koniecpolski imposed a draconian regime. The new Cossack administration, so different from the one Kysil had suggested in 1637, succeeded in suppressing the Cossacks for a decade. But when their discontent burst forth again, it had behind it a pent-up force far greater than any represented by the Cossack revolts of the 1630s.

In the meantime Kysil had become adept in maneuvering in the quickly changing world of Zaporozhian politics in which his talents in bribery, organizing spy networks, and swaying the masses were all put to good use. His sympathies lay with his own order, and he sought to manipulate the Cossacks to the nobility's advantage; but he also insisted that trustworthy Cossacks existed who were guided by the same sentiments about liberty and duty to the fatherland as any noble and who were therefore worthy of concessions and rewards. His goal was to create a Cossack elite from the officers and "honorable segment," and to isolate them from the non-registered Cossacks, as we can see when, after the 1637 rebellion, he took the Cossacks to task for inciting the "peasants," in which category he included the non-registered Cossacks.

Kysil's religious and national bonds with the Cossacks were useful. Through his references to their common blood and membership in the Ruthenian nation and his appeals to their loyalty to the Orthodox church, he could get a hearing, just as his enlistment of the Orthodox church against Cossack rebels deprived them of a potent rallying cry. Kysil's presence as a major functionary of the Commonwealth's administration did much to disarm Skydan's charge that the confrontation of 1637 was a "Polish" assault against the "Christian Ruthenian nation." His Orthodox faith and Ruthenian descent were his major advantages as Cossack commissioner. Had he been a Catholic and a Pole, he would have been just another wealthy landowner and official in the Ukraine; as defender of the Orthodox faith and "scion of a six-hundred-year-old Rus' family" he wielded impressive diplomatic weapons.

The Defense of Orthodoxy in the Diet (1633–1641)

The election of a new monarch in 1632 had provided Kysil and the other Orthodox nobles with an opportunity to restore the legality of the Orthodox church. Instead of obtaining the abolition of the Union of Brest, the Orthodox nobles ended up with a partition of the Ruthenian church. The Orthodox hierarchy, consisting of the metropolitan in Kiev and four suffragan bishops in Lviv, Przemyśl, Luts'k and Mstsislaŭ (a newly created Belorussian see), retained control of all the churches and monasteries in Kiev, except the Vydubets' monastery, and received rights to specified churches in Vilnius and in a number of cities in the Belorussian lands.[83] The Orthodox church was also given the right to establish schools, printing presses, and brotherhoods.

The Uniate church retained the remainder of the bishoprics. It was to be headed by a metropolitan of Kiev, but that office would be merely symbolic because Kiev was an Orthodox stronghold (Ruts'kyi continued to reside in the Grand Duchy of Lithuania in Vilnius and Navahrudak).[84] That metropolitan would have five suffragan bishops in Polatsk, Chełm, Volodymyr-Volyns'kyi, Pinsk, and Smolensk.[85] The Uniate bishops of the two sees granted to the Orthodox, Iov Pochapivs'kyi of Luts'k and Atanazii Krupets'kyi of Przemyśl, were granted compensation for their losses in revenue.[86] Except for the churches and monasteries specifically assigned, religious institutions were to be allowed to choose the denomination to which they wished to belong,[87] and special commissions were created to determine what those preferences were.[88]

The "Pacification of the Greek Faith," far from being a final settlement, simply gave legal sanction to competition and struggle. The division of the dioceses reflected the relative strength of the two factions in the Commonwealth—resistance to the Union of Brest was stronger in the Ukrainian lands of the Kingdom of Poland than in the Belorussian lands of the Grand Duchy of Lithuania.[89] Although Orthodox resistance to the union in the Grand Duchy had had its violent manifestations, such as the murder of Iosafat Kuntsevych in Vitsebsk in 1623, the Orthodox nobles in the Grand Duchy were neither sufficiently powerful nor sufficiently numerous to provide consistent pro-Orthodox Diet delegations comparable to those of the Ukrainian incorporation lands.[90] Support from great Protestant magnates, such as Krzysztof Radziwiłł, certainly strengthened the Orthodox position in the Grand Duchy; however, even in the first years after the union no Orthodox protector of the church in the Grand Duchy was as powerful as Volhynia's Prince Konstantyn Ostroz'kyi. Later the decline of the Protestant faction in the Grand Duchy deprived the Orthodox of their most powerful allies, while the increasingly important faction of Catholic magnates advanced the Uniate cause.[91] In the 1620s and 1630s the few Uniates serving as delegates in the Diet were from the Grand Duchy. Included among them was one of Kysil's major antagonists at the 1632 Election Diet, Mykola Tryzna, steward of the Grand Duchy.[92]

The Belorussian lands, and their cultural capital Vilnius, felt the influence of the Renaissance and Reformation much earlier than the incorporation lands did, and while that influence made Vilnius the major center of Orthodox and Ruthenian culture in the sixteenth century, it also served to effect a closer integration with the officially Catholic Grand Duchy.[93] Those close contacts with Lithuanians and with Polish culture weakened the Rus' Orthodox community far more than parallel processes did later in the incorporation lands.[94] Even though the latter were part of the Kingdom of Poland after 1569, their Orthodox elite proved more resistant to Polish culture and Roman Catholicism. Although the Belorussian lands continued to supply the Orthodox church with leaders, and while the burghers of Hrodna, Polatsk, Vitsebsk, Vilnius, and other cities resisted the union, the Orthodox ecclesiastical and political center shifted to the Ukrainian lands. Vilnius remained a center of Orthodox culture in the first decades of the seventeenth century, but in the late sixteenth, Lviv had gradually become more and more important in its Orthodox publishing and educational activities, and after the union, the loyalty of the bishop of Lviv, Iarema Tysarovs'kyi, to Orthodoxy assured the city's place as an Orthodox stronghold.[95] The Stauropegial Brotherhood of Lviv had no Uniate rival as the Orthodox brotherhood of the Holy Ghost had in Vilnius, where the brotherhood of the Holy Trinity provided Uniate competition. Furthermore, Lviv had no Uniate churches in the first half of the century, while in Vilnius the Uniates even had a seminary to train their clergy.[96] The opposition of the bishops of Lviv and Przemyśl to the Union of Brest and the support of numerous Orthodox petty nobles preserved Orthodoxy's position in the Ruthenian palatinate, while first, the patronage of Ostroz'kyi, and later, the activities of the middle nobility and the support of the Zaporozhian Cossacks, guaranteed the survival of Orthodoxy in the incorporation lands.[97]

Through the strength and determination of the Orthodox nobles, burghers, Cossacks, and clerics, Kiev had also developed as a major Orthodox cultural, educational, artistic, and ecclesiastical center by the 1620s. Unlike the Orthodox metropolitans of the sixteenth century, who avoided this city in ruins, maintaining their residences in the Grand Duchy, Metropolitan Borets'kyi and his successors made Kiev their residence.[98] Unlike most of the bishops consecrated in 1620, who did not actually reside in their sees because of Catholic opposition, Borets'-kyi was able to use Kiev and its surrounding Cossack and noble population as a base of support for his "illegal" hierarchy.[99]

In 1632–1633 the division of sees took all these developments into account. The Orthodox retained the sees of Lviv, whose bishop was the only Orthodox hierarch recognized by the government before 1632, and regained Przemyśl, which had remained Orthodox after the Union of Brest and had resisted the appointment of the Uniate Atanazii Kru-pets'kyi in 1611.[100] They were also given the Luts'k see, which encompassed the central and eastern Volhynian lands, and the metropolitan see of Kiev, which included a large swath of territory in the Kingdom of Poland (the palatinates of Kiev and Bratslav) and in the Grand Duchy, including Vilnius. In practice, however, the Orthodox had little authority in Vilnius and the Uniates little in Kiev; the division approximated a demarcation of spheres of influence, because each metropolitan's authority was greater in areas nearest to his residence.[101]

The Uniates had bishops in Polatsk, Pinsk, and Smolensk, in addition to their metropolitan in the Grand Duchy.[102] They were also given the bishopric of Volodymyr-Volyns'kyi, which included territories both in

the Grand Duchy and the Kingdom in the Polissian region, and Chełm
on the Ukrainian-Polish ethnographic border, the only Uniate bishopric
entirely in the Kingdom and an area in which there were also many
Roman Catholics.[103]

The "pacification" articles that allowed parishes to choose which
jurisdiction they wished to join left Orthodox and Uniates endlessly
struggling for the properties of the "Rus' Church."[104] The 1620 restoration of the Orthodox hierarchy had created rival claimants for sees held
by Uniates, and the struggle in the ensuing decade was not one between
two hierarchies of two distinct ecclesiastical organizations, but between
two groups of competitors, each of whom claimed to be the only holders
of the sees. The 1632 "pacification" tried to solve that problem by
assigning some dioceses to Orthodox and some to Uniates, and by
demanding that new Orthodox candidates be proposed to the king, so
that the claims of competing bishops could be avoided. But there were a
number of obstacles to this plan. At first, the "illegal" Metropolitan
Kopyns'kyi refused to relinquish his claims to Mohyla, causing strife
among the Orthodox. The Uniate bishops of Luts'k and Przemyśl
refused to hand over their dioceses and revenues to the new Orthodox
appointees. Atanazii Krupets'kyi continued to struggle for his rights to
the Przemyśl see throughout the 1630s, and the Orthodox claimant,
Semen (Sylvestr) Hulevych-Voiutyns'kyi, resorted to force to take over
episcopal properties.[105]

But the major problem was that the pacification articles in effect
abolished the territorial dioceses of the Ruthenian church; if an individual parish had the right to choose whatever faith it wished, it could
easily choose one different from that of the nearest bishop and thus
remove itself from his jurisdiction. In the territorial diocese of Lviv, for
example, parishes choosing to be Uniate had to refuse to recognize the
authority of the local bishop and to turn either to the Uniate metropolitan or to the nearest Uniate bishop (Chełm or Volodymyr-Volyns'kyi).
Correspondingly, a parish in the Volodymyr-Volyns'kyi diocese which
declared itself Orthodox rejected the rule of the local bishop, and had to
submit itself instead to the neighboring Orthodox bishop of Luts'k.

The 1632 "pacification" therefore really represented an attempt not to
pacify, but to sever permanently the ecclesiastical traditions and institutions of the Ruthenian church by dividing it into separate Uniate and
Orthodox churches that had no geographical coherence. In practice,
however, it encountered great resistance. Since the articles were vague
in redefining diocesan boundaries and jurisdictional hierarchies, and
since the traditions of territorial dioceses and of a united church were
strong, local bishops continued to claim jurisdiction over all the

churches in their diocese, regardless of choice, and this claim extended even to churches specifically assigned in a royal charter.[106] Local bishops had the authority of tradition and the power of close geographic proximity on their side when it came to the unassigned churches, helping them keep parishes under their control. Since the dioceses had been assigned according to the relative strengths of the two factions to begin with, this was for the most part not difficult to accomplish even though no area was totally unanimous in its support. In general, the Uniates appear to have had less popular backing, and therefore to have had to impose their will on local Orthodox parishes more often than the other way around. Bishop Metodii Terlets'kyi of Chełm was particularly aggressive in securing submission of parishes, notably the church of the Lublin brotherhood, in his diocese. The Orthodox also used force, as Semen (Sylvestr) Hulevych-Vointyns'kyi and the Przemyśl nobility did against Krupets'kyi. Church officials, courts, and nobles often refused to comply in carrying out the specific provisions of the 1632–1633 royal diplomas, and the Orthodox had great difficulty in converting privileges into real gains.[107]

The major cause of friction, then, was the division of parishes not specifically assigned. In rural areas, the will of the landlords and the local magnates, who were often patrons of the church, was decisive, but when a substantial number of petty nobles attended a rural church, a situation common in the Ruthenian palatinate, struggle often ensued. In cities, the commissioners took into account the opinions of the local burghers, but no clear guidelines existed to define how the decision was to be made. The commissions could only deal with major cities and disputed areas, a small percentage of the thousands of parishes in the Commonwealth. In some cases, notably the Chełm diocese, the bishop gained the support of local notables and hampered the commissioners' activities.[108]

In the decentralized Commonwealth, with its weak governmental administration, control of properties usually depended on the balance of local power. Where the Orthodox nobles and burghers were numerous, they took control of parishes. Where Uniate bishops could enlist the support of the local Roman Catholic hierarch, landowners, and rich city dwellers, they retained control. The Commonwealth's intricate legal structure and the "freedom" enjoyed by the nobles ensured that no Orthodox gains would go uncontested and that no decisions would be final.[109]

The Uniate hierarchy, the Roman Pope, and many Catholic nobles did not accept the compromise as binding.[110] The Uniates registered protests after the Election and Coronation Diets, and many Catholic nobles inserted the clause *salvis iuribus Ecclesiae Catholicae* in their consent to the Diet decisions of 1632 and 1633.[111] Pope Urban VIII, the papal nuncio, Honoratio Visconti, and the officials of the Congregation for the Propagation of the Faith warned against making any concessions to the Orthodox.[112] However, Władysław pointed out that concessions were unavoidable in view of the impending Muscovite war and convinced the Pope not to denounce the provisions publicly or to forbid Catholics to assent to them.[113] A special papal commission decided not to forbid concessions on the grounds that this would put the papacy in a position to secure greater gains for Catholicism after Władysław had been elected, Muscovy had been vanquished, and the Swedish throne had been secured.[114] The Holy See assumed that the king need not abide by the 1632 provisions once he had achieved his purpose.[115]

In the course of the 1630s, almost all church properties were contested. The central forum of the struggle remained the Diet, but the Orthodox position had changed significantly. In the 1620s, Orthodox delegates had concentrated on securing recognition of the Orthodox hierarchy and on reversing the policy of regarding the Uniate church as representing all Eastern Christians who had been Orthodox before 1596. Orthodox nobles, Zaporozhian Cossacks, and Orthodox burghers had preserved and even resuscitated the Orthodox church between 1596 and 1632. Diet recognition, however, had been thwarted by the combined ultra-Catholic and Uniate bloc, a comparatively simple matter since the entire parliamentary system of the Commonwealth militated against change or innovation. Only if the Orthodox delegates had been willing to break up Diets by refusal to approve legislation could they have forced concessions, and that course might equally have encouraged the ultra-Catholics into civil strife.

After 1632, the Orthodox task changed from one of acquiring rights to one of defending the legal order and privileges they had finally obtained. Although the Uniate/ultra-Catholic faction maintained that the privileges the Diet had granted were neither legal nor binding, they could not deny the fact that a Diet had authorized the monarch to recognize the Orthodox church and grant it privileges. They could contest these privileges in the courts and obstruct their realization, but now the parliamentary procedure worked against them. In addition, unlike the Orthodox whose liberties had been violated in the 1620s, the staunch Catholic and Uniate delegates did not represent a "wronged" constituency. Their grievances were over the encroachment on the rights of the Catholic church, an issue with which even many Catholic nobles did not have much sympathy and which failed to attract the support of the majority of Ruthenian nobles, burghers, and Cossacks.[116] The Orthodox position was now clearly much stronger, but it still needed able defenders in the Diet. Orthodox nobles had to continue to be elected to the Diet and Orthodox delegates must remain diligent in their defense of their privileges.

Throughout the 1630s, Adam Kysil provided the leadership the Orthodox defense required. He guided the Orthodox faction at the nine Diets that met between the Coronation Diet of Władysław and the Diet of 1641, when he entered the Senate.[117] While information about these Diets varies in completeness, whenever Orthodox activities are mentioned in them at all, Kysil's name figures prominently; Uniates and Catholics ended up referring to him as the "head of the schismatics."[118] As one of the major negotiators in formulating the "pacification" agreement, he had staked his career and reputation on its success, so it is no surprise to find him in the defensive role. He had cooperated with the king in working out the compromise. While the king had no deep commitment to Orthodox rights and often wavered under pressure, he was never actually opposed to them. Thus, as a defender of Orthodoxy, Kysil ran no risk of losing favor at the court.[119] Because Kysil was elected as a delegate from the Volhynian or Chernihiv palatinates, he also had the wishes of his Orthodox constituents to represent.[120] His defense of Orthodoxy may have been strengthened by his close connection with the Orthodox hierarchy, especially with Mohyla, as well.[121] His entrance into the Lviv brotherhood in 1634 represented the marriage of Orthodoxy to his political career.

On the other hand, Kysil had no rivals for the position of Orthodox leader; one might say he assumed it by default. Prince Konstantyn Ostroz'kyi, the undisputed leader of Rus', had died in 1608. With the conversion of the Vyshnevets'kyis and Korets'kyis to Catholicism, leadership in the Orthodox camp had passed to middle-rank families. Lavrentii Drevyns'kyi had led the Orthodox Diet members in the 1610s and 1620s, less so in the thirties as he was growing old (he died in 1640).[122] A leader might have emerged from the Hulevych, Proskura, or Chetvertyns'kyi families, all of whom supported the Orthodox cause, but none of these families seems to have produced a member of stature in the 1630s.[123] Kysil owed his rise partly to his ornate, Ciceronian oratorical style, laced with the classical quotations that seventeenth-century erudition required; it provided him with a useful tool for becoming a parliamentary leader—the ability to persuade.[124]

The relation between Kysil and the Orthodox church proved to be mutually beneficial. To demonstrate that recognizing an Orthodox church was in the interest of king and Commonwealth, Kysil and Mohyla had concentrated on ensuring the loyalty of the Orthodox population during the Smolensk War and the Cossack disturbances. In his report to government officials, Kysil had emphasized the importance that his contacts with the Orthodox church and influence with the hierarchy had had in dealing with those problems. Orthodox clerical and intellectual circles, in their turn, realized they needed Kysil, and they lavished praise upon him for his activities in the Diet. In 1635, the Vilnius Orthodox brotherhood dedicated a prayer book in recognition of his piety and labors on behalf of the glory of the Lord, his generosity in building churches and monasteries and in distributing alms, and his activities at the Diet, dietines, and conferences in defense of Orthodoxy.[125] The relief of the "Orthodox Ruthenian nation," the anonymous author of the dedication maintained, "during the happy rule of the Illustrious and Unconquerable King, His Grace Władysław IV" was mainly owing to Kysil's efforts;[126] he hoped that Kysil would continue that support, and he lauded the Kysil family for its ancient lineage and its services to church and fatherland. Sylvestr Kosiv's *Paterikon,* a Polish translation of the lives of the saints of the Caves monastery in Kiev, which also appeared in 1635, was even more effusive in its praise of the Kysil family.[127] As mentioned earlier, Kosiv declared that in searching through the Rus' chronicles, he had come across a heroic Kysil ancestor named Sventold in the reign of Volodimer, so he added the appellation to Kysil's name. Neither ancestry nor appellation had been alluded to before, but both were subsequently mentioned frequently in heraldic works and government grants, and Kysil styled himself "Świentodycz" ("Sviatoldych") for the rest of his career.[128] Kosiv's "discoveries" had, in fact, more contemporary than antiquarian significance. His history and hagiography had been undertaken to demonstrate conclusively to Catholics and Protestants the sanctity of the Kievan saints and relics, and thereby of the Orthodox church.[129] To encourage Kysil's continued support, he wrote, "While so many others have fallen away, in your [family] is preserved not only an ancient and glorious title, but also the Holy and Ancient Faith of your ancestors."[130] A third Orthodox book, the 1642 *Triodon* of Mykhailo Sliozka, was also dedicated to Kysil. In its preface he is commended for having fulfilled the role of defender of Orthodoxy in the 1630s, and praised at length for his loyalty to the church and able leadership at Diets.[131]

The services that these writers praised increased with religious strife. The 1634 Diet avoided the religious issue, but by the 1635 Diet the struggle had reached fever pitch.[132] Records for this Diet are rather sketchy and do not mention names and statements of the participants in the Orthodox defense, but it is known that Kysil was present. After the Diet, although the king issued a charter to Metropolitan Ruts'kyi clarifying and reaffirming the Uniate position in the Commonwealth, he also reaffirmed Orthodox rights.[133] New commissions for the division of church properties were appointed. Although the Orthodox were obviously not pleased by the confirmation of Uniate rights, they did have some cause for rejoicing when Władysław rescinded his order of the previous year to close the Orthodox "Latin" schools in Kiev and Vinnytsia.[134] Whatever rights the 1635 charter might confer, however, the Orthodox could do little if royal and Diet decrees were violated by Catholic zealots.[135]

After 1635, a clear pattern emerged. Kysil and the other Orthodox delegates would go to the Diet armed with demands from the provincial dietines to rectify the grievances of the church and to secure reaffirmation of the church's privileges, insisting that the Diet turn to no other business until the issue of the "Greek faith" was resolved.[136] The other delegates would condemn the Orthodox for obstructionist tactics that threatened to dissolve the Diet or put off discussion of other issues, including such vital subjects as defense and new appointments. In the end, the Orthodox would not dissolve the Diet, and some sort of accommodation would be reached. At the Diet of 1637 (January 20 to March 4), for example, the Orthodox delegates complained of government officials and Catholic hierarchs who disregarded the privileges granted in 1632–1633 and 1635, and of numerous infractions against the commissioners' decisions concerning the assignment of church properties.[137] A major spokesman for the Catholics, Marcin Koryciński, starosta of Ojców, described what followed in these terms: "We are left no alternative. Since the schismatics refuse to accept our proposed resolution of problems, we must go to the King and charge that the 'Disuniates,' and especially the podkomorzy of Chernihiv [Kysil] who dares to remain obstinate, do not allow us to discuss other matters and wish to dissolve the Diet."[138] Koryciński went on to claim that it had been a mistake to grant privileges to the Orthodox at the Election and Coronation Diets, but his complaints came to nothing.[139]

That reconfirmation was only one of a number of points in contention, however. Kysil protested Uniate seizures of churches in the Chełm and Przemyśl dioceses, demanded that Orthodoxy be tolerated in the Smolensk lands, and argued that Bishop Hulevych and the Orthodox nobles who had taken part in the armed attack against Krupets'kyi, the Uniate bishop of Przemyśl, be pardoned for their role in the attack.[140] Delegates from the Przemyśl land argued against pardoning them. Delegates from the Smolensk area demanded that Orthodoxy be prohibited in Smolensk, because Orthodox complaints against the Commonwealth's religious policy were disloyal and endangered control of

the borderland city.[141] Kysil thus had to defend the interests of the
Orthodox in predominantly Orthodox areas against their own delegates.[142] In so doing, he responded to charges that the ancient privileges
granted the "Greek faith" applied to the Uniate church rather than to
the Orthodox.[143]

Many of these same issues came up again in 1638 at a Diet that was
particularly crucial because the Pavliuk rebellion and the new Cossack
ordinance were discussed there.[144] The dietines in the incorporation
lands sent delegates with many of the same instructions—for example,
the Volhynian dietine wanted the Diet to enforce compliance with the
1633 and 1635 charters, to see that Puzyna, the Orthodox eparch of
Luts'k succeed to all of the Uniate Bishop Pochapivs'kyi's possessions,
to prevent any other Diet action until the Orthodox demands were
satisfied, to insist the Diet affirm the work of the church division
commission, and to commute the sentence of Hulevych.[145]

The Diet was a stormy one for Kysil, who saw his promises to the
Cossacks set aside by a Diet determined to execute Pavliuk. In addition,
he almost lost his position as delegate. Bazilii Soltyk, a delegate from
the Smolensk palatinate, obtained a court decision against Kysil over a
personal insult and demanded that he be removed from the Diet.[146] It is
unclear whether Soltyk's action reflected attempts by Catholic forces to
halt the activities of the able defender of Orthodoxy. Kysil had clashed
with the delegates of the Smolensk palatinate on the religious issue in
1637, and Soltyk may have acted for the powerful Catholic nobility in
that recently acquired Orthodox area.

Kysil kept his seat, however, and continued to engage in sharp
exchanges with delegates who wanted to get on to "more important
matters": the auditing of finances, the discussion of defense, and the
settling of petitions.[147] As a result even the most indifferent Catholic
might well have wished to see Kysil removed. To any such impatience,
he responded, "Although we have little time, I hope to God that we put
aside this battle of wits, for then even a short time will suffice. We
should immediately start reading the constitution [i.e., the reaffirmation
of Orthodox privileges]. If we do not, then we can talk and argue for a
year and even agree to an extension [of the Diet]; nothing will help."[148]

The Volhynian delegates rejected a proposal to extend the session,
following their instructions that nothing—not even extension—could be
discussed until the Orthodox demands had been satisfied.[149] Day after
day, Kysil filled the time with assertions that "nothing is of more value
than religion," and "I will allow discussion of financial accounts as soon
as my religion has been pacified," and charged that the Catholics were
such "obedient sons" of the Pope that they were willing to trample

upon the rights of their fellow nobles.[150] He complained that the courts, particularly the High Tribunal, handed down decisions unfavorable to the Orthodox, and that in the Grand Duchy of Lithuania, the Catholics had won decisions that were counter to the Diet's provisions. He demanded that cases dealing with rights granted by the Diet be tried at the Diet, and not in the courts.[151] He also discussed the case of Bishop Hulevych and the Przemyśl nobles sentenced for their attack upon Krupets'kyi.[152]

Eventually his filibuster was successful. An article favorable to the Orthodox church was adopted; the 1635 privileges were reaffirmed; and it was agreed that Diet decrees could not be contested in the courts.[153] In addition, Władysław issued a privilege to Atanazii Puzyna, bishop of Luts'k, and ordered that Uniates turn over to him the churches that he had been awarded in the 1632–1633 compromise.[154] Only in the Hulevych affair was no concession made—the Przemyśl delegates led by Jakub Fedro had opposed amnesty.[155]

Still, Kysil and the other Orthodox delegates had scored a triumph. Kysil had in fact been so effective in defending the Orthodox church that before the Diet of 1639 a brief was distributed to Uniate delegates in the form of a set of questions and answers designed to help them deal with the next Kysil onslaught. Three likely issues were discussed.[156] One was thought to be the seizure of the Lublin Orthodox brotherhood's church by the Uniate bishop, Metodii Terlets'kyi, of Chełm. Although Władysław had granted a privilege to the brotherhood for this church in 1633, he recognized the legality of Terlets'kyi's seizure.[157] Its possession became a major issue for the Orthodox.[158] The Uniate position paper advised its delegates to parry Kysil's expected protests with claims that it had nothing to do with him; the Lublin delegates should bring up the issue. This argument, if successful, would not only stop Kysil, but would undermine the power of the Orthodox church in areas where the Orthodox no longer controlled delegations to the Diet, since, if other delegates had no right to defend them, they would cease to have a voice.

A second issue would be possession of the churches in Vilnius granted the Orthodox by the 1632–1633 charters. Here the delegates were counseled to reply to Kysil's demand by insisting that the Orthodox churches of Vilnius were already too numerous for the small number of Orthodox faithful. They were also to repeat the standard argument that the Uniates had no right to hand over churches belonging to the Holy See and that their conscience as Catholics could not bear to see the "Holy Union" destroyed. If Kysil demanded that a commission of arbitration be organized in Vilnius, the Uniates were to reply that they had already seen in Volhynia the turmoil that such a commission could cause.[159] The third likely issue would be the reaffirmation of the privileges of the Orthodox church. To that the Uniates were to reply that "all prior constitutions wrung from the Commonwealth by force had been protested by all the estates and were therefore invalid."[160]

As it turned out, the Diet of 1639 did not take up the religious issue at length. It was too involved in the struggle between Vice-Chancellor Jerzy Ossoliński and his enemies to adopt any legislation at all.[161] Still, the instructions make clear how fiercely the Uniates continued to contest their losses and how far the Orthodox were from consolidating the gains of 1632–1633.[162]

At the last two Diets he attended as a delegate, in 1640 and 1641, Kysil was chiefly occupied with the Przemyśl bishopric and the demands for the return of the Lublin brotherhood's church. In 1640 he maintained that, in violation of the *pacta conventa,* the articles signed by the king at the election, and the privilege of 1635, what was due the Orthodox was being given to the Uniates.[163] He complained that the Lublin, Krasnystaw, and other churches the Orthodox had "in use and possession" had been seized by force, and he charged that the Uniates and Catholics had occupied more than three hundred Orthodox churches.[164]

Efforts to mollify the Orthodox resulted in lengthy discussions in the Senate, but Kysil was not satisfied with the half-hearted measures that resulted and continued to demand full compliance with earlier constitutions.[165] His militancy aroused the ire of Mikołaj Ostroróg, the Cupbearer of the Kingdom, who maintained that the Diet should not be troubled with these problems and argued that the churches of Lublin and Krasnystaw were in the diocese of Chełm and should be Uniate in obedience to their bishop.[166] Finally he asserted that since the delegates from Lublin and Chełm had not been given instructions from their dietines to bring up the question, it should not even have been discussed. When attempts to mediate failed, the Orthodox faction as usual announced that no measures would be passed—except those dealing with payment of the troops and the defense of the Ukraine from the Tatars—until their demands were met, and again the Diet was threatened with dissolution. In addition, the Calvinists and the Catholics were fighting over an incident in Vilnius, increasing the likelihood that this Diet would conclude without enacting any legislation.[167]

On May 24, a delegation from the Zaporozhian Host petitioned for the return of seized churches and monasteries, and it demanded that the "Ancient Faith" remain undisturbed.[168] On May 26, a delegate from Przemyśl maintained that the Catholic protests against the constitutions of 1633 and 1635 invalidated the Orthodox privileges.[169] This time, however, the delegates realized that the state could not afford to go through another Diet without deciding anything and insisted on compromise. Over Catholic protests, the Orthodox once again received a reaffirmation of their rights, but the Lublin church was not returned, and the question of the Przemyśl bishopric remained unsettled.[170]

Kysil's last Diet as a delegate, in August–September of 1641, was also troubled by the religious issue.[171] The Volhynian dietine had sent Kysil and its other delegates with instructions to prevent the ratification of any constitutions until the demands of the Orthodox church were settled favorably, measures for regular troops to be stationed in Ukrainian lands were approved, and the rights of the eastern princes to their titles were guaranteed.[172] On September 17, Kysil spoke at length on all these points, asserting that if the Diet did not agree to them, the delegations of the "four border palatinates" (the incorporation lands) would walk out, and the inhabitants of these lands would no longer consider themselves free people.[173] The issues were a matter of religious conscience, personal honor, and the rights of the nobility.[174] When he turned to the problems of the Orthodox church, he dealt almost entirely with abuses taking place in regions other than the incorporation lands. He complained that the Roman Catholic archbishop of Lviv was interfering in ecclesiastical appointments in the Orthodox bishopric, that the Uniates were refusing to return churches to the Orthodox in the Grand Duchy and the Chełm area, that the Orthodox Bishop of Przemyśl still had not been pardoned, and that the Uniates still held the Lublin church.[175] He spoke of monks languishing in chains and of Orthodox Christians dying without benefit of last rites.[176] Catholic delegates responded that the Lublin church rightfully belonged to the Bishop of Chełm, that the Orthodox of Przemyśl had been far more violent than the Uniates, and that the ancient privileges of the Eastern church were now held by the Uniates.[177]

A Diet commission was formed to adjudicate these counterclaims, and, over Catholic protest, drew up a constitution reaffirming Orthodox privileges.[178] The only specific issue resolved was the judgment against the Orthodox faction in the Przemyśl controversy, and the Diet adopted a constitution invalidating the judgment against Bishop Hulevych and his supporters.[179] The reinstatement of their civil rights was obtained in return for the renunciation of Orthodox control of the bishopric. Contrary to the terms of the 1632–1633 pacification, the new constitution required that after Hulevych's death no new appointment was to be made, and therefore the see would revert to the Uniate Krupets'kyi, and that after Krupets'kyi's death, the king was to appoint another Uniate to the see.[180] Krupets'kyi, who in his long tenure as bishop had never exercised much authority because of the firm opposition of the Orthodox nobility, was guaranteed control of a number of churches and monasteries.[181]

Kysil was instrumental in negotiating the settlement, which was opposed by the Catholic nobility of the Przemyśl area who were determined to punish Hulevych and his followers. Despite the remission of sentences against many of their number, the staunchly Orthodox petty nobles of the Przemyśl land were also furious over what they saw as a betrayal of the rights of the Orthodox church. Kysil, usually given lavish praise for his efforts on behalf of Orthodoxy, was this time the subject of derision. Complaints against him were leveled in a poem entitled *Lampoon in the Ruthenian Language, or a Tearful Complaint as if a Sigh of All Orthodox Rus' of the County of Przemyśl Published by the Ihumen Nikifor of the St. Onufrii and Smolnytsia Monasteries at the Request of the Nobles of Przemyśl, Fedir Manastyrs'kyi, Fedir Vynnyts'kyi, Marko Vysochans'kyi, and Fedir Kopystyns'kyi.*[182] It reads in part:

> There has come to us news, O worthy Gentlemen
> Listen, by God, nobles, and you simple men
> What to all of you is beginning to happen.
> All was done to us by your great Lord Kysil,
> The man who believes in many varied ways in the Greek Faith,
> Who, taking money from Christians without measure,
> For a thousand ducats sold our bishopric.
> We have lost our inheritance forever.
> He restored Bishop Sylvestr [Hulevych] to his rights,
> [But] we, Gentlemen, shall never see the bishopric again
>   during our lifetime.
> Wisely into that book Lord Kysil wrote,
> A very wise man, would that he be hanged
> He gave the Orthodox Bishopric to Saint Peter.
> Groan O Gentlemen, groan mournfully
> And beat that Kysil when you can.
> Now we are not Ruthenians [Rus'], nor Poles [Liakhy].
> There appears before a person's eyes horror everywhere.

It goes on to warn the Poles that Kysil is "an old trickster" and an "archtraitor," accuses him of betraying Rus' and going over to the Poles, insults his mother, and charges him with buying estates with the money he had taken from the Przemyśl Orthodox nobles.[183]

The lampoon is the only evidence we have for Kysil's handling of the Przemyśl affair. In fact, until there is corroborating evidence, its authorship must be viewed as uncertain. Its coarseness suggests that it may well have been written not by the Orthodox nobles listed, but by Catholic polemicists who wished to ridicule Kysil and the Orthodox nobles.[184] Whether the lampoon's authors were Orthodox or Catholic, its very existence reveals how precarious Kysil's position was. Any compromise he arranged could arouse the suspicion of his Orthodox followers. Any opportunity to discredit him would be taken by his Catholic opponents.

Why then did Kysil choose to place himself amidst the religious fray? His contemporaries described him as a man of great piety, and he displayed his attachment to Orthodoxy by the foundation of churches and monasteries.[185] Yet in his speeches at the Diet, he insisted that he was not interested in discussing theology, but rather legal rights.[186] The question remains of how committed Kysil really was to the Orthodox faith that he defended so ably at the Diets. To many of his Catholic opponents in the 1630s he was the archetypical Orthodox fanatic.[187] However, even in the early 1630s, he maintained contacts with the Uniate camp and arranged conferences between Orthodox officials and his nephew, the Uniate clergyman Pakhomii Orans'kyi.[188] Why he did not, like so many Ukrainian-Belorussian magnates and nobles, convert to Catholicism is difficult to explain. But if he was determined to remain in the "Rus'" faith, the Uniate church with its plebeian constituency was hardly an acceptable alternative. Kysil had only to observe the continuous setbacks and defeats of the dedicated and energetic Uniate Metropolitan Ruts'kyi, whose death in 1637 was a great loss to the Uniate cause, to see what a poor choice that would have been.[189] Ruts'kyi was unable either to win widespread support or to secure Catholic respect for the Uniate church.[190] It offered few attractions for an ambitious politician like Kysil. However much he had entered the Latin Christian world through his education and court contacts, once he had embarked on a political career as an Orthodox believer he found his faith an asset. As an Orthodox leader, Kysil had at his disposal the not inconsiderable resources in finances and personnel that the church possessed. The discontent of the Ruthenian Orthodox nobility could be channeled through him. Although he might offend Albrycht Stanisław Radziwiłł and the Catholic hierarchy, the king probably regarded him as someone who could keep Orthodox discontent within tolerable limits. Conversion would have deprived him of the support of the Mohylan hierarchy and the Orthodox nobility. He would also have become useless as the royal negotiator for dealing with the Zaporozhian Host.

By determined and skillful parliamentary maneuvering, Kysil and his colleagues realized most of the religious concessions granted in 1632–

1633, despite constant protests from the Catholic hierarchy. Also, despite those same protests, they kept the king from whittling those concessions away. On some issues, notably that of the Przemyśl bishopric and the Lublin church, they were defeated, and however much they raged, it was impossible in a state with so little centralized authority to enforce decisions at the local level. In areas such as the Dnieper Ukraine, this worked to the advantage of Orthodoxy, but in the rest of the Ukraine and Belorussia it did not. Catholics could persecute the Orthodox without fear of reprisal, and, as more and more Orthodox nobles converted to Roman Catholicism, they did so with impunity. For the Orthodox the only defense was their representation in the Diet, and they would lose even that if they were to lose control of the four eastern Ukrainian palatines: as Kysil's confrontations with the Przemyśl and Smolensk delegates demonstrated, they had already lost control of delegations from the western Ukrainian and the Belorussian lands. However successful Kysil might have been, he could not reverse the process of Orthodox decline and Catholic ascension. Even the Diet privileges for which he had fought would be meaningless, if the king should find it expedient to make concessions to ultra-Catholics, to Uniates, or to Rome.

The Regionalism of the Incorporation Lands

Throughout the Commonwealth, nobles had strong attachments to their native regions and palatinates.[191] The unification of the medieval Kingdom of Poland had not fully unified the legal traditions and administrative peculiarities of its various regions.[192] The Grand Duchy of Lithuania also was a conglomerate of lands, each with its jealously guarded local traditions.[193] The separate institutions and traditions of Royal Prussia and Livonia favored regional sentiments among their nobilities. Diet election procedures ensured that delegates were representatives of the palatinates which had sent them, and commissions were often composed according to quotas from the various constituent regions (Little Poland, Great Poland, the Grand Duchy).[194] A noble lacking strong ties to a palatinate or region had little hope of advancement in a state in which dietine and regional politics was a major source of political power and economic gain, and even the magnates were careful to cultivate regional constituencies.

While the solidarity of the noble order counteracted centrifugal tendencies and strengthened loyalty to a common fatherland, local nobilities had strong ties to the ancestral palatinate—and made sure that the king appointed local nobles and not "aliens" to local offices. The absence of a large central bureaucracy, of a powerful court, and of large urban centers militated against the homogenization of the nobility. Nobles did move from one area to another, and land ownership in a number of regions also curbed the development of intense regionalism, but the long-established families in a palatinate formed local societies that kept political and economic power in their own hands.[195] Local society could be penetrated by newcomers, but usually only after long residence and assimilation in an area.[196]

Regional feeling was particularly intense in the incorporation lands. The area had only been a part of the Kingdom of Poland since 1569, and its inhabitants were still keenly aware of differences between themselves and the nobles of the rest of the Kingdom. The transfer from the Grand Duchy to the Kingdom had been carried out only after the maintenance of local political, linguistic, and legal peculiarities had been guaranteed. In the 1630s and 1640s, the dietines of the incorporation lands often had occasion to remind the Diet of their special position in the Kingdom.[197] When they did, they put forth their demands not as separate palatinates of the province of Little Poland, but as the three—or after 1635, four—palatinates of the incorporation.[198] In the 1630s, the indigenous nobles emphasized their distinctness from the nobles of other areas of the Commonwealth and from newcomers to their lands by insisting that Ruthenian remain the area's official language and that local officials, such as scribes, be natives of the area.[199] Their defense of Orthodox privileges was frequently framed as a defense of regional privileges. The problems of security also played a major role in consolidating regional feeling. The area was exposed to foreign attack, particularly Tatar raids, and the palatinates had a common interest in military preparedness. The local elites' fear of Tatar raids and Cossack unrest gave them a common bond not shared by those in less exposed areas or in areas which were more closely tied to the problems of the Baltic rather than of the Black Sea.[200]

In a letter to Hetman Koniecpolski during the Cossack disturbances of 1636, Kysil had offered to render his services "for the good of the Fatherland, especially of our Ukraine."[201] Yet frequently, his understanding of the interests of the Ukrainian lands, or more precisely, of its nobility, led him to protest the policies that the central Diet decided were in the interest of the entire Fatherland. By 1641, his protests over a number of issues prompted him to formulate the legal and political concepts of the nobility of the incorporation land as a coherent statement of regionalism. On September 17, 1641, Kysil began his address to the Diet thus:

Three matters or rather freedoms constitute the free Commonwealth; three opposites of these freedoms bring about slavery. For, where there is free use of inherited dignity, where there is free disposition of possessions, where there is free disposition of conscience, upon which God himself alone rules and over which He alone holds sway, there, too, is free Commonwealth. Where, on the other hand, one believes as one is told to; where one so uses dignities as one has to; where one does not hold one's possessions in such freedom as one wants to; there freedom is already being banished, and replaced by slavery. Such is the conclusion held by all political thinkers. No one can gainsay me, that the latter are the symptoms of slavery, while it is the former that provide proofs of freedom.

Having thus laid down such basis of my speech, my Gracious Lords, I shall present to you in great sorrow the image of the pitiful slavery of my brethren who have remained in their homes, and also come not from one palatinate alone, but from all four Ruthenian palatinates. For we live not in that Commonwealth to which our ancestors hastened and which they joined as free men join free men, as men of liberty join men of liberty, but we live in the state of utmost slavery.

Wishing to prove this to you, my Gracious Lords, so that white would stand out even more so against black, [I ask]: What were the covenants between your ancestors and ours? Which freedoms have been sworn to and how utterly have they been destroyed? I shall remind you of the following three points concerning the relationship between the Ruthenian principalities and the Crown [Kingdom]. First, that our ancestors, the Ruthenian Sarmatians, freely joined you, the Polish Sarmatians; with their spiritual and material possessions they brought the provinces and their ancestral faith that prevailed in them . . .[202]

As with all discussions of nobiliary political thought in the Commonwealth, Kysil's address was based on the assumptions that the liberty of each noble was inviolable, and that the Commonwealth constituted the aggregate of each noble's liberties. Its central purpose was to condemn what the speaker perceived as an assault on the liberty of a region's nobility resulting from the infringement of regional privileges.

In his opening statement, Kysil articulated a number of tenets of regionalism in the Ukrainian lands. That the four incorporated palatinates and their nobilities were a regional bloc was asserted by his insistence that he spoke in the name of the nobility of all four. That Kysil could do so as a delegate from the Volhynian palatinate is evidence of the close relationship of the four palatinates based on common legal interests and geographic exigencies. His identification of the four palatinates as "Ruthenian" designated them as Rus' par excellence.[203] In fact, by limiting the designation "Ruthenian" to the incorporation lands, he excluded the Ruthenian palatinate itself, as well as the Belz and Podolian palatinates, in addition to the Belorussian lands, and chose to identify Rus' with the incorporation lands that shared common laws, privileges, and administrative practices. His characterization of the incorporation as an agreement between the Sarmatian Ruthenians of the incorporated lands and the Sarmatian Poles of the Kingdom of Poland manifested his legal territorial definition of Rus'. It also depicted the incorporation as a bilateral agreement between two equal Sarmatian political nations, forming a permanent constitutional relation between them.

The symptoms of slavery that Kysil decried were all matters that sparked regionalist sentiment in the 1630s and 1640s—the status of the Orthodox church, the retention of princely titles, and the burdens of defense against Tatar raids. In discussing each, Kysil revealed different aspects of his interpretations of regional rights and his views on the inhabitants of the Ukraine and their relation to the Commonwealth.

The religious grievance, which Kysil posed as a regional issue in his address, revealed that despite his emphasis on the legal-territorial definition of Rus' as the four incorporated palatinates, he also saw Rus' as a cultural-religious community living in other areas of the Commonwealth. Such disparate definitions of Rus' were inevitable in any discussion of the persecution of the Orthodox church, a problem not confined to the incorporation lands. The Orthodox issue had been debated at almost all Diets after the Union of Brest. The steadily weakening position of Orthodox nobles in the western Ukrainian lands and Belorussia had placed the burden of defense on the nobles of the incorporation lands, among whom Kysil had figured so prominently throughout the 1630s. Although the Orthodox church throughout the Commonwealth had been granted privileges both before and after the Union of Brest, Kysil focused on the incorporation charters of 1569 as the guarantor of Orthodox privileges. Central to his argument were the assumptions that the nobles of the incorporation lands could speak for the entire Rus' people, and that the guarantees of the acts of incorporation had force outside the incorporation territories.

Kysil argued: "The year was 1569 when the Ruthenians acceded to the Crown, and the year was 1596 when a few Ruthenians instigated the union. Since it was not to those Ruthenians who did not yet exist that the rights were given, it follows clearly that the privileges have been given to us, who are living today, and to our ancestral religion."[204] By resting the Orthodox case on the guarantees of the incorporation, Kysil could avoid the complex issue of whether privileges of the fourteenth and fifteenth centuries had been issued at a time when the Ruthenians could be considered to be in union with Rome. By referring to 1569, he could also largely ignore the tangled web of decrees and privileges issued after the Union of Brest, although he did mention the division of church benefices and buildings between Uniates and Orthodox agreed upon during the election of Władysław IV (1632–1633) and its confirmation in 1635.[205] Kysil chose to point to acts that dealt with a specific territory and to treat them as if they applied to the entire Commonwealth. Hence he brought up the controversy over the Lublin church in his votum, and during the Diet frequently spoke out about the controversy over the bishopric of Przemyśl.[206] Although he did not explain how the agreements of 1569 affected areas outside the incorporation territories, we can assume that he saw the persecution of the Orthodox church anywhere as an infringement on the religious liberty of the Orthodox nobles of the incorporation lands. That for authority he referred to the acts of 1569, rather than to the Confederation of 1573, which guaranteed religious toleration throughout the Commonwealth, illustrates his view that the incorporation charters were the primary regulatory decrees defining the rights of the incorporation lands' nobles in the Commonwealth.

Although Kysil complained primarily about discrimination against Ruthenian Orthodox nobles, he also defended the rights of other strata of the population. He defended the liberty of the commoners of the "Ruthenian nation" as well as of the nobles, and he denounced the ill-treatment of commoners and priests as well as of nobles, thereby defining the Rus' in cultural-religious rather than only in social-territorial terms. This identification of the "Ruthenian nation" as a community composed of a number of orders was accompanied by a differentiation of the community along religious lines. Kysil described the conflict between "old Rus'," the Orthodox, and "new Rus'," the Uniates, thereby revealing his conception of the Rus' community as one that had formerly been monoreligious and whose components still retained Rus' identity.[207] In the name of the nobility of the incorporation lands, he demanded religious rights for the entire community of "old Rus'."

In addressing the question of princely titles, Kysil took up a controversy that affected only the nobility of the incorporation lands—and in fact, only one part of it. In the mid-1630s, Crown Vice-Chancellor Jerzy Ossoliński and the king decided to establish a knightly order named after the Immaculate Conception.[208] First Ossoliński, a staunch Catholic, received authorization for it from the Pope during a trip to Rome in 1633, a trip undertaken to secure papal acquiescence for Władysław's policies toward Catholic church properties and toleration of the Orthodox church.[209] In the process Ossoliński also won considerable trust from papal officials, pleased to find such a loyal Catholic so close to the new king whose own dedication to the church they had so far found wanting.[210]

Knightly honorary orders were in Catholic Europe a common means of rewarding loyal service and building a following, but the plan for establishing one in the Commonwealth could be expected to encounter fervent opposition, since it clearly represented an attempt to strengthen the power of the king and, as a Catholic order, a threat to the religious minorities in the Commonwealth.[211] Already, at the 1637 Diet, Kysil complained that as "obedient sons" of the Pope some Catholic nobles were willing to introduce this innovation into the Commonwealth's structure and denounced it as prejudicial to the Orthodox.[212] The most powerful opposition, however, came from numerous nobles, including many loyal Catholics, who opposed the plan since the granting of titles would introduce gradations into the noble order that were contrary to the Commonwealth's constitution. They attacked Ossoliński for accepting the title of prince of the Holy Roman Empire, a title that he dared to use openly in the Commonwealth.[213] After the stormy Diet of 1638, Ossoliński countered this by offering to renounce his title, but only if the Lithuanian-Ruthenian princes would agree to do the same.[214] The offer, aimed at his political enemies, was applauded by the many delegates who were against all gradations within the nobility.[215] But the proposal clearly contravened the terms of the Union of Lublin and of the incorporation charters. The princes immediately began to campaign for the preservation of their titles, in which they were supported by the delegates from Lithuania and the incorporation lands. Although the Diet excluded the titles "accepted at the Union" from its abolition of foreign titles, the eastern princes thought their position was threatened. Also, no specific mention was made of the titles guaranteed in the incorporation of the Ukrainian lands into the Kingdom.[216]

The Diet's decision caused an uproar among the princes of the eastern lands. Descendants of Gedimin and Rurik, they may have lost their unquestioned control over local nobles, but they still retained their princely titles as symbols of their past authority. The influx of families like the Potocki and Kalinowski, who soon rivaled them in wealth and influence, made the retention of those status symbols seem even more important.[217] Jeremi Wiśniowiecki led the princely families in their campaign against the new threat.[218] Before the 1639 Diet, he distributed a circular defending princely titles in the Commonwealth,[219] and his client, H. Bielejowski, wrote a tract defending the position and rights of the incorporation lands.[220] The Volhynian dietine dispatched its delegates to the Diet with the instruction that families holding their titles before 1569 should retain them, but the breakup of the Diet over other issues prevented any resolution of the matter of titles.[221]

Kysil supported the rights of the eastern princes at the Diets of 1640 and 1641 and threatened to block all legislation until some guarantee was made. In the 1640 Diet, he and Wiśniowiecki insisted that the 1638 decision did not apply to families from the incorporation lands and the Grand Duchy of Lithuania.[222] Kysil maintained that the matter was not one of interest only to the citizens of the Kievan and Volhynian lands and the Grand Duchy of Lithuania, but that it was of concern to all nobles, since it affected rights which had been guaranteed.[223] The defenders of the princely titles encountered strong opposition from the delegates of the Kingdom's old lands, especially from Mikołaj Ostroróg (the Crown cupbearer who had opposed Kysil's demands for the Orthodox church).[224] The constitution was not changed at the 1640 Diet, so Kysil made it a major point of his address to the Diet in 1641.

In defending the right of princes to their titles, Kysil adhered closely to the words of the incorporation charters. He based his argument on the guarantees to the princes at the incorporation and on the services the princes had rendered in defending the region. He maintained that "the orders of princes and noble families" had embarked jointly on the union and that, if the rights of princes were endangered, so soon would be the rights of the entire nobility. Although he emphasized that "the princes accepted equality and parity with our noble order," Kysil maintained, too, that "we swore to hold their names in ancient honor and dignity." He told the Diet: "You, Gracious Lords, accepted two orders in the union and incorporation as an explicit wording." In fact, his discussion of princes and nobles as two separate orders reflected neither the exact words of incorporation charters nor the social divisions intended by that legislation.[225] His insistence that the princes and nobles constituted two separate orders was an archaism that conflicted with the constitutional theory of the Commonwealth and with the very guarantee of nobiliary equality. That in 1641 Kysil could still discuss princes and nobles as distinct orders testifies to the conservatism of political thought in the incorporation lands and to the continuing strength of regional traditions there.

In contrast to the issue of titles, which directly pertained to only a segment of nobles, Kysil's discussion of military affairs affected all nobles and non-nobles in the incorporation lands. The inability of the government of the Grand Duchy to help inhabitants of its Ukrainian lands fend off Tatar attacks had predisposed the nobility of the region toward annexation by Poland. The more powerful Kingdom, with a proven interest in defending its Ukrainian territories of Podillia and the Ruthenian palatinate from Tatar incursions, seemed more likely to deal with the problem effectively. In 1562–1563, the Diet attempted to deal with the defense problem in the southeast by setting up a standing army to be paid from revenue from royal lands. The "Wojsko Kwarciane" (named after the quarter of the revenue of the royal lands allotted for their maintenance) normally numbered between 3,000 and 5,000 men, but was greatly augmented during wartime. The troops' pay often came late and their quartering was a burden on local landowners, whose estates they frequently pillaged. To the nobles the troops often seemed as great a scourge as the Tatars and Cossacks they were intended to control. Tatar attacks, Cossack rebellions, and frontier violence prompted most palatinates to recruit their own troops, and magnates kept private armies that rivaled the standing forces. Therefore the nobles of the Ukraine paid taxes, lost revenue from the army's quartering and pillaging, and expended funds on additional troops.[226]

At the Diet of 1641, Kysil faced a body loath to raise taxes and pacifist because it was fearful that any military activity would lead to the aggrandisement of royal power. In the late 1630s and early 1640s, unlike the nobles of the Ukrainian lands, the nobles of Little and Great Poland, Masovia and the Grand Duchy of Lithuania had little reason to be concerned about military affairs or payments to standing troops. By contrast, in the late 1630s, the nobles of the Volhynian and Kievan palatinates had shown how vitally concerned they were with military issues. When threatening to block all legislation in an effort to secure rights for the Orthodox church, they took care to except the issue of military taxes.[227]

Kysil voiced the frustration and fears of the nobles of the Ukraine when he addressed the Diet. He maintained that the burdens of war, like the benefits of peace, should fall equally on the entire Republic, not on the inhabitants of the Ruthenian territories alone. He likened the situation of the Ukrainian lands to that of those provinces of the Roman republic that were forced to maintain troops. Yet, he argued, while these provinces had been conquered, the "Ruthenian provinces and principalities" had joined the Commonwealth freely. In calling for equal distribution of the burden of maintaining the army, he argued that wintering troops outside the Ukrainian lands was impractical since it would give the Tatars the advantage in mounting attacks. He even went so far as to propose that the Commonwealth abandon the pretense of unity in defense and that each province defend itself, hardly an acceptable alternative for the nobles of the Ukrainian lands. In conclusion, he demanded an equalization of obligations.[228]

Kysil ended his votum with an appeal to his fellow nobles to look upon "these pestilential symptoms of slavery in the body of the Commonwealth." He warned that the "mystical body of the Commonwealth" would decompose if the nobles of the incorporation lands were forced "to drink of slavery." He vowed that his generation and its descendants would continue to demand their rights as long as they were able to do so. Should these rights not be restored, however, inequality would destroy the "free Commonwealth" and all its citizens would come to know the lot of slavery.[229]

Responses to the three grievances lodged in the votum were very different. The problem of princely titles was resolved immediately. The Diet passed a constitution reaffirming the right of the eastern princes to their titles as guaranteed by the Union of Lublin as well as by the incorporation charters.[230] The Diet also reaffirmed previous legislation on the rights of the Orthodox church, but on this matter the legislation was far from decisive.[231] Kysil complained about the exclusion of Orthodox nobles from offices, but such appointments were determined by the king and local dietines, not by the national Diet. Although Władysław IV was relatively tolerant, he was influenced by powerful Catholics at court. About his eventual successor, there could be no guarantee. Local dietines reflected the power relations of the local nobilities: as the Orthodox diminished in numbers and Catholics became more and more influenced by the Counter-Reformation, the dietines were less likely to elect Orthodox candidates to offices. But the essential problem lay in the very practice of the nobiliary freedom that Kysil extolled. Powerful Catholic nobles and bishops could act with relative impunity against Orthodox institutions and commoners. Legal redress seldom resulted in restitution. Ultimately, in 1641, as half a century earlier, the Orthodox church needed powerful protectors to ensure that its rights would be observed. The major difference was that there were fewer and fewer Orthodox nobles who could fill this need. The most difficult of the problems Kysil broached was that of military burdens. The Ukraine, an area that so desperately required a solution to the financial and social problems of the military, found little sympathy or understanding in other areas of the Commonwealth.

As a political statement, the address represented an adamant assertion of regionalist sentiment. While its hyperbolic condemnation of the deprivation of liberties was common in the nobiliary literature of the time, its political-constitutional premises represented a particularly well-developed statement of regionalism. Rus', the incorporation land, was treated as distinct from the older lands of the Crown. Sarmatian Poles and Sarmatian Ruthenians were discussed as two separate political nations. The incorporation charters of 1569 were portrayed as a vital, fundamental constitution deeply embedded in the consciousness of the area's nobility.

In its essence, the votum expressed regionalist sentiments that were shared by strata of the population other than the political nation of the nobility. Its formulation of regionalism provided a conceptualization of the incorporation lands as a political unit. The failure of Kysil and his peers to function as an effective political nation defending regional interests would soon allow new strata of Ukrainian society to champion regional grievances.

But in 1641, when Kysil argued for Ukrainian regional privileges, he had little inkling of how truly explosive the issue would become. He was more likely preoccupied with a personal issue that depended on the assertion of regional rights, his appointment as castellan of Chernihiv. Kysil had been disappointed in not being named palatine when the Chernihiv palatinate was created in 1635—but when a vacancy arose for a castellan in 1639, Władysław chose him.[232]

The act creating the palatinate of Chernihiv conferred upon it all the rights and traditions of the palatinate of Kiev, but its legal status and its position in the order of precedence among the palatinates in the Senate took some years to clarify.[233] When Kysil was named castellan in December, a dispute broke out over what rank and type of castellanship he held.[234] In the old lands of the Kingdom of Poland, each palatinate had a number of castellanships, all of which conferred positions in the Senate, but most of which were of the lowest precedence; they were designated "minor," or "particular."[235] When the Polish administrative system had been adopted in the Grand Duchy of Lithuania, including the incorporation lands in the sixteenth century, one castellanship was created for each palatinate, equal in rank to the oldest of the Kingdom's castellanships; they were designated "major" or "general."[236] Although the Chernihiv palatinate was created with the rights of the Kievan palatinate, whether the Chernihiv castellanship would be "major" or "minor" had not been specified in the act. When an official publication had listed it in the "minor" category, Kysil declined the appointment unless the royal chancery confirmed that it was "major."[237] In doing so he fought not only for his own status, but also for the privileges of the incorporation lands. The Volhynian dietine in its instructions to its delegates for 1641, maintained that by law the palatinates of the incorporation lands were equal to the Kingdom's palatinates, and their counties equal to the Kingdom's counties. Therefore placing the castellanship of Chernihiv among the minor castellanships was a breach of their rights:

Since we do not have in our palatinates "particular" but only "general" castellans, and since the Chernihiv palatinate, as settled upon the territory of the capital of our Rus', Kiev, is incorporated in all its laws and customs to the palatinates of Kiev, Volhynia, and Bratslav and since in its ordinance one castellan is decreed, as is one general palatine, so he [the Chernihiv castellan] should remain among the general castellans. Consequently, we all thank the future castellan of Chernihiv who, having obtained a grant of this castellanship from the king, did not wish to accept it [in a form that would] be prejudicial to our laws, and thus having made his declaration, he has not used his conferral, and he does not wish to use it until the castellanship is restored to that place where it should be by law. We therefore recommend to our delegates that they should bring up the matter of the vacancy of the castellanship at the beginning of the Diet, because this is a matter of public law, not a private affair, and the constitution restoring this castellanship to its rightful place should be enacted so that it should be guaranteed by law for whomever should later accept that dignity.[238]

The Volhynian delegates won their point. A new Diet constitution was passed which affirmed that the Chernihiv palatinate was entitled to all the rights and privileges of the Kiev palatinate, and that the Chernihiv castellan was to be ranked in the Senate immediately after the Livonian castellan and before the county castellans.[239]

On September 25, 1641, Kysil was granted a new privilege as castellan.[240] After listing his services to the king and Fatherland at length, the grant concludes, "and as one general palatine is provided for by legislation, so is one general castellan." The grant conferred a position in the Senate for him before all the county and minor castellans. The writ of conferral also contained a passage asking that these new provisions be called to the attention of the inhabitants of the Kievan, Volhynian, Bratslav, and Chernihiv palatinates.

Chapter 5

The Senatorial Chair

In the Commonwealth, membership in the upper house of the Diet, the Senate, was the sign of a successful political career, since the Senate was an assembly of the most powerful, wealthy, and influential nobles.[1] The Senate, a descendant of the king's council, was one of the three components, along with the king himself and the House of Delegates, necessary in constituting a Diet. In addition, either as a corporate body or through its designated representatives, the Senate was an advisory body to the monarch. When Diets were not in session, the Senate designated a number of its members who were required to reside in Warsaw and confer with the king concerning decisions that had to be made before the next Diet met.[2] The king's selection of a nobleman as a palatine or castellan recognized the recipient's importance in local affairs and gave him a voice in the Senate and in the shaping of national policy.[3] While all 150 Senators of the Commonwealth, with their life tenure of office, had the opportunity to take center stage in the Commonwealth's affairs, in reality, only a small group played a major role in national affairs.[4]

Kysil reached senatorial rank not because of inherited wealth and position, but because of royal favor. In the 1630s he served Władysław well in political and military affairs, and as leader of the Orthodox opposition, he was useful. Władysław's attachment to the Catholic church waxed and waned in rhythm with his ambitions vis-à-vis the Swedish or the Muscovite throne and his campaigns for increasing royal power in the Commonwealth. Orthodox opposition was a trump card that could be played in negotiating with the papacy, whose policy at this time was to support the Union of Brest and oppose "heretic" and "schismatic" influences in the Commonwealth.[5] A responsibly led opposition that did not paralyze the government and remained loyal to the Commonwealth was the royal wish, and that was exactly what Kysil provided.

Still, a position based solely on the favor of even a monarch can be precarious, because it can disappear at the king's whim or, more certainly, at his demise. Only those who used that transitory favor to build an independent power base were secure, so Kysil proceeded to transform himself as quickly as he could from a relatively insignificant Volhynian noble into a magnate. He did so mainly through royal grants and land purchases in the Chernihiv palatinate,[6] an area where burning forests for potash allowed large landowners to amass fortunes.[7] On that basis he then extended his estate holdings into the palatinates of Kiev and Volhynia.[8]

Kysil's cooperation with the Orthodox hierarchy also helped him grow rich. The church lent him ready cash, and, through his contacts with Mohyla, turned over to him in 1642 the city of Hoshcha, in the Luts'k county of Volhynia.[9] That he acquire the city was of importance to the church because an Orthodox academy had been founded there in 1638 by Princess Regina Solomorits'ka on the closing of an Antitrinitarian school, and Mohyla wanted to be sure it had a favorably disposed owner.[10]

In the 1640s, Kysil was most often to be found on his Volhynian estates (Nyzkynychi and Hoshcha) or his Chernihiv estates (his starostwo of Nosivka and his towns Divytsia and Kobyshche).[11] Although the dearth of extant records makes it impossible to judge accurately the size of Kysil's wealth or estates in the 1640s, his offer to the Sapieha family of 200,000 złoty for their Chornobyl' properties certainly suggests that he could rightfully be called a magnate by 1641.[12] It is true that his wealth did not approach that of the fabulously rich Dominik Zasławski and Jeremi Wiśniowiecki or of the influential palatine of Cracow, Stanisław Lubomirski.[13] Also, he was not a member of that inner circle of Władysław's court, which included Adam Kazanowski and Gerhard Denhoff,[14] and he did not possess an office of the first rank, like the most powerful men of the 1640s, Crown Vice-Chancellor—after 1643, Chancellor— Jerzy Ossoliński and Crown Great Hetman Stanisław Koniecpolski.[15] But if Kysil did not belong to the very first rank, he was certainly an influential and active senator, thanks to his contacts with chancellor and king, his willingness to involve himself in new plans, and his careful and able handling of problems. His dedication to the king brought him advances to higher senatorial chairs, the office of castellan of Kiev in 1646, and the office of palatine of Bratslav, just prior to Władysław's death in May 1648.[16]

Yet, Kysil never resided in Warsaw as a courtier, nor did he participate in the numerous public and private issues and affairs that concerned Władysław's entourage.[17] It is not even certain that he lived in Warsaw as senator-in-residence during the first half of 1644,[18] and although he was probably present at all the Diets of the period (1643, 1645, 1646, and 1647), he did not emerge as a major figure in parliamentary debates.[19] He was nevertheless involved in two major projects crucial to Władysław's policies—a plan for a new union of the Orthodox and Catholic churches, and the conclusion of an alliance with the Muscovites against the Crimean Tatars and Ottoman Turks—and through this involvement transformed his less extensive resources and less august position into power and royal favor that surpassed that of the immensely rich Wiśniowiecki or the highly placed Albrycht Stanisław Radziwiłł.[20]

In these years Kysil also became closely associated with the Kingdom's vice-chancellor, and later chancellor, Jerzy Ossoliński. Ossoliński, one of the most energetic and intelligent officials of the Commonwealth, exerted decisive influence on Władysław's policies, though his ambition and willfulness made him unpopular. He was also impatient with the Commonwealth's cumbersome noble democracy, and his consummate skill as plotter and manipulator gave him great power in the Commonwealth, not only in Władysław's reign, but also in the interregnum and Jan Kazimierz's reign that followed. His power lasted until his death in August 1650. One of the reasons for this lasting success was his readiness to abandon allies and change his policies with the prevailing tide.[21]

When Kysil's alliance with Ossoliński began is difficult to establish. In the 1630s they clearly did not agree on a number of major issues: Ossoliński sided with the militant Catholic faction in the Diet, opposed concessions to the Orthodox, and signed petitions protesting the privileges of 1632–1633, while Kysil attacked Ossoliński's project for a knightly order.[22] Still, sometime before 1644, the year of Ossoliński's first known letter to Kysil, the two men got together.[23] They held similar views on foreign policy, especially on the need for war against Tatars or Turks, and on the need for an alliance with Muscovy and the Zaporozhian Cossacks to win such a war.[24] Kysil's pro-Orthodox activities were removed as an obstacle to their partnership when Ossoliński began thinking in terms of a new union, and by 1648 it had reached a stage where Ossoliński could write to Kysil extolling the "public and private friendship" they had formed in their "youth."[25] We know that at least the "public" part of that friendship prospered during the 1640s.

The Attempt at a New Church Union

A desire for a new union was the logical outcome of the wrangling throughout the 1630s, which convinced some among both Orthodox and Uniates that a new solution had to be found to the division in the Ruthenian church. In 1635, Prince Aleksander Sanguszko, a convert to

Catholicism, proposed a union plan.[26] Because of the antipathy between the Orthodox and Uniate factions of the nobility, and between the Orthodox and the Roman Catholic clergy, Sanguszko maintained that he, as a layman and a Roman Catholic, could best serve as a mediator. He also maintained that both Mohyla and the Orthodox bishop of Luts'k, Atanazii Puzyna, were favorably disposed toward such an attempt.[27]

Prince Sanguszko's plan was discussed at the Congregation for the Propagation of Faith, but that body had taken no decision since its members were reluctant to embark on any project until they were sure of Władysław's cooperation.[28] However, even after Władysław expressed support and proposed that—following the recent example of the Muscovite church—the metropolitan see of Kiev be elevated to patriarchal rank, the Congregation refused to condone new discussions between the Orthodox and Uniates. The papal ruling of 1629 against joint Orthodox-Uniate synods was still in force; any plan that might lead to an erection of a patriarchal see in Kiev was opposed as dangerous to Rome's authority.[29] Władysław's support for a Ruthenian patriarchate, therefore, could only sour his relations with the Holy See, which continued to insist that adherence to the Union of Brest was the only solution the Pope could accept. Tensions between Warsaw and Rome had already increased because of Władysław's disputes over other issues with the papal nuncio, Mario Filonardi,[30] and in 1643, the Holy See recalled Filonardi in an attempt to improve relations.[31]

In 1643, Metodii Terlets'kyi, the Uniate bishop of Chełm, wrote to the Congregation for the Propagation of the Faith, again proposing that Rome consider the possibility of a new union.[32] As Sanguszko before him, he asserted that Mohyla and the bishop of Luts'k, Puzyna, were already Catholic in everything but name. He suggested that the Pope appeal to twenty-four influential leaders of the realm, including the Orthodox lay leaders Adam Kysil and Hryhorii Chetvertyns'kyi, to support a union of the churches. This time Pope Urban VIII took Terlets'kyi's advice and addressed letters to Mohyla and Kysil, in which he described them in flattering terms as the most prominent clerical and lay leaders of the Orthodox church and called upon them to unite with the Roman Catholic church.[33] He also wrote to a number of prominent Catholics, urging them to work toward healing the religious breach.[34]

Mohyla and Kysil were both prepared to entertain projects for a new union. Despite Mohyla's successes and Kysil's victories in preserving Orthodox rights, the position of the Orthodox Rus' church was still precarious. One might contest Sakovych's statements in the 1640s that the Rus' church was uncultured and backward, but even the most zealous defender of Orthodoxy could not deny that the Ruthenian Orthodox clergymen were less educated than their Roman Catholic counterparts, that abuses abounded, and that even the best school in Kiev was based on Western models.[35]

The Uniate church, led after 1640 by Metropolitan Antin Seliava, had in the meantime withstood the pressure that the Orthodox had brought to bear, and its hierarchy remained determined to whittle away Orthodox privileges.[36] It retained control of large parts of Belorussia, Polissia, and the Chełm land. Whatever satisfaction the Orthodox hierarchs could take over having been more successful than the Uniate bishops in retaining the allegiance of the nobility and in developing educational and cultural institutions was tempered by the realization that Roman Catholicism was making great advances in the Ukraine and Belorussia at both their expense. The network of Roman Catholic parishes had increased rapidly in the Volhynian, Kiev, Bratslav, and Chernihiv palatinates, until the church penetrated the very core of Orthodox Rus'.[37] In 1637, Aleksander Piaseczyński founded a Jesuit school in Novhorod-Sivers'kyi, in the Chernihiv palatinate, an area where neither Catholics nor Uniates had lived before 1618; and in 1646, under the protection of Janusz Tyszkiewicz, palatine of Kiev, the Jesuits established a collegium in Kiev itself.[38] The Orthodox church was threatened in the very center of Rus', not by the Uniates, but by the Roman Catholics. A compromise with Rome that guaranteed a reunited Ruthenian church with greater privileges than the Uniates enjoyed under the Union of Brest would strengthen the Ruthenian church in its competition with Latin-rite Catholicism.

In 1639 Terlets'kyi had denounced Kysil as the "head of the schismatics."[39] When he wrote the Pope in 1643, he repeated that description, but also remarked that Kysil, who stood out among the "schismatics" for his learning and eloquence, was favorably disposed to conversion to Catholicism.[40] Through Terlets'kyi's letters, Kysil attracted the attention of the Holy See, and for the next ten years, papal nuncios and officials of the Congregation for the Propagation of the Faith continued to regard him as a critical figure in any attempt to win over the Orthodox. Even though Kysil never stopped maintaining that the Catholics must concede that the Union of Brest was a dead letter and must face the reality of Orthodox strength and popular appeal, he somehow succeeded in convincing Roman authorities not only that he was sympathetic to Catholicism, but that in all but a public profession he already was a Catholic.[41]

There is no doubt that, in the 1640s, Kysil was seriously willing to discuss a new union, but for a number of practical reasons, he had to be circumspect in his response to the Pope's overtures. On the one hand, the program he advocated for a war against the Turks and Tatars required papal support,[42] and he had to please his benefactor, Władysław, who backed plans for a union, and Chancellor Ossoliński, who in part conducted the negotations.[43] On the other, his espousal of Orthodoxy, while it had furthered his career, had put him under constant pressure from many sides—any evidence of faltering resulted in condemnation from the militant Orthodox camp. Even when the Orthodox zealots praised Kysil, their approval was not always welcome. For example, a devout Orthodox monk from the Brest area, Afanasii Filipovich, singled Kysil out as a worthy defender of Orthodoxy.[44] However, praise from a fanatic, who broke into a Diet session in 1643, who predicted the destruction of the Commonwealth, and who demanded that Władysław's monument to his father, Zygmunt, be dismantled, must have been discomfiting to Kysil, to say the least. Filipovich's ardor later won him martyrdom in 1648 and reverence as a saint of the Orthodox church, but in the mid-1640s, to Kysil and to Mohyla, who wished to make the Orthodox faith "respectable," he could only have been an embarrassment. Mohyla once even resorted to imprisoning Filipovich in order to restrain his zeal.

Kysil was also forced into the role of defending the Orthodox faith and Ruthenian church against the charges that arose out of religious polemics. The then still Uniate Kasiian Sakovych, Kysil's former tutor, wrote in a 1640 treatise that after he had been made aware of the errors of following the Julian calendar, "I discussed this matter privately and publicly often with various clerics and laymen, and I wrote about this mistake in the calendar to various important personages. For instance, in 1637, I wrote of this to the Diet to Adam Kysil, at that time the podkomorzy, and now castellan, of Chernihiv. His Excellency showed my letter to senior 'Disuniate' clerics and asked that they write back to me about this, but none wrote back."[45] Thus, because of his position as the "head of the schismatics," Kysil was called upon to argue in favor of a calendar less accurate in representing the solar year. Had he possessed Filipovich's certitude in the God-revealed truth with which an Orthodox Christian should alone concern himself, he would have simply dismissed all charges as the works of the Devil. Lacking that single-mindedness, Kysil found himself troubled by the endless theological and ecclesiastical struggles between two churches that both maintained that Christ had intended the Christian church be one. Kysil was clearly no zealot, and his obvious respect for the Pope put his Orthodoxy into question more than once. Both that respect and his devotion to his ancestral faith are evident, for example, in this grant establishing an Orthodox monastery in Nyzkynychi in 1643:

Since I was born in the Holy Faith and my ancestral religion, the Holy Eastern Church of my ancient ancestors of the Greek Rite, in which my ancestor was baptised together with his monarch Volodimer, and in which the ancestors of my house were later incorporated to the Kingdom of Poland, our present Fatherland, I have lived throughout all my life in that faith, and I wish to live to the end of my life [in it] with the help of the Lord. I believe in One God, One Trinity, One Baptism, One Orthodox, or as the Slavs call it, 'Pravoslav' faith, in one Universal Apostolic Church for whom the Holy Martyrs shed their Holy Blood and also in the Heavenly Hierarchy, in various ranks, as the Holy Scripture expresses it, angels, archangels, cherubim, and seraphim under the rule of one Lord and God. I profess an order of God's Church which should in all things accommodate itself to its triumphant capital, and as the Old Testament order prefigured that of the New Testament and had in its order Aaron, the High Priest on earth, and as the entire Commonwealth which is most perfect, has one administrator, so the Commonwealth of the Church, being under the rule of its Lord Founder and God, cannot be in its most perfect form on this earth without an administrator and head, and, as in the time of the Apostles, Our Holy Mother Church professed one head in its hymns, so one leadership of the successors of that head Apostle is necessary for its successors and the succession of the Apostles. But in these unhappy times, God's church is torn asunder with difficulties and sad controversies painful to the Majesty of God, especially in our Fatherland and our Ruthenian nation. . . . Therefore, until the Lord God, on Whose Own Almighty Hand rests this affair, unites all, I, as having always stood for the rights, privileges, and freedoms of my ancestral faith in this Commonwealth, so now make my profession.[46]

Kysil expressed his discontent over the dissension among Christians, at the same time he made clear his primary interest in the ramifications of this dissension for the fatherland and the Ruthenian people. A few years later, when founding a Roman Catholic church for Polish subjects on his estates, he showed how strongly he opposed the schism among Christians by maintaining that as there was "one God, one Faith, one Baptism, there could not be two faiths honored by Latin and Greek rites," and that all means must be employed to bring back the unity that formerly existed.

Kasiian Sakovych was also responsible for making Kysil's sympathies toward Catholicism public. In 1642 Sakovych received permission from the Pope to transfer from the Uniates to Latin Catholicism and, having done so, launched a scathing attack on the "errors, heresies, and prejudices in the Greco-Ruthenian Disuniate Church" (which also criticized the Uniates):

All Uniate Ruthenians and almost all non-Uniate Ruthenians agree with the Holy Roman Church in the above-mentioned matters. But in the following two matters there is agreement [only] of Uniate Rus' with the Romans: on the procession of the Holy Ghost and on the primacy or seniority of the Holy Father, the Roman Pope over all the pastors of the visible Church. 'Disuniate' Rus', however, almost entirely does not wish to believe in these two articles of the Roman Church (excepting Father Puzyna, the bishop of Luts'k and some laymen like Adam Kysil, the castellan of Chernihiv, with whom it has often happened that I have publicly conferred at which time they professed these Catholic articles. Other honorable and important people of the Roman rite know about this.).[47]

The Orthodox response (*Lithos*, 1644) to this comment, possibly written by Mohyla himself, defended the bishop and the castellan as loyal Orthodox believers. Its author asserted that the charge that Kysil and Puzyna did not believe and profess the doctrines of the Orthodox church was a "bold calumny," "for they could not believe otherwise, since one is a bishop and both are sons of the Eastern Church," a categorical tone that indicates how closely Sakovych had come to hitting the mark.[48] In the same year, Kysil responded to Pope Urban's appeal and drafted proposals for a new union.

Kysil and Mohyla appear to have collaborated in drafting this response.[49] Much of the evidence that remains is unsigned, so it is impossible to ascertain which man conceived which part of the proposals, but Kysil may be assumed to have played a major role in their formulation, since they resemble statements he made elsewhere on the problems of religious union.[50] It was Kysil who initially convinced Mohyla to participate in discussions, and who kept up attempts to bring about a union even after Mohyla's death (January 1647).[51] The most detailed discussion of the proposals of 1644, entitled *Sententia cuiusdam nobilis Poloni graecae religionis*, usually attributed to Kysil, agrees in essentials with existing summaries of a document submitted by Mohyla. The proposals can therefore be considered as originating from both men.[52]

They dealt with three issues: the relationship of the Greek and Roman churches, doctrinal and administrative obstacles for union, and practical plans for implementing a new union.[53] The authors adduced several reasons for the failure of previous negotiations for union: they had not been entered into with the proper intention; the procedures followed had conflicted with the political structure of the Commonwealth, particularly since among the Ruthenians the nobles' power was much greater, and the bishops' power much less, than in the Roman church, so that to embark upon any project of union without the nobility's support had been foolhardy; and finally, the Catholics sought *unitas* (uniformity) when they should have been seeking *unio* (union). Since, as the authors assert, the doctrinal differences between Orthodoxy and Catholicism are inconsequential and of interest only to theologians, one need not try to turn Greeks into Romans. The disputes about purgatory, individual judgment, and the Eucharist were already settled, and the difference between the formulas *per Filium* and *a Filio* did not represent an obstacle to union.

The real problem, as far as the Orthodox were concerned, was to interpret the Pope's primacy in a way that would not interfere with the status of the patriarchs. The Ruthenian church must remain loyal to the patriarch of Constantinople, but since that city's occupation by the "barbarian" Turks rendered the patriarch incapable of recognizing the primacy of the Roman see that had existed in ancient times, the Ruthenian church would have to proceed toward union on its own. Once the patriarch of Constantinople was free of bondage and able to approve the union, however, the Ruthenian church would return its obedience to him. At present, the question of obedience to Constantinople would be settled by forwarding a copy of their agreement with the Pope to the patriarch. Should he refuse to recognize it, the Orthodox of the Commonwealth would then be free to conclude their own negotiations with Rome. Since Kysil and Mohyla could be sure that the patriarch would reject the proposals, they could retain a semblance of respect for the patriarchate, and still have a free hand.

The procedures Kysil and Mohyla proposed indicate how wary they were of a merger between the Ruthenian and the Roman Catholic churches. Those procedures called for the metropolitan of Kiev to select the bishops and a synod of bishops to choose the metropolitan. The metropolitan would then be invested with full authority (after his appointment was approved by the king), not by the Popes of Rome or the patriarchs of Constantinople but by the Ruthenian church's bishops. The metropolitan would only be required to send to Rome a pledge of loyalty to the articles of the proposed union.

Kysil and Mohyla also carefully formulated the steps that should be taken to obtain the Orthodox faithful's assent to this new union. The dietines would first arrange meetings between Uniates and Orthodox to discuss religious problems, but no mention of a possible union would be made at that point. The proposal for union would be made public only after a Diet constitution had called for a joint meeting presided over by a Catholic and an Orthodox leader. The king was to forbid interference with that meeting, and transgression would be severely punished. It is obvious that the two men were intent on avoiding the mistakes of the synodal program of 1629, which had failed because no Diet constitution had been passed and because Zygmunt had openly announced that the purpose of the synods was to unite the Orthodox with Rome.[54]

The procedure also avoided issues that the papacy opposed: the subject of the creation of a Ruthenian patriarchate was not even broached, and in place of a synod to discuss religious differences, a meeting convened by lay authorities would merely affirm terms already agreed upon.[55] Differences of belief regarding the Eucharist, purgatory, and individual judgment would be resolved according to the rulings of the Council of Florence and the issue of the *Filioque* would be left to the "theologians."

Less acceptable to Rome were the insistence on the validity of an independent Eastern church tradition and the interpretation of the Pope's primacy as one merely of ceremonial precedence. Kysil and Mohyla wanted a union of two equal parts even if, for the present, one part consisted only of its Ruthenian component. Although the metropolitan was not officially elevated to the rank of a patriarch, he would exercise patriarchal powers. In harmony with their different church governance, the nobles would continue to play a considerable role in making decisions in the Ruthenian church, since one of the reasons why the previous union had failed was thought to be that the bishops had negotiated the union on their own. This emphasis on the nobility's role in the Ruthenian church was probably one of Kysil's contributions.

In March 1645, the Congregation for the Propagation of the Faith examined the proposals.[56] Francesco Ingoli, a major proponent of a conciliatory policy with the Ruthenian Orthodox church, reacted favorably, though he saw in the issue of the *Filioque* a greater obstacle than the Orthodox did, and while independent election of Ruthenian metropolitans might be allowed, he thought the candidates elected should submit themselves to the Pope for confirmation. A more "Roman" view was espoused by another commentator, V. Riccardi, who considered the doctrinal issues far from settled and viewed the Orthodox proposals as antithetical to the unity of the Catholic church.[57]

Despite these reservations, the new papal nuncio, Juan de Torres, was instructed to discuss the project with the king, Chancellor Ossoliński, the Uniate metropolitan, Seliava and Bishop Terlets'kyi.[58] Before they had proceeded very far, however, the situation was radically altered by the illness and death of Mohyla at the beginning of 1647. The papacy thought to capitalize on his removal to dispense altogether with the troublesome procedure of negotiating a new union by simply electing a Uniate as metropolitan, and it secured an assurance from

Władysław to put off any selection to May 1647.[59] No one in the Commonwealth, however, seriously believed that the king would affront the Orthodox and refuse to confirm their candidate.

In accordance with tradition, the councils of Orthodox clergy and laity had met in January and February to choose Mohyla's successors.[60] They proposed Sylvestr Kosiv as metropolitan and Iosyf Tryzna as archimandrite of the Caves monastery.[61] The king, in the meantime, had promised the nuncio that he would wait until Kysil returned from an embassy to Moscow in the summer of 1647 before recognizing any metropolitan.[62] Since Kysil had been present at the election of Kosiv as metropolitan in February 1647, Władysław's statement was merely palliative.[63] In fact, he had confirmed the appointments before Kysil even left for Moscow, and the papal nuncio had to be content with assurances from the king and chancellor that because the new metropolitan was a close associate of Kysil, he would be favorable to the union,[64] and because the position of archimandrite of the Caves monastery, which Mohyla had possessed, had not been conferred on the new metropolitan, his power and wealth would be much curtailed.[65] Kosiv's close relations with Kysil were described by the nuncio as being especially important, since he was convinced that Kysil was actually Catholic, and simply outwardly Orthodox for political reasons.[66] In the end, the selection of Kosiv merely restored the *status quo ante,* except that Kosiv lacked Mohyla's stature.

When Kosiv had been elected, the next question was whether or not he should request the patriarch of Constantinople to supply the chrism, or holy oil, which the metropolitans of Kiev had traditionally received from the patriarch. When he had returned from Moscow in the autumn of 1647, Kysil wrote to Kosiv that he should do nothing, lest he jeopardize the negotiations for union.[67] Kysil's real opinions are difficult to fathom since the only extant copy of this letter is one that the papal nuncio copied from a copy that Kysil sent to Ossoliński, and Kysil undoubtedly conceived the letter as a statement to the government and the Holy See on the terms for a union.[68] In response to Kosiv's proposal that the patriarch of Constantinople should be requested to approve his election and supply the necessary chrism, Kysil insisted that no letter be sent unless it was first shown to the king. He warned the metropolitan of the atmosphere of suspicion and mistrust in the Commonwealth, advised him to explore the possibility of union, and assured him that it would not affect the dogmas or rites of the Ruthenian church. Changes in the Greek church were unthinkable, according to Kysil, since its dogmas and rites predated those of the Roman church and had been adhered to by both before 1054. At the Council of Florence

(1439), the negotiations for union had centered solely on the changes that had been introduced in the Latin church; the Council had accepted those changes and ruled that the Latin formulation on the Trinity did not differ in essence from the Greek. This indicated, Kysil believed, that union was possible only when the two faiths retained their separate institutional structures. The primacy of the Roman pontiffs would be no stumbling block to union at all, according to Kysil, if it were borne in mind that before the schism, the Eastern church had recognized the Roman Pope as the highest dignitary in the Christian church. Eastern Christians would again be willing to recognize that primacy so long as they were allowed to retain their own rite and their patriarchs as their own pastors. Kysil admitted that union was made more difficult by the political situation, which prevented convening a council including all the Orthodox churches, but he asserted that union was possible if the immutability of both rites were recognized. The "so-called Uniates" had breached this principle when they broke with the patriarch of Constantinople and introduced changes in the liturgy and had even accepted the chrism from Rome. He declared the Ruthenian Orthodox church did not wish to make any such concessions, nor should it turn to anyone external for chrism. He proposed that the problem could be solved if the ceremonies for consecrating a patriarch were adopted for consecrating the metropolitans of Kiev, though he also foresaw that the lack of patriarchal chrism would elicit opposition. He ended by advising Kosiv to accept chrism from Constantinople only if Władysław consented.[69]

All this advice was essentially in line with the Orthodox proposals of 1644–1645, except that Kysil placed more emphasis on the independent status that the Ruthenian church must retain in any union with Rome. He undoubtedly composed the letter with both Kosiv and the papal officials in mind, since he assured Kosiv that the traditions and dignity of the Eastern church would be respected and tried to convince Rome that substantial concessions must be made and that the proposed new united Ruthenian church must be virtually independent. De Torres sent the letter without delay, mentioning when he did that the Orthodox were charging the Uniates with abandoning not only Orthodoxy, but also the Greek rite.[70]

By now the prospects for a new union seemed favorable. Orthodox leaders convening in Vilnius adopted a program for union that was in accord with Mohyla's and Kysil's proposals of 1644–1645.[71] One of the reasons for Chancellor Ossoliński's trip to the Ukraine in the summer of 1647 seems to have been to discuss plans for the union with Kysil and the metropolitan.[72] When de Torres forwarded his copy of Kysil's letter in March 1648, he too expressed confidence that an agreement would be reached in a short time, since he thought Kysil's support would guarantee that a conference of Orthodox leaders, scheduled for July, would endorse the union.[73] But before the conference could convene, de Torres, alarmed by reports of a Cossack rebellion, informed his superiors the new union would be delayed.[74] The success of the rebellion later ensured that the delay would be permanent.

Kysil's promotion of union between 1644 and 1648 turned out to be the last effort of the old Ukrainian-Belorussian elite to restore religious unity. Had those plans for union succeeded, Kysil would most probably have been the lay head of the reunited Rus' community, since as the architect of the compromise, he could have derived considerable benefit in the Commonwealth as the de facto head of the reunited Ruthenian "nation." Even without the new union, he emerged with his position in the Ruthenian Orthodox community considerably enhanced, despite his role in the negotiations. The negotiations had, of course, been secret, but it is still unlikely that the Cossack leadership and Orthodox clergy were unaware of them. Sakovych had cast doubt about Kysil's loyalty to Orthodoxy, and the Orthodox meeting in Vilnius had made the new negotiations for union public. How deeply Kysil was involved in them was perhaps less well known, since it was in no party's interest—not even the papacy's—to reveal their particulars. In the end, the Orthodox community may simply have chosen to ignore Kysil's pro-union views, because they needed his support and leadership.

After Mohyla's death, Kysil had no rival as leader of Rus'. The new metropolitan had neither great wealth nor high connections. In addition, Kosiv probably owed his election to Kysil, and certainly was beholden to him for acceptance by the government. Recognition of Kysil as the head of Rus' had already come with his appointment as Kievan castellan in February 1646. Władysław's grant of conferral lauded Kysil's numerous services to the fatherland and chose to elevate his ancestry by declaring it from the "Rus' princes."[75] Without resolution of the Rus' religious issue, however, that leadership held potential for divided loyalty and difficult personal decisions.

When Teodozii Baievs'kyi, a professor of the Kiev collegium, celebrated Kysil's entry into the city as castellan with a Latin panegyric, later published by the Caves monastery, he had no way of knowing that less than three years later the collegium would be celebrating the entry of a Zaporozhian hetman.[76] Baievs'kyi's task was to cultivate Kysil's support for the collegium and the Orthodox church. He, like all the Kievan intellectuals that Mohyla had so carefully gathered worked to ensure Kysil's patronage, as guarantor and creator of an Orthodox church recognized by, and loyal to, the Commonwealth and tolerated by government officials and the Catholic nobility.

Amidst Baievs'kyi's effusive praise of Kysil's services to church, fatherland, army, and family was an allusion to potential contradictions in Kysil's position. Baievs'kyi maintained that a conflict existed between Rus' and Poland over Kysil.[77] Both claimed him as its citizen; whichever would win, the other would lose. The Orthodox cleric proposed that Kysil could resolve this conflict by service to the "Eternal Church." In proposing that Rus' and Poland were two equal competitors for Kysil's loyalty, Baievs'kyi underlined an ambiguity in Kysil's position that became apparent to wider circles only after the rebirth of a Rus' political entity in 1648.

The Commonwealth's Foreign Policy:
The Pact with Muscovy and the
Plans for a War with the Crimean
Khanate and the Ottoman Empire

On September 15, 1644, Chancellor Ossoliński wrote to Kysil. This is the earliest evidence we have of contact between Ossoliński and Kysil and of the influence Kysil's views already had at Władysław's court. The Trubchevsk area was to be ceded to Muscovy, he said; it was cheaper to compensate people for loss of property than it was to pay for a war. Discussing the compensation, he maintained: "His Majesty the King willingly cedes the profits that he receives from those forests to bring peace to the whole Commonwealth, which will then be able to turn both eyes safely to the pagan 'wall,' to the venture that Your Lordship has proposed."[78] Ossoliński's comment indicates that Kysil was not only a supporter of the policy Władysław pursued during the last few years of his reign to extend the Commonwealth's influence and borders to the south, but also that he was an initiator of the discussion of such a program in government circles.[79] During the next twelve months, the chancellor exhorted the Diet to take determined measures against the Tatars; the great hetman, Stanisław Koniecpolski, called for an alliance with Muscovy to conquer the Crimea and the Danubian provinces of the Ottoman Empire; and the king undertook negotiations with Venice and the Pope for subsidies to raise an army against the Ottomans.[80]

When Kysil involved himself with foreign policy, he was entering into one of the more ambiguous areas of the Commonwealth's governance. The formulation and conduct of foreign relations were complex processes involving numerous spheres of influence with overlapping competence. The Diet had the exclusive right to confirm treaties and alliances and to commission and receive major embassies. A legislative body that met both briefly and infrequently was in no position to administer government on a daily basis; therefore, the Senate, important court officials, and the king all acquired considerable power in the conduct of foreign affairs.

In an age when agreements and negotiations between states were looked upon as contracts between monarchs, the king could wield considerable influence. In practice, he maintained his own contacts with foreign powers and with representatives assigned for long periods to Warsaw, and he received foreign delegations and exchanged emissaries. He could thus enhance his authority in guiding the Commonwealth's policies and reduce the power of the Diet to confirming or rejecting his proposals. When the king was acting as the head of the state, and when he was acting as a private person or member of a dynasty, remained ill-defined. The Vasa kings often pursued their policies as claimants to the Swedish throne, though the Diet firmly disavowed those maneuvers. In negotiating treaties, the interests of monarch and Commonwealth could similarly often conflict.[81]

The two Crown and two Lithuanian chancellors also had their own diplomatic contacts. They controlled the seals of state (necessary to validate acts as official) and the chancery books. As the highest officer in the Commonwealth, the Crown chancellor communicated with foreign powers and presented the government's position to the Diet. If the monarch cooperated with one of the chancellors, their combined influence on the Diet could be all the greater.

The Commonwealth's hetmans also exercised influence on foreign policy because they controlled the standing army. The Crown great hetman had particularly broad powers, especially in dealing with the Crimean Tatars and the Ottoman Empire. Finally, the lack of a clear central authority encouraged anyone with sufficient money or influence to conduct his own foreign policy. The Zaporozhian Cossacks, for example, negotiated directly with foreign states, and the magnates of the Commonwealth maintained their own contacts abroad. In addition, through their contacts with co-religionists, religious leaders pursued their own policies on foreign relations.[82]

In some ways the Commonwealth did not differ markedly from any other European state that did not yet have a professional diplomatic corps and had not yet learned how to exercise effective control over an inhabitant's contacts with states, institutions, and people outside its borders. But the Commonwealth admittedly presented an extreme case of diffusion of power and lack of clear procedures for making decisions, especially because it contrasted so strikingly with neighboring Muscovy and the Ottoman Empire, both of which were ruled by an autocrat and by a centralized bureacracy that monopolized foreign contact. In the early seventeenth century, the dangers inherent in the Commonwealth's decentralization were not yet apparent, however. Foreign diplomats might complain bitterly about the complexity of dealing with it, but the pacifist nobles were pleased with a system that discouraged foreign entanglements.[83]

Władysław thirsted for foreign glory and conquest. He conducted major reforms in the military, particularly in improving artillery, and founded a navy on the Baltic.[84] Thwarted in his efforts to embroil the Commonwealth in a war to regain the Swedish throne and thereby in the Thirty Years' War, Władysław decided instead to strengthen his position in the Commonwealth through a foreign campaign on another front. The outbreak of war between Venice and the Ottoman Empire in 1644–1645 provided the opportunity, particularly because Venice would subsidize any help Władysław would provide, so he need not depend on the Diet to support his troops.[85]

Since the Khotyn War, the Commonwealth had faced the danger of an Ottoman invasion a number of times, but the Ottoman Empire was at that time a far from aggressive neighbor and had avoided conflict. The Crimean Tatars posed a far more active threat. In the 1630s the Khanate of Crimea had gone through a period of consolidation and reform that was reflected in its growing military strength and influence in international affairs. The Tatars were able to campaign effectively against the agricultural settlements and the cities of the Commonwealth and Muscovy chiefly because of the enmity between Warsaw and Moscow. So long as the two states remained enemies, the Tatars could alternate alliance and attack to their own advantage. The hostility between the two powers left each state to deal with the Crimean problem in its own manner. The conclusion of the Eternal Peace at Polianovka between Muscovy and the Commonwealth in 1634 had not altered the situation, even though a clause in the agreement called for the two states to stand together against foreign attacks.[86]

Muscovy, defeated in the Smolensk War, had territorial claims against the Commonwealth and had complaints about insults to the tsar due to errors in titulature, incursions of Zaporozhians and border magnates, and the harboring of pretenders to the Muscovite throne. The Commonwealth was equally dissatisfied over Muscovy's harboring of runaway peasants from the newly colonized Left-Bank lands and its refusal to release prisoners of war.[87]

The major impetus for settling these disputes, which had been argued by delegations and commissions throughout the 1630s and 1640s, was the need to form a common defense against the Tatars. Ossoliński reflected these views when he wrote to Kysil about relinquishing Trubchevsk. After its victories and annexations of the Chernihiv and Smolensk lands, the Commonwealth could well afford some concessions to Muscovy; on the other side, however much the Muscovite government smarted over the Commonwealth's intervention in the Time of Troubles and the outcome of the Smolensk War, the Commonwealth was so strong that it would make a better ally than an enemy. Muscovy suffered more from the Tatars than the Commonwealth did in those years. The government was busily building defense lines on its southern frontier to combat the Tatar threat,[88] and unlike the Commonwealth, which appeared to have reduced its Cossack problem in 1638, Muscovy's unruly Don Cossacks had seized the fortress of Azov and had embroiled the tsar in a conflict with the Ottoman Empire by holding off Turkish attempts to recapture it.[89] Cooperation against the Tatars began with exchanging information and blocking Tatar access through either state's territory. After 1645, Muscovy sought a more formal agreement, which coincided with Władysław's plans to involve Muscovy in a Tatar war that would provoke a wider struggle involving both powers against the Ottomans.[90]

Outside his immediate circle the king could expect support action against the Tatars only from the Ukrainian palatinates, because they suffered most from raids, but the nobles even from those areas would oppose involving the Commonwealth in a Turkish war.[91] Since he would in any case have to circumvent the pacifist Diet, the king had to win the eastern magnates over to his plan by arguing that they would stand to gain most from any extension of the Commonwealth's power in the southeast.[92] A Turkish war had already been proposed by Stanisław Koniecpolski, the greatest landowner in the palatinate of Bratslav, and Władysław at least expected support from other eastern magnates.[93]

The king still had to surmount some considerable obstacles, however. Koniecpolski might have proposed an alliance with Muscovy and an offensive war against the Ottomans and Tatars, but there is no indication that he would have agreed to contravene the Commonwealth's laws and antagonize the nobility in the process.[94] He had no interest either in alienating his peers or in increasing the power of the king. In addition, some of the magnates, notably Jeremi Wiśniowiecki, were actually political opponents, and he and others stood to lose territories in any border adjustment with Muscovy.[95] Wiśniowiecki would be deprived of large tracts on the Left Bank were he to accept the decisions of the border commissions.[96] Opposition to border concessions was even more widespread and adamant in the Grand Duchy of Lithuania, far removed from Tatar incursions and far more interested in weakening Muscovy than in allying with it.[97]

Between 1645 and 1648, Władysław tried to overcome all these obstacles, to improve relations with Muscovy, and to secure subsidies from Venice, though the death of Koniecpolski in 1646 upset his plans.[98] Following the usual practice, Władysław appointed Crown Field Hetman Mikołaj Potocki to succeed Koniecpolski, but Potocki neither favored Koniecpolski's proposals, nor was he capable of leading a war. In both that year and the next, the Diets protested any plans for war and demanded that Władysław disband the personal detachments he had already gathered.[99]

The king proceeded all the same. In addition to his personal guard, he believed he could count on the Zaporozhian Cossacks; the Venetians were particularly interested in obtaining their service, since they were famous for their destructive raids in Asia Minor. With support from the Cossacks and the eastern magnates, the king could provoke a Tatar attack that would force the pacifist nobles into war and probably bring the Ottomans into the struggle. This plan could only work if Muscovy were bound by an alliance to assist the Commonwealth.

In a letter of March 16, 1648, Kysil refers to the improvement of Muscovite-Commonwealth relations as being a project to which he had contributed twelve years of arduous labor.[100] No one was more suited for representing the Commonwealth in any negotiations with Muscovy than Kysil was. He had served as an official in the formerly Muscovite Chernihiv lands for over a decade, and he had ample experience in dealing with Muscovite officials on border commissions.[101] Because he favored making territorial concessions, he had earned a reputation in Muscovite diplomatic circles as being a friend of Muscovy; and, of course, he also enjoyed the advantages of being a coreligionist.[102] When electing delegates to the Diet of 1646, the Volhynian nobles had proposed Kysil as best qualified to solve any outstanding differences with Muscovy,[103] and even though that Diet opposed Władysław's plans for a war with the Ottoman Empire, it was apparently willing to send Kysil to Muscovy to negotiate outstanding differences between the two states.[104] The Diet empowered him only to discuss an alliance with Muscovy against the Tatars, however, with the Diet reserving the right to approve the terms.[105] It wanted to make certain that an anti-Tatar alliance with Muscovy would not involve the Commonwealth in any major war.[106]

Even that authorization was owing to Władysław's mollifying those nobles who opposed a settlement with Muscovy. He faced a difficult task because of divergence of interests in a federal state, since the Grand Duchy of Lithuania had to make territorial concessions, while the benefits of a Muscovite alliance against the Tatars would accrue to the Kingdom of Poland, and to its Ukrainian lands in particular. As Ossoliński mentioned, the king was willing to make restitution for the loss of Lithuania's Trubchevsk, but a year later Koniecpolski would still write to Kysil that the Grand Duchy was posing problems.[107]

Kysil was given the task of convincing the recalcitrant nobles that the Commonwealth must abide by its agreements.[108] Combined pressure from the court and threats of war from Muscovy had led the delegates of the Grand Duchy to agree to surrender Trubchevsk in 1645, but the Grand Duchy's representative still refused to join an embassy headed by the castellan of Bratslav, Gabriel Stempkowski, sent to settle the matter. After Trubchevsk was finally handed over, Kysil made some restitution to the Grand Duchy's inhabitants by founding a monastery on his own lands for the monks of the Trubchevsk monastery who did not wish to transfer their allegiance to Muscovy.[109] The Grand Duchy refused to be placated, however, particularly because the delegates of the palatinate of Kiev refused to transfer Chornobyl' to it as compensation for Trubchevsk.[110]

Kysil's next task was to get Wiśniowiecki to agree to relinquish some of his territories on the Left Bank near Nedryhailiv to Moscow. Wiśniowiecki's vast domains constituted an almost independent state, and his claims to the upper reaches of Udai and Sula rivers made him a major antagonist of Muscovy. The Muscovites were well aware of the weakness of the Commonwealth's central government and the consequent ability of men such as Wiśniowiecki to defy the king and the Diet.[111] Yet, as independent as Wiśniowiecki was, there were inducements for him to cooperate. In the mid-1640s, he was involved in a territorial dispute with another eastern magnate, Adam Kazanowski, a favorite of the king.[112] Wiśniowiecki had seized some of Kazanowski's lands, and that had placed him in a vulnerable position. Kazanowski tried to have him expelled from the Diet of 1645, but the king apparently intervened to settle the dispute in Wiśniowiecki's favor.[113] Kysil also rushed to his assistance by issuing a long position paper to save Wiśniowiecki's mandate as a delegate and, when the dispute was settled, by loaning him the 100,000 złotys needed to buy out Kazanowski's claims.[114] The reconciliation of the magnate with the king was marked by his appointment as palatine of Ruthenia in 1646, finally enabling him to enter the Senate.[115]

Still, all that did not make it any easier to find a settlement to the border dispute. Koniecpolski wrote to Kysil in 1645, as he had in 1634, asking that Wiśniowiecki's interests be protected in any territorial settlement, and Kysil used all his diplomatic skills to defend Wiśnio-wiecki's possessions on the upper Sula and Udai.[116] At the same time he tried to comply with Muscovy's insistence for concession in the Nedry-hailiv and Vil'shanka areas.[117] Kysil even arranged a meeting of Wiś-niowiecki with the king to discuss compensation for the territories.[118] In the end Wiśniowiecki must have been placated, however, for in June of 1647, Kysil supervised the transfer of part of the Nedryhailiv region to Muscovy.[119]

In 1645 the castellan of Bratslav, Gabriel Stempkowski, and the Commonwealth negotiators had discussed a possible joint campaign against the Crimea. However, Stempkowski's mission did not resolve all outstanding issues or negotiate an alliance. The death of Tsar Mikhail Fedorovich in 1645 placed the relationship between the Commonwealth and Muscovy in question. Although at the Eternal Peace of Polianovka, the reconfirmation of the terms should one sovereign die had been discussed, it had not been included in the treaty. A Muscovite mission was therefore sent to the king in early 1646 to reaffirm the terms of the Eternal Peace and to reiterate Muscovy's interest in an alliance against the Tatars.[120] The Diet authorized sending a commission to Moscow to renew the Eternal Peace of 1634 and to negotiate the border issue, although it reserved its right to validate any agreement for an alliance drafted at the negotiations.[121] Kysil was selected as chief negotiator to renew the Eternal Peace and was provided with a subsidy of 40,000 złoty to undertake the mission.[122] Nonetheless, throughout the remainder of 1646 and the early months of 1647, Kysil maintained that illness pre-vented his departure.[123] It is true that his attacks of gout had become more acute, but it is, of course, also possible that Władysław's setback in his war plans at the Diet of 1646 contributed to this postponement. The nobles of the Grand Duchy had resented giving up the Trubchevsk territory, and its representatives opposed the very mission itself.[124] Although the Diet of 1647 was no more enthusiastic about Władysław's plans for a war against the Ottomans than it had been the year before, the king devised a strategy to avoid having to gain the Diet's approval. He would negotiate with Venice and begin a war by provoking a Tatar attack. An agreement with Muscovy was now of prime importance, because the king needed cordial relations with Muscovy, desired Musco-vite assistance against the Tatars, and hoped to draw Muscovy into his war against the Ottomans.[125]

Kysil finally departed on his mission to Muscovy on June 28, 1647. The negotiations were highly unusual in that the Lithuanian delegate, Kazimierz Pac, did not accompany Kysil, so determining a final demarcation of the Grand Duchy's border was impossible.[126] Kysil's instructions from the Diet included provisions for a defensive pact against the Tatars, a resolution of the problem of runaway serfs, the establishment of a final border solution, and the satisfaction of complaints concerning the tsar's titles,[127] but he could not conclude a binding alliance against the Tatars.[128]

Kysil's task from the king was to convince the Muscovite negotiators that the Commonwealth was a trustworthy ally.[129] His strategy was then to draw up an informal agreement once he had convinced them that the Commonwealth would come to their aid against Tatar attacks. The terms of the government would hold until the Diet met.[130] He was clearly in a difficult spot, for the Diet had agreed to Kysil's mission, but had severely circumscribed his powers. Therefore, Kysil had to pursue a foreign policy that conflicted with the Diet's instructions, while still protecting himself against accusations that he was overstepping his authority. Empowered by the Diet, he in fact represented the faction around the king that favored a war. He succeeded because in practice negotiators from the Commonwealth were accorded great latitude in implementing instructions, in marked contrast to Muscovite methods of diplomacy, which required negotiators to follow detailed instructions and punished them severely for any deviation from them.[131]

Kysil arrived in Moscow on August 14. He began his mission with a speech before the tsar,[132] in which he compared the Commonwealth and Muscovy to the Cedars of Lebanon, twin states from a single root created by the hand of God.[133] He cited Latin and Greek historians to prove his point, but his main piece of evidence was his assertion that one, uniform Slavic tongue was spoken in both states.[134] The wisdom of an alliance between the two states had been shown by the tsar's father, Mikhail, who had negotiated the Eternal Peace. After discussing the evils of dissension, the benefits of alliance, the king's grief over the death of Mikhail, and his joy over the accession of the present tsar, Kysil called on Aleksei to bring about a new epoch of unity.

Kysil divided Slavic history into three ages. He described the first as a happy one, when the Slavs were united, and thus enjoyed the respect of both empires of Rome and Constantinople. He called the second, present age, an unfortunate one of fratricidal strife, when Slavs shed each other's blood, and thus lost considerable territories to their enemies. He lamented that Perekop, where Volodimer accepted Christianity, was now a stronghold of the Crimean Horde, and other places, where once the ancient Slavs had chastized the Polovtsians, were now the haunts of Tatars. The third age, by God's Grace soon to come, would be another happy one, when brotherly love between two sovereigns would weld eternal peace between their states. Kysil chose some interesting arguments to justify that alliance, including concepts of Slavic linguistic unity and common Slavic origin. He cited historical precedents for a united Slavic front in a campaign to wrest the Black Sea littoral from the control of Turkic nomads.[135] His arguments were very different from the usual statements of the period, including Kysil's own, which emphasized Christian unity and common Sarmatian origin.[136]

Rhetorical flourishes, however, would not win the battle. The Muscovite negotiators, led by Prince Aleksei Nikitich Trubetskoi and Grigorii Gavrilovich Pushkin, were less interested in erudition than they were in titulature and border disputes. They immediately raised the issue of errors in the tsar's titles and demanded death for those nobles and officials of the Commonwealth who had erred. They rebuffed Kysil's explanations that the king's titles were often shortened with the retort that even the Ottomans and the Tatars did not make mistakes in titulature. It took three sessions before Kysil promised that the issue of punishments would be raised at the next Diet and new agreements were reached on titulature.

Kysil's alliance plan was also threatened by Muscovite negotiations with the Crimea.[137] Just before Kysil's arrival, the Muscovites, claiming that they had come to despair of the Commonwealth's interest in an alliance, had taken advantage of Tatar peace overtures.[138] In reporting his mission to the Diet, Kysil later pointed to the danger these negotiations had held for the Commonwealth. The Muscovites argued that the declaration of good faith from the Commonwealth was a year late, and that their decision to renew tribute payments was forced upon them by the Commonwealth's failure to assist them in the past against Tatar raids. Kysil eventually convinced the Muscovites of the Commonwealth's serious intention of forming an alliance,[139] but he later reported to the Diet that he was hampered in not being authorized to conclude a close offensive-defensive alliance on the spot.[140]

All these difficulties were still nothing as compared to those involved in negotiating for the return of runaways. When he complained that runaway peasants from the Commonwealth, including a group which had recently murdered an official of the Commonwealth, were freely accepted on the Muscovite side, the Muscovite negotiators countered with instances of the Commonwealth harboring fugitives and of allowing some Ukrainian Cossacks who were Muscovite subjects to cross the border. Kysil replied that the Cossacks were a free people who could live where they wished, but that peasants were not. The Muscovites continually cited the absence of an article on the return of the peasants in the Eternal Peace of 1634. Kysil admitted this was true, but he maintained that it was nonetheless essential to peace that something be done: he himself had lost 500 of his 3,000 peasants, and Stanisław Koniecpolski and Jeremi Wiśniowiecki had lost a thousand each.[141]

No accommodation was reached. There was too great a difference between their views. Kysil insisted on making a distinction between Cossacks and peasants on the basis of "free" and "unfree" men. The Muscovites were unimpressed by that distinction and charged Kysil with indifference toward religion: "You, Great Ambassador, are of the True Christian Faith and its defender, and these peasants are also of the True Faith, but they lived among people of various faiths, and if we were to give them back, it would mean giving them to a Catholic or Protestant to be persecuted. Is that a Christian act? In such servitude the poor peasant will abandon his faith."[142] Kysil replied: "What do peasants know? They have not the slightest concern for faith, and they flee because they do not wish to pay their landlords even the smallest dues."[143]

Differences also emerged when Kysil broached an issue, not included in his instructions, regarding the attitude of the Muscovite border voevodas who addressed the Commonwealth's senators, officials and nobles without proper titles, just as if they were commoners.[144] The Muscovite negotiators protested that they were only instructed to discuss the titles of the two sovereigns. Kysil responded that if agreements were to be approved by the Senate and the House of Delegates, the Muscovites would just have to address its members correctly, as other governments did. Eventually the Muscovite negotiators came around, but this debate shows the amount of freedom an ambassador from the Commonwealth had in choosing topics for discussion.[145]

The fourth major item on the agenda, the settlement of the border issue, was negotiated without difficulty, partly because it had been under negotiation and in partial settlement since 1634, partly because the Lithuanian delegate was not there. His absence was, however, used later by the Diet delegates from the Grand Duchy as grounds for protesting the results of Kysil's mission.[146]

On September 25, 1647, the negotiators issued an agreement that reaffirmed the Eternal Peace, established the proper form for the sovereign's titles, granted privileges for merchants of each state, and agreed to minor border adjustments.[147] The Commonwealth promised that the Zaporozhian Cossacks would be punished for border incursions and that Tsar Ivan Shuiskii's gravestone, taken by the troops of the Commonwealth during the Time of Troubles, would be returned from Warsaw to Moscow. Demarcation of the border between the Grand Duchy of Lithuania and Muscovy was put off until representatives of the Grand Duchy could be present.[148]

Article Four was the defensive alliance, phrased as a reaffirmation of the provisions of the Peace of 1634. It required each state to come to the aid of the other in the event of a Tatar attack and to prevent the Tatars from crossing its lands. One state could not lay down arms without the other's consent. By drafting the article as a reaffirmation of the Peace of 1634, the negotiators avoided mentioning the need for ratification by the Diet; they simply provided that the king would call a Diet to propose a close alliance should stronger measures prove necessary.[149] The article also said that neither side could be held responsible for what the Zaporozhian or Don Cossacks might do, and that both sides were to avoid provoking the Tatars and were to make clear to the sultan that necessary actions against the Tatars should in no way be construed as hostility toward the Ottomans.[150]

The terms of the alliance had to be kept general; the Diet would otherwise have been able to accuse Kysil of overstepping his authority. How far-reaching the plans for the collective action actually were is impossible to say.[151] They may have included a realignment of alliances in Eastern Europe. In a letter to King Jan Kazimierz in 1650, Kysil claimed that the negotiators had pledged orally to join against the Swedes and to regain control of the Baltic seacoast, but that Władysław's death and the civil war in the Commonwealth had intervened to destroy those plans.[152]

Kysil left Moscow in September 1647, convinced that his negotiations had opened a new period of cordial Muscovite-Commonwealth relations.[153] In late October, he wrote from his estate in Kobyshche to the king's secretary requesting that the government secure the Diet's approval for the alliance as soon as possible. In the meantime, he proposed that the government take the immediate necessary steps to ensure the Muscovites' trust, including issuing decrees to be distributed in the Chernihiv and Smolensk lands specifying the exact titles that were to be used in correspondence with Muscovy.[154] Any correspondence with Muscovy, he said, ought to be checked for correctness by officials.[155] Kysil urged that the final border demarcation, particularly between Muscovy and the Grand Duchy of Lithuania, be made, and that the attacks on Muscovite border patrols along the Tatar campaign route cease. That was most urgent. The king himself should order the border officials and the Zaporozhian commissioner to cease all hostilities.[156] Kysil also asked that Shuiskii's gravestone be sent from Warsaw to Volodymyr, whence he would supervise its transport to the Muscovite border town of Putyvl'.

In the fall and winter of 1647, Kysil was in frequent contact with the neighboring Muscovite voevodas, and he arranged the return of Shuiskii's gravestone after lengthy negotiations over the particulars of the transfer to Putyvl'.[157] He tried to stop infringements of the peace along the border by the Commonwealth's magnates, and he supervised the commissions for border demarcation, whose negotiations were made extremely difficult by the requirement that the Muscovites contact their central authorities in Moscow before any official agreement could be made.[158] Kysil, on the other hand, could act almost completely independently, so the Muscovites regarded him as arbiter in their relations with the Commonwealth and channeled all communications through him.[159] As a reward for his services, the tsar granted him substantial rights to procure potash in the borderlands.[160]

In the winter, Kysil began negotiations with Muscovy for their mutual defense against a possible Tatar attack, passing on whatever information he had been able to collect about internal affairs in the Crimea and about Crimean attempts to secure the sultan's permission to launch an attack.[161] He once more raised the question of "gifts," to which the Muscovite authorities again responded that they had been perfectly within their rights in paying tribute.[162] Kysil's elegant letters discussed the benefit to both states entailed in the alliance and interpreted the treaty obligation as broadly as possible.[163] He was successful in securing Muscovite assurances of support, but the attack that he expected in January and February of 1648 did not occur.[164] Kysil claimed the sultan had forbidden the Tatars from attacking because he feared the alliance between the Commonwealth and Muscovy.[165]

In his official report of the mission to the Diet, intended to counter any charges that he had exceeded his powers, Kysil described the alliance he had concluded with Muscovy as an emergency measure taken to break off Muscovite-Tatar negotiations.[166] In a letter to the king's secretary, however, he was more candid:

> But I conclude that no good citizen could wish upon the Fatherland that this Christian unity, which the Lord God himself has formed, would be dissolved. All the wars that were fought with Moscow did not have as much effect as this alliance of unity of states and nations will have. How much terror this can strike not only in the Horde, but in the Ottoman Porte itself, every perceptive man will comprehend. It is only necessary for us to mollify and not to irritate. Herewith, I assure the alliance is and will be one of action, not of words.[167]

Kysil's expectations were not fulfilled. Between the time the treaty was drawn up in September 1647, and July 1648, when the next Diet convened, the political climate of Eastern Europe changed entirely. After the Cossack revolt, fear that Muscovy would intervene in favor of the Cossacks rekindled hostility, and the treaty was never even ratified by the Diet.[168]

Kysil never wavered from the conviction that the agreement with Muscovy was a great personal triumph. This was reflected in Lazar Baranovych's elegiac praise: "Two monarchs came to an understanding through your person, Great Ambassador."[169] Kysil's "bringing two great monarchs to an understanding" did not have the momentous consequences he had predicted. His successes are not even mentioned in many East European diplomatic histories, which tend to regard the entire period from the mid-sixteenth century to the second half of the seventeenth century as one of continual hostility between the two states.[170] Soviet historians, who view the convergence of interests between the Muscovite state and the Zaporozhian Cossacks as an inevitable historical process, maintain that the negotiations of the 1630s and 1640s were merely a ploy to allow Muscovy to collect the strength needed to "reunite" the lands of Kievan Rus'.[171] The treaty that Kysil negotiated is difficult to fit into that scheme.

Part of the neglect is the result of the limited information available about the mission, the negotiations, and the alliance. In the nineteenth century, Sergei Solov'ev misdated Kysil's mission to 1646, instead of 1647, and the error was still being repeated in Soviet historiography in 1962.[172] Soviet historians who are better informed about the negotiations and initial phases of the alliance see it as insignificant from the very onset of the Ukrainian "national-liberation war," Khmel'nyts'kyi's uprising.

The assumption that conflict between Muscovy and the Commonwealth over the Ukraine was "inevitable" has obscured the considerable importance of Kysil's treaty. However cautious Muscovite authorities may have been in promising assistance against the Tatars, they showed every intention of upholding the terms of the alliance until the summer of 1648.[173] Kysil's successful conclusion of negotiations in 1647 might have turned out to be the high point in Muscovite-Commonwealth cooperation. Had the Commonwealth not pursued this policy, a hostile Muscovy could well have taken advantage of the first sign of the Commonwealth's distress. Thanks to Kysil's efforts, the breakdown in relations between Muscovy and the Commonwealth in 1648 was at least gradual.

Chapter 6

The Khmel'nyts'kyi Uprising*

By early 1648 Kysil had emerged as one of the inner circle of magnates who guided the destiny of the Commonwealth. Like many other first-generation magnates, he had attained his position by winning the favor of the monarch. His ascent was the result of fortuitous circumstances in the late 1640s: as the programs that he espoused for peace with Muscovy, for religious accommodation among Eastern Christians, and for a war against the Tatars and Turks coincided with the policies of the king and his chancellor, Kysil became more and more essential for carrying out these programs. A convergence of events and actors—Władysław's desire for a glorious campaign, the outbreak of the War of Candia, Mohyla's willingness to discuss a new religious solution, Muscovy's desire to solve the Tatar problem—made the Ukraine assume primary importance for the politics of Warsaw. This turn of events strengthened Kysil's position as an initiator, rather than just as an executor of programs.

Kysil's commanding position in Ukrainian affairs also partly resulted from the death of two of the most influential men of the 1630s and 1640s, Crown Great Hetman Stanisław Koniecpolski and Metropolitan Peter Mohyla. Koniecpolski, who had successfully put down the Cossack uprisings of the mid-1630s and imposed the Cossack ordinance of 1638, had been vitally concerned with the security problem of the southeast and had proposed action in league with Muscovy against the Muslim states.[1] His successor Mikołaj Potocki was not his equal either in military expertise or in political vision.[2] With no true successor to Koniecpolski, the usually strong influence of the leader of the army in the Ukraine was undermined. Hence Kysil's importance rose as a local leader who, with his political and diplomatic expertise, might be able to assume some of the power usually associated with the hetman's mace, in particular, in convincing the borderland nobility to back the king's policies.

Mohyla's family background and connections had combined with his personal intellect and energy to give him the authority to transform the Orthodox metropolitan see of Kiev into a major force in the internal life of the Commonwealth and in the entire Orthodox world.[3] Kysil had worked closely with Mohyla for almost two decades and had contributed greatly to the metropolitan's plans as well as benefited materially and politically from his support. Already recognized as the paramount Orthodox layman with his accession to the castellanship of Kiev in 1646, Kysil's position in the church was even further strengthened by the death of Mohyla and the election of Sylvestr Kosiv.

Kysil's importance probably derived from one additional factor, his experience in dealing with the Zaporozhian Cossacks. All plans for a southeastern campaign focused on using the 6,000 registered Cossacks, as well as the thousands of non-registered Cossacks, as the core of the Commonwealth's forces. Venice proposed to provide subsidies to the king in return for Cossack naval raids on Anatolia in order to divert Ottoman forces from Crete. In 1646, Władysław had received a Cossack delegation to discuss war plans. For the Cossacks, the war offered an opportunity to overthrow the harsh Ordinance of 1638. The resistance of the Diet to the king's plans had increased the importance of the Cossacks, since one way to force the Commonwealth into war would be for the Cossacks to provoke a Tatar attack. Regrettably, the conspiratorial relations between the court and the Cossacks remain as mysterious to the modern historian as they were to the Commonwealth's inhabitants in 1648, when many nobles contended that Władysław and his advisers had inspired the Cossacks to insubordination, intending to provoke a war with the Tatars and Ottomans.[4] While Kysil's relations with the Cossacks remain as hidden as those of the king and Ossoliński, the court could have hardly ignored the services of this practiced negotiator at a time when the Cossacks were central to the war policy.

The events of 1647 all point to an unfolding conspiracy to force the Commonwealth into a war in the southeast. In the summer of 1647, Ossoliński had traveled to the Ukraine, where he conferred with local notables and was rumored to have discussed the affairs of the Eastern church. In the fall of 1647, the borderland magnates Aleksander Koniecpolski and Jeremi Wiśniowiecki conducted raids and intelligence gathering operations against the Tatars in the steppe. While there is no definite evidence that the expeditions were part of the court's plans, their provocation of the Tatars makes it appear that one or both of the magnates had been won over to the war plans. Their actions made the Commonwealth brace for a Tatar attack in the winter of 1647–1648. The resistance of the Diet had set back the king's plans and the death of his only son dealt him a great personal blow, but the machinations for war, so long in preparation, went forward, albeit with the king in a weakened position.[5]

The major boost for a war effort was the improvement of relations with Muscovy. Kysil worked assiduously to ensure that the Muscovites would come to the Commonwealth's assistance in the event of a Tatar attack. With an apparent note of regret he wrote to the Putyvl' voevoda, Iurii Dolgorukii, in late February, that the Ottomans had forbidden the Tatars to provoke the allied states, because the Ottomans were at war with the Venetians and, guided "by their pagan cunning," did not wish to face two Christian armies.[6] Kysil informed Dolgorukii that he would soon proceed with plans to visit his Volhynian estates, but that he still believed a Tatar attack would take place in the near future, and he promised to return soon to assist in organizing Muscovy's and the Commonwealth's joint defense.

In late March of 1648, Kysil, recently named palatine of Bratslav, first mentioned trouble with the Cossacks to his Muscovite colleagues, when he reported that professional soldiers (*wojsko kwarciane*) would be stationed in the Cossack areas because the Cossacks of the Chyhyryn regiment had betrayed their colonel.[7] He reported that a thousand Cossacks led by a "peasant" named Khmel'nyts'kyi had fled to Zaporizhzhia, from where they planned to join the Don Cossacks in an attack on the Black Sea that would destroy the Commonwealth's and Muscový's peaceful relations with the Ottoman Empire.[8] Maintaining that he and the great hetman, Mikołaj Potocki, could deal with the situation, he asked the Muscovites to show no mercy should the rebels enter their territory.

Kysil knew well that the Cossack leader was no peasant since Khmel'nyts'kyi had been chancellor of the Host during Kysil's negotiations with the Cossack rebels of the mid-1630s. Although there is no definite proof of subsequent contact between the two men until June 1648, it seems likely that they had dealings during the planning for the Ottoman war. Khmel'nyts'kyi, as a captain under the Ordinance of 1638 that denied Cossacks the higher offices in the registered Host, had taken part in the Cossack delegation to Władysław in 1646. It would have been unlikely that Kysil, who stood so close to the king in the planning for the war and was so well informed about affairs in the Ukraine, would have not been informed about negotiations with the Cossack conspirators. Certainly, the tone of the subsequent correspondence between the two men and Kysil's conviction that he would be able to arrange a settlement with the rebel leader speak for the existence of contacts before the outbreak of the revolt.

Kysil and Khmel'nyts'kyi, who were to deal with each other so frequently after March 1648, shared much in common. They were both of Ruthenian noble descent and of Orthodox faith. Approximately the same age, with Khmel'nyts'kyi probably about five years older, they had both studied in Catholic institutions and served in the campaign against the Ottomans under Hetman Stanisław Żółkiewski at Tsetsora. By the mid-1640s both were mature men, indeed considered old by seventeenth-century standards, who had obtained the success and stability that often breeds conservatism.

In fact, they differed in significant experiences so that one man stood forth to preserve the Commonwealth's administration in the Ukraine, while the other rose up to destroy it. Although the Kysils were in reduced straits at the time of Adam's birth and were subordinates and clients to great magnate families such as the Ostroz'kyis, Zaslavs'kyis, and Zamoyskis, they had an unquestioned ancient family lineage and possessions in the stable noble society of northwestern Ukraine. In contrast Bohdan Khmel'nyts'kyi was born in the rapidly colonizing central-southern steppe zone, where frontier violence forced every man to defend his social status and possessions. His father, Mykhailo, might assert his noble status and possession of Subotiv, but without documents and proofs of nobility, the Khmel'nyts'kyis could only maintain such a position by successfully dealing with the demands and encroachments of the borderland magnates. It appears that Bohdan, like many members of the petty nobility of the borderland, found the profits and opportunities of Cossack life to his advantage. Hence he passed over to the Cossack starshyna with whom Kysil so frequently treated in the 1630s. Khmel'nyts'kyi shared the defeat of the Cossack Host of the mid-1630s and the humiliation of the Ordinance of 1638. As a well-to-do and experienced Cossack leader, he took part in the negotiations with the king in 1646 that offered the chance to throw off the oppressive administration of the Crown hetmans and their appointed colonels. However, just as Khmel'nyts'kyi negotiated the terms under which he and his fellow officers might better their material and social positions, he saw the very existence of his possessions and family placed in jeopardy. The persecutions of Daniel Czapliński, an official of the starosta of Chyhyryn, drove Khmel'nyts'kyi to a fruitless search for rectification. Drawn into the conflict, the starosta of Chyhyryn, Aleksander Koniecpolski, temporarily imprisoned Khmel'nyts'kyi, who, fearful and enraged, then fled to the lower Dnieper at the end of 1647. Raising a standard of revolt as a leader of the Cossacks of the lower Dnieper, Khmel'nyts'kyi took over the Sich and deposed the existing leadership of the Cossack regiment stationed there.[9]

The personal grievances of Khmel'nyts'kyi and the circumstances of his flight became the subject of romantic embellishment from the first years of the revolt. In particular, speculation flourished as to whether the king had issued sweeping privileges to the Cossacks and had counseled Bohdan to seek justice by the sword, possibly in an agreement to use a revolt as the catalyst for the long anticipated war. Certainly, the atmosphere of conspiracy made the entire population of the Ukraine wonder who was behind the revolt, while the earlier negotiations of Khmel'nyts'kyi with the king gave the Cossack leader an aura of legitimacy for his revolt.[10] The first report of the revolt, however, was followed by unexpected news making it doubtful that Bohdan acted in league with the war party. Despite the reluctance of the Ottoman Porte to open up a northern front against the Commonwealth, its vassal Khan Islam Girey had agreed to support the Cossack rebels. Aware of the plans of its northern neighbors to combine forces against it, the Crimean Khanate sought to turn the Cossacks to its advantage. Khmel'nyts'kyi, by seeking Tatar and Ottoman support, perpetrated a diplomatic revolution undoing all the plans that had been laid for establishing a new order in Eastern Europe through a Christian campaign against the Muslim powers.[11]

In March 1648, Kysil remained unaware of the extent of changes that were taking place. Still on the Left Bank, he kept in close touch with Crown Great Hetman Potocki.[12] Initially, their correspondence dealt with outstanding problems with Muscovy, but as the gravity of the situation in Zaporizhzhia became apparent, it centered on how the Zaporozhians could be returned to loyalty.[13] The two men took opposite views: Kysil, believing that the Cossack grievances were legitimate and that the Commonwealth was weak, suggested diverting the rebellious Cossacks to the Black Sea.[14] Potocki, on the other hand, believing that the Cossacks had been a rebellious element for too long and that only defeating them once and for all would make the Commonwealth secure, favored battle.[15] Kysil may also have been privy to plans for cooperation with the Cossacks of which Potocki had no knowledge; in any case he was adamant in warning Potocki that to embark on a campaign to Zaporizhzhia would lead to disaster.[16] Kysil particularly counseled against dividing an already small force for such a campaign, and he proposed instead that Potocki contain the rebels by preventing supplies and recruits from reaching them. This would force the Cossacks into attacking, or retiring to the Don, or launching a campaign on the Black Sea; in each case the present danger would be averted. He chose not to mention that the third possibility would also have provoked an Ottoman response. Potocki ignored all this advice and divided his troops, which included registered Cossacks, for a campaign in Zaporizhzhia. Following mutinies and desertions, the forward detachment, led by the hetman's son Stefan, was surrounded and captured by a united Cossack-Tatar army at Zhovti Vody.[17]

Kysil had reluctantly to agree to Potocki's policies in late April and, while excusing himself from joining Potocki's colors, promised to send him troops.[18] He traveled to his Volhynian estate at Hoshcha where he learned of the army's defeat and passed the news on to Władysław on May 27.[19] He was quick to point out the prudence of his earlier advice:

> It would never have come to this extreme, had the opinions of many of us old servants been taken into account by your Majesty—our opinions not to seek one Cossack in the eddies of Zaporizhzhia; not to dispatch other Cossacks to the Dnieper, but to keep them together with the troops of the Commonwealth and to retain their loyalty in some manner; not to divide so small a contingent by sending part into the field.

Kysil particularly regretted the rash policy that had allowed the Tatars to take advantage of the situation, and he asserted that a settlement had to be made quickly if civil war were to be avoided. If the Cossacks could be diverted to the Black Sea, the Commonwealth, in alliance with Muscovy, would have time to prepare its defense in the event of an Ottoman attack.[20]

In fact, the situation was much more desperate than Kysil imagined. On May 26, the Cossack-Tatar allies had surrounded the main body of the Crown army at Korsun' and taken it captive, along with its hetmans, Mikołaj Potocki and Marcin Kalinowski.[21] Even earlier, on May 20, King Władysław had died suddenly while traveling in the Grand Duchy. The passing of Władysław was for Kysil much more than the inconvenient demise of a favorably disposed monarch. Kysil was in fact devoted to this most personable of Polish kings. He wrote to Ossoliński:

> And therefore he, a particular ruling genius, was worthy not only of ruling us, but the entire Christian world, of which all neighboring nations looked to us, and for the higher good we were all willing to devote our health and fortunes to this so good and happy and beloved a lord. . . . It was good for hetmans to serve under such a lord who was capable of being hetman of all Christendom. . . . It was good for the free Commonwealth, which is not of one custom, one people, and one religion, to have considered the difficulties of citizens of opposing viewpoints.[22]

Kysil appears to have understood that the passing of the tolerant Władysław might bring difficult times for someone not of the dominant religion and people. He was certainly keenly aware that the rapid spread of the rebellion and the political uncertainties of an interregnum endangered his own position.

In May and June, the Cossack revolt expanded into a civil war. Incited by Cossack successes and agitators, disaffected strata in the entire Dnieper basin took up arms. Peasants revolted against their lords, Orthodox clergymen called for vengeance against the triumphant Latins, and Ruthenian burghers plotted against oppressive patriciates. Widespread grievances combined with personal accounts and lawless tendencies as the social order disintegrated. Landlords, Catholic and Uniate clergy, and Jews constituted the major groups of victims, as the revolt took on proportions far beyond Khmel'nyts'kyi's and the Cossacks' grievances.

Kysil wrote on May 31 to the primate archbishop of Gniezno, Maciej Łubieński, the head of state during the interregnum, informing him of the Ukrainian situation and offering his advice.[23] After a lament on the state of affairs in the Commonwealth and the dangers that the Tatars presented, he asserted that Khmel'nyts'kyi meant to establish a new duchy or principality, and that he had already declared Kiev his "capital" and had demanded allegiance from its inhabitants. He claimed the revolt could have been avoided had Cossacks been treated with respect, and not as if they were simple peasants. As a result of this and other mistakes all Rus' was now crazed with the spirit of revolt. He warned that this was a "new Rus'" which would fight not with bows and arrows, but with guns supported by a massive army of peasants, whom he entreated the primate not to confuse with the peasants of the western lands since they were well acquainted with firearms. Kysil requested military assistance, efforts to secure the neutrality of Muscovy, and negotiations with the Ottomans. If the Ottomans intervened, the Muscovite alliance would have to be invoked.

Kysil's letter conveyed that he was as anguished about his own fate as he was for that of the Commonwealth. When he lamented the barbarities committed against the nobles of the eastern lands and their loss of estates, he reported his own loss of 100,000 złotys income from the Chernihiv lands. He carefully prefaced his discussion about the disloyalty of Rus' by an admission that he himself was of Ruthenian blood, in order to preempt accusations of disloyalty.

It is, of course, possible that Kysil overstated the danger of the situation and the extent of the rebels' goals in order to frighten the primate into authorizing negotiations. The earliest known statement by Khmel'nyts'kyi that he sought to establish a Rus' polity was made at the beginning of 1649.[24] Kysil's warning may have reflected more the understanding of the potential of the revolt held by the traditional Ruthenian political nation than it did the goal of the Cossack rebels. In any case, he clearly saw that the Commonwealth was exceptionally weak, the rebels strong, and a compromise had to be reached.

In Warsaw, it was Ossoliński, rather than the aged, infirm primate, who took control of the government during the interregnum. Empowered by Ossoliński, Kysil soon became the executor of the policy he recommended. On June 5, after hearing of the defeat at Korsun', Ossoliński requested Kysil to use his diplomatic skills and influence with the Orthodox clergy to convince Khmel'nyts'kyi not to "lead his nation into servitude to the pagans. . . ."[25] He asked Kysil to assure the Cossacks of the Commonwealth's forgiveness. Kysil had already anticipated Ossoliński's requests. Two days earlier he had written to Ossoliński, reporting the situation in the Ukraine and the information he had gathered through his clerical contacts.[26] Kysil informed Ossoliński that he was ready to take on the role of intermediary, but he reminded the chancellor that his assurances of amnesty to Pavliuk had been betrayed. He obviously wished to be certain that he would not be put in such a position again.

As in the revolts of the 1630s, the government particularly valued Kysil's religious and national affinities with the Cossacks as a means of deflecting their hostility. It also sought to utilize Kysil's wide network of clerical contacts in order to gather information and to employ these clerics as couriers. Fulfilling this expectation, Kysil sent Petro Lasko, the abbot of the monastery at his Hoshcha estate, to Khmel'nyts'kyi with a letter intended to open negotiations.[27] He assured Khmel'nyts'kyi that he believed in his loyalty for three reasons: although the Zaporozhian Army jealously guarded its liberties, it had never broken its oath to the king and the Commonwealth; the Ruthenian nation had always been faithful to the Commonwealth; and whatever blood may have been shed, all were sons of one fatherland, since "everywhere there is servitude, only the Kingdom of Poland is famed for its liberties." He reminded his "old friend" of their common Orthodox faith and of his own position as the only "Christian of the Ruthenian nation" who was a senator in the Kingdom of Poland. Then he asked Khmel'nyts'kyi not to advance further, to send the Tatars away, and to explain the reason for the rebellion, so that Kysil could help "as a son of God's Church and as one whose ancient house is descended by blood from the Ruthenian nation."

Khmel'nyts'kyi, on his part, had begun his revolt in retaliation for injustices against himself and his fellow Cossacks. In doing so, he enlisted the support of dissatisfied peasants and Orthodox believers. However, unlike earlier Cossack leaders who had done the same, he was overwhelmingly successful. In defeating the Commonwealth's armies and military leadership, he then faced the problem of what his next step should be, since he at first was interested only in securing alleviation of personal and Cossack grievances.[28]

On June 16, Kysil recounted to the primate Father Lasko's reception in Khmel'nyts'kyi's camp. Khmel'nyts'kyi had presented Kysil's proposals to a Cossack council of 20,000 men, and, though the Tatars had not yet been sent away, he had invited Kysil to come to negotiate. He wrote to Kysil asking him, as a man who was aware of all the Zaporozhians' grievances, to intercede with the king and the Commonwealth.[29]

Khmel'nyts'kyi mentioned the king, even though he seems to have known that Władysław was already dead. The lack of a monarch impeded negotiations since the Cossacks preferred to view themselves as servitors to the monarch, rather than of the Diet or even of the Commonwealth as a whole. Kysil took this into account when in mid-June he urged Ossoliński to hold the election as soon as possible.[30] He asserted that the Commonwealth meant nothing to the Cossacks who could conceive of allegiance only to the king. His assertion revealed how little truth he really saw in his earlier statements to Khmel'nyts'kyi about the Cossacks' liberties and their demonstrated loyalty to the Commonwealth. In view of the desperate condition of the nobility of the eastern lands, Kysil urged the chancellor to hold the election close to the Ukraine as a sign of support. Since he also advised that the Cossacks be diverted to the Black Sea as soon as possible, he may have been planning a scenario to revive Władysław's Turkish war plan. An assembled nobility and a king near the Ukraine would have to respond to a Tatar or Ottoman attack.

Throughout June 1648 Kysil stood at the center of a network of political maneuverings that stretched from Rome to Moscow. Crown Chancellor Ossoliński spoke for the Warsaw government in urging Kysil to negotiate with Khmel'nyts'kyi, to deflect the Cossacks to the Black Sea, and to prepare Muscovy to fulfill its obligations under the article of alliance.[31] Although the Convocation Diet was called to Warsaw, not near the Ukraine as Kysil advised, Ossoliński did hasten procedures. He also consulted with Kysil on the choice of a candidate and requested Kysil to arrive for personal consultations on affairs of state before the Diet began on July 16.[32]

Kysil's efforts also received approval from the *de jure* leader of the Commonwealth, the primate, Łubieński, who stated, in a letter of June 18, that not only was he himself pleased with Kysil's peace efforts, but so were the senators to whom he had shown Kysil's correspondence.[33] The widespread support for efforts at compromise were due mainly to the recognition that the Commonwealth was woefully unprepared to fight. Because of the papacy's continuing interest in an anti-Turkish league, even the nuncio supported attempts to come to terms with the Cossacks.[34]

The success of any negotiations depended on decisions made in Moscow. From the first, Kysil feared that the Muscovites would take advantage of the rebellion and warned that although the Commonwealth had defeated the Muscovites in the past, it might not be able to do so if they were in league with the rebels. Realizing the all-Ruthenian character of the revolt, he saw the religious and ethnic affinities of the rebels and the Muscovites ("one religion, one blood") as a dangerous potential.[35]

Throughout May and June, Kysil worked to ensure that Muscovy would not use rebellion and interregnum to its advantage and would intervene to fight the Tatars if the Commonwealth requested it. Khmel'nyts'kyi was just as energetically trying to interest Muscovy in the Cossack cause, or, at least, to neutralize the Muscovite army mobilized against the Tatars. Kysil was the more successful of the two, at least at first. An ukase of May 30 guaranteed that, on Kysil's call, an army would march against the Tatars, and the voevoda of Khotmyzh, Semen Bolkhovskii, informed him of this on June 14.[36] When Khmel'nyts'kyi intercepted communications between the Muscovite officials and Kysil in late June, he immediately began to convince the Muscovites that it was not in their interest to intervene, and he obliquely offered the Host's support of the tsar's candidacy in the coming election.[37] The Muscovites did take the candidacy of the tsar seriously, but they realized that it could only be successful through the support of the nobility, not through the support of the rebels. Therefore they were reluctant to side with the rebels.[38]

Fear of Muscovite intervention and uneasiness over his dependence on an alliance with the Tatars increased Khmel'nyts'kyi's willingness to negotiate a truce with Kysil.[39] How seriously he took those negotiations, or whether he even believed he could halt the peasant rebellions he had unleashed is difficult to ascertain. In any event, he needed a respite to take stock of the foreign situation and to organize his hastily assembled forces. When Father Lasko visited Khmel'nyts'kyi for the second time, he was troubled by the hostility of the masses and Khmel'nyts'kyi's negotiations with foreign powers, but he believed that the hetman and the Cossack officers wished to negotiate in good faith.[40] The departure of the Tatar army in late June was viewed in the Commonwealth as a favorable sign, as was Khmel'nyts'kyi's withdrawal eastward to Chyhyryn.[41]

Kysil's position in the Commonwealth was at its height, and he was even influential in securing the appointment of Prince Dominik Zasławski as one of the joint commanders to lead the army while Mikołaj Potocki and Marcin Kalinowski were held captive by Khmel'nyts'kyi's allies, the Tatars.[42] In the expectation that the July Convocation Diet would draw up an agreement to end the war, Ossoliński manipulated the selection of three joint commanders, Zasławski, Michał Ostroróg, the Crown cupbearer, and Aleksander Koniecpolski, the young son of the deceased Hetman Stanisław Koniecpolski.[43] Ostroróg was renowned for his intellect; Koniecpolski descended from a family with great military traditions; and Zasławski was fabulously wealthy. None of the three were experienced military leaders. Their appointment was unpopular. It passed over the Lithuanian hetmans who by tradition led the Kingdom's

armies when the Crown hetmans could not, and it ignored Jeremi Wiśniowiecki, palatine of Ruthenia, and Janusz Tyszkiewicz, palatine of
Kiev, who had campaigned against the Cossacks in the Ukraine after
the capture of the Crown hetmans.[44] But that was essential to negotiations—both men were hated by the Cossacks for their vigorous and often
cruel attempts to suppress the rebellion in the spring of 1648.[45]

Although the wealthy Left-Bank magnate Wiśniowiecki had at first
been out of favor with King Władysław and his inner circle, Ossoliński
and Kysil had striven with some success to win his consent to their
program of a Muscovite alliance and a southeastern war. Kysil had assisted Wiśniowiecki on a number of occasions, and, despite the two
men's different decisions on allegiance to their ancestral faith, there is
no indication of enmity before 1648. However, in the early months of
1648, the two men chose different policies that were to turn them into
bitter foes. While Kysil left the Left Bank early in the revolt and did
not witness the plundering of his estates, Wiśniowiecki fought the rebels
and led his private army and local nobles on a campaign of vengeance.[46]

When Wiśniowiecki and his private army entered Volhynia in June
after fighting their way from the Left Bank, Kysil requested him to
refrain from military maneuvers that might endanger the peace initiative.[47] Wiśniowiecki replied that he saw no use in negotiating with traitors and that he would rather die fighting for a "free" Commonwealth
than live in "servitude" under the rebels.[48] Ossoliński had the Senate
request Wiśniowiecki and Tyszkiewicz to cooperate with the peace mission and Kysil to continue his efforts to reach a compromise with
Khmel'nyts'kyi.[49] By June 1648, the lines dividing the peace and war
parties had been clearly drawn. No longer was the major issue whether
war should be undertaken against the Ottomans. From this time the
camps were a war party that sought a fight to the finish with the rebels
and a peace party that favored compromise.

Although Kysil was at first viewed as a savior in the desperate situation
of June 1648, the opponents of the peace policy and the nobility at large
very soon began to question his loyalty. Wiśniowiecki's remark that he
saw no choice for a loyal noble but to fight was a stone cast at Kysil for
his conciliatory policies. As early as June 19, Kysil protested that the
Orthodox burghers in Luts'k had been imprisoned because of rumors
spread by the Jesuits. He charged that the burghers were being condemned simply because they were of the same nationality and religion
as the rebels.[50] His defense of the Orthodox burghers of Luts'k was at
the same time a plea that his own affiliations not be used against him.
These ties made Kysil useful when negotiations with Khmel'nyts'kyi was
possible, but they made him a suspect in all-out war.

The Convocation Diet and the Second Peace Mission

In late June, Kysil went to the joint dietine that had been called in Luts'k for the four palatinates of Volhynia, Bratslav, Chernihiv, and Kiev.[51] Unlike most of the dietines that met on that day, that of the eastern nobility was willing both to vote subsidies for armament and to back the attempt for a negotiated solution to the civil war.[52] The nobles of the incorporation lands mentioned their gratitude and trust in Kysil and appointed him commander of the troops to be raised. In the event Kysil was engaged in peace negotiations, which the nobility of the dietine pointed out he had begun at the primate's request and heartily applauded, his brother Mykola was to take his place.

The eastern nobles were acutely aware of the grave situation facing the country. By late June, the Cossacks had occupied the entire Left Bank and large areas of the Kiev and Bratslav palatinates on the Right Bank, including the cities of Kiev, Bila Tserkva, Uman', Bratslav and Vinnytsia.[53] The stream of fleeing nobles induced panic among their fellow nobles further west. They were aware that each day increased the chaos in the war zone and the likelihood that their homes and estates would be destroyed. They might applaud Wiśniowiecki's bravery, but they realized that Kysil's policies offered better chances for their return to their homes.

After the dietine Kysil returned to his estate to await the outcome of Father Lasko's second mission. Writing to the primate on June 30, he expressed his apprehension that there could be no effective resistance against the rebels, since the nobility had fled west from Iziaslav, Hoshcha and Polonne to Dubno and Zamość, and many of the burghers had gone over to Khmel'nyts'kyi.[54] Father Lasko did not return to Kysil's Volhynian estate at Hniino until July 7 with new conciliatory letters from Khmel'nyts'kyi, and an offer of a truce.[55] Khmel'nyts'kyi had asked Kysil, who was preparing to leave for the Convocation Diet, to use his offices to secure a settlement.[56] He also sent Cossack emissaries with a list of eleven grievances, expressing dissatisfaction over the government's administrative practices in the Cossack lands and demanding payment of back wages, an increase in the number of registered Cossacks to 12,000 men, and the return of churches to the Orthodox.[57]

By then Ossoliński and Kysil faced considerable difficulties in gaining support for their policies. With the exception of the incorporation lands, most other palatinates had passed instructions unfavorable to Ossoliński and his faction and condemned them for bringing the Commonwealth to near ruin.[58] They were displeased about the irregularities in interregnum procedures during a Warsaw conference of notables, which Ossoliński had convened to assist in conducting the affairs of state.[59] They were equally unwilling to grant concessions to the Cossacks and to provide the money needed to raise an army.[60]

The Diet was poorly attended, but Kysil was present from the first day.[61] Although it is uncertain when he reached Warsaw, the cleverly orchestrated manipulations that he undertook with Ossoliński indicate that the two men had followed Ossoliński's suggestion to meet beforehand to plan strategy. Despite considerable opposition, they carried the day.[62]

The three major issues before the Diet were the procedures for electing a king, an answer to the Cossacks' "requests," and the appointment of military leaders.[63] The primate presented the proposals for negotiations with the Cossacks before the Diet, but left it to Kysil to argue the peace party's case. On July 17, Kysil gave an official report on the results of his embassy to Moscow of the prior autumn and on the origins of the Cossack war.[64] Even before the Diet, he had alarmed many by his "Cossackophile" tendencies. He already had felt obliged to explain his policies to Aleksander Sanguszko, palatine of Volhynia: "I am not enamoured of the Cossacks, but of the Fatherland, and I do not wish to see us all perish."[65] He had also made clear that he was convinced that a settlement must be reached with the Cossacks:

> It is foolish counsel that every peasant is a Cossack and every Cossack a peasant, and it is ridiculous to set up one noble as sufficient to oppose 1,000 commoners in this affair. . . . Even if we are victorious and destroy all the commoners, we will lose our wealth, we will lose our food source and all. [We will sacrifice] the power of the Fatherland and we will prepare a wilderness as a nomadic range for the pagans. Thus, without victors, without vanquished, we sacrifice the Fatherland. . . ."[66]

At the Diet, to the displeasure of many of his listeners, he laid the major blame for the rebellion on the incompetence and abuses of the Commonwealth's military administration.[67] Ossoliński took a much harsher line against the Cossacks, but this appears to have been a stratagem to disarm the hard-line war party.[68]

Except for Vice-Chancellor Andrzej Leszczyński, the major opponents of accommodation, including Tyszkiewicz and Wiśniowiecki, were not present at the Diet, but they were successful in inflaming the delegates' sentiments against the peace party from afar.[69] Stanisław Lubomirski, the palatine of Cracow, wrote a circular letter to the dietines denouncing Ossoliński's policies.[70] Dominik Zasławski, stung by accusations of softness and incompetence, sent a letter to the Diet advocating an anti-Cossack policy.[71] The most eloquent critic was Mikołaj Ostroróg, who had written to Łubieński in early June:

> The only thing I humbly ask your Lordship is to use your authority to
> solicit reinforcements as soon as possible because we should not rely on
> what we are promised by negotiations with a barbarian and savage people,
> and [what] hope can there be for negotiations, and even if they are con-
> cluded what security can there be from them? And even if the treaties
> were firm, it would be impossible to negotiate without an army because
> even the rebellious Khmel'nyts'kyi himself cannot have such authority with
> that mob, which has learned to drown frequently their own het-
> mans. . . ."[72]

At the Diet, however, Ossoliński's and Kysil's opponents were dis-
credited when they charged Władysław and Chancellor Ossoliński with
inciting the uprising, alleging that Władysław had granted the Cossacks
a new charter of privileges. The anti-Ossoliński delegates demanded that
a search be made for the charters, but when they could produce none,
the pro-Ossoliński faction triumphed.[73] Kysil defended Władysław's and
Ossoliński's honor and denounced their opponents, accusing them,
among other things, of intercepting his letters to Khmel'nyts'kyi and to
the Muscovite authorities.[74] He charged that the effort to uncover his
nonexistent treachery had both crippled his mission and affronted his
dignity. He also denied rumors that his estates had been left untouched
by Khmel'nyts'kyi by discussing all the losses he had incurred. He
claimed that his wife had been forced to flee to their last small estate
near Volodymyr; he had only 1,000 złoty left and soon would be forced
to go into service himself.[75]

On July 21, a commission was selected to draw up proposals to
Khmel'nyts'kyi.[76] Kysil argued that in view of the enmity of the Tatars
and the Turks and the possibility Muscovy would use the Commonwealth's distress to its advantage, the Diet should accept negotiations
with the Cossacks as the least of all evils.[77] He denied that the Diet could
not address Khmel'nyts'kyi as a "starszy" because he was a rebel and
had not been appointed to his post by the proper authorities.[78] His most
convincing argument was that the Commonwealth was militarily unprepared, a situation that made any other course of action impossible. The
eighteen commissioners drew up a series of concessions that met some
of the Cossack demands, requiring in return that the Cossacks free their
captives and break with the Tatars. The instructions to negotiators required a return to the Cossack Ordinance of 1638, or at most that of
1630 which authorized 8,000 Cossacks, not the 12,000 Khmel'nyts'kyi
requested. They contained no provision for the back pay that
Khmel'nyts'kyi demanded. The commissioners designated to negotiate
with Khmel'nyts'kyi were given considerable discretionary powers.[79]

Kysil was selected to head the four-man commission, which was voted 10,000 złoty to carry on the negotiations.[80] As a sign of support of Kysil, Ossoliński publicly renounced the Bohuslav starostwo in the Kiev palatinate in Kysil's favor.[81] Finally, over the opposition of the Grand Duchy's delegates and Wiśniowiecki's supporters, the three joint commanders were reappointed, with an advisory board of thirty-two commissioners; Kysil was appointed to that commission as well.[82] Kysil's personal triumph was far from complete, however. It was only with the greatest reluctance that the House of Delegates voted him the usual thanks for his completion of a foreign mission, without, however, ratifying the Muscovite alliance agreement.[83] The Orthodox delegates at the Diet were incensed at the suspicion their fellow nobles displayed toward them, and Kysil objected to the statements about "fides Graeca," an allusion to untrustworthy behavior, being applied to the Ruthenians.[84] He reminded the Diet members that this saying referred to Greeks, not Ruthenians of the "Greek religion."

Kysil reacted strongly to any aspersions against the Orthodox because they undermined his efforts to reconcile the Orthodox and the Uniates during the Diet. Although Khmel'nyts'kyi had included a provision for the return of some Orthodox churches and the reaffirmation of privileges to the Orthodox clergy among the Cossack grievances, religious demands were secondary in the early phase of the revolt, and the Orthodox hierarchy remained aloof from the rebels. Therefore, Kysil, even while in the midst of persuading the Diet to make concessions to the Cossacks, continued to profess confidence to pro-union forces that a new union could be negotiated.[85] Before the Diet opened, Kysil had met in secret with Uniate dignitaries and had promised that he would be able to bring about a union after the Orthodox metropolitan arrived.[86] When Kosiv reached the Diet, the Orthodox clerical and lay leaders held a private colloquium in which they discussed the possibility of inviting Uniates to their meetings. But the Khmel'nyts'kyi uprising had so increased hostility and distrust between Catholics and Orthodox that Orthodox delegates complained that Catholic delegates were accusing them of sympathizing with the rebels, and Kysil had to defend Metropolitan Kosiv against Jesuit charges that he had conspired with the Cossacks. Faced with all this hostility, the Orthodox decided to put off discussions until the Election Diet in October.[87] They could in any case hardly have initiated discussions with the Uniates at a time when the Cossack armies were ascendant, and delay would give them a chance to see how the rebellion ended before committing themselves to a pro- or anti-union policy.

Kysil and his colleagues had been instructed to begin negotiations with Khmel'nyts'kyi by the end of August in Kiev, an almost impossible task,

since by the end of July, Cossack forces had once again advanced west-
ward far into Volhynia.[88] Although the Crown army had just begun to
gather at Hlyniany near Lviv, various military units, including Wiśniowiecki's private army were fighting the advancing Cossacks in Volhynia.[89]
The Zaporozhian hetman claimed that Wiśniowiecki had initiated hostilities, but in reality it was by now almost impossible to halt the social
strife and the expansion of the war zone.[90] The Zaporozhian hetman
risked losing popular support if he did not come to the aid of the rebelling masses. Besides, Khmel'nyts'kyi was well aware of the opposition
in the Commonwealth even to the minor concessions that the Diet had
authorized. Having consolidated his forces, Khmel'nyts'kyi realized that
a new campaign might be needed to retain the support of his Tatar allies,
who demanded chances for obtaining more booty and captives.[91]

The commissioners—Aleksander Sielski, Teodor Obuchowicz, and
Franciszek Dubrawski, and Kysil—departed to negotiate with the Cos-
sacks even before the Diet had ended. On July 31, Kysil wrote to Ossoliński from just outside Warsaw, and by August 3, they had reached
Horodlo on the border of Volhynia.[92] They were empowered to negotiate
only until the beginning of September, so there was no time to waste.
Despite mobilization and distrust, Kysil was initially convinced that
Khmel'nyts'kyi could be won away from the rebelling masses and a campaign could be organized against the Tatars with Muscovite assistance.[93]
By the time he reached Horodlo, however, his optimism was considerably
diminished: massive rebellions in Volhynia had resulted in the plundering of his own estates in Hoshcha.[94]

Throughout August and into September, Kysil and the commissioners
stubbornly attempted to contact Khmel'nyts'kyi, who remained favorably disposed to the negotiations, or so Kysil thought. He believed that
Khmel'nyts'kyi was prevented from negotiating by the rebellious masses
and militants in the Cossack forces, such as Colonel Maksym Kryvonis,
and by the aggressive actions of the Commonwealth's troops and Wiśniowiecki.[95]

But it appears that in fact Khmel'nyts'kyi was only biding his time
until his Tatar allies returned.[96] Although Khmel'nyts'kyi had been unable to win Ottoman support or authorization for full-scale Crimean
attacks on the Commonwealth, Khan Islam Giray had proved willing to
continue to send Tatar forces. At the same time the Muscovite danger
receded, since the government of the Commonwealth had initially been
too suspicious to call its Muscovite allies into the Ukraine, while the
success of the rebels had made the Muscovites reluctant to commit themselves before assessing the new situation.

Kysil was particularly disturbed by the chaos in the countryside, which made communication with Khmel'nyts'kyi difficult and endangered his own life and those of the other emissaries. On August 9, he reported to the chancellor that it was impossible to reach Kiev, because of violence in the Ukraine; even Father Lasko had been assaulted and might not survive.[97] Kysil decided to continue the mission, hoping that, once he could communicate with Khmel'nyts'kyi, the hetman would curb the excesses of the masses. Although by August 11, he still had had no answer from Khmel'nyts'kyi, he could at least relay rumors to Ossoliński that the rebel leader had punished the most belligerent of his colonels, Kryvonis.[98] On August 12, Kysil decided to expand his appeal to the entire starshyna in an attempt to win them over to negotiations.[99] He requested a response as soon as possible, reminding them of his long friendship with the Host and his role as protector of the Orthodox faith. On August 22, Kysil wrote to the chancellor that he had very little progress to report.[100] He was discouraged because Khmel'nyts'kyi had intercepted his letters to Moscow in which he discussed plans for assistance against the Cossacks, but he was determined to complete his mission by the end of August. He complained, however, that attacks upon the Cossacks by Commonwealth forces were undermining his position.

Throughout August, the Commonwealth had been building up its armies and they were now concentrated in two places: the government's army under the leadership of three commanders at Hlyniany near Lviv, and Wiśniowiecki's private army near Zbarazh. In late August and early September, the two armies came together near Chovkans'kyi Kamin', but it was only in mid-September, that the two commands finally united their forces. Throughout August and September, there were skirmishes between the two forces and the Cossacks as they struggled for control of Volhynia and Podillia.[101] Since the military leaders remained opposed to Kysil's mission, the peace mission, as it approached Ostroh, was in mortal danger because of their actions.[102] Kysil and the commissioners had been required to give hostages to Cossack forces in order to proceed on to Khmel'nyts'kyi, but a foray of Wiśniowiecki's troops against the Cossacks breached the truce and a massacre of seven of the hostages ensued. Kysil immediately protested the endangering of his mission to the Senate, to the military commissioners, and to Wiśniowiecki and his cohorts, arguing that, at the very least, the negotiations were providing vitally needed time.[103] Wiśniowiecki scorned the idea of negotiating with Khmel'nyts'kyi since the word of a "peasant" could not be trusted and demanded that Kysil should bring his mission to a close as soon as possible.[104]

After the murder of the hostages, Kysil had protested to Khmel'nyts'kyi that if negotiations were to be undertaken, they must be initiated

immediately.[105] If they were not, he would abandon his mission and join
the Commonwealth's armies. Khmel'nyts'kyi immediately replied that
the unfortunate incident had been provoked by Wiśniowiecki, and he
urged Kysil to persist in his efforts to negotiate.[106]

On August 31, the peace commissioners neared the Cossack camp.
By then many of Kysil's Volhynian military guard had deserted to Wiśniowiecki.[107] Although Kysil continued to use his influence for peace and
contacted the Kievan metropolitan, who was with Khmel'nyts'kyi, the
time limit set for negotiations was rapidly approaching.[108] Even Kysil
realized that war was now unavoidable. Rumors of violence among the
Cossacks left Kysil unsure whether Khmel'nyts'kyi was still alive.

By September 13, the commission had to admit failure. In spite of the
late date, Kysil claimed he still would negotiate with Khmel'nyts'kyi if
the hetman desired to meet him. But, by September 18, he gave up and
went to the army's camp.[109] Kysil's entrance into the Commonwealth's
camp was a personal humiliation. Wiśniowiecki had already publicly
accused him of colluding with Khmel'nyts'kyi and of providing the rebels
with funds in an attempt to secure the vacant crown for himself.[110] More
to the point, he was now accused of raising false hopes and retarding
the process of armament.[111] And once again it was alleged that the reason
Kysil saw justice in the Cossack grievances was that he, like the rebels,
was a Ruthenian.[112]

Soon after Kysil's humiliation, the Commonwealth's forces suffered a
total defeat at the battle of Pyliavtsi.[113] On September 23, tricked into
the belief that Khmel'nyts'kyi had been joined by a large Tatar army,
the discordant Commonwealth forces began a tactical retreat at night
that turned into a rout. The ailing Palatine Kysil had to flee by carriage,
and his enemies later charged him with cowardice.[114]

In the week after Pyliavtsi, Kysil examined the policies he had followed in attempting to reach an accommodation with Khmel'nyts'kyi.[115]
He did not view himself as having been duped by a Cossack hetman
who had never intended to negotiate, but instead believed that the Tatars, the pressures from the Cossacks, and the provocations of leaders
of the Commonwealth's forces had made it impossible for Khmel'nyts'kyi
to negotiate. The most convincing of his justifications for his policies
was that however unsuccessful his peace-seeking activities were, it was
the war party that was ultimately responsible for the disaster. Kysil and
Ossoliński may have overestimated their ability to convince
Khmel'nyts'kyi to cease hostilities and their concentration on negotiations may have diverted attention from war preparations, but at least
the negotiations had given the Commonwealth time to assemble its forces
and the armies gathered at Pyliavtsi ought to have been able to engage

the Cossacks in battle. Instead, the bickering military commanders had simply let their army disintegrate without offering resistance. When, in September and October, Khmel'nyts'kyi marched on Lviv and Zamość, the Commonwealth did not have troops to oppose him.

The Election of Jan Kazimierz

While Kysil was busy trying to negotiate with the Cossacks, his ally Ossoliński had begun the task of deciding on a candidate for the throne and ensuring the selection of his choice.[116] The leading contenders were Władysław's two brothers—Jan Kazimierz and Karol Ferdynand, but the candidacy of both royal brothers weakened the argument for each. In addition, the candidacy of each brother had several drawbacks.[117] Jan Kazimierz was known as a ne'er-do-well adventurer, who had little sympathy for Poland and had often thwarted Władysław's policies. Karol Ferdynand, the unordained bishop of Wrocław, was thrifty, reserved, and taciturn. He was an excellent administrator, but his frugality did not inspire enthusiasm in the nobles, who liked their kings to be generous. Władysław, whose only son had died in 1646, was known to have had reservations about both. Some nobles looked instead to foreign candidates, including the rulers of Transylvania, Muscovy, and Brandenburg.[118]

Foreign candidates had several advantages. Always intent on demonstrating that the monarchy was in no way hereditary, many nobles preferred them to members of the royal family. In addition, foreign monarchs could ensure the Commonwealth military assistance in time of danger. The selection of a non-Catholic, such as the Calvinist prince of Transylvania, György Rákóczi, would appeal to Protestant and Orthodox nobles as a means of curbing Catholic influence. A foreign candidate could secure support from the lower nobility by liberal distribution of funds.[119]

In the period immediately after Władysław's death, Kysil believed that elections should be held as soon as possible, but that the nobility's right to free choice be guarded. He did state that, had Władysław's son lived to be a candidate, he would have respected royal blood and supported him. However, Jan Kazimierz and Karol Ferdynand had not even been approved by Władysław. Because of the dangers facing the Commonwealth, Kysil proposed selecting any candidate, native or foreign, who could bring the country the most tangible benefits.[120]

However, even before Kysil arrived in Warsaw, it had become clear that Jan Kazimierz was Ossoliński's candidate. The chancellor opposed a foreign candidate, and he may have believed that the impetuous Jan Kazimierz would be easier to influence than Karol Ferdynand. Jan Kazimierz's candidacy also appeared weaker, and Ossoliński could be guaranteed more authority for himself if he swung his considerable influence to the election of the weaker candidate.[121] Assuming he would back Ossoliński's choice, commentators listed Kysil as one of the supporters of Jan Kazimierz even before he arrived. In August, the Prussian elector's representative, Andreas Adersbach, reported that because of the Cossack rebellion "Kysil's voice has the weight of three."[122] He mentioned that some nobles suspected Jan Kazimierz of contacting the Cossacks and that Kysil had already made an agreement with Khmel'nyts'kyi and was deliberately drawing out the negotiations so that the Cossacks would have a voice in the election.[123] There is no proof that these rumors were correct, but they do show that Jan Kazimierz was already seen as the peace party's candidate. By October, the lines were clearly drawn.[124] The death of György Rákóczi I, prince of Transylvania, early in the month removed the most serious of the foreign candidates and simplified the contest.[125] The peace faction supported the candidacy of Jan Kazimierz; Vice-Chancellor Leszczyński and advocates of war against the rebels supported Karol Ferdynand.

The Diet that convened on October 6 became an intricate chess game in which issues such as the negotiations with Khmel'nyts'kyi, the selection of military leaders, and the timing and place for calling for a levy of the nobility were related to the struggle over candidates. The military issue was complicated by the fact that after the debacle at Pyliavtsi, the army had on its own authority elected Wiśniowiecki hetman. The Diet had to decide whether this appointment should be legalized or put off until after the election and left to the discretion of the king. The Diet also had to raise a new army and to decide whether a levy of nobles should be called immediately. In the hope that the fanatically Catholic petty nobility of the Masovian region surrounding Warsaw would pour into the capital and opt for the war party candidate, Leszczyński had favored calling a levy to Warsaw even before the election.[126]

Kysil arrived at the Diet on October 9, and the next day he delivered his first major address.[127] He defended himself against charges of cowardice at Pyliavtsi, stoutly maintaining that he had stayed with his troops to the end. He sought to prevent the trial of those responsible for Pyliavtsi in order to divert the Diet from questioning his and Ossoliński's conduct of affairs in the summer of 1648 and to win over those nobles who would be compromised in an inquiry.[128] He next turned to the problem of defense. He admitted that the winter was the ideal season to begin a campaign against the Cossacks, since they would not be able to construct their earthen fortifications, but after suggesting various policies that could be used in dealing with the Cossacks, ranging from toleration to extermination, he proposed resuming negotiations. He claimed that no power in the world could withstand the combined Cossack army and Tatar Horde and asserted, "when one hundred of our Germans [mercenary soldiers] shoot, they kill one man; when a hundred Cossacks shoot, unfailingly they hit fifty."

Kysil proposed that a king should be elected immediately so that negotiations with the Cossacks could be initiated. He reiterated his earlier assertion that the Cossacks had no conception of loyalty to the Commonwealth, and he reminded the delegates that when the Convocation Diet wrote to Khmel'nyts'kyi as "Commander of the Army of the Commonwealth," Khmel'nyts'kyi replied as "Commander of the Zaporozhian Army of His Grace the King." Kysil maintained that the "peasants" had no understanding of the authority of the Commonwealth and would reply "what is the Commonwealth? We are also the Commonwealth. But the king is a lord to us." Although he ostensibly supported the call of a levy of the nobility, he suggested that the levy and the selection of the military leaders be delayed until after the election of a king.

Kysil's suggestion that the Diet elect a new king before discussing other business was not taken, and in the days that followed, various issues were debated. Kysil clarified his policies on numerous occasions. On October 13, he argued that Wiśniowiecki had received the hetman's mace from the hands of a thousand soldiers, not by the will of the Commonwealth, so the Diet need not confirm the action.[129] On October 14, he parried Leszczyński's attempt to call a levy before the election of a king.[130] On the 15th, in an attempt to hasten the election, he proposed that the two Vasa brothers decide between themselves who was to be the sole family candidate, and he ostensibly came out in favor of neither.[131] In fact, Kysil's speech was part of a concerted effort to pressure Karol Ferdynand into withdrawing, and his proposal, interpreted by the Diet members as an espousal of Jan Kazimierz's candidacy, met with strong opposition.[132] Delegates in favor of Karol Ferdynand argued that it was up to the Republic to make a decision, not for the royal brothers to present one as a *fait accompli*.

On October 16, Ossoliński and Kysil met defeat when Wiśniowiecki was acclaimed by the Diet as leader of the Kingdom's armies during the hetmans' captivity. However, Kysil proposed that at least two leaders should be selected, thereby limiting Wiśniowiecki's authority when Andrzej Firlej, castellan of Belz, was appointed as a co-leader.[133]

Kysil and Ossoliński continued to press for election of a monarch.

Kysil lamented the hardship that delay was causing to the nobility of the eastern lands. His lament was motivated by personal experience, since his brother Mykola had just arrived from the battlefront with the news that Khmel'nyts'kyi had reached the Buh River and that the family's last estates were lost.[134] Despite Kysil's urging, the Diet was in no mood to hurry the election, and except for the appointment of the new military leaders, little was resolved.

The forces behind Jan Kazimierz's election were gathering strength, however; his supporters included his cousin, Queen Christina of Sweden, Władysław's widow Maria Ludwika, and just before the election, Bohdan Khmel'nyts'kyi himself. Jan Kazimierz had contacted Khmel'nyts'kyi in October, probably on his own initiative. Despite his stunning successes in August and September, Khmel'nyts'kyi had halted his march within two hundred miles of Warsaw. His decision, the subject of frequent debates by later historians, was partially motivated by practical military considerations—the lack of siege artillery, the problems in provisioning, and outbreaks of the plague. In addition, the Tatar forces, laden with booty and captives, were unprepared for a winter campaign and departed for home in early October. The decision, however, was also determined by the limited nature and goals of Khmel'nyts'kyi's revolt. It did not seek to overturn the existing political and social structure of the entire Commonwealth. Stemming from the grievances of the Ukrainian lands and the Cossack Host, it strove to force Warsaw to compromise, rather than to control Warsaw. Hence, practical considerations and the nature of the revolt combined to form Khmel'nyts'kyi's policy of influencing the outcome of the election.[135]

By early November, Ossoliński's clever manipulations had gathered a preponderance of votes for Jan Kazimierz. Although feelings against the Cossacks and against Ossoliński and Kysil remained strong, the nobles knew as well as anyone that the Commonwealth's troops were helpless in the face of Khmel'nyts'kyi's army, and they were unable, or unwilling, to appropriate funds to raise a large army. The nobles of the western lands showed no enthusiasm to lay down their lives fighting in a levy to save the estates of their eastern brethren. Even the arrival of the popular Wiśniowiecki could not stem the tide. The pro-Karol Ferdynand faction decided at a meeting at Leszczyński's house that its candidate must concede.[136]

Although Jan Kazimierz owed his victory to Ossoliński and supported the chancellor's policy of negotiation, his attitude toward Ossoliński's and Kysil's policies was very different from Władysław's. Władysław had helped formulate the Turkish war plan in cooperation with Ossoliński and Kysil and had enjoyed great popularity with the Cossacks. Jan Kazimierz recognized that the peace party had ensured his election, but he was deeply committed neither to Ossoliński and Kysil, nor to their policies. Although Kysil remained an important adviser, he was no longer a totally devoted one, and unlike Władysław, Jan Kazimierz owed him no debt of gratitude for long years of service.[137] Kysil was dependent upon the continued support of Ossoliński, whose skillful political maneuvering had defeated the numerous enemies of the peace policy. Kysil was indispensable to the Commonwealth and to Ossoliński so long as peace negotiations were seriously considered, but once they were not, he was defenseless against criticism. Such criticism was already voiced at the Election Diet. He had entered the Diet to the cry of "traitor," had publicly been called a Cossack spy, and had almost been assaulted.[138]

Khmel'nyts'kyi's emissaries to Jan Kazimierz demanded amnesty with the restoration of Cossack rights; the Host's subordination to the monarch, not to Crown military authorities; abolition of the Uniate church; and the right of the Cossacks to conduct campaigns on the Black Sea.[139] In three days of stormy Senate sessions in late November, Kysil favored entertaining the proposals and sending negotiators to Khmel'nyts'kyi. The Diet made no decision on accepting or rejecting the Cossack demands.[140] The Cossack emissaries were not even formally received, on a legal technicality—they had been sent to the king on November 17, when there was none, since Jan Kazimierz was elected on November 20. The Diet had considerable reason to assert the proper functions and titles of king and Diet, since Khmel'nyts'kyi had proposed to assist Jan Kazimierz to become an autocrat as other monarchs were.[141] Wary though it might be, the Diet had to face reality, and it empowered the new king to negotiate with the rebels. Jan Kazimierz sent word to Khmel'nyts'kyi that he was willing to accept the conditions, and in early December he appointed a mission, again with Kysil at its head.[142] It was to confirm Khmel'nyts'kyi as hetman, make concessions on the union, and allow a 12,000-man register. The negotiations were scheduled in Kiev for late February, which meant that the extent of the concessions to Khmel'nyts'kyi did not have to be made public until after the Coronation Diet in January, and that the Cossack army would return to the Dnieper basin.[143] Almost all Khmel'nyts'kyi's demands had been met. Not only had he officially been named hetman and granted the insignia of authority, the Zaporozhian mace and standard, but the government accepted the *de facto* abolition of the union in the lands of the revolt and promised to remedy abuses in local officials' treatment of the Cossacks.[144]

From the Pereiaslav Peace Commission to the Zboriv Agreement

The commission that Kysil led into the Ukraine in January 1649 consisted primarily of Ruthenian Orthodox nobles (the castellan of Kiev, Maksymilian Bzhozovs'kyi, Prince Zakharii Chetvertyns'kyi, and Kysil's brother Mykola), in addition to Wojciech Miaskowski, podkomorzy of Lviv, who kept a diary of the commission. Kysil assumed that once having conferred the insignia of the hetmancy upon Khmel'nyts'kyi the civil war would end, and he would return to his estates. He was soon disabused of that notion. In even his first letters back to Warsaw, he wrote of the great changes that had taken place in Khmel'nyts'kyi's outlook.[145] Rebellions in the countryside and Khmel'nyts'kyi's reluctance to begin negotiations had made it difficult even to contact him.[146] Khmel'nyts'kyi received the mission at Pereiaslav rather than in Kiev, but it was treated as just another foreign delegation alongside the Muscovite and Transylvanian groups. Kysil soon found out that Khmel'nyts'kyi no longer acted like a Zaporozhian hetman receiving the symbols of authority from his sovereign, but rather, like an independent ruler negotiating with a foreign power. He described himself as "Autocrat of Rus'." He claimed that he would liberate all of Rus' from "Polish bondage," and he declared that his rule already extended to Chełm, Lviv and Halych.

The change in Khmel'nyts'kyi's goals and self-perception from November 1648 to January 1649 had destroyed any real hope for a settlement. The major source on this question is the report of the commission, kept by Wojciech Miaskowski.[147] It attributes the new attitudes to the influence of the clergy of Kiev and the professors and students of the Kiev collegium. It maintains that they had greeted Khmel'nyts'kyi as "Moses, deliverer, savior, liberator of his people from Polish servitude, well-named *Bohdan* (God given)" and that the visiting patriarch of Jerusalem, Paisius, gave him the title "illustrious prince." This interpretation has been accepted by numerous historians, and it goes far in explaining the religious and national role that Khmel'nyts'kyi proclaimed for himself. However, the degree of influence of the clerical circle and the magnitude of change in Khmel'nyts'kyi's thought and plans are difficult to measure, particularly because so little is known about Khmel'nyts'kyi's aspirations before January 1649. While Khmel'nyts'kyi's declarations in February 1649 were certainly far removed from his demands of November 1648, he may have moderated his statements in November so as to ensure that the Diet selected his candidate as king and refrained from raising troops so as to give him time to consolidate his army and administration. It does appear that a fundamental change in Khmel'nyts'kyi's goals did occur in these months, but the influence of the clergy may have been more to provide religious and national justifications for a policy of continuing the revolt that was determined by other factors.

After his triumphs in August and September, Khmel'nyts'kyi returned to a Dnieper Ukraine in which popular upheavals were stabilizing into a new social order. The Cossack rank and file and the peasant masses demanded that Khmel'nyts'kyi prevent the restoration of the old regime and continue the war. The successes of the revolt had improved the rebels' standing in international affairs and raised Khmel'nyts'kyi's expectations that he might receive foreign support. Once the Muscovites' hopes to have the tsar elected king of Poland were dashed completely, they could reassess their policies toward the Commonwealth and the rebels. György Rákóczi II of Transylvania, also frustrated in his candidacy, now considered what benefits cooperation with the Cossacks might bring, as did the rulers of Moldavia and Wallachia. Although the Ottomans remained unwilling to commit themselves to a new northern policy, the Crimean Tatars displayed readiness to resume Cossack-Tatar operations in the spring. All these factors undoubtedly influenced Khmel'nyts'kyi's policies, but, despite his sweeping statements to the commission, it remains questionable whether he was determined to break away completely from the Commonwealth in February 1649. It is even more unlikely that he had any precise plans for creating a new Ruthenian principality or permanently changing the social order in the Ukraine.

Kysil's long-delayed meeting with Khmel'nyts'kyi revealed how drastic had been the changes in the Ukrainian lands. Accompanied by his wife, Kysil had come expecting to resume his former leading role in Ukrainian affairs. On entering Pereiaslav, he was subjected to derisive accusations from the Cossacks who said, "you, Kysil, bone of our bones, have betrayed us and sided with the Poles." Far from negotiating restoration of the old administration, Kysil found that Khmel'nyts'kyi insisted that an administration existed in Kiev, declaring: "I may judge there, I am lord there, I am the palatine of Kiev." The accounts the commissioners heard of Khmel'nyts'kyi's triumphal entry into Kiev at Christmas illustrated how total the shift in power had been since 1646, when Kysil entered Kiev, acclaimed by the Kiev collegium as a Ruthenian national and religious leader, but still as an official of the Commonwealth.

Although Khmel'nyts'kyi frequently subjected the ill palatine to abuse, Kysil spent several days attempting to convince the hetman to accept a compromise and reach some agreement. He insisted that the hetman's actions would not only destroy the Polish and Lithuanian lands, but also the Ruthenian land and its faith. He argued that just as Poland and Lithuania could not withstand the "pagans" without the Zaporozhians, so the Zaporozhians could not defend themselves without the Polish army. He warned the hetman against leading his people into Muslim bondage, and he appealed to him to break his alliance with the masses so that once again "peasants will plough, and Cossacks will fight." All Kysil's eloquence could not sway the hetman, who insisted that concessions should have come much earlier and that he would resumé hostilities and decisively defeat the Poles.

There was, however, another side to Kysil's relations with Khmel'-nyts'kyi. While waiting at Kysil's estate of Novosilky before proceeding to Pereiaslav to meet with the hetman, Kysil and the Orthodox commissioners took council with the metropolitan of Kiev and representatives of the clergy and brotherhoods. Miaskowski, who complained about being excluded from these meetings, reported that Kysil claimed to have been offered a "Ruthenian principality or a Podolian state," and asserted that he would have accepted one or the other if the Commonwealth would not have condemned him for it.[148] Certainly, the clergymen, who were depicting Khmel'nyts'kyi as a religious and national liberator and plotting with the Orthodox Danubian principalities and with prelates from the Middle East, saw Kysil as a central figure in planning any new Orthodox polity. Kysil had, after all, from the first seen the far-reaching political potential of the revolt for the Ruthenians, and during the negotiations with Khmel'nyts'kyi, he once again mentioned the possibility of the formation of a new state.

Although Khmel'nyts'kyi often taunted Kysil during the negotiations, he conferred with Kysil frequently and tried to convince Kysil's wife to "renounce the Liakhs, and to remain with the Cossacks." What offers Kysil may have received during the negotiations will probably never be known. During his commission numerous Orthodox nobles succumbed to Khmel'nyts'kyi's blandishments. It seems certain, however, that Kysil, like his close collaborator Metropolitan Kosiv, remained cautious and devoted to the Commonwealth.

Kysil and Khmel'nyts'kyi were, nevertheless, able to cooperate in composing a petition to the king that would benefit both the Orthodox church and the Orthodox palatine. A Catholic zealot, the Lithuanian Chancellor Albrycht Stanisław Radziwiłł, later charged Kysil with writing "with his own hand" articles "harmful to the Commonwealth."[149] Indeed the form and content of the petition revealed the hand of Kysil. It claimed that "bloody grievances" had forced the Host to struggle against its servitude and to search for alien lords, but that, on the advice of Kysil, it would refrain from such activities if its petition would be acted on positively.[150] Instead of the usual Cossack demands, the petition dealt almost entirely with church affairs, and its wording reflected the political thought of Kysil's earlier addresses before the Diet. Thus it contained a demand "that the name of the union should not be, but rather only the Roman and Greek observance, as it was when Rus' united to Poland." It requested that the palatine of Kiev be "of the Ruthenian nation and the Greek law" so that he would not persecute the "churches of God," and it complained that the incumbent palatine, Janusz Tyszkiewicz, expelled Orthodox believers from their churches near the palatine's castle. Since Kysil was the most prominent Orthodox noble in the Ukraine, the article could only be construed as a demand that he should be the successor to the elderly Tyszkiewicz. Another point demanded that the Orthodox metropolitan be given a seat in the Senate, and that would give Kysil an ally in the person of his old friend, Metropolitan Kosiv. The Cossacks specifically mentioned that they wished Rus' to have three senators "for the protection of our faith and the rights of the Ruthenian nation."[151] Yet another demand was that Kysil's enemy Wiśniowiecki be removed as commander of the army and from the Ukraine, a demand that turned out to be unnecessary since Jan Kazimierz had already removed him at the Coronation Diet in Cracow.[152] Influenced by the Kievan clergy and Kysil, Khmel'nyts'kyi sought to strengthen the position of the Orthodox in the Commonwealth, even though he refused to accept the commission's proposals for a permanent settlement of the war.

Failing to secure a peace settlement, Kysil succeeded only in obtaining a truce until the end of May, with promises that Khmel'nyts'kyi would receive two commissioners and compile a Cossack register then. A neutral zone was set up in Volhynia and Podillia into which the respective armies were not to advance.[153] There was still no peace settlement, but Khmel'nyts'kyi had for the moment abandoned his western conquests and the Volhynian nobles, including Kysil himself, could return to their estates.

After leaving Pereiaslav, Kysil's commission sent a pessimistic report to the king. It warned that Khmel'nyts'kyi now aspired not only to control of Cossack affairs, but also to sovereignty over the Ruthenian provinces.[154] Yet, the king and Ossoliński continued to profess confidence in an ultimately peaceful resolution of the conflict and avoided calling out a general levy.[155] On March 27, the king wrote to Khmel'nyts'kyi in an attempt to avoid war after the truce would expire and sent an emissary, Jakób Śmiarkowski, on a mission to him.[156] The king maintained that he had already begun to implement the Cossack demands: Tyszkiewicz had died and Kysil would succeed him—the pala-tine of Kiev would now be of the Orthodox faith.[157]

Kysil might have received the highest post in the incorporation lands, but this was not doing him much good in Hoshcha, in the area between the Sluch and the Horyn' that was more of a skirmish zone than a neutral belt, where he resided after completion of his mission. He persisted in his efforts to keep both sides from breaking the truce and to persuade Khmel'nyts'kyi to disengage himself from the rebellious peas-ants and negotiate a peace settlement.[158] He even went as far as to forge a letter from Ossoliński to himself and forward a copy to Khmel'-nyts'kyi in an attempt to convince Khmel'nyts'kyi to negotiate.[159] But as the spring wore on, no concrete response came from Khmel'nyts'kyi.[160] Infractions of the truce became more serious, and the king's emissary Śmiarkowski, sent to Khmel'nyts'kyi's camp, did not return. Kysil despaired of reaching an accommodation; his letters to Ossoliński urged the chancellor to take action since he was sure that Wiśniowiecki soon would goad the Cossacks into open hostilities.[161] By May, it was merely a matter of time before a major clash broke out, and Ossoliński urged Kysil to try to secure an extension of the truce until July.[162] Writing to Ossoliński on May 11, Kysil, now thinking of himself not as a negotiator but as a pawn, regarded his continued presence in Hoshcha as a means of buying time.[163] He lamented that the Commonwealth was prepared neither for war nor for peace:

> I have neither resolutions nor instructions because the demands of Khmel'nyts'kyi have not been decided upon by the king or the Common-wealth. No promises will help, since the enemy is mighty and will demand results. What, then, should a commissioner's position [his own] be on the abolition of the union, about Czapliński, about the place of the metro-politan in the Senate. I don't know.

Four days later, foreseeing the outbreak of hostilities, Kysil wrote that he wished to know where the Commonwealth's armies would establish their line of defense.[164] Although he still requested further information on terms for his mission, he announced that his small band of retainers would join the king's forces in the upcoming battle. By then it became evident that Khmel'nyts'kyi intended to mount a new cam-paign in alliance with the Tatars and it was rumored that he had sworn loyalty to the Ottoman sultan. In an attempt to combat such a policy, Kysil turned to the Zaporozhian colonels, pleading:

> Our ancestors and the ancestors of your Excellencies laid down their brave young heads, profusely shed their blood for so many hundred years for the faith of Christ, for our lords and kings, and for this Christian State,

and now one Hetman brings it about that your Excellencies love a Muslim ruler and his state more than your own natural one.[165]

Kysil went on to advise the Zaporozhians to ask their hetman which state had secured their freedoms, "from which had they received their mothers' milk?" He asked them to think of the Greeks' position; he warned them that if they accepted Ottoman suzerainty, "Christian churches will be turned into mosques and Christian people will groan." Kysil unsuccessfully tried to undermine Khmel'nyts'kyi's almost dictatorial powers with the exclamation: "Happy were the ancient ancestors of the Zaporozhian Army who once to a man knew what had been enacted at a council."

As the end of May and the termination of the truce drew near, Kysil began to worry about his safety. Khmel'nyts'kyi had intercepted a letter Kysil had sent to Moscow requesting assistance against the Cossacks. Although it was clear that the Muscovite government now had no intention of intervening in the Commonwealth's behalf, Khmel'nyts'kyi was nonetheless furious and demanded a new negotiator from the king.[166] Kysil beat a hasty retreat from Hoshcha beyond the Horyn' river, but he continued his attempts undaunted, dispatching the inveterate emissary Father Lasko to Khmel'nyts'kyi.[167] Khmel'nyts'kyi was by now also using negotiations as a means of gaining time until the Tatars arrived, but secret messages from the king's envoy Śmiarkowski, still detained at Khmel'nyts'kyi's camp, convinced Kysil that further negotiation was futile. He was not comforted when he learned from Khmel'nyts'kyi that the Muscovite tsar had interceded in his behalf after the tsar had found out about the intercepted letters.[168] When Khmel'nyts'kyi told him to stay at Hoshcha so he would not perish with the rest of the "high nobility," Kysil called it a trick to capture him. On May 25, he reported his failure and plan to move to his estates near Volodymyr.[169]

Kysil's admitted failure coincided with the nobles' renewed charges that the peace party's policy had brought the Commonwealth near ruin. Although his negotiation with the Ottomans had not gone as far as was rumored, Khmel'nyts'kyi had successfully enlisted Tatars who could take advantage of the spring grass to launch a massive campaign. It was also believed that Khmel'nyts'kyi had obtained support for the Transylvanians, since György Rákóczi II wished to gain the Polish throne by arms, though in fact Rákóczi did not feel himself strong enough to make such a move. The noble levy had still not assembled. Ossoliński had forestalled calling it and even at the Senate sessions in early June 1649, had attempted to put off the third and final call for mobilization, since a levy could easily turn into a rebellious confederation against his rule.[170] Still, Ossoliński's preference for professional troops over the unwieldy levy, however sound in theory, had not produced enough soldiers. Wiśniowiecki, although deprived of leadership of the army, was showing his usual energy in calling up the troops from his own Ruthenian palatinate and this, too, could lead to open rebellion.[171]

Kysil's personal position was desperate—after a year of negotiations, he still had not regained his once numerous estates. His failure to deliver the promised peace had brought him odium from all sides and made him vulnerable to attacks from Leszczyński and Wiśniowiecki. His only gains were the titles of palatine of Kiev and starosta of Bohuslav, and these were small comfort to a palatine who might never see his capital.[172]

As Kysil fled west to the uncertain reception that would meet an unsuccessful negotiator, he felt the need to justify his conduct, and he defended his policy to the powerful Lithuanian vice-chancellor, Kazimierz Leon Sapieha, the greatest Catholic magnate in the Grand Duchy.[173] In discussing the peasant and Cossack rebellions against the nobility, he maintained that logic ordained self-defense in either of two methods: appropriations for a professional army or a levy. He thought the first method was preferable, but since it had not been followed, the nobility could now save itself only by taking to its horses. He cited the war with Sweden of 1625–1629 as a lesser danger against which the nobility had rallied, but lamented that in the present conflict, during which half the fatherland had been lost, only nine or ten thousand troops had been raised. Kysil answered those who blamed him for having promised peace and the chancellor for delaying the levy, by maintaining that he had warned the Commonwealth of danger as soon as the peace negotiations had clearly failed. He reminded Sapieha that his armistice had given the country a respite during which troops could be assembled. Kysil asserted that no one person should be blamed, since the fault was that of the Coronation Diet that had not appropriated funds for an army. Thus, in order to avoid personal blame for the present problems of the Commonwealth, Kysil chose to condemn the Diet at which he was not present. In making recommendations for the present situation, Kysil favored withdrawal in the face of superior forces over giving battle with the Commonwealth's meager forces, and he advised going no further than the Buh, the western border of Volhynia, in the confrontation with Khmel'nyts'kyi.

The weakness of his position also required that he reappraise his political alliances, and he began by seeking the assistance of Kazimierz Leon Sapieha to make peace with his political enemies.[174] He had maintained contact with Sapieha for a number of years.[175] As administrator of the truce, he kept Sapieha informed and sent information to the king and Chancellor Ossoliński through him.[176] In June, he became more and more frustrated as he received no answer from the king or chancellor and, hearing rumors that he was under attack from many sides, Kysil turned to Sapieha for assistance.[177] He first asked him to intercede with the Lithuanian chancellor, Albrycht Stanisław Radziwiłł, about a property dispute over lands near Kobryn', to help his precarious financial condition. Then he asked Sapieha to intercede for him with Crown Vice-Chancellor Leszczyński.[178]

Leszczyński greeted Kysil's overtures with caution. He wrote to Sapieha of Kysil's hitherto baneful influence on the king and maintained "this man is hated in the Republic, partly because of his guarantee of peace and treaties, and because he did not maintain that the Cossacks should be beaten when there was still time, and partly because of his excessive intimacy with the Chancellor." Leszczyński said that Kysil could redeem himself in his eyes only by breaking with Ossoliński, which he might anyway be obliged to do since Ossoliński was publicly ascribing to Kysil errors he himself had made. If Kysil would break with Ossoliński, Leszczyński even offered to "convince Wiśniowiecki to restore friendly relations with him."[179]

Kysil was too cautious to take so radical a step. Even as he negotiated with the war party, he avoided offending Ossoliński since he knew very well that he was so implicated in the policy of placating the Cossacks and serving Ossoliński's plans that he would in any case have been received in the other camp only with the greatest circumspection.[180] As it turned out, he did not take the drastic step; his services were once again needed by Ossoliński and the king. Between the beginning of July and mid-August, Kysil received an order to join the royal forces.[181] Although Ossoliński may have made Kysil the scapegoat in June and July, the unpreparedness of the Commonwealth's military forces probably convinced him that Kysil was more useful to him as friend than foe, since a negotiator with the Cossacks might be needed again.

The Cossack-Tatar army, which had begun to move west in June numbered over a hundred thousand; it was faced by much smaller armies of the Kingdom and reinforcements from the Grand Duchy, whose leaders now viewed the rebellion as so dangerous that they were willing to assist the Kingdom in suppressing it.[182] Ossoliński was still under the misapprehension that the Sultan Mehmed IV had ordered Tatar Khan Islam Girey to refrain from supporting Khmel'nyts'kyi. In early June, armies led by Andrzej Firlej, the castellan of Belz, and Stanisław Lanckoroński, the castellan of Kam"ianets'-Podil's'kyi, had advanced into Volhynia. In mid-June Firlej even wrote to Kysil, assuring him that he could return to Hoshcha,[183] but when the enormous Cossack-Tatar army advanced into Volhynia, the Kingdom's forces, the troops led by Wiśniowiecki and the other private armies closed themselves up in the fortress of Zbarazh.[184]

Their situation seemed hopeless, since there was little chance that they could hold out until reinforcements arrived. The king and Ossoliński had only gotten around to calling a levy on July 20, and had still to gather the army at Lublin and march to the besieged.[185] Despite the government's weak position Khmel'nyts'kyi was officially deposed, and a loyal Cossack, Semen Zabus'kyi, was named to replace him as starszy.[186] As early as April, Kysil had urged Ossoliński to assume command of the army, and in July Ossoliński did so by insisting on serving as the major commander of the levy.[187]

The call-to-arms had produced a force of under 15,000 men.[188] Although nobles of the eastern palatinates attempted to convince their peers in the west that the fate of the fatherland was in the balance—and the western nobles did respond better than they had on previous calls—they by and large regarded the Cossack uprising as an eastern problem. The effectiveness of the levy was also hampered by opposition to Ossoliński's leadership. In crossing the Strypa River near Zboriv on August 15, the levy was encircled by Khmel'nyts'kyi and a Tatar army led by Khan Islam Girey and in the ensuing battle was on the verge of being annihilated.[189] In this seemingly hopeless situation, Ossoliński achieved one of the great triumphs of his career. Whether he had any earlier contacts with the Tatar Khan Islam Girey is not known, but on August 15 he was able to convince Islam Girey to accept tribute and captives in return for forcing Khmel'nyts'kyi to come to terms. Since it was not in the Tatars' long-run interest that the Zaporozhians become too powerful and since Islam Girey was under orders from Istanbul not to provoke the Commonwealth into a full-scale war that could develop into a northern front to the Venetian-Ottoman conflict, the khan decided to negotiate with the Commonwealth. Even in this "betrayal" the Tatars were adamant that the Cossacks should be granted substantial concessions in their negotiations with the Commonwealth, for the khan planned to continue cooperation with the Cossacks against his northern neighbors.[190]

Kysil took an active part in the negotiations in a delegation which included Ossoliński, Albrycht Stanisław Radziwiłł, and Andrzej Firlej.[191] He was instrumental in convincing Khmel'nyts'kyi to accept a promise that religious grievances would be dealt with at the next Diet rather than to demand that the king swear to a specific statement abolishing the union.[192] Kysil also conducted the ceremony of his swearing an oath to the king on August 18.[193]

The agreement betwen Khmel'nyts'kyi and the Commonwealth included eleven provisions known as the Zboriv Agreement, affirming for
the Host privileges that were far greater than those that it had previously held. In practice, the agreement recognized the existence of a
semi-autonomous Cossack political entity in the Ukraine. The privileges
included a Cossack register of fully 40,000, demarcation of the territory
where Cossacks could reside that included almost all of the Kiev and
Chernihiv palatinates and some of the Bratslav, the conferral of the
Chyhyryn starostwo to the hetman's office, an amnesty for Orthodox
and Catholic nobles who had participated in the uprising, a provision
that offices in the Kiev, Chernihiv and Bratslav palatinates were to be
granted only to Orthodox nobles, the expulsion of Jews from Cossack
territory, the closing of the Jesuit school in Kiev, a provision that no
other Jesuit schools were to be permitted in the Ukraine, the establishment of a seat in the Senate for the metropolitan, and a guarantee that
the Orthodox clergy could negotiate the abolition of the union at the
next Diet.[194] Although the articles did not include the Cossack demands
for parts of Volhynia, for immediate abolition of the union, for a
separate Cossack judicial administration, for abolition of the Roman
Catholic bishopric in Kiev, for senatorial positions for three Orthodox
hierarchs, and for oaths by the king, six senators, and six delegates of
the Diet to uphold the privileges to Orthodoxy, they still represented an
undeniable triumph for the Cossacks.[195] In particular the guarantee of a
forty-thousand-man Cossack army ensured Hetman Khmel'nyts'kyi his
place as an almost independent ruler of the Ukraine.

The Zboriv Agreement reflected the indecisive outcome of Khmel'-
nyts'kyi's diplomatic maneuvers and military campaigns. After a year of
victories and negotiations, the Cossack hetman had only been able to
obtain the limited support of the Crimean Tatars. At Zboriv he faced
losing even this support if he did not accede to a compromise with the
Commonwealth. While the articles granted the Host privileges undreamed of at the beginning of the uprising, they fell far short of
creating a separate state ruled by the hetman. They did, however,
reflect the augmentation of power of the Host and of the hetman over
the non-Cossack segments of the populace. In particular, the Host
became the protector of Orthodox interests, including education, and as
such had usurped the role hitherto fulfilled by the Ruthenian nobility.
The articles also went far toward legalizing the establishment of a social
and political order different from that of other areas of the Commonwealth. On royal lands where a Cossack administration would be set up,
an autonomous order was to prevail alien to that of the nobles' Commonwealth. But, though the Zboriv Agreement went far, it did not alter

the right of nobles to repossess their lands. With their return to their estates, the old social order and political administration would be restored in much of the Ukraine, albeit in modified form because of the guarantee that three senators would be Orthodox and eventually the union would be abolished. The palatinates of Bratslav, Chernihiv, and Kiev were to be a territory possessing conflicting social and political systems. Yet, though the Zboriv Agreement guaranteed substantial restoration of the Commonwealth's administration, its provision for a Cossack army of 40,000 left effective power in the hands of the hetman.

From the outbreak of the revolt, Kysil had struggled to save the policies of Władysław and to restore the pre-March 1648 political and social order. On a number of issues, he soon counseled acceptance of change. He called for recognizing the Cossack leadership as legitimate, for returning internal autonomy to the Host through election of officers, and for expanding the number of Cossacks. He abandoned plans for a new religious union, urged compliance with Orthodox demands, and used the revolt to strengthen the position of the Orthodox hierarchy and nobility. At the core of his policies were the convictions that the rebels could be won over and that Black Sea war plans could be revived. Very early in the revolt he became convinced that the rebels were too strong for the Commonwealth to suppress, and that if they were not placated, the rebellion would develop into a Ruthenian separatist movement. By Zboriv, many of Kysil's fears had proven correct, yet Kysil's policies had in the end failed because of his overestimation of his own and Ossoliński's abilities to control the nobles of the Commonwealth and to win over Khmel'nyts'kyi. The renewal of hostilities in the spring of 1649 and the Zboriv Agreement demonstrated this failure. From then on, Kysil had to deal not with a rebel movement, but with an emerging new polity, the Cossack Hetmanate.

Chapter 7

Mediator between the Commonwealth and the Cossack Hetmanate

After the negotiation of the Zboriv Agreement, Kysil served as an intermediary between the government in Warsaw and the newly formed Cossack polity in the Ukraine. Although legally the Zboriv articles were confined to granting privileges, albeit extensive ones, to the Zaporozhian Cossacks, in practice, Khmel'nyts'kyi exercised almost complete control over a large area comprising the palatinates of Kiev, Chernihiv and Bratslav. Kysil's task was therefore twofold. He had to act as an official of the Commonwealth in his capacity as the palatine of Kiev, and this involved asserting the rights and powers of the pre-1648 social and administrative order in a new situation. However, since Khmel'nyts'kyi effectively ruled the Ukraine, Kysil also functioned as the Commonwealth's ambassador to the fledgling Cossack polity.

The Ratification of the Zboriv Agreement

Although Ossoliński, Kysil, and the other negotiators had somewhat reduced the scope of the Cossack demands, no amount of official propaganda on the king's "great victory" at Zboriv could make the Zboriv Agreement really acceptable to the Commonwealth's nobility.[1] Attacks on the negotiators soon appeared. An anonymous pamphlet included a satirical sketch in which the king and the khan sit together on a throne while Ossoliński points to Kysil and sings out: "Behold the Savior of the Fatherland! Arise my chosen one, you will be crowned," the metropolitan of Kiev addresses Kysil as the "ornament of the Ruthenians, . . . the glory of the schismatics," and Kysil tells the metropolitan, "You also will sit above the twelve tribes of Israel."[2] A virulent attack upon Ossoliński, blaming him for the entire Khmel'nyts'kyi debacle, included in its charges that he was "the one who, at Zbarazh, wanted the flower of the nobility, the power of the army, destroyed because of his private interests, held in common with the Lord Kysil, palatine of Kiev."[3]

Ossoliński now had to answer these charges to prepare a suitable climate so that the Diet that was to sit in late November would accept the Zboriv articles. Kysil's task was to make sure the Cossacks complied with the provisions for compiling the register, to restore order in the Kiev palatinate, and to return the eastern nobles to their estates. Without Cossack compliance, the chances for obtaining the Diet's approval were nil; achieving it would not be easy.[4]

Despite the remarkable gains they represented, Khmel'nyts'kyi was also not satisfied with the Zboriv terms. Instead of being recognized as the ruler whose territory extended to Lviv, Halych, and Chełm, he was designated by the Zboriv articles as merely a Zaporozhian hetman in the service of the Polish king, and his Cossack units were not even allowed in Volhynia. Furthermore, organizing the return of the Commonwealth's nobility and its administration to Cossack territory would not be an easy undertaking, nor would selecting 40,000 Cossacks from his armies and returning the rest to their masters.

In September, Kysil sent one of his servitors, Ivan Sosnyts'kyi, to Khmel'nyts'kyi's camp to discuss his plans and tasks.[5] Writing from Kiev on September 28, Sosnyts'kyi described the difficulties Kysil would face in dealing with the "disorderly mob" in the Ukraine. Sosnyts'kyi contacted Ivan Vyhovs'kyi, the Host's General Chancellor, but was not allowed to see Khmel'nyts'kyi himself. Vyhovs'kyi warned him that the hetman had no intention of allowing the eastern nobles to return to their estates until after the Diet had confirmed the Zboriv articles, and Sosnyts'kyi himself advised Kysil to stay out of the Ukraine until the peace terms had been published.

Sosnyts'kyi's contact with Vyhovs'kyi established a connection between Kysil and this major functionary in the Khmel'nyts'kyi administration. Vyhovs'kyi, an Orthodox Volhynian noble, belonged to the conservative faction of the Cossack elite, who wished to curb social disorder and Cossack anarchy. Like many of the Orthodox nobles who had joined the Khmel'nyts'kyi movement, he had respect for the Commonwealth's political and social institutions and sought to introduce them into the Hetmanate. Kysil and Vyhovs'kyi were thus men of similar attitudes and backgrounds, even though on different sides in the civil war.[6] Through his contacts with Vyhovs'kyi and the Orthodox clergy, Kysil sought to convince Khmel'nyts'kyi to execute the Zboriv articles. He also wished to gain personal advantages. Sosnyts'kyi asked Vyhovs'kyi to intercede with Khmel'nyts'kyi to restore some of Kysil's estates and to allow Kysil to sell potash from his forests in the Chernihiv palatinate. The tactic had some success. Vyhovs'kyi responded warmly, calling himself a "longtime servant" of Kysil and urging that he not attempt to enter the Kiev palatinate without assurances from Khmel'nyts'kyi.[7] Vyhovs'kyi also dispatched Sosnyts'kyi to the Left Bank to look after Kysil's economic interests and provided him with documents from Khmel'nyts'kyi.[8] Subsequently, Khmel'nyts'kyi assured Kysil that he would receive respect due to a palatine as soon as the Cossack register was completed.

The dietines for the November Diet were supposed to meet on October 11.[9] On the eighth, Khmel'nyts'kyi informed Kysil that he had sent out universals to calm the masses so that the Kievan dietine could meet at Zhytomyr, and he asked Kysil's help in gaining Diet approval for the demands of the Host and the Orthodox church, promising in return to restore Kysil's private estates and royal lands.[10] Khmel'-nyts'kyi's universals were of course too late to protect the Kievan dietine that gathered on October 11.[11] Even in Zhytomyr, in the western part of the Kievan palatinate, the dietine was unable to function normally, so the Kievan nobles withdrew to meet in the open air at Ziatkivtsi, near the Sluch River on the border of the Volhynian and Kievan palatinates.[12] The nobles were so desperate to return to their estates and the sources of their income that they wrote to Khmel'nyts'kyi they were willing to renounce their claims over those peasants who wished to be Cossacks.

After receiving Khmel'nyts'kyi's tardy authorization for the dietine, Kysil attempted to obtain permission for the nobles to return to their estates under almost any terms, and he requested that at least starostas and podstarostas be allowed on royal and private lands during the compilation of registers.[13] For himself, he complained that he had received none of the income he was due as palatine, and that he had not been allowed to take up residence in the castle in Kiev. He then requested a meeting with Khmel'nyts'kyi to discuss plans for the Diet.

Kysil's request was soon granted. On November 6, he went to Kiev; three weeks later he informed the king that he had met with Khmel'-nyts'kyi and had been given considerable authority to carry out his functions as palatine.[14] On November 24, he signed an agreement with the burghers of Kiev defining his rights as palatine.[15] He was particularly pleased that he was allowed to perform a palatine's office as judge: a Cossack who had murdered a nobleman was executed on his orders in front of a crowd of 20,000 Cossacks.[16] The compilation of the register was also well advanced.

Kysil attempted to ensure that the Cossack emissaries to the Diet would be given instructions favorable to a peace settlement; and the king, in his proclamations to the dietines, had requested the nobility to draft instructions favorable to the Zboriv Agreement.[17] But convincing the Diet to ratify the agreement would still be difficult. The articles on the Eastern church were particularly controversial. Anything less than

an abolition of the union was unacceptable to Khmel'nyts'kyi's supporters, while the Uniate hierarchy had behind it both the tradition of
religious freedom and, more significantly, the support of the papal nuncio and the ultra-Catholic delegates.[18] Restricting offices in the Kiev,
Bratslav, and Chernihiv palatinates to Orthodox nobles would be another
thorny issue.[19] For this reason, and undoubtedly through Kysil's urging,
Khmel'nyts'kyi instructed his Cossack delegates to limit their demands
to the return of Orthodox properties.[20] Even that, however, had potential
for conflict, because the determination of which churches were originally
Orthodox would be extremely difficult. Kysil could be pleased that Metropolitan Kosiv, who was to receive a seat in the Senate, was entrusted
by Khmel'nyts'kyi to negotiate for compliance with Cossack-Orthodox
demands.[21]

Kysil did not arrive at the Diet with the Cossack delegates and the
metropolitan until December 11, twenty days after it had started.[22]
Therefore, he did not take part in the complex proceedings through
which Jan Kazimierz and Ossoliński convinced the Diet that it had no
alternative but to approve the Zboriv Agreement. They hoped that the
Tatars had broken permanently with the Cossacks and that Khmel'-
nyts'kyi would now be willing to accept the Zboriv Agreement as the
best he could obtain and to join in a renewal of the Turkish war plan.
Their chief interest was to reorganize the army and finances, for whatever would come of the Zboriv Agreement, the Commonwealth needed
to restore its position of power. While the Diet debated the Zboriv
articles, Kysil held a series of private conferences to try to settle the
church question.[23]

The Catholic and Uniate factions used every argument of religious
freedom and of the inviolability of Catholic church property to keep
from relinquishing any sees, properties, or churches to the Orthodox,
while Metropolitan Kosiv and the Orthodox clergy argued for total abolition of the union on the basis of the ancient rights of the Orthodox
church. The Orthodox also pleaded that they must secure the abolition
because Khmel'nyts'kyi threatened to drown the clergy in the Dnieper
if they did not succeed in fulfilling his wishes. Kysil sided with the Orthodox, but maintained that it was not total abolition that was necessary,
but rather, a series of transfers of property and offices. Kysil's strategy
was to steer the discussion away from issues of dogma and to restrict it
to the problems of jurisdiction and rights. He quite openly affirmed that
he saw no differences in the interpretations of the Holy Spirit's relation
to the other persons of the Trinity, and he labeled as "academic," arguments over purgatory and the form of eternal punishment. Even in
front of an assembly of Orthodox clerics, he stated that papal precedence

was a right inherited from St. Peter, but he defiantly professed loyalty to Constantinople and he dared any Catholic to say that there was error in the Eastern church. The metropolitan is reported to have been displeased with Kysil's remarks, but he merely insisted that religious dogmas should not even be mentioned at the conference. Kysil's attitudes emerged most clearly in a debate over whether Prince-Saint Volodimer had been Orthodox or Uniate. A Uniate answered an Orthodox participant's statement that only the Orthodox had retained the faith of Volodimer by asserting that the Uniates traced their faith not only to Volodimer, but also to Christ and St. Peter. Kysil interjected that it was not their faith, but their privileges, that the Orthodox traced to Volodimer.

He often disagreed, however, with the Orthodox clerics' arguments. When they claimed they would be afraid to return if the union were not abolished, he charged them with being sheep rather than the shepherds of their flock. He was disturbed by their total submission to Cossack power:

> We should not make our faith (*blahochestie*) dependent on Cossack strength, because when a faith rises by the sword it will perish by the sword. We must establish everything by the decision of the Commonwealth, for if this matter were to come to a great war, if the Poles were to win, we would perish, if the Cossacks were to triumph, you would, as earlier, be the servants of your servants. I advise you therefore not to break up the Diet [over the religious articles], for this would also be damaging to the liberty of the Zaporozhian Host, which has not yet been confirmed [by the Diet], and in truth we would lose their [the Cossacks'] favor and loyalty. . . . We would cause a sudden war, and eternal ill-will from the Poles would be [directed] against our faith. If the Poles triumph we [Orthodox] will perish; if the Cossacks win, we will, as of old, be in servitude to them, and if the state cannot rule itself or maintain itself, we will fall into some third party's hands.[24]

Kysil urged the Orthodox clergy not to prevent a ratification of the articles of Zboriv by their intransigence: "It is better to return to your regions with comfort and with Holy Peace, to go to the Zaporozhian Host with liberties, and to those poor Christians who now live in slavery, with freedom." He claimed that Khmel'nyts'kyi placed Zaporozhian liberties above all else, and he insisted that the hetman would be angry if the clergy made the confirmation of those liberties impossible. The compromise he eventually worked out was included in a royal charter of January 12, which was issued secretly to avoid Catholic protests.[25] It turned many churches and estates over to the Orthodox, but it did not abolish the union totally.

Although the Diet was willing to allow the king to make concessions to the Orthodox to preserve peace, the Senate refused to accept the Kievan metropolitan as a member, and over that the king had no control. Kysil had a hard time convincing the metropolitan to accept this turn of events without breaking up the negotiations.[26]

Realizing that the Commonwealth did not have either a ready army or the funds to raise one, the Diet reluctantly agreed to ratify the Zboriv Agreement. In order to make this bitter pill more palatable, it did not pass the agreement as a Diet constitution, but rather authorized the king to fulfill the terms negotiated at Zboriv. At the same time the Diet called for raising an army of 16,200 soldiers and provided for its financing. While the execution of this legislation would take considerable time, the Diet had begun the process of rebuilding the Commonwealth's power.

The royal charter affirming the Zboriv articles gave Kysil, who was to reside in Kiev, full authority from the Commonwealth to keep the peace and to adjudicate conflicts between the Cossacks and the rest of the population. Kysil returned to the Ukraine in January 1650, to begin that difficult assignment.[27] His finances improved slightly by the conferral of the starostwo of Nowy Targ, which he had demanded and to which he sold the rights soon after it had been conferred.[28] However, any real recouping of his position rested on his success in implementing the provisions of the Zboriv Agreement.

From the Ratification of the Zboriv
Agreement to the Bila Tserkva Agreement
(January 1650–September 1651)

In 1650, the only year of Khmel'nyts'kyi's hetmancy when the Zaporozhian Host was not in open conflict with the Commonwealth's armies, Kysil tried to reestablish elements of the old political and social order in the face of widespread hostility on the part both of the peasantry and of the rank-and-file Cossacks, not to mention the vengeful excesses of the returning nobles. His authority depended totally on his good relations with the hetman, since Kysil had only a small military detachment at his command.[29]

As a result of the agreement, the Crown hetmans were released from Tatar captivity. Their return greatly strengthened the adamantly anti-Cossack faction in the Commonwealth and made Kysil's task even more difficult. Khmel'nyts'kyi was aware that the diehard anti-Cossack faction in the Commonwealth saw Zboriv as but a temporary setback.

Even those in the Commonwealth who favored accommodation with the Cossacks and compliance with the Zboriv articles realized that the chances for internal peace were not good, and might depend on providing the Cossacks and their Tatar allies with someone else to fight—Muscovy or the Ottoman Empire. Otherwise, Khmel'nyts'kyi would have to face peasant rebellions and Cossack mutinies against the restoration of the old order. Foreign powers now began to look upon the Cossack polity as a separate state on the international scene. Sweden, Muscovy, the Ottoman Empire, Transylvania, Moldavia and Venice were vitally interested in the policies originating in Chyhyryn and Kiev. Both Khmel'nyts'kyi and Warsaw sought to break the stalemate by finding new allies. Until they succeeded, both sides tried to keep the fragile peace without making too many concessions.[30]

In January 1650, Kysil departed for the Ukraine to attend the post-Diet dietine of the Kievan palatinate scheduled for February 21 in Zhytomyr, but not held until early March.[31] The assembled nobility complained of Cossack failures to comply with the king's universals and looked to Kysil for leadership and for the protection of their lives and properties.[32] Together with the nobles from the dietine, Kysil entered Kiev in mid-March, intending to secure Khmel'nyts'kyi's compliance with the Zboriv articles that allowed the nobles to return to their estates.[33]

Kysil's first dispatch to the king, written a week after he arrived in Kiev, reported the difficulties of his situation.[34] He delineated four sources of Cossack discontent: rumors that Commonwealth troops were marching on the Ukraine, apprehension over the release of Mikołaj Potocki, the decline of Khmel'nyts'kyi's authority following a revolt in Zaporizhzhia, and dissatisfaction, directed toward himself, because the Union of Brest had not been abolished. He reported that a general assembly of Cossacks, which could reverse the hetman's decisions, had almost been called. Kysil believed that the quashing of the revolt against Khmel'nyts'kyi in Zaporizhzhia made it possible for the hetman and the officers to enact the articles of the Zboriv Agreement. Because of this, Kysil had been able to set up an administration and had begun his duty of dispensing justice. He was fearful of new revolts, however, and above all begged for financial assistance. Although he had no income from his office and lands, he had to dispense funds to the Cossacks and the indigent nobility.

Kysil reported that Khmel'nyts'kyi had made clear that the nobles would not be allowed to return to their estates if the Commonwealth's armies advanced toward Cossack territory. Kysil had promised that no troops would advance, that taxes would not be collected, and that if the petty and middle nobles would be allowed to return to their estates, they would behave with restraint toward their subjects. He had had to promise Khmel'nyts'kyi that the magnates would not return, but that they would send their estate agents, though only Ruthenians were to be permitted.

Although the situation Kysil depicted in Kiev was far from stable, he retained his trust that Khmel'nyts'kyi and the Cossack officers wished to comply with the settlement. At the end of March, he reported to the king the departure of Cossack delegates for Warsaw with the final registers of the names of the forty thousand Cossacks.[35] He asserted that the Cossack officers who visited him daily desired to maintain peace and that the peasantry was the real problem. Kysil admitted that only a minority of those excluded from the registers were willing to return to their landlords. Nevertheless, Kysil did not want to give the Cossacks an excuse for war. He urged that the king treat Khmel'nyts'kyi's professed willingness to comply with the Zboriv Agreement as a sign of his good faith. This must be done, he stated, even if such a policy resulted in the "servitude" of the Ukraine's nobles—that is, even if their peasants continued to disobey them. He also feared the reaction of the masses, if provoked by the Commonwealth's troops, and begged to be informed before any expeditions were launched so that he and the nobility could find a pretext to flee to safety.

In the same letter, Kysil reported to the king that emissaries from Moldavia, Wallachia and Transylvania were with Khmel'nyts'kyi. His attention to Cossack diplomatic relations reflected the importance of the East European alliance system in deciding the success or failure of his role as commissioner. The Commonwealth's major concern was that Muscovy would intervene in the civil war.[36] A Muscovite mission to Warsaw, in March 1650, posed a number of demands to the Commonwealth and protested against infringements of the Peace of 1634. Complaining of mistakes in titulature in letters addressed to the tsar and of insults to Muscovy in books published in the Commonwealth, Grigorii Pushkin and other Muscovite emissaries demanded death sentences for those who offended the tsar and the burning of the offensive books. These predictable grievances were accompanied by the totally unexpected demand that the Commonwealth return Smolensk to Muscovy. To convince the Commonwealth's leaders that the demands were serious, the emissaries maintained further that they had negotiated with the Swedes to join them in a campaign and that they had under consideration responding favorably to Khmel'nyts'kyi's pleas for assistance.[37]

As soon as the Muscovite demands were made, the king and Ossoliński turned to their expert on Muscovite affairs, Kysil, for advice on dealing with the demands of the emissaries. On April 21, Kysil replied from Kiev with a long brief on foreign policy.[38] He asserted that a Muscovite-Swedish alliance would be a great danger, but was highly unlikely.[39] He dismissed Muscovite grievances about the border with an explanation that the Peace of 1634 contained a provision that forbade using the border as an excuse for hostilities. He asserted that questions of titulature had already been settled and, in any case, that complaints against the Commonwealth's officials and magnates were unfounded because it was the scribes who were guilty, not their masters. He rejected complaints of insults made in published works, because these had not been covered by the treaty.

After suggesting the obvious step of coming to terms with the Swedes and negotiating with the Tatars, Kysil discussed the problem of securing Khmel'nyts'kyi's loyalty. He requested that the king draft letters immediately to the Cossack hetman, assuring him that no royal troops would approach the Cossack lands. In discussing Orthodox Muscovy's threats, Kysil dealt with the issue of religious discontent among the Orthodox. He asserted that the government must renounce its support of the Uniates. He claimed that

> No one has worked for it [the union] and wishes it more than I, or has suffered as much from both sides, about which the Chancellor well [knows], but when the Lord God has allowed such times, it is already necessary to negotiate not the articles of faith, but rather the retention of Rus', and not to think of conversion.[40]

In conclusion, Kysil proposed defensive measures for Smolensk and the Chernihiv lands. He counseled that the Kingdom's armies go no further than the Horyn' and Sluch rivers and that after Khmel'nyts'kyi had become convinced of the benefits of serving the Commonwealth and not allying with Muscovy, Cossack forces be used on the Left Bank.

The king apparently followed Kysil's suggestion quickly and authorized negotiations to secure Khmel'nyts'kyi's loyalty to the Commonwealth in the event of war with Muscovy. In the next few months, the Commonwealth's government attempted to convince the hetman to undertake an attack on Muscovy. For a number of reasons, Khmel'nyts'kyi was willing to entertain this proposal. The Muscovite government had not offered real assistance to the Cossacks and seemed merely to be using the Cossack problem to wring concessions from the Commonwealth. Khmel'nyts'kyi was under pressure from the Tatars to embark on new campaigns. They had received favorable concessions at Zboriv from the Commonwealth. Consequently, they preferred to retain the *status quo* with the Commonwealth and to attack Muscovy.

Without certain allies, the hetman had to retain good relations with the Commonwealth. By showing interest in an expedition against Muscovy, he strengthened the position of the faction favoring peace with him.[41]

In mid-April, Kysil wrote to Khmel'nyts'kyi, attempting to win him over to an anti-Muscovy policy.[42] He described in detail the efforts of the "perfidious" Muscovites to ensnare the Commonwealth in a war with the Swedes and Transylvanians. These efforts had met with no success, he confided, so that if the Muscovites initiated hostilities, they would meet the combined Commonwealth, Zaporozhian and Tatar forces. The detail with which he described the Muscovite activities must have been intended to impress the hetman with how well-informed the authorities were and how capable they were of isolating Muscovite aggression.

Throughout the spring of 1650, Khmel'nyts'kyi avoided antagonizing either the Commonwealth or Muscovy. In March, he wrote to profess his loyalty to the king, although his pledge included a demand for the abolition of the union.[43] In May, the hetman responded favorably to Kysil's proposals for a united attack against Muscovy.[44] But while alarmed Muscovite border voevodas were filing reports that a Zaporozhian attack against Muscovy was imminent, Cossack delegates in Warsaw were convincing the Muscovite mission that Muscovy should stand firm and that their Orthodox brothers, the Zaporozhians, would stand behind them.[45]

In June, Kysil met with Khmel'nyts'kyi at Cherkasy to discuss the possibility of a Muscovite war.[46] Khmel'nyts'kyi assured Kysil at that time of the khan's support in a campaign against Muscovy, but he advised the Commonwealth to send remuneration to the Crimea before the Muscovites could buy the Tatars off with their tribute. Kysil believed that Khmel'nyts'kyi would be willing to attack Muscovy, and that if a decision were made to begin a war with Muscovy, the government should attempt to maintain Khmel'nyts'kyi's support with financial subsidies. In order to neutralize Muscovite efforts to win support in the Ukraine, Kysil proposed that the Cossack delegates should be sent away from Warsaw as soon as possible and that they should not be allowed to communicate with the Muscovite emissaries. Moreover, new concessions should be made to the Rus' faith and nation, and the king should issue universals to the nobility of the Kiev and Bratslav palatinates ordering them not to antagonize the Cossacks.

Kysil continued to fear Muscovite intervention throughout the summer of 1650. In fact, the Muscovite government sent new emissaries to Warsaw in July who were empowered to reconfirm the Eternal Peace of 1634. They also rescinded the demand for Smolensk and settled for minor concessions. Although the Muscovite government had not decided to support the Cossacks, it had threatened the Commonwealth with intervention. Muscovy had not yet abandoned its anti-Tatar policy in favor of a renewal of antagonism with the Commonwealth and had not yet succeeded in gaining allies against the Commonwealth. Consequently, Muscovy and Khmel'nyts'kyi continued to view each other with distrust. After 1650, however, it became clear that Muscovy was biding its time.[47]

As the Muscovite threat subsided, Ossoliński returned to his former plans for a war against the Ottoman Empire. He still hoped to direct Cossack restlessness away from the Commonwealth. Missions from the Balkan Christians to Warsaw in the winter of 1649–1650 rekindled interest in a Turkish war. In the spring of 1650, Venetian officials in Vienna and Papal Nuncio de Torres in Warsaw, with the knowledge and compliance of the king and Ossoliński, dispatched an emissary, Alberto Vimina, to Khmel'nyts'kyi to discuss Zaporozhian enlistment in the Venetian cause against the Ottomans. Kysil, as usual, served as an intermediary. The hetman received Vimina politely, but was unwilling to commit himself. He was, in fact, simultaneously contemplating acceptance of Ottoman protection to counterbalance the Commonwealth's influence in the Ukraine.[48]

Ossoliński's revival of the anti-Turkish plan came almost at the end of his political career. He died in August 1650, just as it was becoming clear that Khmel'nyts'kyi was deeply involved in negotiations with the Ottomans.[49] The death of the chancellor marked a turning point in Kysil's career. Andrzej Leszczyński, a Roman Catholic bishop, a proponent of a hardline policy against the Cossacks and a long-time political enemy of Kysil, replaced Ossoliński as chancellor. Kysil's power had derived from his oratorical and diplomatic skills and from his contacts among the Orthodox and the Cossacks, but it was Ossoliński who held the position of influence at court and who outmaneuvered their enemies through his contacts with the monarch and through the prerogatives of his position. After the chancellor's death, Kysil had no close powerful ally at the center of power. He continued to serve the king and Commonwealth in the Ukraine, but he had little voice in the formulation of policy in Warsaw. He was often not even informed about important decisions. Without the powerful Ossoliński as an ally, Kysil found it increasingly difficult to answer critics of accommodation with the Cossacks.

Just prior to the chancellor's death, in early August Kysil attended a conference at Irkliïv near Chyhyryn with Khmel'nyts'kyi.[50] In a report to Jan Kazimierz about the conference, he elaborated on the problems he had encountered because of the aggressive policies of both the Cossack colonel, Ivan Bohun, and the Crown hetman, Potocki.[51] He was especially concerned over the respect shown to the delegates from the Ottomans, which contrasted markedly with the disrespect shown the Commonwealth's delegation.[52] Kysil reported the measures which he had undertaken to counteract Ottoman influence. He even summoned Kosiv to the conference to dissuade Khmel'nyts'kyi, who had stated that he had one foot in the Commonwealth and the other in the Ottoman Empire. Although Khmel'nyts'kyi maintained that he did not wish to betray the king, he threatened to do so if Potocki's hostilities did not cease, if the Commonwealth's military camp were set closer than Lviv, and if churches were not returned to the Orthodox.

Although Kysil had advised making concessions to Khmel'nyts'kyi, in August 1650, the anti-Cossack party chose to insult the Zaporozhian hetman. Crown Hetman Potocki sent a letter to Khmel'nyts'kyi chastising him for his relations with foreign powers and demanding that the Cossacks relinquish control of much of the Chernihiv and Bratslav palatinates.[53] When Kysil wrote the king on August 24, he complained that Potocki's letter had unnecessarily antagonized Khmel'nyts'kyi and he pleaded with the monarch to reassure Khmel'nyts'kyi and to hold Potocki back.[54]

Despite the affront, Khmel'nyts'kyi was not yet ready to confront the Commonwealth directly because he was unsure of the outcome of his negotiations with the Ottomans. However, he and his Tatar allies did find a field of action. In September they turned against Moldavia rather than Muscovy. The Cossacks and Tatars launched their long-awaited campaign against Vasile Lupu, an ally of the Commonwealth. The successful outcome of the campaign allowed the hetman to negotiate the betrothal of Vasile Lupu's daughter, Roxanda, to his son, Tymish, and this action further established Cossack Ukraine as an independent polity with Khmel'nyts'kyi as its ruler.[55]

Neither Khmel'nyts'kyi nor the Commonwealth's government wanted the Moldavian expedition to set off renewed conflict between them. The hetman had publicly instructed his Cossacks to refrain from attacking the nobility on the Right Bank during the campaign, and Kysil issued explanations that the Cossack troop movement was not directed against the nobility or Crown forces.[56] In mid-September, he also counseled the Kievan dietine to await the outcome of events and further information from the king, Potocki and Khmel'nyts'kyi.[57]

Relations between Warsaw and Chyhyryn became more strained during the winter of 1650. Although Khmel'nyts'kyi's attempts to gain support from the Muscovite government had been unsuccessful, the

Commonwealth's government was concerned by his negotiations with Rákóczi of Transylvania and by his relations with the Porte. It sought to win the Tatars away from him. It was in the interest of Warsaw that Khmel'nyts'kyi be unable to launch a new campaign until a new Crown army could be raised, and Kysil was useful to allay the hetman's suspicions of duplicity on the part of the Commonwealth—suspicions that might drive him completely over to the Ottomans.[58]

Kysil realized how little support there was in Warsaw for his activities. In mid-October, he wrote the king to outline what he understood to be the dangers of current policies in the Ukraine.[59] He described the Cossack viewpoint and devoted considerable attention to claims that Potocki had broken the Zboriv Agreement. Cataloguing his attempts to dissuade Khmel'nyts'kyi from these views, which Kysil obviously felt had considerable justification, he described the consternation of the nobility in the Ukraine over the violence that would result if Potocki's troops neared the demarcation line. He openly declared that he hoped the upcoming Diet would renew the peace policy adopted by the last Diet, and he especially urged that a civil war be avoided until the implications of the Moldavian campaign could be studied. Comparing the present political situation with that of previous years, Kysil admitted that he was particularly disturbed by the Commonwealth's attempt to ally with the Tatars against the Cossacks. He feared that such a policy would drive Khmel'nyts'kyi into alliance with the Ottomans.

As usual, Kysil saw resolution of the religious issue as essential to ending the conflict. He maintained that in order to preserve the fatherland, the triumph of Orthodoxy must be accepted, and he complained that even those concessions made at the last Diet, particularly those pertaining to the Grand Duchy of Lithuania, were not being implemented. He claimed that he wished it were not necessary to abolish the Uniate church, and he recalled his own work of more than a decade with the former chancellor, Ossoliński, to further the interests of the union. But he insisted that the union created such antipathy among the Cossacks that they had refused to allow Latin-rite Catholic churches to function in territories under their control, and he argued that, for the good of the Catholic church, the Union of Brest should be sacrificed. He maintained that he could not justify losing Rus' for the sake of twenty or thirty Uniate churches. His solution was that those among the Uniate clergy and faithful who wished to remain Catholic should pass over to the Latin rite, since "to change from rite to rite is only to take off one robe and to put on another."

Kysil also proposed measures designed to lessen hostility between Cossacks and nobles over the use of lands in the Ukraine. He urged that the government grant more royal land to the registered Cossacks so that they might resettle from private to state lands, a policy that would reduce friction between the Cossacks and the nobility.

Kysil's estrangement from the dominant policy-makers in Warsaw became obvious in the following month. Without his knowledge, the king had dispatched a mission to the Tatars to draw them away from their alliance with the Cossacks and to ally them with the Commonwealth in a joint anti-Cossack campaign.[60] When the Tatars informed Khmel'nyts'kyi of this mission, he expressed his anger to Kysil. Kysil then protested to Warsaw that he had not been forewarned of the mission.[61] He described his attempts to convince Khmel'nyts'kyi that such a mission could not have been sent. The incident showed that Kysil could no longer be viewed as a negotiator who was informed of his government's policies.

In November, Kysil's declining influence was reflected in the hetman's treatment of him. Khmel'nyts'kyi wrote to the Volhynian dietine, denouncing governmental noncompliance with the guarantees made to the Orthodox church and castigating Kysil for having deceived the Zaporozhians into believing that their demands for freedom for the Orthodox church would be met.[62] Kysil, who had so long been the lay leader of Orthodoxy, found that the hetman challenged his position even before the Orthodox nobles of his ancestral palatinate. Thus, as the December Diet approached, Kysil was distrusted by both Khmel'nyts'kyi and the Commonwealth's policy makers.

The December Diet was intended to ready the Commonwealth for the inevitable conflict with Khmel'nyts'kyi.[63] Part of its objective was to resolve some of the outstanding points of friction with Muscovy. It was symbolic of the decline of his position that Kysil only went as far west as Hoshcha while the Diet met and he sent a votum outlining his views.[64] He analyzed the Commonwealth's policies toward the Cossacks after 1648, tracing the development of the pro-peace and pro-war policies toward the Zaporozhian hetman. He maintained that the pro-war policy had been unsuccessfully tried after Korsun' and had resulted in Pyliavtsi. After that failure, a pro-peace policy had been successfully followed under the Zboriv Agreement. Kysil's account was not entirely accurate, for he ignored the responsibility both he and Ossoliński bore for the disasters of 1648, which had taken place despite the pro-peace policy then being pursued.

Kysil described his mission during 1650 as twofold: to keep watch over the rebellious masses, and to continue the period of peace so that the nobles might return to their estates. He considered both tasks as having been successfully carried out, despite the numerous "difficulties" that he had encountered. His conclusions were that a comparison of the pro-peace and the pro-war policies illustrated the superiority of the former. He explained the deterioration of Cossack-Commonwealth relations as chiefly the result of actions of the pro-war party in the Commonwealth.

Kysil asked the members of the Diet to consider three factors. First, did they possess the means to destroy their internal and external enemies? He reminded them that, even if they were to win in battle, they could never achieve a final victory, because this would only be possible by annihilating the rebellious masses. Second, if sufficient forces were not at hand, then they must take into account the time necessary to raise them. Third, they must consider the danger of pushing the masses into the arms of the Turks and Tatars. He warned that rash action might result in the Commonwealth's border shifting from Ochakiv, on the Black Sea, to the Sluch River, in Volhynia. He pointed to the lack of military preparedness in the Commonwealth, the readiness of its enemies, and the threat of Tatar and Turkish intervention. His conclusion was that the Commonwealth should choose peace.

He further outlined the conditions of peace acceptable to the Cossacks. They expected the Kingdom's troops to be withdrawn from the borders of Cossack territory, the Zboriv Agreement to be upheld, important persons to be offered as hostages, bishoprics to be granted to the Orthodox, and Cossack administration and justice to be permitted in their territories. As difficult as he admitted these conditions were, Kysil did not view them as intolerable, and he explained how they could be met. He described only the last demand as one beyond the prescriptions of Zboriv and therefore to be rejected.

Kysil proposed a consolidation of the autonomous Orthodox Cossack entity established at Zboriv at a time when the government and most nobles were planning to defeat the Cossacks and to restore the pre-1648 political order and religious configuration. His letters were greeted with public derision at the Diet.[65] The seventeenth-century historian Kochowski describes the scene as one in which a great cry arose in the Diet, that

> as a goat will never be a ram, so a schismatic will not be an honest defender of Catholicism, and being of one faith with the peasant-rebels, he cannot defend Catholic liberties.[66]

Despite the hostility against Kysil at the Diet, he was appointed to a commission to negotiate with Khmel'nyts'kyi.[67] Although the commission was designed to stall until troops authorized by the Diet could be assembled, every effort was made to give it credibility, since in the event that the Cossacks were to gain the upper hand, the commission might be used to negotiate a new settlement. Bishop Andrzej Zaremba, one of the members, even consulted with de Torres concerning his moral obligations if ordered to make concessions on the religious issue.[68] Jan Kazimierz requested an opinion by the nuncio concerning the possibility of abolishing the union and transferring Uniates to the Latin rite. The nuncio was apprehensive of any major concessions on the religious issue, but he remained calm because he did not believe that the Commonwealth's leaders intended to negotiate.[69]

The careful measures to allay Khmel'nyts'kyi's suspicions apparently included the need to deceive Kysil as well. In mid-January, when secret Senate sessions were mapping out a war plan, Leszczyński wrote Kysil to convince him that the Commonwealth was truly interested in negotiating. Assuring Kysil of the king's and his own hope for peace, the chancellor promised Kysil to send both public and private instructions. Leszczyński confided:

> You will find out from these instructions that we honestly desire peace. One should not wonder that it has been deliberated to hire troops and call up a levy, because we have been destroyed a number of times.[70]

Jan Kazimierz also wrote to Kysil to convince him that the Commonwealth was negotiating in good faith.[71] The king particularly stressed the necessity of having Khmel'nyts'kyi renounce foreign alliances. However, he forbade Kysil to discuss the abolition of the Union of Brest, because he maintained it was impossible for him, as king, to order a Ruthenian to be Orthodox if he wished to be a Uniate. Finally, he asked Kysil for advice on the steps necessary for negotiations with Khmel'-nyts'kyi, but requested that he await his fellow commissioner, Stanisław Lanckoroński, before proceeding with negotiations.

Kysil remained at Hoshcha in January and February, and he took an active role in the negotiations.[72] His contacts were frequent with Marcin Kalinowski, the field hetman and palatine of Chernihiv, and Heronim Radziejowski, the vice-chancellor who had succeeded Leszczyński.[73] Kysil's strained relations with Hetman Potocki and Chancellor Leszczyński made a search for other allies imperative, and both Kalinowski and Radziejowski seemed likely allies for his policies in the Ukraine.[74] Although Kalinowski's attempt to regain the eastern lands appeared every bit as militant as Potocki's, the Cossacks regarded him as favorable to them.[75]

Kysil's correspondence with the newly appointed vice-chancellor had a more specific goal. Radziejowski was the favorite of the Queen Maria Ludwika, but in early 1651, the vice-chancellor was a new force at court, a relatively insignificant figure raised to a high post through his influence with the queen and through marriage to a wealthy heiress.[76] Kysil turned to him to secure the queen's support in retaining for himself the starostwo of Bohuslav.[77] In addition, Kysil thought Radziejowski a man who would listen to reason in solving the Cossack-Commonwealth conflict, including the religious issue. He expressed his frustration:

> But let us speak the truth. The churchmen divide us from both sides, otherwise things might remain peacefully in their place, and the Republic might be preserved. As I wrote to Khmel'nyts'kyi, of the Rus' faith there will be nothing, if we Ruthenians no longer exist.[78]

Kysil's attempts to cultivate ties with Kalinowski and Radziejowski had no long-term results. Within a year Radziejowski, who had indeed considered championing a new program of accommodation with the Cossacks, was deprived of his position because of conflicts with the monarch. Kalinowski's differences with Potocki did not signify a willingness to back Kysil and his pro-Cossack policy.

Kysil's search for political allies was particularly expedient after the final failure of his pro-peace policy.[79] By mid-March, he had to admit defeat in his efforts to prevent hostilities when border conflicts had developed into open warfare.[80] Hostilities brought much more than the failure of Kysil's attempts to find a peaceful solution of the situation. In the storming of Vinnytsia, his brother, Mykola Kysil, starosta of Cherkasy, was killed. Kysil's lament over his brother's death was expressed in a letter to his colleague, Maksymylian Bzhozovs'kyi, castellan of Kiev:

> My only dearest brother! Rather that I should lay in the tomb, because he was a blooming rose in my house, and I am already a thorn; he has laid down his life like his grandfather, his great-grandfather, the father of his great-grandfather, his two uncles, his two cousins. . . . But impious and jealous people in the Fatherland, who slandered the ancient honor, faith and glory of my house, are no less the cause that, of his own accord, my dearest brother was shamed at that place by their aspersions and sought death and sealed [his fate] with profusely flowing blood.[81]

Kysil expressed the wish that he himself would soon meet death. Struck by grief, he insisted that one day the correctness of his policies would be recognized, and he condemned those who were sending so many nobles to their deaths.

Deprived of an active role in government affairs and shaken by the loss of his brother and heir, Kysil was also pessimistic about the outcome of the war. By mid-April, he had withdrawn to his westernmost Volhynian estate of Hniino.[82] He had forfeited the confidence of Khmel'nyts'kyi as well, for the latter had charged that

The Lord Palatine guaranteed a commission and peace, but instead sent his brother with Kalinowski and Lanckoroński to make war. For this injustice his brother laid down his life.[83]

Kysil was even more concerned by the antipathy shown him by the nobility of the Commonwealth. As early as January 1651, he complained to the king about insults against him at the Diet.[84] He justified his activities and declared that he gave his advice not to further the interests of the "Ruthenian" faith, nor those of the peasantry and Cossacks, because as a Polish noble and senator, he had nothing in common with Cossacks and peasants. He wished only to fulfill his oath of loyalty to the Commonwealth and to maintain its unity.

Public attacks against him were becoming more common, and these were now dangerous, since he had no major protector at court. An anonymous diatribe warned of Kysil's treachery:

Poles, watch out, lest there be a snake in the grass or lest Kysil purloin a vessel through soft words. He has gotten the Palatinate of Kiev, and the sly man wants to get the Rus' Duchy.[85]

Rumors that circulated questioning his loyalty now resulted in action by the government. As early as February 1651 his requests to carry on negotiations without waiting for the full commission to assemble were denied, apparently because Kysil was held in suspicion for his opinions, especially for his complaints against Potocki.[86]

After over a year of intricate diplomatic maneuverings, the two opponents had not changed the configuration of alliances. The Commonwealth had been unable to win away the Tatars from their alliance with Khmel'nyts'kyi, but Khmel'nyts'kyi had not succeeded in gaining outright Ottoman assistance through his offers to become a vassal, or in drawing the Transylvanians into the struggle. There had, however, been major changes within the Commonwealth. The Diet had authorized the necessary expenditures to field a well-equipped army and had recruited regular troops at home and abroad. The return of the hetmans had solved the confusion over military leadership and had even permitted better coordination with private armies such as that of Wiśniowiecki, as well as with the Lithuanian army led by Janusz Radziwiłł. Therefore, the Crown army, which met the combined Cossack-Tatar forces at Berestechko in Volhynia, represented the maximum effort of which the Commonwealth was capable. For three days in June the battle swayed back and forth; finally, despite their desperate resistance, the Cossacks were defeated. Seeing the battle as lost, Khan Islam Girey accepted Polish bribes and retreated even before the final defeat. The Battle of Berestechko appeared to be a final vindication of the pro-war policy.[87]

For a time the Cossacks were even unsure whether Khmel'nyts'kyi was alive. With troops of the Grand Duchy of Lithuania advancing upon, and then taking, Kiev, the triumph of the Commonwealth armies seemed complete. In the aftermath of the victory at Berestechko, the confident pro-war party even excluded Kysil from Senate sessions.[88]

Although Kysil had been incorrect about the outcome of open battle, his conviction that the Commonwealth could not subdue the enemy unless it annihilated a large segment of the population of the Ukraine proved to be accurate. Two factors made a complete military conquest impossible. First, Khmel'nyts'kyi was not captured, and he easily replenished his forces with Cossacks and peasants who feared the victorious armies of the Commonwealth. Second, there was not enough money to pay the Commonwealth's army for an extended campaign. Faced with disease and the onset of autumn in a hostile and denuded countryside, the Commonwealth military command knew that a quick resolution of the Cossack problem was necessary. The death of Wiśniowiecki during the campaign and the willingness of the aged and sickly Potocki to settle for less than total victory made possible a favorable response to Khmel'nyts'kyi's peace overture in September.[89]

As always, when negotiations between the Commonwealth and the Cossacks were contemplated, both sides valued Kysil's talents. Thus, Khmel'nyts'kyi addressed his proposals for peace not only to Potocki, but also to Kysil.[90] Potocki requested Kysil's assistance, and Kysil served well in the dangerous series of missions to the Cossacks. On one occasion, as the peace negotiators were returning from Khmel'-nyts'kyi's camp, they were attacked by peasants and Tatars, and Kysil lost 18,000 złoty in gold, silver and equipage, and very nearly lost his life as well.[91]

The negotiations dealt with the size of the new Cossack register, the alliance with the Tatars, the stationing of troops in the Ukraine and private property rights. Kysil faced a difficult task, for he had to convince the Cossack negotiators to accept the harsh demands imposed by the victors. The Bila Tserkva Agreement, signed in September 1651, provided for a register of only 20,000 Cossacks, who would be permitted to live only on royal lands of the Kievan palatinate. The register was to be completed by Christmas. Royal troops were not to be stationed in the Cossack military centers; the nobility was to return to its lands, but was to hold off collection of dues until the new register was completed; the Orthodox church was guaranteed its privileges; amnesties were extended to rebels; Jews were to have the right to return to their tax farms and leaseholds; if the Tatars did not become an ally of the Commonwealth, the Zaporozhians were to break with them; and in the capital and judicial center of Kiev, as few Zaporozhians as possible were to be accepted into the new register.[92]

As a result of the Bila Tserkva Agreement, Kysil was obligated to return once again to the capital of his palatinate, albeit a capital in ruins after the Lithuanian occupation. He could expect the eventual restoration of his personal estates. Nevertheless, it was unlikely that the Bila Tserkva Agreement could be easily imposed upon a hostile Ukrainian populace. Moreover, the Commonwealth's victory made it unlikely that the agreement would be accepted by its nobility as a final resolution of the conflict.

The Last Years

By early October, Kysil had taken up residence in the Dnieper Ukraine as a guarantor of the peace and as an overseer of compliance with the articles of the Bila Tserkva Agreement. He also began to report to Potocki on the course of his activities.[93] Although the overall tone of his letters was optimistic, Kysil admitted difficulties he had encountered in reestablishing the Commonwealth administration, particularly on the Left Bank. The Chernihiv palatinate was an especially volatile area, since under the terms of the Bila Tserkva Agreement, all Cossacks fortunate enough to be included in the register had to retire to the Kievan palatinate, and the Chernihiv palatinate was to be returned to the Commonwealth's administration and nobility. However, unlike the situation in the Bratslav palatinate, there were no royal troops present to enforce this provision. Kysil asserted that the Cossacks excluded from the register were preparing to emigrate to Muscovite territories. Although this migration would entail a loss to the economy of the area, Kysil thought it preferable to the trouble that unregistered Cossacks could cause on the Left Bank.

In early October, Khmel'nyts'kyi avowed his determination to enforce the Bila Tserkva Agreement and his satisfaction with Kysil's appointment as intermediary.[94] Whatever his long-term plans, Khmel'nyts'kyi was in no position, in the autumn and winter of 1651–1652, to provoke a confrontation with the Commonwealth armies. During the winter the Cossacks were at their greatest disadvantage in fighting. In addition, the passing of time could only further disorganize and disperse the Crown and Lithuanian armies. Khmel'nyts'kyi found it difficult, however, to accede to the Crown hetmans' demands. Potocki, Field Hetman Kalinowski and Kysil had to provision the Crown armies and to complete the register of 20,000 Cossacks by Christmas. They also had to ensure that the Cossacks migrated to the royal lands of the Kievan palatinate, and that the nobility returned to the eastern lands unhindered. Khmel'nyts'kyi had to force these measures on a resentful people.

Jan Kazimierz and even the Chancellor Leszczyński were convinced that ratifying the agreement, at least as a temporary compromise, was necessary because the Commonwealth was unable to maintain an army for a longer period of time.[95] The king would have to persuade the Diet scheduled to convene in January to confirm the agreement, yet only immediate and tangible implementation in the Ukraine could overcome the nobility's antagonism. Rapid compliance with these articles was exactly what Khmel'nyts'kyi did not want. Rebellions against the terms of the agreement and mutinous challenges to his authority had already broken out.[96] The death of Potocki, who had negotiated the agreement and was committed to making it succeed, further worsened the situation.[97] Although his successor, Field Hetman Kalinowski, had formerly had the reputation of being the more moderate of the two hetmans toward the Cossacks, he now refused to allow Khmel'nyts'kyi any latitude in implementing the agreement, despite the threats to the authority of Hetman Khmel'nyts'kyi among the Cossack ranks.

From November through May, Kysil resided in Kiev and attempted to facilitate rapid Cossack compliance with the Bila Tserkva Agreement. He served as an intermediary between Khmel'nyts'kyi and Field Hetman Kalinowski, and was in close contact with the Lithuanian Field Hetman Janusz Radziwiłł.[98] Khmel'nyts'kyi assured Kysil of his intention to compile the register as soon as possible, but claimed that the murder of Colonel Mykhailo Hromyka of Bila Tserkva and the rebellion of the Colonel Lukia Mozyria of Korsun' were retarding the pace of the compilation.[99] In order to gain time the Cossack hetman also resorted to subterfuges: he interpreted the Christmas deadline to mean the "Ruthenian" Christmas (i.e., ten days later), and pleaded for a delay in the order that the Cossacks migrate to the Kievan palatinate.

Kysil's faith in, and distrust of, Khmel'nyts'kyi alternated in rapid succession throughout these months. Always cautious, he urged Hetman Kalinowski not to provoke the masses to a desperate resistance.[100] On January 5, 1652, Kysil wrote to Kalinowski, urging him to be patient with tardy registers and the failure of the Cossacks to break with the Tatars.[101] Proposing a policy of peaceful vigilance, he maintained that by accepting Khmel'nyts'kyi's request to limit the presence of the Crown army on the Left Bank to the Chernihiv palatinate, a tactical advantage could be gained without inciting the populace to warfare.[102] Therefore, writing to Leszczyński on January 11, Kysil recommended

Khmel'nyts'kyi's proposal, that the army confine its activities to Chernihiv and not enter the "farther" Ukraine (Kievan palatinate), be accepted.[103] On his part Khmel'nyts'kyi promised to break with the Tatars
as soon as possible, but could not do so at present because of pressure
from the masses. Kysil was uncertain of the truth of this, but found
considerable evidence supporting it. Therefore, Kysil sought to convince Leszczyński that the peace policy should be pursued.

As news of massive dissatisfaction with the Bila Tserkva Agreement
in the Ukraine and the reluctance of Khmel'nyts'kyi to break with his
Tatar allies reached Warsaw, the king increasingly became interested in
using the Diet called for January 1652 to built up the army.[104] Late in
December, the king addressed a threatening letter to Khmel'nyts'kyi
demanding immediate compliance with the Bila Tserkva terms and a
break with the Tatars. The hetman wrote to Kysil of the "bitter and
unpalatable dishes" that the king had served him and claimed them to
be unjustified.[105] He, in turn, threatened that, while he did not wish
events to take this course, he was obliged to respond by finding appropriate means. He boasted that he need not seek Tatars in the open
steppe, but that they would of their own accord come to him, and that
he only awaited the Diet's outcome to take final action. In response to
the first indication of the Commonwealth's new hard-line policy toward
Cossack relations with the Tatars in a universal from Hetman Kalinowski, Kysil complained that although messages were exchanged
almost daily between Kiev and Kalinowski's headquarters, he was not
being kept informed.[106] While he doubted the likelihood of a Tatar
attack, and thought rather that Tatar movements were an internal
matter of preparation for a new campaign against Moldavia, he was
shocked that the king and fatherland for whom he had gathered so much
information had not informed him of new policies.

On January 23, Kysil sent a sharp note to the king himself.[107] He
feared that his loyalty was again being questioned, and that he was being
called a traitor to the fatherland. Never modest in spelling out his
services, he compared his situation to a stigmatic. He stated that the
hard-line letters from the king had caused considerable difficulty, and
that whenever Khmel'nyts'kyi had asked for advice, he had always
urged calm, although he had no idea what action the Cossacks would
take. He enclosed Khmel'nyts'kyi's letter, in which the hetman vowed
to seek Tatar assistance. He pointed out that the willingness of the
Tatars to begin new campaigns, as well as rumors that the Diet would
take an anti-Cossack stance, created an unfavorable climate for negotiation. Referring to dissension within the Cossack camp, Kysil asserted his
faith in Khmel'nyts'kyi and his surprise that royal troops had not

intervened in support of the hetman against the Cossack rebels. Kysil predicted that the Cossack emissaries to the king might be recalled.

If the king's letters and instructions were prompted by fear of an imminent Cossack-Tatar attack, they overestimated Khmel'nyts'kyi's readiness to begin a new war. Instead, Khmel'nyts'kyi had a new register delivered to Kysil, and on February 24, Kysil could write to the king emphasizing the success of the peace policy—the register had been compiled, Cossack delegates had been sent to the Diet, and troops had been stationed beyond the Dnieper.[108] Kysil cited, as another proof of the success of the peace program, the large number of nobles who had been able to return to their estates.

Still dedicated to a peaceful resolution of the conflict, Kysil described the situation as one in which achievements must be carefully tended and preserved. He believed that the best guarantee of peace was a large army maintained in the Bratslav palatinate, far from the Cossack land, and he proposed that the troops now stationed beyond the Dnieper be removed. He advised that provisions for the troops be obtained from the entire Kingdom, since the Ukrainian palatinates were already completely devastated. According to Kysil, Khmel'nyts'kyi should be treated well, in order to encourage dissension with the Tatars, after which a Cossack campaign against the Tatars or Turks might be incited. Kysil argued that if the Cossacks were assured of their ancient privileges, the masses would understand that no possibility existed of securing Cossack assistance in a rebellion. The Tatars, always in search of loot, would soon enough attack either the Ukraine or Muscovy, leading inevitably to Cossack attempts to obtain part of the spoils, and thus to hostilities between them. The Crown troops could then intervene and the long-planned campaign against the Muslim states could be launched. Thus, despite the tremendous changes of the past four years, Kysil clung to the program he had espoused in the reign of Władysław IV.

At least parts of Kysil's long-standing solution for the Commonwealth's Cossack problem were in accord with the international situation at the time. After the Bila Tserkva Agreement, representatives of the Venetian Republic, which was still involved in its lengthy struggle against the Ottoman Empire, offered to provide a substantial subsidy to engage the Zaporozhians in a war against the Turks. In response to Venetian inquiries, during the winter of 1651–1652, the government asked Kysil to investigate the acceptability of such a proposal among the Cossacks. Kysil reported that 100,000 florins would secure Cossack support, and the Venetians agreed to this sum. In the early months of 1652, the Venetian government and Papal Nuncio de Torres treated the possibility of Cossack assistance against the Turks as a matter of great importance.[109]

Khmel'nyts'kyi, willing to entertain this proposal, in March of 1652 instructed Semen Savych, the colonel of Kaniv, to meet with Kysil to discuss the conditions under which the Cossacks could begin an anti-Turkish campaign.[110] He, however, pointed out the need for preparation before the campaign could be launched. In fact, this may have been only a delaying tactic until a new campaign could be initiated against the Commonwealth. Khmel'nyts'kyi emphasized the privations the Host had endured through the winter, the need to build boats, and the necessity of gathering an adequate military force to accompany the naval expedition. He also expressed his fears about the lack of preparation of the Crown's army. The answer from the Cossack Council, which Khmel'nyts'kyi signed, avowed the desire to campaign against the "pagans" and to retain the trust of the king, but stalled for time.

However, the anti-Turkish war plans had little chance for success. Despite the progress in Cossack compliance with the peace provisions, the Diet which met from January to March refused even to confirm the Bila Tserkva Agreement. The meeting was extremely stormy, since the delegates seemed united only in their opposition to Bila Tserkva, and on February 18 they passed a resolution condemning the Bila Tserkva commissioners because the Cossack register exceeded the number suggested by the last Diet. For the most part, other issues, above all the struggle between the royalist faction and the supporters of the deposed Vice Chancellor Radziejowski, dominated the proceedings. Despite the Diet's refusal to confirm peace with the Cossacks, it passed no measures to provide for the Commonwealth's defense. For the first time in the history of the Commonwealth, the protest, or *liberum veto,* of one of the delegates broke the Diet. The spring Diet of 1652 demonstrated not only the inability of the Commonwealth's governing structure to deal with the Cossack problem, but also the complete paralysis of the government.[111]

The Bila Tserkva Agreement remained unconfirmed, and the Cossack delegates who brought the new register to the Diet received only royal privileges: an answer to Cossack "requests" on religious grievances, confirmation of Khmel'nyts'kyi's control of Chyhyryn, and permission to build boats. The privileges mentioned a figure of 20,000 for the Zaporozhian army and assured the Cossacks of their right to the Trekhtymiriv hospital, but these privileges were not confirmed by the Diet.[112]

Even after the conclusion of the first Diet of 1652, Kysil did not accept the inevitability of the outbreak of hostilities. Although March and April were marked by bitter conflicts between the Polish troops and the Ukrainian Cossacks and populace, Khmel'nyts'kyi allayed Kysil's apprehensions by cooperating in late April in a joint Commonwealth-Cossack judicial commission in Korsun'.[113] When Kysil wrote to Leszczyński on May 1, he praised Khmel'nyts'kyi's efforts to suppress disturbances among the Cossack masses.[114] In order to secure peace, Kysil proposed that Crown troops be removed from the Left Bank and he predicted that peace would encourage the return of refugees who had fled to Muscovy because of dissatisfaction with the Bila Tserkva Agreement. Resurrecting his proposals of the 1630s, he suggested that a supervisor for the Kingdom's troops be stationed in the Bratslav and Podillia palatinates and that this supervisor negotiate with the Zaporozhian hetman through an assistant in the Dnieper lands. He considered a permanent army of 8,000 to 10,000 adequate, as long as both the nobility and the royal commissioners were required by the Diet to live in the Dnieper lands, and were not absentee officials.

Kysil, who had hoped to be present at a new Diet scheduled for late July, saw the fulfillment of these terms as the best guarantee of peace. In any event, he emphasized that the troops raised by that Diet could not possibly take the field until November—too close to the winter season to begin a campaign. Kysil was especially concerned that the troops would be without food. To facilitate the implementation of his suggestions, Kysil requested letters and universals from the king to the Zaporozhian hetman.

As so often before, Kysil overestimated the willingness of the opposing sides to compromise. In early 1652, Khmel'nyts'kyi once again turned to Muscovy to secure protection against the Commonwealth and to his Tatar allies, who were eager for a new campaign. However, the disorderly conduct of the famine-stricken army enraged the Ukrainian populace, and Hetman Kalinowski, having given up any hope of peace, filed numerous reports that contradicted those of Kysil.[115]

In May 1652, a council of Cossack colonels supported Khmel'nyts'kyi's decision to wage campaign against Moldavia, enforcing Hospodar Vasile Lupu's agreement to allow his daughter, Roxanda, to marry Khmel'nyts'kyi's son.[116] Until that time, the hospodar had pursued a policy favorable to the Commonwealth. Roxanda's hand in marriage was much sought after by numerous magnates, including Dymitr Wiśniowiecki and possibly the elderly Hetman Kalinowski himself.[117] In order to prevent the marriage with Tymish, Kalinowski attempted to block the routes of the Cossack and Tatar detachments marching on Moldavia. Grossly underestimating the strength of his enemy, Kalinowski led the Crown troops stationed in Bratslav and Podillia to a total defeat at Batih at the end of June 1652. Kalinowski, as well as numerous other magnates and nobles, died in the battle.[118]

However unrealistic Kysil's plans for an accommodation with the Cossacks may have seemed, his appraisal of the Commonwealth's military strength had proven accurate. In the debacle of the military campaign, Kysil had to flee from Kiev for the last time. The Diet which assembled in late July attempted to raise an army against the triumphant Cossack forces.[119] Kysil's reports on the causes of the Batih debacle were a major source of information to the Diet delegates on the military situation in the Ukraine, but he did not attend the Diet in person.[120]

Little is known about Kysil's activities after Batih. Although that military disaster made war inevitable, the second Diet of 1652 failed to raise a new army. Nevertheless, in the early months of 1653, a series of small offensives were launched against the Cossack forces by the new Crown hetman, Stanisław Potocki. Meanwhile, the Cossack missions to Muscovy finally yielded political results, for in March 1653, the Muscovite authorities decided to take the Zaporozhians under the tsar's protection. The Commonwealth's leaders were no more united than in the past. Janusz Radziwiłł and a group of Lithuanian senators formed a new peace party as well as a senatorial council called in Hrodna in February 1653, but decisions were delayed until the Diet met in March at Brest. Whether or not Kysil attended the consultation session is not known, but he was present at the late March–early April Diet.[121] Although the Diet was prolonged, the king still could not secure substantial funds for armament.[122]

Kysil died soon after the Diet in Brest. His will, inscribed in the books of the Brest palatinate, is testimony both to his successes and to his failures.[123] Although he left the bulk of his estates in the Volhynian, Kievan and Chernihiv palatinates to his wife for use during her lifetime, Kysil wished that they be divided eventually among his numerous relatives in both the Volhynian and Lithuanian branches of the family.[124] Despite the considerable debts that he mentions and the loss of the real centers of his wealth, the forests of Chernihiv, Kysil left his family considerable property; nonetheless, the Kysils were never to rise to prominence again.[125]

Kysil's will is important as his last statement on the religious and political problems of the period. He maintained, "I have lived in the ancient Orthodox Catholic religion of my Mother, the Holy Eastern Church of God, in which my ancestors have remained immutably for six hundred years, and in which I now wish to remain to my last breath." However, he appealed both to saints Western and Eastern to intercede for his salvation. He again called for the unity of the nations and religions in the Commonwealth, and justified his own activities once more:

I throw my unworthy endeavors which were always faithful to bringing peace to peoples and religions, and therefore to the fatherland, and all my numerous sufferings and losses of health and fortune undergone on these occasions, at the feet of God's Majesty, before whom all secrets will be revealed and each will render an accounting of acts and deeds. I forgive everyone's envy and hatred and detraction of loyal and industrious services, those who have in any way hurt me who was innocent.[126]

In contrast to 1648–1649, when the entire Commonwealth and many foreign powers carefully followed Kysil's statement and actions, by 1653 few saw his passing as affecting the course of events. Comment about Kysil's death centered on speculation as to whom he had really served[127] The new papal nuncio, Pietro Vidoni, perhaps best summarized Kysil's contemporaries' discomfort with his views. Describing Kysil's death in a report to Rome, he said:

He died in accordance with the way he lived. Just as it was never possible to be sure whether he was a traitor or a true son of the Fatherland, so in death it is not known whether he died a member of the Holy Church or a schismatic.[128]

To the end Kysil had tried to reconcile the unreconcilable—he refused to give the Jesuit fathers who surrounded his deathbed a clear sign that he renounced Orthodoxy in favor of Catholicism. Buried in his ancestral estate in Nyzkynychi, in the church he had erected, rather than in his capital of Kiev, Kysil returned to the provincial backwater from which he came. With him was buried the old Ruthenian nobility of the Commonwealth.

Chapter 8

The Unresolved Dilemma

In the year of Kysil's death, the Cossack captain of Hlukhiv Company, Pylyp Umanets' responded to the Muscovite voevoda of Sevsk, who had rebuked him for writing directly to so highly placed a Muscovite official:

> Your Grace wrote to us not long ago in a charter, that it is not proper for simple people to write to a voevoda. We, by the Grace of God, are not now simple, but we are knights of the Zaporozhian Host. It is true that the now deceased great ambassador of the Kingdom, Adam Kysil, enacted with the Great Sovereign and the great boyars that it is only permitted for palatines, starostas, judges, and land and castle scribes to correspond with voevodas. And now with us, by the Grace of God, as long as it be his Holy Will, here in the whole Siverian land, there is no palatine, no starosta, no judge, no scribe. God grant that the lord Bohdan Khmel'nyts'kyi, hetman of the entire Zaporozhian Host, be in good health. The lord colonel is now in our land the palatine, the captain–the starosta, and the otaman (horodovyi)–the judge.[1]

Umanets' described the new political order in the Ukraine which had emerged after the Cossack uprising swept away the rule of the Commonwealth. Subsequently the Commonwealth continued to fill the post of palatine of Kiev, as it did all the posts of the lost lands of the Kievan and Chernihiv palatinates, but a Kievan palatine never took up residence in the city. The hill on which the palatine's castle had stood became known as the "Kysilivka," in memory of the last of the Commonwealth's resident palatines of Kiev.[2]

The Commonwealth refused to accept loss of control over the Ukrainian lands and, less than a year after Kysil's death, this policy forced Khmel'nyts'kyi to sign the Pereiaslav Agreement with Muscovy. The legal definition of the agreement (submission, incorporation, protectorate, military alliance) has been the subject of considerable dispute.[3] Whatever Khmel'nyts'kyi's intentions were, the Pereiaslav Agreement brought the Muscovites fully into the conflict and gave the Muscovite tsar claims to sovereignty over the Ukraine.

After 1654, the fledgling Cossack Ukrainian state became a center of attention and dispute in the foreign policies of Sweden, Muscovy, the Commonwealth, and the Ottoman Empire. New circumstances changed the political alliance system: the Commonwealth allied with the Tatars; Sweden, Transylvania, and Muscovy invaded the Commonwealth's territories; and Lithuanian leaders betrayed the Kingdom of Poland. At the center of the vortex stood the founder of the Hetmanate, the wily diplomat Bohdan Khmel'nyts'kyi. Although he was dissatisfied with his relation with Muscovy, he remained determined to destroy permanently the power of the Commonwealth in the Ukraine. Just before his death in 1657, his anger over the Muscovite truce with the Commonwealth in 1656 led him to explore breaking his link to the tsar and entering into a closer relationship with Sweden.

Only after Khmel'nyts'kyi's death did the leadership of the Hetmanate and the Commonwealth seek to return to the path of accommodation that Kysil had espoused. Five years after his death, another Ukrainian magnate, Iurii Nemyrych (Jerzy Niemirycz), and another Zaporozhian hetman, Ivan Vyhovs'kyi, negotiated the Treaty of Hadiach with the Warsaw government. Far surpassing the limited provisions of the Zboriv Agreement, Hadiach provided for the restructuring of the Commonwealth into a triune state, including a Rus' Principality or Duchy comprising the Kiev, Bratslav, and Chernihiv palatinates. The agreement recognized the abolition of the Union of Brest in the Rus' Principality, assured toleration for Orthodoxy throughout the Commonwealth, granted Senate seats to the metropolitan and three bishops, and reserved some of the major posts in the Rus' Principality for Orthodox nobles. Not only was a Cossack register of 30,000 men to be paid by the government, but the Zaporozhian hetman was to command a standing army of 10,000 men. The Hadiach Agreement recognized the Kiev Orthodox school as an academy and allowed for the establishment of another Orthodox higher institution in the Principality. Most important, one hundred men from each Cossack regiment were to be ennobled. In short, the Hadiach Agreement was a reform of the Union of Lublin that granted privileges to a Cossack political entity largely by including Cossack elements in the nobility. The Zaporozhian polity was to be integrated into the Commonwealth's institutions and the Zaporozhian hetman was to be named palatine of Kiev. The new polity was to represent Rus' religious and national interests, although provisions such as toleration of Orthodoxy and the bishops' entry into the Senate provided for Rus' interests in the other Ukrainian and Belorussian lands.[4]

Although substantial segments of the Commonwealth's nobility opposed the compromise and Rome attempted to save the position of the Uniate church, the Diet ratified the Hadiach Agreement. However, Vyhovs'kyi and Nemyrych did not have the power or authority to secure the rank-and-file Cossacks' acceptance of a new link with Poland or to eject Muscovy from Ukrainian internal affairs. The aftermath of the Hadiach policy, a period known as the "Ruin," was a turbulent time in which the Commonwealth, Muscovy, Crimea, and the Ottoman Empire supported rival Zaporozhian hetmans. The order which Khmel'nyts'kyi had forged during his long hetmancy was destroyed in endless dissensions and wars, and the Zaporozhian hetmans were unable to avoid the division of the Hetmanate's territories along the Dnieper between the Commonwealth and Muscovy in 1667, and the subsequent recognition of this division as permanent in 1686.[5]

Proponents of the Hadiach tradition have seen it as a solution to the Commonwealth's structural flaws, maintaining that it would have preserved a united Cossack Rus'-Ukraine had it not, regrettably, been enacted too late. They assert that if only the solution of a Ruthenian Principality had been initiated at the time of the Union of Lublin or at the beginning of the Khmel'nyts'kyi uprising, the Commonwealth would have been strengthened and spared the ruinous mid-century wars and the Ukraine would have become an equal partner in a viable federation. Instead, they maintain, the decade of war weakened the power of the Commonwealth, decimated the nobility of the Ukrainian lands, and embittered the rank-and-file Cossacks and masses against Polish rule. This made the success of the Hadiach Agreement impossible.[6]

Such views overlook basic problems.[7] A Hadiach solution could not have been undertaken in 1569 and the decades that followed because no articulate body of public opinion in the Ukraine demanded the creation of a new Ruthenian political entity. It would have been a farsighted policy indeed that could have endowed the Ukraine with a political structure that its political elite had not yet even envisioned. The Commonwealth's nobility, therefore, had no potential partner with which it might form a Rus' polity. The nobility of the Ukrainian territories was assimilating into the Kingdom's nobility and was not even united in its perception of issues such as the religious controversy.

The Zaporozhian Host was no more likely a prospect as a suitable partner.[8] Before 1648, the Host was interested in preserving the peculiarities of the social and political structure of the Dnieper lands as a means of ensuring the continuation of its own privileged status. Cossack issues became intertwined with religious grievances and the discontent of the peasantry in the first half of the century, but it was only gradually, after 1648, that the Cossacks became a ruling order, and the leadership of the officers of the Host a conscious elite of a Rus' political entity.[9] Only the inability of the Commonwealth to suppress the uprising, the visible moderating effects which administration had on the Host's leadership and the influx of a considerable number of nobles (including Vyhovs'kyi) into the Cossack army and administration made recognition of the Cossack elite possible. Most important, the *de facto* existence of a Rus' state under Khmel'nyts'kyi from 1648 to 1657 gave the Cossack leadership a legitimacy undreamed of in 1648.

Yet, in explaining why the Hadiach plan finally arose, the role of the individual remains important. The events of the period were, of course, rooted in long-term socioeconomic and political processes, but at a time when society was ready to consider a new relationship, the inspiration for the Hadiach Agreement came to a considerable degree from Iurii Nemyrych, a magnate who sided with the Cossacks. It is inevitable to question why the program of a separate Rus'-Cossack Principality within the Commonwealth came from Nemyrych, and not Kysil. Kysil, after all, was a major statesman of the first half of the century specializing in Ukrainian affairs. He was an adherent of the Eastern church and was deeply involved in resolving religious controversy. He was close to Kosiv and the other clerical leaders who had rekindled interest in Rus' history. He enjoyed authority and respect among almost all the major elements of Ukrainian society, the Orthodox nobility whom he had led at so many Diets, the hierarchy and clergy with whom he had worked closely, and the Zaporozhian Cossack officer class who saw him as a moderate on Cossack affairs. He had influence with the ruling circles of government and was trusted by the papacy. Kysil, moreover, was certainly aware of the concept of creating a Rus' Principality. In early 1648, he warned the Polish authorities that Khmel'nyts'kyi sought to form a Rus' Principality and contemporaries charged Kysil with seeking to set himself up as the head of a restored Rus' state, and even of having encouraged Khmel'nyts'kyi's ambitions.

Kysil, however, never made any far-reaching proposal comparable to the Hadiach Agreement. Instead, the plan came from Nemyrych, a man who, although from a wealthy and noble family of the Kievan palatinate, had been brought up as an Antitrinitarian Protestant, had no long-term contacts with the Orthodox hierarchy or Zaporozhian Host, and who, because of his "heretical" beliefs, was suspect to both Orthodox and Catholics—particularly since his "blasphemies" had caused political controversy in the 1640s.[10]

Timing was, of course, extemely important. Certainly the difficulties which Kysil faced in securing the acceptance of the Zboriv and Bila Tserkva articles show that no one would have been ready to consider seriously the creation of a separate political entity in the Dnieper Ukrainian lands in the late 1640s and early 1650s. By the late-1650s, when Nemyrych was politically active, the necessity for compromise was more universally recognized. In addition the virtual dissolution of the Commonwealth during the "Deluge," which included magnates siding with foreign powers, had greatly changed concepts of what was permissible for a magnate to plan and for the Commonwealth to entertain.

But it is also the difference in character, background, and experience which helps explain why Nemyrych offered bold solutions while Kysil limited himself to piecemeal measures. Nemyrych—the scion of a magnate family, born into one of the most intellectual of faiths, the Polish Antitrinitarians, educated at the best European universities, author of historical, literary, and poetic works—displayed brilliance, inventiveness, as well as inconstancy in his career. His unique 1658 tract, arguing that the Protestants could find a resolution of their problems of conscience in the Orthodox church, reflected issues and a creativeness of approach that is lacking in Kysil's monotonous, legalistic discussions on the Eastern church.[11]

Kysil was a man of more humble origin, who had achieved considerable success by careful and cautious service. His loyalty to the system in which he achieved success was not a trait which lent itself to daring and dramatic thought. For all his much-acclaimed eloquence, the perception of his political commentary, and his pragmatic ability to analyze situations and arrive at compromises, Kysil was not an original thinker, or an independent, daring politician. The outlines of his career show the remarkable consistency of his policies concerning major domestic and foreign policy issues, tempered at times to fit changes in circumstances. His basic conservative and stable world view led him to favor mediation and compromise whenever possible. Such were his programs about the Rus' church, the customs and rights of the incorporation lands, recognition of Cossack power, and settlement of outstanding grievances with Muscovy. Even Kysil's most daring plan, the anti-Turkish alliance, was an attempt to settle the two major sources of instability in the Ukraine, Tatar raids and Zaporozhian turbulence. He sought to break Tatar power and to harness the turbulence of the Zaporozhians by directing them outward. Inclusion of the Ottomans in the war plans was based on the sovereign's known desire to embark upon such an enterprise, the cooperation of Muscovy, and an international situation in which the Commonwealth could obtain military and financial support from Venice. Even if Kysil did first propose the Turkish war plan, he did not put it forth as a new idea, but merely asserted that the time was right for a program which had long been considered.

To maintain that Kysil was not an innovative thinker does not detract from his stature as a statesman. For in the face of the failures of the Commonwealth's policies in the Ukraine during the first half of the seventeenth century, Kysil's proposals displayed a considerable grasp of reality and showed the gravity of the area's problems and discontent. Yet, though Kysil's programs provided an alternative to the disaster course the Commonwealth was on in its policy in the Ukraine, the constant rebuffs and setbacks they encountered demonstrated that he lacked the consensus for a satisfactory resolution of the problem of the Eastern church and that the Commonwealth was unable to formulate a consistent foreign policy or to accept a compromise solution on the Cossack presence in the Ukraine. His programs were always patchwork solutions in the face of great pressures. As such, they disintegrated rapidly as soon as danger passed. But he, of course, never wielded sufficient power, even during the height of his alliance with Ossoliński, to impose his policies.

Kysil's stature as a statesman, in the end, must be measured in terms of the effectiveness and practicality of his policies. Did he pursue programs which had a reasonable chance of success, given the attitudes and power configuration of the time? This question is of particular importance for the Cossack issue during the Khmel'nyts'kyi period—a time when Kysil had decisive influence.

Vice-Chancellor Andrzej Leszczyński accused Kysil of having lulled the Commonwealth into inactivity "when it was time to beat the Cossacks."[12] It can be maintained that in a conflict in which real lasting compromise was impossible, Kysil's numerous promises of results from negotiations and peace plans undercut the one way for the Zaporozhian problem or the Cossack War to be dealt with effectively—that is, a determined struggle to obliterate the Host. On the basis of the military situation of 1648, Kysil's peace policy was a reprieve, but the psychological climate that Ossoliński and Kysil created was not one which encouraged full-scale military preparation. Distrust of military leaders such as Wiśniowiecki certainly weakened the Commonwealth's military stance. Kysil did gain time in 1648–1650. But in the initial phase of the conflict, he and Ossoliński viewed the Zaporozhian revolt as a problem which they could easily manage, and they therefore may be accused of deluding the Commonwealth. Yet, though Kysil undoubtedly overestimated his own power to end the conflict, he correctly predicted the unwillingness and unreadiness of the nobility to pay the price necessary to conquer the rebels.

Kysil justified his policies by maintaining that they had averted certain disaster, and that his negotiations had saved the Commonwealth in the wake of the disasters of 1648 and 1649. However, after the conclusion of the Zboriv Agreement it became apparent that neither the Commonwealth nor Khmel'nyts'kyi found the agreement acceptable and that each side viewed the other with too deep a distrust to allow for a lasting peace. Less is known about Khmel'nyts'kyi's real plans and goals, but it is certain that from the start Zboriv had too little support in the Commonwealth to be anything more than a temporary expedient. Therefore by 1650, Kysil became a politician without a viable program since his policy became to maintain peace at all cost. Before Berestechko at least his assessment of the Commonwealth's inability to defeat the Cossacks was correct; afterward he did not even have this justification.

The more straightforward policy of Wiśniowiecki was that of a less perceptive analyst of the problems of the Commonwealth's rule in the Ukraine, but also that of a better representative of the thinking of the nobility. The nobility at large was convinced that the Cossack attack on what was, in essence, magnate rule in the Ukraine was an assault on the entire noble estate's position. Although in practice numerous nobles, both Orthodox and Roman Catholic, joined the uprising and the new Cossack order, there was no countervailing ideology of the middle and petty nobility directed against the magnates' dominance. Wiśniowiecki, Kalinowski, Koniecpolski, Lanckoroński and other hard-line war proponents were therefore able to represent what was their cause as that of the entire nobility as a whole and of the Commonwealth. They could conceive only a settlement in which the Zaporozhians would be defeated decisively and the old order restored in full.

Ultimately the bickering factions in the Commonwealth's leadership undermined each other's policies, and both policies proved failures. Like any leader who fails, Kysil can hardly be seen as a great statesman. But at the base of his policy was a willingness to attempt a new solution or at least to accept change. Kysil was also interested in preserving magnates' and nobles' landholdings in the Ukraine, but he was convinced that this could be done only through accommodation with the Zaporozhian Host and the Orthodox church. In addition, he differed from a man such as Wiśniowiecki in that he was able to conceive of higher interests of state that would supersede the interests of his economic peer group (the magnates) and his order (the nobility) because these were dependent on the Commonwealth's power. Therefore, for the good of the state, the Commonwealth's rule, and the retention of at least part of his order's economic rights in the Ukraine, Kysil was willing to negotiate a shift in the economic and political power in the Ukraine. His policy was thus one of saving as much as possible. Although he may have overestimated the possibilities of compromise, it is difficult to conceive of any other course that he might have taken. For a man who had dealt all his life with the conflicts of the Ukrainian lands and who had observed the inability of the Commonwealth to resolve them, the war party's program appeared mad.

Kysil's difficulties in reconciling the combatants in the Khmel'nyts'kyi uprising were but part of a larger problem. The Catholic nobles, increasingly intolerant, viewed the "intransigence" of the Orthodox Ukrainian nobles on religious issues as sabotage of the Diet. The nobility as a whole refused to permit the formation of a large standing army that might defend the Ukraine and do away with the need to use the Zaporozhian Army. At the same time, however, it would not allow any compromise that would integrate the warrior Zaporozhians into the Commonwealth's political noble nation. With the outbreak of the Khmel'nyts'kyi uprising all the weaknesses of the Commonwealth's government in the Ukraine were exposed, as the nobles' democracy proved incapable of forming a decisive policy toward the rebels.

To be an Orthodox Ruthenian in the Ukraine was to have the best vantage point for seeing the inadequacies of the Commonwealth's administration. Kysil was devoted to the essence of the Commonwealth's political and social system, but he foresaw the disastrous consequences of its failure to come to terms with the Eastern church conflict, the dissatisfaction of the Cossacks, the danger of the Tatars and Muscovy, and the defense needs of the Ukrainian lands. While his constant lament that failure to deal with Ukrainian problems would lead to ruin for the Commonwealth and that the fatherland could not survive the loss of the Ukraine may seem merely a repetition of the obvious, it stands out as the most sweeping and consistent assessment of Ukrainian problems in the Commonwealth in the second quarter of the seventeenth century.[13] In fact, Kysil seemed to be calling his peers back to the Commonwealth's age of greatness, by urging religious toleration, recognition of legitimate rights of at least part of the non-noble strata of population, and decisiveness in dealing with military and foreign problems. He saw the Commonwealth as composed of many peoples and many faiths. At the same time, his respect for the interest and power of the state, including the king, recalled the healthier body politic of the sixteenth century rather than the political culture of the Commonwealth of the 1630s through 1650s. His ideal Commonwealth was that of the Golden Age, but his career was fated to be in the Commonwealth of the Silver Age, with its hardening barriers between social orders, its religious intolerance, and its declining political culture and institutions.

Kysil's dilemma was that he came to lead a Ruthenian "nation" that, particularly for its Ukrainian part, could find no stable relationship in the Commonwealth or with Poland. That dilemma might be summed up by the phrase "gente Ruthenus, natione Polonus." It is a phrase that has been avoided in this work, partially because it has been used so imprecisely to describe Kysil, as well as a large number of Ruthenian nobles of remarkably different political cultural and national characteristics. Also it was never used by Kysil himself or by his contemporaries in depicting his situation. In fact, while he never described the Poles as his "gens," he did at times refer to the Ruthenians as his "natio." But while the phrase "gente Ruthenus, natione Polonus" may be seen as a cliché that has impeded understanding of Polish-Ukrainian relations, it does suggest the problem of the division between political loyalty and national descent. It does not imply any clear cultural characteristics, hence allowing for its use for so many Ruthenian nobles. In exploring these three questions, a more precise understanding of Kysil's dilemma over the relationship of Rus' and Ukraine to Poland and the Commonwealth can emerge.

Kysil had been acculturated into the Polish nobility and had come to view the Commonwealth in general and the Kingdom of Poland in particular as his beloved Fatherland. Together with this political loyalty, he assumed Polish cultural traditions and the Polish language, which he used to such great effect in his oratory. Yet, however similar Kysil became to his noble brothers of Little and Great Poland, he never ceased to view himself as a Ruthenian. He perceived himself as a member of a Rus' community that was defined in religious, cultural and historical ways. This community was in danger of dissolving under Polish and Latin Christian impact. It had no clearly defined unified political structure such as the Kingdom of Poland or the Grand Duchy of Lithuania. Still, Kysil, imbued with the political culture of the nobles' Commonwealth, saw himself and other Ruthenian Orthodox nobles as a Rus' "political nation" responsible for the whole community. This mission was difficult, both because the Rus' community was dispersed among so many lands in the Commonwealth (from Vilnius and Vitsebsk to Kamianets'-Podil's'kyi, Lviv and Kiev), and because so many Ruthenian great nobles eschewed their Rus' heritage. But assimilation was not for Kysil, who took pride in his Kievan Rus' ancestor Sventoldych and knew that the "Kingdom of Poland," however dear to him, was merely his "present fatherland," having replaced the earlier fatherland of the Principality of Kievan Rus'. Not the least of Kysil's motivations for this loyalty to the Rus' heritage was, of course, that the situation called for a noble Ruthenian to mediate between the amorphous Rus' community and the nobiliary Commonwealth. This, after all, may be seen as the reason for Kysil's spectacular rise.

In assuming leadership of Rus', Kysil in many ways furthered the transformation of the Rus' *gens* into a Rus' *natio* with its own territory and corporate political traditions. He accepted and adapted the political tenets of his age in his leadership of the Ruthenian community—above all, in interpreting the articles of the incorporation of the Ukrainian lands into the Kingdom of Poland as an agreement between the Ruthenian and Polish nobilities. Hence he founded his arguments more and more frequently on Rus' being represented by the nobles of the incorporation lands. His identification of these Ukrainian lands as a Rus' territorial *"patria,"* a political Rus' *par excellence,* can be explained by the late stage at which Polish culture and Latin Christianity penetrated them, by their steadfast adherence to Orthodoxy (partially because of the nearness of the Zaporozhians), and by the cultural-ecclesiastical leadership and historical traditions of Kiev. Even more important for Kysil here was the center of Ruthenian Orthodox nobility resistance to the Union of Brest and here was his homeland. It was these incorporation lands that Kysil portrayed as the land of the Sarmatian Ruthenians who entered into an agreement with the Sarmatian Poles. Applying the political concepts of his age, Kysil advocated the right of a political "nation"—the nobility—to lead Rus' and maintained that the incorporation lands constituted a Rus' historical-political entity.

These views, advanced at a time when knowledge of the history of Kievan Rus' was increasing, gave a new meaning to the concept of the Ruthenian "nation." It did not supplant the idea of Rus' as a cultural-religious community dispersed throughout the Commonwealth, but it did provide bases for a new thinking about the Ukraine, or at least its major part, as a political entity. This came at a time when the dynamic Ukraine, with its rapid economic growth, high levels of violence and large segments of arms-bearing population, and regional interests frequently divergent from those of Warsaw, was not yet fully integrated into the Kingdom of Poland. Hence Kysil, who in theory sought to buttress the Commonwealth's control of the Ukraine, in practice undermined the Commonwealth's position and Polish influence through his tenacious defense of Orthodoxy, his furthering of Ruthenian consciousness, and his propagation of regional awareness and political thought. In the long run, the issues and concepts he espoused were to be integrated into the program of the rebels, as the Cossacks came to see themselves as the political nation of the Ukraine and the defenders of Rus' traditions and Orthodoxy.

The emergence of the Ukraine as a political entity stemmed from important economic and social factors, above all the economic boom and the unrest among an armed frontier population of Cossacks and peasants who were excluded from so many rights. Still, in explaining the rise of Cossack Ukraine, religious sentiments, Rus' historical traditions, and political concepts must be seen as important. Kysil played a major role in shaping these, as he did in influencing the middle and lesser

Ruthenian Orthodox nobility, who in considerable numbers joined the Cossack revolt and brought their political culture to the Cossack camp.

The key to Kysil's dilemma lies in his relationship to the Ruthenian "nation" that he presumed to lead. That relationship, as well as the changing nature of the Ruthenian "nation," are best seen by comparing Kysil to his predecessors and successors as leaders of the Ruthenian nobility. Preceding him was the towering figure of Konstantyn Ostroz'kyi, the Rurikid princely magnate who stood at the head of a homogenous Rus' society in the Lithuanian period, but who lived to see the disintegration of the old ways. After him came Ivan Vyhovs'kyi, the Volhynian noble who became Cossack Hetman, and Iurii Nemyrych, who espoused a compromise between the Cossack Hetmanate and the Commonwealth in the entirely changed situation after the great revolt. Between the old Rus' of the Lithuanian past and the new Rus' of Cossack Ukraine was the tumultuous period of Kysil's life. As the old was dissolving and the new was forming, Kysil sought to preserve Rus', but like so many conservatives he did so by employing new concepts. He thus propounded views that the Ruthenians should be led by a noble political nation and that the Ukraine was a Rus' *patria*. In the end, these concepts, lacking a universally recognized Rus' polity as their focus, could not succeed in the seventeenth century Commonwealth. Integration of the Ruthenian elite into the Polish nobility had gone too far and there was insufficient support for the still amorphous views put forth by Kysil, who himself did not reject allegiance to the Polish political nation in its broadest sense. Certainly Kysil did not wish to embark on drastic violent measures to ensure the place of Rus' in the Commonwealth. Even more so, he never sought to enlist the non-noble Ruthenian orders, although he did at times exploit Cossack, clerical and burgher discontent in arguing his cause.

Ultimately, Kysil's nobiliary Ruthenian political nation could not resolve the internal problems of Rus'. As his own religious policies showed, Kysil was a tolerant man who sought above all to end the controversy over the Ruthenian church and to restore the unity of Ruthenians. Caught, however, between staunch Catholics who could no longer support toleration for Orthodoxy and passionate Orthodox determined to eradicate the union, he could find no solution to the division in the Rus' church. Just as he developed Rus' political and historical consciousness, so Kysil expressed Rus' discontent with the nobiliary Commonwealth's religious policies. His programs, however, provided no solutions for the Rus' community, declining and divided as it was. The continuing conversion and assimilation of more Ruthenian nobles and the growing strength of the Counter-Reformation, which could always hope that Władysław's successor would abandon toleration, predicted a disaster for Rus' in the nobiliary Commonwealth. Unbeknownst to Kysil, in searching for an answer to Ruthenian problems and expressing Ruthenian discontent, he was preparing the way for new Ruthenian leaders who would overturn the very social and political system that he sought to preserve. He could not halt the conversions and assimilation of Ruthenian nobles that weakened the Ruthenian political position. He could not prevent the discrimination against Orthodoxy that enraged the Ruthenian masses and led Orthodox burghers, clergymen, and peasants later to turn to the Cossacks for defense of their rights. He could not find a resolution for the religious divide between Orthodox Ruthenians and Uniate Ruthenians. He, the devoted son of the nobiliary Commonwealth, expressed the Rus' community's discontent with the "Lachs" and the Commonwealth, but he could not find a solution for this discontent.

The Polish penetration of the Ukraine and the Ruthenian-Ukrainian reaction did not represent the clash of two modern nations. The Commonwealth was, after all, the republic of a "noble nation," but it was in the Ukraine that the formation of this noble nation faced its most difficult test. As the leader of the old Ruthenian nobility in the Ukraine, who lived to see the rise of the new Cossack Ukraine, Kysil frequently expressed the burden of his intermediary position between Poles and Ruthenians.[14] With the rise of the new Cossack Ukraine, the tensions between Poland and Rus' that Kysil had striven to resolve took on a new degree of intensity.

In the end there was to be no place for Adam Kysil. From the uprising of 1648 there emerged a solidly Catholic and Polish Commonwealth of the nobility and a staunchly Orthodox and Cossack Ukraine. Declare as he would that as a senator and a loyal citizen of the fatherland he had nothing in common with the rebels, Kysil's contemporaries correctly saw that the leader of Rus' was inextricably connected with the rebels, however much he might wish otherwise.[15] After all, Kysil himself said that the war was between religions and peoples.[16] The Cossack colonel Fylon Dzhalalyi voiced the problem most directly, asking "And you, Kysil, bone of our bone, why have you betrayed us and sided with the Poles?"[17] As early as 1646, Father Baievs'kyi had understood that Rus' and Poland contended for Kysil's loyalty. But in the matrix of political, class, religious and national loyalties of seventeenth-century Eastern Europe, there could be no answer to Kysil's dilemma.

Appendix A

The Creation of a Magnate's Economic Power: A Chronological List of the Acquisition of Adam Kysil's Estates and Offices

Unlike most other magnates in the Commonwealth, Adam Kysil did not leave intact his estates to subsequent generations of magnates who descended from him. His loss of revenue in the last years of his life due to the Khmel'nyts'kyi uprising forced him to mortgage domains in order to survive. The Khmel'nyts'kyi uprising eventually tore away his holdings in the Chernihiv palatinate not only from the Commonwealth, but also from his heirs. His failure to produce a direct heir resulted in the division of his other estates between various branches of his own and his wife's family after his death. Therefore, although Kysil must have been an excellent economic manager to amass such wealth, there are almost no records about his farflung estates. Family estate records for the seventeenth-century Commonwealth are in general rare, and they usually survive in families who maintained magnate status for generations, particularly in the more pacific areas of the Commonwealth. The numerous petty and middle noble claimants to Kysil's estates fought long and hard for their rights, but they preserved few documents describing the estates during Adam Kysil's life. The social revolution of the Khmel'nyts'kyi uprising destroyed private and government records on the old order in the Chernihiv palatinate. Although some economic records exist for Kysil's Volhynian estates in the *aktovi knyhy* or *akta ziemskie i grodzkie* of the Tsentral'nyi Derzhavnyi Istorychnyi Arkhiv URSR (Central State Historical Archive of the Ukr.SSR) in Kiev, Soviet denial of access to these collections has prevented a study of even these estates. Fortunately, I was able to obtain registers of the Volhynian *aktovi knyhy* held by the L'vivs'ka naukova biblioteka im. V. Stefanyka AN URSR (V. Stefanyk Lviv Scientific Library of the Academy of Sciences of the Ukrainian SSR) in the Radzimiński Collection (Zbirka Radzimins'koho) of fond 5.* Hence, from published and archival materials, it has been

---

* LBN, MS 42 I.4. Summaryusz z akt Włodzimierskich z lat 1569–1813. 7 vols. contains a register of documents dealing with the Kysil family in its alphabetical register of families. Information from this source is listed as Summaryusz. For other references the abbreviated forms used elsewhere are employed.

possible to establish the chronology of Kysil's economic rise. The following table traces the acquisition of private lands and government offices that culminated in Kysil's ascent to magnate status. Although no attempt is made to describe the estates and royal lands, information is provided, when available, on the sums expended (in Polish złoty, z.p.). Even taking into account the inflation in the seventeenth-century Commonwealth, they illustrate the rapid increase in Kysil's economic position.

The following information is provided, when available: A. earliest evidence of possession; B. place; C. from whom; D. financial terms, and E. reference.

    1.A. 1616–1621
      B. Nyzkynychi (part) (Volodymyr county, Volhynia)
      C. Father, Hryhorii Kysil
      D. Inheritance
      E. "Try test." p. 50
    2.A. 23 January 1625
      B. Pidhaitsi (Volodymyr county, Volhynia)
      C. Volodymyr capitula
      D. Purchase
      E. Summaryusz, fol. 162
    3.A. 1 March 1627
      B. Butiatychi (part) (Volodymyr county, Volhynia)
      C. Stefan and Anastaziia Wetryha
      D. Transfer of possession
      E. Summaryusz, fol. 163
    4.A. 1628
      B. Zorenychi (Kiev palatinate)
      C. Filon Bohushevych, father-in-law
      D. Purchase
      E. ODAZUM, I, 207
    5.A. 1629
      B. Polupanshchyna (Volodymyr county, Volhynia)
      C. —
      D. —
      E. *Zaliudnennia*, pp. 77, 84
    6.A. 1629
      B. Tyshkovychi (Volodymyr county, Volhynia)
      C. —
      D. —
      E. *Zaliudnennia*, pp. 77, 84

7.A. 1620s
  B. Perekop, Sloboda, Novyi Brusyliv and other settlements (Chernihiv lands)
  C. Zygmunt III
  D. Grant
  E. Met. Kor. MS 185, fols. 391–392; record of their transfer in 1641 to Mikołaj Broniewski
8.A 12 January 1631
  B. Nyzkynychi (part), Kurevychi, Pidhaitsi (Volhynia)
  C. Mykola Kysil, brother
  D. Purchase, 17,500 z.p.
  E. Summaryusz, fol. 165
9.A 1632
  B. Vytkiv (Belz palatinate)
  C. Zygmunt III
  D. Grant
  E. Pułaski, "Pierwsze lata," 198
10.A. 13 February 1633
  B. Nosivka starostwo (Chernihiv lands)
  C. Władysław IV
  D. Grant
  E. Met. Kor., MS 180, fols. 14–15
11.A. October 1633
  B. Divytsia (Chernihiv lands)
  C. Mykola Soltan
  D. Purchase
  E. Met. Kor., MS 180, fols. 234–235
12A. 1635
  B. Podkomorzy of Chernihiv
  C. Władysław IV
  D. Grant
  E. AGAD, Metryka Ruska, fol. 47
13A. 1635–1638
  B. Kobyshche, Kozarhorod (Chernihiv palatinate)
  C. —
  D. —
  E. Shamrai, "Misto Kobyshcha," pp. 229–232; "Try test.," p. 49
14.A. 9 June 1638
  B. Hniino, Mohyl'no, Smilianka, Turiia, Iurii (Volodymyr county, Volhynia)
  C. Alexander Łysakowski
  D. Transfer of property
  E. Summaryusz, fol. 168

15.A. 19 July 1638
   B. Dorohynychi (2/3) (Volodymyr county, Volhynia)
   C. Petro Kalushovs'kyi's wife nee Sukhodol'ska (1/3) & Andrii and Halyna Kysilivna Sukhodol'ski (1/2)
   D. Purchase, 20,000 z.p.
   E. Summaryusz, fol. 168
16.A. 1 December 1639
   B. Castellan of Chernihiv
   C. Władysław IV
   D. Grant
   E. Met. Kor., MS 185, fols. 221–222
17.A. 23 December 1642
   B. Hoshcha, Seniv forest (1/4) (Luts'k county, Volhynia)
   C. Peter Mohyla, Metropolitan of Kiev
   D. On 3 February 1643 Kysil paid Princess Regina Solomorits'ka, the former owner, 12,000 z.p. as part of the agreement
   E. Golubev II-2, pp. 285–287; PAN MS. 3022, fol. 33
18.A. 25 June 1642
   B. Hubin, Tumyn (Volhynia)
   C. Adam Burchacki
   D. Collateral for loan (converted into sale June 1645)
   E. Summaryusz, fols. 171, 172
19.A. 23 July 1644
   B. Lubovychi, Veryna (Kiev palatinate)
   C. Border agreement with Teodor Ielets'
   D. —
   E. Summaryusz, fol. 170
20.A. 29 December 1644
   B. Svoichiv and Vol'ka (Volhynia)
   C. Danylo Ialovyts'kyi, podkomorzy of Krem"ianets'
   D. Mortgage, 100,000 z.p.
   E. Summaryusz, fol. 171
21.A. 16 May 1645
   B. Terentyiv, Luts'k county (Volhynia)
   C. —
   D. Given as dowry to Halyna Kysilivna on her marriage to Daniel Stempkowski, starosta of Volodymyr
   E. Summaryusz, fol. 10
22.A. 29 April 1645
   B. Makoshyn (Chernihiv palatinate)
   C. Adam Kazanowski

D. Purchase
E. Summaryusz, fol. 172
23.A. 1646
  B. Novosilky, Zamostychky, Bohushivka, Dzvyn, Lobachivshchyna (Kiev palatinate)
  C. Filon Bohushevych, father-in-law
  D. Purchase
  E. Rulikowski, "Nowosiołki," p. 283
24.A. 5 February 1646
  B. Castellan of Kiev
  C. Władysław IV
  D. Grant
  E. *Arkhiv IuZR,* pt. III, vol. I, 401–406
25.A. 22 December 1646
  B. Vepryn, Kukhary (Kiev palatinate)
  C. Witowski, podsędek kijowski
  D. Purchase
  E. Summaryusz, fol. 9
26.A. mid-March 1648
  B. Palatine of Bratslav
  C. Władysław IV
  D. Grant
  E. Rawita-Gawroński, *Sprawy,* pp. 79–82. Letter of 16 March.
27.A. July 31, 1648
  B. Starostwo of Bohuslav
  C. Jerzy Ossoliński
  D. Promise of transfer after election
  E. BO, MS 3564, fols. 78–80
28.A. March-April, 1649*
  B. Palatine of Kiev
  C. Jan Kazimierz
  D. Grant
  E. BK, MS 991, fols. 106–107
29.A. 29 May 1649
  B. Orany, Laskiv (Volhynia)
  C. Mykola Kysil
  D. Inheritance
  E. Summaryusz, fol. 9–10
30.A. 15 December 1649
  B. Sukhodoly, Iakovychi, Voiskovychi, Khvorostiv, Lynshchyna (Volhynia)
  C. Prince Dymitr Wiśniowiecki

*On the starostwo of Cherkasy, held for a short time after January 16, see p. 332, n. 145.

D. Mortgaged for 55,000 z.p., increased by 16,500 on 13 January 1651. Reaffirmed with the addition of Dehtiv on 16 May 1651 for an additional 37,500 z.p. in the name of Prince Konstanty Wiśniowiecki

E. Summaryusz, fols. 9, 175–176

31.A. 1650
   B. Starostwa of Tovmach and Nowy Targ
   C. Jerzy Ossoliński
   D. Transfer
   E. Oświęcim, p. 222, Radziwiłł, *Memoriale*, IV, 156, BOZ, MS 1217, fols. 186–187

32.A. 1652
   B. Krasnosile
   C. Princess Regina Solomorits'ka
   D. Purchase
   E. "Try test.," p. 52

33.A. 1653
   B. Krasyliv, Chudynky, Volodymyrivka, Mnishyn (Volhynia)
   C. Princess Regina Solomorits'ka
   D. Purchase
   E. "Try test.," p. 52

34.A. 1653
   B. Sataniv, Kharbkiv (Belz palatinate)
   C. —
   D. —
   E. "Try test.," p. 52

35.A. 1653
   B. Koil'no, Vil'ky (Volhynia)
   C. Ialovyts'kyi, podkomorzy of Krem"ianets'
   D. Purchase
   E. "Try test.," pp. 53, 63

36.A. 1653
   B. Ozdiutychy (Volhynia)
   C. —
   D. —
   E. Summaryusz, fol. 177, "Try test.," p. 54

37.A. 1653
   B. Novyi Brusyliv (Volhynia)
   C. Ialovyts'kyi, podkomorzy of Krem"ianets' or Adam Burkhots'kyi
   D. Purchase
   E. "Try test.,"pp. 52–54

38. A. 1653
    B. Transdnieper estates along Desna, Mina forest, Kysil'horod forest
    C. —
    D. —
    E. "Try test.," p. 64
39. A. July 1653
    B. Novyi Volodymyr, Kysilevychi, Makarevychi, Vyrva, Mukosilevychi, Hymy, Lenchary, Ryznia (Kiev palatinate)
    C. At that time mortgaged to Maksymiliian Bzhozovs'kyi for 60,000 z.p.
    D. Bought from Zmijowskie
    E. "Try test.," pp. 63–64; Summaryusz, fol. 178
40. A. 13 January 1664
    B. Vadkiv, Pastukhiv islands (Kiev palatinate)
    C. —
    D. —
    E. Kataloh kolektsiï dokumentiv Kyïvs'koï arkheohrafichnoï komisiï, Doc. 173

Appendix B

Biographies and Secondary Literature*

Although Adam Kysil occupied an important position in the affairs of the seventeenth-century Commonwealth, only a few articles and sketches were devoted to his life and political activity. Most of the works are not concerned with all periods and aspects of his life and are based only on a limited range of sources. They do, however, usually express strong opinions about Kysil's political, national, religious and class affiliations. Frequently their authors sought to use Kysil's life to propagate views on Polish-Ukrainian and Orthodox-Catholic relations.

Of the significant works, the earliest is Julian Bartoszewicz's "Adam Kisiel, Wojewoda Kijowski," published in *Tygodnik Illustrowany* in 1860. This short sketch deals mainly with Kysil's activities in 1648–1649. Its major sources are Grabowski's *Ojczyste spominki, Pam.*, heraldic books (Niesiecki's *Herbarz* and Okolski's *Orbis Polonus*), memoirs and seventeenth-century histories. Bartoszewicz planned a full-scale biography of Kysil, the unfinished, 700-page manuscript of which is located in Arch. Łodz., Arch. Bart. MS 1768 under the title, "Adam Kisiel, Wojewoda Kijowski." The source base of this unfinished work is not much greater than that of his article. The Polish scholar Bartoszewicz evaluates Kysil highly as a statesman, and as a Ruthenian who was loyal to the Commonwealth. In later works, Bartoszewicz was to express his alarm over the Ukrainian national movement and cultural advances of his own time. Hence his portrayal of Kysil should be seen as that of an exemplary Ruthenian, Polish in political loyalty and in culture.

In 1865 Ludwik Powidaj published "Adam Świętoldycz Kisiel, wojewoda kijowski, nosowski, bohusławski starosta," in *Dziennik Literacki*. He based his work on correspondence published in the Michałowski collection, and other unspecified materials. Written from a prison cell in Cracow, the work was the product of a revolutionary of 1863 who wished to counteract Russian claims to the eastern borderlands of the old Commonwealth and Russian charges that the Poles had always per-

---

* For the sake of brevity, works cited in this appendix will appear in the shortened format adopted in the footnotes. When only one work is listed in the bibliography under the name of the author, the title generally will not appear in this introduction.

secuted the Orthodox. Powidaj condemned the religious intolerance of the seventeenth century, but saw Poland as no worse than other European countries. He viewed the abolition of the Cossacks as necessary to establish the "modern" way of life, but he condemned the nobility for its many mistakes. He praised Kysil as a patriot of the Commonwealth and an enlightened proponent of central power. In sum, he argued for the establishment of a progressive Commonwealth within 1772 borders and cast Kysil as an adherent of such a program.

In 1874 Kazimierz Pułaski, a historian who devoted numerous studies to Right-Bank Ukraine, published "Pierwsze lata publicznego zawodu Adama Kisiela (1628–1635)," in *Przewodnik Naukowy i Literacki* (the work was republished in 1887 in *Szkice i poszukiwania historyczne* as "Pierwsze lata zawodu publicznego Adama Kisiela [1622–1635]"). These items are listed as published sources in the bibliography because they consist mostly of twenty documents and fragments from the Kysil family archive, located at that time in the Biblioteka Zawadyniecka in Podillia. Pułaski mentioned that the archive was in very poor condition and that he had published all the documents that he could decipher. This work is significant, therefore, because it published part of the family archive, which later disappeared.

In 1874, Kysil came in for praise from another side. S. Baranovskii paid tribute to Kysil as a defender of Orthodoxy in the article "Pravoslavnyi, volynskii pomeshchik A. Kisel' kak pol'skii diplomat v epokhu B. Kmel'nitskogo" in the unofficial section of *Volynskie eparkhial'nye vedomosti*. The Volhynian priest's didactic purpose was to prove to the nobility of Volhynia that Orthodoxy had not always been the "peasant's faith."

The most comprehensive biography of Kysil as well as the most thorough discussion of his character and the problems of the time is the work of the Ukrainian scholar Ivan Novitskii (Ivan Novyts'kyi) "Adam Kisel', Voevoda kievskii 1580(?)–1653 g." which was published in *Kievskaia starina* in 1884. The author undertook the biography to rectify attitudes then current about Kysil in Ukrainian historiography. Novyts'kyi was especially concerned about contradictory passing remarks on Kysil in Mykola Kostomarov's biography of Khmel'nyts'kyi. He was troubled by Kostomarov's lack of understanding of the difficult position in which Kysil had found himself and his condemnation of Kysil for the latter's failure to join with Khmel'nyts'kyi. Novyts'kyi sought to explain these aspects of Kysil's career viewed by many as contradictions in his political, religious and national loyalties. His work differentiates between "narodnyi" (ethnic-national) and "natsional'nyi" (state-national) patriotism. According to Novyts'kyi, Kysil's allegiance to Rus' can be explained by the former type of patriotism, while his simultaneous loyalty to the Commonwealth was an outgrowth of the latter type.

With an eye to nineteenth-century Polish, Ukrainian, Russian problems, Novyts'kyi illustrated the dichotomy in Kysil's loyalties in the following manner:

> In order to understand the difference better we have pointed out in Kysil's "narodnyi" and "natsional'nyi" patriotism (so often and with no basis confused—we should note—in contemporary local life), we will attempt to point out a corresponding parallel, taking as a basis conditions surrounding us. We posit the following situation. The governor of Galicia is a local Ruthenian (*Rusin*) Uniate, while the governor of the Podolian or Volhynian province is a Catholic of Polish nationality, although a Russian citizen. We posit further, that in case of a war between Russia and Austria, a movement might arise among the people of Eastern Galicia in support of the former state, while among the landowners of Podillia and Volhynia [a movement might arise] in support of the latter. It would be clear to anyone that the governors we have posited could refuse to take part in any hostile actions against their kinsmen and their fellow believers, yet remain loyal citizens of their government and work in its interest, while each would seek by peaceful means to pacify and maintain control of that part of the local population that was ready to side with the enemy. Were it to be otherwise—if either aided such a movement or even joined it, he would be a traitor to his state. (p. 636)

Novyts'kyi viewed Kysil as a man loyal to his state, his people, and his estate. He praised Kysil as a model public figure. In his defense of Kysil, Novyts'kyi represented the anti-populist trend in Ukrainian historiography that stemmed from the work of Iurii Maksymovych. As for Kysil's religious allegiances, Novyts'kyi portrayed him as primarily interested in solving the problems of Uniate-Orthodox divisions, but not deeply committed to either variant. He did not know about Kysil's negotiations for a new union. In fact, Novyts'kyi's biography was based on a limited numer of published sources. He knew little of Kysil's career prior to 1648. Novyts'kyi's perspective was nevertheless reflected in nineteenth-century Russian encyclopaedias, such as *Entsiklopedicheskii slovar'* and *Russkii biograficheskii slovar'*.

In 1886 Rudolf Ottman discussed Kysil's activities in 1648–1649 in an article published in *Przegląd Powszechny*. The materials for this work were published sources and several original letters found in Baron Ludwik Kronenberg's collection, which were published by Rawita-Gawroński in *Sprawy* in 1914. Like Novyts'kyi, Ottman was interested in the question of Kysil's political ethics, in particular in his having received grants from the Muscovite tsars.

In 1905, J. T. Lubomirski published a popular pamphlet discussing Kysil's loyalty to the Polish state and his Ruthenian heritage. The pamphlet uses few sources and its chief value is its publication of Kysil's will of 1621 and the inscriptions on his burial monument. It also contains an interesting list of great outstanding Ruthenians according to Lubomirski's views:

1. An anonymous Cossack officer, who in 1651 questioned Mikołaj Potocki why he did not permit a struggle against the Turks.

2. Bohdan Khmel'nyts'kyi, who in defending Rus' brought about Poland's fall.

3. Jeremi Wiśniowiecki, who, the living embodiment of the princes praised in the "Lay of the Host of Igor," was a soul which would be the embellishment of any nation.

4. Adam Kysil, who was a true successor to Prince Ostroz'kyi, a representative of holy Rus' and the metropolitans and clergy who did not take part in the revolt.

Several articles by Bugoslavski, Stecki, and Urbanowicz provided significant details on the church Kysil built in Nyzkynychi and on his burial monument.

In 1927, B. M. Leliavskii published a sketch which is the most flagrant attempt to use Kysil as a political symbol. The author was one of the followers of Galician Russophilism, an almost defunct movement by the 1920s which was thrown into confusion by the fall of tsarist Russia. Leliavskii extolled Kysil as a true "Russian," a defender of the Orthodox faith, and yet a loyal son of the Polish state. Addressing himself to more contemporary problems, Leliavskii described Kysil as the spiritual ancestor of the remnant Russophile movement of the 1920s, which cooperated with the Polish government. He described the followers of UNDO (Ukrainian National Democratic Alliance), the largest legal Ukrainian party in interwar Poland, as the spiritual descendants of the Cossack-traitors.

A terse, though comprehensive account of Kysil's career, was published in 1965 by Zbigniew Wójcik. This short entry in *Polski słownik biograficzny* provides considerable information on both published and unpublished sources. Unlike all the other authors of sketches on Kysil, Wójcik does not display a desire to use Kysil to discuss modern Polish-Ukrainian relations.

Kysil has received more serious scholarly attention in general works on the Polish-Lithuanian Commonwealth and its various problems in the seventeenth century than he has in biographic literature. His career and policies have often been examined in monographs and articles on the Khmel'nyts'kyi uprising, on the Eastern Church, on the relations be-

tween Muscovy and the Commonwealth, and on the historical consciousness of the Ukrainian nobility of Rus' and the incorporation lands.
Histories of the 1648–1653 period contain information concerning Kysil's
actions and opinions. Such comments are scattered and often consist of
quotations of remarks that Kysil made concerning certain events or issues. Less frequently do authors actually evaluate Kysil's programs.
Most historians credit Kysil highly as a negotiator and analyst of the
political situation and, consequently, cite his letters frequently. Indeed,
Johann Christian von Engel, author of one of the first scholarly histories
of the Ukraine, described Kysil as the Richelieu of his time and place
(Engel, *Geschichte*, p. 187).

The earliest discussions of Kysil in Ukrainian historical literature are
in the Cossack Chronicles, whose conservative authors praised Kysil for
his Orthodox piety and political wisdom, and ignored the difficult question, for them, of why he did not side with Khmel'nyts'kyi. See in particular Hrabianka's description of Kysil at his death as "a pious man, a
great zealot of the Greco-Ruthenian faith, delightful in speech, friendly
to the Ukraine, a descendent of the ancient and illustrious house of
Sviatoldych who was the Ruthenian Hetman in 1128" (p. 118).

Kysil figures as a skillful negotiator in the major nineteenth-century
histories of the Khmel'nyts'kyi period. Bantysh-Kamenskii's *Istoriia Malorossii*, Kulish's *Otpadenie*, Szajnocha's *Dwa lata*, Solov'ev's *Istoriia
Rossii* and Pavlishchev's *Pol'skaia anarkhiia* all mention Kysil's activities
but do not thoroughly examine his thought or policies. Kulish, the great
critic of Khmel'nyts'kyi, sees Kysil as a "Little Russian" who did more
to save Poland than did the Poles themselves. In contrast, Kostomarov,
as Novyts'kyi asserted, did little to explain Kysil's position and criticized
him by innuendos. These early histories were surpassed both in depth
of coverage and extent of source materials on the Khmel'nyts'kyi period
by Hrushevs'kyi's *Istoriia Ukraïny-Rusy*. This work is impressive as a
feat in digesting and organizing archival and published sources. Although written over sixty years ago, it remains the basic reservoir of
information about the period, to which subsequent specialized studies
and new archival finds have added information.

To a considerable degree, the narrative of Hrushevs'kyi often assumes
the character of a recounting of available sources. Only in his interpre-
tive essay, "Khmel'nyts'kyi, Khmel'nychchyna" and in his conclusion to
volume 9, part 2 of his history, does Hrushevs'kyi analyze the period.
True to his populist convictions, he was extremely critical of elites and
leaders, including Bohdan Khmel'nyts'kyi. He was sympathetic to the
masses and their struggle for freedom. Korduba's "Der Ukraine Nie-

dergang" provides an extensive critique and summary of Hrushevs'kyi's views.

I have drawn substantially from Hrushevs'kyi's description of events and sources. The material he cites is particularly valuable because it often comes from archives and libraries in the Soviet Union, to which I was denied access. Notwithstanding the mass of material that he gathered about Kysil, Hrushevs'kyi never studied Kysil's career and his views. He considered Kysil an important figure who had not received the attention from scholars that he merited. (IX–1, 510).

Of nineteenth-century studies on the 1648–1653 period, those that comprise the *Szkice historyczne* of Ludwik Kubala retain great importance because of the extensive source material used by the author and his considerable talent in analyzing events. His detailed biography of Kysil's political ally, Jerzy Ossoliński, is extremely useful because it contains material on the activities of the two men in the early years of the Khmel'nyts'kyi uprising. Kubala did not pay particular attention, however, to evaluating Kysil's historical importance.

After Hrushevs'kyi, the two most important Ukrainian historians of the Khmel'nyts'kyi period have been Viacheslav Lypyns'kyi and Ivan Kryp"iakevych. Lypyns'kyi's studies established how widespread support for Khmel'nyts'kyi was among the Ukrainian nobility and examined the Ruthenian consciousness and the political culture of the nobility before 1648. Lypyns'kyi devotes considerable attention to Kysil, in particular to the difficulties that Kysil faced as a Ruthenian on the side of the government. Lypyns'kyi, who wished to underline the conservative elements in the Khmel'nyts'kyi uprising, is troubled by Kysil's person, and explains his failure to go over to the Khmel'nyts'kyi camp as due to his negative experience in the first bloody stage of the revolt and to his advanced age. (*Z dziejów Ukrainy*)

Ivan Kryp"iakevych, like Lypyns'kyi, a representative of the conservative "statist" school in Ukrainian historiography, was transformed into a Soviet Marxist after his native city of Lviv had been annexed to the USSR. His biography of Khmel'nyts'kyi is a pastiche of his new and old views and should be used in conjunction with his prewar "Studiï." The biography is more a description of the effects of the uprising on Ukrainian political, social and economic life than a true biography. Kryp"iakevych writes little about Kysil and, in line with Soviet views, condemns his role, but does so in a relatively moderate tone. (*Bohdan Khmel'nyts'kyi*, p. 131)

In Polish twentieth-century works the most interesting characterization of Kysil is in Rawita-Gawroński's two-volume study, *Bohdan Chmiel-*

nicki. Written in the first decade of the twentieth century, it reflects the increasing influence of nationalism on historical studies in Eastern Europe. The work is a bitter denunciation of Khmel'nyts'kyi and the Cossacks and a glorification of Wiśniowiecki. As such, it stems from an old and influential Polish literary tradition which had its roots in the seventeenth-century epic poem by Twardowski, *Wojna domowa,* and which was reinforced by Sienkiewicz's nineteenth-century novel, *Ogniem i mieczem.* Rawita-Gawroński viewed the struggle between the Cossacks and the Commonwealth as one between barbarity and civilization. He saw Kysil as having made the tragic mistake of underestimating the evil of the Cossacks, although he maintained a certain respect for the culture of Kysil, the assimilated Ruthenian (I, p. 223).

A more moderate reflection of this view is to be found in Tomkiewicz's *Jeremi Wiśniowiecki,* which is a sympathetic treatment of Wiśniowiecki, the "Polish national hero" or "Ukrainian national traitor." This positive evaluation of Wiśniowiecki's policies contains a large number of sources and treats a number of incidents in which both Kysil and Wiśniowiecki took part.

Interwar Polish historiography produced a lively exchange about the influence of Sienkiewicz on Polish historical thought. Olgierd Górka, in his *Ogniem i mieczem,* attacked the entire Sienkiewicz tradition. Górka considered Kysil a far more worthy "hero" than Wiśniowiecki. The political changes after World War II forced Polish historians officially to praise the cause of the Cossacks and to describe the war as one of national liberation. For a critical evaluation of prewar Polish historiography by the postwar Polish historians Baranowski and Libiszowska, see "Problem narodowo-wyzwoleńczej walki."

The imposition of an official line in Poland may be the reason that the period has fallen into neglect since the 1950s. Few studies about this period—once so favored by Polish historians—have appeared. The only exceptions are the excellent works by Zbigniew Wójcik and the popular studies of Podhorecki. The grip that Sienkiewicz holds over the Polish reading public is evident from the large editions of Marceli Kosman's *Na tropach bohaterów Trylogii.* Kosman tries to give the reader historically accurate sketches of the characters in Sienkiewicz's novels, including Kysil (pp. 73–82).

Kysil is a *persona non grata* in Soviet historical circles. The official line, expressed in the article, "Kysil', Adam Hryhorovych," in *Ukraïns'ka radians'ka entsyklopediia,* is that Kysil was "a Ukrainian magnate, a sympathizer with Poland. . . . Kysil played a particularly shameful role when the Cossack peasant rebellion of 1637 broke out in the Ukraine. . . . For his treason Kysil received large estates in the Ukraine and became a magnate. . . . Ukrainian and Polish bourgeois nationalist historiographies, falsifying historical facts, characterize Kysil as a defender of Orthodoxy and remain silent on his treasonous activities." (VI, 379) Although Kysil is designated a traitor and avoided as a research topic, his activities have been illuminated by Soviet research. Soviet scholars have produced a number of works which clarify his actions during the Khmel'nyts'kyi years. The works of Shevchenko and Isaievych are particularly well researched. M. Petrovs'kyi, another specialist on the Khmel'nyts'kyi revolt, published *Vyzvol'na viina* during the Stalinist period, before the imposition of the "Reunification ideology," represents an earlier Soviet viewpoint.

Literature and views on Kysil's church activities and role in foreign affairs are discussed extensively in the footnotes.

Appendix C

Sources*

Primary sources for a biography of Kysil may be divided into several categories. Manuscript and published works exist in each of the following categories:

1. Official governmental and private records, including grants, court decisions, deeds and tax rolls;
2. Correspondence and speeches;
3. Diet diaries;
4. Diplomatic reports and correspondence of foreign envoys;
5. Contemporary literature, including memoirs, chronicles, book dedications, newsreports and seventeenth-century histories.

The specific sources on which the biography of Kysil has been based were cited in the notes. The bibliography includes a complete listing of the manuscripts and publications which contain source materials on Kysil. The purpose of this note is to analyze the significant types of source materials and the major repositories in which they are located.

The first category, government and private records, includes appointments to office, land grants, matriculation books at the Zamość Academy (BN, BOZ, MS 1598), membership rolls of the Lviv Brotherhood (published in *Pamiatniki*), financial records and judicial decisions. The *Metryka koronna,* the official state archive of the Kingdom of Poland, includes a number of land grants and official appointments. The foreign chancery books of the *Metryka, Libri Legationum,* are another major source. These also include domestic correspondence from war zones, and *Libri Legationum* 32 (1634–1635) contains considerable correspondence to, from, and about Kysil during the Smolensk War. Because of loose supervision of state archives and dislocations resulting from the partitions of Poland, many state records exist in other collections (e.g., BJ, MS 94 which are the chancery records of P. Gębicki from 1634–1636). The state chancery books for the four provinces of the incorporation lands remain in Moscow, but these documents have been surveyed

---

* Works cited in this appendix appear in the shortened format adopted in the footnotes.

by means of the register held in AGAD, *Tak zwana Metryka litewska VIII–1, Index Actorum Publicorum,* which was compiled by Stefan Hankiewicz in 1673.

More significant are the *Akta ziemskie* and *Akta grodzkie,* or official court and registry books of the palatinates. They include official documents of the dietines, proceedings of the courts of the nobility and acts which local nobles wished to register as official. They provide information about Kysil's activities at the Diets, his family connections, land holdings, tax rolls and registry of charters. Much of the material from this source was published in the series, *Arkhiv Iugo-Zapadnoi Rossii.* Although I was denied access to these books for the incorporation lands now held in Kiev's *Tsentral'nyi derzhavnyi istorychnyi arkhiv,* a considerable amount of the material is described in the series of pamphlets entitled *Opis' aktovoi knigi Kievskogo Tsentral'nogo arkhiva* and in the registers of the Volhynian lands in the LBN, Zbirka Radzymyns'koho.

Material from the *Akta ziemskie* and *Akta grodzkie* is also available in copies in manuscript collections, particularly in the form of summaries for property disputes. A substantial amount of such material on Kysil exists in the PANK as a result of the numerous property disputes among Kysil's heirs. (PANK, MSS 2925, 2943, 2950, 3002, 2977, 2978, 3022, and 3099.) This material, which is invaluable for the family's genealogy, reflects partisan claims and must be used with caution. Tax rolls from the *Akta ziemskie* and *Akta grodzkie* and the central archives have been published extensively in *Arkhiv Iu. Z. R., Źródła dziejowe, Pam.* and the excellent publication of the 1629 register for Volhynia in Baranovych, *Zaliudnennia.*

The judicial records of the Lublin Tribunal were largely destroyed during World War II, but summaries were published in *Źródła dziejowe* (especially volumes XIX, XXI and XXII) in the nineteenth century. The Kingdom's military records and financial archives contain only sporadic information for this period. The listing for the levy of 1621 in AGAD, Zbiory z Biblioteki Narodowej, MS 5422 is particularly important for early seventeenth-century Volhynia. Both volumes of Golubev's *Kievskii Mitropolit* contain a collection of important documents and sources. These addenda are separately entitled *Materialy dlia istorii Zapadno-Russkoi tserkvi.* Both of these volumes include official documents and correspondence on Kysil, the Diets and church affairs.

The most important source for a biography of Kysil consists of his letters, speeches and writings. Kazimierz Pułaski used the remnants of the Kysil family archive for his publication, "Pierwsze lata." I have been unable to locate any additional parts of a family archive dating to the first half of the seventeenth century. The lack of an extant family archive or remnants of Kysil's own collections means that all materials survived only in other family collections, in registries of correspondence and in copy books.

Kysil's writings, primarily in the form of letters, provide the major source for this biography. Other than the anonymous pamphlet attributed to Kysil by Golubev in "Neizvestnoe polemicheskoe sochinienie," a *votum* published by Sysyn, "Regionalism," and a speech before the tsar, LBN, MS 225, almost all of Kysil's extant writings are letters. I exclude the accounts of his speeches at the Diets, which will be discussed under the category of "Diaries of Diets." Hundreds of Kysil's letters survive primarily in copies, in official inscription books and in *silvae rerum*. Almost all of his letters discuss public affairs and most are written with care and elegance according to the standards of the time, because they were meant to serve as position papers.

Before dealing with the predominant form of Kysil's correspondence, it would be best to deal with the exceptions. Only a small number of original letters by Kysil dealing with economic and political affairs survive in the two major seventeenth-century family archives. (AGAD, Arch. Radz. V, Korespondencya do Radziwiłłów, and Arch. Zamoyskich, Teka 338, 727 and 943.) Other parts of Kysil's correspondence exist in inscription books kept by the recipient. Major collections of this type are AGAD, Arch. Radz. VI, nr. 36, Dyaryusz Janusza Radziwiłła; PANK 1819, Kopiariusz korespondencyi hetmana St. Koniecpolskiego 1634–1639 [in a nineteenth-century copy] and BN, BOZ, MS 931, Listy do Lwa Sapiehy 1644–1649. In these collections are letters which were intended for the specific recipient. Finally, a large number of Kysil's original letters to Muscovite officials are preserved in Moscow's archives and were published by the St. Petersburg Archaeographic Commission in *Akty Iugo-Zapadnoi Rossii*, III.

The majority of Kysil's letters survive in multiple copies in seventeenth-century manuscripts. Some of these manuscripts were inscription books kept by individuals and institutions during the Khmel'nyts'kyi years. Important documents were copied for the purpose of preservation by the West Prussian estates into inscription books. (Arch. Gdańsk, "Recesy stanów zachodniopruskich") Examples of collections of documents gathered by contemporaries are Arch. Kr., "Pinocciana," MS 363, Arch. Kr. Zbiory Rusieckich, MSS 31 and 41, PANK, MSS 2254 and 2257, in part published in Michałowski, BO, MSS 188–189, and LBN MS 225 and 231. The multiple copies are the result of the "public" nature of so many of Kysil's letters. The letters were copied and sent on to convey news from the front or to inform friends of the debates of the day. Often letters that struck the fancy of a provincial nobleman were copied into his *silva rerum*. These manuscripts, including copies of poems, speeches, letters, and parts of books, exist in thousands of manuscripts in Polish archives and libraries. These compilations have for the most part not been inventoried and the compilers of most are not known. Numerous copies of Kysil's letters exist in these volumes. In addition to these seventeenth-century copies, Kysil's letters also exist in eighteenth- and nineteenth-century collections compiled by scholars. Often the manuscripts that the copies were made from no longer exist. The most important are the volumes of the Teki Naruszewicza in the BCz, which were commissioned by the eighteenth-century Polish historian, Adam Naruszewicz.

A considerable amount of Kysil's correspondence from the Khmel'-nyts'kyi period has been published. Some publications have been made from a single manuscript or related manuscript groups: Michałowski *Księga pamiętnicza* publishes substantial parts of the manuscripts PANK, MSS 2251, 2252, 2253, 2254, 2255, 2256 and 2257. The source addendum to Szajnocha's *Dwa lata* are from BO, MS 225, now in the Ukrainian Academy of Sciences Library in Lviv. Grabowski's *Ojczyste spominki* appears to be based on Arch. Kr., "Pinocciana," MS 363, and Rawita-Gawroński's *Sprawy i rzeczy* is from a collection of original letters in the collection of Baron Ludwik Kronenberg. Other published collections, such as *Arkhiv Iu. Z. R.* (part III, vol. IV published in 1914 and entitled *Akty, otnosiashchiesia k epokhe Bogdana Khmel'nytskogo (1648–1654)*), *Zherela* (vol. VI, XII) and *Pam.* include letters from various manuscripts dealing with a single event or period. This is also true of the three-volume series, *Voss.*, published in 1954. A major addition to the published correspondence was the *Dokumenty ob osvoboditel'noi voine ukrainskogo naroda (DOVUN)*, which includes three hundred previously unpublished documents found in Polish libraries and archives during an archeographic search. Particularly important for the study of Kysil's life is the publication of all known documents issued by Khmel'-nyts'kyi in *Dokumenty Bohdana Khmel'nyts'koho* by Ivan Kryp"iake-vych and Ivan Butych. This collection is unique in that the compilers tried to gather all copies of the documents. Other publications represent the copy that the editors had at hand, and therefore require comparison with other manuscript copies.

Many manuscripts were destroyed in the twentieth century and others are now inaccessible. Catalogues and descriptions therefore assume the function of sources. For example, *Vyzvol'na viina ukraïns'koho narodu v 1648–1654 rr. Vozz"ednannia Ukraïny z Rosieiu. Anotovanyi pokazh-*

chyk describes letters in the libraries of Lviv and Franciszek Puławski's *Opis* describes the materials of the Krasiński Library destroyed during World War II.

Kysil's activities and political positions are also reflected in the diaries of the Diets. Although no institution was more important to the inhabitants of the old Commonwealth and the materials about Diets are voluminous, no central record-keeping institutions existed. The correspondence of the period is replete with comment on the Diet and *silvae rerum* contain numerous copies of *vota* or speeches, but the Diet kept no official record of its proceedings. It was not even until the eighteenth century that the laws or constitutions of the Diets were collected and published together in consecutive volumes. We must depend on information on the Diets or *Diariusze* (here called diaries), which are chronological notes of the discussions by observers and participants. These diaries were commissioned by magnates or institutions, or were taken down for personal interest. The Lithuanian Grand Chancellor Albrycht Stanisław Radziwiłł kept a personal diary in which he noted the proceedings of each Diet, and his notes are classified as *Diariusze* for the Diets of Władysław's reign. The estates of West Prussia made a policy of gathering information on the Diet and for most of the Diets of this period, one or more diaries exist in the manuscript collections, Arch. Gdańsk, Recesy. A large number of diaries for the 1630s and 1640s exist in the large collections of seventeenth-century material in the manuscript division of the University of Wrocław, MSS Akc. 1949/KN 439; Akc. 1949/KN 440 (cited in footnotes as Steinwehr II and Steinwehr III). These diaries were not used by nineteenth-century historians and are a particularly important source about Kysil's defense of the Orthodox church. The majority of diaries are anonymous documents, and their commissioner is also unknown. Diets of the early seventeenth century have at least one diary, but the number of diaries for each varies greatly as does the degree of detail.

It is only recently that registers of diaries and their locations are available (see under "Published Sources" registers by Konopczyński, Olszewski and Radwański). Other than a few publications of excerpts, mostly done in the nineteenth century, almost all the diaries are in manuscript form. Systematic source study and publication of diaries is not being conducted. The only positive development has been the study of specific Diets, and publications of articles and monographs. Czapliński's monograph *Dwa sejmy* is an outstanding example.

Kysil's activities and speeches at the Diet are particularly important for his biography. The possibility for bias or error by the diarist in describing his activities always remains open. In the case of Albrycht Stanisław Radziwiłł, the diarist's antagonism to Kysil as "schismatic" is apparent. Although each diarist was interested in some issues more than others and favored certain views, the diaries were intended as a faithful record of what happened. At times *vota* exist which can be compared with a diarist's account, and the use of a number of diaries for one Diet reduces the chance that a fallacious account is accepted.

Materials relating to Diets—diaries of dietines, instructions to delegates, reports—are even more poorly studied than the diaries. The publication of some of the instructions of the dietine of Volhynia in *Arkhiv Iu. Z. R.*, part II, vol. I affords some material about Kysil and his constituency's wishes. Instructions are also published for the Ruthenian and Cracow palatinates (in *Akta grodzkie* and *Akta sejmikowe*). Though they offer little information about Kysil, they provide material on the political climate.

Reports of foreign ambassadors and emissaries provide a particularly important source of information. This was a source studied with considerable diligence in the nineteenth century by scholars such as Czermak and Kubala. Archaeographic commissions collected copies of *Polonica* from foreign libraries and archives. The most important are the "Teki rzymskie" and "Teki londyńskie" at Zakład Dokumentacji Instytutu Historii PAN w Krakowie and the "Teki Lukasa" from French collections in BO. Of these collections, only a few documents in the "Teki rzymskie" from the Holy See not included in the publications by Šmurlo, *Le Saint-Siège, Zherela* XVI or the numerous publications of the Basilian Fathers under the series *Analecta* OSBM series II, section III were of importance for work about Kysil. I also found material from the Venetian archives, in "Teki rzymskie," vols. 105 and 106 and "Teki Cieszkowskiego," vols. 17 and 18. No relevant material exists in "Teki Czermaka" and "Teki Wołyńskiego."

Material from the Vatican archives has been extensively published. In addition to vol. XVI of *Zherela* and Šmurlo, *Le Saint Siège*, the modern scholar has at his disposal the 18,000 documents published in the Basilian *Analecta* series II, section III, and the 3,000 documents of the thirteen volumes of *Monumenta Ucrainae Historica*. The *Litterae Nuntiorum* has been of particular importance to my work about Kysil. Additional documents from the Papal Nuncio Santa Croce are published in Kryp"iakevych, "Novi materiialy."

Reports of Muscovite emissaries and missions can be found in the three volumes of *Voss.* and in the third volume of *Akty Iu. Z. R.* Reports from Swedish archives are published in *Arkhiv Iu. Z. R.*, part III, vol. VI (1908). Extremely valuable reports by the Prussian representatives are published in vol. I of *Urkunden und Actenstücke*. Some foreign emissaries' reports are found in vol. XII of *Zherela* (= *Materiialy do istoriï ukraïns'koï kozachchyny,* vol. V, part I, *Akty do Khmel'nychchyny (1648–1657),* comp. Myron Korduba [Lviv, 1911]).

The last category of sources, "Contemporary Literature," is extremely varied. It includes the highest percentage of published materials. Books dedicated to Kysil, newspapers and leaflets, political poetry and tracts and contemporary histories were published during Kysil's life or soon after. Early histories (Rudawski, Pastorius, Kochowski, Vimina, Bisacconi, etc.) are included as primary sources, since the authors often had personal contact with the people and events that they describe and they often include testimony of eyewitnesses. The works often reflect seventeenth-century political biases and literary tastes, and information in them must be carefully evaluated. It is indicative of the period that Twardowski's *Wojna domowa,* an epic poem, was accepted as an authoritative history of the period.

In the nineteenth century, historians published numerous seventeenth-century memoirs, chronicles and diaries from manuscripts. Some, such as Temberski's Latin *Annales* (*Roczniki*) were official histories of an institution (the Cracow Academy). Others were private diaries, such as those by Oświęcim, Jemiołowski, and Jerlicz. These works were probably not intended for publication and are an excellent source of contemporary rumors and public opinion. The major source of this type is Radziwiłł's *Memoriale,* which remained unpublished in its Latin original until the 1960s. For evaluation of the major diaries and memoirs, see Czermak's article, "Kilka słów o pamiętnikach polskich." An additional source often published at this time were the chronicles of various religious institutions and monasteries. See Józefowicz's chronicle about Lviv, the texts published in *Sbornik letopisei,* the chronicle published by Sadok Barącz, and the compilations published by Petrushevich.

Lengthy book dedications to Kysil form a major source about his life. Dedications are noted in the bibliography. Because of Kysil's involvement in church affairs, polemic literature is a major source for his life. See in particular the works by his tutor Sakowicz [Sakovych], by Orański, and the pamphlets *Prawa y przywileje* and *Jedność święta.* Dedications of the publications of the Kiev academy are published in Titov's *Materiialy.* Major collections in which polemic literature is republished are *Pamiatniki polemicheskoi literatury v Zapadnoi Rusi,* 3 vols. St. Petersburg, 1878–1903 (= *Russkaia istoricheskaia biblioteka,* VI, VII, XIX) and *Arkhiv Iu. Z. R.,* part I, vols. VII, VIII, and IX.

The late seventeenth- and early eighteenth-century Cossack chronicles (for example *Litopys Samovydtsia*) were also viewed as primary sources in the nineteenth century, although subsequent scholarship has shown them to be more important sources for the history of their time than for the early seventeenth century. For discussions and evaluations of histories, memoirs, diaries, and major leaflets, see Hrushevs'kyi , VIII–3, 199–211, note 3, "Dzherela do istoriï Khmel'nychchyny i istorychna tradytsiia ïi."

In conjunction with the publication of correspondence, smaller, unpublished literary and memorial works began to appear. Some of this material exists as rare leaflets, often bound into manuscripts. Other items are in manuscript copy, although some appear to be copies of prints. These items pose the same problems of dispersal and multiple copies as correspondence. Each must be evaluated as a source for the type of information sought.

This survey presents the major sources for Kysil's biography. Additional detailed information on documents and the contents of each source can be found in the notes.

Notes

Introduction

1. Mykhailo Hrushevs'kyi, *Istoriia Ukraïny-Rusy IX*, pt. 1, reprint (New York, 1958), 509. Hereafter Mykhailo Hrushevs'kyi, *Istoriia Ukraïny-Rusy*, reprint, vols. I–X (New York, 1954–58) will be referred to as Hrushevs'kyi I, etc. and vol. VIII, pts. 1, 2, 3 as VIII–1, VIII–2, VIII–3.

2. For biographies of Kysil, see Appendix B.

3. *Ukraïns'ka radians'ka entsyklopediia* VI (Kiev, 1961), 379.

4. See the following articles: "Ukrainian-Polish Relations in the Seventeenth Century: The Role of National Consciousness and National Conflict in the Khmelnytsky Movement," in Peter J. Potichnyj (ed.), *Poland and Ukraine: Past and Present* (Edmonton-Toronto, 1980), pp. 58–82; "Stosunki ukraińsko-polskie w XVII wieku: rola świadomości narodowej i konfliktu narodowościowego w powstaniu Chmielnickiego," *Odrodzenie i Reformacja* (Warsaw), XXVII (1982), 67–92; "A Contemporary's Account of the Causes of the Khmel'nyts'kyi Uprising," *Harvard Ukrainian Studies*, V, no. 2 (June, 1981), 254–267; "Seventeenth-Century Views on the Causes of the Khmel'nyts'kyi Uprising: An Examination of the 'Discourse about the Present Cossack-Peasant War'," *Harvard Ukrainian Studies*, V, no. 4 (December, 1981), 430–466; "The Problem of Nobilities in the Ukrainian Past: The Polish Period, 1569–1648," in Ivan L. Rudnytsky (ed.), *Rethinking Ukrainian History* (Edmonton-Toronto, 1981), pp. 29–102; "Regionalism and Political Thought in Seventeenth-Century Ukraine: The Nobility's Grievances at the Diet of 1641," *Harvard Ukrainian Studies*, VI, no. 2 (June, 1982), 167–190.

5. For Kysil's estates, see Appendix A. For archival sources, see Appendix B. I was not allowed to carry on research on Kysil in the Soviet Union under an IREX grant in 1972–73. In 1980 while working on another topic in seventeenth-century Ukrainian history during an IREX grant, I was denied access to all libraries and archives in Moscow and Leningrad and all archives in Kiev and Lviv.

Chapter 1

1. For discussion of periods in Polish history, see Władysław Czapliński, *O Polsce siedemnastowiecznej: Problemy i sprawy* (Warsaw, 1966) and Tadeusz Ulewicz, "Zagadnienie sarmatyzmu w kulturze i literaturze polskiej (Problematyka ogólna i zarys historyczny)," *Zeszyty Naukowe Uniwersytetu Jagiellońskiego*, no. 59, *Prace Historycznoliterackie*, no. 5, *Filologia*, no. 9 (1963), pp. 29–92.

2. For the sixteenth century, see *Polska w epoce Odrodzenia: Państwo, społeczeństwo, kultura*, ed. Andrzej Wyczański (Warsaw, 1970).

3. For the periodization of the "seventeenth century," and its characteris-

tics, see *Polska XVII wieku: Państwo, społeczeństwo, kultura,* ed. Janusz Tazbir (Warsaw, 1969).

4. The best discussion of the state and society in this period is Zdzisław Kaczmarczyk and Bogusław Leśnodorski, *Od połowy XV wieku do r. 1795,* vol. II of *Historia państwa i prawa Polski,* 4th ed. (Warsaw, 1971) hereafter Kaczmarczyk, *Historia*), which contains bibliographies about almost all the topics discussed in this section. Also see Ireneusz Ihnatowicz, Antoni Mączak, and Benedykt Zientara, *Społeczeństwo polskie od X do XX wieku* (Warsaw, 1979), pp. 227–455. For institutional history, see Stanisław Kutrzeba's classic studies, *Historia ustroju Polski w zarysie,* I, *Korona,* 5th ed. (Lviv, 1920), II, *Litwa,* 2nd ed. (Lviv, 1921). For a general history of the period, see Andrzej Wyczański, *Polska-Rzeczą Pospolitą Szlachecką 1454–1764* (Warsaw, 1965) and Norman Davies, *God's Playground: A History of Poland,* 2 vols. (New York, 1982), I, 159–476.

5. Kaczmarczyk, *Historia,* pp. 38–39. Major studies about the union are Oskar Halecki, *Dzieje Unii Jagiellońskiej,* I (Cracow, 1919); II (Cracow, 1920) and Stanisław Kutrzeba, *Unia Polski z Litwą: Polska i Litwa w stosunku dziejowym* (Cracow, 1913). On the problem of foreign policy, see Władysław Konopczyński, "Udział Korony i Litwy w tworzeniu wspólnej polityki zagranicznej, 1569–1795," *Pamiętnik VI Powszechnego Zjazdu Historyków Polskich w Wilnie 17–20 września 1935 r.,* I (Lviv, 1935), 78–81. For sources to the Union of Lublin see *Akta Unji Polski z Litwą, 1387–1791,* ed. Stanisław Kutrzeba and Władysław Semkowicz (Cracow, 1932).

6. The retention of separate identity is discussed in V. Druzhytz, "Palazhenne Litoŭska-Belaruskai dziarzhavy paslia Liublinskai Vunii," *Pratsy Belaruskaho Dziarzhavnaho universytetu,* 1925, nos. 6–7, pp. 216–251 and Henryk Wisner, *Najjaśniejsza Rzeczpospolita: Szkice z dziejów Polski szlacheckiej* (Warsaw, 1978), pp. 13–42. For a discussion of literature on the Grand Duchy in this period, see Ryszard Mienicki, "Przegląd badań nad dziejami Litwy 1569–1696," *Pamiętnik VI Powszechnego Zjazdu,* I, 26–36. On the internal structure and federal ties of the Grand Duchy to the kingdom, see Kutrzeba, *Litwa,* and L. Lappo, *Velikoe Kniazhestvo Litovskoe za vremia ot zaklucheniia Lublinskoi Unii do smerti Stefana Batoria* (St. Petersburg, 1901). For a discussion of the impact of the Union of Lublin, see Oscar Halecki, "Why Was Poland Partitioned?," in *The Development of the USSR: An Exchange of Views,* ed. D. Treadgold (Seattle, 1964), pp. 296–305.

7. See Kaczmarczyk, *Historia,* pp. 31–34, and Stanisław Grodziski, *Obywatelstwo w Szlacheckiej Rzeczypospolitej* (Cracow, 1963).

8. For the development of the *szlachta,* see Juliusz Bardach, *Historia państwa i prawa Polski do połowy XV wieku* (Warsaw, 1957), pp. 422–430. The section contains a bibliography of the major literature. Also see Hans Roos, "Der Adel der Polnischen Republik im vorrevolutionären Europa," in Rudolf Vierhaus, ed., *Der Adel vor der Revolution. Zur sozialen und politischen Function des Adels im vorrevolutionären Europa* (Göttingen, 1971), pp. 41–76; the special issue "Etudes sur la noblesse," of *Acta Poloniae Historica* XXXVI (1977), and Jarema Maciszewski, *Szlachta polska i jej państwo* (Warsaw, 1969).

9. For the multinational nature of the *szlachta* and the process of the formation of the elite of the eastern lands as a Polish *szlachta*, see Kaczmarczyk, *Historia,* pp. 35–40. On unions of nobilities, see Gotthold Rhode, "Staaten-Union und Adelstaat: Zur Entwicklung von Staatsdenken und Staatsgestaltung in Osteuropa, vor allem in Polen/Litauen im 16. Jahrhundert," *Zeitschrift für Ostforschung* IX, no. 2/3 (July 1960), 184–213. On the *szlachta*'s ideology see Andrzej Zajączkowski, *Główne elementy kultury szlacheckiej w Polsce: Ideologia a struktury społeczne* (Wrocław, 1961); Janusz Tazbir, *Kultura szlachecka w Polsce: Rozkwit-upadek-relikty* (Warsaw, 1978); Józef Andrzej Gierowski, ed., *Dzieje kultury politycznej w Polsce* (Warsaw, 1977), and Jarema Maciszewski, "Społeczeństwo," in *Polska XVII wieku,* pp. 120–150. The percentage of nobles is an approximation accepted in the scholarly literature, but not based on reliable computations. See, for example, Maciszewski, *Szlachta polska,* p. 35.

10. For a discussion of both liberty and equality, see Jarema Maciszewski, *Szlachta polska,* pp. 156–168.

11. For Sarmatism, see Stanisław Cynarski, "Sarmatyzm—ideologia i styl życia," *Polska XVII wieku,* pp. 220–243; Tadeusz Ulewicz, *Sarmacja: Studium z problematyki słowiańskiej XV i XVI wieku* (Cracow, 1950); Tadeusz Mańkowski, *Genealogia sarmatyzmu* (Warsaw, 1946), and the special issue of the Warsaw journal, *Teksty* (1974), no. 4.

12. On the ideological aspects of equality see Zajączkowski, *Główne elementy,* pp. 35–49. On the struggle for equality, particularly the "execution of the laws" movement, see Anna Sucheni-Grabowska, "Walka o demokrację szlachecką," *Polska w epoce Odrodzenia,* pp. 9–67, and the bibliography, pp. 304–306.

13. For a description of the oligarchy of the magnates and literature on the topic, see Kaczmarczyk, *Historia,* pp. 189–192, and his discussion on the magnate oligarchy's control of the state in "Oligarchia magnacka w Polsce jako forma państwa," *VIII Powszechny Zjazd Historyków Polskich w Krakowie 14–17 września 1958,* VII, ed. Zdzisław Kaczmarczyk, (Warsaw, 1959), 61–76. For a discussion of the definition of "magnate" see Władysław Czapliński and Adam Kersten, ed., *Magnateria polska jako warstwa społeczna* (Toruń, 1974). Andrzej Kaminski has recently called for abandoning the term "magnate" because it covers too large a group of nobles of very different levels of power and wealth. He proposes that a small group of prominent families identified by Włodzimierz Dworzaczek be called "aristocrats." Although Kaminski correctly draws attention to the ambiguity of the term "magnate," he does not really make a sufficiently strong case for why the introduction of "aristocrat" will improve discussion on the nobility. I have decided to use the more usual term "magnate." See Andrzej Kaminski, "The *Szlachta* of the Polish-Lithuanian Commonwealth and Their Government," *The Nobility in Russia and Eastern Europe,* ed. Ivo Banac and Paul Bushkovitch (New Haven, 1983), pp. 25–27. For a discussion of the various aspects of the magnates' lives, see Władysław Czapliński and Józef Długosz, *Życie codzienne magnaterii polskiej w XVII wieku* (Warsaw, 1976). For an analysis of how magnate families rose and fell, see Teresa Zielińska, *Magnateria polska epoki saskiej* (Wrocław, 1977).

14. The most comprehensive study on the seventeenth-century Diet is Henryk Olszewski, *Sejm Rzeczypospolitej epoki oligarchii: Prawo, praktyka, teoria, programy* (Poznań, 1966). Also see Stanisław Kutrzeba, *Sejm walny Rzeczypospolitej polskiej* (Warsaw, 1923) and Władysław Czapliński, "Z problematyki sejmu polskiego w pierwszej połowie XVII wieku," *Kwartalnik Historyczny,* LXXVII, no. 1 (1970), 31–45. For the theory of representation in the Diet, see Konstanty Grzybowski, *Teoria reprezentacji w Polsce epoki Odrodzenia* (Warsaw, 1959). On dietine politics, see Władysław Czapliński, "Wybór posła w dawnej Polsce," in *Dawne czasy; Opowiadania i szkice historyczne z XVII wieku* (Wrocław, 1957), pp. 215–235.

15. On the evolving operation of the Diet, see Kaczmarczyk, *Historia,* pp. 118–128. The increasingly important role of the Senate is discussed in Władysław Czapliński, "Senat za Władysława IV," in *Studia historyczne ku czci Stanisława Kutrzeby,* I (Cracow, 1938), 81–104. For an excellent, but popular study of the Diet and dietines, see Marek Borucki, *Sejmy i sejmiki szlacheckie* (Warsaw, 1972).

16. For the Diet in its decline, see Kaczmarczyk, *Historia,* pp. 237–242.

17. For the *liberum veto,* see Władysław Konopczyński, *Liberum veto* (Cracow, 1918); Władysław Czapliński, *Dwa sejmy w roku 1652* (Wrocław, 1955).

18. On the power of the king, see Kaczmarczyk, *Historia,* pp. 110–118. For a discussion of the nobility's discontent with attempts at extending royal power in Zygmunt III's reign, see Jarema Maciszewski, *Wojna domowa w Polsce (1606–1609),* I (Wrocław, 1960).

19. On the offices the king distributed see Kaczmarczyk, *Historia,* pp. 129–135; for the incomes derived, see Władysław Pałucki, *Studia nad uposażeniem urzędników ziemskich w Koronie do schyłku XVI wieku* (Warsaw, 1962). On the powers and court of the king see Władysław Czapliński, *Na dworze Władysława IV* (Warsaw, 1959).

20. On the rights of the burghers, see Kaczmarczyk, *Historia,* pp. 57–74 and 203–213.

21. The standard study on cities is Jan Ptaśnik, *Miasta i mieszczaństwo w dawnej Polsce,* 2nd ed. (Warsaw, 1949). On the unique situation of Gdańsk, see Maria Bogucka, "Gdańsk—polski czy międzynarodowy ośrodek gospodarczy?" *Polska w epoce Odrodzenia,* pp. 100–125.

22. For a survey of the scholarly literature about the grain trade, the increase of demesne farming and of peasant labor obligations, see Andrzej Kaminski, "Neo-Serfdom in Poland-Lithuania," *Slavic Review,* XXXIV, no. 2 (June, 1975), 253–258. On the important problem of Baltic trade, see Marian Małowist, "The Economic and Social Development of the Baltic Countries from the Fifteenth to the Seventeenth Centuries," *Economic History Review,* 2nd ser., XII, no. 2 (1959), 177–189. For the Vistula traffic in the seventeenth century, see Honorata Obuchowska-Pysiowa, *Handel wiślany w pierwszej połowie XVII wieku* (Wrocław, 1964). For general economic developments, see Antoni Mączak, "Problemy gospodarcze," *Polska XVII wieku,* pp. 324–326. For the competition of Russian grain, see Maria Bogucka, "Zboże rosyjskie na rynku amsterdamskim w pierwszej połowie XVII wieku," *Przegląd Historyczny,* LIII, no. 4 (1962), 612–628.

23. For a characterization of foreign policy, see Zbigniew Wójcik, "Międzynarodowe położenie Rzeczypospolitej," in *Polska XVII wieku*, pp. 13–51 and his comments on the gentry's fear of an army in royal hands, in "Poland and Russia in the 17th Century: Problems of Internal Development," *Poland at the 14th International Congress of Historical Sciences in San Francisco: Studies in Comparative History* (Wrocław, 1975), pp. 131–132. See the discussion on Polish-Lithuanian foreign policy in *VIII Powszechny Zjazd Historyków Polskich w Krakowie 14–17 września 1958*, III, ed. Kazimierz Lepszy (Warsaw, 1960), 70–119.

24. For a discussion of the magnates' role in initiating military ventures, see Kaczmarczyk, *Historia*, 179–180. For their intervention in the Muscovite Time of Troubles, see Jarema Maciszewski, *Polska a Moskwa: 1603–1618: Opinie i stanowiska szlachty polskiej* (Warsaw, 1968), pp. 9–38.

25. For an analysis of the nobility's pacifism, see J. Maciszewski, *Polska i Moskwa: Opinie i stanowiska szlachty polskiej.* The discussants at the Eighth Congress of Polish Historians (see footnote 23) treat the increasing pacifism in the second quarter of the seventeenth century. See *VIII Powszechny Zjazd*, III, 93–119.

26. For a discussion of Zygmunt's and Władysław's claims, see Władysław Czapliński, *Władysław IV i jego czasy* (Warsaw, 1972), pp. 2–51. For a survey of the Commonwealth's wars, see Wójcik, "Międzynarodowe położenie Rzeczypospolitej" and the bibliography in *Polska XVII wieku*, pp. 321–322. For the Commonwealth's position during the Thirty Years War, see Władysław Czapliński, *Władysław IV wobec Wojny 30-Letniej (1637–1645)* (Cracow, 1937).

27. For the military, see Jan Wimmer, "Wojsko," *Polska XVII wieku*, pp. 151–189 and the bibliography, pp. 328–330. For a more detailed account, see *Zarys dziejów wojskowości polskiej do roku 1864*, I (Warsaw, 1965), II (Warsaw, 1966). For a discussion of the military in this period, see Bohdan Baranowski, *Organizacja wojska polskiego w latach trzydziestych i czterdziestych XVII wieku*, Prace Komisji Wojskowo-Historycznej Ministerstwa Obrony Narodowej, ser. A, X (Warsaw, 1957). On financial matters and the military, see Jan Wimmer, "Wojsko i skarb Rzeczypospolitej u schyłku XVI i w pierwszej połowie XVII w." *Studia i Materiały do Historii Wojskowości*, XIV, pt. 1 (1968), 3–91.

28. On confederations, see Kaczmarczyk, *Historia*, p. 128, pp. 243–245. For the legality of confederations, see A. Rembowski, *Konfederacja i rokosz w dawnym prawie polskim* (Warsaw, 1896). The major armed rebellion of the nobility for this right was led by Zebrzydowski between 1606 and 1609. See Maciszewski, *Wojna Domowa.*

29. On the Commonwealth's religious tolerance see Jan Tazbir, *Państwo bez stosów: Szkice z dziejów tolerancji w Polsce XVII wieku* (Warsaw, 1958). For confessional problems in the seventeenth century, see Janusz Tazbir, "Problemy wyznaniowe," *Polska XVII wieku*, pp. 189–220 and bibliography, pp. 330–331.

30. The legal status of the Orthodox church in Poland, Lithuania and the Commonwealth up until 1632 is treated in detail in Kazimierz Chodynicki, *Kościół Prawosławny a Rzeczpospolita Polska 1370–1632* (Warsaw, 1934). On the

granting of equality to Orthodoxy, see Kazimierz Chodynicki, "Geneza równouprawnienia schyzmatyków w W. Ks. Litewskiem: Stosunek Zygmunta Augusta
do wyznania grecko-wschodniego," *Przegląd Historyczny,* XXII (1919–1920),
54–135. For a discussion of the legislation on Orthodoxy, see V. Bednov, *Pravoslavnaia tserkov v Pol'she i Litve po "Volumina Legum"* (Ekaterinoslav, 1908).

31. On the Reformation, see Janusz Tazbir, "Społeczeństwo wobec Reformacji," *Polska w epoce Odrodzenia,* pp. 197–224, and the bibliography, pp. 312–
313. The series publications, *Reformacja w Polsce,* I–XII (1921–1956) and *Odrodzenie i Reformacja w Polsce* (1956 to present) are devoted to the problems
of the Reformation.

32. On the Confederation of Warsaw, see Mirosław Korolko, *Klejnot swobodnego sumienia: Polemika wokół konfederacji warszawskiej w latach 1573–
1658* (Warsaw, 1974).

33. On the Jewish population of the Commonwealth, see Salo Wittmayer
Baron, *A Social and Religious History of the Jews,* 2nd ed. XVI: *Poland-Lithuania 1500–1650* (New York-London, 1976). Bernard Weinryb, *The Jews of Poland: A Social and Economic History of the Jews of Poland from 1100 to 1800*
(Philadelphia, 1972) and Maurycy Horn, *Powinności wojenne Żydów w Rzeczypospolitej w XVI i XVII wieku* (Warsaw, 1978). On Jews in the Ukrainian lands,
see Maurycy Horn, *Żydzi na Rusi Czerwonej w XVI i pierwszej połowie XVII w.
Działalność gospodarcza na tle rozwoju demograficznego* (Warsaw, 1975).

34. The depth of belief in freedom for the nobility is evident in a pro-Uniate
polemic against the Orthodox at the Luts'k dietine in 1632 *Antimaxia albo Dyskurs na Dyskurs wydany od kogoś pod czas rellatiej P. P. Posłów Wołhinskich
w Łuczku pro die 16 Aug. Anno. 1632.* BCz, Ms 373, pp. 470–481. Although
the polemic is directed against granting rights to Orthodoxy, after discussing the
political rights of the nobility the author discusses liberty of religion as a cherished right. He contrasts the Commonwealth's religious peace to the wars in
surrounding states.

35. On the Socinian movement in the Commonwealth see Orest Levitskii,
"Sotsinianstvo v Pol'she i Iugo-Zapadnoi Rusi," *Kievskaia Starina,* 1882, no. 4,
pp. 25–57, no. 5, pp. 193–225, no. 6, pp. 401–432; Janusz Tazbir, *Arianie i katolicy* (Warsaw, 1971); and Stanisław Kot, *Socinianism in Poland: The Social
and Political Ideas of the Polish Antitrinitarians in the Sixteenth and Seventeenth
Centuries,* trans. Earle Morse Wilbur (Boston, 1957).

36. On the status of the Catholic church in the Commonwealth, see *Kościół
w Polsce,* II, *Wieki XVI–XVIII* (Cracow, 1970), and Janusz Tazbir, *Historia
Kościoła Katolickiego w Polsce, 1460–1795* (Warsaw, 1966).

37. The problems of tolerance and intolerance in the seventeenth-century
Commonwealth are discussed in *Kościół w Polsce,* II, 31–39, and by Władysław
Czapliński, "Parę uwag o tolerancji w Polsce w okresie Kontrreformacji," *O
Polsce siedemnastowiecznej* (Warsaw, 1966).

38. For the Commonwealth's ethnic diversity, see Henryk Samsonowicz, *Historia Polski do roku 1795* (Warsaw, 1973), pp. 168–169.

39. For the linguistic situation among the Eastern Slavs, see Antoine Martel,

La langue polonaise dans les pays Ruthenes: Ukraine et Russie Blanche, 1569–1667, Travaux et Mémoires de l'Univérsité de Lille, Nouvelle Serie: Droit et Lettres, XX (Lille, 1938), 11–13.

40. On the use of the term *Ukraine,* see W(acław) L(ipiński), "Nazwy Ruś i Ukraina i ich znaczenie historyczne," *Z dziejów Ukrainy,* pp. 47–54.

41. For a description of the various Ukrainian lands at the end of the sixteenth and beginning of the seventeenth centuries, see [Aleksander Jabłonowski], *Pisma . . . ,* 4 vols. (Warsaw, 1910–1911), III, IV; Michał Hruszewski, "Szlachta ukraińska na przełomie XVI i XVII wieku" in *Z dziejów Ukrainy,* pp. 1–46. (A translation of Mykhailo Hrushevs'kyi, "Vidnosyny kul'turni i natsional'ni: natsional'nyi sklad i natsional'ni elementy," Hrushevs'kyi VI, 235–293. (Notes from Jabłonowski's work are added by Lypyns'kyi [Lipiński],) and Antoine Martel, *La langue polonaise,* pp. 20–27. Also see A. I. Baranovich, *Ukraina nakanune osvoboditel'noi voiny serediny XVII v.* (Moscow, 1959), and D. I. Myshko, *Sotsial'no-ekonomichni umovy formuvannia ukraïns'koï narodnosti* (Kiev, 1963). Section I, "Ukraïna naperedodni vyzvol'noï viiny, 1648–1654" of I. P. Kryp"iakevych's *Bohdan Khmel'nyts'kyi* (Kiev, 1954), pp. 13–60, is a summary of socio-economic relations in seventeenth-century Ukraine. For a discussion of the nobility in the Ukraine, with extensive bibliographic notes, see Frank Sysyn, "The Problem of Nobilities in the Ukrainian Past: The Polish Period, 1569–1648," in Ivan L. Rudnytsky, ed. *Rethinking Ukrainian History* (Edmonton, 1981), pp. 29–102.

42. Other than the works cited in footnote 41, on Galicia or the Ruthenian palatinate see I. A. Linnichenko, *Cherty iz istorii soslovii v Iugo-Zapadnoi (Galitskoi) Rusi XIV–XV vv.* (Moscow, 1894); Henryk Paszkiewicz, *Polityka ruska Kazimierza Wielkiego* (Warsaw, 1925); W. Abraham, *Powstanie organizacyi Kościoła Łacińskiego na Rusi* (Lviv, 1904). For social relations in seventeenth-century Red Rus', see Władysław Łoziński, *Prawem i lewem: Obyczaje na Czerwonej Rusi w pierwszej połowie XVII wieku,* 5th ed., 2 vols. (Cracow, 1957). For a bibliographical sketch on all the Ukrainian lands of the Polish kingdom, see, "Studiï nad suspil'no-politychnym ustroem ukraïns'ko-rus'kych zemel' Pol'shchi i ïkh literatura," Hrushevs'kyi, V, 634–642.

43. On Podillia, see N. Molchanovskii, *Ocherk izvestii o Podolskoi zemle do 1434 goda* (Kiev, 1885). For comparison of Volhynia and Podillia, see Aleksander Jabłonowski, "Wołyń i Podole pod koniec w. XVI-go.," *Pisma,* IV (Warsaw, 1911), 144–233.

44. On the annexation of these lands, see Oskar Halecki, *Przyłączenie Podlasia, Wołynia i Kijowszczyzny do Korony w roku 1569* (Cracow, 1915). Baranovich, *Ukraina,* contains a good description of the society and economy of the incorporation lands.

45. On the decentralized structure of the Lithuanian state, see M. Liubavskii, *Oblastnoe delenie i mestnoe upravlenie Litovsko-Russkogo Gosudarstva* (Moscow, 1892).

46. V. Picheta, "Pol'sko-litovskie unii i otnoshenie k nim litovskoi shliakhty," *Sbornik statei, posviashchennykh V. O. Kliuchevskomu* (Moscow, 1909), pp. 605–632.

47. For a description of the privileges of the annexed territories, see Halecki, *Przyłączenie*, and Jarosław Pelenski, "The Incorporation of the Ukrainian Lands of Old Rus' into Crown Poland (1569): Socio-material Interest and Ideology— A Reexamination," *American Contributions to the Seventh International Congress of Slavicists (Warsaw, August 21–27, 1973)*, III (The Hague and Paris, 1973), pp. 19–52. Podlasie is not included in my discussion because of the great differences from the other incorporated lands before the union and the different terms of its incorporation.

48. On the legal position of the Chernihiv lands, see Mykola Vasylenko, "Pravne polozhennia Chernyhivshchyny za pol's'koï doby (1618–1648)," *Chernyhiv i pivnichne Livoberezhzhia*, Zapysky Ukraïns'koho naukovoho tovarystva v Kyievi, XXIII (Kiev, 1928), 290–300.

49. For a description of the religious and ethnic make-up of the area, see Halecki, *Przyłączenie*, pp. 217–245.

50. On the institutional and social changes in the Grand Duchy prior to the Union of Lublin, see M. Liubavskii, *Litovsko-russkii seim* (Moscow, 1901); for the prior social structure see his *Ocherk istorii Litovsko-Russkogo Gosudarstva do Liublinskoi Unii vkliuchitel'no* (Moscow, 1910). See also F. I. Leontovich, "Boiare i sluzhilye liudi v Litovsko-Russkom Gosudarstve," *Zhurnal Ministerstva Iustitsii*, no. 5, 1907, pp. 221–292, no. 6, 1907, pp. 193–264; F. I. Leontovich, *Soslovnyi tip territorial'no-administrivnogo sostava Litovskogo Gosudarstva i ego prichiny* (St. Petersburg, 1895). For a collection of essays on the political, cultural, and economic history of the Grand Duchy, see V. I. Picheta, *Belorussiia i Litva XV–XVI vv.: Issledovaniia po istorii sotsial'no-ekonomicheskogo, politichesko i kul'turnogo razvitiia* (Moscow, 1961).

51. On the problem of the boiars in the Ukraine, see Kryp''iakevych, *Bohdan Khmel'nyts'kyi*, pp. 48–49.

52. The harmful influence of the magnates of the eastern lands on the Polish social and political development is a frequent theme in Polish historiography. See, for example, Maciszewski, "Społeczeństwo," p. 141.

53. Computations for the percentage of the nobility are very imprecise, but Kryp''iakevych's estimates of landed nobility for the Kiev and Bratslav palatinates are under 1 percent of the population. Kryp''iakevych, *Bohdan Khmel'nyts'kyi*, p. 16.

54. On the origins of the Cossacks, see G. Stökl, *Die Entstehung des Kosakentums*, Veröffentlichungen des Osteuropa-Institutes, III (Munich, 1953). See the general studies on Cossacks, Leszek Podhorecki, *Sicz zaporoska* (Warsaw, 1960): V. Golobutskii, *Zaporozhskoe kazachestvo* (Kiev, 1957); and Zbigniew Wójcik, *Dzikie pole w ogniu: O kozaczyźnie w dawnej Rzeczypospolitej* (Warsaw, 1960). For a bibliographical essay about the problem, see "Pochatky kozachyny," Hrushevs'kyi, VII, 563–569.

55. Władysław Tomkiewicz, "O składzie społecznym i etnicznym kozaczyzny ukrainnej na przełomie XVI–XVII wieku," *Przegląd Historyczny*, XXXVII (1948), 249–260.

56. For a bibliography on innovations of Batory and the myths surrounding

them, see "Batoriieva reforma," Hrushevs'kyi VII, 577–581. On the importance of the Batory period for Cossack legitimism, see Aleksander Jabłonowski, "Kozaczyzna a legitymizm: Dwie legendy polityczno-historyczne Ukrainy: Batoryańska i baturyńska," *Pisma,* II, 210–241.

57. For a discussion of the position of the registered and unregistered Cossacks, see Jabłonowski, "Kozactwo," *Pisma,* I, 120–209

58. For a discussion of the Cossacks' role in international relations, see Zbigniew Wójcik's introduction in Zbigniew Wójcik, ed., *Eryka Lassoty i Wilhelma Beauplana Opisy Ukrainy,* trans. Zofia Stasiewska and Stefan Meller (Warsaw, 1972), pp. 5–51.

59. For a bibliographical essay on the Zaporozhian Cossacks in the early part of the seventeenth century, see "Kozachyna v pershykh dvokh desiatilitakh XVII v.," Hrushevs'kyi VII, 581–584. Also see Władysław Serczyk, "The Commonwealth and the Cossacks in the First Quarter of the Seventeenth Century," *Harvard Ukrainian Studies,* II, no. 1 (March 1978), 73–93.

60. For economic and social relations in this period, see Baranovich, *Ukraina,* pp. 51–132, and I. D. Boiko, *Selianstvo Ukraïny v druhii polovyni XVI-pershii polovyni XVII st.* (Kiev, 1963), and Hrushevs'kyi V, 1–385.

61. The colonization of the Dnieper lands in the late sixteenth and early seventeenth century has been the subject of considerable debate. The depopulation of these lands prior to the sixteenth century and the role played by the Polish nobility have been two major issues of dispute. Jabłonowski, *Pisma,* III, is the major scholarly work asserting that the Ukrainian steppe was largely depopulated in the sixteenth century. M. F. Vladimirskii-Budanov, in "Naselenie Iugo-Zapadnoi Rossii ot vtoroi poloviny XV v. do Lublinskoi unii (1596)," *Arkhiv Iugo-Zapadnoi Rossii . . . ,* 8 parts, 34 vols. (Kiev, 1859–1914) (hereafter *Arkhiv Iu. Z. R.*), pt. VII, vol. II (Kiev, 1890), asserted that a large population existed there prior to the Union of Lublin. Soviet historians have asserted that the Ukraine had a considerable population and have denied any "beneficial" influences of Polish nobles' colonization. See A. I. Baranovich, "Naselenie predstepnoi Ukrainy v XVI v.," *Istoricheskie zapiski AN SSR,* XXXII (1959), 198–232; Mykola Tkachenko, "Narysy z istoriï selian po Livoberezhnii Ukraïni v XVII–XVIII vv.," *Zapysky istorychno-filol'ohichnoho viddilu Vse-Ukraïns'koï akademiï nauk* (hereafter ZIFV), XXVI (1931), 31–179. For bibliographical essays on the problem, see "Literatura suspil'no-ekonomichnykh i kol'onizatsiinykh obstavyn skhidno-ukraïns'koho zhytia XV–XVI vv.," Hrushevs'kyi VI, 562–563, and "Ukraïns'ka kol'onizatsiia na skhid vid Dnipra (Livoberezhe, Slobids'ka Ukraïna)," Hrushevs'kyi VIII, 197–199. Also see Zenon Guldon, "Badania nad zaludnieniem Ukrainy w XVII wieku," *Kwartalnik Historii Kultury Materialnej* XIII (1965), 561–566 and O. S. Kompan, "Do pytannia pro zaselenist' Ukraïny v XVII st.," *Ukraïns'kyi istorychnyi zhurnal* 1960, no. 1, pp. 65–77. On the settlement and economic role of Jews, see Baron, *A Social and Religious History,* XVI. On cities, see P. V. Mykhailyna, *Mista Ukraïny v period feodalizmu (Do pytannia pro stanovyshche mist v umovakh inozemnoho ponevolennia v kintsi XVI-pershii polovyni XVII st.)* (Chernivtsi, 1971).

248 Notes to pages 25–27

62. For a short account of the Cossack rebellions of the period, see Golobutskii, *Zaporozhskoe kazachestvo*, pp. 100–146. For more detailed study, see Hrushevs'kyi VII.

63. For the problem of the Commonwealth's eastern foreign policy, see Zbigniew Wójcik, "Niektóre zagadnienia polityki wschodniej Rzeczypospolitej w końcu XVI i w XVII wieku w literaturze zagranicznej lat ostatnich," *Rocznik Lubelski*, V (1962), 7–43. For relations with the Tatars and Ottomans, see Bohdan Baranowski, *Polska a Tatarszczyzna w latach 1624–1629* (Łódz, 1943); Bohdan Baranowski, *Stosunki polsko-tatarskie w latach 1632–1648* (Łódz, 1949). For a discussion of the Crimea, see V. D. Smirnov, *Krymskoe khanstvo pod verkhovenstvom Ottomanskoi Porty* (St. Petersburg, 1887); Alexandre Bennigsen *et al*, *Le khanat de Crimée dans les Archives du Musée du Palais de Topkapi* (Paris-The Hague, 1978), and Alan W. Fisher, *The Crimean Tatars* (Stanford, 1978). Tatar-Muscovite relations are discussed in A. A. Novosel'skii, *Bor'ba Moskovskogo gosudarstva s tatarami v pervoi polovine XVII veka* (Moscow, 1948).

64. For a discussion of Polish-Russian relations in the seventeenth century, see Bohdan Baranowski and Zofia Libiszowska, "Problematyka stosunków polsko-rosyjskich XVII wieku," *Zeszyty Naukowe Uniwersytetu Łódzkiego*, series I, Nauki humanistyczno-społeczne, XVI (1958), 41–58. For border problems, see Władysław Godziszewski, *Granica polsko-moskiewska wedle pokoju polanowskiego wytyczona w 1. 1634–1648* (Cracow, 1934). On Muscovite foreign relations with the Habsburgs, see Walter Leitsch, *Moskau und die Politik des Kaiserhofes im XVII Jahrhundert, pt. 1 1604–1654* (Graz-Cologne, 1960) Wiener Archiv für Geschichte des Slaventums und Osteuropas. Veröffentlichungen des Institut für osteuropäische Geschichte und Südostforschung der Universität Wien IV.

65. For a discussion of foreign policy in the south-east, see Czapliński, "Polityka Rzeczypospolitej Polskiej w latach 1576–1648," *VIII Powszechny Zjazd*, III, 95–100, and Józef Tretiak, *Historia wojny chocimskiej* (Cracow, 1921).

66. The Commonwealth was unable to support its forces even though it spent 90 percent of its budget on the military. This sum was only one half of what Denmark or Sweden spent on their armies. The reason for this was the limited taxing powers of the government. Wimmer, "Wojsko," p. 169. On the power of the hetmans, see Wimmer, "Wojsko," p. 174, and Wacław Zarzycki, *Dyplomacja hetmanów w dawnej Polsce* (Warsaw-Poznań, 1976) Bydgoskie Towarzystwo Naukowe. Prace Wydziału Nauk Humanistycznych, ser. E, no. 8.

67. The best general discussion of estate, religious and national identifications in the seventeenth-century Commonwealth is Wyczański, *Polska*, pp. 263–364. Literature on national consciousness is cited in my article, "Ukrainian-Polish Relations in the Seventeenth Century," and in its revised version in Polish, "Stosunki ukraińsko-polskie w XVII wieku: Rola świadomości narodowej i konfliktu narodowościowego w powstaniu Chmielnickiego," *Odrodzenie i Reformacja* XXVII (1982), 67–92.. These studies serve as the basis of this section.

68. Tazbir, "Problemy wyznaniowe," p. 196 and Wójcik, "Poland and Russia in the Seventeenth Century," pp. 122–123.

69. These uses of "Greek" and "Eastern" occur in the full title of a very important source for religious and national attitudes, the *Supplikatia do przeoświeconego i Jaśnie Wielmożnego Senatu Przezacnej Korony Polskiej i W. X. Litewskiego*. (Hereafter *Supplikatia*), republished in *Z dziejów Ukrainy,* pp. 99–111.

70. Often the "Rus' faith" is used as a synonymn for the "Greek" or "Eastern faith." *Supplikatia* in *Z dziejów Ukrainy,* p. 101. At times authors were more explicit in identifying the source of their faith and the local church. See, for example, *Supplikatia,* p. 101.

71. Two major articles deal with the problem of the development of national consciousness in the Commonwealth of this period. Stanisław Kot, "Świadomość narodowa w Polsce XV–XVII," *Kwartalnik Historyczny,* LII, no. 1 (1938), 15–33, and Janusz Tazbir, "Świadomość narodowa," *Rzeczpospolita i świat. Studia z dziejów kultury XVII wieku* (Wrocław, 1971), pp. 23–43. Neither of these scholars deals with the problem of Rus' identity. The widespread occurrence of the view that the nobility was the totality of the nation is emphasized by both authors. On the medieval period, also see Konstantin Symmons-Symonolewicz, "National Consciousness in Medieval Europe: Some Theoretical Problems," *Canadian Review of Studies in Nationalism* VIII, no. 1 (Spring 1981), 151–166.

72. For a discussion of the use of *Rus'* and *Malorossiia, Ukraina,* and *Rossiia,* see Omeljan Pritsak and John S. Reshetar, Jr., "The Ukraine and the Dialectics of Nation-Building," in *The Development of the USSR: An Exchange of Views,* ed. Donald W. Treadgold (Seattle, 1964), pp. 248–249, 255–259. Note that in the seventeenth century, the term *Rossiia* was preferred to *Rus'* by Kievan clerical circles as a designation for the Ukraine. The limitation of *Rus'* as a designation for the Ukrainians and Belorussians can be seen, for example, in Kassian Sakovych's discussion on the calendar: "That more peoples retain the old calendar than the new, such as the Greeks, Moldavia, Rus', Moscow and some of the heretics in the German cities." Kassian Sakowicz, *Kalendarz stary, w którym jawny y oczywisty błąd okazuie się około święcenia Paschi* (Warsaw, 1641), p. 20. Sakovych's plea to Rus' to accept the new calendar also contains criticism of the intellectual level of the other Orthodox nations and singles Muscovy out for an attack on its political system. Sakovych criticized Muscovy for the tyrannical nature of its government (pp. 32–33). He asserted: "But you, happy Rus' and Polish nation, born in golden freedom, can decide for yourself and choose that which is best for your soul and body." For literature on the formation of the Russian nation, see *Voprosy formirovaniia russkoi narodnosti i natsii: Sbornik statei,* ed. N. M. Druzhinin (Moscow, 1958) and Günter Stökl, "Die Entstehung der russischen Nation," in his *Der russische Staat in Mittelalter und früher Neuzeit* (Wiesbaden, 1981), pp. 58–73.

73. On the problems of differentiating Belorussian and Ukrainian texts, see Uladzimir Anichenka, *Belaruska-ukrainskaia pis'mova-mounyia suviazi* (Minsk, 1969). In discussing seventeenth-century Rus', it must be remembered that Moldavia was closely connected with the Rus' cultural and religious sphere. The fact that Moldavians were non-Slavs had little importance in a period during which

a small religious elite wrote its works in an international Slavonic. For problems of the formation of the Belorussian and Ukrainian nations, see the bibliography "Discussions on the Origins of the Ukrainian Nation," in Myron Korduba, *La litterature historique sovietique-ukrainienne: compte-rendu 1917–1931.* Reprint of the Warsaw 1930 edition, Harvard Series in Ukrainian Studies, X (Munich, 1972), xxxiv–xxxvi. For literature on the formation of the Belorussian nation and the origin of the name "Belorussia," see *Bibliiahrafiia pa historyi Belarusi: Feadalizm i kapitalizm* (Minsk, 1969), p. 90.

74. I have found these various definitions and concepts of the term in a number of seventeenth-century documents. I have used two documents published in Lipiński, ed., *Z dziejów Ukrainy*. They are, Jan Szczęsny Herburt's "Zdanie o narodzie ruskim," pp. 92–97, a pamphlet published in 1623 entitled "Supplikatia do przeoświeconego . . . obojego stanu duchownego i świeckiego Senatu . . . od obywatelów koronnych i W. X. Litewskiego wszystkich wobec i każdego z osobna ludzi zawołania szlacheckiego, religii starożytnej greckiej, posłuszeństwa wschodniego" (pp. 100–111). The *Supplikatia* uses the phrase "Rus' rzymskiego nabożeństwa." The concept of Rus' as the nobility of the incorporation lands is particularly pronounced in a petition to the Diet by the Volhynian nobility of August 21, 1632. Lipiński, ed., *Z dziejów*, pp. 127–128.

75. For a discussion of stagnation in Ukrainian literature, see Dmytro Čyževs'kyj, *A History of Ukrainian Literature (From the 11th to the End of the 19th Century)*, trans. Dolly Ferguson, Doreen Gorsline and Ulana Petyk, ed. George S. Luckyj (Littleton, Colo., 1975), pp. 226–235. Čyževs'kyj maintains that "The period extending from the end of the thirteenth to the end of the sixteenth centuries represents a distinct pause in the development of Ukrainian literature, but such pauses have occurred periodically in the spiritual, cultural, and literary life of Ukraine." (p. 235). For an interpretative essay on the "intellectual silence" of Rus' culture, see Georges Florovsky, "The Problem of Old Russian Culture," *The Development of the USSR*, pp. 125–129. Florovsky sees a crisis of Russian Byzantinism as a major problem of "Old Russian" culture. He maintains "The crisis consisted in that the Byzantine achievement had been accepted, but Byzantine inquisitiveness had not. For that reason the achievement itself couldn't be kept alive." (p. 138).

76. For discussions of Polish cultural development in this period, see Paweł Czartoryski, "Rodzime źródła kultury umysłowej polskiego Odrodzenia," *Polska w epoce Odrodzenia*, pp. 266–283; Jerzy Ziomek, "Z dziejów myśli i literatury Renesansu," *Polska w epoce Odrodzenia*, pp. 283–304; and Czesław Hernas, *Barok* (Warsaw, 1973).

77. On the crisis and response of Orthodox Rus', see William K. Medlin, "Cultural Crisis in Orthodox Rus' in the Late 16th and Early 17th Centuries as a Problem of Socio-Cultural Change," in Andrew Blane, ed., *The Religious World of Russian Culture*, 2 vols. (The Hague, 1975), II, 173–188.

78. On the influence of Polish monarchs on the church, see Chodynicki, *Kościół Prawosławny*, pp. 76–171. Chodynicki, however, aserts that the church existed with more autonomy from secular rulers than in Orthodox states and that the relationship cannot be described as one of persecution.

79. On the authority of the Eastern patriarchs, see Izydor Szaraniewicz, "Patryjarchat wschodni wobec Kościoła Ruskiego w Polsce i Rzeczypospolitej Polskiej," *Rozprawy i Sprawozdania z Posiedzeń Wydziału Historyczno-Filozoficznego Akademii Umiejętności*, VIII (1878), 255–344. For the deposition of Divovych see Chodynicki, *Kościół Prawosławny*, pp. 128–130. Also, see I. I. Sokolov, "Pro vidnosyny ukrains'koï tserkvy do hrets'koho skhodu na prykintsi XVI ta na pochatku XVII st. za novovydanymy materiialamy: Istorychnyi narys," *ZIFV*, 1919, no. 1, pp. 53–84.

80. Soviet scholars have attempted to study all aspects of Russian assistance to Ukrainians prior to 1648. They have shown considerable interest by Ukrainians and Belorussians in receiving financial and other assistance, but relatively little assistance rendered. See, for example, F. P. Shevchenko, *Politychni ta ekonomichni zv"iazky Ukraïny z Rossieiu v seredyni XVII st.* (Kiev, 1959). For later contacts, see Vitalii Eingorn, *Snosheniia malorossiiskogo dukhovenstva s moskovskim pravitel'stvom v tsarstvovanie Alekseia Mikhailovicha* (Moscow, 1899). Discussion of Russian intellectual assistance has concentrated on Fedorov and Kurbskii. These examples may be viewed as isolated cases, and, in fact, they probably reflect a misconception about the two men. For discussion of the different cultural environments of the Ukraine and Muscovy in the sixteenth and seventeenth centuries, see Edward L. Keenan, *The Kurbskii-Groznyi Apocrypha: The Seventeenth-Century Genesis of the "Correspondence" Attributed to Prince A. M. Kurbskii and Tsar Ivan IV* (Cambridge, Mass., 1971), pp. 53–58.

81. For assistance from Moldavia to the Lviv Brotherhood, see Ia. D. Isaievych, *Bratstva ta ïkh rol' v rozvytku ukraïns'koï kul'tury XVI–XVIII st.* (Kiev, 1966).

82. On lay participation in the Kievan metropolitanate, see V. Zaikin, *Uchastie svetskogo elementa v tserkovnom upravlenii, vybornoe nachalo i sobornost' v Kievskoi mitropolii v XVI i XVII v.* (Warsaw, 1930) and Orest Levitskii, "Cherty vnutrennago stroia zapadno-russkoi tserkvi," *Kievskaia starina*, 1884, no. 8, pp. 627–654. Roman Catholic polemicists often charged that in the Orthodox church the laity controlled the clergy. Piotr Skarga, *O jedności Kościoła Bożego* in *Russkaia istoricheskaia biblioteka*, VII (St. Petersburg, 1882), 465, 487. Also see Józef Tretiak, *Piotr Skarga w dziejach i literaturze unji brzeskiej* (Cracow, 1912) and Janusz Tazbir, *Piotr Skarga: Szermierz kontrreformacji* (Warsaw, 1978). For a bibliographical essay, see "Tserkovnyi ustrii i vidnosyny XIV–XVI vv.," Hrushevs'kyi, V, 655–657. For a discussion of attempts at union of the Orthodox and Catholic churches in the fifteenth and sixteenth centuries and the Union of Brest, see Oskar Halecki, *From Florence to Brest (1439–1596)* (New York, 1959). For a bibliographical essay on the union, see "Tserkovna Uniia," Hrushevs'kyi V, 657–661.

83. For the struggle against the Union of Brest, see P. Zhukovich, *Seimovaja bor'ba pravoslavnogo zapadnorusskogo dvorianstva s tserkovnoi uniei do 1609*, no. 1 (St. Petersburg, 1901); no. 2 *(1609–1619 gg.)* (St. Petersburg, 1904); no. 3 *(1620–1621 gg.)* (St. Petersburg, 1906); no. 4 *(1623–1625 gg.)* (St. Petersburg, 1908); no. 5 *(1625–1629 gg.)* (St. Petersburg, 1910); no. 6 *(1629–1632 gg.)*

(St. Petersburg, 1912). The dissatisfaction of the Uniate church with its position is discussed in Mirosław Szegda, *Działalność prawno-organizacyjna Metropolity Józefa IV Welamina Rutskiego (1613–1637)* (Warsaw, 1967). For the problem of conversions to the Latin rite, see Martel, *La langue polonaise,* pp. 250–258. For a bibliographical sketch on cultural developments in this period and the restoration of the hierarchy, see "Kyïvs'ke kul'turne zhytie pershykh desiatylit XVII v. i vidnovlenne pravoslavnoï erarkhiï," Hrushevs'kyi VII, 584–588.

84. On the brotherhoods, see Isaievych, *Bratstva.*

85. On the schools founded in this period, see K. V. Kharlampovich, *Zapadno-russkiie pravoslavnye shkoly XVI i nachala XVII veka, otnoshenie ikh k inoslavnym, religioznoe obuchenie v nikh i zaslugi ikh v dele zashchity pravoslavnoi very i tserkvi* (Kazan', 1898); S. T. Golubev, *Istoriia Kievskoi dukhovnoi akademii: Period do-mogilianskii* (Kiev, 1888); Aleksander Jabłonowski, *Akademia Kijowsko-Mohilańska*; Khvedor Titov, *Stara vyshcha osvita v kyïvs'kii Ukraïni XVI-poch. XIXv.* Zbirnyk istorychno-filolohichnoho viddilu Ukraïnskoï Akademiï Nauk, XX (Kiev, 1924), and E. N. Medynskii, *Bratskie shkoly Ukrainy i Belorussii XVI–XVII vv.* (Kiev, 1954). For sources about educational and printing institutions, see Ia. D. Isaievych, *Dzherela z istoriï ukraïns'koï kul'tury doby feodalizmu XVI–XVIII st.* (Kiev, 1972), pp. 51–109. For a bibliographical essay on schools, see "Shkil'nytstvo," Hrushevs'kyi VI, 612.

86. For remarks on the level that studies of Greek reached in Kiev prior to 1648, see Ihor Ševčenko, *Ljubomudreišij Kyr "Agapit Diakon: On a Kiev Edition of a Byzantine "Mirror of Princes,"* Supplement to *Recenzija,* V, no. 1 (1974), 17–18 and his "Byzantium and the Eastern Slavs after 1453," *Harvard Ukrainian Studies,* II, no. 1 (March 1978), 5–25. For this cultural struggle, see Martel *La langue polonaise,* pp. 259–288. The major proponent of total rejection of Latin culture was the most talented of the Ukrainian polemicists, Ivan Vyshens'kyi. For Vyshens'kyi's stance see the chapter "Skarga i Wiszeński," in Józef Tretiak, *Piotr Skarga,* pp. 233–287, and Ivan Franko, *Ivan Vyshens'kyi i ioho tvory* (Lviv, 1895). For the "Westernizers'" defense of their teaching of Latin and Polish, see *Lithos, abo kamień z procy prawdy cerkwie świętey prawosławney Ruskiey . . .* (Kiev, 1644) (attributed to P. Mohyla), republished in *Arkhiv Iu. Z. R.,* pt. I, vol. IX (Kiev, 1893), 375–377. (Subsequent citations of page numbers are to this reprint edition.) For Władysław's 1634 order to cease the teaching of Latin and the defense of Latin in schools, see Martel, *La langue polonaise,* p. 283.

87. The best work on Mohyla is S. Golubev, *Kievskii mitropolit Petr Mogila i ego spodvizhniki,* 2 vols. in 2 pts. (Kiev, 1883–1898) (hereafter Golubev I–1, I–2, II–1, II–2). Two relatively new works on Mohyla and his collegium, with bibliographies of the vast earlier literature are Arkadii Zhukovs'kyi, *Petro Mohyla i pytannia iednosty tserkov* (Paris, 1969) and Alexander Sydorenko, *The Kievan Academy in the Seventeenth Century* (Ottawa, 1977). Also see the Soviet work by Z. I. Khyzhniak, *Kyevo-Mohylians'ka akademiia* (Kiev, 1970).

88. Antoine Martel includes a listing of the polemical literature (seventeenth-century books and manuscripts), grouped according to language. From 1628 to 1648 no works are extant in Cyrillic script, and Polish had already surpassed

Cyrillic works by 1610. *La langue polonaise*, pp. 132–141. For Orthodox justifications of the use of Polish and Latin, see *Lithos*, pp. 375–377. Martel has shown that the Uniates were more conservative and retentive of Slavonic than were the Orthodox, p. 142. Martel discusses the increased use of Polish in all forms of literature and official documents. In particular, see the chapter "La langue des écrivains ruthènes," pp. 67–160. Martel views the preference of Slavonic and the rejection of "Ruthenian" as a fatal error that resulted in the increased use of Polish, pp. 76–79, 89–97. On the polemic literature and the increasing use of Polish, see Aleksander Brückner, "Spory o unię w dawnej literaturze," *Kwartalnik Historyczny*, X (1896), 578–644, and Tadeusz Grabowski, *Z dziejów literatury unicko-prawosławnej w Polsce 1630–1700* (Poznań, 1922).

89. For a description of the cultural and intellectual revival of the period, see Mykhailo Hrushevs'kyi, *Kulturno-natsional'nyi rukh na Ukraïni XVI–XVII st.*, 2nd ed. (n.p., 1919) and A. Savych, *Narysy z istoriï kul'turnykh rukhiv na Ukraïni ta Bilorusi v XVI–XVII v.*, Zbirnyk Istorychno-filolohichnoho viddilu Vse-Ukraïns'koï Akademiï Nauk XC (Kiev, 1929). For a bibliography of the literature on this period, see Georgii Florovskii, *Puti russkogo bogosloviia* (Paris, 1937), pp. 326–330, and "Literatura tserkovnykh i natsional'nykh vidnosyn druhoï chetvertyny XVII v.," in Hrushevs'kyi VIII–1, 318–320. For an evaluation of seventeenth-century literary and linguistic developments, see Čyževs'kyi, *A History*, pp. 355–362. Hrushevs'kyi criticized Mohyla's cultural policies as blind imitations of Polish-Latin models. VIII–2, 99. As a populist, Hrushevs'kyi viewed the Mohylan period as of little value "from the standpoint of Ukrainian life," because it was not based on the national culture and did not provide for the needs of the masses. Florovsky criticizes the Mohylan period from a totally different perspective, its "Latinization" of Orthodoxy and what he sees as its negative influence on Orthodox thought and institutions. *Puti*, pp. 44–56.

90. Some Polish historians have described the process as almost a sacred mission of civilization and portrayed the process as an irreversible advance of "Polish Western Culture" in the east. There are elements of such attitudes in Aleksander Jabłonowski, *Akademia Kijowsko-Mohilańska*, and in his response to F. Titov's criticism, "W sprawie 'Akademii Kijowsko-Mohilańskiej'," *Pisma*, II, 281–344. Titov's criticism was largely a defense of "Russian national honor," F. T[itov], "Urok s zapada," *Trudy Kievskoi dukhovnoi akademii*, March, 1902, pp. 450–479, and "K voprosu o znachenii Kievskoi akademii dlia pravoslaviia i russkoi narodnosti v XVII–XVIII vv.," *Trudy Kievskoi dukhovnoi akademii*, November, 1903, pp. 375–408 and January, 1904, pp. 59–101.

91. For the Ukrainian elite's insistence that the "Ruthenian" language be used, see W. Semkowicz, "Po wcieleniu Wołynia: Nielegalny zjazd w Łucku 1569 i sprawa językowa na Wołyniu," *Ateneum Wileńskie*, V–VI (1924), 183–190.

92. On the problem of discrimination against the Orthodox in cities, see Jan Ptaśnik, "Walka o demokratyzację Lwowa od XVI w. do XVIII w." *Kwartalnik Historyczny*, XXXIX, no. 2 (1925), 228–257, Maurycy Horn, *Walka klasowa i konflikty społeczne w miastach Rusi Czerwonej w latach 1600–1647 na tle sto-*

sunków gospodarczych (Wrocław, 1972), and O.S. Kompan, *Uchast' mis'koho naselennia u vyzvol'nyi viini ukraïns'koho narodu 1648–1654 rr.* (Kiev, 1954).

93. On governmental policy and the union see K. Lewicki, "Sprawa unji Kościoła Wschodniego z Rzymskim w polityce Rzplitej," *Sprawy Narodowościowe,* VII (1933), 491–508, 650–671, and Chodynicki, *Kościół Prawosławny,* pp. 194–418. For comparisons with the Greek position under the Turks unfavorable to the Commonwealth, see excerpts of Zakharii Kopystens'kyi, *Palinodiia . . .* in Bilets'kyi, ed., *Khrestomatiia,* p. 169, and the polemical work *Supplikatia,* p. 100. For a succinct description of the problems of Orthodox faithful after 1596, see Baranovich, *Ukraina,* pp. 118–122.

94. For the influence of the Counter-Reformation on Polish culture, see the essays in *Wiek XVII: Kontrreformacja-Barok. Prace z historii kultury,* ed. Janusz Pelc (Wrocław, 1970). For examples of the type of charges leveled by Polish proponents of the Union, see Józef Tretiak, *Piotr Skarga,* pp. 53–82. For an example of persecution, see the account of Anna Ostrogska-Chodkiewicz's action against the burghers of Ostroh in the chronicle account in O. A. Bevzo, *L'vivs'kyi litopys i Ostrozhs'kyi litopysets: Dzhereloznavche doslidzhennia* (Kiev, 1970), pp. 137–140. For an excellent discussion of this problem, see Martel's chapter "Le fiat général: rupture d'équilibre entre deux civilisations," *La langue polonaise,* pp. 161–193. In some ways, criticism was just as severe against the Uniate church. See, for example, the attack of the convert to Latin-rite Catholicism Kasian Sakovych on the Uniates for the low level of their schools. Kassian Sakowicz, *Epanorthosis albo perspectiwa . . .* (Cracow, 1642), pp. 111–113. For a discussion of rising hatred against the Ruthenians in the Commonwealth see the publication of the "Dyskurs o teraźniejszej wojnie kozackiej albo chłopskiej," and analysis of the text in Sysyn, "A Contemporary's Account of the Causes of the Khmel'nyts'kyi Uprising," and "Seventeenth-Century Views on the Causes of the Khmel'nyts'kyi Uprising."

95. On the limited political aspirations of the Ukrainian elite at Lublin, see Pelenski, "The Incorporation . . ." and Halecki, *Przyłączenie.*

96. For problems of assimilation and the political culture of the Ukrainian nobility, see Sysyn, "The Problem of Nobilities in the Ukrainian Past," pp. 65–71 and Teresa Chynczewska-Hennel, "Świadomość narodowa Kozaczyzny i szlachty ukraińskiej w XVII wieku" (Ph.D. dissertation, Polish Academy of Sciences, Institute of History, 1982). Chynczewska-Hennel treats the religious, linguistic, and historical aspects of national consciousness among the Ukrainian nobility.

97. In the context of cultural contact and conflict, even the Julian and Gregorian calendars, both of which were used by a number of nations in Europe in the seventeenth century, took on "national coloration." The Julian calendar holidays were called "the Ruthenian holidays," as they were in areas of Polish-Ukrainian and Polish-Belorussian contact until the twentieth century. See Kassian Sakowicz, *Kalendarz stary, w którym jawny y oczywisty błąd okazuie się około święcenia Paschi . . .* (Warsaw, 1641).

98. The symbol of Wiśniowiecki as a renegade, so popular in nineteenth-

and twentieth-century Ukrainian historiography, is foreshadowed in the seventeenth-century Lviv Chronicle, which describes Wiśniowiecki as "from Ruthenian ancestry, a Pole" (*z rus'koho pokolinnia liakh*), O. A. Bevzo, *L'vivs'kyi litopys,* p. 122. Also, see Metropolitan Isaia Kopyns'kyi's plea to Wiśniowiecki to remain true to Orthodoxy, published in Lipiński, *Z dziejów Ukrainy,* pp. 121–123, from a copy entitled, "Letter to Prince Jeremi Korybut Wiśniowiecki who at the time, from a Ruthenian became a Pole" (*z Rusyna Lachom został*). Numerous examples of charges of treason against Sakovych from both Orthodox and Uniates are included in Golubev's discussion of the religious polemics of the 1640s. Golubev II–1, 320–462..

99. The necessity for the Orthodox church to defend itself against charges that it was a peasant's faith is apparent in Kopyns'kyi's plea to Wiśniowiecki to remain Orthodox. Kopyns'kyi maintained that "Although adversaries unfavorable to us maintain that the Greek faith is a peasant's faith, if what they say is true, then the Greek tsars and great monarchs were of peasant faith." Lipiński, *Z dziejów,* p. 122.

Chapter II

1. This discussion of Volhynia is based on Władysław Tomkiewicz, "Wołyń w Koronie (1569–1795)," *Rocznik Wołyński,* II (1931), 26–45, P. N. Batiushkov, *Volyn: istoricheskie sud'by iugo-zapadnogo kraia* (St. Petersburg, 1888), and Jabłonowski, "Ziemia wołyńska w połowie XVI-go w.," "Zamki wołyńskie w połowie XVI-go w.," and "Wołyń i Podole pod kon. XVI-go w." in *Pisma,* IV, 1–252.

For a discussion of Polish influences in Volhynia, see Anna Dembińska, *Wpływy kultury polskiej na Wołyń w XVI wieku (Na łonie warstwy szlacheckiej),* Prace Komisji Historycznej Poznańskiego Towarzystwa Przyjaciół Nauk, XVI (Poznań, 1930). For the position of the Orthodox church, see K. Chodynicki, "Z dziejów prawosławia na Wołyniu (922–1596)," *Rocznik Wołyński,* V–VI (1937), 52–106.

2. On the support for Švitrygaila, see Oskar Halecki, *Ostatnie lata Świdrygiełły i sprawa wołyńska za Kazimierza Jagiellończyka* (Cracow, 1915).

3. For a description of Volhynian land holding at the time of the Union of Lublin, see Jabłonowski, "Ziemia wołyńska," *Pisma,* IV, 1–72.

4. For church holdings, see Chodynicki, "Z dziejów prawosławia," p. 69.

5. For a listing of Orthodox monasteries and their dates of founding, see Max Boyko, *Bibliography of Church Life in Volhynia,* Publications of the Volhynian Bibliographic Center, IX (Bloomington, Indiana, 1974), 51–73.

6. On the nobility's influence in the Orthodox church, see Chodynicki, "Z dziejów prawosławia," pp. 52–60.

7. For the terms of incorporation, see Pelenski, "The Incorporation of the Ukrainian Lands," pp. 48–52. Religious rights and the granting of szlachta status were in fact the results of a number of reforms which were undertaken in the Grand Duchy in the decade prior to the Union of Lublin.

8. In the first half of the seventeenth century, the male lines of the Ostroz'-

kyi and Zbaraz'kyi families died out, and major estates passed to the Leszczyński and Opaliński families of Great Poland, the Firlej and Sobieski families of Little Poland, and the Grand Duchy of Lithuania's Daniłłowicz and Radziwiłł families. Tomkiewicz, "Wołyń," pp. 44–45.

9. No statistics exist on the number of minor Polish nobility who entered Volhynia and leased estates or were granted them for services by the great landowners. However, an examination of the landholder register of Volhynia in 1629 reveals a large number of petty Polish nobles as "possessors." Oleksander Baranovych, *Zaliudnennia volyns'koho voievodstva v pershii polovyni XVII st.* (Kiev, 1930), pp. 30–89.

10. The royal lands of Volhynia, *korolivshchyna*, were only 4.7 percent of the total hearths. Baranovych, *Zaliudnennia*, p. 23. After the Union of Lublin, they could be distributed according to royal wishes, and while, for example, in 1629 the Volodymyr starostwo was held by Roman Hois'kyi, a member of a prominent Volhynian family, Stanisław Koniecpolski, field-hetman and a member of the Little Polish nobility, held most of the Kovel' starostwo. Baranovych, *Zaliudnennia*, p. 75.

11. The process of reshaping the Volhynian elite is discussed in Dembińska, *Wpływy kultury polskiej.*

12. For Orthodox control of the Diet, see the dietine instructions in *Arkhiv Iu. Z. R.*, pt. II, vol. I. For dietine politics, see Czapliński, "Wybór posła."

13. Tomkiewicz, "Wołyń," 43. Detailed information on conversions is in P. G. Viktorovskii, "Zapadnorusskie dvorianskie familii, otpavshie ot pravoslaviia v kontse XVI i XVII vv.," *Trudy Kievskoi dukhovnoi akademii*, 1908, no. 9, pp. 17–60; no. 10, pp. 189–206; no. 11, pp. 344–360; no. 12, pp. 502–524; 1909, no. 6, pp. 178–214; 1910, no.3, pp. 339–392; no. 11, pp. 409–420; 1911, no. 2, pp. 259–273; no. 6, pp. 257–272; nos 7–8, pp. 396–424.

14. Tomkiewicz, "Wołyń," 43. Boyko, *Bibliography of Church Life in Volhynia*, pp. 182–183, contains a list of some of the Roman Catholic churches erected in this period. By 1629, landholdings of the Roman Catholic church equalled those of the Eastern church. Baranovych, *Zaliudnennia*, p. 23. The number of Roman Catholic churches in the Luts'k diocese increased from about 110 to 175 from the end of the sixteenth century to 1648. Ludomir Bieńkowski, "Organizacja Kościoła wschodniego w Polsce," *Kościół w Polsce*, II, 961.

15. For Protestant denominations in Volhynia, see Aleksander Kossowski, *Zarys dziejów protestantyzmu na Wołyniu w XVI i XVII w.* (Rivne, 1933). Also see bibliography in Boyko, *Bibliography of Church Life in Volhynia*, pp. 211–212.

16. The rapid decrease of use of the Ruthenian chancery language in the incorporation lands is discussed in Martel, *La langue polonaise*, pp. 54–66.

17. The Ostroh Academy was the only institution of higher education in Volhynia prior to 1600. In the period 1600–1648, four Orthodox, three Catholic, and four Antitrinitarian schools were active. For indication of the increase of Jesuit and other Western Christian institutions, see the maps in Ambroise Jobert, *De Luther à Mohila; La Pologne dans la crise de la chrétienté 1517–1648*, Collection Historique de l'Institut d'Etudes Slaves, XXI (Paris, 1974), 244–245.

18. For a bibliography on Ostroz'kyi, see Boyko, *Church Life in Volhynia*, 109–114. For a discussion of the Ostroh school, see K. Kharlampovich, "Ostrozhskaia pravoslavnaia shkola," *Kievskaia starina*, 1897, no. 5, pp. 117–207; no. 6, pp. 363–388.

19. The Ostroz'kyi family and their close relatives, the Zaslavs'kyi family, owned one-third of all Volhynia. Tomkiewicz, "Wołyń," p. 32. Prince Konstantyn's estates included twenty-five cities, ten towns, 670 settlements with twenty monasteries, and 600 Orthodox churches. Chodynicki, "Z dziejów prawosławia," p. 77. The Ostroz'kyi estates were legally treated as a unit called an *ordynacja* and this almost independent state was responsible for maintaining an army of 6,000 men. Wimmer, *Wojsko polskie*, p. 21.

20. The major study of Ostroz'kyi's role in the church union is K. Lewicki, *Książę Konstantyn Ostrogski a Unia Brzeska, 1596 r.* (Lviv, 1933).

21. For a bibliography of the religious polemics, see Makhnovets', ed., *Ukraïns'ki pys'mennyky*, I, 447–461.

22. For listings of the pro-Orthodox faction among the Volhynian nobility at the beginning of the seventeenth century, see the nobility's protest in defense of the Lublin brotherhood (1601) in *Arkhiv Iu. Z. R.*, pt. II, vol. I, 35–39, and the documents in support of the Luts'k brotherhood in M. A. Maksimovich (Maksymovych), *Sobranie sochinenii*, I (Kiev, 1876–1880), 200–213.

For lists of Uniate supporters in 1598 and 1603, see Wacław Lipiński, "Echa przeszłości," *Z dziejów Ukrainy*, 119–120. The fluidity of support is demonstrated by Hryhorii Chetvertyns'kyi's signature as a Uniate in 1603. He had signed the 1601 defense of the Lublin brotherhood and was an ardent supporter of the Orthodox church throughout the first half of the century.

23. One of the last conversions of a magnate in Volhynia was that of Iurii Chortorys'kyi (Czartoryski) in about 1610. M. Iuzefovich, "Predislovie," *Arkhiv Iu. Z. R.*, pt. IV, vol. I (Kiev, 1867), xix.

24. Of the thirty-seven land holders who owned more than 300 hearths in 1629, two of the Chetvertyns'kyi princes (Stefan and Iurii) owned 387 and 302 hearths. In comparison, two members of the Hois'kyi family had over 2,000, and the combined Zaslavs'kyi holdings were over 20,000. The well-known defender of the Orthodox church, Lavrentii Drevyns'kyi, possessed 99; Iurii Puzyna, 211; and the future Orthodox bishop, Semen Hulevych-Voiutyns'kyi, 32. Baranovych, *Zaliudnennia*, pp. 25–27, 56.

25. See Chodynicki, "Z dziejów prawosławia,". pp. 102–106.

26. For the role of the family in this period, see Jan Stanisław Bystroń, *Dzieje obyczajów w dawnej Polsce: Wiek XVI–XVIII*, II (Warsaw, 1960), 119–157, and Władysław Czapliński, "Rodzina szlachecka," in *Dawne czasy* (Wrocław, 1957), pp. 120–128. For a discussion of kinship ties in medieval Poland, see Maria Koczerska, *Rodzina szlachecka w Polsce późnego średniowiecza* (Warsaw, 1975).

27. Władysław Czapliński demonstrates that even the fervent Catholicism of Albrycht Stanisław Radziwiłł was not sufficient to influence him to support Catholic candidates for posts in preference to his Calvinist relatives or to concur in

attempts to punish Krzysztof Radziwiłł for alleged blasphemies. "Sprawiedliwy Magnat," in *Dawne czasy,* p. 175.

28. On inheritance laws, see Kaczmarczyk, *Historia,* pp. 292–296.

29. For Polish heraldic practices, see Włodzimierz Dworzaczek, *Genealogia* (Warsaw, 1957).

30. For examples of the extremes that genealogical claims reached, see Kazimierz Bartoszewicz, *Radziwiłłowie* (Warsaw, 1928), pp. 1–16.

31. Family tradition names Oleksander or Olekhno Kysil, the son of the "Princess Sviatopolkovna Chetvertyns'ka," as the founder of an unbroken family line and maintains that his bravery in the struggle between Švitrygaila and Władysław-Jogaila led to the granting to his son of Nyzkynychi and Dorohynychi in Volhynia and confirmation of land titles in the Kievan lands.

Although all genealogies and records of family tradition trace the family to Oleksander-Olekhno, the accounts of him vary considerably. See Silwester Kossów (Kosiv), "Praefacya do Iegomości," in *Paterikon* (Kiev, 1635). Although the side Oleksander took is not mentioned, one would implicitly assume he was with Władysław-Jogaila, the winner. He is described as the son of a Chetvertyns'ka and the husband of a Nemyrychivna. A copy of testimony given by Iurii Kysil "Dorohinicki" (Jerzy Kisiel), who claimed to be over 90 years of age on August 5, 1697, asserts that Olekhno was the husband of Chetveryns'ka and that his son Mykyta, owner of Brusyliv and Noryns'k, received Nyzkynychi and Dorohynychi in a 1401 charter from Švitrygaila. The Polish Academy of Sciences Library in Cracow (hereafter PANK), MS 3022, fol. 40. This variant of family tradition is interesting because: 1. it mentions Mykyta, who is left out of the Kosiv genealogy in an implausible jump to Adam Kysil's great-grandfather (unnamed, but obviously Tykhno) as the son of Olekhno; 2. it mentions Noryns'k, in the palatinate of Kiev as a hereditary property of the Kysil family. The grant of Nyzkynychi and Dorohynychi is ascribed as being from Švitrygaila on the basis of "documents." There may be a basis to this assertion. A manuscript currently in the Volhynian Oblast' Archive contains a copy of such a grant. *Volyns'ka oblast': Istoriia mist i sil Ukrains'koi RSR* (Kiev, 1970), p. 558. Iurii Kysil's testimony is in a packet of genealogical charts stemming from the Lenkiewicz, Voronych, and Kysil families' struggle for Adam's inheritance in the eighteenth century. PANK, MS 3022, fol. 40.

Family tradition about Olekhno Kysil is of considerable interest. Intermarriage with the princely Chetvertyns'kyi family would have been relatively rare between middle nobility and the numerous (though often far from wealthy) princely families of the fifteenth century, and is therefore an assertion of upward social mobility as well as of a link to the family which in the seventeenth century was the very symbol of the Rus' Orthodox tradition. The land grant claims place the Kysil family within a definite geographic context. The Volhynian villages of Nyzkynychi and Dorohynychi were the basis of the Kysil family estates throughout the sixteenth century.

The confirmation of lands in the Kiev area undoubtedly refers to the area called in the sixteenth century the "Kysilivshchyna"—a tract of land in the

Ovruch area that the family claimed in the mid-sixteenth century. For a description of both the lands and settlements included in the "Kysilivshchyna," as well as the sixteenth-century charters presented by the family in a 1604 court case with the Lozka family, see *Źródła dziejowe,* 24 vols. (Warsaw, 1876–1915), XXII, 475–476.

It is in the fifteenth century that we find the first Kysil recorded in contemporary documents: Mykyta Kysil, Adam's great-great grandfather and the probable son of Olekhno. Z. L. Radzimiński, comp., *Monografia XX Sanguszków oraz innych potomków Lubarta-Fedora Olgerdowicza, X. Ratneńskiego,* I (L'viv, 1906), 124. Kosiv's description of Adam Kysil's great-grandfather would indicate that Mykyta was married to a Nemyrych. For additional information on the Kysils' genealogy, see the work by Wacław Rulikowski in manuscript "Zbiór notat genealogiczno-heraldycznych," III, pt. 1, pp. 365–368 in Lvivs'ka Naukova Biblioteka Akademiï Nauk (hereafter LBN), MS 7444 (also listed as part of the Radzimiński collection).

32. Jabłonowski, "Zamki wołyńskie," *Pisma,* IV, 95.

33. Franciszek Rawita-Gawroński, "Kisielowie, ich ród-pochodzenie-posiadłości," *Przewodnik Naukowy i Literacki,* XL (1912), 1008–1023, 1116–1124.

34. A fairly comprehensive list of Tykhno's activities as witness to land sales, judge and arbitrator to various disputes, and testator to wills is included in Rawita-Gawroński, "Kisielowie," pp. 1118–1119.

35. For information on Maryna Kysilivna Chortorys'ka, see *Arkhiv Iu. Z. R.,* pt. II, vol. I, 11, and Józef Wolff, *Kniaziowie litewsko-ruscy od końca czternastego wieku* (Warsaw, 1895), p. 39.

36. The 1570 Volhynian tax register lists Dorochynychi as divided almost equally between Tykhno's sons, Andrii and Petro, *Źródła dziejowe,* XIX, 23. The 1577 tax register has a listing for Oleksander Kysil (presumably Andrii's son, who inherited his part of Dorohynychi after Andrii's death) *Źródła dziejowe,* XIX, 70, while the listing for Petro is "Urzędnik p. Piotra Kisila, horodniczego Witebskiego z połowicy imienia Dorohinickiego," 75. The title "horodnychyi of Vitsebsk" indicates Petro's move to the Grand Duchy of Lithuania. In the 1583 register, Oleksander Kysil's holdings in Dorohynychi increased and no mention is made of Petro's holdings in the settlement (although Oleksander's holding is still referred to as a part) and Hryhorii paid on land for his father's brother, Petro. *Źródła dziejowe,* XIX, 79.

Petro received the provincial honor of the title "horodnychyi" of Vitsebsk in 1567 and received lands in the area. He was married to Maryna Sovianka. On October 29, 1583, his sons Ivan, Vasyl' and Illia took part in a court case without him. This indicated that he was already deceased. Since he is listed in the Volhynian tax register of that year, he probably died in 1583. For additional information on Petro, see Rawita-Gawroński, "Kisielowie," p. 1120; *Arkhiv Iu. Z. R.,* pt. VIII, vol. III (Kiev, 1909), 219–220. Adam Boniecki, *Herbarz Polski,* 10 vols. (Warsaw, 1901–1913), X, 97 (hereafter, Boniecki, X), and PANK, MS 2943, fols. 38–39.

It was this "Lithuanian" branch of the Kysil family which survived longest in the male line. In Adam Kysil's generation the most prominent member of this branch of the family was Mykola, scribe of the Vitsebsk land, later its judge. Numerous letters of Mykola Kysil are located in PANK, MS 3604 and MS 6007.

Petro's brother, Andrii, who remained on the family estate in Dorohynychi, had two sons, Oleksander and Ivan. Andrii appears to have died between 1570 and 1577. In 1569 he swore the Union of Lublin oaths for his nephews Hryhorii and Tymish. Boniecki maintains, on the basis of Volhynian court records, that Andrii and his wife Maria had a daughter whom they married to Fedir Krupets'-kyi in 1575, as well as two sons, Oleksander and Ivan. Boniecki, X, 96. Ivan is not included in the genealogical chart of PANK, MS 2978, fol. 40. Iurii Kysil mentions Ivan and Oleksander as sons of Andrii by two different mothers. PANK, MS 3022, fol. 40.

At the turn of the sixteenth century, Ivan and Oleksander joined the legal processes with Adam's father, Hryhorii, to secure rights to the "Kysilivshchyna" tract in the Kievan palatinate against the claims of the Lozka and Butovych families. *Źródła dziejowe*, XXI, 43. Oleksander received Andrii's share of Dorohynychi, *Źródła dziejowe*, XIX, 23–24, 70. No descendants of Ivan are known. When Oleksander died in 1619, he left his estate to his wife Anna Svishchovs'ka, his sons Pavlo, Havrylo, and Andrii, and his daughters Halyna and Maria. PANK, MS 2943, fols. 38–39. Although both Pavlo and Havrylo are mentioned as having laid down their lives during Adam's campaign in the Prussian expedition (Kosiv, *Paterikon*), in 1629 Havrylo was still listed as the owner of half of Dorohynychi. Baranovych, *Zaliudnennia*, p. 84.

Hnevosh, Adam's grandfather, is relatively little known to us. In 1545 he was already the major owner of the southeastern Volhynian settlement of Khreniv and was responsible for a *horodnia* (watchtower) in Krem"ianets'. *Pamiatniki, izdannye Vremennoiu kommissieiu dlia razbora drevnikh aktov, vysochaishe uchrezhdennoiu pri Kievskom voennom, Podol'skom i Volynskom general-gubernatore*, 4 vols. (Kiev, vol. I, 1845; vol. II, 1846; vol. III, 1852; vol. IV, 1859), vol. IV, section II, 17–18 (hereafter *Pam.*).

At his father's death he inherited Nyzkynychi. Family tradition has Hnevosh a courtier of Zygmunt I, married to a Maria Tryzna (of a Lithuanian Rus' family), and dying in 1568 at the battle of Orsha. That Hnevosh's wife was Maria Tryznianka is proven by a June 19, 1566 mention of a document on the mother and her son Hryhorii. PANK, MS 2943, fol. 38. The last two assertions are also supported by the 1569 Union of Lublin affirmation in Volhynia, at which Hnevosh was not present and Andrii, Hnevosh's brother, swore for his two nephews, "Timofei" and Hryhorii, who were away with their mother in the Grand Duchy of Lithuania. *Zhizn' kniazia Andreia Mikhailovicha Kurbskogo v Litve i na Volyni*, I (Kiev, 1849), 25. In all other sources Hnevosh's sons are called Ivan and Hryhorii. Ivan divided Hnevosh's estates with Hryhorii on October 2, 1572. PANK, MS 2943, fols. 38–39. There is no indication of what his other possessions were, but it is certain that Hryhorii received Nyzkynychi. Ivan is not mentioned in the 1600–1604 court cases with the Butovych and Lozka families and thus was probably already deceased. *Źródła dziejowe*, XXI, 43.

Ivan was the father of Matvii and Oleksander, contemporaries of Adam. Matvii, who rose only to the rank of *stol'nyk* of Chernihiv, and Oleksander, eventually *podstolii* of Chernihiv, closely followed their illustrious cousin's career. For informationn on Matvii and Oleksander, see Boniecki, X, 95. In 1629 Matvii and Oleksander owned one half of Dorohynychi—presumably Petro Tykhnovych's original share in the settlement. Baranovych, *Zaliudnennia*, p. 84. In 1621 Matvii participated in the Volhynian levy "for himself and for his brother": Archiwum Główne Akt Dawnych, Warszawa (hereafer AGAD), Zbiory Biblioteki Narodowej (hereafter BN), MS 5422. Both cousins followed Kysil to the eastern lands, where they became active in the affairs of the Chernihiv palatinate as well as numerous commissions. Oleksander even served on Kysil's 1647 mission to Moscow. *Arkhiv Iu. Z. R.,* pt. I, vol. I (Kiev, 1859), 341.

37. A register of family documents contains an entry on the division of property in 1572 between Hryhorii and his brother Ivan. PANK, MS 2943, fols. 38–40. For the Kysil family holding in Nyzkynychi, see *Źródła dziejowe,* XIX, 23, 24, 73, 79. *Arkhiv Iu. Z. R.,* pt. I, vol. I, 373, on the holdings of the Volodymyr eparchy mentions Hryhorii Kysil's tenancy of Tyshkovychi. Baranovych's classification of the nobility designates owners of estates with less than 50 hearths as small holders, since Nyzkynychi had only 32 hearths in 1629, only the addition of Tyshkovychi and Polupanshchyna made the Kysils middle landholders, according to Baranovych's classification. *Zaliudnennia,* pp. 77, 84. Including Dorohynychi, the entire Kysil family owned only 93 1/2 hearths in Volodymyr county in 1629.

38. *Źródła dziejowe,* XXI, 43, 475–476. One of the major towns bordering this tract was Brusyliv, owned by the Butovych family. Later Adam Kysil used the appellation "of Brusyliv" in his signature.

39. Family tradition described him as *rotmistr,* or military leader, and field secretary in Stefan Batory's 1580s campaigns against Muscovy. Kosiv, "Praefacya," *Paterikon.* Hryhorii served as judge of Volodymyr as early as 1593, a post he held as late as 1616. The last mention of Hryhorii is for February 3, 1616. *Arkhiv Iu. Z. R.,* pt. VIII, vol. III, 535–537. Information on Hryhorii is plentiful from the 1590s to 1616. Nothing could be more inaccurate than Rawita-Gawroński's statement: "Gregor-Hrehory did not make any significant mark in the history of the family. We only know of his life about one border dispute with his neighbor Vasyl' Zahorovs'kyi" (from 1577). "Kisielowie," p. 1121. For documents signed by Hryhorii or about him, see *Arkhiv Iu. Z. R.,* pt. VI, vol. I, 190–199 (1588); pt. VIII, vol. III, 226–229 (1570); pt. III, vol. I (Kiev, 1863) 44 (1593); pt. I, vol. I, 91 (1579); pt. VIII, vol. IV (Kiev, 1887), 54 (1582), and Mykhailo Chortorys'kyi's will appears on p. 118 (1593); *Zhizn' Kniazia Andreia Mikhailovicha Kurbskogo v Litve in na Volyni,* I, 200. Hryhorii was one of five signatories of Kurbskii's will.

40. See Boniecki, VIII, 65 and Kasper Niesiecki, *Herbarz Polski . . . ,* Jan Nep. Borowicz, ed., 10 vols. (Leipzig, 1839–1846), IV, 98. For Socinian contacts, see Levitskii, "Sotsinianstvo," *Kievskaia starina,* 1882, no. 5, p. 206.

41. For Kysil's comments, see his will of 1621, J. T. Lubomirski, *Adam Kisiel, Wojewoda Kijowski* (Warsaw, 1905), pp. 8–9.

42. The last mention of Hryhorii is in 1616 (see footnote 39). In Adam Kysil's will of 1621, he describes his father as deceased. J. F. Lubomirski, *Adam Kisiel*, pp. 8–9. The last mention of Ianush is in 1623 in the Zamość Academy's matriculation book. BN, Biblioteka Ordynacyi Zamojskich (hereafter BOZ), fol. 117. Kysil's birth date as 1600 can be derived from his tombstone, which contains an inscription that he lived fifty-three years. Lubomirski, *Adam Kisiel*, p. 31.

43. Kazimierz Pułaski, *Kronika polskich rodów szlacheckich Podola, Wołynia i Ukrainy*, I (Brody, 1911), 134–141. Adam Kysil mentions an Orans'kyi as his sister's son in his 1621 will. Lubomirski, *Adam Kisiel*, p. 10. *Arkhiv Iu. Z. R.,* pt. VIII, vol. III, 226–229, contains the complaint of the Volodymyr judge Havrylo Iakovyts'kyi, November 7, 1570. The *Metryka* for the incorporation lands contains an agreement between the Orans'kyi and Kysil families in 1585–1586, AGAD, Register of *Metryka Rus'ka,* book 8, fol. 230.

44. Kosiv, "Praefacya," *Paterikon.*

45. *Arkhiv Iu. Z. R.,* pt. III, vol. I, 50–51.

46. Kosiv, "Praefacya," *Paterikon.* Kosiv maintained in the book's dedication that while searching among Rus' and other chronicles he encountered information about the founder of Adam Kysil's family, "Sventoldych," "Hetman Wojsk ruskich" who in the reign of Volodimer the Great, saved Kiev by the ingenious subterfuge of convincing besieging Pechenegs that the city was well supplied with food reserves by digging similar holes and placing water and bread in them and then extracting "kysil'" (sour custard) from the ground. This family legend has some basis in the early chronicles. The name in the chronicle most similar to Sventoldych is Svenald—a figure active in the reigns of Ihor and Sviatoslav. For a study of the scholarly literature about Svenald, see Andrzej Poppe, "Ze studiów nad najstarszym latopisarstwem ruskim I. Sweneld-ojciec Mściszy, czy Sweneld-ojciec zemsty?" *Studia Źródłoznawcze,* XVI (1971), 85–102. The chronicle account for 997 on the "kysil'" incident closely resembles Kosiv's account, but does not mention the name of the elder who proposed the stratagem. Also, the incident takes place in Bil'horod, not Kiev. *Polnoe sobranie russkikh letopisei,* 2nd ed. (St. Petersburg, 1908), II, 112–113. Kosiv states that he found information on the Kysil family when studying those chronicles which had been carried off "from the Rus' principalities to Moscovy" and this induced him to dedicate his works to one of the last faithful Orthodox nobles of Rus'. The hypothesis of a fortuitous coincidence is backed up by a marginal note linking the Kysils to the incident in the Ermolaev copy of the Hypatian Chronicle next to the 997 notation "There was one 'starets' who was not at that 'veche'"—"predok Pana Kiseliuv." Omeljan Pritsak has posited that a copy of the chronicle was made under the patronage of Adam Kysil in the 1630s or 1640s. Omeljan Pritsak, "The External History of the Texts of the Hypatian Chronicles," *Minutes of the Seminar in Ukrainian Studies,* III (1972–1973), 20. It is only after 1635 that "Sventoldych" was added by Adam and the other Kysils to their family name. While a family tradition may have linked the family to a follower of the popular Prince Volodimer—the evidence seems to indicate that the "Sventoldych

link" was a creation of the Orthodox intellectual Kosiv, who happened upon a fortuitous passage while preparing his *Paterikon* for publication. The credibility of the entire account is increased slightly due to the name of Kysil's Volynian estate—Nyzkynychi and its similarity to Niskina, a name used by Długosz for Mal, the father of Svenald. Poppe, "Ze studiów," pp. 90–91. Hrushevs'kyi I, 438–439, fn. 2.

47. Kosiv, "Praefacya," *Paterikon*. An example of a considerable distortion of the Kysil family's claims and an elevation to princely ranks can be found in Kysil's privilege from Władysław IV to the Kievan castellanship (February 5, 1646), which mentions the Kysil family's loyalty to the Polish Crown as from the time of Bolesław. *Arkhiv Iu. Z. R.,* pt. III, vol. I, 402. The Chrobry story later became intertwined with that of Sventoldych and the siege of Kiev. Niesiecki, *Herbarz Polski,* IV, 95. The elevation of the Kysils to equal status with the princely families can also be seen in the placement of them among the princely families in the synodic of the Saint Sophia Cathederal, Tsentral'na Naukova Biblioteka Akademii Nauk v Kyievi, VIII, MS 377–705, fols. 146–147.

48. On attitudes toward education, see J. Freylichówna, *Ideał wychowawczy szlachty polskiej w XVI i początku XVII wieku* (Warsaw, 1938).

49. Freylichówna, *Ideał,* pp. 85–88.

50. Freylichówna, *Ideał,* pp. 65–68.

51. Zahorovs'kyi's will was published in *Arkhiv Iu. Z. R.,* pt. I, vol. I (Kiev, 1859), 67–94. For a discussion of the will, see Mykhailo Vozniak *Istoriia ukraïns'koï literatury,* 3 vols. (Lviv, 1920–1924), II, pt. I, 30–33.

52. See Kharlampovich, "Ostrozhskaia pravoslavnaia shkola."

53. Kysil registered as the first student during the rectorship of Szymon Birkowski in 1609. BN, BOZ, MS 1598, *Album Univers. generalis studii Zamoscensis,* p. 51. Students of either the lower school or of the academy courses usually registered when first entering the program. It appears, however, that a student may have studied at the Academy some time before being enrolled. Although Adam wrote of his two brothers in his will of June 11, 1621 as studying at the academy (Lubomirski, *Adam Kisiel,* p. 10), his younger brother Ivan is not inscribed in the *Album* until 1623. BN, BOZ, MS 1598, p. 117.

54. On Zamoyski's vast domains, see Ryszard Orłowski, "Ordynacja zamojska," *Zamość i Zamojszczyzna w dziejach i kulturze polskiej,* Kazimierz Myślinski, ed. (Zamość, 1969), 105–124. For the planning and architecture of the city, see Stanisław Herbst, *Zamość* (Warsaw, 1954). Also see Adam Andrzej Witusik, *O Zamoyskich, Zamościu i Akademii Zamojskiej* (Lublin, 1978).

55. J. K. Kochanowski, *Dzieje Akademii Zamojskiej (1594–1784),* Fontes et Commentationes Historiam Scholarum Superiorum in Polonia Illustrantes, VII (Cracow, 1899–1900), 59–64. For Jan Zamoyski's attitudes and influence in the Commonwealth, see Stanisław Łempicki, *Działalność Jana Zamoyskiego na polu szkolnictwa, 1573–1605* (Cracow, 1921).

56. For the complete syllabus of the plan of study, see Kochanowski, *Dzieje,* pp. 33–40. The best discussion of education at the academy is Adam Andrzej Witusik, *Młodość Tomasza Zamoyskiego: O wychowaniu i karierze syna magnackiego w Polsce w pierwszej połowie XVII wieku* (Lublin, 1977), pp. 40–96.

57. On Jesuit education in this period, see Bronisław Natoński, "Szkolnictwo jezuickie w dobie kontrreformacji," *Wiek XVII*, ed. J. Pelc, pp. 309–339. On the differences in program, see Witusik, *Młodość Tomasza Zamoyskiego*, pp. 43–46, 95.

58. Kochanowski stresses the academy's training of notaries and commoners' sons. Kochanowski, *Dzieje*, p. 22.

59. Witusik, *Młodość Tomasza Zamoyskiego*, pp. 91–92.

60. AGAD, Archiwum Zamoyskich, MS 727, fols. 69–72. Adam Kysil to Tomasz Zamoyski, June 12, 1635. Kysil discussed his youth spent at Tomasz's side and the principle of szlachta liberty they believed in at that time.

61. BN, BOZ, MS 1598, fols. 90, 99, 117, 261.

62. Paulus Radoszchicki, *Laurea Palaestrae Philosophicae Excellent. D. D. Academiae Zamoscensis Professoribus . . .* (Zamość, January 2, 1620), fol. 1.

63. Kochanowski, *Dzieje*, pp. 19–49.

64. Petr Mohyla, *Triodion sy est' trypisnets'* (Kiev, 1631). Preface reprinted in Kh. Titov, *Materiialy dlia istorii knyzhnoi spravy na Ukraini v XVI–XVIII vv.* (Kiev, 1924) Zbirnyk Istorychno-filolohichnoho viddilu UAN XVII, 133.

65. Golubev asserts on the basis of a manuscript in the Kiev Lavra Collection that Kosiv and Trofimovych-Kozlovs'kyi attended the Zamość Academy. Golubev II, 322. Regrettably, the *Album studiosorum* was not kept for a period from 1598 to 1606. Since this was very likely the period when these two men entered the academy, the absence of their names in the *Album* is not surprising.

66. For Drevyns'kyi's son's studies, see BN, BOZ, MS 1598, fol. 27.

67. Concerning the Orthodox institutions and inhabitants of Zamość, see V. Budilovich, *Russkaia pravoslavnaia starina v Zamost'e* (Warsaw, 1886).

68. See footnote 65.

69. In Sakovych's 1642 work *Epanorthosis albo perspektiwa . . .* , he stated during a critique on Communion in the Eastern Rite that: "So a priest in the village of Batiatychi near Kryliv, in Volhynia, gave me [Communion], when I was going from Zamość on holidays with His Lordship Adam Kysil, the present Castellan of Chernihiv, to His Lordship's parents, while I was His Lordship's tutor," 20.

For bio-bibliographical information on Sakovych, see Makhnovets', ed., *Ukraïns'ki pys'mennyky*, I, 511–513.

70. Kasian Sakovych, *Virshi na zhalosnyi pohreb zatsnoho rytsara Petra Konashevycha Sahaidachnoho* (Kiev, 1622), reprinted in Titov, *Materialy*, pp. 37–51.

71. *Lithos*, and Pachomiusz Oranski-Wojna, *Zwierciadło albo zasłona naprzeciw uszczipliwey Perspektywie X. Kassyana Sakowicza, złożonego archimandryty Dubienskiego* (Vilnius, 1645).

72. See footnote 60.

73. Zamoyski was palatine of Podillia, and after 1618 palatine of Kiev, from 1629–1635 he was vice-chancellor, and then chancellor until his death in 1638. Niesiecki, *Herbarz*, X, 66–68. For detailed information on Zamoyski, see Stanisław Żurkowski, *Żywot Tomasza Zamoyskiego, Kanclerza W. Kor.* (Lviv, 1860) and Witusik, *Młodość Tomasza Zamoyskiego*.

74. See, for example, Kysil's letters of September 30, 1635, AGAD, Archiwum Zamoyskich, MS 727, fols. 73–74 and March 24, 1637, AGAD, Archiwum Zamoyskich, MS 338.

75. The nomination of Kysil as castellan of Kiev, February 5, 1646, is published in *Arkhiv Iu. Z. R.*, pt. III, vol. I, 405. Kysil is not listed in the card-file of the Polish Academy of Sciences in Cracow, *Kartoteka Polaków studiujących zagranicą*, or in Domet Oljančyn's register in his article "Aus der Kultur und Geistesleben der Ukraine," *Kyrios*, 1936, no. 3, pp. 264–278, and no. 4, pp. 351–366. I have been unable to find his name in published matriculation books of Western European institutions.

76. On the structure of the Commonwealth's army in this period, see *Zarys dziejów wojskowości polskiej do roku 1864*, I (Warsaw, 1965), 365—384. For Czarniecki's career, see Adam Kersten, *Stefan Czarniecki, 1599–1665* (Warsaw, 1963).

77. For Polish military history in the period of the "Great Hetmans," see Jan Wimmer, *Wojsko polskie w drugiej połowie XVII wieku* (Warsaw, 1965), pp. 11–37, and his article "Wojsko," in *Polska XVII wieku*.

78. The problem of Kysil's participation in the Muscovite wars of the 1610s is a complex one. His presence is proven by Władysław IV's comment in the grant of the Kievan castellanship, February 5, 1646. He characterized Kysil's military exploits as "Beginning from our first Muscovite expedition," *Arkhiv Iu. Z. R.*, pt. III, vol. I, 403. The grant of the castellanship of Chernihiv to Kysil on December 1, 1639, referred to unspecified "Turkish, Muscovite, and other expeditions," AGAD, Metryka Koronna (hereafter Met. Kor.), MS 185, fols. 221–222. A February 12, 1633 grant of the Nosivka starostwo includes a phrase, presumably about the 1617–1618 Muscovite expedition, "And taking into account the considerable merits in Moscow of the well-born Adam of Brusyliv Kysil, . . . and of his house and his two brothers, the two who then laid down their service of the Commonwealth in Prussia." AGAD, Met. Kor., MS 180, fols. 14–15. The "Prussian war" was in 1626, and by the context the presence of Kysil and his two "brothers" (cousins) in the Muscovite expedition must have been prior to that date.

Although Władysław did accompany his father Zygmunt on the unsuccessful campaign of 1612–1613, he would have hardly referred to this campaign as "our" first expedition. However, Władysław stated that Kysil began his career in the Muscovite expedition, and then mentioned the Busha (Iaruha) campaign, which ended in the truce of September 23, 1617. Hrushevs'kyi VII, 359. Władysław left for his march on Muscovy in April, 1617 and reached Viazma by late October. It was not until the summer of 1618 that Sahaidachnyi came to Władysław's support. Hrushevs'kyi VII, 376. If the "first expedition" does refer to that of the 1617–1618 campaign, it is difficult to accept that Kysil began his career with the April 1617 Muscovite expedition, but was at Busha in October 1617. It is possible that Kysil joined the Muscovite expedition after some service at Busha in 1617, but one would have to assume that he returned before the culmination of the expedition (Władysław's attempt to take Moscow in October 1618) had been reached. Kysil is reported as having served at Orynyn in November and December 1618. This sequence seems more likely than placing an earlier date to Kysil's involvement in the Muscovite wars and presuming that Władysław called his 1612–1613 presence with the army "our expedition." Although Władysław maintains that Kysil served from his earliest youth, if 1600 is accepted as Kysil's birth date, he would have been only twelve or thirteen years of age in 1612–1613.

79. For Kysil's participation in the Busha, Orynyn, Tsetsora and Khotyn campaigns, see Kosiv, "Praefacya," *Paterikon*, fol. 6; Władysław's grant of the Kievan castellanship, February 5, 1646, *Arkhiv Iu. Z. R.*, pt. III, vol. I, 405, and his conferral of Chernihiv castellanship, September 25, 1641, AGAD, Met. Kor. MS 185, fols. 407–409. For a detailed account of the Tsetsora campaign, see Ryszard Majewski, *Cecora: Rok 1620* (Warsaw, 1970). On Khotyn, see Leszek Podhorodecki and Noj Raszba, *Wojna chocimska 1621 roku* (Cracow, 1979). Also see Jerzy Pietrzak, *Po Cecorze i podczas wojny chocimskiej: Sejmy z lat 1620–1621* (Wrocław, 1983).

80. See his will of June 11, 1621, published in Lubomirski, *Adam Kisiel*, 9, and "Try testamenty Adama Kysilia," *Ukraïna*, 1918, nos. 1–2, 62. In the October 1621 Volhynian levy register Kysil's mother was required to field one horse. Kysil's cousin Matvii appeared in the levy. AGAD, BN, MS 5422.

81. Kysil mentions in his will that he has a detachment of five horses under Jerzy Zasławski. "Try testamenty," p. 59. It seems likely that Kysil served with Jerzy Zasławski before Khotyn, but no detachment led by Zasławski appears to have taken part in the Tsetsora debacle, and I have been unable to find evidence of Zasławski's participation on the Turkish and Muscovite fronts. Zasławski is not mentioned in the detailed study: Majewski, *Cecora: Rok 1620*. Some information on Jerzy Zasławski is included in Niesiecki, *Herbarz*, X, 95. In one *comput* on the Khotyn war, Zasławski is listed as heading 200 horses, PANK, MS 1051, fols. 431–435, while another describes his unit as 150 horses under the Fifth Regiment led by Chodkiewicz. BCZ, MS 110, p. 652. Kysil's last contact recorded with Zasławski was his election from Zasławski's regiment in February 1622 to the Khotyn Confederation, Biblioteka Raczyńskich (hereafter BR), MS 2, pp. 1117–1123.

82. Kysil made no mention of losses at Tsetsora in his will, but rewards a man whose brother was killed at Orynyn. "Try testamenty," 59.

83. April 28, 1621 in Kazimierz Pułaski, "Pierwsze lata publicznego zawodu Adama Kisiela (1622–1635)," *Szkice i poszukiwania historyczne*, 3 vols. (Cracow, 1877–1909), I, 194.

84. For materials on the Confederation, including Kysil's election from Jerzy Zasławski's regiment, see BR, MS 2, p. 1117–1123. For the confederation's demands, see *O konfederacyi lwowskiej, w roku 1622 uczynionej*, ed. Kazimierz Józef Turowski (Cracow, 1858).

85. Kysil's role in the Khotyn confederation is praised by Mikhail Sliozka in his dedication to Kysil of *Triodion si est' trypisnets'* . . . (Lviv, 1642), fol. 3.

86. Lubomirski, *Adam Kisiel*, p. 8.

87. Pułaski, "Pierwsze lata," pp. 195–196. Zygmunt's letter appointing Kysil a delegate stresses the need for secrecy, "in order to have the best influence on the spirit of the nobility, so that they might stand up for the fatherland during the sudden and serious dangers to the Commonwealth." Kysil's value as a royal delegate was often praised, as his later appointment to the 1629 Orthodox Synod illustrated. Władysław singled out his abilities as a delegate when appointing him castellan of Chernihiv in 1639. Met. Kor., MS 185, fols. 221–222.

88. While there is evidence of Kysil's participation in almost all Diets after 1629, there is little documentary proof for the 1620s. Since the Volhynian dietine instructions are not published for this period and since most delegates are not mentioned in the extant diaries, the silence on Kysil's participation should not be thought to indicate that he had not entered the Diet. The first definite proof of his election as a delegate to the Diet are the Volhynian dietine instructions of 1624. Biblioteka Zakładu Narodowego im. Ossolińskich we Wrocławiu (hereafter BO), MS 1926, fol. 63. A royal grant in 1646 mentioned that he had participated in twenty-four Diets as a delegate. Nomination as Kievan castellan February 5, 1646 *Arkhiv Iu. Z. R.*, pt. III, vol. I, 405. This would indicate he served in all the Diets from 1621 to 1641.

89. For the Volhynian dietine' religious demands, see Tomkiewicz's article "Wołyń," pp. 26–45.

90. For the events of this period, see Chodynicki, *Kościół Prawosławny,* pp. 431–479, and Zhukovich, *Seimovaia bor'ba,* nos. 4 and 5.

91. See *Supplikatia,* in Lipiński, *Z dziejów Ukrainy,* pp. 99–101. It is usually attributed to Drevyns'kyi, Hrushevs'kyi VII, pp. 480–508.

92. On the 1630 rebellion and its consequences, see Mykhailo Antonovych, "Pereiaslavs'ka kampaniia 1630 r.," *Pratsi Ukraïns'koho istorychno-filolohich-noho tovarystva v Prazi,* V (1943), pp. 5–41. Antonovych lists Kysil as assisting in putting down the 1630 rebellion. "Pereiaslavs'ka kampania," p. 19. While this is likely, Antonovych cites Pułaski, "Pierwsze lata," p. 198, as a source, but no specific information on the 1630 campaign is on that page. The only mention is of Kysil's military services.

93. See Zygmunt's grant of the village of Vytkiv to Kysil, Pułaski, "Pierwsze lata," p. 198. It mentions the intervention of Zamoyski.

94. Kysil's contacts with Tomasz Zamoyski are documented by a number of his letters to Tomasz and to his wife Katarzyna Ostrogska-Zamoyska. These letters, currently in the Archiwum Zamoyskich, AGAD, are the only major collection of letters in Kysil's own hand. For Kysil's requests for assistance, see Kysil to Tomasz Zamoyski, June 12, 1635. AGAD, Archiwum Zamoyskich, MS 727, pp. 61–72. In his most personal letters to Zamoyski, Kysil discusses their youth, equality of all nobles, and problems of his brother Mykola in making use of the grants made in the Chernihiv lands. The Kysils had problems in assuming control of lands granted to them, but seized by Aleksander Piaseczyński, the starosta of Novhorod-Sivers'kyi. Kysil calls upon Zamoyski as chancellor to assist his brother in straightening out problems of claims. Mykola was granted a military post in Novhorod-Sivers'kyi on December 12, 1635 (AGAD,

Met. Kor., MS 182, fols. 3–4); Aleksander Piaseczyński was granted considerable land rights in Siveria on December 12, 1635 (AGAD, Met. Kor., MS 182, fols. 10–11). Oleksander Kysil received estates (*boiarszczyny*) on March 16, 1635, in a grant mentioning his participation in the Prussian expedition (1626) (AGAD, Met. Kor., MS 181, fol. 95). Also see the following letters of Kysil to Zamoyski: Kysil to Tomasz Zamoyski, September 30, 1635, AGAD, Archiwum Zamoyskich, MS 727, pp. 73–74. Kysil discusses problems of offices. Kysil to Tomasz Zamoyski, March 23, 1637, AGAD, Archiwum Zamoyskich, MS 338. The letter deals with position of judge of Volodymyr, which Kysil had secured for his brother through Zamoyski's intercession. He states that "storms" had broken out against this election and requests that his cousin should receive the post in the Chernihiv lands that his brother would vacate. He reminds Zamoyski of his services to him in military ventures.

95. See footnote 93 and 94. Zamoyski appears to have suggested Kysil's appointment as delegate to the dietine held in Zhytomyr in 1628. Zygmunt wrote to ask for his suggestion for a delegate. Czapliński, "Wybór posła," pp. 220–221. Kysil was selected as the delegate. Pułaski, "Pierwsze lata," p. 196.

96. Kysil was requested to aid in forming opinion at the Volhynian dietine by Tomasz Zamoyski. (Undated, probably December 1625, Zamoyski to a number of nobles whose support he sought, BN, BOZ, MS 1602, fol. 323.) Six people were selected for this letter including the Volhynian palatine, Prince Jerzy Zasławski. For Kysil's services in economic dealings, see: Kysil to Katarzyna Zamoyska, August 15, 1626, AGAD, Archiwum Zamoyskich, MS 943 (about Zamoyski family financial affairs) and Kysil to Tomasz Zamoyski, March 30, 1626, AGAD, Archiwum Zamoyskich, MS 727, 62–63 (financial reports). For Zamoyski's gratitude for Kysil's assistance in the 1626 campaign, see Tomasz Zamoyski to Kysil, December 16, 1627, Archiwum Zamoyskich, MS 891. (A letter thanking Kysil for his military assistance. It discusses a commission to the Swedes and preparations for the Diet.)

97. Seweryn Gołębiowski, "Pamiętnik o Tomaszu Zamoyskim, Kanclerzu W. Kor.," in *Biblioteka Warszawska*, LII (1853), 223.

98. Tomasz Zamoyski to Kysil, August 5, 1626, AGAD, Archiwum Zamoyskich, MS 891, pp. 1–2. He thanks Kysil for his willingness to serve in the Prussian war and discusses monetary problems.

99. Kysil to Tomasz Zamoyski, July 9, 1626, AGAD, Achiwum Zamoyskich, MS 727, 64–66. He relates problems in recruiting pancers and hussars.

100. Kysil's participation in the Prussian war was mentioned by Kosiv in the *Paterikon*. Kosiv praised him for his heroic services before the view of Władysław while under Zamoyski's colors. The king also mentioned Kysil's bravery at Gniew when granting Kysil the positions of castellan of Chernihiv, AGAD, Met. Kor., MS 185, fols. 407–409, and castellan of Kiev, *Arkhiv Iu. Z. R.,* pt. III, vol. I, 405. On August 5, 1626, Zamoyski wrote to Kysil thanking him for agreeing to recruit a detachment and discussing monetary problems. AGAD, Archiwum Zamoyskich, MS 891, pp. 1–2. Zamoyski discussed his rejection of the king's proposal that he assume the post of hetman in this letter. Kysil was granted

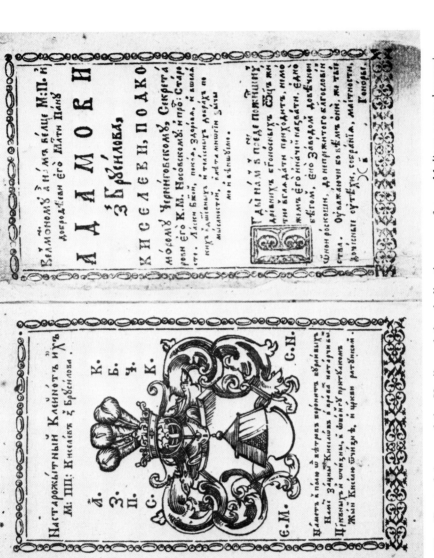

The Coat of Arms of the Kysils and the dedication page from *Molitvy povsednevnyi*.

Abraham van Westerveldt, *Janusz Radziwiłł Receiving the Envoys of Bohdan Khmel'nyts'kyi in Kiev, 1651* (18th-century copy). The castle of the palatine of Kiev on the hill called Kisilivka is pictured on the right.

Church of the Protectress. Nyzkynychi.

Bust of Kysil in the Church of the Protectress in Nyzkynychi.

Sarcophagus of Mykola Kysil in the crypt of the Church of the
Protectress, Nyzkynychi. It contains the remains of Adam Kysil.

estates as the result of his bravery in the Prussian war. Zygmunt made a land grant to Kysil for his services as *rotmistrz* during the campaign in Prussia. Puła-ski, "Pierwsze lata," p. 195. For Kysil's participation, see Seweryn Gołębiowski, "Pamiętnik o Tomaszu Zamoyskim," p. 223. The battle of Gniew is discussed in detail in Jerzy Teodorczyk, "Bitwa pod Gniewem (22.IX—29.IX 1626)," *Studia i Materiały do Historii Wojskowości,* vol. XII, pt. II (1966), 70–172.

101. Pułaski, "Pierwsze lata," p. 195.

102. The last known mentions of Hryhorii were in 1616. *Arkhiv Iu. Z. R.,* pt. VIII, vol. III, 537, and LNB, Zbirka Radzymyns'koho (hereafter ZR), MS 42 I.4. Summariusz z akt Włodzimierskich z lat 1569–1813, 7v., Kisiel entry, fol. 158, September 28, 1616. He was deceased at the time of Adam Kysil's June 1621 will. Since Kysil mentioned that his father died without a will, it is unlikely that it will ever be possible to establish the exact date of Hryhorii's death. "Try testamenty," pp. 57–60.

103. Only careful study of the Volhynian *aktovi knyhy* can clarify why Kysil called Chetvertyns'kyi his "brother" in the will. The influence of Hryhorii Chet-vertyns'kyi on Kysil is difficult to determine but was probably a decisive element in Kysil's development. Besides Kysil's designation of Chetvertyns'kyi as exe-cutor of his will in 1621, the only definite indications of contacts between the two men are his mention of "Prince Chetvertyns'kyi" as his "brother" in a 1629 letter to Tomasz Zamoyski (AGAD, Archiwum Zamoyskich, BS 338) and a letter Kysil wrote to Chetvertyns'kyi in January 1653 (BO, MS 7249, pp. 7–9). Chetvertyns'kyi was considerably older than Kysil. Although he never rose higher than the rank of podkomorzy of Luts'k, he was influential through his close familial connections with the Zbarazki family. His defense of Orthodoxy in the 1620s and 1630s was unswerving, and almost alone of the Orthodox no-bility, he raised sons who were also defenders of Orthodoxy. He, like Kysil, often served as a delegate from the Volhynian palatinate (1627, 1630, 1632, 1638, 1639), and the two men must have worked closely together in the defense of Orthodoxy. Kysil's ties with the Chetvertyns'kyis were also cemented by the families' avowed genealogical connection. It is also possible that the Kysil's adoption of "Sventoldych" was an imitation of the princely Chetvertyns'kyi fam-ily's appellation of "Sviatopolk." In any event, the influence of a member of the most zealous of all Ukrainian families in the defense of Orthodoxy, the preser-vation of Slavonic, and the rebirth of the Rus' historical tradition may be pre-sumed to have been great at the crucial early phase of Kysil's career. On Chetvertyns'kyi, see the article by Wanda Dombrowska in *Polski Słownik Bio-graficzny,* 16 vols. to date (Cracow, 1935 to present), IV, 362. The 1653 letter from Kysil to Hryhorii calls Dombrowska's designation of 1651 as Hryhorii's death into question.

104. Kysil mentioned four Volhynian nobles as his executors: Petro Kalu-shovs'kyi, Petro Lashch from Tuchap, Illiia Malyshchyns'kyi, and his "brother" Prince Hryhorii Chetvertyns'kyi. "Try testamenty," pp. 57–68. Other than Chet-vertyns'kyi, all were from minor Volhynian families. His father's creditor, Ivan Ivanyts'kyi, mentioned in the will, was from a more prominent family of Volo-

dymyr county and was probably his uncle. His witness, Mykhailo Orans'kyi, was probably his brother-in-law.

105. Kysil may be presumed to have married Anastaziia in the mid-1620s. In his 1653 testament he states that Anastaziia has been his wife for twenty-six years. "Try testamenty," p. 62. The earliest mention of Anastaziia as Kysil's wife is for March 27, 1627. LNB, ZR, MS 42.I.4, fol. 163.

106. For information on Bohush, see Edward Rulikowski, "Nowosiołki," *Słownik Geograficzny Królewstwa Polskiego i innych krajów słowiańskich,* 15 vols. (Warsaw, 1880), VII, 283 and Jabłonowski, *Pisma,* III, 162–163.

107. Bohush purchased Novosilky in 1585, but by 1630 it was in the hands of Filon, Anastaziia's father. In 1646 Filon sold Novosilky to Kysil. Rulikowski, "Nowosiółki," p. 283.

108. In 1628 Filon sold the castle and the village of Zorenychi to Kysil. *Opisanie dokumentov Arkhiva zapadnorusskikh uniatskikh mitropolitov,* ed. S. G. Runkevich, 2 vols. (St. Petersburg, 1897), I, 207. (Hereafter *ODAZUM.*)

109. He mentioned his wife's barrenness, but praised her for her piety, love, and services in his last will. "Try testamenty," 62.

110. According to the Orthodox nobleman Ioakhym Ierlych (Joachim Jerlicz), Anastaziia was the widow of Mykhailo Butovych, the owner of Brusyliv. [Joachim Jerlicz], *Latopisiec albo kroniczka Joachima Jerlicza,* ed. K. Wł. Wójcicki, 2 vols. (Warsaw, 1853), I, 81. The earliest known use of "of Brusyliv" by Kysil is March 1, 1627, the month in which Anastaziia is first mentioned as his wife. LNB, ZR, MS 42.I.4, fol. 163. On New Brusyliv, see "Try testamenty," p. 62.

111. Pułaski, "Pierwsze lata," p. 198.

112. AGAD, Met. Kor., MS 185, fols. 391–392. For Władysław's administration, see Vasylenko, "Pravne polozhennia," pp. 292–294.

113. In the 1630s, Kysil sought offices for his family and granted them lands. See AGAD, Met. Kor., MS 181, fols. 3–4, 95, 171–172.

114. The most extensive discussion of Kysil's participation in the synod is in Zhukovich, *Seimovaia bor'ba,* no. 6, pp. 9–33. I have discussed Kysil's participation in the synods in "Adam Kysil and the Synods of 1629: An Attempt at Orthodox-Uniate Accommodation in the Reign of Sigismund III," *Harvard Ukrainian Studies,* III–IV (1979–1980), 826–842 and most of this section comes from this article. Also see Ivan Khoma, "Ideia spil'noho synodu 1629r.," *Bohosloviia,* XXXVII (1973), 21–64 and Teofil Długosz, "Niedoszły synod unicko-prawosławny we Lwowie 1629 roku," *Collectanea Theologica,* XIX (1938), 479–506.

115. On Ruts'kyi's dissatisfaction see Mirosław Szegda, *Działalność organizacyjna Metropolity Józefa IV Welamina Rutskiego (1613–1637)* (Warsaw, 1967), pp. 177–186. For the problems facing the Uniate church, see A. H. Velykyi, *Z litopysu khrystyians'koï Ukraïny,* V (Rome, 1972), 27–32.

116. For a description of this period, see Chodynicki, *Kościół Prawosławny,* pp. 431–439.

117. For the problem of the Orthodox hierarchy, see Hrushevs'kyi VII, pp. 497–508.

118. On Kuntsevych, see M. Solovii and A. H. Velykyi, *Sviatyi Iosafat Kuntsevych: Ioho zhyttia i doba* (Toronto, 1967).

119. On Borets'kyi's contacts with Muscovy, see Chodynicki, *Kościół Prawosławny*, pp. 541–543.

120. For Kiev's rise as a cultural center in this period, see Hrushevs'kyi, *Kul'turnyi-natsional'nyi rukh*, pp. 208–230.

121. The scholarly literature on Mohyla is considerable. For his works and scholarly literature on him, see Makhnovets', *Ukraïns'ki pys'mennyky*, I, 415–427.

122. Chodynicki, *Kościół Prawosławny*, pp. 107–109.

123. *Prawa, konstytucye y przywileie Królewstwa Polskiego, y Wielkiego Xięstwa Litewskiego, y wszytkich prowincyi należących: Na walnych seymiech koronnych od Seymu Wiślickiego roku Pańskiego 1347 az do ostatniego seymu uchwalone,* comp. Stanisław Konarski, 8 vols. (Warsaw, 1732–1782), III, 282. (Hereafter *Volumina legum.*)

124. On Smotryts'kyi's defection, see Golubev I–1, 188–201; Zhukovich, *Seimovaia bor'ba*, no. 6, pp. 157–159; Hrushevskyi VIII–1, 77–78; Bohdan Kurylas, *Z"iedynennia Arkhyepyskopa Meletiia Smotryts'koho v istorychnomu i psykholohichnomu nasvitlenni* (Winnipeg, 1962), and Tadeusz Grabowski, "Ostatnie lata Melecjusza Smotryckiego," *Księga pamiątkowa ku czci Bolesława Orzechowicza* (Lviv, 1916), pp. 297–327.

125. For the Orthodox obstruction of the Diet, see Zhukovich, *Seimovaia bor'ba*, nos. 5 and 6.

126. For Ruts'kyi's complaints to Rome about Latin-rite Catholic attitudes toward Uniates, see his letter of 1624 in Theodosius T. Haluščynskyj and Athanasius G. Welykyj, ed., *Epistolae Josephi Velamin Rutskyj Metropolitae Kioviensis Catholici (1613–1637)*, series II, Analecta OSBM, section III; vol. I of Epistolae Metropolitarum Archiepiscoporum et Episcoporum (Rome, 1956), 136–141. (Hereafter Rutskyj, *Epistolae.*)

127. For the nuncio's activities during this period, see Athanasius G. Welykyj, ed., *Litterae Nuntiorum Apostolicorum Historiam Ucrainae Illustrantes (1550–1850), V, 1629–1638,* in Analecta OSBM, Series II, Section III (Rome, 1961).

128. For the Congregation for the Propagation of the Faith's rulings, see Athanasius G. Welykyj, ed., *Acta S. C. de Propaganda Fide Ecclesiam Catholicam Ucrainae et Bielarusiae Spectantia, I, 1622–1667,* in Analecta OSBM, Series II, Section III (Rome, 1953).

129. For Roman policy in this period, see E. Šmurlo, *Le Saint-Siège et l'Orient Orthodoxe Russe: 1609–1654,* in 2 parts (Prague, 1928), 52–69. (Hereafter cited as Šmurlo, I and II.)

130. For Ruts'kyi's attempt to obtain Vatican approval for a "Ruthenian" patriarchate, see Szegda, *Działalność prawno-organizacyjna*, pp. 193–200. This section is a summary of Father Szegda's chapter in his thesis. I would like to express my thanks to him for having allowed me to read his manuscript. Also, see D. Tanczuk, "Quaestio Patriarchus Kioviensis tempore conaminum Unionis

Ruthenorum (1582–1632),'' *Analecta OSMB*, series II, vol. I (1949), 128–144, J. Krajcar, "The Ruthenian Patriarchate—Some Remarks on the Project for its Establishment in the 17th Century," *Orientalia Christiana Periodica*, XXX, nos. 1–2 (1960), 65–84 and the negative evaluation of the effort by Długosz, "Niedoszły synod," pp. 484–485.

131. For the reaction to Smotryts'kyi's discussions, see Kurylas, *Z"iedynennia Arkhyepyskopa Meletiia Smotryts'koho,* pp. 65–73.

132. Ruts'kyi to Congregation, January 9, 1629; Ruts'kyi, *Epistolae,* p. 225. Ruts'kyi, in some of his correspondence with Rome also attributed the initiative to the Orthodox. See his letter to the Congregation, March 25, 1629 Rutskyj, *Epistolae,* pp. 229–230. The papal nuncio was negative from the outset and viewed calling the synods as an usurpation of papal authority. Santa Croce to Cardinal Bandini, March 17, 1629, *Litterae Nuntiorum*, V, 11–13.

133. Ruts'kyi, *Epistolae*, p. 225. Ruts'kyi, in some of his correspondence with Rome, also attributed the initiative to the Orthodox: see his letter to the Congregation, March 25, 1629, in Ruts'kyi, *Epistolae*, pp. 229–230.

134. For Kysil's thanks to Ruts'kyi for proposing him as a delegate, see his letter of July 14, 1629, in Ivan Kryp"iakevych, "Novi materiialy do istorii soboriv v 1629 r.," *ZNTSh*, CXVI (1913), 29. For Ruts'kyi's praise of Kysil, see his letter of July 27, 1629, to the papal nuncio, Antonio Santa Croce. Ruts'kyi, *Epistolae*, p. 232.

135. For the projected constitution, see P. Zhukovich, *Materialy dlia istorii kievskogo i l'vovskogo soborov 1629 goda,* Zapiski Imperatorskoi Akademii nauk, VIII, no. 15 (St. Petersburg, 1911), 19–20. On negotiations at the Diet, see Anna Filipczak-Kocur, *Sejm zwyczajny z roku 1629* (Warsaw-Wrocław, 1979), pp. 92–94.

136. The Diet constitution project concludes with a statement: "The delegate of the Palatinate of Volhynia wrote this copy with his own hand, Adam Kysil." Zhukovich, *Materialy,* p. 19. For an account of the discussions, see Drevyns'kyi's and Kropyvnyts'kyi's protest after the Synod (undated), see Zhukovich, *Materialy,* pp. 22–24.

137. Zhukovich, *Materialy,* p. 23.

138. *Arkhiv Iu. Z. R.,* pt. I, vol. VI, 598–599. The document is dated February 28, 1629, while another copy is dated February 16 (*Arkhiv Iu. Z. R.,* pt. I, vol. VI, 598). Santa Croce sent a copy to Bandini on March 17, 1629, *Litterae Nuntiorum,* V,, 11–13.

139. The protest of the Orthodox clergy on July 12, 1629 charged that the delegates to the diet had not been empowered to convene a synod. Zhukovich, *Materialy,* p. 21. Drevyns'kyi and Kropyvnyts'kyi maintained that discussions had taken place after their official functions as delegates had terminated. Zhukovich, *Materialy,* p. 23.

140. See footnote 138 for citation of universals. This was protested by Drevyns'kyi and Kropyvnyts'kyi, Zhukovich, *Materialy,* p. 23.

141. For Zygmunt's appointment of Kysil, undated, see Pułaski, "Pierwsze lata," p. 197.

142. Golubev describes Kysil as an Orthodox nobleman and ignores the 1632 conversion problem, I–1, 212. Zhukovich's document publication proved definitely that Kysil was the king's delegate to the Kiev synod, not Prince Aleksander Zasławski, as had been earlier postulated on the basis of manuscripts of the eighteenth-century Uniate metropolitan, Lev Kishka (Zhukovich, *Materialy*, p. 5). In fact, although Pułaski's 1874 publication on the king's mandate to Kysil proved this, the document was unknown to historians of the synod. Zhukovich maintained that Kysil was still a Uniate, but possibly already favorable to accepting Orthodoxy. Chodynicki accepted this view in his work, *Kościół Prawosławny*, p. 485, but in a series of corrections replaces Uniate with "zealous Orthodox," p. 631. He postulates that Radziwiłł's comment deals with Adam Franciszek Kisiel. This hypothesis is spurious since Adam Franciszek was a generation younger than Adam Kysil and was active in the second half of the seventeenth century. PANK, MS 2878, fol. 40. Adam Franciszek could not have been at the 1632 Diet. Kryp"iakevych took the noncommmittal stand of calling Kysil "in the middle between Uniates and Orthodox," "Novi materiialy," p. 9.

143. Albrycht Stanisław Radziwiłł, *Memoriale Rerum Gestarum in Polonia 1632–1656*, 5 vols., Polska Akademia Nauk-Oddział w Krakowie, Materiały Komisji Nauk Historycznych, XV, XVIII, XXII, XXV, XXVI (Wrocław, I, 1968; II, 1970; III, 1972; IV, 1974; V, 1975), III, 66. (Hereafter Radziwiłł, *Memoriale* I, II, III, IV, V.)

144. For the older tradition, see S. Baranovskii, "Pravoslavnyi volynskii pomeshchik, A. Kisel' kak pol'skii diplomat v epokhu B. Khmel'nitskogo," *Volynskie eparkhial'nye vedomosti*, November 1, 1874, no. 21, pp. 747–766.

145. This assertion is made on the basis of his comment to Mohyla (as reported by him to Ruts'kyi) that he was of the same faith as Mohyla, Zhukovich, *Materialy*, p. 10.

146. Rutskyj, *Epistolae*, p. 232.

147. For Ruts'kyi's views on Smotryts'kyi's conversion see his letter to the Congregation for the Propagation of the Faith on January 9, 1629. Rutskyj, *Epistolae*, pp. 223–225.

148. Although Kysil praised Borets'kyi for his efforts in reaching an agreement, Ruts'kyi was suspicious of Borets'kyi's real intentions. Ruts'kyi to Santa Croce, July 27, 1629. Rutskyj, *Epistolae*, pp. 231–233.

149. Szegda, *Działalność*, p. 196.

150. This account of the synod is based chiefly on Kysil's report to Metropolitan Ruts'kyi, published in Zhukovich, *Materialy*, pp. 8–18. Another copy is in Kryp"iakevych, "Novi materiialy," pp. 25–28. Relevant material is in Šmurlo, II, 44–72. The course of the synod is described in all of these works, but the best general discussion of the events of 1629 is Chodynicki, *Kościół Prawosławny*, pp. 479–512. Also, see Petr Orlovskii, "Kievskii sobor v 1629 g." *Kievskaia starina*, XC (July–August 1905), 168–173.

151. Zhukovich, *Materialy*, pp. 10–11, 14–16. For Boryskovych's objections, see the protests of the Orthodox clergy, July 12, 1629, Zhukovich, *Materialy*, p. 21.

152. Zhukovich, *Materialy*, pp. 11–12.
153. Zhukovich, *Materialy*, pp. 12–13.
154. Zhukovich, *Materialy*, pp. 12–13.
155. Golubev I–2, 368–369.
156. Zhukovich, *Materialy*, pp. 20–22. Kryp"iakevych asserts that in the protest registered in the Kiev court books a militant anti-Uniate position was taken by the clergy, who went so far as to demand the abolition of the union. Kryp"iakevych, "Novi materiialy," p. 12. In the papers of Santa Croce, Kryp"iakevych found a more moderate translation of the protest which the clergy gave to Kysil, and a letter from the clergy to the king, Kryp"iakevych, "Novi materiialy," pp. 24–25. He postulates that the militant public protest was for home consumption, and the conciliatory message was for the king. I can find no support in the Zhukovich copy for Kryp"iakevych's assertion that the clergy demanded the abolition of the union.
157. Zhukovich, *Materialy*, pp. 22–24.
158. Zhukovich, *Materialy*, pp. 13–14.
159. Kryp"iakevych, "Novi materiialy," p. 29.
160. Zhukovich, *Materialy*, p. 10; Rutskyj, *Epistolae*, p. 232.
161. Zhukovich, *Materialy*, p. 17.
162. Zhukovich, *Materialy*, p. 1. Kysil also reported having attempted to win over the Cossacks by calling them "men necessary to the fatherland." Zhukovich, *Materialy*, p. 10.
163. Golubev I–2, 364. Radziwiłł's letter of June 20, 1629.
164. See Šmurlo, II, 44–72; Rutskyj, *Epistolae*, pp. 225, 229–237; *Litterae Nuntiorum*, V, 27–33; *Acta S. C. De Propaganda*, I, 78–80; Kryp"iakevych, "Novi materiialy," pp. 18–19. The Congregation rejected the request to hold a joint synod on June 4 and June 22. *Acta S. C. De Propaganda*, I, 78–80.
165. For Kysil's favorable comments, see Zhukovich, *Materialy*, p. 13.
166. Kysil quoted Morokhovskyi's opinions in discussing the Synod. Zhukovich, *Materialy*, p. 13. Morokhovs'kyi had even been proposed as a Uniate liaison to the Kiev synod, Šmurlo, I, 64. Morokhovs'kyi's will is in *Arkhiv Iu. Z. R.*, pt. I, vol. VI, 634–637.
167. Rutskyj, *Epistolae*, p. 232.

Chapter III

1. The problem of the interregnum is treated in Czapliński, *Władysław*, pp. 93–116.
2. On the rivalry for the Swedish throne, and Gustavus Adolphus's intervention, see Czapliński, *Władysław*, pp. 77–92, 101–102. For a detailed discusion of the role of Gustavus Adolphus in the election, see Adam Szelągowski, "Układy Królewicza Władysława i dysydentów z Gustawem Adolfem w r. 1632," *Kwartalnik Historyczny*, XIII (1899), 683–733. Also see Adam Szelągowski, *Rozkład Rzeszy i Polska za panowania Władysława IV* (Cracow, 1907), pp. 40–64, for relations with Sweden and the Habsburgs. The major study on Gustavus

Adolphus's policy toward the Commonwealth is David Normann, *Gustaw Adolfs politik mot Ryssland och Polen under Tyska kriget* (Uppsala, 1943).

3. Hrushevs'kyi VIII–1, 139–142.

4. On Gustavus Adolphus's contacts with Muscovy, see B. F. Porshnev, "Bor'ba vokrug shvedsko-russkogo soiuza v 1631–1632 gg.," *Skandinavskii sbornik*, I (Talin, 1956), 11–71, and "Gustav Adolf i podgotovka Smolenskoi Voiny," *Voprosy istorii*, 1947, no. 1, pp. 53–82.

5. For a discussion of Muscovite plans and objectives during the Smolensk War, see B. F. Porshnev, "Sotsial'no-politicheskaia obstanovka vo vremia Smolenskoi Voiny," *Istoriia SSSR*, 1957, no. 5, pp. 112–140. For the expectations of the Commonwealth's leaders, see Czapliński, *Władysław*, p. 94.

6. Czapliński, *Władysław*, p. 98. Szelągowski, "Układy," pp. 694–695.

7. Czapliński, *Władysław*, pp. 98–99. Szelągowski, "Układy," pp. 683–686.

8. Szelągowski, "Układy," pp. 732–733.

9. Czapliński, *Władysław*, p. 99. Szelągowski, "Układy," pp. 683–684.

10. Hrushevs'kyi VIII–1, 135–136, 201.

11. Chodynicki, *Kościół*, pp. 541–544.

12. Hrushevs'kyi VIII–1, 134–135.

13. Hrushevs'kyi VIII–1, 135.

14. Chodynicki, *Kościół*, pp. 537–540.

15. Hrushevs'kyi VIII–1, 130–131.

16. See Czapliński's analysis of Władysław's problems in securing his election, *Władysław*, pp. 93–98.

17. For a comparison of the two monarchs' religious policies, see Czapliński, *Władysław*, pp. 98–99.

18. For an analysis of the problems Władysław faced, see Chodynicki, *Kościół*, p. 557.

19. Radziwiłł's diary entry of October 19, 1632 mentions that Kysil had renounced the union on Easter day, 1632 (April 11). *Memoriale*, I, 66. His entry of March 15, 1635 describes this event as having occurred after Zygmunt's death, April 30. *Memoriale*, II, 779.

20. Radziwiłł was particularly incensed over this apostasy and mentioned it during his negative evaluations of Kysil. See *Memoriale*, II, 79.

21. Kysil's role at this Diet is not known, but his presence at the Diet is testified to by *Volumina legum*, III, 338. For a description of the Diet, see Chodynicki, *Kościół*, pp. 537–540.

22. See footnote 19 for the contradictory evidence as to whether Kysil's announcement took place prior to or after Zygmunt's death.

23. Hrushevs'kyi VIII–1, 140.

24. On May 12, Mohyla wrote to Radziwiłł asking for assistance in restoring the privileges of the church. *Arkheologicheskii sbornik dokumentov, otnosiashchikhsia k istorii Severnozapadnoi Rusi*, VII (Vilnius, 1870), 90–91. On June 6, 1632, Mohyla thanked Radziwiłł for his response and reiterated his plea. *Arkheologicheskii sbornik*, VII, 300–301. The Catholics often accusingly charged the Orthodox of joining with the heretics. See Fabian Birkowski, *Exorbitancje*

ruskie (Cracow, 1632), and K. Skupiński, *Rozmowa albo rellatia rozmowy dwóch Rusinów, schismatika z unitem* (Vilnius, 1634), republished in *Arkhiv Iu. Z. R.,* pt. 1, vol. VII, 650–733.

25. Pułaski, "Pierwsze lata," pp. 199–200.

26. *Arkhiv Iu. Z. R.,* pt. II, vol. I, 162–182; BN, MS 4848, pp. 99–106. Kysil did sign the June 3, 1632 dietine decisions.

27. I have found no information about Kysil in the diaries of the Convocation, in Radziwiłł, *Memoriale,* I, in the account of the debates on religion in the *Supplementum Synopsis albo zupełnieysze obiaśnienie krótkiego opisania praw, przywileiów, świebod i wolności . . .* (Vilnius, 1632), reprinted in *Arkhiv Iu. Z. R.,* pt. 1, vol. VII (Kiev, 1877), 577–649. He was not a delegate from the Volhynian palatinate; *Arkhiv Iu. Z. R.,* pt. 2, vol. I, 162–182. He did not sign the Confederation articles. Wojewódzkie Archiwum Państwowe w Gdańsku, Recesy stanów zachodniopruskich (hereafter Recesy), MS 300, 29/112, fols. 186–195 (print bound in manuscript), *Confoederacya Generalna,* July 16, 1632.

28. The *Supplementum Synopsis* is a summary of these discussions; *Arkhiv Iu. Z. R.,* pt. 1, vol. VII, 577–649. On this period see A. H. Velykyi, *Z litopysu khrystians'koï Ukraïny,* V (Rome, 1972), 56–58 and Šmurlo, I, 87–88. For the demands made by the Orthodox, see Golubev, I–2, 408–413.

29. For the Cossacks' participation in the Diet, see the entry under October 11 in BCz, MS 363, fols. 141–145. For their petitions and the Diet's answer, see BCz, MS 365, pp. 1419–1426 and Golubev I–2, 403–405.

30. Šmurlo, I, 90. For the agreement, see Recesy, MS 300, 29, 112; fol. 82.

31. Prior to the Convocation Diet, the Orthodox Vilnius brotherhood published the Orthodox case in *Synopsis albo krótkie opisanie praw, świebod y wolności . . . ,* republished in *Arkhiv Iu. Z. R.,* pt. 1, vol. VII, 533–576. This work is usually attributed to Lavrentii Drevyns'kyi; Makhnovets', *Ukraïns'ki pys'mennyky,* I, 336. After the Diet, the brotherhood published an account of the negotiation commission at the Convocation: *Supplementum Synopsis,* reprinted in *Arkhiv Iu. Z. R.,* pt. 1, vol. VII, 577–649. The Vilnius Uniate brotherhood answered the *Synopsis* on September 1, 1632 in a pamphlet entitled, *Jedność Święta Cerkwie Wschodniey y Zachodniey . . . Przeciw skryptowi synopsis nazwanemu,* and defended the Uniate position at the Election Diet in a pamphlet issued October 1, 1632 entitled *Prawa y przywileie od Naiaśnieyszych Królów . . . Obywatelom Korony Polskiey y Wielkiego X. L. Religiey Greckiey w jedności z S. Kościołem Rzymskim będącym.*

32. For an account of the disturbances at the Luts'k dietine, see BCz, MS 2086, pp. 253–254. The opposing sides also issued position papers. The Uniate answer to the Orthodox pamphlet: *Antimaxia albo Dyskurs wydany od kogoś pod czas Rellatiej pp. Posłów Wolhinskich w Luczku. pro die 16 Aug. 1632,* manuscript copies in BCz, MS 373, pp. 470–481, and BCz, MS 124, pp. 587–601.

33. The instructions of the dietine are in BCz, MS 365, pp. 1722–1727.

34. August 16, 1632, BCz, MS 365, pp. 1728–1729. On September 4, the

Uniate hierarchy protested the Volhynian dietine's rejection of the Uniates' proposals at the Volodymyr-Volyns'kyi court. Golubev I–2, 447–449.

35. BO, MS 5972, fol. 5.

36. For Kysil's activities at this Diet, see Radziwiłł, *Memoriale*, I, 60–66. Czapliński recounts the events on the basis of Diet diaries in Merseburg, *Władysław*, pp. 101–115. The most detailed account, with considerable information on Kysil is BCz, MS 363, fols. 113–302. Another copy of the MS 363 manuscript is in Muzeum Narodowe, MS 302, fols. 113–196. For Kysil's arguments, see BCz, MS 363, fols. 139, 155, 158, 161, 163, 245. Kysil's arguments against the need for papal consent are in BCz, MS 363, fol. 365. Fragments of another copy of this diary are published in Golubev I–2, 454–505. For additional information on Kysil's role at the Election Diet, see Biblioteka Kórnicka (hereafter BK), MS 1317, pp. 154, 157. On religious problems at the Diet, see Zacharias ab Haarlem, *Unio Ruthenorum a morte Sigismundi III usque ad coronationem Laislai 1632–1633* (Tartu, 1936).

37. BCz, MS 363, fols. 139–140. The protest was also signed by Leon Sapieha, palatine of Vilnius, Albrycht Stanisław Radziwiłł, and numerous other Lithuanian dignitaries. Krzysztof Radziwiłł was particularly adamant in attacking the protest.

38. Radziwiłł, *Memoriale*, I, 63.

39. Radziwiłł, *Memoriale*, I, 64.

40. Radziwiłł, *Memoriale*, I, 64–65. For his threatening tactics, see BCz, MS 363, fol. 167.

41. BCz, MS 363, fols. 164–170,

42. For the articles of compromise, see Golubev II–2, 4–9. For a Latin copy of the articles, see *Litterae Nuntiorum*, V, 120–123.

43. The articles were read on November 16, 1632, BCz, MS 363, fol. 268.

44. See Czapliński, *Władysław*, pp. 109–110. For Krzysztof Radziwiłł's role in assisting the Orthodox, see BCz, MS 363, fols. 138–140, 167–168, 240.

45. Hrushevs'kyi VIII–1, 134–135. For a characterization of the factions in the Orthodox church in the early 1630s, and the contrasts between Mohyla and Kopyns'kyi, see S. Golubev, "Priskorbnye stolknoveniia Petra Mogily s svoim predshestvennikom po mitropolii i kievo-nikol'skimi inokami," *Trudy Kievskoi dukhovnoi akademii*, 1897, no. 10, pp. 209–226.

46. For a discussion of historians' evaluations of Mohyla's ambition, see Hrushevs'kyi VIII–1, 171.

47. Kysil first used the title "Secretary of His Royal Majesty" in signing Władysław's *pacta conventa*:Lipiński, *Z dziejów Ukrainy*, p. 129. On May 19, 1633, Władysław wrote to him using the title, "courtier." Pułaski, "Pierwsze lata," p. 205. On the significance of these posts, see Czapliński, *Na dworze*, pp. 133–141.

48. M. A. Maksimovich, "Akt izbraniia Petra Mogily v mitropolity kievskie," *Sobranie sochinenii*, I (Kiev, 1876), 390.

49. Pułaski, "Pierwsze lata," pp. 202–204.

50. See the signatures in the *pacta conventa*, BCz, MS 363, fols. 277–300.

51. BCz, MS 363, fol. 245. For the actions of the Catholic party to prevent concessions, see Velykyi, *Z litopysu*, V, 60–64. Šmurlo I, 88–95. For documentation on the Uniate church and the Vatican's activities, see Šmurlo II, 88–109; Rutskyj, *Epistolae*, pp. 259–269; *Litterae Nuntiorum*, V, 88–142. For Pope Urban VIII's intercession to save the Uniate position, see Athanasius G. Welykyj, ed. *Documenta Pontificum Romanorum Historiam Ucrainae Illustrantia (1075–1953)*, I, Analecta OSBM, Ser. II, Section III (Rome, 1953), 485–492.

52. For Kysil's activities at the Coronation Diet, see BCz, MS 363, fols. 322, 340, 354–355, 359, 362–365. An attempt was made to have Kysil's status as delegate annulled because he had been elected to other functions by the Volhynian dietine. This attempt was led by Mikołaj Koryciński, starosta of Ojców, who was one of Kysil's major opponents in the religious controversies. BCz, MS 363, fols. 339–341. During the Diet, an anonymous pamphlet entitled *Rzym albo Stolica Rzymska ieśli co ma do praw Korony Polskiej y W. X. Litewskiego politickich, krótkie uważenia, roku 1633 stanom koronnym na seym koronatiey podane* appeared. According to S. Golubev, the anonymous author argues against the papacy's influence in the Commonwealth, and cites Western models such as France as examples of states where its influence is limited. Golubev attributes authorship of the pamphlet to Kysil. S. Golubev, "Neizvestnoe polemicheskoe sochinenie protiv papskikh pritiazanii v Iugo-Zapadnoi Rossii (1633 goda)," *Trudy Kievskoi dukhovnoi akademii*, 1899, no. 2, pp. 300–341. Golubev's attribution (p. 325) is in accordance with the arguments Kysil put forth at the Election Diet, BCz, MS 363, fol. 365. However, I have been unable to gain access to the Moscow archives, where this pamphlet probably exists. Without a comparison of the text with other texts known to be written by Kysil, it is impossible to establish his authorship of the pamphlet.

53. February 16, 1633, BCz, MS 363, fol. 342. For the Zaporozhians' support of Orthodoxy at the Election Diet, see BCz, MS 363, fols. 142–143, and Golubev I–2, pp. 452–453.

54. The mission was headed by Jerzy Ossoliński. For an account of the mission, see Ludwik Kubala, *Jerzy Ossoliński*, 2nd ed. (Warsaw, 1924), pp. 46–63, in *Dzieła Ludwika Kubali: Wydanie zbiorowe*, I.

55. Radziwiłł, *Memoriale*, I, 184.

56. *Arkhiv Iu. Z. R.*, pt. 1, vol. XI (Kiev, 1904), 395.

57. *Arkhiv Iu. Z. R.*, pt. 1, vol. XII (Kiev, 1904), 485.

58. M. A. Maksimovich, "Rodoslovnye zapiski kievlianina," *Sobranie sochinenii*, I, 210.

59. On February 15, 1633, Kysil was elected as one of the seven delegates from Little Poland (Deputaci do namowienia o wojnie Moskiewskiey y ad disciplinam militarem). Kropyvnyts'kyi was also named to the delegation. BCz, MS 363, fol. 340.

60. AGAD, Met. Kor., MS 180, fols. 14–15.

61. Kysil's appointment as Chernihiv podkomorzy was inscribed in the *Metryka Rus'ka*, which is now located in the Moscow Central Historical Archive. For a register of the act, Stefan Hankiewicz, *Index Actorum Publicorum albo*

Regestr Xięg . . . od roku Pańskiego 1569 aż do roku 1673, AGAD, Tak zwana Metryka Litewska, VIII–1, fol. 47. (Metryka Rus'ka)

62. For the international situation at the beginning of the war, see Porshnev, "Bor'ba vokrug shvedsko-russkogo soiuza v 1631–1632 gg." and "Gustav Adolf i podgotovka Smolenskoi Voiny." For the situation in Muscovy during the war, see Porshnev, "Sotsial'no-politicheskaia obstanovka." Also see O. L. Vainshtein, *Rossiia i Tridtsatiletniaia Voina 1618–1648 gg.* (Leningrad, 1947). For the actual course of the campaign, see the series of articles by Wacław Lipiński in *Przegląd Historyczno-Wojskowy:* "Początek działań rosyjskich w Wojnie Smoleńskiej (1632–1634)," V (1932), 29–61; "Stosunki polsko-rosyjskie w przededniu Wojny Smoleńskiej 1632–1634 i obustronne przygotowania wojskowe," V (1932), 235–272; "Działania wojenne polsko-rosyjskie pod Smoleńskiem od października 1632 do września 1633 r.," V (1932), 165–206; "Organizacja odsieczy i działania wrześniowe pod Smoleńskiem w 1633," VI (1933), 173–227; "Bój o Żaworonkowe wzgórza i osadzenie Szeina pod Smoleńskiem (16–30 października 1633r.)," VII (1934), 217–254. The Zaporozhian role in the war, above all on the Siverian front, has been given little attention, largely due to the lack of sources other than those in *Akty Moskovskogo gosudarstva,* I (St. Petersburg, 1890) and Kysil's correspondence published by Pułaski. The only work on the subject is Oleh Tselevych, "Uchast' kozakiv v Smolens'kii Viini 1633–34 rr.," *ZNTSh.,* XXVIII (1899), 1–72., which deals with the Siverian front only briefly and almost entirely on the basis of *Akty Moskovskogo gosudarstva,* I, and does not utilize Pułaski, "Pierwsze lata."

63. For a discussion of the structure of the Muscovite army see E. Stashevskii, *Smolenskaia Voina 1632–1634 gg.: Organizatsiia i sostoianie moskovskoi armii* (Kiev, 1919).

64. For the problems the Commonwealth faced at the outset of the Smolensk War, see Czapliński, *Władysław,* pp. 153–166.

65. Pułaski, "Pierwsze lata," p. 205.

66. Hrushevs'kyi VIII–1, 201.

67. On June 11, 1633 Piaseczyński reported his problems with the Zaporozhians. AGAD, Libri Legationum (hereafter LL), MS 32, fols. 93–95. Koniecpolski wrote to the king on June 25, including Piaseczyński's letter and informing the king of Turkish complaints of Cossack incursions. AGAD, LL, MS 32, fols. 95–96. Piaseczyński had problems with the Zaporozhians from the very beginning of the campaign. See his letter to Tomasz Zamoyski of February 10, 1633. AGAD, Arch. Zamoyskich, t. 737.

68. *Akty Moskovskogo gosudarstva,* I, 448.

69. For Mohyla's consecration in late April 1633, see Hrushevs'kyi VIII–1, 183–185.

70. For Mohyla's actions in this period, see Golubev II–1, 1–15. The fact that the two men were in Lviv in the spring of 1633 (the Lviv brotherhood recorded expenditures for a reception for Kysil on June 10, 1633), *Arkhiv Iu. Z. R.,* pt. 1, vol. XI, 395, and their subsequent closely coordinated activities makes this hypothesis probable.

71. For Mohyla's struggle with Kopyns'kyi, see Golubev, "Priskorbnye stolknoveniia," pp. 209–226.

72. On July 9, 1633, Władysław wrote to Koniecpolski informing him that he had sent emissaries to Piaseczyński to order that he and the Cossacks come up to Smolensk. He simultaneously wrote to the Zaporozhians ordering them not to embark on a Black Sea campaign, and to the starostas of the Ukraine ordering that they prevent the Zaporozhians from campaigning on the Black Sea. AGAD, LL, MS 32, fols. 95–97. Presumably, Kysil was one of the emissaries he mentioned. On July 19, the king, after having received notification of the Zaporozhian retreat from Putyvl', wrote ordering them back to Piaseczyński's service and then on to Smolensk. AGAD, LL, MS 32, fol. 98. On July 25, Koniecpolski wrote to the king of the continued danger on the Turkish front caused by Cossack incursions, and he reported that he had sent the king's orders to the Cossacks and was waiting for an answer. Kysil may have gone from Lviv in June directly to the siege of Putyvl' (since the Lviv brotherhood book may in fact be recording the funding of Kysil's reception after it occurred). This supposition is based on Pawłowski's report that "Kysil also promised them [the Zaporozhians] money at the border," but that they did not receive the promised payment. AGAD, LL, MS 32, fol. 105. Kysil thus may have arrived in June, just before or at the same time the Cossacks deserted Piaseczyński. The only other possible time this may have occured was in January, prior to the Coronation Diet, when Kysil was on his eastern trip to the Kiev dietine.

73. The embassy of Kysil and Pawłowski appears to have taken place in late July or early August. Pawłowski's account of the episode is undated. However, Koniecpolski wrote on July 25 that he had sent the king's message to the Zaporozhians, but had not yet received a response (AGAD, LL, MS 32, fols. 99–100), and the king wrote thanking Kysil on August 9, for his success (Pułaski, "Pierwsze lata," p. 206). The Zaporozhians were already reported to be back in battle and nearing Smolensk by August 27 (AGAD, LL, MS 32, fol. 104). Therefore, the Cossack council must have taken place about August 1. The only complicating factor of the dating is that the first letter to the Cossacks in AGAD, LL, MS 32 from the king on the issue of their return is dated August 22, 1633 (fols. 98–99). Since the Cossacks wrote to the king on August 22 that they were returning to the campaign due to the intercession of Kysil, but were held back due to transportation problems, it is certain that the episode took place no later than the middle of August. But the Zaporozhians' letter makes August 1 appear to be too early a dating. While approximately the August 1 date is the most likely time, it is possible that: 1. the August 9 date on the letter published by Pułaski is a mistake (possibly should be August 19); or 2. though the episode did take place around August 1, further negotiations were necessary before the Cossacks returned. The Pawłowski report is from AGAD, LL, MS 32, fols. 104–106. It is published in part by Lipiński, Z dziejów Ukrainy, pp. 195–196, and in Ukrainian translation by Hrushevs'kyi VII–1, 186–187, 204–205, from a copy (probably from the LL) in BCz, MS 141, pp. 601–603.

74. For Kysil and Pawłowski's problems, see Hrushevs'kyi VIII–1, 203–205.

75. AGAD, LL, MS 32, fol. 106.

76. AGAD, LL, MS 32, fol. 105.

77. Pułaski, "Pierwsze lata," p. 206. On August 22, Władysław wrote to the Zaporozhians. On the basis of information that Kysil had sent, he expressed pleasure that the Cossacks were returning to the war effort and would appear before Smolensk. AGAD, LL, MS 32, fol. 104. On August 22, the Zaporozhians wrote to the king that though they had abandoned the siege of Putyvl' for "certain reasons," as soon as they received his order from Kysil they decided to return to battle. They expressed their dissatisfaction at not having received the payment promised at Władysław's coronation, and reminded him that they expected him to keep the promises that their salaries would be paid. AGAD, LL, MS 32, fols. 106–107.

78. For the Zaporozhians' role before Smolensk, see Wacław Lipiński, "Organizacja odsieczy," pp. 207–208.

79. An exact dating of the Cossack council described by Pawłowski would add considerably to our information on the struggle between Kopyns'kyi and Mohyla. It would appear that under pressure Kopyns'kyi resigned from the metropolitan see, but after Mohyla's entry into Kiev, refused to give up his position. Mohyla imprisoned him for his obstinacy. In the second half of 1633, Kopyns'kyi was abbot of the Monastery of St. Michael. Golubev II–1, 14–16. Since dates are lacking for this sequence, a dating of the Cossack council would clarify problems. It would appear that Kopyns'kyi fled to the Cossacks after his imprisonment and that the renunciation Kysil obtained was in fact not the first Kopyns'kyi made. It is possible, however, that the imprisonment incident took place after the Cossack council. The close proximity of Kiev and Pereiaslav makes either of these hypotheses possible.

80. The role of the Orthodox clergy in Władysław's war effort is also evident in his use of the Bishop Iosyf Bobrykovych in late August as an emissary to the Zaporozhians. AGAD, LL, MS 32, fols. 106–107. Bobrykovych was the delegate from the Vilnius brotherhood who followed a pro-Uniate course in 1629 and was rewarded by his appointment as bishop in the 1632–33 recognition of Orthodoxy.

81. Pułaski, "Pierwsze lata," p. 208. Letter of September 8, 1633, Pułaski, "Pierwsze lata," p. 209.

82. Pułaski, "Pierwsze lata," pp. 209–210.

83. Pułaski, "Pierwsze lata," pp. 211, 214–215.

84. Pułaski, "Pierwsze lata," pp. 212–213.

85. Pułaski, "Pierwsze lata," p. 216. Pułaski found this "Relatio przyścia Ałłabiowa pod Czernichów i odejścia," in Kysil's papers, pp. 216–222. Another copy is in the AGAD, LL, MS 32, fols. 119–121.

86. Pułaski, "Pierwsze lata," p. 218. The manifesto is described by Kysil and translated into Polish and probably paraphrased.

87. See Kysil's circular of October 20, 1633 to the inhabitants of the border area. Pułaski, "Pierwsze lata," p. 223.

88. Pułaski, "Pierwsze lata," p. 223.

89. See Kysil's circular of October 20, 1633, Pułaski, "Pierwsze lata," pp. 221–225.

90. Pułaski, "Pierwsze lata," p. 226. AGAD, Met. Kor., MS 180, fol. 245.

91. This campaign is described in detail in Władysław Tomkiewicz, *Jeremi Wiśniowiecki*, pp. 11–17, but mistakenly dated 1633 instead of 1634.

92. Kysil's recruitment of 20,000 Cossacks is mentioned in Władysław's conferral of the castellanship of Kiev, February 5, 1646. *Arkhiv Iu. Z. R.*, pt. 3, vol. I, 402.

93. For Kysil's participation in the spring campaign, see *Akty Moskovskogo gosudarstva*, I, 585–586, 611–613.

94. For the terms of the Polianovka Treaty, see S. M. Solov'ev, *Istoriia Rossii s drevneishikh vremen*, V (Moscow, 1960), 174–181. On the negotiations, see B. F. Porshnev, "Na putiakh k Polianovskomu miru," in *Mezhdunarodnye otnosheniia: Politika-Diplomatiia XVI–XX veka. Sbornik statei k 80-letiiu akademika I. M. Maiskogo* (Moscow, 1964), pp. 512–537.

95. He pressed the right of his *podkomorstwo* in relation to the neighboring Novhorod-Sivers'kyi. Pułaski, "Pierwsze lata," p. 211. He also made explicit his rights to the town Divytsia that he had acquired from Mykola Soltan. AGAD, Met. Kor., MS 180, fols. 234–235.

96. For a discussion of the border problem in the reign of Władysław IV, see Władysław Godziszewski, "Granica polsko-moskiewska wedle pokoju polanowskiego (wytyczona w latach 1634–1648)," *Prace Komisji Atlasu Historycznego Polski*, III (Cracow, 1935), 1–96.

97. Godziszewski, "Granica polsko-moskiewska," pp. 8–10.

98. Godziszewski, "Granica polsko-moskiewska," pp. 18–20.

99. For the king's requests to delay and discussion of the problem of border magnates, see Pułaski, "Pierwsze lata," pp. 228–230.

100. Pułaski, "Pierwsze lata," p. 231.

101. Pułaski, "Pierwsze lata," p. 228.

102. Pułaski, "Pierwsze lata," pp. 228–229.

103. Kysil was thanked for his services on the Muscovite border in a letter of December 6,, 1634 from Koniecpolski, Pułaski, "Pierwsze lata," p. 235. Kysil was renamed to the commission, but as the junior colleague. Godziszewski, "Granica polsko-moskiewska," p. 20.

104. Godziszewski maintains that the new appointments were made because of the magnates' military strength in the region. Godziszewski, "Granica polsko-moskiewska," p. 20.

105. Godziszewski, "Granica polsko-moskiewska," p. 20.

106. For Kysil's later negotiations with Muscovy, see Godziszewski, "Granica polsko-moskiewska," pp. 39–41. Sixteen years later, Kysil advised the government on how to deal with Pushkin; April 11, 1650, Kysil to Jan Kazimierz, BCz, MS 402, pp. 5–12.

107. For Kysil's growing interests in the area, see AGAD, Met. Kor., MS 182, fols. 59–60; AGAD, Met. Kor., MS 186, fol. 94.

108. For examples of Kysil's reward from the Muscovite court, see *Akty,*

otnosiashchiesia k istorii Iuzhnoi i Zapadnoi Rossii, III (hereafter *Akty Iu.Z.R.*) (St. Petersburg, 1861), 107.

109. Radziwiłł, *Memoriale,* II, 78–79.

Chapter 4

1. Kysil was definitely the delegate from the Chernihiv palatinate in 1639 and probably for the four other Diets after the creation of the palatinate (although only his title and not his delegate status is mentioned for these Diets, the election of the demarcation commission in 1638 and the absence of his name from the Volhynian lists make it likely that he represented Chernihiv). PANK, Komisja historyczna, Kartoteka posłów do Sejmu.

2. *Volumina legum,* III, 863. His cousin Oleksander was elected at the second 1635 Diet. *Volumina legum,* III, 914.

3. *Volumina legum,* III, 895.

4. *Volumina legum,* III, 788, 987; *Volumina legum,* IV, 44.

5. *Volumina legum,* III, 947. Demarcation of Kiev and Chernihiv palatinates. Mykola, Oleksander and Matvii Kysil were also named. *Volumina legum,* III, 951. Demarcation of Chernihiv and Smolensk palatinates. Mykola was also named.

6. *Volumina legum,* III, 25. Mykola and Oleksander were also named.

7. *Volumina legum,* III, 939–941.

8. For background on this period, see Hrushevs'kyi VIII–1, 56–139, 200–258.

9. For an account of Commonwealth–Turkish-Tatar relations in the reign of Władysław IV, see Bohdan Baranowski, *Stosunki polsko-tatarskie w latach 1632–1648.* Prace Instytutu Historycznego Uniwersytetu Łódzkiego I (Łódź, 1949).

10. *Volumina legum,* III, 833.

11. Kysil to Żółkiewski, July 10, 1636,BCz, MS 132, p. 115.

12. Koniecpolski wrote to Kysil on November 20, 1634 about the pact which had been negotiated with Shagin Aga and mentioned that Kysil restrained the Cossacks from provoking war, as well as that instructions were separately included in the letter (they have not survived). Pułaski, "Pierwsze lata," p. 233. On December 2, Koniecpolski wrote to Kysil that he was not sure the matter was well under hand, but asking him to wait upon the arrival of Żółkiewski before making final decisions, and on December 6 he wrote a letter of thanks to Kysil for his efforts. The king also sent a letter praising Kysil's service. Pułaski, "Pierwsze lata," pp. 234–235.

13. For Władysław's Swedish war plans, see Czapliński, *Władysław,* pp. 173–199.

14. For a general discussion of the Commonwealth's foreign and Cossack policy in 1635–1638, see Hrushevs'kyi VIII–1, 200–289. Cossack affairs between 1635–1638 and particularly the 1637–1638 Pavliuk rebellion have two major sources. The first is the contemporary history written by Szymon Okolski, a preacher for Mikołaj Potocki, one of the participants in the Polish forces, and

dedicated to Stanisław Potocki. Both of his seventeenth-century works were republished in the nineteenth century. Szymon Okolski, *Dyaryusz Transakcyi wojennej między wojskiem koronnem i zaporoskiem w r. 1637* and *Kontynuacya Dyaryusza wojennego odprawiona w roku 1638 . . .* , K. J. Turowski, Biblioteka polska. Seria IV, nos. 1 and 2 (Cracow, 1859). Okolski's history is obviously written to glorify his patrons.

More important as a source is the chancery volume of Hetman Stanisław Koniecpolski for 1634–1638. This is the manuscript which Hrushevs'kyi bases his account of the Polish campaign on, citing it as *Imp. Pub. Bib. Pol.* F. IV, no. 94. After 1921 the manuscript was returned to Poland in a "revindication" program to restore to Poland those manuscript collections which had been seized in the late eighteenth century by the Imperial Russian government. The manuscript was destroyed with most of the "rewindykaty" during the German occupation of Warsaw. Bohdan Baranowski, *Stosunki polsko-tatarskie w latach 1632–1648*, pp. 3–5. Many of the documents of the chancery were copied in *Teki Naruszewicza* held in the Czartoryski Library in Cracow. A copy of almost the entire manuscript was made by Panteleimon Kulish, who planned to publish Koniecpolski's chancery. He had many of the documents translated into Russian, and subsequently loaned or given to Ludwik Kubala. It survives as MS 1819 at the Polish Academy of Sciences in Cracow. The manuscript begins in 1635, not 1634, and is missing the first 63 folios. Kubala, *Jerzy Ossoliński*, p. 389.

Vsevolod Holobuts'kyi's citation of this manuscript to the Kiev Central Scientific Library as "IV Pol. 94" seems inexplicable, barring a second copy by Kulish which happens to have the same call number in Kiev as the original had in St. Petersburg. Holobuts'kyi's citations may be to documents translated or recounted in Hrushevs'kyi. Golobutskii, *Zaporozhskoe Kazachestvo*, pp. 222–249. Most of the documents of Koniecpolski's chancery, including some from the 63 folios missing in the Cracow copy, are included in the unpublished volume by Panteleimon Kulish, *Materialy dlia istorii vossoedineniia Rusi*, II in TsNB in Kiev, II 13402.

15. Hrushevs'kyi VIII–1, 212. *Volumina legum,* III, 403.

16. Hrushevs'kyi VIII–1, 221–225.

17. Kysil discussed Żółkiewski's and his own role in his 1637 "Discourse," BCz, MS 133, p. 140. See also PANK, MS 1819, pp. 127–130.

18. For the problems of this period, see Hrushevs'kyi VIII–1, 213–219. For the Crimean civil war, see Hrushevs'kyi VIII–1, 228 and Benningen *Le Khanat de Crimée,* pp. 149–155, 339–340.

19. Throughout 1636, especially during the Cossack negotiations, the Commonwealth authorities feared that Muscovy would take advantage to resolve border conflicts in its favor. Kysil was assigned by Koniecpolski and Żółkiewski to observing Muscovite actions and heading off a confrontation. Kysil was specially requested by Koniecpolski in the summer of 1636 to return to Siveria from the Lublin Tribunal to gather information on the border problem. Kysil contacted the Muscovite border voevodas and carried on intelligence work. Kysil to Żółkiewski, July 10, 1636, BCz, MS 132, pp. 113–117.

20. Kysil to Koniecpolski, July 29, 1636, BCz, MS 132, pp. 173–177; PANK, MS 1819, pp. 41–43.

21. For an account of the first Pereiaslav council see Żółkiewski to Koniecpolski, July 24, 1636. BCz, MS 132, pp. 149–152.

22. For a description of these problems, see Hrushevs'kyi VIII–1, pp. 230–239.

23. Kysil's description of the second council centers on the need for funds. In a report to the king on August 6, he also called for alleviating the justifiable Cossack grievances against officials in the Ukraine and reported on the information he had received from his spies with the Tatars and the Muscovites. BCz, MS 132, pp. 175–177; PANK, MS 1819, pp. 44–47.

24. On August 18 Władysław responded to Kysil. BCz, MS 132, pp. 203–205; PANK, MS 1819, pp. 81–82. The king requested that Kysil return to the Cossacks to demand obedience from them and to promise that the money would arrive.

25. Two copies of the "Discourse" exist: BCz, MS 132, pp. 451–454; PANK, MS 1819, pp. 78–81.

26. For another account by Kysil of his falsification of documents in the king's name, see BCz, MS 132, p. 224.

27. BCz, MS 132, p. 454; PANK, MS 1819, p. 81.

28. Kysil to Koniecpolski, August 25, 1636, BCz, MS 132, pp. 223–226; PANK, MS 1819, pp. 75–77.

29. BCz, MS 132, p. 224.

30. BCz, MS 132, pp. 227–230; PANK, MS 1819, pp. 83–86.

31. BCz, MS 132, p. 227.

32. Hrushevs'kyi VIII–1, 237.

33. Żółkiewski wrote of the grave state of his health throughout the summer and autumn of 1636. See Żółkiewski to Koniecpolski, September 2, 1636, BCz, MS 132, pp. 207–208.

34. For the Diet's answer to the Cossack grievances see the letter issued in June 1637. BCz, MS 133, p. 285. For the Diet's answer to Cossack demands, see BCz, MS 133, pp. 143–145.

35. Potocki and Kysil to Koniecpolski, May 10, 1637, BCz, MS 133, p. 147. The Rusavka council is recounted on the basis of this letter. BCz, MS 133, pp. 147–150, 179–182 and PANK, MS 1819, pp. 120–129.

36. BCz, MS 133, p. 147.

37. BCz, MS 133, p. 180.

38. BCz, MS 133, pp. 181–182.

39. BCz, MS 133, p. 181.

40. BCz, MS 133, p. 182.

41. BCz, MS 134, pp. 139–142; PANK, MS 1819, pp. 127–130.

42. BCz, MS 134, p. 142.

43. See his description of his financial position in his first "Discourse." BCz, MS 132,, pp. 451–454.

44. The Cossack Ordinance of 1638 is discussed in detail in Władysław

Tomkiewicz. "Organiczenie swobód kozackich w roku 1638," *Kwartalnik Historyczny,* XLIV (1930), 125–175.

45. BCz, MS 133, pp. 143–145.

46. For the interaction of foreign policy and the Cossack problem in this period, see Hrushevs'kyi VIII–1, 245–254.

47. Letter of the nonregistered Cossacks to the registered, June 16, 1637, BCz, MS 133, pp. 209–214.

48. Hrushevs'kyi VIII–1, 245–254.

49. Hrushevs'kyi VIII–1, 250–258.

50. Zaporozhians to Koniecpolski, September 21, 1637, BCz, MS 133, pp. 527–533.

51. Hrushevs'kyi VIII–1, 258–261.

52. Okolski, *Dyaryusz,* p. 17.

53. For Pavliuk's answer on September 7, see BN, BOZ, MS 1173, fols. 500–501.

54. On Pavliuk's demands, see Hrushevs'kyi VIII–1, 255–256.

55. For Koniecpolski's response, see Hrushevs'kyi VIII–1, 257.

56. Hrushevs'kyi VIII–1, p. 259 from the St. Petersburg Imperial Public Library, MS 94, p. 461, October 11, 1637 (O.S.); BCz, MS 133, pp. 607–608.

57. Pavliuk to Kysil, September 7, 1637. BN, BOZ, MS 1173, fols. 500–501.

58. Hrushevs'kyi VIII–1, 261.

59. Okolski, describing Potocki's movements on December 9, mentions moving out with the troops of Adam Kysil. *Dyaryusz,* p. 34.

60. Hrushevs'kyi VIII–1, 261.

61. Difficulties with the Crown troops forced Potocki to attempt arbitration even at the last minute. Okolski relates that on December 10, Potocki had Kysil send his servant to the Cossacks to try to return them to obedience. *Dyaryusz,* p. 42. In early December, Potocki was negotiating with the Crown troops to perform three more weeks' service. BCz, MS 133, pp. 773–777.

62. Okolski, *Dyaryusz,* p. 51.

63. Hrushevs'kyi VIII–1, 270.

64. Potocki to Koniecpolski, December 19, 1637, BCz, MS 133, p. 794 reports Kysil's heroic actions with a few hundred of his men. Okolski reports Kysil's unit's losses as six men. Okolski, *Dyaryusz,* p. 55.

65. Kysil even before becoming the intermediary in negotiations appears to have been central in information gathering. A number of prisoners-hostages taken before Kumeiky (including an Orthodox priest) were spared and handed over to Kysil. Okolski, *Dyaryusz,* p. 48.

66. On December 23, Mikołaj Potocki wrote to Koniecpolski about the Cossack submission. He described Kysil as his intermediary.

67. Koniecpolski was committed to a hard line with the Cossacks by the autumn of 1637. See, for example, his letter of November 29 to the king. BCz, MS 133, pp. 745–748. On December 31, he wrote to the king of his plans for resolving the Cossack problem at the next Diet. He maintained that the king should appoint a commissioner instead of a starszy and that starostas should replace colonels. BCz, MS 133, pp. 819–821.

68. For a description of the administration of the oath by Kysil, see Okolski, *Dyaryusz*, pp. 65–66 and Mikołaj Potocki's report to Koniecpolski, December 31, 1637. BCz, MS 133, pp. 823–828.

69. For Khmel'nyts'kyi's role at Kumeiky, see Kryp''iakevych, *Bohdan Khmel'nyts'kyi*, pp. 73–74.

70. Hrushevs'kyi VIII–1, 276–282.

71. For a description of Kysil's reception of Potocki, see Okolski, *Dyaryusz*, p. 70.

72. For Potocki's activities in Kiev and Kysil and Stanisław Potocki's administration of the oath see Okolski, *Dyaryusz*, p. 72.

73. Kysil to Ossoliński, June 3, 1648, Karol Szajnocha, *Dwa lata dziejów naszych, 1646, 1648,* 3 vols. in *Dzieła Karola Szajnochy,* VIII–X (Warsaw, 1877), IX, 281. (Hereafter Szajnocha I, II, III.)

74. BCz, MS 135, pp. 63–64.

75. For the campaign see the instructions given on February 21, 1638. BCz, MS 133. The instructions call for setting up a guard to keep the dissident element from Zaporizhzhia. The instructions included a secret portion on the apprehension of Skydan and the limitation of the register.

76. In addition to the account in Radziwiłł, *Memoriale,* III, the 1638 (March 10 to May 1) Diet is described in diaries in: BJ, MS 2274, fols. 5–28 (partially published in Golubev II–2, 143–149); BCz, MS 390, pp. 389–412; and BK, MS 1318. This account is based on the Jagiellonian Library diary. The course of the 1638 Diet is recounted from Tomkiewicz, "Ograniczenie," who used as his major source the diary BJ, MS 274, fols. 6–28.

77. Tomkiewicz, "Ograniczenie," pp. 142–144.

78. Tomkiewicz, "Ograniczenie," p. 144.

79. For Kysil's defense of Orthodoxy, see Golubev II–2, 144.

80. Kysil's defense of Pavliuk is not mentioned in the Diet diaries, but is in *Pamiętniki do panowania Zygmunta III i Władysława IV* (Warsaw, 1846), p. 252. See also *Kronika Pawła Piaseckiego, Biskupa Przemyskiego* (Cracow, 1870), p. 418. Whether Kysil spoke at the Diet or not, contemporary opinion saw the execution of Pavliuk as the compromising of Kysil's honor. See for example Ks. Sadok Barącz, *Pamiętniki zakonu W.W.O.O. Bernardynów w Polszcze* (Lviv, 1874), p. 87.

81. Hrushevs'kyi VIII–1, 286.

82. Kysil to Primate Maciej Łubieński, June 30, 1648, *Jakuba Michałowskiego, wojskiego lubelskiego, a później kasztelana bieckiego Księga pamiętnicza z dawnego rękopisma będącego własnością Ludwika Hr. Morsztyna wydana staraniem i nakładem C. K. Towarzystwa Naukowego Krakowskiego* (Cracow, 1864), p. 67. (Hereafter Michałowski.)

83. For the terms of the agreement, see the Orthodox requests and the royal concessions at the Election Diet, published in Golubev II–2, 4–9. Latin texts of this agreement are published in Augustinus Theiner, ed., *Vetera Monumenta Poloniae et Lithuaniae Gentiumque Finitimarum Historiam Illustrantia,* III (Rome, 1863), 399–401, and Rutskyj, *Epistolae,* pp. 266–269. *Litterae Nun-*

tiorum, V, 120–123. For Władysław's charter of March 14, 1633, see *Arkhiv Iu. Z. R.,* pt. II, vol. I, 223–227. The Orthodox were guaranteed two churches in Mstsislaŭ, one monastery and four churches in Mahilioŭ, two churches in Orsha, one in Dzisna, and one church in Polatsk.

84. For Ruts'kyi's places of residence after 1633, see Rutskyj, *Epistolae,* pp. 271–386.

85. For the composition of the Uniate Metropolitanate, see Ludomir Bieńkowski, "Organizacja Kościoła Wschodniego w Polsce," in *Kościół w Polsce,* II, 847–849. For a description of the Uniate church, see Luzhnytskyi, *Ukraïns'ka tserkva,* pp. 355–368.

86. *Arkhiv Iu. Z. R.,* pt. II, vol. I, 226.

87. Golubev II–2, 8.

88. Golubev II–2, 7.

89. Władysław Tomkiewicz, "Dzieje unji kościelnej w Wielkiem Księstwie Litewskiem (1596–1795)," *Pamiętnik VI Zjazdu,* I, 325–326.

90. Tomkiewicz, "Dzieje unji," p. 326. For the papal nuncio's disappointment that the Volhynian dietine defended Orthodoxy, despite the large numbers of Catholics in the palatinate, see his letter of June 23, 1632, *Litterae Nuntiorum,* V, 91–92. For his description of Volhynia as the center of Orthodox resistance, September 20, 1632, *Litterae Nuntiorum,* V, 111–112.

91. Tomkiewicz, "Dzieje unji," p. 326.

92. BCz, MS 398, fols. 155–159.

93. Tomkiewicz, "Dzieje unji," p. 326. See the discussion on Protestantism in the Grand Duchy in *Pamiętniki VI Zjazdu,* I: Kazimierz Hartleb, "Zagadnienie reformacji na ziemiach polsko-litewskich," pp. 329–337; Aleksander Kossowski, "Stan dotychczasowych badań nad dziejami protestantyzmu na ziemiach Wielkiego Księstwa Litewskiego w XVI–XVII w.," pp. 338–343; Kazimierz Kolbuszewski, "Polskie piśmiennictwo reformacyjne na ziemiach dawnego W. Księstwa Litewskiego," pp. 344–352, and Kot, *La Réforme dans le Grand-Duché de Lithuanie.*

94. Tomkiewicz asserts this seemingly paradoxical situation in the following way: "Despite its traditions of independence, the Grand Duchy of Lithuania was in basic matters more connected internally to the rest of the Commonwealth and much more penetrated by the influences of Western culture in comparison to the still forming processes in the Ukraine, which were full of contradictions." "Z dziejów unji," p. 326. For the role of Vilnius as an Orthodox publishing center, see N. Anushkin, *Vo slavnom meste Vilenskom: Ocherki iz istorii knigopechataniia* (Moscow, 1962) and N. Anushkin, *Na zare knigopechataniia v Litve* (Vilnius, 1970).

95. Tomkiewicz, "Dzieje unji," p. 326. For the development and decline of the Vilnius Orthodox brotherhood, see D. Stsepuro, "Vilenskoe Sv. Dukhovskoe Bratstvo v XVII i XVIII st.," *Trudy Kievskoi dukhovnoi akademii,* 1898, no. 7, pp. 75–96; no. 8, pp. 345–373; 1899, no. 3, pp. 546–577; no. 5, pp. 225–262; no. 6, pp. 523–563; no. 7, pp. 30–52. On the Uniate Seminary, see R. R. Holowackyj, *Seminarium Vilnense SS. Trinitatis (1601–1621)*

(Rome, 1957). For the rise of Lviv as a cultural center in the latter half of the sixteenth century, see E. L. Nemirovskii, *Nachalo knigopechataniia na Ukraine: Ivan Fedorov* (Moscow, 1974), pp. 14–30.

96. For a discussion of the brotherhood and the city's role as an Orthodox stronghold, see Ia. D. Isaievych, *Bratstva ta ïkh rol'*. For a discussion of the refusal of the bishops of Lviv and Przemyśl to support the union, see Chodynicki, *Kościół*, pp. 401–404.

97. Tomkiewicz, "Dzieje unji," p. 326.

98. On the metropolitans' residence prior to the seventeenth century, see Bieńkowski, "Organizacja," p. 791. On the development of Kiev in the 1620s, see Hrushevs'kyi, *Kul'turno-natsional'nyi rukh*, pp. 208–244 and *Istoriia Kyieva*, I (Kiev, 1960), 143–177.

99. For the problems faced by the illegal hierarchy, see Makarii, *Istoriia russkoi tserkvi*, XI (St. Petersburg, 1882; reprinted at Dusseldorf, 1969), 265–396 and Ivan Vlasovs'kyi, *Narys istorii ukrains'koi pravoslavnoi tserkvy*, II (New York, 1956), 115–128.

100. On Krupets'kyi's tenure as bishop, see Antonii Dobrianskii, *Istoriia episkopov trekh soedinennykh eparkhii, Peremyshl'skoi, Samborskoi i Sanotskoi, ot naidavneishkikh vremen do 1794 g.*, 3 vols. (Lviv, 1893), 11, 12–40.

101. Tomkiewicz, "Dzieje unji," p. 326, Bieńkowski, "Organizacja," p. 848.

102. Bieńkowski, "Organizacja," p. 848.

103. For a description of the Chełm diocese's borders, Bieńkowski, "Organizacja," p. 863.

104. Golubev II–2, 78.

105. On Krupets'kyi's refusal, see Dobrians'kyi, *Istoriia*, II, 17–21. For Pochapovs'kyi's refusal to recognize his Orthodox successor's claims, see Pochapivs'kyi's protest against the commissioners designated to divide church properties in Volhynia, October 16, 1635, Golubev II–2, 92–96. Władysław's grant of the Przemyśl bishopric to Hulevych-Voiutyns'kyi, March 14, 1635 is published in Golubev II–2, 79–81. His grant of March 15, 1633 to Oleksander Puzyna as bishop of Luts'k, is published in *Arkhiv Iu. Z. R.*, pt. 1, vol. VI, 660–661.

106. The charter guaranteed that those who wished to differ with the local bishop's faith had the right to do so, and gave an example that a Uniate in the bishopric of Mstsislaŭ would treat the Archbishop of Polatsk as his bishop, and an Orthodox Christian in the Polatsk Archdiocese, the Bishop of Mstsislaŭ. It concluded, however, with a passage that similar arrangments should be made in other areas of the Kingdom of Poland and Grand Duchy of Lithuania. Golubev II–2, 8.

107. For Terlets'kyi's activities, see Golubev II–1, 77–134 and his description of his resistance to the commissioners of March 10, 1636. Golubev II–2, 99–109. See the detailed description of this struggle in Łoziński, *Prawem i lewem*, I, 257–263.

108. Terlets'kyi was extremely proud of his ability to halt the work of the commission. See his letter to Metropolitan Rafail Korsak. A. G. Welykyj, ed.

Litterae Episcoporum Historiam Ucrainae Illustrantes (1600–1900), I, series II, Analecta OSBM, section III (Rome, 1972), 298.

109. Hrushevs'kyi describes the period: "The acts of Władysław in reality inaugurated a new period of stubborn, not so much struggle, as war between Orthodox and Uniates. After a time when, due to the tactics of Zygmunt, the Orthodox were drummed out of their positions, and almost all possibility of struggle was taken away from them, it understandably was a great success that the acts of Władysław gave the Orthodox a legal basis and real circumstances in which they could struggle with the pressure of the union with certain chances for success." Hrushevs'kyi VIII–1, 187–188.

110. See the Uniate hierarchy's reports to Rome in March or April 1633, Rutskyj, *Epistolae,* pp. 272–277, 279–280; for the Uniate hierarchy's activities during the election, see Rutskyj, *Epistolae,* pp. 290–292. For Rafail Korsak's advocacy of the Uniate cause in Rome in this period, see Athanasius G. Welykyj, ed. *Epistolae Metropolitarum Kioviensium Catholicorum Raphaelis Korsak, Antonii Sielava, Gabrielis Kolenda (1637–1674),* series II, Analecta OSBM, section III (Rome, 1956), pp. 97–114. For a discussion of Vatican attitudes toward the compromise, see Šmurlo, I, 88–95.

111. See the Uniate hierarchy's protest of November 8, 1632, Theiner, *Vetera,* III, 402, and Rutskyj, *Epistolae,* p. 264, and the Catholic and Uniate hierarchy's protest of March 16, 1633, Theiner, *Vetera,* III, 403.

112. See the Nuncio Visconti's reports on the Convocation and Election Diet, Theiner, *Vetera,* III, 394–399 and *Litterae Nuntiorum,* V, 95–141. For Pope Urban VIII's letters to Władysław and other officials in the Commonwealth see Athanasius G. Welykyj, ed. *Documenta Pontificum Romanorum Historiam Ucrainae Illustrantia (1075–1953),* I, series II, Analecta OSBM, section III (Rome, 1953), 485–494. For the instructions and letters of the Congregation for the Propagation of the Faith, see Athanasius Welykyj, ed. *Litterae S.C. de Propaganda Fide Ecclesiam Catholicam Ucrainae et Bielarusiae Spectantes,* I, series II, Analecta OSBM, section III (Rome, 1954), 118–128. See Urban VIII's letters in Theiner, *Vetera,* III, 402, 403.

113. For a discussion of practical politics as an influence on papal policy, see Šmurlo, I, 93–95.

114. See Ossoliński's report to the Holy See, December 6, 1633, Theiner, *Vetera,* III, 405–408. For the Congregation for the Propagation of the Faith's discussion an eventual condemnation of the concessions to the Orthodox, see Athanaius Welykyj, ed., *Acta S.C. de Propaganda Fide Ecclesiam Catholica Ucrainae et Bielarusiae Spectantia,* I, series II, Analecta OSBM, section III (Rome, 1953), 120–122, 123–124, 128–138.

115. See the instructions of March 1634 of the Congregation for the Propagation of the Faith to the papal nuncio, *Litterae S.C. De Propaganda Fide,* I, 132–135.

116. For opposition to all concessions to the Orthodox, see the protest of the Uniate hierarchy against the 1635 charter to the Orthodox, March 18, 1635, *Litterae Episcoporum,* I, 264–265 and the protest of March 8, 1635 of the Roman Catholic hierarchy, nobility and the Uniate clergy, Golubev II–2, 74–78.

117. The following regular and extraordinary Diets were held between 1633 and 1641:
1. Extraordinary, July 19–August 1, 1634;
2. Regular, January 31–March 17, 1635;
3. Extraordinary, November 21–December 9, 1635;
4. Regular, January 20–March 4, 1637;
5. Extraordinary, June 3–June 18, 1637;
6. Regular, March 10–May 1, 1638;
7. Regular, October 5–November 16, 1639;
8. Regular, April 19–June 1, 1640;
9. Regular, August 20–October 4, 1641,

All Diets are described in Radziwiłł, *Memoriale* II and III, and diaries for most exist in Archiwum Gdańsk, Recesy 300, 29. There are diaries for four Diets (1635, II, 1638, 1640, 1641) in the Steinwehr codex, in Biblioteka Uniwersytetu Wrocławskiego, Akc. 1949 Kn 439, and KN 440 (hereafter, Steinwehr II and III). For listings of diaries see Władysław Konopczyński, *Chronologia sejmów polskich 1483–1793* (Cracow, 1948) with additions in Henryk Olszewski, "Nowe materiały do chronologii sejmów polskich," *Czasopismo Prawno-Historyczne*, IX, no. 2 (1957), 229–258.

118. On January 5, 1639 Terlets'kyi wrote Korsak about problems of the Orthodox and stated: "Neque aliud in haec tempestate inter schismaticos remanet, nisi continuus timor et horror; pauci eorum in suis pernoctant domibus, expectantes in momenta meos missionarios. Tanto magis quod etiam capita sua Kisiel nullo consilio reperto scribant suis . . ." *Litterae Episcoporum*, I, 298. Albrycht Stanisław Radziwiłł in *Memoriale*, II, 336 called Kysil the delegate of the schismatics and disturber of discussions.

119. For Władysław's religious views, see Czapliński, *Władysław*, pp. 98–99. For Władysław's tendency to waver, see his decree of April 10, 1636. He ordered that churches in the Grand Duchy of Lithuania assigned by the commissioners to the Orthodox be returned to the Uniates. Golubev II-2, 118–119.

120. At most Diets after 1635, with the exception of 1640, Kysil represented the Chernihiv palatinate. In 1641, Kysil was the Volhynian delegate. Komisja historyczna, Polska Akademia Nauk w Krakowie, Kartoteka posłów do sejmu. For the Volhynian dietine instructions ordering the defense of Orthodoxy, see *Arkhiv Iu. Z. R.*, pt. II, vol. I, 228–251 (1638), 251–266 (1639), 267–282 (1641).

121. Kysil's relations with Mohyla were not only in religious and cultural affairs. There are a number of instances in which Kysil had economic dealings involving Orthodox church lands with Mohyla. The most important of these was the town of Hoshcha which formerly belonged to the pious Orthodox princess Regina Solomirits'ka. PANK, MS 3022, fol. 33. See [Jan Marek Giżycki], *Z przeszłości Hoszczy na Wołyniu* (Cracow, n.d.), pp. 24–25.

122. For Drevyns'kyi's career, see the article in *Polski Słownik Biograficzny*, V (Cracow, 1939–1946), 423–424 by Kazimierz Chodynicki.

123. For a list of the major Orthodox families in the 1630s and 1640s, see the

lists of nobles who signed Mohyla's election in 1632, Maksimovich, *Sochineniia,* I, 393–394 and Iosyf Tryzna's election as Archimandrite of the Caves monastery in Kiev, January 25, 1647, *Arkhiv Iu. Z. R.,* pt. II, vol. I, 348–349.

124. For example, Mykhailo Sliozka discusses Kysil's eloquence in his 1642 *Triodion . . .* dedication. He attributes it partially to "the reading of important works, not the least of these being the addresses of important people, which as is the custom are given at the dietines, convocations, and above all at the General Diets which your Excellency has often attended." He praises Kysil as having fulfilled his office subtly, wisely, and adroitly and in a manner arousing the astonishment of all." *Triodion si est trypisnets* (Lviv, 1642), fol. 3.

125. *Molitvy povsednevnyi . . .* (Vilnius, 1635), "Predmova," fols. 1–6.

126. *Molitvy povsednevnyi . . . ,* fol. 5.

127. Kossów, *Paterikon* "Praefacya."

128. See, for example, Szymon Okolski, *Orbis Polonus, Splendoribus Caeli . . . Authore R. P. Fr. Simone Okolski,* 2 vols. (Cracow, 1641), I, 307–308 and Władysław's grant of the castellanship of Kiev, February 5, 1646, *Arkhiv Iu. Z. R.,* pt. III, vol. I, 401–406. Kysil's descent from Sventold was even inscribed on his sarcophagus. Lubomirski, *Adam Kysil,* pp. 32–34.

129. Kossów, *Paterikon,* pp. 1–16.

130. Kossów, *Paterikon,* "Praefacya," fol. 4.

131. *Triodion si est' trypisnets',* fols. 2–4.

132. For a discussion of Uniate dissatisfaction with the Diet of 1634, see Ruts'kyi's letter of January 19, 1635. Rutskyj, *Epistolae,* pp. 309–310.

133. The major sources for the 1635 I. Diet are: Radziwiłł, *Memoriale,* II, 60–75. Recesy, 300, 29/115. Discussion of the Orthodox church on fols. 103–107, 138, 203–205. Kysil was a delegate from Chernihiv palatinate. *Volumina legum,* III, 409, 425. Golubev II–1, 115–118 contains Russian translations of the privileges and citation to all publications of the two privileges. A Catholic protest to the Diet constitution on the Greek faith is published in Golubev II–2, 74–78. The Diet constitution reaffirming the 1632–1633 pacification. *Volumina legum,* III, 407. Hrushevs'kyi views the issue of the two decrees as a defeat for the Orthodox since the privilege to the Orthodox was merely one of toleration, while that to the Uniates was one of protection. Hrushevs'kyi VIII–1, 192–194.

134. Władysław had issued a decree on November 27, 1634 closing the "Latin" schools of Vinnytsia and Hoshcha. BJ, MS 94, p. 95.

135. Władysław was not above setting aside decisions and privileges granted the Orthodox when Catholic pressure was brought to bear. See Golubev II–2, 118–122.

136. For the dietine instructions ordering the defense of Orthodoxy, see *Arkhiv Iu. Z. R.,* pt. II, vol. I, 228–251 (Volhynia, 1638); 251–266 (Volhynia, 1639); 267–282 (Volhynia, 1641).

137. The account of this Diet is based on the most complete of the diaries on the religious issue, BCz, MS 390, pp. 277–333. Recesy 300, 29/118, fols. 12–38 is less detailed on the religious issue. See also Radziwiłł, *Memoriale,* II, 201–213.

For Kysil's protests on these problems, see BCz, MS 390, p. 319. For a discussion of the complaints of the Orthodox church, see BCz, MS 390, p. 285.

138. BCz, MS 390, p. 302.

139. For a discussion of dealing with the Orthodox church's requests, see BCz, MS 390, p. 319.

140. BCz, MS 390, pp. 301–304. The final decree of "infamy" against Hulevych and a large number of petty nobles by the Piotrków Tribunal was issued in March 1637 after the closing of the Diet. Golubev II-2, 124–129.

141. BCz, MS 390, pp. 301–304.

142. BCz, MS 390, pp. 300, 303. The authorities of the Commonwealth were particularly apprehensive concerning their control of Smolensk and therefore a policy of rapid introduction of Catholicism was attempted. See Šmurlo, I, 70–76.

143. BCz, MS 390, pp. 303–304.

144. The 1638 Diet has an unusually large number of extant descriptions. The religious issue is dealt with in the most detail in BJ, MS 2274, fols. 5–28 (published in part in Golubev II-2, 143–149, though mistakenly cited as MS 2285); in Recesy 300, 29/121, two copies, fols. 104–137; fols. 139–171; and Steinwehr II, fols. 468–476.

145. *Arkhiv Iu. Z. R.,* pt. II, vol. I, 234–236.

146. Golubev II-2, 144.

147. Golubev II-2, 144–148. For Soltyk's and Kysil's struggle at the 1639 Diet, see BCz, MS 390, p. 447 and Radziwiłł, *Memoriale,* II, 336. The case originally arose because Kysil questioned Soltyk's szlachta status. The case was decided in Soltyk's favor at the Lublin Tribunal in 1642. PANK, MS 2253, fol. 526. Soltyk received support in his struggle from the nobility of the Smolensk lands. BCz, MS 2102, pp. 97–98.

148. Golubev II-2, 147–148.

149. Golubev II-2, 148. Also see Steinwehr II, fols. 472, 474.

150. Golubev II-2, 146–147.

151. Golubev II-2, 145 and Steinwehr II, fol. 472. Kysil complained about fines being levied against the Orthodox by the courts.

152. Golubev II-2, 146.

153. The Diet constitution stated: "Warowany iest pokoy rozróżnionych w Religii Greckiej Konstytucyą anni 1635. Przetoż aby im posterum Dekreta w Tribunałach tak Koronnych iako y W.X. Lit., które vim sapiunt legis nie były ferowane, authoritate praesentis Conventus waruimy, reassumuiąc w tym Konstytucyą anni 1627." *Volumina legum,* III, 933.

154. Golubev II-2, 157.

155. Golubev II-2, 146.

156. Golubev II-2, 167–168. The document is entitled "Information for their Excellencies the Uniates" but does not include names of the authors or recipients.

157. For Władysław's privilege of March 15, 1633, see Golubev II-2, 9–11. Also see Golubev II-2, 168–169, 205–206.

158. For a discussion of the Lublin church issue during this period, see Ar. Longinov, *Pamiatnik drevnego pravoslaviia v Liubline: Pravoslavnyi khram i suschchestvovavshee pri nem bratstvo* (Warsaw, 1883), pp. 29–32. Lublin was an especially sensitive issue, because the nobility from all over the Commonwealth visited it for Tribunal sessions.

159. Golubev II–2, 167–168.

160. Golubev II–2, 168. See the April 24, 1638 protest of Catholic and Uniate Diet delegates against the concessions made at that Diet. Golubev II–2, 155–156.

161. The issue of the Orthodox faith was only mentioned at the Diet of 1639 once (November 3), Recesy 300, 29/122, fol. 125.

162. See for example, the king's order of October, 1638 against Atanazii Puzyna for having taken possession of the properties that were to go to him after the death of his Uniate rival Iov Pochapivs'kyi. Golubev II–2, 139–141.

163. This account of the Diet is based on the diary in Steinwehr III, fols. 24–31. Also see the two diaries in the Gdańsk archive. Recesy 300, 29/123, fols. 151–174, and fols. 176–204. There is also considerable information in Radziwiłł, *Memoriale*, III, 2–20.

164. Steinwehr III, fol. 24.

165. Steinwehr III, fol. 24.

166. Steinwehr III, fols. 25–26.

167. Kysil had mentioned the payment of the troops and defense of the Ukraine as the only constitution the Orthodox would allow until their religious grievances were satisfied at the 1638 Diet. Steinwehr II, fol. 474. For this demand at the 1640 Diet, see Steinwehr III, fol. 26.

168. Steinwehr III, fol. 28.

169. Steinwehr III, fol. 29.

170. For the reading of the constitution on the Orthodox church, see Steinwehr III, fol. 29.

171. This description of the Diet is based on Steinwehr III, fols. 78–84. Considerable material on the religious aspects of this Diet are in the Gdańsk archive's Recesy 300, 29/124 fols. 90–123. Also see Radziwiłł, *Memoriale*, III, 52–70.

172. *Arkhiv Iu. Z. R.,* pt. II, vol. I, 273–276.

173. Steinwehr III, fol. 82.

174. Steinwehr III, fol. 82.

175. Steinwehr III, fol. 83.

176. Steinwehr III, fol. 83.

177. Steinwehr III, fol. 82.

178. Steinwehr III, fol. 82. The confirmation is published in *Volumina legum,* IV, 6–7.

179. *Volumina legum,* IV, 6–7.

180. *Volumina legum,* IV, 6–7.

181. For Krupets'kyi's difficulties in functioning as bishop, see Dobrianskii, *Istoriia,* II, 12–40. For a detailed discussion of the Przemyśl bishopric affairs, see Łoziński, *Prawem i lewem,* I, 257–263. The problem was especially complex

because the first royal charter in 1633 was granted to the Przemyśl nobleman Ivan Popel' (March 18, 1633) (charter in Golubev II–2, 14–15), but the election was invalidated. Mohyla then supported the candidacy of Semen (Sylvestr) Hulevych-Voiutyns'kyi, an official of the Volhynian palatinate, and a well-known defender of Orthodoxy at the Election and Coronation Diets. It was not until 1635 that Hulevych received a final conferral of the bishopric and Popel' agreed to vacate the see. Hrushevs'kyi VIII–1, 181–183. Hulevych received a March 14, 1635 decree of conferral which granted him rights to three monasteries. Golubev II–2, 79–81.

182. BR, MS 25, fols. 59–60. *Paszkwil Ruskim językiem albo pożałowanie płaczliwe butto takoie wzdychanie wsiey Prawosławney Rusi Powiatu Przemyskoho, k podaniu, k czytaniu, y k pieniu prawednym Chrestianom Starozakonney Wiry Hreczkoiey a wydane z welikoiu pieczenciu czeresz Oscza Nikiphora Humena Onofroyskoho y Smolnickoho w horach w pulmili od Swiatoiey Beskiedy za prozboiu usilnoiu Ich. Mci. Pana Fedora Manastyrskoho y P. Fedora Winnickoho y P. Marka Wysoczanskoho Kuryłowa, y P. Fedora Kopystynskoho Obywatelow Ziemli Premyskoiey.* Marko Vysochans'kyi and Fedir Vynnyts'kyi were named in the "Infamy" decree of March 13, 1637. Golubev II–2, 124.

183. BR, MS. 25, fol. 60.

184. The content and tone of the lampoon were unlikely to bring credit to the ostensible authors. Therefore it probably originated in Catholic circles who wished to ridicule the Orthodox. Polish authors, including Jesuits, are known to have used Ruthenian for comic effect. See Paulina Lewin, "Problematyka społeczna intermedium polskiego," *Pamiętnik Literacki* LII, no. 1 (1961), 18 and Alodia Kawecka-Gryczowa, "*Tragedia ruska*: Zabytek z początku XVII wieku," *Pamiętnik Teatralny* 1973, no. 2, pp. 273–289.

185. For praise of Kysil's piety, see Sliozka, *Triodon si est trypisnets'*, fols. 2–4. Kysil used his wealth for the restoration of his ancestral church in Nyzkynychi and the foundation of a monastery there in 1643. The stone church is of considerable architectural significance. See Eugenjusz Urbanowicz, "Cerkiew w Niskiniczach na Wołyniu," *Ziemia*, XVI, no. 5 (1931), 91–95, and Grigorii Bugoslavskii, "Kievskii voevoda Adam Kisel' i vystroennaia im. v s. Niskinnichakh, Vladimir-Volynskago uezda, tserkov'," *Sbornik statei v chest' grafini Praskovii Sergeevny Uvarovoi* (Moscow, 1916), pp. 232–248. Kysil's foundation charters for the monastery in Nyzkynychi is published in part in Golubev, I–1, 235–236. In 1646 Kysil founded St. Nicholas nunnery on his Volhynian estate of Hniino, under the stipulation that his mother be appointed abbess. *ODAZRM* I, 282. His foundation charter stated that he was motivated by the realization that many noblewomen wished to enter the religious life, but that there was a lack of suitable institutions. Kysil was also extremely active in founding Orthodox religious establishments in the Chernihiv lands. Considering the rapid penetration of Catholicism in these lands in the 1630s and 1640s, Kysil's support of Orthodoxy was of particular importance. In 1640 he founded a nunnery in Makoshyn. Filaret, *Istoriko-statisticheskoe opisanie Chernigovskoi eparkhii* (Chernihiv, 1861), IV, 151. Kysil also endowed Makoshyn St. Nicholas monastery,

Filaret, IV, 139–141, and donated the land for and founded a monastery in Maksakiv, Filaret, IV, 69–73. Maksakiv monastery was founded for those monks from a monastery in Trubchevsk who wished to remain in the Commonwealth when the city was handed over to Muscovy in 1646. Kysil provided them with the lands to stay in the Commonwealth and a September 26, 1646 charter from the king granted them the lands perpetually. PANK, MS 272, fols. 10–11. Kysil's grant is published in Filaret, IV, 72–73. A portrait of Kysil as a patron of the monastery at Maksakiv has survived. See Platon Bilets'kyi, *Ukraïns'kyi portretnyi zhyvopys XVII–XVIII st.: Problemy stanovlennia i rozvytku* (Kiev, 1969), pp. 111, 114–117. For Kysil's patronage in Volhynia, also see H. N. Lohvyn, "Mykhailivs'ka tserkva v Hoshchi," *Ukraïns'ke mystetstvoznavstvo,* no. 4, 1970, pp. 92–93.

186. BCz, MS 363, fol. 139.

187. See Radziwiłł, *Memoriale,* II, 336.

188. Letter of Iosyf Ruts'kyi to Rafail Korsak, February 5, 1634, Rutskyj, *Epistolae,* p. 296.

189. For his contemporaries' evaluation of the Uniate metropolitan see, Rutskyj, *Epistolae,* pp. xii–xxii.

190. For a description of Ruts'kyi's last efforts and the problems of the Uniate church, see Rafail Korsak's letter to Francisco Ingoli of the Congregation for the Propagation of the Faith, March 8, 1637, *Epistolae Metropolitarum Kioviensium Catholicorum: Raphaelis Korsak . . . ,* pp. 134–139. A memorandum sent in 1644 by Korsak's successor, Antonii Seliava, to the Congregation published in the same volume discusses Latin Rite Catholics' refusal to treat the Uniates as equals, pp. 192–194.

191. For a discussion of regional loyalty, see Tazbir, "Świadomość narodowa," pp. 40–42 and Frank E. Sysyn, "Regionalism and Political Thought in Seventeenth-Century Ukraine: The Nobility's Grievances at the Diet of 1641," *Harvard Ukrainian Studies,* VI, no. 2 (Summer 1982). This article discusses regionalism in the history of the Commonwealth and in the Ukraine in particular. Parts of the article serve as the base for this section.

192. Bardach, *Historia,* pp. 383–392.

193. For a discussion of the formation of the Grand Duchy from separate lands and principalities, see Kutrzeba, *Historya,* II, *Litwa,* 28–33.

194. For the election process, see Czapliński, "Wybór posła w dawnej Polsce." In the seventeenth century separate consultations for delegates and senators from Great Poland, Little Poland, and the Grand Duchy of Lithuania were held at the Diet. Kutrzeba, *Historya,* I, *Korona,* 144. These regional divisions were also reflected in the court system. The tribunal for Great Poland was held at Piotrków and for Little Poland at Lublin. Wyczański, *Polska,* p. 99.

195. Wyczański discusses the moderating factor of migration on regional particularism in this period. *Polska,* pp. 276–277.

196. For a study of regional society and ties, see Łoziński's study, *Prawem i lewem* about the Ruthenian palatinate.

197. The Volhynian nobility reminded the Diet of its special privileges under

the Lithuanian Statute. Instructions of January 27, 1638. *Arkhiv Iu. Z. R.,* pt. II, vol. I, 234–235. They insisted that, according to the Union of Lublin, church properties were to be administered only by natives of the palatinate, p. 237.

198. See, for example, the Volhynian nobility's Diet instruction, August 27, 1639. *Arkhiv Iu. Z. R.,* pt. II, vol. I, 259.

199. See the instruction of Volhynian nobility to their delegates, January 27, 1638, *Arkhiv Iu. Z. R.,* pt. II, vol. I, 238. Also see the instructions of July 13, 1641, *Arkhiv Iu. Z. R.,* pt. II, vol. I, 273.

200. See the Volhynian nobility's instructions of January 27, 1638 to its delegates to the Diet. *Arkhiv Iu. Z. R.,* pt. II, vol. I, 231. The delegates were ordered to assure that in the event of a possible Turkish attack, support would come from "palatinates which are distant from these dangers." Also, see the Volhynian nobility's discussion of Tatar, Turkish and Cossack problems in their instructions of August 27, 1639. *Arkhiv Iu. Z. R.,* pt. II, vol. I, 256–258. Even when delegates from these palatinates adamantly maintained that no measures would be passed unless Orthodox demands were met, they excepted measures for the defense of the Ukraine. Steinwehr II, fol. 474.

201. BCz, MS 132, pp. 153–154; PANK, MS 1819, pp. 41–43.

202. "Votum of Adam Kysil before the Diet of 1641" is published in its Polish original as an appendix to Sysyn, "Regionalism," pp. 186–190. The beginning of the votum had been published earlier in Golubev II–2, 153–154. The votum has no date, but its date can be determined because it is summarized in a Diet diary in Steinwehr III, fol. 82.

203. One discrepancy between the text of the votum and the description in the diary of the Diet is the use of "Ukrainni" in the diary: Steinwehr III, fol. 82. This usage reveals the other significant development in nomenclature of the period, the conversion of *Ukrainne województwa* and *Ukraina* into a specific geographic designation and their extension to all the incorporation lands.

204. The manuscript copy is corrupt, giving 1564 and 1576 as the dates, but the context makes clear that these are a copyist's error.

205. Steinwehr III, fol. 84.

206. Steinwehr III, fol. 84.

207. Sysyn, "Regionalism," pp. 187.

208. For discussion of this problem, see Kubala, *Jerzy Ossoliński,* pp. 104–110; Czapliński, *Władysław,* pp. 225–239.

209. Kubala, *Jerzy Ossoliński,* p. 104.

210. For Ossoliński's trip to Rome, see Kubala, *Jerzy Ossoliński,* pp. 46–63.

211. Czapliński, *Władysław,* p. 227.

212. Golubev II–2, 146.

213. Kubala, *Jerzy Ossoliński,* pp. 119–120.

214. Kubala, *Jerzy Ossoliński,* pp. 119–20.

215. See Tomkiewicz, *Jeremi Wiśniowiecki,* p. 134.

216. *Volumina legum,* III, 931.

217. For the struggle between the "new" and "old" princes, see Tomkiewicz, *Jeremi Wiśniowiecki,* p. 134.

218. Tomkiewicz, *Jeremi Wiśniowiecki,* pp. 134–135.

219. Published by Tomkiewicz in *Jeremi Wiśniowiecki,* p. 135.

220. Hieremias Bielejowski, *Obrona tytułów Xiążęczych od Rzeczypospolitey uchwałą seymową pozwolonych* (July 20, 1641). The work is dedicated to Wiśniowiecki. Bielejowski warned in his short pamphlet that any attack on "old" princely titles would threaten the Union of Lublin, fol. 16.

221. Instructions of August 27, 1639. *Arkhiv Iu. Z. R.,* pt. II, vol. I, 255–256. The dietine of Volhynia interpreted the constitution as an infringement of the Union of Lublin. In 1638 the dietine opposed "foreign titles." *Arkhiv Iu. Z. R.,* pt. II, vol. I, 238.

222. Steinwehr III, fol. 26. For Kysil's relations with Wiśniowiecki in the 1640s see Tomkiewicz, *Jeremi Wiśniowiecki,* pp. 144–145. Kysil put forth the major defense position to save Wiśniowiecki's mandate at the 1645 Diet during Wiśniowiecki's bitter dispute with Adam Kazanowski "Rationes stabilendae dignitatis Ks. J. Mości Wiśniowieckiego, żeby z izby poselskiej nie był rugowany. Koncept J. M.P. Kisiela, kasztelana czernihowskiego." BCz, MS 1657, p. 504.

223. Steinwehr III, fol. 26; Radziwiłł, *Memoriale,* III, p. 16.

224. Steinwehr III, fol. 26; Radziwiłł, *Memoriale,* III, p. 16.

225. On the wording of the charters, see Stanisław Kutrzeba and Władysław Semkowicz, *Akta Unji Polski z Litwą, 1385–1791* (Cracow, 1932), pp. 300–319. The most similar wording occurs in the order that the Volhynian populace swear allegiance to the Kingdom of Poland, p. 298.

226. On the military in this period, see Jan Wimmer, *Wojsko polskie w drugiej połowie XVII wieku* (Warsaw, 1965), pp. 11–37.

227. See the instructions of the Volhynian nobility to delegates to the Diet dated January 27, 1638 and August 27, 1639, *Arkhiv Iu. Z. R.,* pt. II, vol. I, 231, 256–258. For exceptions made on military issues, see the Diet diary of 1638 in Steinwehr II, fol. 474.

228. Sysyn, "Regionalism," p. 189. Kysil asserted: "A jako pieniężna płata wojsku Rptej colligitur ze wszytkiej Rptej, tak prowiant temuż wojsku, suadet ratio, iubet aequalitatis, non unius Russiae, sed totius Reipublicae."

229. Sysyn, "Regionalism," p. 190.

230. *Volumina legum,* IV, 8–9.

231. *Volumina legum,* IV, 6–7.

232. Marcin Kalinowski's appointment of March 16, 1635 as palatine of Chernihiv is in Met. Kor., MS 180, fols. 440–441. Kalinowski also received a right for burning forest products for two years in the starostwo of Chernihiv. Met. Kor., MS 180, fol. 542. For Kysil's discontent, see Radziwiłł, *Memoriale,* II, 78–79. Kysil actively sought advancement. In 1638 the instructions for the Volhynian dietine requested that he be rewarded for his many services. *Arkhiv Iu. Z. R.,* pt. II, vol. I, 245. Kysil was granted the position of castellan of Chernihiv on December 1, 1639, Met. Kor., MS 185, fols. 221–222.

233. *Volumina legum,* III, 865–866. At the 1638 Diet, Kysil became involved in disputes about the order of precedence of the new palatinate. Steinwehr, II, fol. 471.

234. The dispute is discussed in the Volhynian dietine's instructions of July 13, 1641. *Arkhiv Iu. Z. R.*, pt. II, vol. I, 270–271.
235. Kutrzeba, *Historya*, I, *Korona*, 96–97.
236. Kutrzeba, *Historya*, II, *Litwa*, 88–89.
237. *Arkhiv Iu. Z. R.*, pt. II, vol. I, 271.
238. *Arkhiv Iu. Z. R.*, pt. II, vol. I, 271.
239. *Volumina legum*, IV, 11.
240. Met. Kor., MS 185, fols. 407–409.

Chapter 5

1. For a discussion of the position of the Senate and senators in Władysław IV's reign see Władysław Czapliński, "Senat za Władysława IV," *Studia historyczne ku czci St. Kutrzeby* (Cracow, 1938), I, 81–104; Kutrzeba, *Historya*, I, *Korona*, 142–144, 150–151.
2. Czapliński, "Senat," pp. 81–90.
3. For a discussion of the competence and rights of palatines and castellans, see Kutrzeba, *Historya*, I, *Korona*, 96–103.
4. For a discussion of the Commonwealth's parliamentary development in this period and the power of the Senate, see Władysław Czapliński, "Z problematyki sejmu polskiego w pierwszej połowie XVII wieku," *Kwartalnik Historyczny*, LXXVII, no. 1 (1970), 31–45.
5. For a summary of Władysław's changing foreign policy see Czapliński, *Władysław*, pp. 17–200. Roman policy is discussed in Šmurlo I, 96–125.
6. In 1645 Kysil made extensive purchases of property from Adam Kazanowski, AGAD, Met. Kor., MS 190, fols. 69–76.
7. For a discussion of magnates' colonization of the Left-Bank lands, see Tomkiewicz, *Jeremi Wiśniowiecki*, pp. 57–114. For a listing of landlords and their holdings on the Left Bank, see Aleksander Jabłonowski, "Zadnieprze," *Pisma*, III, 8–80; also see, Tkachenko, "Narysy," pp. 75–119.
8. The most complete listing of Kysil's acquisitions in these palatinates is in [Jan Marek Giżycki], *Z przeszłości Hoszczy na Wołyniu* (Cracow, n.d.), pp. 36–42.
9. Kysil borrowed the substantial sum of 55,000 złoty from Mohyla. Mohyla left this money to the Kiev collegium when he died in early 1647. Mohyla's will of December 22, 1646, published in Zhukovs'kyi, *Petro Mohyla*, p. 244.
10. [Giżycki], *Z przeszłości*, pp. 24–25.
11. For an indication of Kysil's various residences in the 1640s, see the inventory of his letters to Kazimierz Leon Sapieha, BJ, MS 3573, fols. 1–6. Although the evidence is limited, it appears that Kysil resided primarily in the Chernihiv palatinate. For information about his main residence, Kobyshche, see S. Shamrai, "Misto Kobyzhcha v XVIII st.," *ZIFV VUAN*, XXVI (1930), 229–232.
12. BJ, MS 3573, fol. 1. For other financial transactions of Kysil in this period involving sums as large as 40,000 złoty, see PANK, MS 3022, pp. 7–10.
13. Zasławski inherited most of the Ostroz'kyi fortune. He owned almost

15,000 hearths in Volhynia. Baranovych, *Zaliudnenia,* p. 146. For information on Wiśniowiecki's massive Left-Bank domains, see Tomkiewicz, *Jeremi Wiśniowiecki,* pp. 57–114. For information on Lubomirski's great wealth in the Cracow palatinate, see Czapliński, *Władysław,* pp. 138–139 and Józef Długosz, "Mecenat kulturalny Stanisława Lubomirskiego (1583–1649)," *Wiek* XVII, pp. 339–362.

14. For a discussion of the king's inner circle, see Czapliński, *Władysław,* pp. 280–297.

15. For a discussion of Ossoliński's power at the court, see Czapliński, *Władysław,* pp. 213–216. On Koniecpolski's role during Władysław's reign, see Czapliński, *Władysław,* p, 138.

16. For Kysil's grant of the Kiev castellanship, on February 5, 1646, see *Arkhiv Iu. Z. R.,* pt. III, vol. I, 401–406. Kysil mentioned his elevation in a letter to Crown Hetman Potocki in late March or early April. *Dokumenty ob osvoboditel'noi voine ukrainskogo naroda 1648–1654* (Kiev, 1965), pp. 21–22. (Hereafter *DOVUN*).

17. Although there is little information about Kysil's contacts with Władysław, the pattern of his advances and actions indicates that Kysil was in favor. A Kievan monk reported to the Muscovite authorities in 1646 that Kysil had gone with Wiśniowiecki to the king to settle the problem of Wiśniowiecki's claims. March 2, 1646 (OS), *Akty Iu.Z.R.,* III, 82–83. One of the few letters from Władysław to Kysil in this period is that of June 3, 1642, BCz, MS 138, pp. 419–420. In discussing the king's circle at court, Czapliński does not even mention Kysil. *Władysław,* pp. 280–296.

18. Kysil was designated as a senator in residence for the first half of 1644. *Volumina legum,* IV, 73. But he did not take part in any of the Senate consultations of that period. In the records of the twenty-five Senate consultation sessions held from April 1643 to June 1645, Kysil's name occurs in the list of senators present only on March 28, 1645 in a session immediately after the Diet. The session was devoted chiefly to Muscovite affairs. BK, MS 347, pp. 408–411.

19. Kysil was appointed a senator in residence at the 1643 Diet and was at the Senate consultations after the Diet in 1645. At the 1646 Diet he was appointed to the commission to negotiate with Muscovy. *Volumina legum,* IV, 88. No information exists on his participation in the 1647 Diet.

20. Wiśniowiecki remained out of favor throughout Władysław's reign and was by-passed for senatorial office until 1646. Tomkiewicz, *Jeremi Wiśniowiecki,* pp. 157–158. Also see Tomkiewicz's evaluation of Wiśniowiecki's lack of the qualities of a statesman, p. 387. For discussion of Radziwiłł's lack of interest in affairs of state, see Czapliński, "Sprawiedliwy magnat."

21. For an evaluation of Ossoliński's policies and talents, see Kubala, *Jerzy Ossoliński,* pp. 1–3, 383–385.

22. Kubala, *Jerzy Ossoliński,* pp. 46–49. Ossoliński signed the March 16, 1633 protest against the recognition of the Orthodox church. Theiner, *Vetera,* III, 403. For Ossoliński's struggle against the Orthodox at the 1633 Coronation Diet, see BCz, MS 363, fol. 363.

23. September 15, 1644. BCz, MS 1657, p. 129.

24. In his 1644 letter, Ossoliński mentioned that the border concessions were a small price compared to the great sums that would be lost in a war with Muscovy. BCz, MS 1657, p. 129.

25. June 16, 1648, Ossoliński to Kysil, *DOVUN*, p. 50.

26. For a discussion of plans for a new union in the 1630s and 1640s, see Šmurlo I, 96–125. For a discussion of the 1636–1643 attempts at a compromise see Mikołaj Andrusiak, "Sprawa patriarchatu kijowskiego za Władysława IV," *Prace historyczne w 30-lecie działalności profesorskiej Stanisława Zakrzewskiego* (Lviv, 1934), pp. 271–276, and A. Wojtyła, "De tentaminibus novae 'Unionis Universalis' in Polonia-Lithuania anno 1636 factis," *Orientalia Christiana Periodica*, XVIII, no. 1–2 (1952), 158–197. For the documents of Sanguszko's project, see Šmurlo II, 111–116.

27. Šmurlo II, 114, 116.

28. Vatican documents concerning Sanguszko's project are published in Šmurlo II, 116–150. A letter of July 10, 1636 from Pope Urban VIII, lauding Sanguszko's efforts, is published in Theiner, *Vetera*, III, 412 and *Documenta Pontificum Romanorum*, I, 510–511. Also see *Acta S. C. De Propaganda Fide*, I, 163–168. On April 11, 1636 the Congregation instructed the papal nuncio to put off the whole matter. Šmurlo II, 125–127.

29. The rulings of 1638 are published in *Acta S. C. De Propaganda Fide*, I, 163–168. Urban VIII's initial response to Władysław is published in *Documenta Pontificum Romanorum*, I, 512. The king's initiative and the issues involved are discussed by Metropolitan Rafail Korsak in a letter to Francesco Ingoli, Secretary of the Congregation, March 24, 1638, *Epistolae Metropolitarum Kioviensum Catholicorum: Raphaelis Korsak*, pp. 151–153. Instructions to the papal nuncio, Mario Filonardi, reaffirmed the 1629 decisions. *Litterae S. C. De Propaganda Fide*, I, 142–143, 146–151. For Władysław's and Metropolitan Ruts'kyi's efforts, see Šmurlo II, 132–136; and I, 253–255, footnotes 227 and 228, and Wojtyła, "De tentaminibus," pp. 176–197.

30. For Filonardi's complaints against Władysław, see his report to the Holy See of March 18, 1642, *Litterae Nuntiorum Apostolicorum Historiam Ucrainae Illustrantes (1550–1850)*, VI, ed. Athanasius Welykyj, series II, Analecta OSBM, section III (Rome, 1962), 118–121.

31. For a discussion of relations between Rome and Warsaw in this period, see Andrusiak, "Sprawa patriarchatu," pp. 275–276.

32. See Šmurlo I, 101, published in part, p. 255, footnote 230, and II, 255.

33. For the letters to Mohyla and Kysil dated November 3, 1643, see *Documenta Pontificum Romanorum*, I, 530–532. In planning to send the letters, a major obstacle was the problem of referring to the "false metropolitan" Mohyla as a metropolitan. Šmurlo I, 256–257.

34. See *Documenta Pontificum Romanorum*, I, 524–530, 532–537 for letters to the king and other notables, dated November 3, 1643. These letters, including the letter to Kysil and Mohyla, are also published in A. I. Turgenev, ed., *Akty istoricheskie, otnosiashchiesia k Rossii, izvlechennye iz inostrannykh arkhivov i bibliotek*, 2 vols. (St. Petersburg, 1841–1842), II, 209–220.

35. For Sakovych's attacks and Mohyla's defense, see Golubev II–1, 320–462. For an evaluation of the period, see Florovskii, *Puti*, pp. 44–56.

36. For a characterization of the Uniate church during Seliava's tenure as metropolitan, see Velykyj, *Z litopysu*, V, 106–110. For examples of the protests against privileges to the Orthodox by the nuncio, Filonardi, Metropolitan Seliava and Catholic notables, see Theiner, *Vetera*, III, 418–422.

37. The spread of the Roman Catholic church into the eastern areas of the Commonwealth is indicated by the marked increase of monastic houses between 1600 and 1650. Jerzy Kłoczowski, "Zakony męskie w Polsce w XVI–XVIII wieku," *Kościół w Polsce*, II, 603–606 and the map by Adam Chruszczewski, "Zakony męskie w Polsce XVII–XVIII wieku," in the volume *Mapy: Wiek XVI–XVIII* of *Kościół w Polsce*, II. Tomkiewicz discusses Wiśniowiecki's patronage of Roman Catholic churches in the Left Bank of the palatinate of Kiev and his curtailment of patronage to Orthodox institutions, *Jeremi Wiśniowiecki*, pp. 102–110.

38. On the spread of Jesuit schools in the Ukraine, see Natoński, "Szkolnictwo jezuickie w Polsce w dobie Kontrreformacji," pp. 319–322. For the schools in Novhorod-Sivers'kyi and Kiev, see Józef Łukaszewicz, *Zakłady naukowe w Koronie i w Wielkim Księstwie Litewskim od najdawniejszych czasów aż do roku 1794*, 2 vols. (Poznań, 1851), II, 87–88, 121–123.

39. *Litterae Episcoporum*, I, 298, January 5, 1639.

40. Šmurlo I, 255.

41. During discussions (September 28, 1643) which led to the drafting of the Pope's and Congregation's letters, Kysil was described on the basis of Terlets'kyi's letter as 'layco scismatico castellano di Cernovich et potentissimo in opere e sermone et in credito grande presso li scismatici per la sua prudenza e sapere, e se questo col detto Mohilla colle persuasioni di Sua Santità inchinassero all'unione" (in Francesco Ingoli's hand), Šmurlo I, 256, fn. 233. For later comment on Kysil as a "Catholic" see Nuncio Juan de Torres' report of July 13, 1647. *Litterae Nuntiorum*, VI, 223–244 and March 12, 1648, *Litterae Nuntiorum*, VI, 247.

42. For the papacy's role in the Turkish war plans, see Wiktor Czermak, *Plany wojny tureckiej Władysława IV* (Cracow, 1895), pp. 41–42. For papal interest in the Ottoman Empire see the nuncio's reports from June 1645 to July 1647, *Litterae Nuntiorum*, VI, 172–224.

43. For a description of Ossoliński's central role in efforts for a new union, and his contacts with Kysil concerning this matter, see the nuncio's report of March 12, 1648 in *Litterae Nuntiorum*, VI, 247. The instructions to de Torres from the Congregation advised him to consult with Ossoliński in planning procedures for a new union. March 17, 1645. *Litterae S. C. De Propaganda Fide*, I, 181–182.

44. Aleksander F. Korshunov, *Afanasii Filippovich: Zhizn' i tvorchestvo* (Minsk, 1965).

45. Kassian Sakowicz, *Kalendarz stary . . .* (Warsaw, 1641), back cover.

46. Golubev II–1, 286.

47. Sakowicz, *Epanorthosis albo perspectiwa*, p. 117.

48. *Lithos* (reprint), p. 381.

49. The documents of the proposals are published in Šmurlo II, and consists of: 1. A letter of the intermediary Father Valeriano Magno, January 28, 1645, pp. 156–157. 2. A document "Compendio del negotio dell'unione de' Rutheni universale," which Šmurlo entitled "Mémoire de Métropolite Pierre Mohila." The publication is based on five copies of the text and includes notes made by officials of the Congregation, pp. 157–163. 3. A document entitled "Sententia cuiusdam nobilis Poloni graecae religionis," which Šmurlo entitled "Mémoire du Palatin Adam Kisiel" pp. 163–169.

For information on the March 16, 1645 session that discussed the proposals, see Šmurlo I, 257, footnotes 240 and 241. The sensitivity of the religious problems of the seventeenth century assures that the participants' secretiveness makes any study of projects and proposals extremely difficult. In the case of the 1644 plans for union, we are also faced with problems of attribution of specific documents and roles. All surviving documents are in Vatican archives. Two of the documents discussed by the Congregation for the Propagation of the Faith are proposals from the Orthodox conditions under which union would be considered. One is an Italian summary, extant in a number of copies of a document submitted by Mohyla. The second is a more extensive document, complementary in content, entitled "Sententia cuiusdam nobilis Poloni graecae religionis." Šmurlo attributed this proposal to Kysil. This view is supported by the following facts: 1. Urban VIII had written to Kysil asking him to propose conditions for a union. 2. Kysil had expressed favorable attitudes toward union in his 1643 and 1646 donations to religious institutions. 3. In 1647, Kysil wrote to Metropolitan Kosiv, urging him to support efforts for establishing a new union. This letter is similar in essentials to the proposals of 1644. Kysil's letter of December 13 (1647) is published in Šmurlo II, 173–177.

Recently, Father Athanazius Welykyj has proposed that the lack of an original for Mohyla's proposal (footnote 59, document 2) can be explained by assuming that the "Sententia" was in fact the larger brief from which the Italian summaries were abstracted and that the title "cuiusdam nobilis Poloni" was merely appended to protect Mohyla's identity. A. H. Velykyj, "Anonimnyi proekt Petra Mohyly po z'iedynenniu ukraïns'koï tserkvy 1645 r." *Zapysky ChSVV* 4 (10) (1963), 484–497. Welykyj's argument provides an explanation of the fate of Mohyla's broader project and of the similarity of the two documents. However, Welykyj presumes that Mohyla wrote the document in collaboration with Kysil and that the more secular aspects of the proposal, especially on the inclusion of the nobility in the preparatory steps of a union, may be attributed to Kysil. Velykyi, "Anonimnyi proekt," p. 61. Welykyj points out that Kysil, a cautious politician, would hardly have ignored a direct appeal from the Pope.

Although Kysil's name does not appear on any of the proposals or in the discussions of the proposals, the proposals can be assumed to reflect Kysil's viewpoints. First, Kysil's December 13, 1647 letter is in accord with the earlier proposals. Second, it appears that it was Kysil who convinced Mohyla to react favorably to attempts to form a new union. Pietro Saracino wrote to the secretary of the Congregation, Francesco Ingoli in circa 1647: "il suddetto Adamo Kisiel convenendo co'l mitropolita schismatico l'habbi essortato fortemente al ricevimento dell'unione, con dire che lui gia era disposto all'istesso, et a dichiararsi catolico, anchorche il suddetto mitropolita schismatico volesse perservare nel suo errore." *Monumenta Ucrainae Historica,* 13 vols., comp. Metropolitan Andrei Sheptyts'kyi (Rome, 1964–1975), II, 321.

The two men may have responded jointly because the papal authorities viewed them as a pair. See Cardinal Antonio Francisco Fipolo's letter to Mohyla (letter dated November 14, listed by Golubev as November 9). The letter begins: "Reverendissimus Methodius Chelmensis Episcopus Ruthenus unitus tot tantaque de moribus, doctrina et zelo Amplitudinus Tuae et domini Adami Kisiel Castellani Czernihoviensis huic Sacrae Congregationi de propaganda fide retulit, ut merito Eminentissimi Patres, vobis cooperantibus, spem non modicam conceperunt vivendi tandem renovatam illam totius Russiae cum hac Sancta Sede Catholica et Apostolica Romana Unionem," Golubev II–2, p. 285.

50. Welykyj's suppositions that it was on Kysil's insistence that the importance of the lay nobility in the Ruthenian church was mentioned seem probable, but are not derived from documentary evidence. Velykyi, "Anonimnyi proekt," p. 63.

51. See his statement when founding the monastery in Nyzkynychi, p. 188 and his December 13, 1647 letter to Kosiv, Šmurlo II, 173–177.

52. Welykyj quotes a letter of Pietro Saracino of August 20, 1648 asserting that plans for a new union were first inspired by books which Metodii Terlets'kyi had brought from Rome. Saracino asserted that Kysil had given these books to Mohyla. "Anonimnyi proekt," p. 61.

53. Welykyj has pointed out that the *Sententia* has received relatively little attention, even though it is more detailed than the proposal usually ascribed to Mohyla. "Anonimnyi proekt," pp. 56–57. For an analysis and Ukrainian translation of the document, see Zhukovs'kyi, *Petro Mohyla,* pp. 147–164.

54. See Šmurlo II, 163–169 on Mohyla's and Kysil's proposals.

55. The Congregation's subsequent instructions to Papal Nuncio de Torres list the demand for a patriarch and a joint synod as the reason for earlier failures. They continue that the Orthodox metropolitan now appeared to be favorably inclined to a union and ordered the nuncio to provide additional information on his character and views, to gather information on Atanazii Puzyna, the bishop of Luts'k, and to study the possibilities for a union. The Congregation was still concerned the Orthodox might under the guise of negotiation merely be attempting to destroy the Union of Brest. March 17, 1645, *Litterae S. C. De Propaganda Fide,* I, 181.

56. *Acta S. C. De Propaganda Fide,* I, 213–214. Also see Šmurlo I, 257–258, footnote 240 and his discussion on 119–120.

57. For Ingoli's comments, see Šmurlo II, 161–163. For Riccardi's, see Šmurlo II, 162,

58. The instructions to de Torres of February 26, 1645 and March 17, 1645, are published in *Litterae S. C. De Propaganda Fide,* I, 177–184.

59. See Šmurlo I, 119–120, and the letter of de Torres to Cardinal Camilo Pamphili, February 23, 1647, *Litterae Nuntiorum*, V, 215–216.

60. *Arkhiv Iu. Z. R.*, pt. II, vol. I, 337–348.

61. Kosiv was nominated on February 25, 1647, *Arkhiv Iu. Z. R.*, pt. II, vol. I, 337–342 and Tryzna on January 25, 1647, *Arkhiv Iu. Z. R.*, pt. II, vol. I, 342–348.

62. De Torres, May 4, 1647; *Litterae Nuntiorum*, VI, 218.

63. Kysil entered his name first among the lay electors of the metropolitan and archimandrite. *Arkhiv Iu. Z. R.*, pt. II, vol. I, 341, 346.

64. Šmurlo II, pp. 171–173. June 8, 1647. Father Valeriano Magno to Francesco Ingoli, July 13, 1647. De Torres to Cardinal Giovanni Panzirolo Doc. 33 (97): "Ha smembrato pero in tre persone le rendite che haveva il defonto metropolita, dal che nascera che non possa fondar e mantener le scuole come faceva l'altro, et essendo amico del castellano di Chiovia, dovevano ambedue esser qui in breve, et haveva inditii assai efficaci della loro conversione, poiche questo cavaliere achorche scismatico s'era dischiarato piu volte col. sign. gran cancelliere del regno ch'egli era catolico; ma alcuni rispetti humani lo tenevano in quella religione perversa." The letter to Panzirolo is published in *Litterae Nuntiorum*, VI, 223–224.

65. De Torres to Panzirolo, July 13, 1647. Šmurlo II, 172, and *Litterae Nuntiorum*, VI, 223–224.

66. See the letter of de Torres to Cardinal A. Capponi of July 13, 1647. *Litterae Nuntiorum*, VI, 224. He stated about Kysil: "il quale ha piu volte detto che sebene nel di fuori si professava scismatico, nell' interno pero teneva la nostra Religione Cattolica, alla professione della quale non era mai venuto per mondani rispetti, ma ne dava ogni giorno piu nuovi segni, e nuove speranze, e con la conversione di questo S. M. si persuade, che vi debba venir ancor il Metroplita."

67. This letter of December 13 (1647) is published in Šmurlo II, 173–177. The copy of the letter does not include the year, but merely the month and day, December 13, and the place Kolyschi, a distortion of Kobyshche. The year can be established from the context, Kysil's place of residence, and a mention of the letter by the papal nuncio when he forwarded it on March 13, 1648. *Litterae Nuntiorum*, VI, 249–250.

68. For de Torres's discussion of Kysil's letter and the problem of the chrism, see *Litterae Nuntiorum*, VI, 247, 249–250.

69. Šmurlo II, 176–177. Kysil's arguments that confirmation by the patriarch would be necessary to establish Kosiv's authority convinced Ossoliński to issue documents approving such a step. De Torres reported disapprovingly on Ossoliński's decision and rationalization of this step. March 12, 1648, *Litterae Nuntiorum*, VI, 249–250. In late November, Kysil maintained that although he favored union, it was necessary to show obedience to the patriarch of Constantinople in order to retain the masses' support. Pietro Saracino to Francesco Ingoli, November 14, 1648, Šmurlo I, 260, footnote 251.

70. Report of Papal Nuncio de Torres, March 12, 1648, *Litterae Nuntiorum*, VI, 246–250. De Torres was optimistic about the chances for a union chiefly

because of his high regard for Ossoliński and Kysil. See p. 248 for his comments on Orthodox attitudes toward Uniates.

71. The decisions of the colloquium are discussed by the contemporary chronicler [Joachim Jerlicz], *Latopisiec albo kroniczka Joachima Jerlicza*, ed. K. Wł. Wójcicki, 2 vols. (Warsaw, 1853), I, 54–55. He dates the colloquium as on April 25, 1647. Jerlicz's dating was accepted by Šmurlo, who maintained that information about the conference reached Rome very late, in August 1648. Šmurlo I, 259. Kubala also accepted Jerlicz's dating. *Jerzy Ossoliński*, p. 254. Both these historians assert that the conference was held with the permission of the papal nuncio, but the nuncio's correspondence to Rome from this period contains no information about the conference. *Litterae Nuntiorum*, VI, 215–222. Some of the documents of August 1648 that Šmurlo refers to are published in *Litterae Nuntiorum*, VI, 282–284. It is possible they pertain to subsequent discussions held between Uniates and Orthodox in Vilnius in the spring of 1648. But it is just as likely that the date in Jerlicz is incorrect and should be 1648, not 1647. In the spring of 1648, just prior to Władysław's death, both the nuncio and the king were in Vilnius. *Litterae Nuntiorum*, VI, 253–260. A conference in early 1648 is described in a contemporary pamphlet, *Relacya sprawy przez Władysława IV odbytej Unitów z Grekami* (Vilnius, 1648). This pamphlet is mentioned in K. Estreicher's bibliography, *Bibliografia polska*, 34 vols. (Cracow, 1872–1951), VIII (= Part II, *Spis chronologiczny*, vol. I, *Stulecia XV–XVII*), 267. Estreicher, however, gives no library location for the pamphlet, and I have been unable to find it.

72. See [Stanisław Oświęcim], *Stanisława Oświęcima Dyaryusz 1643–1651*, ed. Wiktor Czermak, Scriptores Rerum Polonicarum, XIX (Cracow, 1907), 205. Oświęcim claims that an agreement to hold a conference on July 16, 1648 was decided upon at that time, but that the whole affair was kept secret. For more information about Ossoliński's trip, see Kubala, *Jerzy Ossoliński*, pp. 255–257. Also see Miron Costin, *Letopisetul Ţarii Moldovei*, ed. P. P. Panaitescu (Bucharest, 1961), p. 161.

73. *Litterae Nuntiorum*, VI, 247. De Torres wrote that the conference would take place on July 15.

74. April 29, 1648, *Litterae Nuntiorum*, VI, 256.

75. *Arkhiv Iu. Z. R.*, pt. III, vol. I, 401–406.

76. Fr. Theodosius Wasilewicz Baiewski, *Tentoria Venienti Kioviam cum novi Honoris fascibus Illustrissimo Domino, D. Adamo de Brusiłow Sventoldicio Kisiel Castellano Kiovi: Nossov: & Capitaneo (n.p. Typis Pieczariensibus, 1646)*.

77. Baiewski, *Tentoria*, fol. 7.

> Rossia Te Patrem canit atque Polonia Patrem,
> Rossia Te Civem Sarmata Teque suum
> Lis de Te: veniat Polus has componere lites,
> Ast veniens lites conciliare nequit.
> Si Rossis cedat Civem, Civemque dolebit
> Sarmata; sufficiet Solus utrique simul
> ludicat; at queritur Divina Ecclesia, poscit

Cedite vester erit: si meus inquit erit.

78. BCz, MS 1657, fol. 207.

79. Although Ossoliński's comment indicates that Kysil at least initiated a dicussion of a war against the Tatars, it is insufficient to prove that Kysil first conceived the plan for a major war against the Tatars and Ottomans. Władysław Godziszewski argues against such a hypothesis, and points out that a war with the Ottomans had been considered by Władysław long before. "Granica polsko-moskiewska wedle pokoju polanowskiego 1634 (wytyczona w latach 1634–1648)," *Prace Komisji Atlasu Historycznego Polski,* III (1935), 33. Ossoliński's letter does not even refer specifically to the Ottomans, and Kysil's proposal may have been only about the Tatars. Without more concrete evidence, we can only speculate whether Kysil influenced Koniecpolski's proposal for an alliance with Muscovy in a campaign to annex the Crimea and the Danubian vassals of the Ottomans. On this plan, see Kubala, *Jerzy Ossoliński,* pp. 182–184. Wiesław Majewski has speculated that Kysil may have renewed discussion of war against the Ottomans at Władysław's court and that he proposed the idea of a Muscovite alliance to Koniecpolski. "Plany wojny tureckiej Władysława IV a rzekome przymierze kozacko-tatarskie z 1645 r," *Przegląd Historyczny,* LXIV, no. 3, pp. 271, 280.

80. See Majewski, "Plany," pp. 271–272. For a detailed description of this period, see Wiktor Czermak, *Plany wojny tureckiej Władysława IV* (Cracow, 1895), pp. 1–62.

81. For discussions of spheres of competence in making the Commonwealth's foreign policy, see Kaczmarczyk, *Historia,* pp. 126, 134–135, 242, 248. The role of the Senate in foreign policy is discussed in Czapliński, "Senat za Władysława." The Commonwealth's diplomacy under the Vasas is treated in Czapliński, "Dyplomacja polska w latach 1605–1648," in *Polska służba dyplomatyczna XVI–XVIII w.* ed. Z. Wójcik (Warsaw, 1966), pp. 203–256. The functions of various officials and institutions are discussed in an article in the same collection by Zbigniew Wójcik, "Z dziejów organizacji dyplomacji polskiej w drugiej połowie XVII wieku," pp. 256–277.

82. The competence of chancellor and hetman are discussed in Kaczmarczyk, *Historia,* pp. 130–131, 247–248. Also see Czapliński, "Dyplomacja," pp. 217–218, 233–238, and pp. 231–232 on the Cossacks.

83. On changes in European diplomacy in this period, see Sir George Clark, *The Seventeenth Century,* 2nd ed. (London, 1947, paperback, 1961), pp. 124–153. For a contemporary discussion of the difficulties of negotiating with the Commonwealth, see the report of the Venetian ambassador, Giovanni Tiepolo, who was commissioned to negotiate an alliance against the Ottomans in 1645–1647. A Polish translation is published in J. U. Niemcewicz, ed., *Zbiór pamiętników historycznych o dawnej Polszcze z rękopismów tudzież dzieł w różnych językach o Polszcze wydanych oraz z listami oryginalnemi królów i znakomitnych ludzi w kraju naszym,* 5 vols. (Leipzig, 1839–1840), V, 1–34. For Muscovite diplomatic practices, see, S. A. Belokurov, *O posol'skom prikaze* in *Chteniia v Imperatorskom obshchestve istorii i drevnosti rossiiskikh pri Moskovskom universitete* (hereafter *Chteniia* [Moscow]), 1906, no. 3 (= vol. CCXVII).

84. On Władysław's reforms, see Bohdan Baranowski, *Organizacja wojska polskiego w latach trzydziestych i czterdziestych XVII w.* (Warsaw, 1957), Władysław Czapliński, *Polska a Bałtyk w latach 1632–1648* (Wrocław, 1952), and Tadeusz Marian Nowak, "Polish Warfare Technique in the 17th Century, Theoretical Conceptions and their Practical Applications," in *Military Technique, Policy, and Strategy in History* (Warsaw, 1976), pp. 11–94..

85. On Władysław's foreign policy in this period, see Czapliński, *Władysław,* pp. 332–377.

86. For an evaluation of Ottoman and Tatar policy toward Eastern Europe in this period, see Zbigniew Wójcik, *Historia powszechna XVI–XVII wieku* (Warsaw, 1973), pp. 440–444 and Josef Matuz, *Krimtatarische Urkunden im Reichsarchiv zu Kopenhagen* (Freiburg, 1976), pp. 1–19. For the terms of the Peace of Polianovka, see N. N. Bantysh-Kamenskii, *Perepiska mezhdu Rossieiu i Pol'sheiu po 1700 god, sostavlennaia po diplomaticheskim bumagam,* 3 parts (Moscow, 1862), III, 65. The background of the Polianovka peace is discussed in B. F. Porshnev, "Na putiakh k Polianovskomu miru 1634 g."

87. Bantysh-Kamenskii's *Perepiska,* III, 122–124, contains detailed accounts of documents in Muscovite archives on negotiations until 1645. The gaps in Polish archives on foreign relations makes research on the problem difficult. For a survey of the Commonwealth's relations with Muscovy during Władysław IV's reign, see Władysław Godziszewski, *Polska a Moskwa za Władysława IV* (Cracow, 1930) (= Polska Akademja Umiejętności, *Rozprawy Wydziału Historyczno-Filozoficznego,* series II, vol. XLII, no. 6).Godziszewski concentrates on the 1630s and devotes relatively little attention to the 1640s. The problem of border commissions is treated in detail in Godziszewski, "Granica polsko-moskiewska." L. V. Zaborovskii, *Rossiia, Rech' Pospolitaia i Shvetsiia v seredine XVII v.* (Moscow, 1981) contains only a cursory discussion of the period before 1648.

88. The most comprehensive work about Muscovite-Tatar relations in the period is A. A. Novosel'skii, *Bor'ba Moskovskogo gosudarstva s tatarami v pervoi polovine XVII veka* (Moscow-Leningrad, 1948). See pp. 293–307 and 367–372 for a discussion of the defense line. For Commonwealth-Tatar relations in this period, see Baranowski, "Stosunki polsko-tatarskie."

89. For the Azov problem see Novosel'skii, *Bor'ba,* pp. 256–300 and N. A. Smirnov, *Rossiia i Turtsiia v XVI–XVII ss.,* 2 vols. (= Uchenye zapiski: Moskovskii Ordena Lenina gosudarstvennyi universitet, no. XCIV), II, 43–125.

90. Novosel'skii discusses Muscovite foreign policy interests in this period, *Bor'ba,* pp. 326–332. Baranowski deals with the first unsuccessful attempts at cooperation, "Stosunki polsko-tatarskie," pp. 164–179; Godziszewski includes a very schematic account of this period, *Polska a Moskwa,* pp. 66–71. Also see, Zbigniew Wójcik, *Dzieje Rosji: 1533–1801* (Warsaw, 1971), pp. 121–124. An unpublished dissertation by Zbigniew Świtalski, "Sojusz polsko-rosyjski z roku 1647" (Warsaw, 1970) deals with the 1630s and 1640s, but the author did not use Soviet archives. The abstract of the thesis is in the Institute of History's library of Warsaw University.

91. For an indication of the damage done to the Ukraine by Tatar raids, see

Maurycy Horn, "Chronologia i zasięg najazdów tatarskich w latach 1600–1647," *Studia i Materiały do Historii Wojskowości,* vol. VIII, pt. 1 (1962), 3–71. Even in the threats to break the Diets over the rights of the Orthodox church, the delegates from the Ukrainian palatinates excluded the issue of defense of the Ukraine and payment of the troops. See, for example, Kysil's speech of May 5, 1640 at the Diet. Steinwehr III, fol. 25. However, the Volhynian nobility demanded that peace be maintained at the dietines of January 7, 1645 and of September 13, 1646. *Arkhiv Iu. Z. R.,* pt. II, vol. 1, 284, 315–316.

92. Władysław's plans to win over a group of magnates are discussed in Kubala, *Jerzy Ossoliński,* pp. 177–178.

93. For the importance of Koniecpolski to Władysław's plans, see Czermak, *Plany,* pp. 67–69. Czermak quotes part of Tiepolo's dispatch of April 27, 1647 in which he reported that the king assured him a number of detachments from the eastern magnates in any struggle. *Plany,* p. 270. The campaigns of Jeremi Wiśniowiecki and Aleksander Koniecpolski to the steppe indicate support for the king's policies. Tomkiewicz, *Jeremi Wiśniowiecki,* pp. 179–180.

94. See Majewski, "Plany," pp. 272–273 for a discussion of Koniecpolski's stance.

95. Tomkiewicz, *Jeremi Wiśniowiecki,* pp. 156–158 discusses the magnate's problems with the king.

96. Wiśniowiecki's territorial claims and the work of border commission are discussed in detail in Tomkiewicz, *Jeremi Wiśniowiecki,* pp. 75–81.

97. The problem with the Grand Duchy over lands is discussed in Godziszewski, "Granica polsko-moskiewska," pp. 35–39.

98. For an evaluation of the successes and failures of Władysław's policies, see Czapliński, *Władysław,* pp. 353–377.

99. Władysław's difficulties with Potocki are treated in Czermak, *Plany,* pp. 168–170. The Diets of 1646 and 1647 are described in Czermak, *Plany,* pp. 222–242, 272–299, and Kubala, *Jerzy Ossoliński,*

100. March 16, 1648. Kysil to Mikołaj Potocki, Rawita-Gawroński, ed., *Sprawy i rzeczy,* pp. 79–80.

101. For Kysil's work on border commissions, see Godziszewski, "Granica polsko-moskiewska," pp. 19–20, 39–40.

102. Afanasii Lavrent'evich Ordin-Nashchokin described the Diet of 1643 in a letter to Fedor Ivanovich Sheremetev. He asserted that Wiśniowiecki and Adam Kazanowski wished to stop Muscovy from receiving the lands due it, but that Kysil had written to the Diet "standing up for justice." His letter also contains a statement that the two magnates had conspired to have Kysil granted the office of castellan of Chernihiv in order to keep him from attending the Diet. Although there is no corroboration for Nashchokin's charges, his letter indicates Muscovite antagonism toward the border magnates who claimed lands demanded by Muscovy. I. V. Galaktionov, *Ranniaia perepiska A. L. Ordina-Nashchokina (1642–1645 gg)* ([Saratov], 1968), pp. 64–65. At the 1643 Diet it was suggested that Kysil was a good candidate for dealings with the Muscovites. BCz, MS 390, pp. 565–566.

103. September 13, 1646, *Arkhiv Iu. Z. R.*, pt. II, vol. 1, 316–317.

104. *Volumina legum*, IV, 88.

105. The Diet constitution only mentions the border issue. A summary of the instructions exists in the mission's report. "Relatia Moskiewskiey Legatiej," but the terms of Kysil's mission emerge from the report. The "Relatia" exists in at least six copies; BJ, MS 49, pp. 85–91, BCz, MS 141, pp.290–302, BCz, MS 2102, pp. 226–231, Wojewódzkie Archiwum Państwowe w Gdańsku (hereafter Arch. Gdańsk.), MS 300, 53/71, pp. 129–136, Wojewódzkie Archiwum Państwowe w Łodzi (hereafer Arch. Łodz.), Archiwum Bartoszewiczów (hereafter Arch. Bart.), MS 127, pp. 65–72, and LNB, fond Ossolins'kykh 2, MS 225, fols. 42–46. All copies agree in content, although differences in wording exist. For purposes of citation, I will use Arch. Gdańsk., MS 300, 53/71. Kysil is spoken of in the third person throughout the "Relatia." It is almost certain, however, that he was himself the author since writing such a report was an obligation for each ambassador. Adam Przyboś and Roman Żelewski, eds., *Dyplomaci w dawnych czasach* (Cracow, 1959), pp. 41–42. See a letter from Franciszek Isajkowski to Kazimierz Sapieha (November 11, 1647) in which he mentioned that the king had received a copy of the "Relatia" and Kysil's oration before the tsar. BN, BOZ, MS 931, fols. 31–32. In a letter to one of the king's secretaries (the copy does not specify whom), on October 24, 1647, Kysil mentioned the "Relatia" as "Relatia moia," "My Report." Arch Łodz., Arch. Bart., MS 127, p. 85. See Arch. Gdańsk., MS 300, 53/71, p. 130 for Kysil's discussion of the limitation of his powers to conclude an agreement.

106. The Diet's suspicions about the king's intentions were reflected in numerous demands for control and information. Czermak, *Plany,* pp. 227–228.

107. July 20, 1645, BCz, MS 1657, p. 106.

108. Copies of a number of letters in which Kysil argues for an accommodation with Muscovy exist in BCz, MS 1657, but without addressees. June 29, 1645, p. 129, August 2, 1645, p. 106, September 1, 1645, p. 91. For the Trubchevsk issue, see Godziszewski, "Granica polska-moskiewska," pp. 35–39.

109. On September 26, 1646, Władysław confirmed the right of the Trubchevsk monks to the lands that Kysil granted them in the palatinate of Chernihiv, PANK, MS 272, fols. 10–11. Kysil founded a monastery in Maksakiv for the monks from Trubchevsk. Summaries of Władysław's confirmation and Kysil's subsequent grants are in Filaret, *Istoriko-statisticheskoe opisanie*, IV, 70–74.

110. For the protests of the delegates from the palatinate of Kiev at the Diet of 1646, see BJ, MS 49, p. 171.

111. Nashchokin's letters provide commentary on the Muscovite view of the Commonwealth's government. In one letter he calls it a state without a head and one in which important men do not listen to the king. He ends by asking where justice-truth (*pravda*) can exist amidst such instability. December 30, 1642 (O.S.), Nashchokin to Sheremetev, Galaktionov, *Ranniaia perepiska,* p. 29.

112. In the dispute over possession of the Left-Bank center of Romny, Wiśniowiecki opposed the king's favorite. Tomkiewicz, *Jeremi Wiśniowiecki,* pp. 138–146.

113. Tomkiewicz also discusses the possibility that Ossoliński intervened in Wiśniowiecki's favor, *Jeremi Wiśniowiecki,* pp. 145–147.

114. Kysil's successful address to save Wiśniowiecki's mandate is entitled "Rationes stabiliendae dignitatis Ks. J. Mości Wiśniowieckiego, żeby z izby poselskiej nie był rugowany. Koncept J. M. P. Kisiela, kasztelana czernihowskiego," BCz, MS 1657, pp. 504–505. The documents of Kysil's loans to Wiśniowiecki are in AGAD, Met. Kor., MS 190, fols. 85–86. Kysil also bought lands from Kazanowski at that time. AGAD, Met. Kor., MS 190, fols. 69–76. Adam and his brother Mykola also served on the Diet commission that adjudicated the dispute between Wiśniowiecki and Kazanowski. O. Nikolaichik, "Materialy po istorii zemlevladeniia kniazei Vishnevetskikh v Levoberezhnoi Ukraine," *Chtenia v istoricheskom obshchestve Nestora Letopistsa,* vol. XIX, no. 3 (1900), 168–174.

115. Tomkiewicz, *Jeremi Wiśniowiecki,* p. 157.

116. July 20, 1645. Koniecpolski to Kysil, BCz, MS 1657, p. 106.

117. A Polish translation of a speech that Kysil delivered before Muscovite negotiators, probably during Kysil's negotiations in 1645, makes a strong case for the Commonwealth's rights to the upper Udai and upper Sula, BCz, MS 1657, pp. 503–504.

118. Irynach, a Kievan monk, visiting Moscow in March 1646, reported that Kysil had gone to see the king with Wiśniowiecki in order to discuss compensation. *Akty Iu.Z.R.,* III, 82–83. An original copy of this report was also in the Wiśniowiecki family's archives, Arch. Łodz., Arch Bart. Inwentarz archiwum w Wiśniowcu, fol. 215.

119. Godziszewski, "Granica polsko-moskiewska," pp. 40–41. The terms of Kysil's commission of June 1647, which handed over Nedryhailiv, are published by V. I. Kholmogorov in "Akty, otnosiashchiesia k Malorossii," *Chteniia* (Moscow) 1885, no. 2, pp. 1–12.

120. Bantysh-Kamenskii, *Perepiska,* III includes a description of Muscovite archival material up until 1645. See pp. 65–66 for the Polianovka peace and pp. 128–144 for negotiations in 1644–1645. After 1645, we must depend on the sketchy treatment in N. N. Bantysh-Kamenskii, *Obzor vneshnikh snoshenii Rossii,* 4 vols. (Moscow, 1894–1902), III, 126–127.

121. The assertion by Kubala that a formal agreement for an alliance had already been concluded by Stempkowski in his 1645 mission was shown to be mistaken by Czermak. Czermak, *Plany,* pp. 384–391. Kysil had the first mandate from the Diet, albeit a limited one.

122. For the financial provisions, see "Summariusz rachunków skarbowych przedstawiony na sejmie konwokacyjnym w 1648 roku." AGAD, Archiwum Skarbowe Koronne, oddz. III, no. 6. For the royal proposal of March 4, 1647 to the Diet, see BJ, MS 49, p. 280.

123. Kysil to one of the king's secretaries, October 4, 1647. Arch. Łodz., Arch. Bart., MS 127, p. 82.

124. There was considerable reluctance by the Grand Duchy's officials to appropriate the funds necessary for Pac's mission. The problem is discussed in

the letters of February 17, 1647 and March 23, 1647 from Franciszek Isajkowski (*referendarz y pisarz* of the Grand Duchy) to Kazimierz Leon Sapieha, BN, BOZ., MS 931, fols. 29–31. The king turned to Kazimierz Leon Sapieha to expedite the mission, January 29, 1647, PANK, MS 349, fol. 1. On March 21, 1647 the king requested Sapieha to send information from the Grand Duchy's archives on Muscovite affairs. PANK, MS 349, fol. 7. Also see his letters of September 26 and September 29, 1647, PANK, MS 349, fols. 13, 15. The nobles and magnates of the Grand Duchy, who were little interested in the southern frontier and were much more concerned with keeping the gains on the Muscovite border, were hostile to an alliance at the Diet of 1646 and demanded that tribute to the Tatars be paid. BJ, MS 49, p. 157. Also see the king's instructions to the Diet of 1647, BCz, MS 375, p. 1028.

125. Władysław's instructions to the dietines were anti-Tatar. BJ, MS 49, pp. 279–289. His proposals of March 4 to the Diet stress the tsar's continued interest in a defensive alliance. He makes no mention of an offensive alliance. BJ, MS 49, p. 280. For Władysław's plans in this period, see Czermak, *Plany,* pp. 272–299.

126. In the "Relatia," Kysil claimed to have waited to have informed Pac of his plans, and to have awaited his arrrival in Moscow for six weeks. Arch. Gdańsk., MS 300, 53/71, p. 129. Pac arrived in Moscow, but in October, after Kysil's departure (Novosel'skii, *Bor'ba,* p. 366). Novosel'skii states that the Muscovites refused to negotiate and delegates reluctantly affirmed the treaty. For a description of Pac's negotiations, see Bantysh-Kamenskii, *Obzor,* III, 125–126. Also see, Aleksandr Barsukov, *Rod Sheremetevykh,* 8 vols. (St. Petersburg, 1881–1914), III, 364–365.

127. Kysil's eight-part instructions also included private citizens' claims on Muscovy. See his short summaries in the "Relatia," Arch. Gdańsk., MS 300, 53/71, p. 129.

128. See his complaints over the difficulties this caused him, "Relatia," Arch. Gdańsk., MS 300, 53/71, pp. 130–131.

129. In the "Relatia," Kysil describes his difficulties in securing the Muscovite negotiators' confidence in the Commonwealth and his need to justify earlier indifference to Muscovy's requests for cooperation. Arch. Gdańsk., MS 300, 53/71, pp. 130–132. The course of negotiations is difficult to reconstruct without access to Muscovite records from the "posol'skii prikaz." This material was used by S. M. Solov'ev in his *Istoriia Rossii,* book V, vol. X, 471–474, and Solov'ev quoted considerable parts of the negotiations in modern Russian translation. See p. 688 for the editors' updated information about the sources used. Solov'ev mistakenly described the negotations as taking place in 1646. He made no mention of the agreement concluded and stated that the Muscovites were unable to convince the Commonwealth's negotiators to join in an offensive alliance.

Adam Darowski's "Zatargi o starostów pogranicznych 1618–1654: Szkic historyczny, skreślony na podstawie rosyjskich źródeł historycznych," in his *Szkice historyczne,* series III (St. Petersburg, 1897), pp. 185–287 contains long quotations from the negotiations but all are also in Solov'ev, pp. 276–280. Darowski also mistakenly dated the mission as taking place in 1646. It would appear that despite the article's title, Darowski merely translated sections of Solov'ev into Polish.

The only recent historian to use the Moscow archives about the negotiations is Novosel'skii, *Bor'ba,* pp. 365–367. Barsukov, *Rod Sheremetevykh,* III, 345, 361–365 includes some information from "Razriadnyi Prikaz" records.

130. For Kysil's optimism that the Muscovites would abide by the agreement, see his letter to the king's secretary, October 24, 1647, Arch Łodz., Arch. Bart., MS 127, p. 86.

131. Kysil expressed fear that his actions would be interpreted badly in his October 24, 1647 letter to the king's secretary. Arch. Łodz., Arch. Bart., MS 127, p. 85. For his support of the war policy, see p. 86. The divergence between his powers from the Diet and his real goals emerge in his "Relatia," in which he asserted that the alliance was necessary to forestall a Muscovite-Tatar alliance. Kysil described Muscovite foreign policy to Mikołaj Potocki, the Crown great hetman, in a letter of March 16, 1648. Rawita-Gawroński, ed., *Sprawy i rzeczy,* p. 80.

132. Kysil had left the Commonwealth on June 27, 1647. For his journey to Moscow, see the "Relatia," Arch. Gdańsk., MS 300, 53/71, p. 129. Kysil made a will prior to his departure, but there is no copy of its text. PANK, MS 3022, fol. 38. The only published version of the speech is in Solov'ev, *Istoriia Rossii,* book V, vol. X, 471–472. Although some of the sections have quotation marks, it is likely they are paraphrase translations into modernized Russian. Kysil sent a copy of the speech to Władysław. Franciszek Isajkowski to Kazimierz Leon Sapieha, BN, BOZ, MS 931, fols. 31–32 mentions that Władysław had received a copy. I have not had access to the copy of the speech in Moscow used by Solov'ev. I have depended on a Latin-script copy, which is apparently a Polish translation, in LNB, fond Ossolyns'kych 2, MS 225, fols. 104–106.

133. Solov'ev quotes Kysil as calling the states "the great Polish kingdom with its great Principalities and the great Russian state." Solov'ev, *Istoriia Rossii,* book V, vol. X, 471. The comment is of importance for its concept of common interest of states and peoples, not sovereigns. The terms used for the two states are especially intriguing—the Kingdom of Poland with an oblique reference to Lithuania—not the Commonwealth, and the "Russian," not Muscovite state. The text in LNB, fond Ossolyns'kykh 2, MS 225, fol. 104 reads: "Wielkie Kró-lewstwo Polskie z Xięstwy swoiemy, Którym szczęśliwie panuie Naiaśnieyszy Wielki Hospodar Król, Pan mój, y Waszego Carskiego Wieliczewstwa Wielkie Ruskie Hospodarstwo, iako dwa cedry Libańskie z iednego wynikłe korzenia, tak z iednego narodu Słowiańskiego Państwa obiedwie Wszechmocna Boska ręka zgromadziła y ufundowała."

134. Solov'ev's Russian text is: "osobenno istinnyi svidetel' est' sam iazyk, oboim velikim gosudarstvam, kak edinomu narodu, obshchii i nepremennyi." Solov'ev, *Istoriia Rossii,* book V, vol. X, 471. The text in LNB, fond Ossolyn-s'kych 2, MS 225, fol. 104 reads: "ale nayprawdziwszym jest świadkiem ten sam język obudwom Państwom." Later Kysil maintains (fols. 105–106): "Gdy się to

jusz na początku jaśnie pokazało, że oboie Państwa z jednych początków narodów y krwie słowieńskiej idą, przypatrzyć się jest potrzebna y uważyć."

135. For a discussion of historical and linguistic views in the late Middle Ages and early modern period, and the relation of Sarmatism to the concept of Slavic communality, see Tadeusz Ulewicz, *Sarmacja: Studium z problematyki słowiańskiej XV i XVI w.* (Cracow, 1950).

136. Another speech by Kysil, probably delivered before the Muscovite border commissioners in 1645 and translated and reworked for the Commonwealth's public, concentrates on Sarmatian and Christian unity: "Szczęśliwa constellatio była, kiedy dwaj wielcy Monarchowie Panowie naszy krwie niesyte boie y iej dziedziczne hostilitates między Sarmatami a Sarmatami y między Chrześciany a Chrześciany zakrwawione bronie swoie do pochew włożywszy na wieczny sobie od P. Boga Państw powierzonych zezwolili pokój y przyiąwszy go świątobliwemi swemi y przednieyszych w Państwach swych osób przysięgami na potomne zezwolili czasy, narodom wszytkim Chrześciańskim uciechą, pogańskim wielkim stał się ten węzeł dwóch narodów y państw chrześciańskich postrachem." BCz, MS 1657, p. 503.

137. Solov'ev, *Istoriia Rossii,* book V, vol. X, 472; "Relatia," Arch. Gdańsk., MS 300, 53/71, pp. 129–130.

138. Novosel'skii discusses Muscovite-Tatar negotiations in *Bor'ba,* pp. 397–401, but makes no mention of them in his discussion of Kysil's mission, pp. 365–366. For Kysil's account of the danger of Tatar-Muscovite agreement, see "Relatia," Arch. Gdańsk., MS 300, 53/71, pp. 130–131. Kysil may have been alarmist in the "Relatia" in order to justify his conclusion of an agreement with Muscovy. Nevertheless, his account undoubtedly has some substance. The Muscovites were treating Tatar overtures seriously. Novosel'skii seems intent on emphasizing the title of this work and only discussing Muscovy's "struggle" with the Tatars. Although it is difficult to evaluate Novosel'skii's account of the negotiations without comparing it with the Muscovite diplomatic records that he used, it is possible that he overlooked the issue of Muscovite-Tatar negotiations purposely when discussing Kysil's mission. At the very least, he gives no indication of understanding Władysław's and Kysil's tactics.

139. Novosel'skii, *Bor'ba,* p. 366. "Relatia," Arch. Gdańsk., MS 300, 53/71, p. 130.

140. Novosel'skii summarizes an answer given by the *Dumnyi d'iak,* N. Chistoi, *Bor'ba,* pp. 365–366. It includes a number of complaints about the inability of the king to obtain the Diet's approval for a war against the Tatars. Among the complaints is an accusation that the Commonwealth was incapable of controlling the Zaporozhian Cossacks' attacks on Muscovy. Novosel'skii does not describe the discussions, except for a comment that Kysil agreed that an offensive alliance was to be preferred to a defensive one but could not be concluded at that time because of the terms of his instructions. The "Relatia" presents a more detailed account, but obviously was intended for a wider audience, and may not reflect the actual proceedings. "Relatia," Arch. Gdańsk., MS 300, 53/71, pp. 130–132. Kysil maintains that the Muscovite officials argued

for a long time over whether to accept his proposal; finally they decided to pay the usual tribute to the Tatars, therefore avoiding a break with them, but to inform them of the new alliance. In his "Relatia" Kysil writes about Muscovite justification of contacts with the Tatars on the grounds of the Commonwealth's reluctance to cooperate against the Tatars. He complains that had the Commonwealth been ready to undertake the "Tatar venture" an agreement would have been readily concluded. "Relatia," Arch. Gdańsk., MS 300, 53/71, p.130.

141. For the problem of the runaways, see Solov'ev, *Istoriia Rossiia,* book V, vol. X, 472–473; "Relatia," Arch. Gdańsk., MS 300, 53/71, pp. 134–135.

142. Solov'ev, *Istoriia Rossii,* book V, vol. X, 473.

143. Solov'ev, *Istoriia Rossii,* book V, vol. X, 473.

144. "Relatia," Arch. Gdańsk., MS 300, 53/71, p. 134.

145. "Relatia," Arch. Gdańsk., MS 300, 53/71, p. 135.

146. At the Convocation Diet in July 1648, delegates from the Grand Duchy protested against thanking Kysil for the completion of his embassy (July 19), BO, MS 3567, fol. 73. Pac delivered a separate report of his mission, in which he complained that Kysil had negotiated with the Muscovites, without waiting for the delegates from the Grand Duchy, Kysil maintained that he had taken four weeks to travel to Moscow and that he had waited for Pac seven weeks. He insisted that, for the good of the Commonwealth, he had to begin negotiations. July 22, 1648, BO, MS 3567, fol. 75. For discussion of the border problem, see "Relatia," Arch. Gdańsk., MS 300, 53/71, p. 133. A deadline of June 11, 1648 was set for drawing a final line of demarcation between the Grand Duchy and Muscovy.

147. An official text of the treaty is in the Central State Archive of Ancient Acts (TsGADA) in Moscow, *Pol'skie dela,* 1647 g. no. 4, fols. 4–6 and is cited by Novosel'skii, *Bor'ba,* p. 366. Article 4, the alliance pact, is published in *Akty Iu.Z.R.,* III, 128–129 from this text. Two copies of the treaty exists in Poland. Bo, MS 3566, fols. 210–215, and Arch. Łodz., Arch. Bart., MS 127, pp. 72–82.

148. The treaty includes thirteen articles about the following subjects: 1. Titles of the tsar; 2. Border problems between the Grand Duchy of Lithuania and Muscovy; 3. Border problems between the Grand Duchy of Lithuania and Muscovy and a June 1, 1648 (O.S.) deadline for complying with the terms of the settlement; 4. The defensive alliance; 5. Exchange of prisoners; 6. Agreement on trade; 7. Border incursions by inhabitants of the Commonwealth; 8. Disputes about Pavel Ivanovich Soltyk; 9. A summary of opposing views on runaways; 10. Border problems between the kingdom of Poland and Muscovy; 11. Attacks on Muscovite border patrols by Zaporozhian Cossacks; 12. Titles of the Commonwealth's and Muscovy's officials; 13. Request by the tsar that Shuiskii's memorial stone be sent to Muscovy.

149. The article calls for the Commonwealth's hetmans and Muscovy's military leaders, "as is written in the eternal peace and affirmed by the kissing of the cross," to warn each other about Tatar movements, not allow the Tatars to traverse their lands and to stand as one against Tatar attacks. *Akty Iu.Z.R.,* III,

129; BO, MS 3566, fol. 212; Arch. Łodz., Arch. Bart., MS 127, p. 76. The treaty provided that should the Tatars display greater enmity, the king to call a Diet to strengthen the terms of the alliance. Kysil maintained in his "Relatia" that he had been able to avoid Muscovite-Tatar rapprochement by his negotiation of the treaty, but that the Commonwealth was free to accept the alliance if the Diet would agree. Arch. Gdańsk., MS 300, 53/71, p. 132. This interpretation differs from the terms of the treaty, which imply that the defensive alliance would go into effect from the moment that the negotiators signed the treaty. The statements in the "Relatia" that a Muscovite-Tatar alliance was avoided by the negotiating of the Commonwealth-Muscovite agreement and emphasizing the power of the Diet to accept or reject the alliance were intended to silence potential complaints that Kysil had exceeded his authority.

150. A major issue not mentioned in the alliance is that of Muscovy's payment of monetary gifts to the Tatars. The treaty merely states that the two sovereigns and states were to give the Tatars no cause to attack and that they were to conduct themselves "according to prior custom." *Akty Iu.Z.R.,* III, 128; BO, MS 3566, fol. 211; Arch. Łodz., Arch. Bart., MS 127, pp. 75–76. In the "Relatia," it is stated that the Muscovites decided to ally with the Commonwealth, but to continue payment of agreed-upon gifts, which the Tatars demanded. Arch. Gdańsk., MS 300, 53/71, p. 130. Later Kysil claimed in his dealings with the Muscovite voevodas that the terms of the treaty forbade the payment of gifts, which he labeled as tribute. March 30, 1648, Kysil to Nikifor Iurevich Pleshcheev, Voevoda of Putyvl', *Akty Iu.Z.R.,* III, 168–170. This may have been part of an oral agreement that Kysil made with the Muscovite negotiators, but does not accord with the treaty terms or his statement to the Diet in the "Relatia." It is also unclear why the Muscovite government, which initially demanded an offensive alliance, paid the "gifts." It is likely that this was due to awareness that the alliance with the Commonwealth was still far from firm.

151. Novosel'skii's description of the negotiations confirms an indication that Kysil had extensive discussions with the Muscovite negotiators which may have included more detailed planning for cooperation between the king and the tsar. These indications are Kysil's explanation of the Diet's obstruction of a plan for an offensive alliance and his admission that he would have preferred to conclude an offensive alliance immediately. Novosel'skii, *Bor'ba,* p. 365. Kysil's later optimism that a firm agreement had been concluded suggests that the negotiations included more than his "Relatia" and the treaty reveal. His revelation concerning dicussions about the Swedes suggests that the *Posol'skii prikaz* books may contain considerable additional information about discussions for a firm Muscovite-Commonwealth alliance.

152. The original of the letter, dated April 7, 1650 is in BCz, MS 402, pp. 5–12. The discussion of the Swedish problem is on p. 6. Parts of it are published in Godziszewski, "Granica polsko-moskiewska," p. 42. Kysil maintained that he had secretly discussed the alliance against the Swedes with Pushkin and Trubetskoi and that they had demanded an oral pledge from him. Kysil's comment that Władysław's death had destroyed these plans indicates how deeply Kysil

was involved in Władysław's plans and how widesweeping the foreign policy plans of Władysław's circle were.

153. See his letter of October 24, 1647. Kysil to the king's secretary, Arch. Łodz., Arch. Bart., MS 127, p. 86.

154. October 24, 1647. Kysil to the king's secretary, Arch. Łodz., Arch. Bart., MS 127, pp. 82–86.

155. These universals were drawn up. See, Arch. Łodz., Arch. Bart., MS 127, pp. 86–88 (January 10, 1648) and *Akty Iu.Z.R.*, III, pp. 89–90. November 27, 1647. (N.S.?) Władysław mentioned that various titulature omissions which gave offense to the tsar had been brought to his attention by Kysil. He also discussed the problem of border demarcation. The problem of titulature was not easily resolved. See the lengthy complaints of Trubetskoi, Pushkin, and Chistoi to Kysil of March 15, 1648 (O.S.), *Akty Iu.Z.R.*, III, pp. 160–163. The Muscovite authorities were also upset over the additions to the Polish king's titles. Wiśniowiecki and Ossoliński were included in the list of offenders. See a letter from the above officials to Kysil of March 17, 1648 (O.S.), *Akty Iu.Z.R.*, III, Doc. 162, pp. 164–165.

156. The king followed Kysil's advice and threatened in his universal to the inhabitants of the border areas to punish any Cossacks who attacked Muscovite patrols. *Akty Iu.Z.R.*, III, pp. 89–90. November 27, 1647 (N.S.?)

157. On December 18, 1647, Kysil wrote to the officials Z. S. Leont'ev, *Namestnik* of Kashirsk, and I. S. Kobyl'skii, voevoda of Sevsk, about the return of Shuiskii's monument, *Akty Iu.Z.R.*, III, pp. 93–97. On January 23, 1648, Kysil wrote to the voevoda of Putyvl', Prince Iurii Alekseevich Dolgorukii that the monument had been sent to his estate in Novosilky near Kiev and that as soon as the ice was solid enough on the Dnieper, it would be delivered. *Akty Iu.Z.R.*, III, pp. 108–109. The final details of the transfer are described in a report of Dolgorukii to the tsar, February 19, 1648 (O.S.), *Akty Iu.Z.R.*, III, pp. 137–139.

158. See letters from Kysil to Dolgorukii, March 5, 1648, *Akty Iu.Z.R.*, III, pp. 139–140, and to Leont'ev, March 16, 1648 (O.S.?), *Akty Iu.Z.R.*, III, pp. 163–164.

159. For an example of Kysil's frustration in dealing with his Muscovite colleagues, see his letter of February 23 (O.S.?) to Trubetskoi, Pushkin, and Chistoi, *Akty Iu.Z.R.*, III, pp. 140–141.

160. Kysil's acceptance of favors offended the nineteenth-century historian Ottman's sense of ethics. It is the only negative element in Ottman's glowing evaluation of Kysil as a statesman. See R. Ottman, "Adam z Brusiłowa Kisiel, wojewoda kijowski. Kartka z lat 1648–1649," *Przegląd Powszechny*, vol. IX (1886), 182–205.

161. For Kysil's warnings and provisions of information, see *Akty Iu.Z.R.*, III, pp. 104–106, January 14, 1648, Kysil to Dolgorukii and January 23, 1648, pp. 108–109, Kysil to Dolgorukii. Kysil's information and demands were carefully forwarded to Moscow. See *Akty Iu.Z.R.*, III, pp. 112–113, January 23, 1648 (O.S.).

162. For Kysil's attempts to interpret the treaty in the broadest possible context, see his letter to Dolgorukii, of February 26, 1648, *Akty Iu.Z.R.*, III, pp. 127–128. Kysil defended the Commonwealth's policies toward the Tatars and claimed it was the Tatars who had first worsened relations. In a letter to Nikifor Iurovich Pleshcheev, Voevoda of Putyvl', March 30, 1648, he chided the Muscovites with paying tribute. *Akty Iu.Z.R.*, III, pp. 168–170. For discussion and interpretation of the treaty from the Muscovite view, see Dolgorukii's letter to Kysil (February, 1648, O.S.). *Akty Iu.Z.R.*, III, pp. 119–120.

163. For an example of Kysil's elegant style see his letter to Pleshcheev, March 30, 1648, *Akty Iu.Z.R.*, III, pp. 168–170.

164. In February 1648 (O.S.) Dolgorukii assured Kysil that the Khotmyzh and Sevsk voevodas had been ordered to provide assistance to the Commonwealth in the event of a Tatar attack. *Akty Iu.Z.R.*, III, pp. 119–120.

165. For Kysil's explanation of the Tatars' decision to attack, see his February 1648 (O.S.?) letter to Dolgorukii, *Akty Iu.Z.R.*, III, pp. 131–132, and his letter of February 23, 1648 (O.S.?), *Akty Iu.Z.R.*, III, pp. 142–143. Kysil listed the substantial forces that the Commonwealth had assembled, including 6,000 Cossacks and numerous contingents from magnates. He claimed to have 1,000 of his own men ready.

166. "Relatia," Arch. Gdańsk., MS 300, 53/71, p. 132.

167. October 24, 1648, Arch. Łodz., Arch. Bart., MS 129, p. 86.

168. For an analysis of Muscovy's objectives and difficulties in this period, see Wójcik, *Dzieje Rosji*, pp. 131–138. For the last attempt to ratify the alliance, see Jan Kazimierz's December 6, 1648 instructions to the dietines. Michałowski, p. 216.

169. Łazarz Baranowicz, *Lutnia Apollinowa w każdey sprawie gotowa, na błogosławiąca rękę iako na takt iaki patrząc Iaśnie w Bogu przeoświęconego Iego Mości Oyca Łazarza Baranowicza, Archiepiskopa Czernichowskiego, Nowogrodskiego y wszytkiego Siwierza* (Kiev, 1671), pp. 49–76.

170. B. F. Porshnev states, "Russian-Polish relations became worse and worse in the second half of the 1640s; a breach of the Polianovka Peace became more and more certain." "K kharakteristike mezhdunarodnoi obstanovki osvoboditel'noi voiny ukrainskogo naroda 1648–1654 godov," *Voprosy istorii*, 1954, no. 5, p. 44. N. A. Smirnov sees the period as one in which the Commonwealth sought to draw closer to the Ottoman Empire. "Bor'ba russkogo i ukrainskogo narodov protiv agressii sultanskoi Turtsii v XVII veke," *Voprosy istorii*, 1954, no. 3, p. 92.

171. One finds this view even in the best Soviet work on Commonwealth-Muscovite relations, G. M. Lyzlov, "Pol'sko-Russkie otnosheniia v nachal'nyi period osvoboditel'noi voiny ukrainskogo naroda, 1648–1654 gg. (do Zborovskogo mira)," Akademiia Nauk SSSR, Institut slavianovedeniia, *Kratkie soobshcheniia XXI* (1957), 58–59. For a more dogmatic approach, see O. K. Kasymenko, *Rosiis'ko-ukraïns'ki vzaemovidnosyny 1648-pochatku 1651 r.* (Kiev, 1955), p. 103.

172. V. Golobutskii (Holobuts'kyi), *Diplomaticheskaia istoriia osvoboditel'noi voiny ukrainskogo naroda 1648–1654 gg.* (Kiev, 1962), p. 70.

173. See Lyzlov, "Pol'sko-russkie otnosheniia," p. 62 and Shevchenko, *Politychni ta ekonomichni z"viazky*, pp. 78–81.

Chapter 6

* The massive scholarly literature and source material to the Khmel'nyts'kyi
years can best be approached through the historiographic essays in Hrushevs'kyi
VIII-2, 199–224, the extensive Soviet bibliography *Metodicheskie ukazaniia i
bibliografiia po izucheniiu spetskursa "Osvoboditel'naia voina ukrainskogo naroda 1648–1654 gg. i vossoedinenie Ukrainy s Rossiei"* pt. 1 (Dnipropetrovs'k,
1980), and John Basarab, *Pereiaslav 1654: A Historiographical Study* (Edmonton, 1982). For Polish historiography, see Bohdan Baranowski and Zofia Libiszowska, "Problem narodowo-wyzwoleńczej walki ludu ukraińskiego w XVII w.
w historiografii polskiej," *Kwartalnik Historyczny,* LXI, no. 2 (1954), 197–217.
For a discussion of seventeenth century West European accounts as sources to
the period, see D. S. Nalyvaiko, "Zakhidnoevropeis'ki istoryko-literaturni
dzherela pro vyzvol'nu viinu ukraïnskoho narodu 1648–1654 rr.," *Ukraïns'kyi
istorychnyi zhurnal,* 1969, no. 3, pp. 137–144; no. 9, pp. 137–143; no. 10,
pp. 134–145; no. 11, pp. 131–136; no. 12, pp. 128–132.

The most comprehensive work on the Khmel'nyts'kyi period is Hrushevs'kyi
VIII-2, VIII-3, IX-1, IX-2. For his evaluation of Khmel'nyts'kyi and the period, see Mykhail Hrushevs'kyi, "Khmel'nyts'kyi-Khmel'nyshchyna-Istorychnyi
eskiz," *ZNTSh,* XXIII–XXIV (1898), 1–30. Also, see the extensive review of
Hrushevs'kyi's work by Korduba. Miron [Myron] Korduba, "Der Ukraine Niedergang und Aufschwung," *Zeitschrift für Osteuropäische Geschichte,* VI (New
Series II) (1932), 36–60, 193–230, 358–385. Of the older historiography, Kulish
is of particular interest because of all Ukrainian historians he alone violently
condemned the Khmel'nyts'kyi movement. Panteleimon Kulish, *Otpadenie Malorossii ot Pol'shi, 1340–1654,* 3 vols. (Moscow, 1888). For recent Soviet interpretations of the period, see the collection, Akademiia Nauk SSSR, Institut
istorii, Institut slavianovedeniia. Akademiia Nauk Ukr. SSR, Institut istorii,
Vossoedinenie Ukrainy s Rossiei 1654–1954. Sbornik statei (Moscow, 1954) and
Akademiia Nauk Ukrainskoi SSR, Institut istorii, *Osvoboditel'naia voina 1648–
1654 gg. i vossoedinenie Ukrainy s Rossiei* (Kiev, 1954). For a Marxist study that
appeared before the current cult of the "Reunion," see Mykola Petrovs'kyi,
*Vyzvol'na viina ukraïnskoho narodu proty hnitu shliakhets'koi Pol'shchi i pryed-
nannia Ukraïny do Rossii, 1648–1654 rr.* (Kiev, 1940). For an interpretation of
the period by a member of the "Statist" school (*dershavnyts'ka shkola*) see
Oleksander Ohloblyn, *Dumky pro Khmel'nychchynu* (New York, 1957). Also
see his *Problema derzhavnoï vlady na Ukraïni za Khmel'nychchyny i Pereiaslavs'ka uhoda 1654 roku* (Munich, 1966). Kysil, as a major leader of the period,
is mentioned in almost all studies, including seventeenth-century histories of the
movement. See, for example, S. Oświęcim, *Dyaryusz,* pp. 46, 49, 111, 205, 222,
265–266, 269, 273, 285, 307, 344, 370–371; Ks. Sadok Barącz, ed., *Pamiętnik
zakonu WWOO Bernardynów w Polszcze* (Lviv, 1874), pp. 140–148, 181;
S. Temberski, *Roczniki,* pp. 91, 153, 164–165, 168; Joachim Pastorius, *Bellum
Scythico-Cosacicum seu de conjuratione tartarorum cosacorum et plebis Russicae
contra Regnum Poloniae . . .* (Gdańsk, 1652), pp. 20–21, contains a Latin summary of Kysil's first letter to Khmel'nyts'kyi; Albertus Wiiuk Koialowicz, *De
rebus anno 1648 & 1649 contra Zaporovios Cosacos gestis* (Vilnius, 1651),

pp. 96–97, Maiolino Bisaccioni, *Historia delle guerre civili di questi ultimi tempi scritta dal Conte* . . . (Venice, 1663), pp. 291–294, 303, 315, 323–325. Other contemporary accounts and histories will be cited in the footnotes.

For foreign policy in the Khmel'nyts'kyi period, see Golobutskii, *Diplomaticheskaia istoriia*. Although this study is tendentious and far from exhaustive, it has a useful historiographical introduction, pp. 3–33. Also see F. P. Shevchenko, "Dyplomatychna sluzhba na Ukraïni pid chas vyzvol'noï viiny 1648–1654 rr.," *Istorychni dzherela ta ïkh vykorystannia* I (1964), 81–113; and Porshnev's "K kharateristike," pp. 44–58. The major discussions of the national and religious factors in the Khmel'nyts'kyi movement are Viacheslav Lypyns'kyi's studies, Wacław Lipiński, "Stanisław Michał Krzyczewski," in Wacław Lipiński, ed., *Z dziejów* and Viacheslav Lypyns'kyi, *Ukraïna na perelomi, 1657–1659* (Vienna, 1920) and Frank E. Sysyn, "Ukrainian-Polish Relations in the Seventeenth Century." Lypyns'kyi also demonstrated the considerable participation of the nobility in the Khmel'nyts'kyi movement. A persuasive case against interpreting the Khmel'nyts'kyi movement solely as a struggle between classes or social orders is made by Ivan Franko in "Khmel'nyshchyna 1648–1649 u suchasnykh virshakh," *ZNTSh*, XXIII–XXIV (1898), 1–114. For a discussion of interpretations of the war, see Frank E. Sysyn, "Seventeenth-Century Views on the Causes of the Khmel'nyts'kyi Uprising: An Examination of the 'Discourse on the Present Cossack or Peasant War.'" For the development of institutions and administration in Cossack Ukraine, see Ivan Kryp"iakevych, "Studiï nad derzhavoiu Bohdana Khmel'nyts'koho," in *ZNTSh*, CXXXVIII–CXL (1925), 67–81; CXLIV–CXLV (1926), 109–140; CXLVII (1927), 55–80; CLI (1931), 111–156.

For the violence of 1648, see the outdated, but well-written study by Karol Szajnocha, *Dwa lata dziejów naszych, 1646, 1648* (Szajnocha II, III) and Hrushevs'kyi VIII–2, 140–195, VIII–3, 7–101. The major source about the violence against Jews is the Hannover Chronicle. Nathan Hannover, *Abyss of Dispair: The Famous 17th Century Chronicle Depicting Jewish Life during the Chmielnicki Massacres of 1648–49,* trans. Abraham J. Mesch (New York, 1950). Also, see Bernard D. Weinryb, "The Hebrew Chronicles on Bohdan Khmel'nyts'kyi and the Cossack-Polish War," *Harvard Ukrainian Studies*, I, no. 2 (June 1977), 153–177. The destructive aspects of 1648 are emphasized in Franciszek Rawita-Gawroński, *Bohdan Chmielnicki do elekcyi Jana Kazimierza* (Lviv, 1906), pp. 236–249.

1. On Koniecpolski's career, see Leszek Podhorodecki, *Stanisław Koniecpolski ok. 1592–1646* (Warsaw, 1978).

2. On Potocki, see the entry in *Polski słownik biograficzny*.

3. The best discussion of Mohyla's place in the Commonwealth is in Halina Kowalska's "Piotr Mohiła," *Polski słownik biograficzny* XXI/3 (1976), 568–572.

4. Sources on contacts between the king and the Cossacks are examined in Czermak, *Plany wojny tureckiej Władysława IV.*

5. On the campaigns of Wiśniowiecki and Koniecpolski, see Tomkiewicz, *Jeremi Wiśniowiecki*, pp. 177–179.

6. The letter is dated February 23 without any indication of calendar. Usu-

ally Kysil added "Roman date" to the letters he sent to Muscovy and used the new style. The editors of *Akty* assume that the date is Old Style. If this assumption is correct, the letter was sent on March 5 (N.S.), *Akty Iu.Z.R.*, III, pp. 142–143.

7. *Akty Iu.Z.R.*, III, pp. 166–169.

8. For an account of Khmel'nyts'kyi's career, see Ivan Kryp"iakevych, *Bohdan Khmel'nyts'kyi*. Other major biographies are: Nikolai Kostomarov, *Bogdan Khmel'nitskii, Istoricheskaia monografiia*, 3 vols., 4th ed. (St. Petersburg, 1884) (= *Istoricheskie monografii i issledovaniia N. Kostomarova*, IX, X, XI); Franciszek Rawita-Gawroński, *Bohdan Chmielnicki do elekcyi* and *Bohdan Chmielnicki od elekcyi Jana Kazimierza do śmierci (1648–1657)* (Lviv, 1909). For an evaluation of Khmel'nyts'kyi, see Olgierd Górka, "Bohdan Chmielnicki, jego historycy, postać i dzieło," in Polska Akademia Nauk, *Sesja naukowa w trzechsetną rocznicę zjednoczenia Ukrainy z Rosją. 1654–1954. Materiały* (Warsaw, 1956), pp. 65–103, and Tadeusz Korzon, "O Chmielnickim: Sądy PP. Kulisza i Karpowa," *Kwartalnik Historyczny*, IV (1892), 34–79. Concerning Khmel'nyts'kyi's social and political views, see I. P. Kryp"iakevych, "Sotsial'no-politychni pohliady Bohdana Khmel'nyts'koho," *Ukraïns'kyi istorychnyi zhurnal*, 1957, no. 1, pp. 94–105. Also see George Vernadsky, *Bohdan: Hetman of Ukraine* (New Haven, 1941).

9. For sources on the early stages of the revolt, see Wiesław Majewski, "Krytyczny przegląd źródeł do dziejów powstania Chmielnickiego w okresie początkowym (jesień 1647-maj 1648)," *Studia Źródłoznawcze*, XXVI (1981), 141–164.

10. This was the original, but unanswered problem of W. Czermak, *Plany wojny tureckiej Władysława IV.* For a discussion of contacts between the Zaporozhians and the king, see Czermak, *Plany*, pp. 299–326. Kubala, *Jerzy Ossoliński*, pp. 251–265.

11. On Khmel'nyts'kyi's alliance, see Bohdan Baranowski, "Geneza sojuszu kozacko-tatarskiego z 1648 r.," *Przegląd Historyczny*, XXXVII (1948), 276–287. For Cossack-Ottoman relations, see Omeljan Pritsak, "Das erste türkisch-ukrainische Bündnis (1648)," *Oriens*, VI (1953), 266–293. For a major source in Polish translation concerning Tatar politics, see Hadży Mehmed Senai, *Historia Chana Islam Gereja III*, ed. Zygmunt Abrahamowicz (Warsaw, 1971), which has extensive notes and Benningsen, *Le Khanat de Crimée*, pp. 167–197.

12. Five letters from Potocki to Kysil and three letters from Kysil to Potocki from March to June 1648 survive in copies in BO, MS 206, fols. 72–95. Many of these are undated. BJ, MS 49, pp. 449, 455–456 contains two additional letters written in March by Potocki as well as a letter from that month written by Kysil to the king. Five of the eight letters in the Ossolineum codex are published in *DOVUN*. A letter from Kysil to Potocki of March 16 is published in Rawita-Gawroński, ed., *Sprawy*, pp. 79–82.

13. Kysil to Potocki, BO, MS 206, fols. 72–75. Potocki to Kysil, March 6, 1648, BJ, MS 49, pp. 447–448; March 14, 1648, BJ, MS 49, p. 449. Potocki to Kysil, March 25, 1648, BJ, MS 49, pp. 455–456.

14. See BO, MS 206, fols. 75–77, and BO, MS 206, fols. 77–79. These undated letters are published in *DOVUN*, pp. 16–22.

15. Potocki to Kysil, April 14, 1648, BO, MS 206, fols. 79–80 (published in *DOVUN*, pp. 24–26), also BO, MS 206, fols. 80–81, 81–82 (published in *DOVUN*, pp. 26–27).

16. *DOVUN*, pp. 16–18.

17. On the defeats at Korsun' and Zhovti Vody, see E. M. Apanovich, "Pobedy ukrainskogo naroda nad pol'sko-shliakhetskimi voiskami na nachal'nom etape osvoboditel'noi voiny (1648 g.)," *Vossoedinenie Ukrainy s Rossiei, 1654–1954*, pp. 78–105.

18. BO, MS 206, fols. 77–79 (published in *DOVUN*, pp. 26–27); BO, MS 206, fols. 80–81.

19. Szajnocha II, 272–275 (published from BO, MS 231, fols. 146–148, now in LNB); BO, MS 206, fols. 82–85; BK, MS 991, fols. 369–370.

20. Szajnocha II, 274. Kysil particularly feared the Muscovites' reaction if a civil war broke out in the Commonwealth. Also, see his letter to Ossoliński of May 26, 1648 in LNB, MS 231, fols. 158–159.

21. Hrushevs'kyi VIII–3, 189.

22. Kysil's letter of May 31, 1648 to Chancellor Ossoliński, BO, MS 206, fols. 88–90.

23. Published in *Voss.* II, 25–30; *Pam.* I, 26–42; Michałowski, pp. 26–31. Manuscript copies: AGAD, Arch Rad., Dział II, Ks. 14, pp. 26–34; BO, MS 189, pp. 73–77; BO, MS 206, fols. 82–85; BO, MS 3564, fols. 23–27; Arch. Gdańsk., MS 300 R/ Ee 32, pp. 238–243; BCz, MS 2576, pp. 105–109; BCz, MS 377, pp. 735–738; BK, MS 991, fols. 370–372; Recesy, MS 300, 29/129, fols. 104–106; LNB, MS 231, fols. 161–164.

24. The best discussion of Khmel'nyts'kyi's political motivations is Ivan Kryp"iakevych, "Sotsial'no-politychni pohliady." For Khmel'nyts'kyi's historical consciousness see F. P. Shevchenko, "Istorychne mynule v otsintsi B. Khmel'nyts'koho," *Ukraïns'kyi istorychnyi zhurnal*, 1970, no. 12, pp. 126–132. Kysil was so uncomfortable about his "being descended from Ruthenian blood" that he mentioned his ancesters' services to their present Fatherland. *Voss.* II, 26.

25. *DOVUN*, pp. 36–37 (published from BO, MS 206, fols. 95–96). Primate Łubieński wrote requesting Kysil's services, in particular in Muscovite affairs, on June 8. *DOVUN*, pp. 44–47 (from BO, MS 206, fols. 96–97). Kysil had requested Muscovite assistance long before Łubieński's authorization. He had written to the border voevodas in May. Kysil's letter is mentioned in Prince Semen Bolkhovskoi's letter of June 4 (O.S.), *Akty Iu.Z.R.*, III, 204–205. This action is evidence of the great power Kysil appropriated for himself in deciding the Commonwealth's Muscovite policy.

26. Arch. Gdańsk., MS 300, R/Ee 32, pp. 237–238.

27. The letter's copies are undated, but mistakenly dated as June 12 by the editor of Michałowski. It had to be earlier, since Khmel'nyts'kyi replied on June 13. Michałowski, pp. 46–48; BO, MS 206, fols. 90–92; BO, MS 189,

pp. 104–107; LBN, MS 205, fols. 58–59, 53–54 (mentioned in *Vyz.*, pp. 23–24). For Khmel'nyts'kyi's letter, see *DKh.*, pp. 39–41. Kysil's comment that he was the only "Christian of the Ruthenian Nation" who was a senator in the Commonwealth was not correct. Although he was the only palatine, Maksymilian Bzhozovs'kyi was castellan of Kiev. See Władysław Tomkiewicz, "Brzozowski, Maksymilian," *Polski słownik biograficzny,* III, 66. Kysil undoubtedly found it easier to write to Khmel'nyts'kyi about a common "Fatherland" because Khmel'nyts'kyi was himself a noble. On Khmel'nyts'kyi's descent, see Kryp"iakevych, "Sotsial'no-politychni pohliady," pp. 94–95.

28. For a discussion of Khmel'nyts'kyi's goals at this time, see Hrushevs'kyi VIII–3, 3–21 and the extensive review of Hrushevs'kyi's work, by Miron [Myron] Korduba, "Der Ukraine Niedergang und Aufschwung," *Zeitschrift für Osteuropäische Geschichte,* VI (new series II) (1932), 53–57. The Papal Nuncio de Torres reported that it was said that Khmel'nyts'kyi was willing to negotiate in order to avoid submission to the Tatars, but he himself saw the move as a ploy. June 17, 1648, *Litterae Nuntiorum*, VI, 264. Most of the documents cited from 1648 to 1653 in *Litterae Nuntiorum* were published by Stepan Tomashivs'kyi in *Vatykans'ki materiialy do istorii Ukraïny*, vol. 1, pt. 1 (Lviv, 1919), as volume XVI of *Zherela do istorii Ukraïny*, 16 vols. (Lviv, 1895–1919). Hereafter *Zherela.*)

29. Michałowski, p. 50; *Pam* I, 88–92; BCz, MS 379, pp. 19–20; BCz, MS 2576, p. 127; BCz, MS 400, p. 10; BO, MS 5768, fols. 202–217 (now in Lviv Academy, *Vyz.*, p. 25); Recesy MS 300, 29/129, fol. 111. Date July 18 is in Steinwehr III, fol. 247. For Khmel'nyts'kyi's letter of June 13, 1648, see *D.Kh.*, pp. 39–41.

30. See the letters of June 3, 1648. Kysil to Ossoliński, Szajnocha II, 281. Arch. Gdańsk., MS 300, R/Ee 32, pp. 237–238 and Recesy, MS 300, 29/129, fol. 111, and the undated letter, BO, MS 206, fols. 9–95; Arch. Gdańsk., MS 300, R/Ee 32, p. 331. For his exposition on the need for a king, see his undated letter, BO, MS 206, fols. 94–95; Arch. Gdańsk., MS 300, R/Ee 32, p. 331.

31. He did so because the *interrex,* Maciej Łubieński, was infirm and almost eighty years of age. See Wacław Urban, "Łubieński, Maciej (1572–1652)," *Polski słownik biograficzny,* XVIII, 491–493.

32. *DOVUN,* pp. 50–52. Ossoliński was particularly critical of the tsar's candidacy.

33. June 18, 1648, Arch. Gdańsk., MS 300, R/Ee 32, 265.

34. For a discussion of papal policy in this period, see Eduard Winter, *Russland und das Papsttum*, 3 parts (Berlin, 1960–1972) (= Quellen und Studien zur Geschichte Osteuropas VI), I, 315–332.

35. See Kysil's letter to the primate of May 31, 1648 (cf. fn. 23). For his use of "one blood, one religion," see *Voss.* II, 26.

36. The final order that a Muscovite army would support the Commonwealth against the Tatars came in late May. Bolkhovskoi reported his readiness on June 4, 1648 (O.S.), *Akty Iu.Z.R.,* III, 203–204. By July the Muscovite govern-

ment expressed its growing reluctance, particularly in light of the absence of a monarch in the Commonwealth. Letter of the tsar and boyars to Kysil, July 13 (O.S.), 7156 [1648], LNB, MS 225, fols. 172–174.

37. See Khmel'nyts'kyi's letter to the tsar, *DKh.*, pp. 48–49. For Khmel'nyts'kyi's fear of Muscovy's intentions, see Seredyka, "Stosunki ukraiń-sko-rosyjskie w 1648," pp. 169–172. For Khmel'nyts'kyi's position, see Hrushevs'kyi VIII–3, 9–12.

38. The Soviet scholar Kasymenko, strongly rejects this interpretation of the letter, and insists that Khmel'nyts'kyi intended the "reunion of the Ukraine with Russia," *Rosiis'ko-ukraïns'ki, vzaiemovidnosyny* pp. 89–94. He criticizes Kryp"iakevych for interpreting the letter as referring to the election.

39. For Khmel'nyts'kyi's policies in this period, see Hrushevs'kyi VIII–3, 7–23.

40. *Voss.* II, 44–46; *Zherela* XII, 66 (= *Materiialy do istoriï ukraïns'koï ko-zachchyny,* vol. V, part 1, *Akty do Khmel'nychchyny [1648–1654],* ed. Myron Korduba [Lviv, 1911]) (From BO, MS 225, pp. 85–87 now in LNB); BCz, MS 142, pp. 479–484; Arch. Gdańsk., MS 300, R/Ee 32, pp. 346–348.

41. Hrushevs'kyi VIII–3, 18–21.

42. See his suggestions to Kysil, July 1, 1648, Szajnocha II, 292–293.

43. Kubala, *Jerzy Ossoliński,* pp. 270–273.

44. See Tomkiewicz, *Jeremi Wiśniowiecki,* pp. 190–192 on the problem of appointments of commanders and Kubala, *Jerzy Ossoliński,* p. 272.

45. For a more critical evaluation of Wiśniowiecki's activities than that of Tomkiewicz, see Miron Korduba, "Jeremias Wisniowiecki im Lichte der neuen Forschung," *Zeitschrift für Osteuropäische Geschichte,* VIII (new series IV) (1934), 221–238.

46. For Kysil's evaluation of Wiśniowiecki as a hothead who lacked intelligence and prudence, see his letter of the following year to Ossoliński. April 24, 1649. Arch. Kr., Pinocciana, MS 363, pp. 305–310.

47. Kysil to Wiśniowiecki (undated), Michałowski, pp. 54–55.

48. Wiśniowiecki to Kysil, June 21, 1648, Michałowski, pp. 55–56; BCz, MS 1656, pp. 122–123, 153–154; BO, MS 3564, fols. 49–50. Rawita-Gawroński maintains that a letter by Kysil he published dated June 22 and without an adressee was an answer to Wiśniowiecki. I would doubt this hypothesis since this letter does not answer any of the questions posed. *Sprawy,* pp. 82–84.

49. June 24, 1648 (to Wiśniowiecki), BCz, MS 2576, pp. 128–129; June 24, 1648 (to Tyszkiewicz), LNB, MS 225, fols. 64–66.

50. *Arkhiv Iu. Z. R.,* pt. III, vol. IV (Kiev, 1914), 18–20. This volume is entitled, *Akty, otnosiashchiesia k epokhe Bogdana Khmel'nitskogo.*

51. Ossoliński referred to a joint dietine that the "four palatinates" would hold. Letter of June 16, 1648, *DOVUN,* p. 52. Kysil had written to Ossoliński in an undated letter that his presence at the dietine in Luts'k depended on the situation in the Ukraine. BO, MS 206, fols. 88–90. For a report on the course of the dietine see Kysil's letter to Ossoliński from Luts'k on June 29, Rawita-Gawroński, ed., *Sprawy,* pp. 84–87. Kysil was unsure whether he should return

to Hoshcha in order to begin negotiations with the Cossacks or proceed through Hniino to the Convocation. In this letter he reported on the Cossacks' eleven points and mentioned that a return to the Kurkuriv ordinance (1625) could be expected, since it was inconceivable that the Cossacks would accept the ordinance of 1638.

52. See the Volhynian dietine's instructions, BN, BOZ, MS 931, fols. 177–182. At the Convocation Diet, the palatinates of the incorporation lands were especially interested in restoring peace. Steinwehr III, fol. 257.

53. See the map in Kryp"iakevych, *Bohdan*, facing p. 132.

54. June 30, 1648, Kysil to Łubieński from Hoshcha, Michałowski, pp. 65–68. For Łubieński's correspondence to Kysil at this time, see his letter of July 1, LBN, MS 225, fols. 73–74.

55. Kysil apparently left for Warsaw after July 7. He wrote from Hoshcha reporting on Lasko's second mission. *DOVUN*, pp. 71–73, and Lasko did not return until July 7, Szajnocha II, pp. 192–195, *Voss.* II, 44–48; BCz, MS 142, pp. 479–484.

56. Khmel'nyts'kyi wrote to Kysil on June 27 asking for his continued support, *D.Kh.*, pp. 51–53.

57. June 12, 1648, *D.Kh.*, pp. 36–38.

58. Kubala, *Jerzy Ossoliński*, pp. 281–282.

59. Ossoliński had attempted to have the Convocation Diet declared an Election Diet, and there was considerable dissatisfaction that Ossoliński was tampering with election procedures. June 10, 1648, Report of Michał Behm. Recesy, MS 300, 29/129, fols. 83–84. Also see Behm's comment in his letter of June 14, Recesy, MS 300, 29/129, fols. 89–90.

60. Kubala, *Jerzy Ossoliński*, pp. 281–282.

61. The most detailed description of the Convocation Diet is in Kubala, *Jerzy Ossoliński*, pp. 281–300. For Kysil's attendance, see Steinwehr III, fol. 256.

62. See Kubala, *Jerzy Ossoliński*, pp. 287–289 for examples of the two men's cooperation. Also see Ossoliński's letter to Kysil of July 2, 1648, LNB, MS 231, fols. 175–177.

63. The account of the Convocation Diet is based on the following diaries: Published: 1. Michałowski, pp. 101–144; 2. Radziwiłł, *Memoriale*, IV, 20–43; 3. *DOVUN*, pp. 79–82 (fragment from BJ 90, fol. 506). Unpublished: 1. BO, MS 3564, fols. 71–80; 2. BCz, MS 378, pp. 580–605; 3. PANK, MS 367, fols. 87–95; 4. Arch. Gdańsk., MS 300, R/Ee 32, pp. 41, 42, 47, 55, 101–102; 5. Steinwehr III, fols. 256–264; 6. Recesy, MS 300/29, 129, fols. 436–461; 7. Recesy, MS 300/29, 129, fols. 486–529. One of the best contemporary analyses of the Convocation Diet is a letter written on June 22, 1648 by Jan Wojakowski. He reports the small attendance at the Diet and that almost all the senators present favored peace. He recounts the reception of the Cossack delegates and the search for secret communications between Władysław and the Zaporozhians. Wojakowski also reports a debate over how Khmel'nyts'kyi should be addressed, during which Kysil argued for recognition of him as "starszy" despite the fact that he had not formally received the title from the gov-

ernment. Finally, the report includes a discussion of the problem of selecting a military leadership. Wojakowski also reports that the Orthodox delegates complained of the treatment of their faith. Arch. Kr. Zbiory Rusieckich, MS 41, pp. 31–34.

64. Michałowski, pp. 104–105; Radziwiłł, *Memoriale*, IV, 21; Steinwehr III, fol. 256; Recesy MS 300/29, 129, fol. 436.

65. Kysil to Sanguszko, June 19, 1648, BCz, MS 142, pp. 273–276. Published in *Arkhiv Iu. Z. R.*, pt. III, vol. IV, 18–20 without an addressee.

66. June 22, 1648. Letter of Kysil to unknown addressee. Rawita-Gawroński, ed., *Sprawy*, p. 83.

67. Michałowski, p. 105; BO, MS 3567, fol. 72; Recesy, MS 300/29, 129, fol. 492.

68. Kubala maintains that Ossoliński's "hard line" at the Diet was merely a pose. *Jerzy Ossoliński*, pp. 283–284.

69. Kubala, *Jerzy Ossoliński*, pp. 283–287. For Wiśniowiecki's activities, see Tomkiewicz, *Jeremi Wiśniowiecki*, pp. 211–225.

70. A letter to a dietine on June 24. Michałowski, pp. 56–62. Lubomirski's response to Kysil's attempt to win his favor is published in *DOVUN*, pp. 47–50 (June 14, 1648).

71. For Zasławski's views see his letter of July 26. Michałowski, pp. 89–90. For its impact on the Diet, see Steinwehr III, fol. 257.

72. Ostroróg to Łubieński, June 6, 1648. Arch. Gdańsk., MS 300, R/Ee 32, p. 331.

73. Michałowski, p. 105. Kubala, *Jerzy Ossoliński*, pp. 288–289.

74. In answering demands to see the letters of the king presumed to be in a box the Cossack delegates had brought to the Diet, Kysil discussed three major causes of the military disasters: the preparation of hostilities by the Tatars, the discontent and vexation of the Cossacks, and the rash policies of Potocki. Kysil discussed his role in negotiations and reminded the Diet of the Pavliuk incident. Steinwehr III, fol. 256. His letters had been intercepted by a servitor of Prince Dominik Zasławski and held for two weeks. Recesy, MS 300/29, 129, fol. 458. A delegate from the Sandomierz palatinate defended Zasławski, and Ossoliński had to intervene to restore calm.

75. One of Kysil's major themes was the loss of his fortune. In a letter which he wrote on June 22 (incorrectly attributed to Wiśniowiecki by Rawita-Gawroński) Kysil discussed the loss of 100,000 złoty income from his Left-Bank lands, the plundering of his estates in the Kiev palatinate, the fact that his Volhynian properties could not possibly support him and the 300,000 złoty debt he had incurred. Rawita-Gawroński, ed., *Sprawy*, p. 83.

76. See Kysil's speech before the special committee in BO, MS 3567, fols. 76–77. He put forth his suggestions for the commission in this talk. Also see Recesy, MS 300/29, 129, fol. 495; Radziwiłł, *Memoriale*, IV, 25–26, and BO, MS 3567, fols. 76–77. For a summary of Kysil's argumentation at the Convocation Diet see "Rationes veniam dandam esse Cozacis rebellibus z Sentimentu Jemści Pana Kisiela, Woiewody Bracławskiego." Point 9 includes the phrase "they should choose the lesser of two evils." BO, MS 3564, fol. 49.

77. During the entire summer of 1648, rumors spread of a Muscovite invasion into the Siverian lands and Smolensk and at times the loyalty of the inhabitants of the Grand Duchy was questioned. Letter of Zasławski to Łubieński, July 23, 1648, Arch. Gdańsk., MS 300, 53/71, pp. 163–164.

78. BO, MS 3567, fols. 76–77.

79. For the Diet's instructions to the commissioners, see *DOVUN,* pp. 87–91.

80. See Ludwik Weiher, letter of July 31, 1648, BO, MS 3564, fols. 78–80. Also, see BO, MS 3567, fols. 77–78.

81. Ludwik Weiher, July 31, 1648, BO, MS 3564, fols. 78–80.

82. Kubala, *Jerzy Ossoliński,* pp. 297–298.

83. At the Convocation Diet, Pac levied a protest against Kysil for not having waited for him before negotiating in Moscow. BO, MS 3567, fol. 75. Jerzy Sornell charged in a letter to Jerzy Grabowski that Khmel'nyts'kyi had Kysil on his side "about this one should not doubt although at the Convocation he was publicly praised and thanked." He made these charges on the basis of a prisoner's confession. Arch. Gdańsk., MS 300, R/Ee 32, pp. 433–434.

84. At the Convocation Diet some delegates maintained within hearing distance of Kysil that they did not know whom to trust "when they are of one faith and one baptism with them (the rebels)," Steinwehr III, fols. 257–258.

85. In 1647, Papal Nuncio de Torres had accepted Kysil's statements that only "human considerations" held him back from conversion. Dispatches of July 13, 1647, *Litterae Nuntiorum,* VI, 223–224. When reporting events at the Convocation Diet to Cardinal Francesco Ingoli, Pietro Saracino, a Uniate priest from Italy assigned to the Diocese of Chełm, concurred with de Torres' views. Saracino added the qualifying statement "according to external signs." Excerpts of a letter of August 2, 1648, Šmurlo I, p. 259, footnote 250. For de Torres' evaluation of Kysil's importance during this period, see his dispatches of August 12, 1648. *Litterae Nuntiorum,* VI, 282–283, 284–285.

86. Saracino to Ingoli discusses negotiations before and during the Diet, August 2, 1648, Šmurlo I, 259, footnote 250. For the religious turmoil at the Diet, see the diary published in Michałowski, pp. 122–123, BCz, MS 378, fol. 591 and BO, MS 3567, fol. 74. Also see Wacław Lipiński, "Stanisław Krzyczewski," in *Z dziejów Ukrainy,* pp. 172–173.

87. De Torres, Dispatches of August 12, 1648, *Litterae Nuntiorum,* VI, 282–283, 284–285.

88. For the course of the rebellion in this period, see Hrushevs'kyi VIII–3, 27–65.

89. On Wiśniowiecki's activities in this period, see Tomkiewicz, *Jeremi Wiśniowiecki,* pp. 213–236.

90. For a description of the social strife, see Kryp"iakevych, *Bohdan,* pp. 135–144 and Apanovych, "Pobedy," pp. 163–169. Khmel'nyts'kyi's antagonism to Wiśniowiecki led the Cossack hetman to declare the prince's estates confiscated. Letter to Samuel Łaszcz, July 29, 1648, *D.Kh.,* pp. 59–60.

91. On Khmel'nyts'kyi's motivations, see Hrushevs'kyi VIII–3, 49–52.

92. Kysil to Ossoliński, July 31, 1648, Rawita-Gawroński, ed., *Sprawy,* pp. 87–89. Kysil to Łubieński, August 4, 1648, Szajnocha III, 209; BO, MS 3564, fols. 82–83; BN, BOZ, MS 1217, fols. 294–295; Recesy, MS 300, 29/ 129, fol. 162.

93. Kysil to Ossoliński, July 31, 1648, Rawita-Gawroński, ed., *Sprawy,* pp. 87–89.

94. See Kysil's letter of August 9 to Ossoliński, Michałowski, pp. 151–153; *Pam.* I, 190–198; Arch. Gdańsk., MS 300, R/Ee 32, pp. 437–439; LBN, MS 225, fols. 115–117. (*Vyz.* p. 46).

95. Michałowski, pp. 151–153 (cited in note 94).

96. For hypotheses on Khmel'nyts'kyi's motives, see Hrushevs'kyi VIII–3, 59–65.

97. See citation, footnote 94.

98. *DOVUN*, pp. 97–99; *Vyz.*, p. 47; Arch. Gdańsk., MS 300, R/Ee 32, pp. 431–433, 440–441; BO, MS 3564, fol. 94; mistakenly dated August 2 in Michałowski, pp. 149–150.

99. Szajnocha III, 210–213.

100. Michałowski, pp. 159–160; *Pam.* I, 216–218; BCz, MS 379, p. 80; Stein-wehr III, fol. 275; Arch. Gdańsk., MS 300, R/Ee 32, p. 397. Also see his letter of August 24, 1648 to Primate Łubieński, LNB, MS 225, fol. 110.

101. For the armies' activities in this period, see Tomkiewicz, *Jeremi Wiśnio-wiecki,* pp. 225–241.

102. The best account of the Ostroh incident is Kysil's commission's diary for August 30, Michałowski, pp. 170–174; *Vyz.* p. 31; BCz, MS 379, pp. 89–93; Arch. Gdańsk., MS 300, R/Ee 32, pp. 557–560, 573—576; Recesy, MS 300, 29/ 129, fols. 183–184.

103. Kysil to senators, Michałowski, pp. 161–163; *Pam.* I, 231–238; (n.d.) AGAD, Arch. Rad., dział II, book 14, pp. 133–136; BK, MS 991, fol. 386. The reaction of the Senate in Warsaw to events in Volhynia in late August and early September is recorded in Senate Consultation minutes, Arch. Gdańsk., MS 300, R/Ee 32, pp. 161–164. Considerable attention was paid to Tatar affairs. The letters exchanged between Kysil, Wiśniowiecki, and the military commissioners were read at the Senate meetings. Wiśniowiecki's letter of August 27 accused Kysil of not defending Ostroh, even though he had considerable military forces. This letter is published in Michałowski, pp. 160–161, and *Pam.* I, 219–226 as from the military commissioners, but it is identical in content to the letter sum-marized in the Senate minutes as from Wiśniowiecki himself. Kysil's answer to Wiśniowiecki, his letter of August 31 to the primate raising hopes for negotia-tions, and a diary of August 30 of the peace commissioners were read. In another report of the Senate meeting of September 16, Wiśniowiecki's accusations against Kysil are mentioned. Arch. Gdańsk., MS 300, R/Ee 32, p. 178. Some senators were concerned over the lack of information from the military camp. On September 17, Vice-Chancellor Leszczyński lauded Wiśniowiecki, but even he was not ready to take the step of calling out a levy of the nobility. Ossoliński also spoke on the uncertain situation and maintained that Kysil had given the

Commonwealth time to gather troops. Arch. Gdańsk., MS 300, R/Ee 32, pp. 173–185. Also see, Kysil to military commissioners, Michałowski, p. 169; *Vyz.*, p. 31; Arch. Gdańsk., MS 300, R/Ee 32, pp. 408–410, 425–427.

104. August 27, 1648. Military commissioners to Kysil, Michałowski, pp. 160–161; *Pam.* I, 219–226; BCz, MS 379, pp. 88–89; *Vyz.*, p. 31; BK, MS 991, fol. 386.

105. August 25, 1648, Kysil to Khmel'nyts'kyi, *Pam.* I, 238–248, Michałowski, pp. 164–166 (mistakenly dated August 27); LNB, MS 225, fols. 132–135 (*Vyz.*, p. 31).

106. See Khmel'nyts'kyi's letter to the commissioners of August 19 and 28, 1648, *DKh.*, pp. 65–68.

107. Kysil also faced problems in mid-September with his troops due to lack of funds. Arch. Gdańsk., MS 300, R/EE 32, pp. 415–416. Delegates from the commissioners also questioned Kysil about his supervision of the negotiations. He was bluntly asked to name the traitor who was reporting on the Commonwealth's secrets to Khmel'nyts'kyi. When he did not make a direct response, it was presumed that he himself was the traitor. The delegates made final agreements over the terms on which Kysil would conclude his negotations. Relations were far from cordial. Kysil was on the defensive in these consultations and to questions of whether the negotations had any chances or not he replied, "I do not have any prophetic spirit to know whether they will be or not." Dzierslaw Slugocki went so far as to write: "Who cannot understand by now how God has punished us with this person," Dzierslaw Slugocki, Stolnik of Lublin, to Niezabitowski, Michałowski, pp. 182–184. On September 6, Kysil wrote to Tyszkiewicz, regretting that he had not encountered him at the camp, and reporting the near hopelessness of the peace mission. Kysil also denied the rumors which were circulating about him. BCz, MS 143, pp. 31–32. Dated September 5 in BCz, MS 2576, p. 245.

108. Kysil and commissioners to Łubieński and Commonwealth, September 13, 1648. Michałowski, pp. 184–186; BCz, MS 379, pp. 94–96; AGAD, Arch. Rad., II, book 14, pp. 147–152; BO, MS 189, pp. 144–145. Steinwehr III, fols. 274–275; Arch. Gdańsk., MS 300, R/Ee 32, pp. 413–415, 561–563.

109. See the contemporary account of the camp at Pyliavtsi in *DOVUN*, pp. 117–122. For allegations that Kysil arrived first in Warsaw, see BO, MS 189, pp. 149–151. A letter of Sebastian Walmirski, September 23, 1648, describes the flight from Pyliatvsi, Arch. Gdańsk., MS 300, 53/Ee 82 (Nowa teka 418), fol. 104. Also, see Temberski, who calls Kysil the prime head of the schism in Rus' and a patron of Cossack sedition, *Roczniki*, p. 91.

110. Early in September Kysil came into contact with Wiśniowiecki's camp at Cholhans'kyi Kamin'. Wiśniowiecki sent an emissary to meet him, and according to one report, charged that the Cossacks had promised their own and the Tatar troops to put Kysil on the throne. The Dominican Father Ciekliński also maintained that the 2,000 Volhynian soldiers Kysil led, "seeing that he was suspected of treason, left his service." Michałowski, pp. 179–180, September 2,

1648, Report of Rev. Ciekliński, Dominican. Also in PANK, MS 1056, fol. 10; BCz, MS 2576, pp. 238–239; Arch. Gdańsk., MS 300, R/Ee 32, p. 571.

111. September 19, 1648, *Pam.* I, 290–292.

112. Mikołaj Krosnowski, Archbishop of Lviv to Stanisław Zadorski, September 1, 1648. Michałowski, pp. 177–178. For another version of this statement from BCz, MS 143, see Lipiński, "Stanisław Michał Krzyczewski" in Lipiński, *Z dziejów,* p. 176. Lipiński cites numerous examples of accusations against Kysil as a "Rusin," pp. 175–178.

113. For an account of Pyliavtsi, see Szajnocha III, 69–124; Hrushevs'kyi VIII–3, 66–78; Tomkiewicz, *Jeremi Wiśniowiecki,* pp. 237–250.

114. For an attack on Kysil for his role at Pyliavtsi, see "Z Warszawy relacja pogromu wojska polskiego pod Pilawcami. Anno Domini 1648," *DOVUN,* pp. 117–119. The anonymous author accuses Kysil of cowardice and treachery. Kysil described his part in the consultations and his infirmity in a September 29, 1648 letter to Łubieński. Michałowski, pp. 203–207. Recesy, MS 300/29, 130, fols. 372–373 and LNB, MS 225, fols. 181–183.

115. Kysil to Łubieński, September 29, 1648. Michałowski, pp. 203–207. (Full citation in footnote 114.)

116. For Ossoliński's activities, see Kubala, *Jerzy Ossoliński,* pp. 301–337.

117. For a discussion of the two brothers' characters, see Władysław Czapliński, "Karol Ferdynand Waza (1613–1653)," *Polski słownik biograficzny,* XII, 85–87 and "Jan II Kazimierz Waza," *Polski słownik biograficzny,* X, 410–413.

118. The best discussions of the election struggle are Kubala, *Jerzy Ossoliński,* pp. 301–328; Myron Korduba, "Borot'ba za pol'skyi prestil po smerti Volodyslava IV," *Zherela,* XII, 1–60; Adam Andrzej Witusik, "Elekcja Jana Kazimierza w 1648 roku," *Annales Univ. M. Curie-Skłodowska,* Sec. F. *Nauki filoz. humanist,* XVII, *1962* (Printed 1965), 119–153.

119. For a discussion of the foreign candidacies, particularly that of György Rákóczi of Transylvania, see Korduba, "Borot'ba," pp. 1–27.

120. Kysil discussed his views on the factors important in choosing a new monarch in undated letters to Stanisław Lubomirski, the palatine of Cracow (BO, MS 206, fols. 85–88) and Ossoliński (BO, MS 206, fols. 88–90). Lubomirski's answer of June 14 (BO, MS 206, fols. 98–99), is published in *DOVUN,* pp. 47–48. Lubomirski stood firmly for supporting all the regulations even if they retarded the election process. In his letter to Lubomirski, Kysil expressed his concern over rumors that heredity was to be the primary consideration in the selection of the successor. Among other matters, he discussed the problems of Jan Kazimierz's claim to the Swedish throne and Swedish-Commonwealth relations. In writing to Ossoliński he was even more explicit. He discussed his disapproval of the actions of the two royal brothers and was fearful that the principle of elective monarchy would be undermined. Ossoliński's answer of June 16, 1648 is published in *DOVUN,* pp. 50–52 (published from BO, MS 206, fols. 99–102).

121. Kubala, *Jerzy Ossoliński,* pp. 306–307 and Korduba, "Borot'ba," pp. 36–37.

122. *Urkunden und Actenstücke. Geschichte des Kurfürsten Friedrich Wilhelm von Brandenburg,* 23 vols. (Berlin-Leipzig, 1864–1930), I, 279. Andreas Adersbach to Friedrich Wilhelm, August 22, 1648. He counts Kysil as Jan Kazimierz's supporter.

123. Andreas Adersbach to Friedrich Wilhelm, August 30, 1648. *Urkunden* I, 285–286.

124. The discussion of the Election Diet is based on the diary published in Michałowski, pp. 219–260 and Radziwiłł, *Memoriale,* IV, 48–89, on the articles by Witusik and Korduba, and the diaries in Recesy, MS 300, 29/130, fols. 250–335 and 342–369.

125. Rákóczi had attempted to enlist support from the Protestants, particularly Janusz Radziwiłł. He also sought to negotiate with the Cossacks and Orthodox through Kysil's intermediacy. Korduba, "Borot'ba," pp. 21–22.

126. Kubala, *Jerzy Ossoliński,* p. 317. For Kysil's opposition, see Michałowski, p. 248. For the division of parties, see Korduba, "Borot'ba," pp. 36–38.

127. For Ossoliński's and Kysil's tactics, see Kubala, *Jerzy Ossoliński,* pp. 316–321. For Kysil's arrival at the diet, see Michałowski, p. 228. For Kysil's address, see Michałowski, pp. 235–238; Radziwiłł, *Memoriale,* IV, 53–54; Recesy, MS 300, 29/130, fols. 270–271.

128. Many of Karol Ferdynand's supporters demanded a trial of the military commanders. Kubala, *Jerzy Ossoliński,* p. 317. Michałowski, pp. 235–236.

129. Radziwiłł, *Memoriale,* IV, 56.

130. Michałowski, pp. 244–245.

131. Michałowski, pp. 249–250. The Imperial Court's representative Lizola reported on Kysil's speech and the negative reaction to it. October 17, 1648. *Zherela* XII, 87–88.

132. Michałowski, p. 250.

133. Radziwiłł, *Memoriale,* IV, 59.

134. Michałowski, p. 259. See Mykola's letter to Adam of October 14, 1648 published in *DOVUN,* pp. 166–171.

135. Korduba, "Borot'ba," pp. 31–54. Kubala argues that Khmel'nyts'kyi's support of Jan Kazimierz in November 1648 was crucial to the election. *Jerzy Ossoliński,* pp. 322–324. Korduba, however, views it as having come too late to affect the selection. "Borot'ba," pp. 54–60. Also see Hrushevs'kyi VIII–1, 101–112. For Khmel'nyts'kyi's activities in this period, particularly his contacts with the Rákóczi family, see Myron Korduba, "Mizh Zamostem ta Zborovom (Storinky znosyn Semyhorodu z Ukraïnoiu i Pol'sheiu)," *ZNTSh,* CXXXIII (1922), 39–56.

136. Korduba, "Borot'ba," pp. 44–50.

137. The major study and assessment of Jan Kazimierz is Wiktor Czermak, *Z czasów Jana Kazimierza.* Studya historyczne (Lviv, 1893).

138. Kubala, *Jerzy Ossoliński,* p. 317.

139. November 15, 1648, *D.Kh.,* pp. 83–84.

140. Michałowski, pp. 354–360.

141. See *D.Kh.*, p. 80.

142. For Jan Kazimierz's December letter to Khmel'nyts'kyi see Arch. Gdańsk., MS 300, 53/83 (Nowa teka 660), fol. 41. He also wrote of his acceptance on December 11. Arch. Gdańsk, MS 300, 53/83 (Nowa teka 660), fol. 44.

143. For the instructions to the peace commissioners, see Arch. Gdańsk., MS 300, R/Ee 32, pp. 741–742.

144. The problem of the concessions about the union was considered extremely difficult. See the report of the Prussian diplomat Johann von Hoverbeck to Friedrich Wilhelm, December 15, 1648. *Urkunden*, I, 331–333.

145. Kysil wrote from Wiczki to the king on December 26, just prior to joining the other peace commissioners. His primary complaint was the lack of funds to carry out his mission. At this time Kysil was already concerned about the growing anarchy in these lands. Rawita-Gawroński, ed., *Sprawy*, pp. 89–91. A response to Kysil's complaint may have been the conferral of the starostwo of Cherkasy at the Coronation Diet (January 16, 1649). *Arkhiv Iu. Z. R.*, pt. III, vol. IV, pp. 323–324. Kysil, however, soon transferred it to his brother Mykola, *Arkhiv Iu. Z. R.*, pt. III, vol. IV, 320–323. Also see, commissioners to king, February 11, 1649, Ambroży Grabowski, ed., *Ojczyste spominki w pismach do dziejów dawnej Polski . . .*, 2 vols. (Cracow, 1845), II, 10–12 (hereafter Grabowski II) (published from Arch. Kr., "Pinocciana," MS 263, pp. 251–252 and MS 363, pp. 239–240); *DOVUN*, pp. 201–204, and LNB, MS 225, fols. 199–202. Kysil emphasized that the union would be a real "knot" and the Cossacks would demand its total abolition.

146. On the basis of his experiences in earlier peace missions, Kysil was very concerned that his position not be undermined by attacks of the Commonwealth's forces. He issued a series of "universals" to prevent this from happening in February 1649. *Arkhiv Iu. Z. R.*, pt. III, vol. IV, 43–44; AGAD, Arch. Rad., II, book 14, pp. 238–240; BCz, MS 144, pp. 99–100; Grabowski II, 11–12. (Published from Arch. Kr. "Pinocciana," MS 363, p. 254) and LNB, MS 225, fol. 203.

147. There is no critical edition of the diary. It has been published in: *Pam.*, I (2nd ed.), 314–329; Michałowski, pp. 369–385; *Voss.* II, 104–114; and exists in the following manuscript copies: BO, MS 189, pp. 221–232; BCz, MS 379, pp. 163–175; BCz, MS 964, pp. 7–48; BCz, MS 1651, pp. 301–314; BCz, MS 966, pp. 153–161; BCz, MS 394, pp. 3–20; Arch Gdańsk., MS 300, 29/129, fols. 223ff.; BN, BOZ, MS 950, fols. 137–143; Steinwehr III, fols. 661–667; LBN, MS 225, fols. 203–211 (noted in *Vyz.*, p. 52). Unless otherwise specified, information on the negotiations in Pereiaslav comes from the diary.

148. Miaskowski's report of January 31, 1649, published in part in Lipiński, *Z dziejów*, p. 177 from Arch. Kr., "Pinocciana," MS 363, pp. 247–248. Also see LNB, MS 225, fols. 189–199. In a report of March 8, the commissioners point out the great changes which had occurred in Khmel'nyts'kyi's thinking. They maintain that he now thought not just about the Cossacks, but about overlordship of the Ruthenian provinces. Arch. Kr., "Pinocciana," MS 363, pp. 262–264.

149. Radziwiłł, *Memoriale*, IV, 115.

150. The "Supplication" of February 24, 1649 is published in *D.Kh.*, pp. 105–106.

151. The three senators were to be the palatine, castellan and metropolitan of Kiev. Bzhozovs'kyi was already castellan.

152. Tomkiewicz, *Jeremi Wiśniowiecki*, pp. 292–297.

153. For the terms of the armistice see *D.Kh.*, pp. 103–105; *Pam.* I, 377–382. AGAD, Arch. Rad., II, book 14, pp. 235–238; Arch. Kr., "Pinocciana," MS 363, pp. 260–262; BO, MS 189, pp. 217–219; Steinwehr III, fols. 318–319. For the commissioners' call to the hostile armies to keep the peace, see Grabowski II, 13–14; Arch. Kr., "Pinocciana," MS 363, p. 255; Arch. Kr., Zbiór Rusieckich, MS 41, p. 85; Steinwehr III, fol. 319.

154. Kysil and commissioners to king, March 8, 1649, Arch. Kr., "Pinocciana," MS 363, pp. 262–264. Kysil maintained that Khmel'nyts'kyi spoke "de Dominio et Ducatu prowincij ruskich."

155. Kubala, *Jerzy Ossoliński*, pp. 346–347 for the struggle between Ossoliński and Leszczyński about whether the Commonwealth should continue to negotiate or to embark on an open policy of war. Mykola Kysil reported the terms to a small circle of court officials and the king on March 17. Albrycht Stanisław Radziwiłł to K. L. Sapieha, March 17, 1649. BN, BOZ, MS 931, fol. 247.

156. Grabowski II, 113–117. For information about Śmiarkowski, see A. Krauzhar [Aleksandr Kraushar], "Posol'stvo Iakova Smiarkovskogo k Bogdanu Khmel'nitskomu vo vremia osady Zamost'ia v 1648 g. (po rukopisnym istochnikam)," *Kievskaia starina*, 1894, no. 12, pp. 445–460.

157. An undated copy of the conferral. BK, MS 991, fols. 106–107. The papal nuncio reported the appointment on March 13. *Litterae Nuntiorum*, VII, 18. Khmel'nyts'kyi wrote a letter of congratulations on the appointment on April 24, *D.Kh.*, pp. 114–115.

158. Kysil's method to cajol Khmel'nyts'kyi can be seen in the early period of the post-Pereiaslav negotiations in a letter written in the spring of 1649. He queried whether he should continue to assure the king and the Commonwealth of Khmel'nyts'kyi's good intentions. He both complained of the way he was treated and expounded on his "credentials," "On me, like on an ass, His Royal Majesty places all [burdens] and to me therefore, from Rus' there is woe, and from the Poles (*Lachowie*) no peace. . . . Have mercy, as a son of the Mother Church of God, that I, in may gray years, in my status as a senator, and on my prior good will toward you and the Zaporozhian army . . ." *Arkhiv Iu. Z. R.*, pt. III, vol. IV, 171–174.

159. Kysil persisted, even though he was not informed of all the activities undertaken by the court. For example, he complained on April 15 that an emissary had been sent to Khmel'nyts'kyi and because he had not been shown the instructions his mission was impeded. Arch. Kr., "Pinocciana," MS 363, pp. 287–293. He reported to the chancellor about the forged letter and enclosed a copy of it as well as the letter he had sent to Khmel'nyts'kyi on April 15, 1649. Arch. Kr., "Pinocciana," MS 363, pp. 287–293. It is my hypothesis that the two

letters mentioned are those published in *Arkhiv Iu. Z. R.,* pt. III, vol. IV, 169–174. I maintain this because the letter from Kysil to Khmel'nyts'kyi contains the statement that Kysil is showing his faith in Khmel'nyts'kyi by including a letter from Ossoliński which he asks Khmel'nyts'kyi to keep secret. Also, the two undated letters come from the same manuscript. (Pol. Rukopis' I. P. Bib. IV, F, no. 129, fols. 280–363.) The "Ossoliński" letter emphasizes the Commonwealth's military preparedness (the recruitment of 60,000 foreign troops, the authorization of a levy), but asserts considerable trust in Khmel'nyts'kyi's intentions. The very explicitness of the instructions seems to be intended more for Khmel'nyts'kyi than for Kysil. Also, Khmel'nyts'kyi is spoken of in very respectful terms. If my hypothesis is correct, the comment that the Kievan palatinate was conferred on Kysil immediately after learning of the death of Janusz Tyszkiewicz, even though numerous senators, including Wiśniowiecki, sought it, is of some significance. Kysil may have wished to convince Khmel'nyts'kyi that the king and chancellor were working hard to appease Khmel'nyts'kyi. Hrushevs'kyi had no doubts of the letter's authenticity and quotes it at length, VIII–3, 157–158.

160. Khmel'nyts'kyi's first known response was not until April 24, and while he congratulated Kysil on his appointment as Kievan palatine, he complained of infractions of the truce by the Commonwealth's forces and did not propose steps to prolong the peace. *D.Kh.,* pp. 114–115. On May 13, Khmel'nyts'kyi still claimed to be searching for a safe place to hold a meeting with the commissioners. *D.Kh.,* pp. 118–119.

161. For an example of Kysil's urging of military preparedness, see his letter of April 24 to Ossoliński. Arch. Kr., "Pinocciana," MS 363, pp. 308–310. He was particularly upset by the divergence between the official counts of units and the actual state of the units. He still had some hope that Khmel'nyts'kyi would follow his suggestions for separating the Cossacks from the peasantry, but he believed time was too short to bring about a peace settlement. He discussed the lack of Commonwealth forces in contrast to the power of the foe. The situation of the Commonwealth was critical because of the importance of the lands it had lost or, as he expressed it: "This is not about Livonia, the loss of which was not beneficial to the fatherland, but without us [the Ukrainian lands and their nobility] the fatherland will no longer exist as we have known it." (Literally, the fatherland will not be the fatherland). He appealed as the first senator among his afflicted brothers for help to be sent quickly. Kysil was especially disturbed by the confusion in the military. He urged Ossoliński to take over leadership, particularly to keep it out of Wiśniowiecki's hands. He claimed that a leader of intelligence and prudence was necessary, not one of fury.

162. Ossoliński to Kysil (no date; approximately the end of April). *Arkhiv Iu. Z. R.,* pt. III, vol. IV, 169–172.

163. See his letter of May 11, 1649 to Ossoliński. Grabowski II, 21–23. (Published from Arch. Kr., "Pinocciana," MS 363, pp. 321–324.) BO MS 189, pp. 250–252.

164. Grabowski II, 24–26 (published from Arch. Kr., "Pinocciana," MS 363, pp. 325–327).

165. May 18. Grabowski II, 26–29. (Published from Arch. Kr., "Pinocciana," MS 363, pp. 329–332, dated May 10, presumably Old Style.)

166. De Torres reported that Khmel'nyts'kyi wrote to Firlej demanding Kysil to be removed. May 22, 1649, *Litterae Nuntiorum*, VII, 34–35. Also see the June 12, 1649 report of the papal nuncio in Vienna, Camillus de Melzi. *Litterae Nuntiorum*, VII, 42.

167. Obuchowicz to K. L. Sapieha, May 22, 1649, *Pam.* I, 396–398; Grabowski II, 29; Michałowski, pp. 394–395; Kysil sent his last letter on May 23 (Grabowski II, 118–119). (Published from Arch. Kr., "Pinocciana," MS 363, pp. 333–334.) Father Lasko filed a complete report of the adventures of his mission when he returned to Hoshcha on June 13. *DOVUN*, pp. 230–232; Arch. Kr., "Pinocciana," MS 363, p. 375. Lasko brought information on the execution of Śmiarkowski and the other delegates. The ties which existed in the Orthodox establishment were demonstrated by Lasko's depositing documents with Metropolitan Kosiv.

168. For the events of this period, see the two letters sent by Kysil and Obuchowicz to Ossoliński on May 25. Michałowski, p. 395; *Pam.* I, 399–401; May 26, Grabowski II, pp. 35–36. (Published from Arch Kr., "Pinocciana," MS 363, p. 351.) For the secret relations mentioning Khmel'nyts'kyi's anger, see *Voss.* II, 203; Grabowski II, pp. 36–37.

169. Kysil commented that Khmel'nyts'kyi wished to have him in his hands. May 25, 1649, *Pam.* I, 399–401.

170. The diary of the Senate sessions is published in Michałowski, pp. 399–405.

171. See Tomkiewicz, *Jeremi Wiśniowiecki,* p. 304.

172. Kysil complained that it was no use to be palatine of Kiev, when Kiev was in alien hands. June 12, 1649, Kysil to Sapieha, BN, BOZ, MS 1217, fols. 299–300.

173. Among the numerous letters from Kysil to Sapieha during this period (predominantly in BN, BOZ, MS 1217), the most extensive justification by Kysil is in an undated letter published in *DOVUN*, pp. 237–238 from a copy in AGAD, Arch. Radz. The same letter, dated July 23, but mistakenly identified as "apparently to the Crown Chancellor [Ossoliński]," is published in Michałowski, pp. 418–421. The letter, dated July 3, 1649, exists in BN, BOZ, MS 1217, fols. 302–306 and an undated letter fols. 306–307.

174. Obuchowicz had arrived at Kysil's camp with a letter from Sapieha in late May. Kysil replied on June 12 reporting the failure of the commission. BN, BOZ, MS 1217, fols. 299–300. On June 19, he wrote that "The Lord Palatine of Kiev is gravely troubled by the lack of any responses from his confidant the Lord Chancellor," and that he was upset over the charges against him. BN, BOZ, MS 1217, fols. 323–324.

175. The negotiations centered around Kysil's purchase of Sapieha's estates in Chornobyl'. BJ, MS 3573 contains synopses of fourteen letters from Kysil to Sapieha.

176. June 12, 1649, BN, BOZ, MS 1217, fols. 299–300. For Sapieha's role as

a source of information on the commission see the April 11, 1649, letter from A. S. Radziwiłł to him. BN, BOZ, MS 931, fol. 254.

177. As late as July 9, 1649, Kysil wrote to Sapieha that he had not received a response from the king and was surprised that the king had not issued an order calling him to his side. BN, BOZ, MS 1217, fols. 320–321. Kysil was prepared to move to Lublin.

178. June 12, 1649, Kysil to Sapieha, BN, BOZ, MS 1217, fols. 299–300. Kysil discussed his former services to Radziwiłł as well as his loss of income in the Ukraine. Writing in late June that he had received no word from the chancellor or the king in over four weeks, Kysil expressed his dissatisfaction and his need to be rewarded for his services. BN, BOZ, MS 1217, fols. 306–307.

179. Andrzej Leszczyński to K. L. Sapieha, July 11, 1649; BN, BOZ, MS 931, fols. 291–293. Leszczyński complained of Ossoliński's arrogance and his blocking of Leszczyński's advice. He was especially concerned over the failure to call the levy. Leszczyński's comment about Ossoliński appears to be correct. At the Coronation Diet, Ossoliński accused Kysil of being too conciliatory with the "peasants" (the rebels). Cited by Lipiński, "Stanisław Michał Krzyczewski," *Z dziejów,* pp. 175–176 from a document entitled "Dyaryusz czynności I. P. senatorów zgromadzonych przez U. KM. na konwokacyą R. 1649" in BCz, MS 144, fol. 741.

180. Kysil, obviously worried about Ossoliński's attitude toward him, sent a letter to the king through Sapieha, requesting him personally to hand the letter to the king. He added, however, that he was also writing to the Crown chancellor to avoid offending him, July 9, 1649, BN, BOZ, MS 1217, fols. 320–321. While there is no copy of Kysil's letter to the king extant, it was probably a justification of his activities that he feared might be intercepted by the Crown chancellor.

181. The king left Warsaw on June 24 and arrived in Lublin on July 3. On July 17, news arrived that Zbarazh was besieged and on July 20 the third call to a levy was issued. Kubala, *Jerzy Ossoliński,* pp. 356–357. For the military aspects of the Zboriv campaign, see Ludwik Frąś, "Bitwa pod Zborowem w r. 1649," *Kwartalnik Historyczny,* XLVI, no. 3–4 (1932), 344–370. By August 13 Kysil was present with a detachment of 100 men as the royal levy reached Zolochiv. Ludwik Kubala, " Oblężenie Zbaraża i pokój pod Zborowem," *Szkice historyczne,* Seria I i II (= *Dzieła Ludwika Kubali. Wydanie zbiorowe,* 2 vols. [Warsaw-Lviv, 1923–24], II) (Warsaw-Lviv, 1923), p. 112, fn. 78.

182. Frąś lists BCz, MS 144, pp. 707, 713 as containing other registers.

183. June 17, 1649. Grabowski II, 46–47 (published from Arch. Kr., "Pinocciana," MS 363, p. 379), LNB 225, fol. 231 (see *Vyz.,* 257, p. 58).

184. On June 10, 1649, Kysil wrote to Lanckoroński of his own and his brother's readiness to serve the fatherland with their troops. BN, BOZ, MS 1217, fols. 301–302. On June 24, 1649, Mykola wrote describing the Crown army's maneuvers. BN, BOZ, MS 1217, fols. 309–314. Adam's brother, Mykola, was with the Crown army at Zbarazh. *DOVUN,* pp. 249–259.

185. Frąś, "Bitwa pod Zborowem," pp. 338–339.

186. Hrushevs'kyi VIII–3, 195–196.

187. April 24, 1649, Kysil to Ossoliński, Arch. Kr., "Pinocciana," MS 363, pp. 305–310. For discussion about a levy, see Kubala, *Jerzy Ossoliński*, pp. 322–358.

188. Frąś, "Bitwa pod Zborowem," p. 349.

189. For the international situation that Khmel'nyts'kyi faced, see Izydor Edmund Chrząszcz, *Stosunki kozacko-tatarskie z uwzględnieniem stosunków z Turcją, Mołdawją i Siedmiogrodem w I połowie 1649* (Lviv, 1929). Chrząszcz emphasizes Khmel'nyts'kyi's hopes that the Rákóczi family would intervene in his favor, p. 9.

190. For the khan's motivations, see Hrushevs'kyi VIII–3, 198–209. Eugeniusz Latacz has proposed that the primary consideration of the king and Ossoliński at Zboriv was the revival of plans for a war against the Ottomans and that the matter was discussed with the khan and Khmel'nyts'kyi. Eugeniusz Latacz, "Ugoda Zborowska a plany tureckie Jana Kazimierza," *Historia*, III (1933), 1–10.

191. There is little documentation about the Zboriv negotiations. Other than accounts in the seventeenth-century histories of the Cossack wars, there are only a few reports from members of the Miaskowski family, an anonymous report, and some official panegyrics. See Hrushevs'kyi VIII–3, 198, footnote 1. The accounts vary in many details and contain errors in publication (Michałowski, pp. 435–439 appears to be particularly faulty). Arch. Kr., "Pinocciana," MS 363, pp. 411–414 and Kubala, "Oblężenie," pp. 119–122, which appear to be copies of the same letter to Karol Ferdynand, differ greatly in details. Among the contemporary histories, Kysil's role is discussed at the greatest length in Albertus Wiiuk Koiałowicz, *De rebus anno 1649 contra Zaporovios Cosaccos gestis* (Vilnius, 1651), pp. 96–97. For the course of negotiations with the khan and Khmel'nyts'kyi, see Kubala, "Oblężenie," pp. 97–109.

192. Kysil took credit for this in a letter to the king, dated October 26, 1650, in Michałowski, pp. 583–589. The letter is dated October 29, in BO, MS 3564, fols. 248–257.

193. The scene of Kysil leading Khmel'nyts'kyi to take the oath is described in Koiałowicz, *De rebus*, p. 97.

194. There is no scholarly edition of the Zboriv Agreement. For citations of the extant copies and a Ukrainian translation, see Hrushevs'kyi VIII–3, 215–217. A special privilege to the Cossacks was issued, defining their rights, particularly for judicial autonomy, and forbidding them from interfering with the functioning of the royal officials. Michałowski (undated), pp. 442–443. For a Polish text, see *Sobranie gosudarstvennykh gramot i dogovorov, khraniashchikhsia v Gosudarstvennoi Kollegii inostrannykh del*, 5 vols. (Moscow, 1813–1894), III, 450–454.

195. August 17, 1649, *D.Kh.*, pp. 128–130.

Chapter 7

1. An example of the propaganda campaign after Zboriv is the *Relatio Gloriossimae expeditionis, . . . Joannis Casimiri, Regis Poloniae & Sveciae* (1649).

2. Kubala, *Jerzy Ossoliński,* p. 369. BCz., MS 417, p. 135 contains a slightly different text. Also, see Samuel Grondski de Grond, *Historia Belli Cosacco-Polonici . . . Conscripta Anno MDCLXXVI,* ed. Carolus Koppi ([Pest], 1789), pp. 112–113.

3. Stanisław Przyłęcki, ed., *Pamiętniki o Koniecpolskich* (Lviv, 1841), p. 427.

4. For the peace party's activities in this period, see Kubala, *Jerzy Ossoliński,* pp. 364–385.

5. September 28, 1649, Michałowski, pp. 497–498. Sosnyts'kyi appears to have been a long-time servitor of Kysil, and it was he who registered Kysil's will in 1653. "Try testamenty," p. 61.

6. On Vyhovs'kyi and his policies, see Vasyl' Herasymchuk, "Vyhovs'kyi i Iurii Khmel'nyts'kyi. Istorychni studiï," *ZNTSh,* LIX (1904), 1–40; LX (1904), 41–70 and "Vyhovshchyna i Hadiats'kyi traktat," *ZNTSh,* LXXXVII (1909), 5–36, LXXXVIII (1909), 23–50; LXXXIX (1909), 46–90.

7. Vyhovs'kyi to Kysil, September 29, 1649, Michałowski, pp. 448–450.

8. Vyhovs'kyi to Kysil, October 9, 1649. Grabowski II, 64. (Published from Arch. Kr., "Pinocciana," MS 363, pp. 470–471.) Michałowski, p. 508.

9. The instruction for the dietines is published in Michałowski, pp. 498–508.

10. *D.Kh.,* pp. 139–140. Also see Khmel'nyts'kyi's second letter to Kysil of October 11.

11. For an account of the dietine and sources about it, see Hrushevs'kyi VIII–3, 230–232. The protest of Anna Chodkiewicz against the dietine for damages to her property is published in *Arkhiv Iu. Z. R.,* pt. III, vol. IV, 436–437. The chief source of information of the dietine is Kysil's letter of October 16 to Ossoliński. Michałowski, pp. 509–510. The instruction of the Kiev palatinate has not been found, but that of neighboring Bratslav dietine included a provision for compensating Kysil for his services. October 11, 1649, *Arkhiv Iu. Z. R.,* pt. III, vol. IV, 334–342.

12. Kysil to Ossoliński, October 16, 1649, Michałowski, pp. 509–510.

13. Grabowski II, 123–127 (Arch. Kr., "Pinocciana," MS 363, pp. 471–474); LNB, MS 225, fols. 275–277 (see *Vyz,* 295, p. 65).

14. Hrushevs'kyi accepts the November 6 date given in Jerlicz's account, principally because Jerlicz was present in Kiev in this period.

15. The original was in the Krasiński Library and was destroyed during World War II. It is mentioned in Franciszek Pułaski, *Opis 815 rękopisów Biblioteki Ordynacji hr. Krasińskich* (Warsaw, 1915), item 232.

16. Kysil to king, November 25, 1649. Grabowski II, 65–66. Also see, Kysil to Khmel'nyts'kyi, October 20, 1649. Grabowski II, 126–127, where he pleads: "Let there be an end to this war between religions and peoples, the woeful effects of which we have seen so many proofs."

17. The king's instructions are published in Michałowski, pp. 498–508. The king discussed Zbarazh and Zboriv as great victories.

18. The nuncio, de Torres, and the ultra-Catholics such as Sapieha, were

extremely active in pressuring the court not to make major concessions to the Orthodox. See the nuncio's reports in *Litterae Nuntiorum,* VII, pp. 36–87 (all page numbers in this note refer to this volume). October 2, 1649 (Nuncio reports that both Ossoliński and the king have assured him that the peace will bring no setbacks to the Faith and in fact may result in the conversion of Kosiv. The king also has assured him that it will be the Diet that will decide the provisions of the peace, and that offices will not be restricted to Ruthenians), November 20, 1649 (Nuncio reports conversation with the king in which he has been assured that the Diet will not enact any provisions detrimental to Catholicism), January 1, 1650, pp. 113–114, and two dispatches on January 9, 1650, pp. 115–116 (Deal with attempt by the Orthodox metropolitan to receive seat in Senate), January 15, 1650, pp. 120–121 (Nuncio reports rumors of issuing of the January 12 privilege to the Orthodox, and the opposition of Sapieha and Albrycht Stanisław Radziwiłł. Mentions Kysil's arguments for need for concessions as well as the king's negative response to them in public), pp. 143–146, March 26, 1650 (Reports that privilege to the Orthodox was sent secretly with compliance of Ossoliński and Kysil and that the papal nuncio had protested and urged the Catholic bishops to do so). These and other documents in the volume show both the nuncio's active policy and the equivocation of the king and Ossoliński. Ossoliński later maintained to the nuncio that he had been duped by Kysil; *Litterae Nuntiorum,* VII, 143–146. This report by the nuncio gives a summary of his efforts to prevent concessions to the Orthodox.

19. The nuncio was particularly pleased that the restriction of offices was almost immediately disregarded and Stanisław Lanckoroński was appointed palatine of Bratslav. *Litterae Nuntiorum,* VII, 101. November 20, 1649.

20. *D.Kh.,* pp. 151–152 (end of November).

21. This was in accordance with the terms of the Zboriv Agreement. Hrushevs'kyi VIII–3, 216. For Khmel'nyts'kyi's later charges against Kysil for failing in this mission, see his November 1, 1650 (O.S.) letter to the Volhynian nobility, *D.Kh.,* pp. 192–194.

22. For a detailed account of this Diet, see Łucja Cześcik, *Sejm warszawski w 1649/50 roku* (Wrocław, Warsaw, Cracow, Gdańsk, 1978). Almost all other secondary literature, including Hrushevs'kyi, is based solely on the reports in Radziwiłł, *Memoriale,* IV, 152–161. A copy of the diary exists in Recesy, MS 300, 29/133, fols. 197–288, as well as a number of fragments, fols. 344–347, 360–384. Kysil is not mentioned in this diary until December 23, fol. 264. But only after January 3 is he mentioned frequently at Diet sessions. Kysil's name first appears on December 20 in Radziwiłł, *Memoriale,* IV, 152, when an attempt by the primate to thank him was shouted down by a delegate, but Kysil's presence is not specifically mentioned, p. 399. Some of the most detailed information on the Diet is provided by the papal nuncio's reports, but the arrival of Kysil seems to be reported in a number of rumors. On December 11, 1649 he reported that Kysil had arrived with Cossack delegates, *Litterae Nuntiorum,* VII, 108 and on December 18, 1649 that the metropolitan and Khmel'nyts'kyi's son had arrived (together with Kysil), *Litterae Nuntiorum,* VII, 109.

23. The major source on church matters is a report from the Orthodox mission to the Diet, which was sent to Moscow and translated partially into Russian. It was published by Hrushevs'kyi IX 62, 1509–1523, but was not utilized for his discussion of the Diet in VIII–3. Hrushevs'kyi discussed the January meetings in brief in vol. IX–1, 25–29. It is a particularly interesting source as a representative of the Orthodox clerical establishment's viewpoint, but undoubtedly Kysil's actions and speeches are distorted in the recounting and by translation into Russian of Kysil's speeches.

24. Hrushevs'kyi IX–2, 1515–1516.

25. The privilege is published in *Arkhiv Iu. Z. R.*, pt. III, vol. IV, 382–386.

26. Radziwiłł, *Memoriale*, IV, 160–161.

27. January 12, 1650, *Litterae Nuntiorum*, VII, 117; January 19, 1650, *Arkhiv Iu. Z. R.*, pt. III, vol. IV, 386–389.

28. On the Nowy Targ starostwo and its sale, see Oświęcim, *Dyaryusz*, p. 222; Radziwiłł, *Memoriale*, IV, 156; J. Prażmowski to K. L. Sapieha, January 19, 1650. BOZ, MS 1217, fols. 186–187. Kysil sold his rights to the starostwo for 120,000 zł.

29. On the difficult situation that Kysil faced in carrying out the Zboriv Agreement, see Hrushevs'kyi VIII–1, 269–288.

30. For the situation after Zboriv, see Korduba, "Der Ukraine Niedergang," pp. 58–60, 193–196. On the reaction to Potocki's return, see Hrushevs'kyi IX–1, 7–13. For a discussion of the Ukraine's international position after Zboriv, see Golobutskii, *Diplomaticheskaia istoriia*, pp. 213–266. For a different view of the Ukraine's foreign contacts, see Hrushevs'kyi IX–1, 9–138.

31. On the uncertain situation Kysil encountered prior to the dietine see two reports from Zhytomyr of February 9 and February 17, 1650, Arch. Kr., Zbiór Rusieckich, MS 31, pp. 73–74. Kysil issued a universal calling the dietine on February 18. *Opis' aktovoi knigi Kievskogo Tsentral'nogo arkhiva*, 60 vols. (Kiev, 1867–1914), no. 19 (1878), Item 27, pp. 6–7. On Kysil's expected arrival for a dietine in Zhytomyr on February 21 see Szymon Pawsze to Janusz Radziwiłł, February 21, 1650. BK, MS 1558, item 7.

32. The dietine's decisions are published in *Arkhiv Iu. Z. R.*, pt. III, vol. IV, 410–416.

33. For Kysil's entry into Kiev and the difficult negotiations of March 1650, see Hrushevs'kyi VIII–3, 281–284. A Muscovite report on the March meetings is published in Hrushevs'kyi IX–1, 15–17. Hrushevs'kyi did not, however, use the detailed report of Szymon Pawsze, sent to Janusz Radziwiłł on April 9, 1650. BK, MS 1558, item 10.

34. The dispatch is published without a date in Rawita-Gawroński, *Bohdan* II, 91–95. The letter exists in numerous copies: N. D. "Relatio"BCz, MS 398, pp. 21–27; March 23 (no year), AGAD, Arch. Rad., II, book 10, pp. 313–315; March 23, 1650, BCz, MS 378, pp. 640–644; March 22, 1650, BN, MS 3091, fols. 12–13.

35. March 29, 1650. *Pam.* II, 19–35; AGAD, Archiwum Zamoyskich, 3052, pp. 13–15.

36. For a discussion of Muscovite-Commonwealth relations in this period, see G. M. Lyzlov, "Pol'sko-russkie otnosheniia v period do zemskogo sobora 1651 g.," Akademiia Nauk SSSR. Institut slavianovedeniia, *Kratkie soobshcheniia*, XXVII (1959), 45–67.

37. On the Muscovite March to July mission, see Ludwik Kubala, "Poselstwo Puszkina w Polsce w r 1650," *Szkice historyczne*, Seria I i II (Warsaw, 1923), pp. 125–142. Also see Lyzlov, "Pol'sko-russkie otnosheniia v period ot Zborovskogo mira," pp. 49–65.

38. BCz, MS 402, pp. 5–14 (original signed by Bzhozovs'kyi for Kysil with an explanation that Kysil could not sign because of his gout).

39. In discussing Swedish relations, Kysil pointed out that during his negotiations in Moscow in 1647, he had secretly discussed the possibility of a joint Commonwealth-Muscovite alliance against the Swedes in order to regain the Baltic littoral for both states. He cited this little-known diplomatic intercourse as evidence that real Muscovite-Swedish cooperation was unlikely. BCz, MS 402, pp. 5–6. For a discussion of Swedish relations with the Commonwealth in this period, see Tadeusz Nowak, "Geneza agresji szwedzkiej," in *Polska w okresie drugiej wojny pólnocnej 1655–1660,* ed. Kazimierz Lepszy, 3 vols. (Warsaw, 1957), I, 102–105. For Muscovite-Swedish relations, see G. V. Forsten, "Snosheniia Shvetsii i Rossii vo vtoroi polovine XVII veka (1648–1700)," *Zhurnal Ministerstva narodnogo prosveshcheniia*, CCCXV (February, 1898), 210–277; CCCXVI (April 1898), 321–354; CCCXVII (May 1898), 48–103; CCCXVII (June 1898), 311–350.

40. BCz, MS 402, p. 11.

41. Hrushevs'kyi IX–1, 45–46, Lyzlov, "Pol'sko-russkie otnosheniia v period ot Zborovskogo mira," pp. 55–56.

42. Letters from Kysil to Khmel'nyts'kyi dated either April 14 or April 17, probably identical, are cited in Hrushevs'kyi IX–1, 38–39 as existing in BO, MS 221, fol. 9, BO, MS 1453, p. 373. Both of those manuscripts are now in LNB. (*Vyz.* p. 67 provides a summary of the copy in LNB, MS 1453.) A letter dated April 17 is in AGAD, Branicki z Suchej 155/181, pp. 235–238.

43. March 20, 1650, *D.Kh.,* pp. 157–159.

44. May 20, 1650. *D.Kh.,* pp. 167–168; May 26, 1650, *D.Kh.,* pp. 168–169.

45. See Shevchenko, *Politychni . . . zv"iazky,* p. 308 for reports about a Cossack attack, and Hrushevs'kyi IX–1, 40–41 for Khmel'nyts'kyi's proposals to Muscovy.

46. Michałowski, pp. 548–550. The editor has mistakenly dated the letter "about May 6." Kysil gives dates for the conference in early June.

47. See Lyzlov, "Pol'sko-russkie otnosheniia v period ot Zborovskogo mira," p. 60.

48. On Vimina's mission, see Myron Korduba, "Venets'ke posol'stvo do Khmel'nyts'koho (1650)," *ZNTSh*, LXXVIII (1907), 51–89. The article includes an appendix of documents about Vimina's mission.

49. For the last phase and an evaluation of Ossoliński's career, see Kubala, *Jerzy Ossoliński,* pp. 380–385.

50. For information on the Irkliïv conference, see Hrushevs'kyi IX–1, 66–67.

51. Kysil to the king on August 12, 1650. *Voss.* II, 385–390.

52. For the political situation in this period, particularly increasing Ottoman influence, see Hrushevs'kyi IX–1, 59–68 and N. I. Kostomarov, "Bogdan Khmel'nitskii, dannik Ottomanskoi Porty," *Vestnik Evropy,* 1878, no. 12, pp. 806–817 and Bennigsen, *Le Khanat de Crimée,* pp. 177–197. Also see Kysil's letter to the king, August 28, 1650, LNB, MS 225, fols. 305–306.

53. BCz, MS 144, pp. 935–940.

54. Steinwehr III, fol. 434; and AGAD, Arch. Rad., Oddział VI, MS 36, "Dyaryusz Janusza Radziwiłła," unpaginated sections of Radziwiłł's chancery from 1649 to 1652. Referred hereafter as Diary of Janusz Radziwiłł with the date of the letter. Khmel'nyts'kyi both bitterly complained to Kysil of Potocki's letter and militant activities (Diary of Janusz Radziwiłł, August 26, 1650, inscribed under October 14) and issued universals which convinced Kysil of his peaceful intent (August 26, 1650, Diary of Janusz Radziwiłł). Kysil did list the breaches of the peace in length when writing to Khmel'nyts'kyi (Diary of Janusz Radziwiłł, September 5, 1650, Kysil to Khmel'nyts'kyi).

55. For Ukrainian-Moldavian relations in this period, see A. F. Ermolenko, "Ukrainsko-moldavskie otnosheniia v gody osvoboditel'noi voiny ukrainskogo naroda (1648–1654)," in *Vossoedinenie Ukrainy s Rossiei 1654–1954. Sbornik statei,* pp. 223–241, and Hrushevs'kyi IX–1, 80–97.

56. Kysil issued a universal to calm the nobility and inform the king and Potocki on September 7, 1650. *Arkhiv Iu. Z. R.,* pt. III, vol. IV, 502; *Pam.* II, 36–39; Diary of Janusz Radziwiłł. Khmel'nyts'kyi's universal was issued on September 7, *D.Kh.,* pp. 185–186.

57. A votum dated September 8 to the dietine which met in Zhytomyr is in the Diary of Janusz Radziwiłł. Another copy is in BCz, MS 144, pp. 961–966.

58. For the international situation in this period, see Hrushevs'kyi IX–1, 121–138.

59. This letter has been published dated October 26 in Michałowski, pp. 583–589. Other copies are dated October 16, Arch. Kr., "Pinocciana," MS 363, pp. 523–529; BCz, MS 417, pp. 89–92; BCz, MS 2519, pp. 69–74; and LNB, MS 225, fols. 323–327.

60. Hrushevs'kyi IX–1, 147–148.

61. *DOVUN,* pp. 357–358 (undated). The letter is cited from another copy by Hrushevs'kyi IX–1, 147–148. It also exists in LNB, MS 225, fols. 337–338.

62. November 1, 1650 (O.S.), *D.Kh.,* pp. 192–195.

63. For the political climate of this period, see Hrushevs'kyi IX–1, 144–159. In a recent unpublished study on Hieronym Radziejowski, Adam Kersten argues that even at this time the king and queen remained interested in a Turkish war, if an agreement could be reached with Khmel'nyts'kyi. "Hieronim Radziejowski, 1612–1667" (1979), pp. 295–296.

64. Kysil's votum is published in *DOVUN,* pp. 361–367 from a copy in Recesy, MS 300, 29/134. Other copies exist in BCz, MS 417, fols. 100–109, BCz,

MS 144, pp. 1095–1107; Steinwehr III, fols. 443–444. For Kysil's attitudes at this time, see his letter of December 5 to the king, Recesy, MS 300, 29/134, fols. 449–451 and LNB, MS 225, fols. 341–345.

65. The short Diet diary in BCz, MS 417, pp. 199–218, only contains mention that Kysil's letters were read. The evaluation is based on Kochowski (see footnote 66) and Kysil's subsequent complaint to Jan Kazimierz, January 18, 1652. Diary of Janusz Radziwiłł.

66. Vespasianus a Kochow Kochowski [Wespazjan Kochowski], *Annalium Poloniae ab obitu Vladislai IV. Climacter Primus* (Cracow, 1683), pp. 209–211.

67. The king wrote to Kysil on December 20 and maintained that he wished to abide by the Zboriv articles and requested Kysil's assistance in dealing with the Cossacks. Recesy, MS 300, 29/134, fol. 448; BCz, MS 417, p. 194.

68. January 7, 1651. De Torres, *Litterae Nuntiorum,* VII, 220–221.

69. December 31, 1650. De Torres, *Litterae Nuntiorum,* VII, 217–218.

70. January 13, 1651. Leszczyński to Kysil, Michałowski, pp. 602–603; BCz, MS 1657, p. 300.

71. King to Kysil. Michałowski, pp. 600–601.

72. He expressed his acceptance of his role as a mediator in his January 18, 1651 letter to the king. Diary of Janusz Radziwiłł.

73. Kysil wrote to Kalinowski on March 3, 1651. BCz, MS 145, pp. 73–78; AGAD, Arch. Rad. II, teka 9, item 1246; *Vyz.* 340, p. 74. Kalinowski to Radziejowski, Michałowski, pp. 609–611. Radziejowski wrote to Kysil on January 13 (BCz, MS 1657, pp. 299–300). Kysil replied on January 22 (Michałowski, pp. 603–604; BO, MS 189, p. 443); Kysil to Radziejowski, February 23 and 26 (Michałowski, pp. 607–609; p. 611) and March 16, BO, MS 189, pp. 454–455.

74. Kalinowski led the military campaign in the Bratslav palatinate, and his contacts with Radziejowski seem to have disturbed Potocki. See Potocki's letter of March 16 to Radziejowski questioning the meaning of universals calling troops to Kalinowski's side, Michałowski, pp. 618–619; and Kalinowski's letter of reassurance to Potocki of March 4, *DOVUN,* pp. 390–391. Radziejowski replied sharply to Potocki's letter on March 26, Michałowski, pp. 626–627. Polish emissaries to Khmel'nyts'kyi in January reported in full to Radziejowski (*DOVUN,* pp. 376–378). Khmel'nyts'kyi replied favorably to Radziejowski on January 27, 1651. *D.Kh.,* pp. 210–211. Radziejowski's attempts to play an intermediary role between the court and the Cossacks backfired and served to bring on his dismissal after Khmel'nyts'kyi's chancery fell into the Commonwealth's army's hand at Berestechko. See Kersten, "Hieronim Radziejowski," pp. 315–316.

75. A report by Polish emissaries to Chyhyryn in January mentioned that "There is tremendous antipathy to the Lord of Cracow [Potocki], there is not a dinner during which he is not mentioned with malice. They hold the Chernihiv palatine [Kalinowski] to be their friend." *DOVUN,* p. 378. On February 10 Khmel'nyts'kyi wrote to Kysil to thank both him and Kalinowski for their efforts to prevent friction on the armistice line. *D.Kh.,* pp. 211–212.

76. On Radziejowski, and his later problems with the king, see Ludwik

Kubala, "Proces Radziejowskiego," *Szkice historyczne,* Seria I, II, 5th ed. (Warsaw, 1923), pp. 223–259 and Kersten, "Hieronim Radziejowski," pp. 320–330.

77. January 22, 1651. Michałowski, pp. 603–604; BO, MS 189, p. 443.

78. February 23, 1651, Kysil to Radziejowski, Michałowski, p. 608.

79. On the outbreak of hostilities in this period, see Hrushevs'kyi IX–1, 191–202. For Kysil's realization that war was inevitable, see his letter to Maksymylian Bzhozovs'kyi, February 11, 1651, Diary of Janusz Radziwiłł.

80. Kysil to Radziejowski, March 16, 1651, BO, MS 189, pp. 454–455.

81. Oświęcim, *Dyaryusz,* pp. 273–274.

82. This is the place given in his letter of April 14, 1651. Kysil to unknown addressee. Michałowski, pp. 631–632.

83. April 14, 1651, Kysil to an unknown addressee, Michałowski, p. 632.

84. January 18, 1651. Kysil to the king. Diary of Janusz Radziwiłł.

85. Michałowski, pp. 612–613. For a discussion of this poem in the context of the political poetry of the period, see Juliusz Nowak-Dłużewski, *Okolicznościowa poezja polityczna w Polsce. Dwaj młodsi Wazowie* (Warsaw, 1972), pp. 149–150.

86. Report by an unknown correspondent from Warsaw, February 21, 1651, Arch. Kr., Zbiór Rusieckich, MS 41, pp. 143–144.

87. For a description of the Battle of Berestechko, see Ludwik Kubala, "Bitwa pod Beresteczkiem," *Szkice historyczne,* Seria I i II (Warsaw, 1923), pp. 153–201.

88. After the Berestechko Battle, Stanisław Ślesiński, a nobleman (captured), who claimed to have been with Khmel'nyts'kyi since the Battle of Korsun', charged that he had witnessed a number of suspicious meetings between Kysil and Khmel'nyts'kyi lasting up to three hours, and that each time Kysil received more gold. Józef Kobierzycki, *Przyczynki do dziejów ziemi sieradzkiej,* 2 vols. (Warsaw, 1915–1916), I, 47–48. For Kysil's exclusion from the Senate sessions see a report of June 30 by a Swedish agent in the Crimea, *Arkhiv Iu. Z. R.,* pt. III, vol. VI, 39 and Oświęcim, *Dyaryusz,* p. 344.

89. For the difficulties of the Commonwealth's armies after Berestechko, see Hrushevs'kyi IX–1, 335–337.

90. Hrushevs'kyi IX–1, 345.

91. For a contemporary account of the negotiations see "Relacye z obozu pod Beresteczkiem," published in Ambroży Grabowski, ed., *Starożytności historyczne polskie, czyli pisma i pamiętniki do dziejów dawnej Polski . . . ,* 2 vols. (Cracow, 1840), II, 271–314. For Kysil's description of the attacks on his entourage, see his letter to his wife Anastaziia, September 30, 1651. BCz, MS 145, pp. 313–315.

92. For copies of the Bila Tserkva treaty, see *Pam.* II, 118–139; Arch. Kr., "Pinocciana," MS 363, pp. 637–641; BCz, MS 966, pp. 149–152; *Vyz.* 400, p. 85; Arch. Kr., Zbiór Rusieckich MS 31, pp. 151–153. A Ukrainian translation is in Hrushevs'kyi IX–1, 365–366.

93. On October 9, Khmel'nyts'kyi wrote to Potocki about Kysil's presence

in Bohuslav. *D.Kh.,* pp. 227–228. See Kysil's letters of October 27, 1651 in BCz, MS 145, pp. 303–308 and October 28, 1651 in BCz, MS 145, pp. 337–338.

94. See Khmel'nyts'kyi's letter to Potocki, October 9, 1651. *D.Kh.,* pp. 227–228.

95. For the political situation after Bila Tserkva, see Władysław Czapliński, *Dwa sejmy w roku 1652* (Wrocław, 1955), pp. 37–66.

96. On the rebellions against Khmel'nyts'kyi, see Hrushevs'kyi IX–1, 391–393.

97. For Potocki's espousal of a "soft" line toward Khmel'nyts'kyi, see his letter to Andrzej Leszczyński, November 2, 1651. *Arkhiv Iu. Z. R.,* pt. III, vol. IV, 623–627; also in BCz, MS 145, pp. 339–347.

98. The most important source for this period is the Diary of Janusz Radziwiłł, in AGAD, Arch. Rad. VI, MS 36. No pages are given for this manuscript because the manuscript had not received final pagination when this research was conducted. Hrushevs'kyi did not use the diary and complains about the paucity of sources for this period.

99. December 14, 1651, Khmel'nyts'kyi to Kysil from Chyhyryn, Diary of Janusz Radziwiłł.

100. January 1, 1652. Kysil to Kalinowski, Diary of Janusz Radziwiłł.

101. Kysil to Kalinowski, January 5, 1652, Diary of Janusz Radziwiłł.

102. See the letter of Khmel'nyts'kyi to Kysil, January 9, 1652. Diary of Janusz Radziwiłł, also in BK, MS 1286, pp. 372–374.

103. January 11, 1652, Kysil to Leszczyński, Diary of Janusz Radziwiłł; BK, MS 1286, pp. 381–385. BK, MS 1286 includes a set of copies made from the Diary of Janusz Radziwiłł.

104. For a detailed account of preparation for the January Diet, see Czapliński, *Dwa sejmy,* pp. 51–66.

105. Khmel'nyts'kyi's letter is published in *D.Kh.,* pp. 243–245.

106. January 19, 1652, Kysil to Kalinowski, Diary of Janusz Radziwiłł; BK, MS 1286, p. 401.

107. January 23, 1652, Kysil to the king, Michałowski, pp. 653–654; Arch. Kr., "Pinocciana," MS 363, pp. 714–715, Recesy, MS 300, 129/135, fols. 461–462, BO, MS 3564, fols. 266–269 (mistakenly dated 1651).

108. *Pam.* III, 1–7.

109. See the report of the papal nuncio in Venice of November 25, 1651, *Litterae Nuntiorum,* VII, p. 325; that of Warsaw of December 17, *Litterae Nuntiorum,* VII, p. 327; January 6, 1652, *Litterae Nuntiorum,* VIII, 12–13; February 24, 1652, *Litterae Nuntiorum,* VIII, 13. For the Venetian plan, see the report of March 9, 1652 *Litterae Nuntiorum,* VIII, 16–17. The report discusses the willingness of Cavazza to agree to the 100,000 florin sum that Kysil had reported necessary. A letter by Kysil of February 22 to the chancellor is mentioned, and special attention is devoted to the importance of Vyhovs'kyi in the negotiations. A letter of Khmel'nyts'kyi to Kysil of February 16 is also discussed, March 16, 1652, *Litterae Nuntiorum,* VIII, 18–19.

110. Khmel'nyts'kyi wrote a letter to Kysil on March 12 which agrees essen-

tially with the "instructions" to Savych. The letter is only known from a Latin translation in the Vatican archives. *D.Kh.*, pp. 256–258. On April 6, de Torres reported that the instruction of Khmel'nyts'kyi's emissary to Kysil had been received in Warsaw and that he had translated them from Polish to Latin. *Litterae Nuntiorum*, VIII, 22. These instructions in the papal nuncio's archives are not yet published, but a copy exists. PAN, Zakład Dokumentacji, Teki Rzymskie, MS 76, Załączniki, pp. 1–5. A Polish version is in BJ, MS 3595, fols. 7–8. For information on this period, see Hrushevs'kyi IX–1, 431.

111. The most thorough account of the Diet is Czapliński, *Dwa sejmy*, pp. 51–131.

112. The royal privilege is published in *DOVUN*, p. 636.

113. Hrushevs'kyi IX–1, 413–419.

114. *DOVUN*, pp. 640–644.

115. On May 25, 1652, the papal nuncio wrote that the chancellor claimed to be driven to desperation by the contradictions in Kysil's and Kalinowski's letters. *Litterae Nuntiorum*, VIII, 29.

116. Hrushevs'kyi IX–1, 426–430.

117. For an account of this period, see Ludwik Kubala, "Krwawe swaty," *Szkice historyczne*, Seria 1 i 2, 3rd ed. (Warsaw, 1923), pp. 309–323.

118. Kysil reported on the outcome of the Batih battle in a letter to K. L. Sapieha (n.d.), BCz, MS 1657, p. 367.

119. For a detailed account of the 1652 Diet, see Czapliński, *Dwa sejmy*, pp. 139–178.

120. Arch Kr., "Pinocciana," MS 363, p. 794, Czapliński, *Dwa sejmy*, p. 171.

121. For information on this Diet, see Hrushevs'kyi IX–1, 503–504, 508. Kysil's activities are briefly mentioned by Radziwiłł, *Memoriale*, IV, 277.

122. The developments of the post-Batih period are discussed in Hrushevs'kyi IX–1, 489–490.

123. The will has been published in "Try testamenty Adama Kysilia," *Ukraïna*, 1918, books 1–2, pp. 61–65. Copies or summaries of the will exist in the following manuscripts: BJ, MS 5491, vol. III, fols. 33–36; PAN, MS 2915, fols. 1–4; PAN, MS 3099, fol. 7; PANK, MS 2943, fols. 3–7; and BCz, MS 146, pp. 1149–1152.

124. In Kysil's will of 1653, over 50 towns and villages are mentioned. "Try testamenty," p. 55. His substantial Left-Bank estates are mentioned only with general descriptions. For an attempt to reconstruct the extent of Kysil's estates see [Jan Marek Giżycki], *Z przeszłości*, pp. 36–42. Although Giżycki is very precise in describing Kysil's extensive Volhynian holdings, he discusses Kysil's enormous Chernihiv holdings only in general terms. Many of his Chernihiv estates appear to have been feudal holdings, and at his death were granted by the king to Crown Chancellor Stefan Koryciński, BCz, MS 127, pp. 193–195.

125. For a discussion of the complex court case between the descendants of Kysil's niece and those of his paternal cousins, see Edward Rulikowski, "Nowosiołki," *Słownik Geograficzny Królewstwa Polskiego . . .*, VII (Warsaw, 1886), 285–286.

126. "Try testamenty," p. 62.

127. Marcin Goliński reported Kysil's death in the following manner: "Adam Kysil, the old Palatine of Kiev, a Schismatic of the Ruthenian Faith, died. It was believed about him that he was on the side of the Cossacks and had his secrets with them, but this is a misconception since he negotiated honestly and served on commissions to the Cossacks." BO, MS 189, p. 622. Also Radziwiłł, *Memoriale,* IV, 282.

128. For Vidoni's statement, see his dispatch of May 19, 1653, *Litterae Nuntiorum,* VIII, p. 95. Albrycht Stanisław Radziwiłł mentions that Kysil indicated that he wished to convert on his deathbed. *Memoriale,* IV, 106.

Chapter 8

1. This excerpt of a letter from the *Posol'skii prikaz* archives is published in Hrushevs'kyi IX–1, 148.

2. *Istoriia Kyieva,* I, 148.

3. For a discussion of various interpretations, see Andrii Iakovliv, *Dohovir Bohdana Khmel'nyts'koho z Moskvoiu* (New York, 1954) and Basarab, *Pereiaslav 1654.*

4. For a discussion of the Hadiach Agreement, or Union, see Hrushevs'kyi X, 310–359 and the unpublished doctoral dissertation of Andrew Pernal.

5. For an outline of this complex period, see Dmytro Doroshenko, *Narys istorii Ukrainy,* 2nd ed., 2 vols. in 1 (Munich, 1966), II, 51–94.

6. This view is put forth most strongly by Stanisław Kot, *Jerzy Niemirycz: W 300-lecie ugody hadziackiej* (Paris, 1960). Also see Aleksander Jabłonowski, *Historya Rusi południowej do upadku Rzeczypospolitej Polskiej* (Cracow, 1912), pp. 259–260.

7. For discussion of the genesis of Hadiach, see Andrzej Kaminski, "The Cossack Experiment in *Szlachta* Democracy in the Polish-Lithuanian Commonwealth: The Hadiach (*Hadziacz*) Union," *Harvard Ukrainian Studies,* I, no. 2 (June 1977), 178–197.

8. The Cossacks' lack of respect for the Commonwealth as their sovereign was pointed out by Kysil at the Election Diet of 1648. Michałowski, p. 238. On November 15, 1648, the Cossacks demanded that they be directly subordinated to the king, and not be under the control of the Crown hetmans *D.Kh.,* pp. 83–84.

9. In the early stages of the revolt, Khmel'nyts'kyi offered to assist Jan Kazimierz in increasing the king's power. November 15, 1648. Khmel'nyts'kyi to Jan Kazimierz, *D.Kh.,* p. 80.

10. For a biography of Nemyrych see Kot, *Jerzy Niemirycz,* For a negative evaluation of Nemyrych, see Janusz Tazbir's review of Kot's book, "Prawdziwe oblicze Jerzego Niemirycza," *Przegląd Historyczny,* LI (1960), 721–726. Tazbir's negative evaluation of Nemyrych's motives does not conflict with the image of Nemyrych as a daring and creative thinker. Also see Tazbir, "The Political Reversals of Jurij Nemyryč," *Harvard Ukrainian Studies,* V, no. 3 (September 1981), 306–319.

11. Nemyrych's original text has been lost, but the general aspects of his proposal are known because of a rebuttal by Samuel Przypkowski. See Kot's discussion in *Jerzy Niemirycz*, pp. 59–63.

12. July 11, 1649, A. Leszczyński to K. L. Sapieha, BN, BOZ, MS 931, pp. 291–293.

13. Kysil clearly maintained that while the Commonwealth could survive the loss of Livonia, it could not survive the loss of the Ukraine. As he put it, "the Fatherland will not be the Fatherland." Letter of April 24, 1649, Kysil to Ossoliński, Arch. Kr., "Pinocciana," MS 363, pp. 308–310.

14. Kysil once said to Khmel'nyts'kyi "to me, therefore, from Rus' there is woe, and from the Poles no peace." Spring, 1649, *Arkhiv Iu. Z. R.,* pt. III, vol. IV, 171–174.

15. A frequently cited speech of Kysil, which was included in manuals of oratory, includes the passage: Civis ac Senator sum plena fide Patriam, integerrimo Reges meos veneratus obsequio. Ac si cui genus, si virtus & innocenter gesti honores fiduciam augere possunt, certe mihi, qui sanguine & fide Rutheno, exiis tamen descendam Swietuldyciis, quorum auxilio & consilio, corpori Regni nobilis Roxolania accessit. Mihi cum Rebellibus, prater eadem sacra commune nihil. . ." *Orator Polonus . . .* (Warsaw, 1740), p. 597.

16. October 20, 1649, Kysil to Khmel'nyts'kyi, Grabowski II, 126–127.

17. *Voss.* II, 106.

Frequent Abbreviations of Published Works

Arkhiv Iu. Z. R. Arkhiv Iugo-Zapadnoi Rossii, izdavaemyi Vremennoiu kom-missieiu dlia razbora drevnikh aktov, vysochaishe uchrezhdennoiu pri Kiev-skom voennom, podolskom i volynskom general-gubernatore, 8 parts, 34 v. Kiev, 1859–1914.

Akty Iu. Z. R., III. *Akty, otnosiashchiesia k istorii Iuzhnoi i Zapadnoi Rossii, sobrannye i izdannye Arkheograficheskoiu komissieiu,* 15 v. St. Petersburg, 1863–1892.

Boniecki. Boniecki, Adam. *Herbarz Polski,* 10 vols. Warsaw, 1901–1913.

Chteniia (Moscow). Chteniia v Imperatorskom Obshchestve istorii i drevnostei rossiiskikh pri Moskovskom universitete.

D. Kh. Dokumenty Bohdana Khmel'nyts'koho 1648–1657, comp. I. Kryp''ia-kevych and I. Butych, published by Instytut suspil'nykh nauk Akademiï Nauk Ukraïns'koi RSR and Arkhivne upravlinnia pry Radi ministriv Ukraïns'koï RSR. Kiev, 1961.

DOVUN. Dokumenty ob osvoboditelnoi voine ukrainskogo naroda 1648–1654 gg., ed. A. Z. Baraboi *et al.* Kiev, 1965.

Golubev I-1, I-2, II-1, II-2. Golubev, S. *Kievskii Mitropolit Petr Mogila i ego spodvizhniki (Opyt tserkovno-istoricheskogo issledovaniia),* 2 v. Kiev, 1883–1898.

Grabowski, I and II. Grabowski, Ambroży, ed. *Ojczyste spominki w pismach do dziejów dawnej Polski. Diaryusze, relacye, pamiętniki, i. t. p., służyć mo-gące do objaśnienia dziejów krajowych i tudzież listy historyczne do panowania królów Jana Kazimierza i Michała Korybuta oraz listy Jana Sobieskiego, Mar-szałka i Hetmana Wielkiego Koronnego,* 2 v. Cracow, 1845.

Hrushevs'kyi, I etc., and VIII-1, VIII-2, VIII-3. Hrushevs'kyi, Mykhailo. *Istoriia Ukraïny-Rusy,* vols. I–X (vol. VIII, 1, 2, 3). New York, 1954–1957.

Kaczmarczyk. Kaczmarczyk, Zdzisław and Leśnodorski, Bogusław. *Od połowy XV wieku do r. 1795,* vol. II of *Historia państwa i prawa Polski,* 4 ed. Warsaw, 1971.

Litterae Nuntiorum, V, VI, VII, VIII. *Litterae Nuntiorum Apostolicorum His-toriam Ucrainae illustrantes (1550–1850),* Analecta OSBM series II, sec-tion III, ed. A. G. Welykyj, 13 v. to date. Rome, 1959–1969.

Michałowski. [Michałowski, Jakub]. *Jakuba Michałowskiego, wojskiego lubel-skiego, a później kasztelana bieckiego księga pamiętnicza z dawnego rękopisma*

350   **Between Poland and the Ukraine**

będącego własnością Ludwika hr. Morsztyna, ed. Antoni Zygmunt Helcel. Cracow, 1864.

ODAZUM. Opisanie dokumentov Arkhiva zapadnorusskikh uniatskikh mitropolitov, comp. S. G. Runkevich, 2 v. St. Petersburg, 1895.

Pam. I, II, III, IV. *Pam"iatniki, izdannye Vremennoiu kommissieiu dlia razbora drevnikh aktov, vysochaishe uchrezhdennoiu pri Kievskom voennom, podolskom i volynskom general-gubernatore,* ed. N. Ivanishev. 4 v. Kiev, 1845–1859.

Radziwiłł, *Memoriale,* I, II, III, IV, V. Albrycht Stanisław Radziwiłł, *Memoriale Rerum Gestarum in Polonia 1632–1656,* 5 vols. Polska Akademia Nauk. Oddział w Krakowie, Materiały Komisji Nauk Historycznych, XV, XVIII, XXII, XXV, XXVI. Wrocław, I, 1968; II, 1970; III, 1972; IV, 1974; V, 1975.

Šmurlo. Šmurlo, E. *Le Saint Siège et l'Orient Orthodoxe Russe 1609–1654.* Publication des Archives du Ministère des Affairs Étrangères, Series I, no. 4, 2 parts. Prague, 1928.

"Try test." "Try testamenty Adama Kysilia," *Ukraïna,* 1918, books 1–2, pp. 49–67.

Volumina legum. Prawa, konstytucye y przywileie Królewstwa Polskiego y Wielkiego Xięstwa Litewskiego, y wszytkich prowincyi należących: na walnych seymiech koronnych od Seymu Wiślickiego roku Pańskiego 1347 aż do ostatniego seymu uchwalone, comp. Stanisław Konarski, 8 v. Warsaw, 1732–1782.

Voss. I, II, III. *Vossoedinenie Ukrainy s Rossiei. Dokumenty i materialy 1620–1654,* comp. P. P. Gudzenko *et al.,* published by Akademiia Nauk SSSR, Institut istorii and Akademiia Nauk USSR, Institut istorii. 3 v. Moscow, 1953–1954.

Vyz. Vyzvol'na viina ukrains'koho narodu v 1648–1654 rr. Vozz"ednannia Ukraïny z Rosieiu. Anotovanyi pokazhchyk rukopysnykh materialiv biblioteky, published by L'vivs'ka biblioteka Akademiï Nauk URSR, Viddil rukopysiv. Lviv, 1954.

Z dziejów Ukrainy, II. Wacław Lipiński (Viacheslav Lypyns'kyi), ed., *Z dziejów Ukrainy. Księga pamiątkowa ku czci Włodzimierza Antonowicza, Paulina Święcickiego i Tadeusza Rylskiego.* Kiev-Cracow, 1912.

Zaliudnennia. Ol. Baranovych, *Zaliudnennia volyns'koho voevodstva v pershii polovyni XVII st.,* published by Vseukraïns'ka akademiia nauk, Sotsial'no-ekonomichnyi viddil, Komisiia istorychno-heohrafichna, Kiev, 1930.

Zherela. Zherela do istoriï Ukraïny, 16 v. (Lviv, 1895–1919).

ZIEV. Zapysky istorychno-filol'ohichnoho viddilu Vseukraïnskoï Akademii Nauk.

ZNTSh. Zapysky Naukovoho tovarystva imeni Shevchenka.

Bibliography

Unpublished Sources

AGAD—Archiwum Główne Akt Dawnych w Warszawie
    Metryka Koronna (Met. Kor.) MSS. 180, 181, 182, 185, 190, 191.
    Libri Legationum (LL), MS. 32, 33, 35.
    Archiwum Skarbowe Koronne, dział III, księga 6.
    Tak zwana Metryka Litewska, VIII-1, Stefan Hankiewicz, Index Actorum
        Publicorum Albo Regestr Xięg . . . od roku Pańskiego 1569 aż do roku
        1673. (Metryka Rus'ka)
    Archiwum Radziwiłłowskie (Arch.Rad.)
        dział II, teka 9.
        dział II, księga 10. Miscellanea acta publica, 1607–1640
        dział II, księga 14. Kopiarnia różnych pism.
        dział V, teka 148.
        dział VI, nr 36, Dyaryusz Janusza Radziwiłła.
    Archiwum Zamoyskich
        dział I Korespondencja, teki 306, 338, 727, 841, 943, 3052.
    Archiwum Branickich z Suchej
        MS. 155/181, 19th century. Ukrainne sprawy (zbiory S. Przyłęckiego).
    Zbiory Biblioteki Narodowej (BN)
        MS 5422, 17th century. Reiestr popisu na pospolitem ruszeniu Woje-
        wództwa Wołyńskiego . . . 1621.
Arch. Gdańsk.—Wojewódzkie Archiwum Państwowe w Gdańsku
    Recesy stanów zachodniopruskich (Recesy)
        300,29/112 for the year 1632
        300,29/115 for the year 1635
        300,29/118 for the year 1637
        300,29/119 for the year 1637
        300,29/120 for the year 1638
        300,29/121 for the year 1638
        300,29/122 for the year 1639
        300,29/123 for the year 1640
        300,29/124 for the years 1641–1642
        300,29/125 for the years 1643–1644

300,29/126 for the year 1645
300,29/127 for the year 1646
300,29/128 for the year 1647
300,29/129 for the year 1648
Interregnum
300,29/130 for the year 1648
Acta Interregni
300,29/131 for the year 1648
Acta Interregni
300,29/133 for the year 1649
300,29/134 for the year 1650
300,29/135 for the year 1651
300,29/136 for the year 1652
300,29/137 for the year 1652
300,29/138 for the year 1652
300,29/139 for the years 1653–1654
Korespondencja m. Gdańska po r. 1525
300,53/71
300,53/82 (Nowa teka 418)
300,53/83 (Nowa teka 660)
300,53/101 (Nowa teka 1185)
Rękopisy
MS. 300 R/Ee32, 17th century.
(Materiały do sejmu 1648).
Arch.Łodz.—Wojewódzkie Archiwum Państwowe w Łodzi
Archiwum Bartoszewiczów (Arch.Bart.)
MS. 127, 17th century.
Silva rerum
MS. 40, 19th century.
Inwentarz archiwum w Wiśniowcu, 1560–1664.
Arch.Kr.—Archiwum Miasta Krakowa i Województwa Krakowskiego
Archiwa podworskie i zbiory
Zbiory Rusieckich
MS. 31, 17th century.
Miscellanea 1626–1654
MS. 41, 17th century.
Miscellanea 1645–1652.
Pinocciana
MS. 361, 17th century.
Akta polityczne z czasów Władysława IV . . .
MS. 363, 17th century.
Acta publica Regni Poloniae, 1632–1654.

BCz—Biblioteka Muzeum im. Ks. Czartoryskich w Krakowie
Teki Naruszewicza MSS., 18th century.
MS. 110 for the years 1617–1620
MS. 124 for the year 1632
MS. 127 Reign of Zygmunt III
MS. 132 for the year 1636
MS. 134 for the year 1637
MS. 138 for the years 1641–1643
MS. 141 for the year 1647
MS. 142 for the year 1648
MS. 143 for the year 1648
MS. 144 for the years 1649–1650
MS. 145 for the year 1651
MS. 146 for the year 1652
MS. 147 for the years 1653–1654
MS. 363, 17th century.
Bezkrólewie 1632. Acta interregni
MS. 365, 17th century.
Akta za panowania Zygmunta III, 1630–1633
MS. 373, 17th century.
Akta za panowania Władysława IV, 1632–1646
MS. 375, 17th century.
Akta za Zygmunta III, Władysława IV, 1606–1648
MS. 377, 17th century.
Szczegóły niektóre za panowania Zygmunta III i Władysława IV
MS. 378, 17th century.
Akta za Zygmunta III i Władysława IV wraz z początkiem pano-
wania Jana Kazimierza
MS. 379, 17th century.
Akta za Jana Kazimierza, 1648–1649
MS. 390, 17th century.
Akta od 1618 do 1661
MS. 394, 17th century.
Akta za Jana Kazimierza, 1648–1655
MS. 400, 17th century.
Akta za panowania Jana Kazimierza od 1648 do 1668
MS. 402, 17th century.
Oryginały za Jana Kazimierza
MS. 417, 17th century.
Manuskrypt zebrany staraniem szlachcica polskiego, 1645–1683.
Georges Szornel

MS. 2576, 17th century.
Akta z czasów Władysława IV i Jana Kazimierza
MS. 964, 18th century.
Kopie historyczne z dawnych panowań oraz o indygentach, nobilitacyach, urzędach (podobno z tek Naruszewicza)
MS. 966, 18th century.
Pisma różne za Stanisława Augusta. Diversa acta, notae, commentarii necnon epistolae, quae ad historiam Poloniae saecolorum XIV–XVIII spectant . . .
MS. 1651, 17th century.
Opisanie konfederacyi wojska koronnego. Acta diversa annorum 1612–1652
MS. 1656, 17th century.
Pisma 1665–1667. Silva rerum. Epistolae, orationes, lauda, diarii, acta diversissima . . . praesentim vero annorum 1632, 1648, 1655–1667
MS. 1657, 17th century.
Manuscriptum varia continens. Wiek XVII. Epistolae, orationes, lauda diversaque acta annorum 1501, 1530, 1548, 1573, 1583–1673 (silva rerum)
MS. 2086, 17th century.
Listy i pisma 1632
MS. 2102, 17th century.
Transakcya z Moskwą w roku 1635
MS. 2519, 16th and 17th centuries.
Akta za Wazów i listy królewskie
MS. 2576, 17th century.
Akta z czasów Władysława IV i Jana Kazimierza.
Muzeum Narodowe
MS. 302, 17th century.
Breve Compendium Electionis Nov. I Regis Varsavia A. 1632 celebrata.
BJ—Biblioteka Jagiellońska w Krakowie
MS. 49, 17th century.
Akta do panowania Władysława IV, 1633–1648
MS. 90, 17th century.
Listy i scripta różne podczas interregni 1648
MS. 94, 17th century.
Akta kancelarii królewskiej Władysława IV, za sekretariatu P. Gembickiego. 1634–1636
MS. 116, 17th century.
Kod. pap. z w. XVII różnymi pisany rękami

MS. 2274, 17th century.
Kodeks pap. z r. 1638
MS. 3573, 19th century.
Treść listów Adama Kisiela, 1641–1650
MS. 3595, 17th century.
[Part of "Dyaryusz Janusza Radziwiłła," June 15–July 21, 1652, AGAD, Arch. Rad.VI, nr 36]
MS. 5491, Vol. 3
Akta oryg. i odpisy oraz notatki dotyczące różnych rodzin i osób, XV–XIX w.
MS. 7513, 17th century.
[Part of "Dyaryusz Janusza Radziwiłła," May–June 8, 1651, AGAD, Arch.Rad.VI, MR.36].
BK—Biblioteka PAN w Kórniku
MS. 1317, 17th century.
Pisma do panowania Władysława IV
MS. 1558, 17th century.
Akta do panowania Jana Kazimierza, 1649–1668 [originals and copies]
MS. 1286, 19th century.
Listy B. Chmielnickiego, Kisiela . . .
MS. 347, 17th century.
Akta za panowania Władysława IV, 1632–1648 [originals]
MS. 991, 17th century.
Silva rerum Zygmunta III, Władysława IV i Jana Kazimierza.
BN—Biblioteka Narodowa w Warszawie
MS. 3091, 17th century.
Listy i papiery dotyczące panowania Jana Kazimierza.
Biblioteka Ordynacji Zamoyskiej (BOZ)
BOZ, MS. 858, 17th century.
Awizy, listy, mowy . . .
BOZ, MS. 931
Odpisy listów różnych osób do Lwa Kazimierza Sapiehy, podkanclerzego litewskiego, z lat 1644–1649. Czynności bezkrólewia po śmierci Władysława IV. [Polish mid. XVII w.]
BOZ, MS. 934, 17th century.
Mowy . . .
BOZ, MS. 950, 18th century.
Listy, mowy 1591–1736
BOZ, MS. 1173, 17th century.
Listy, mowy, instrukcye na seymy, lauda sejmikowe, 1622–1635

BOZ, MS. 1217
Silva rerum 1600–1750. XVIII cent.
BOZ, MS. 1598
Album Univers. generalis studii Zamoscensis, 1595–1659.
MS. 1602, 17th century.
Kopiariusz korespondencyi Tomasza Zamoyskiego.
BO—Biblioteka Zakładu Narodowego im. Ossolińskich we Wrocławiu
MS. 188, II, 17th century.
Kodeks papierowy XVII (Marcina Golińskiego)
MS. 189, II, 17th century.
Kodeks Marcina Golińskiego, rajcy kazimierzowskiego
MS. 206, 17th century.
Kodeks papierowy XVII w.
MS. 3564, II, 17th century.
Listy i diariusze 1648–1674
MS. 3566, II, 17th century.
Instrukcye i lauda ruskie oraz sprawy sejmowe itp. 1628–1651
MS. 3567, II, 17th century.
Mowy i woty oraz listy rozmaite IMP Jakuba Sobieskiego in anno
1646 na sejmach i inszych publicznych aktach
MS. 5972, II, 17th to 19th centuries.
Autografy monarchów 1612–1818
MS. 7249, II, 17th to 20th centuries.
Papiery Bolesława i Marii Wysłouchów, Tom LXXV. Miscellanea.
BR—Biblioteka im. Raczyńskich w Poznaniu
MS. 2, 17th century.
Sprawy publiczne w Polsce w roku 1619, 20, 21 i 1622 (1623)
MS. 25, 17th century.
Rozmaitości obejmujące listy, relacye, wiersze itp. Akta urzędowe
od r. 1609–1641.
BUW—Biblioteka Uniwersytetu Wrocławskiego
MS. Akc. 1949, KN 439, 17th century.
Polonica Varia I–II (Steinwehr)
MS. Akc. 1949, KN 440, 17th century.
Polonica Varia I–III (Steinwehr)
LNB—Lvivs'ka Naukova Biblioteka im. Stefanyka Akademiï Nauk Ukraïns'koï
RSR
Fond Ossolyns'kykh (5)
MS. 225 (17th century Polish manuscript)
MS. 231 (17th century Polish manuscript)
MS. 7444, Wacław Rulikowski "Zbiór notat genealogiczno-heraldycz-
nych"

Zbirka Radzymyns'koho
MS. 42 I.4 Summariusz z akt Włodzimierskich z lat 1569–1813. 7 vols.
159. III.5 Summariusz z akt Łuckich 1592–1739
PANK—Biblioteka PAN w Krakowie (Dawniej PAU)
MS. 272, 17th and 18th centuries.
Akta rusko-polskie 1618–1786
MS. 349, 17th century.
Listy do Sapiehów etc. Tomus VIII (orygin.)
MS. 367, 17th century.
Dyaryusze, mowy, listy 1622–1656
MS. 1051, 17th century.
Without title.
MS. 1056, 19th century.
Edward Kotłubaj, "Listy, Dijariusze i Relacije od początków wojen kozackich do obioru Jana Kazimierza 1648." Z rękopisów archiwum Radziwiłłowskiego w Nieświeżu wydał i przypisami objaśnił . . .
MS. 1819, 19th century.
Kopiariusz korespondencyi hetmana St. Koniecpolskiego, 1634–1639
MSS. 2251, 2252, 2253, 2254, 2255, 2256, 2257, 17th century.
Księga pamiętnicza Jakuba Michałowskiego
MSS. 2915, 2943, 2977, 2978, 3022, 3099, 3604, 6007.
[Genealogical tables and summaries of documents. Evidence of 17th and 18th centuries court cases concerning the ownership and boundaries of Kysil's estates.]
Zakład Dokumentacji Instytutu Historii PAN w Krakowie
Teki Rzymskie, 19th century, nr 76, 105.
Recesy—See Arch. Gdansk
Steinwehr—See Biblioteka Uniwersytetu Wrocławskiego (BUW)
TsNB—Tsentral'na Naukova Biblioteka Akademii Nauk Ukraïns'koï RSR (Kiev)
II 13402 P. Kulish, Materialy dlia istorii vossoedineniia Rusi, II
Arkhiv O. I. Levyts'koho, fond 81, nr. 30
"Adam Kysil" [copies from inscription books from the Chernihiv and Volhynian palatinates]
Biblioteka Sofiis'koho Soboru
VIII 377–705—Synodic of the Kiev St. Sophia's Cathedral
Pochaïvs'ka Biblioteka
MS. 48 [formerly 66]
Shors'ka Biblioteka Khreptovycha
I MS. 6012 [17th century Polish manuscript]

Published Sources

Acta S. Congregationis de Propaganda Fide Ecclesiam Ucrainae et Bielarusiae Spectantia, Analecta OSBM, series II, section III, ed. A. G. Welykyj, 4 vols. Rome, 1953–1955.

Akta grodzkie i ziemskie z czasów Rzeczypospolitej Polskiej z Archiwum tak zwanego Bernardyńskiego [*Archiwum Ziemskiego*] *we Lwowie*, 15 vols. Lviv, 1868–1935.

Akta sejmikowe województwa krakowskiego, 4 vols. Cracow, Wrocław, 1932–1964.

Akty istoricheskie, otnosiashchiesia k Rossii, izvlechennye iz inostrannykh arkhivov i bibliotek, ed. A. I. Turgenev, 2 vols. St. Petersburg, 1841–1842.

Akty Moskovskogo gosudarstva, izdannye Imperatorskoi Akademieiu nauk, 3 vols. St. Petersburg, 1890–1901.

Akty, otnosiashchiesia k istorii Zapadnoi Rossii, sobrannye i izdannye Arkheograficheskoiu komissieiu, 5 vols. St. Petersburg, 1846–1853.

Akty, otnosiashchiesia k istorii Iuzhnoi i Zapadnoi Rossii, sobrannye i izdannye Arkheograficheskoiu komissieiu, 15 vols. St. Petersburg, 1863–1892.

Arkheograficheskii sbornik dokumentov, otnosiashchikhsia k istorii Severozapadnoi Rusi, 14 vols. Vilnius, 1867–1904.

Arkhiv Iugo-Zapadnoi Rossii, izdavaemyi Vremennoiu komissieiu dlia razbora drevnikh aktov, vysochaishe uchrezhdonnoiu pri Kievskom voennom, podol'skom i volynskom general-gubernatore, 8 parts, 34 vols. Kiev, 1859–1914.

Baiewski, Thodosius Wasilewicz [Baevs'kyi, Teodozii Vasylevych]. *Tentoria Venienti Kioviam cum novi Honoris fuscibus Illustrissimo Domino, D. Adamo de Brusiłow Sventoldicio Kisiel Castellano: Nosov: & Capitaneo a Collegio Mohil. Kiou.—expansa opera Fr. Theodosii Wasilewicz Baiewski. Kiev, 1646.

Baliński, Michał, ed. *Pamiętniki historyczne do wyjaśnienia spraw publicznych w Polsce XVII wieku posługujące, w dziennikach domowych Obuchowiczów i Cedrowskiego pozostałe*. Vilnius, 1859.

Bantysh-Kamenskii, N. N. *Obzor vneshnikh snoshenii Rossii*, 4 vols. Moscow, 1894–1902.

———. *Perepiska mezhdu Rossieiu i Pol'sheiu po 1700 god, sostavlennaia po diplomaticheskim bumagam*, 3 parts. Moscow, 1862.

Barącz, Sadok, Ks., ed. *Pamiętniki zakonu WW. OO. Bernardynów w Polszcze*. Lviv, 1874.

Baranovych, Ol. *Zaliudnennia Volyns'koho voevodstva v pershii polovyni XVII st.*, pub. by Vseukraïns'ka Akademiia Nauk, Sotsial'no-ekonomichnyi viddil, Komisiia istorychno-heohrafichna. Kiev, 1930.

Baranowicz, Łazar. *Lutnia Apollinowa w każdey sprawie gotowa, na błogosławiąca rękę iako na takt iaki patrząc* . . . Kiev, 1671.

Bevzo, O. A., *L'vivs'kyi litopys i Ostroz's'kyi litopysets': Dzhereloznavche doslidzhennia*. Kiev, 1970.

Bieleiowski, Hieremias. *Obrona tytułów Xiążęczych od Rzeczypospolitey uchwałą seymową*. n.p., 1641.

Bisaccioni, Maiolino. *Historia delle guerre civili di questi ultimi tempi scritta dal conte* . . . Venice, 1663.

[Chevalier, Pierre] Sheval'e P'er. *Istoriia viiny kozakiv proty Pol'shchi*, intro. by A. Z. Baraboi. Kiev, 1963.

Costin, Miron. *Chronicon Terrae Moldavicae ab Aarone Principe*, ed. Eugeniusz Barwinski. Bucharest, 1912.

Daneykowicz, Jan, ed. *Swada Polska y Łacińska albo Miscellanea Oratorskie Seymowe, Weselne, Kancellaryine, Listowne, Kaznodziejskie, Pogrzebowe, Statystyczne, Panegiryczne, Inskrypcyine, y inne różne, w oboim języku Prozą y Wierszem* . . . 2 vols. Lublin, 1745–1747.

Documenta Pontificum Romanorum Historiam Ucrainae illustrantia, Analecta OSBM, series II, section III, ed. A. G. Welykyj, 2 vols. Rome, 1953–1954.

Documente privitore la Istoria Romanilor, 19 vols., 2 supplements. Bucharest, 1885–1922.

Dokumenty Bohdana Khmelnyts'koho 1648–1657, comp. I. Kryp"iakevych and I. Butych, pub. by Instytut suspil'nykh nauk Akademiï Nauk Ukraïns'koï RSR and Arkhivne upravlinnia pry Radi ministriv Ukraïns'koï RSR. Kiev, 1961.

Dokumenty ob osvoboditel'noi voine ukrainskogo naroda 1648–1654 g.g., ed. A. Z. Baraboi et al. Kiev, 1965.

Dopolneniia k aktam istoricheskim, otnosiashchimsia k Rossii, sobrannye v inostrannykh arkhivakh i bibliotekakh; izdany Arkheograficheskoiu komissieiu, eds. Ioann Grigorovich and V. Komovskii. St. Petersburg, 1848.

Epistolae Metropolitarum Archiepiscoporum et Episcoporum. Analecta OSBM, series II, section III, ed. A. G. Welykyj, 8 vols. to date. Rome, 1956–1970.

Franko, Ivan. "Khmel'nychchyna 1648–1649 u suchasnykh virshakh," *ZNTSh*, XXIII–XXIV (1898): 1–114.

Galaktionov, I. V. *Ranniaia perepiska A. L. Ordina-Nashchokina (1642–1645 gg)*. [Saratoy], 1968.

Gazotti, Pietro. *Historia delle Guerre d'Europa arrivate dell'Anno 1643 sino al 1680*. Venice, 1681.

Golubev, S. *Materialy dlia istorii Zapadno-Russkoi tserkvi*, 2 parts. Kiev, 1883–1898. (= *Prilozheniia* to S. Golubev, *Kievskii Mitropolit Petr Mogila i ego spodvizhniki* [*Opyt tserkovno-istoricheskogo issledovaniia*], 2 vols. Kiev, 1883–1898.

Grabowski, Ambroży, ed. *Ojczyste spominki w pismach do dziejów dawnej Polski. Diaryusze, relacye, pamiętniki i. t. p., służyć mogące do objaśnienia dziejów krajowych i tudzież listy historyczne do panowania królów Jana Ka-*

zimierza i Michała Korybuta oraz listy Jana Sobieskiego, Marszałka i Hetmana Wielkiego Koronnego, 2 vols. Cracow, 1845.

———. *Starożytności historyczne polskie, czyli pisma i pamiętniki do dziejów dawnej Polski*, 2 vols. Cracow, 1840.

———. *Władysława IV króla polskiego listy i inne pisma urzędowe*. Cracow, 1845.

Grondski de Grond [Grądzki], Samuel. *Historia Belli Cosacco-Polonici authore Samuele Grondski de Grondi conscripta anno MDCLXXVI*, ed. Carolus Koppi. [Pest], 1789.

Gründliche und denckwürdige Relation der neulichen Cosaken-Revolte wider die Cron Polen, unter Commando Gen. Chmielnicki . . . (n.p., 1649).

Hannover, Nathan. *Abyss of Despair. The Famous 17th Century Chronicle Depicting Jewish Life During the Chmielnicki Massacres of 1648–49*, translated from the Hebrew by Abraham J. Mesch. New York, 1950.

Istoricheskie sviazi narodov SSSR i Rumynii v XV—nachale XVIII v. Dokumenty i materialy v trekh tomakh, ed. Ia. S. Grosul, 3 vols. Moscow, 1965–1970.

Jedność święta Cerkwie wschodniey y zachodniey od początku Wiary S. Katholickiey obficie rozkrzewiona w ruskie kraie od przyięcia Krztu S. szczęśliwie zawitała prawami y przywileiami od Naiaśnieyszych K. I. M. Polskich potężnie warowana przeciw skryptowi synopsis nazwanemu, . . . Przez Bractwo Wileńskie Przenaświętszey Troycy w jedności z S. Kościołem Rzymskim będące. [Vilnius], 1632.

[Jemiołowski, Mikołaj]. *Pamiętnik Mikołaja Jemiołowskiego, towarzysza lekkiej chorągwi, ziemianina województwa bełzkiego, obejmujący dzieje Polski od roku 1648 do 1679 spółcześnie, porządkiem lat opowiedziane*, ed. August Bielowski. Lviv, 1850.

[Jerlicz, Joachim]. *Latopisiec albo kroniczka Joachima Jerlicza*, ed. K. W. Wójcicki, 2 vols. Warsaw, 1853.

Józefowicz, Tomasz Jan. *Kronika miasta Lwowa od roku 1634 do 1690 obejmująca w ogólności dzieje dawnej Rusi Czerwonej a zwłaszcza historyja arcybiskupstwa lwowskiego w tejże epoce*, ed. and tr. M. Piwocki. Lviv, 1854.

Kholmogorov, V. I. "Akty, otnosiashchiesia k Malorossii," *Chteniia* (Moscow) 1885; no. 2, pp. 1–46.

Kobierzycki, Stanisław. *Historia Vladislai IV. Poloniae Sveciaeque Principis, usque ad excessum Sigismundi III.* Gdańsk, 1655.

Kochowski, Wespazjan. *Annalium Poloniae ab Obitu Vladislai IV. Climacter Primus.* Cracow, 1683.

Kojałowicz, Wijuk Wojciech [Kojalowicz, Albertus Wiiuk]. *De rebus anno 1648 et 1649 contra Zaporovios Cosacos gestis.* Vilnius, 1651.

[Koniskii, Georgii]. *Istoriia Rusov ili Maloi Rossii.* Moscow, 1846.

Konopczyński, Władysław. *Chronologia sejmów polskich, 1493–1793.* Cracow,

1948. (= Archiwum Komisji Historycznej, Polska Akademia Umiejętności, series II, vol. IV, no. 3.)

Korduba, M. "Venets'ke posol'stvo do Khmel'nyts'koho (1650r.)," *ZNTSh,* LXXVIII (1907), 51–89.

Korshunov, Aleksandr F. *Afanasii Filippovich: Zhizn' i tvorchestvo.* Minsk, 1965.

Kossów, Sylwester (Kosiv, Sylvestr). *Paterikon abo żywoty SS. Oycow Pieczarskich. Obszyrnie słowienskim ięzykiem przez Świętego Nestora, zakonnika y latopisca ruskiego przedtym napisany. Teraz zaś z graeckich, łacińskich, słowienskich y polskich pisarzow obiaśniony y krocey podany,* przez Wielebnego w Bogu Oyca Silvestra Kossowa, Episkopa Mścisławskiego, Orszańskiego y Mohylewskiego. Kiev, 1635. Contains a dedication to Adam Kysil.

Kryp"iakevych, Ivan. "Novi materiialy do istorii soboriv v 1629 r.," *ZNTSh,* CXVI (1913): 5–39.

Kuczarewicz, Marcin. *Relacyja ekspedyciey zbaraskiej w roku Pańskim 1649.* Lublin, 1650.

Kurdiumov, M. F. *Opisanie aktov, khraniashchikhsia v arkhive Imperatorskoi Arkheograficheskoi komissii.* St. Petersburg, 1907.

Lazarevskii, Aleksandr Matveevich. *Opisanie staroi Malorossii: Materialy dlia istorii zaseleniia, zemlevladeniia i upravleniia,* 2 vols. Kiev, 1888–1893.

Linage de Vauciennes. *L'origine du soulevement des cosaques contre la Pologne . . .* Paris, 1674.

Litopys Samovydtsia, ed. Iaroslav Dzyra. Kiev, 1971.

Litterae Episcoporum Historiam Ucrainae illustrantes (1600–1900), Analecta OSBM, series II, section III, ed. A. G. Welykyj, 2 vols. to date. Rome, 1972–1973.

Litterae S. Congregationis de Propaganda Fide Ecclesiam Catholicam Ucrainae et Bielarusiae spectantes, Analecta OSBM, series II, section III, ed. A. G. Welykyj, 7 vols. Rome, 1954–1957.

Litterae Nuntiorum Apostolicorum Historiam Ucrainae illustrantes (1550–1850), Analecta OSBM, series II, section III, ed. A. G. Welykyj, 13 vols. to date. Rome, 1959–1969.

Łoś, [Jakób]. *Pamiętnik Łosia, towarzysza chorągwi pancernej Władysława Margrabi Myszkowskiego, wojewody krakowskiego, obejmujące wydarzenia od r. 1646 do 1667, z rękopisu współczesnego, dochowanego w zamku podhorodeckim, wydane,* ed. Żegota Pauli. Cracow, 1858.

Lunig, Johann Christian, ed. *Orationes Procerum Europae, Eorundemque Ministrorum ac Legatorum, ut & Virorrum Celeberrimorum, in multifariis, tam Laetitiae, quam Tristitae casibus, nec non Belli ac Pacis negotiis, itemque Religionis causa, Ab aliquot Seculis, usque ad Annum 1713, Latina Lingua habitae . . . ,* 3 vols. Leipzig, 1713.

Manchester [Henry Montague, Earl of Manchester]. *Al mondo contemplatio mortis et immortalitatis. Rozmyślanie o śmierci y nieśmiertelności z angielskiego yęzyka na polski przetłumaczone przez I. A. Załuskiego,* n.p., 1648. Contains dedication to Kysil by Fra. Victorinus Euthanasius, in Collegio Mohil. Kiou. S.S.T.

[Michałowski, Jakub]. *Jakuba Michałowskiego, wojskiego lubelskiego a później kasztelana bieckiego księga pamiętnicza z dawnego rękopisma będącego własnością Ludwika hr. Morsztyna,* ed. Antoni Zygmunt Helcel. Cracow, 1864.

Molitvy povsednevnyi, ot mnohikh i S[via]tykh Ot[e]ts' sobrannyi, s pilnostiu przezrenyi, na nekotory[kh] mesttsakh" popravlenyi i z druku osmyi raz vydanyi . . . Trudoliubiem Inokov S[via]tyia obshchezhitelnyia obiteli Soshestviia Pre[svia]taho i Zhivotvoriashchaho D[u]kha. Vilnius, 1635. Contains dedication to Kysil.

Monumenta Hungariae Historica. Diplomataria, 28 vols. Budapest, 1857–1888.

Monumenta Ucrainae Historica, comp. Andrei Sheptyts'kyi, 13 vols. Rome, 1964–1975.

Mytsyk, Iu. A., "Tri neizvestnykh pis'ma Bogdana Kmel'nitskogo Adamu Kiseliu," *Sovetskie arkhivy* 1982, no. 4, pp. 45–47.

Niemcewicz, J. U., ed. *Zbiór pamiętników historycznych o dawnej Polszcze z rękopismów, tudzież dzieł w różnych językach o Polszcze wydanych, oraz z listami oryginalnemi królów i znakomitych ludzi w kraju naszym,* 2nd ed., 5 vols. Leipzig, 1839–1840.

Nikolaichik, O. "Materialy po istorii zemlevladeniia kniazei Vishnevetskich v Levoberezhnoi Ukraine," *Chteniia v istoricheskom obshchestve Nestora Letopistsa,* vol. XIV, no. 3 (1900): 91–192.

O konfederacyi lwowskiej w roku 1622 uczynionej nauka. Ed. Kazimierz Józef Turowski. Cracow, 1858.

Okolski, Szymon. *Dyaryusz transakcyi wojennej między wojskiem koronnem i zaporoskiem w r. 1637, tudzież kontynuacya dyaryusza wojennego w roku 1638 przez . . . ,* ed. Kazimierz Józef Turowski. Cracow, 1859. (= Biblioteka Polska, Sekcja na r. 1859, nos. 1–2.)

[Okolski, Szymon]. *Orbis Polonus, Splendoribus Caeli: Triumphis Mundi: Pulchritudine Animantium: Decore Aquatilium: Naturae Excellentia Repitilium, Condecoratus. In Anti Sarmatorum Gentilitia, Pervetustae Nobilitatis Polonae Insignia, Vetera & Nova Indigenatus Meritorum Praemia & Arma; Specificantur & Relucent . . .* Authore R. P. Fr. Simone Okolski, 2 vols. Cracow, 1641.

Olszewski, H. "Nowe materiały do chronologii sejmów polskich," *Czasopismo Prawno-Historyczne,* IX, no. 2 (1957): 229–258.

Opis' aktovoi knigi Kievskogo Tsentral'nogo arkhiva, oznachennoi po spisku onogo pod . . . , pub. by Kievskii Tsentral'nyi arkhiv, 60 vols. Kiev, 1869–1913.

Opisanie dokumentov Arkhiva zapadnorusskikh uniatskikh mitropolitov, comp. S. G. Runkevich, 2 vols. St. Petersburg, 1895.

Orański-Wojna, Pachomiusz. *Zwierciadło albo zasłona naprzeciw uszczypliwej*

Perspektywie X. Kassyana Sakowicza, złożonego archimandryty Dubienskiego. Vilnius, 1645.

Orator Polonus . . . Warsaw, 1750.

[Ordin-Nashchokin, Afanasii L.]. *Ranniaia perepiska A. Ordin-Nashchokina (1642–1645),* ed. I. V. Galaktionov. Saratov, 1968.

[Oświęcim, Stanisław]. *Stanisława Oświęcima Dyaryusz 1643–1651,* ed. Wiktor Czermak. Cracow, 1907. (= Scriptores Rerum Polonicarum, XIX.)

Pamiętniki do panowania Zygmunta III i Władysława IV. Warsaw, 1846.

Pamiatniki, izdannye kievskoiu komissieiu dlia razbora drevnikh aktov, 2nd ed., 3 vols. Kiev, 1898.

Pamiatniki, izdannye Vremennoiu komissieiu dlia razbora drevnikh aktov, vysochaishe uchrezhdennoiu pri Kievskom voennom, podolskom i volynskom general-gubernatore, ed. N. Ivanishev, 4 vols. Kiev, 1845–1859.

Pamiętniki historyczne do wyjaśnienia spraw publicznych w Polsce XVII wieku posługujące, w dziennikach domowych Obuchowiczów i Cedrowskiego pozostałe, ed. Michał Baliński. Vilnius, 1859.

Pamiętniki o wojnach kozackich za Chmielnickiego przez nieznanego authora, 2nd ed., ed. Zygmunt Schletter. Wrocław, 1842.

Pastorius, Joachim. *Bellum Scythico-Cosacicum seu de Coniuratione Tatarorum, Cosacorum et Plebis Russicae contra Regnum Poloniae . . . ,* Gdańsk, 1652.

[Pastorius, Joachim]. *Relatio Gloriosissimae Expeditionis, Victoriossimi Progressus & Eaustissimae Pacificationis cum Hostibus . . .* n.p., 1649.

Petrushevich, A. S. comp. *Dopolneniia ko svodnoi galitsko-russkoi letopisi s 1600 po 1700 god.* Lviv, 1891.

———. *Svodnaia galitsko-russkaia letopis' s 1600 po 1700.* Lviv, 1874.

[Piasecki, Paweł]. *Kronika Pawła Piaseckiego, biskupa przemyskiego . . . ,* intro. by J. Bartoszewicz, ed. K. W. Wójcicki. Cracow, 1870.

Polnoe sobranie russkikh letopisei, 2nd ed., II, St. Petersburg, 1908.

Povest' vremennykh let, prepared by D. S. Likhachev; ed. V. P. Adrianova-Perets, 2 vols. Moscow, 1950.

Prawa y przywileje od Najaśnieyszych Królów . . . Polskich y W. X. L. nadane Obywatelom Korony Polskiey y Wielkiego X. L. Religiey Greckiey, w Iedności z S. Kościołem Rzymskim będącym. Przez Bractwo Wileńskie Przenaświętszey Troycy w Jedności s. Cerkiewnej będące na świat wydane. [Vilnius], 1632.

Przyłęcki, Stanisław, ed. *Pamiętniki o Koniecpolskich. Przyczynek do dziejów polskich XVII wieku.* Lviv, 1842.

Pułaski, Franciszek. *Opis 815 rękopisów Biblioteki Ordynacji hr. Krasińskich.* Warsaw, 1915.

Pułaski, Kazimierz. *Kronika polskich rodów szlacheckich Podola, Wołynia i Ukrainy,* 1 vol. Brody, 1911.

P[ułaski], K[azimierz]. "Pierwsze lata publicznego zawodu Adama Kisiela (1628–1635)," *Przewodnik Naukowy i Literacki,* 1874, no. 1, pp. 98–124.

Pułaski, Kazimierz, "Pierwsze lata zawodu publicznego Adama Kisiela (1622–1635)," *Szkice i poszukiwania historyczne,* vol. I, Cracow, 1887, pp. 191–236.

Radoszchicki, Paulus. *Laurea Palaestrae Philosophicae Excellent D. D. Academiae Zamoscensis Professoribus. Iacobo Skwarski Płocen. Gasparo Tradkowski, & Stanislao Roszynski Magisterij & Doctoratus in Philosophia insigniae ab Excellentis D. Urbano Bryllio Phil. Doct. eiusdem Acad. Pub. Professore feliciter accipientibus.* Mensis Iannuarij die 2 Anno D. 1620. In Typogr. Acad. Zamoss. Contains a dedication to Kysil.

Radwański, Zbigniew. "Uzupełnienie do chronologii sejmów polskich," *Czasopismo Prawno-Historyczne,* II (1949): 449–451.

Radzimiński, Z. L., comp. *Monografia XX. Sanguszków oraz innych potomków Lubarta-Fedora Olgerdowicza X. Ratneńskiego,* vol. I. Lviv, 1906.

Radziwiłł, Albrycht Stanisław. *Memoriale Rerum Gestarum in Polonia 1632–1656,* 5 vols., Polska Akademia Nauk. Oddział w Krakowie. Materiały Komisji Nauk Historycznych, XV, XVIII, XXII, XXV, XXVI. Wrocław, I, 1968; II, 1970; III, 1972; IV, 1974; V, 1975.

Rawita-Gawroński, Fr[anciszek], ed. *Sprawy i rzeczy ukraińskie. Materyały do dziejów kozaczyzny i hajdamaczyzny.* Lviv, 1914.

Relacye nuncjuszów apostolskich i innych osób od r. 1548 do 1690, comp. E. Rykaczewski, 2 vols. Poznań, 1864.

Relatio glorissimae expeditionis, . . . Joannis Casimiri, Regis Poloniae & Sveciae (1643).

Rudawski, Laurentius. *Historiarum Poloniae ab excessu Vladislai IV ad pacem Olivensem usque libri IX.* Warsaw, 1755.

Russkaia istoricheskaia biblioteka, pub. by the Arkheograficheskaia komissija, 39 vols. St. Petersburg, Petrograd, Leningrad, 1872–1927.

Sakowicz, Kassian [Sakovych, Kasiian]. *Epanorthosis albo perspectiwa y obiaśnienie błędów, herezyey y zabobonów w Greko-Ruskiey Cerkwi Disunitskiey tak w artykułach wiary, iako w administrowaniu sakramentów, y w inszych obrządkach y ceremoniach znayduiących się.* Cracow, 1642.

––––––. *Kalendarz stary, w którym jawny y oczywisty błąd okazuie się około święcenia Paschi y responsa na zarzuty starokalendarzan y co za pożytki ruskiemu narodowi z przyięcia nowego kalendarza a iakie szkody z trzymania się starego y iako się ma rozumieć poprawa kalendarza.* Warsaw, 1641.

––––––. *Okulary kalendarzowi staremu, przy których y responsa katolickie na obiectie starokalendarzan są położone y pożytki ruskiemu narodowi z przyięcia rzymskiego kalendarza ukazane, y o ogniu graeckim zmyślonym, iakoby z nieba do Grobu Pańskiego zstępuiącym, y czymby się miała różnić Unia od Disuniey.* Cracow, [1644].

Sbornik letopisei, otnosiashchikhsia k istorii Iuzhnoi i Zapadnoi Rusi, ed. V. Antonovich. Kiev, 1888.

Senai z Krymu, Hadzy Mehmed. *Historia Chana Islam Gereja III,* eds. Zygmunt Abrahamowicz *et al.* Warsaw, 1971.

Šmurlo, E. *Le Saint-Siège et l'Orient Orthodoxe Russe 1609–1654.* Publication des Archives du Ministère des Affairs Étrangères, series I, no. 4, 2 parts. Prague, 1928.

Sobranie gosudarstvennykh gramot i dogovorov, khraniashchikhsia v Gosudarstvennoi kollegii inostrannykh del, 5 vols. Moscow, 1813–1894.

Sysyn, Frank E.."Documents of Bohdan Xmel'nyc'kyj," *Harvard Ukrainian Studies* II, no. 4 (December 1978): 500–524.

Szajnocha, Karol. *Dwa lata dziejów naszych* (= vols. VIII, IX, X *Dzieła Karola Szajnochy* [Warsaw, 1877]).

Szilágyi, Sándor, ed. *Erdély és az északkeleti háború. Levelek és okíratok (1648–1660),* 2 vols. Budapest, 1890–1891.

[Temberski, Stanisław]. *Stanisława Temberskiego roczniki 1647–1656,* ed. Wiktor Czermak. Cracow, 1897 (= *Scriptores Rerum Polonicarum,* vol. XVI).

Theiner, Augustin, ed. *Vetera Monumenta Poloniae et Lithuaniae Gentiumque Finitimarum Historiam Illustrantia,* 4 vols. Rome, 1860–1864.

Threnos, to jest Lament jedyney św. powszechney Apostolskiej Wschodniej Cerkwie z objaśnieniem dogmat wiary pierwszey z greckiego na słowiański, a teraz z słowiańskiego na polski przetłomaczony przez Teophila Orthologa, teyże świętey Cerkwie Wschodniej syna. Vilnius, 1610. Attributed to Meletii Smotryts'kyi.

Titov, Kh[vedir]. *Materialy dlia istoriï knyzhnoï spravy na Vkraïni v XVI–XVIII vv. Vsezbirka peredmov do ukraïns'kykh starodrukiv.* Kiev, 1924 (= Zbirnyk istorychno-filolohichnoho viddilu, Vseukraïns'ka Akademiia Nauk, XVII).

Triodion si est trypisnets' . . . Typography of Mikhail Sliozka. Lviv, 1642. Contains dedication by Sliozka (Slioska) to Kysil.

"Try testamenty Adama Kysilia," *Ukraïna,* 1918, books 1–2, pp. 49–67.

Twardowski, Samuel. *Wojna domowa z Kozaki i Tatary, Moskwą potym Szwedami i z Węgry, przez lat dwanaście za panowania Najjaśniejszego pana Jana Kazimierza, Króla Polskiego, tocząca się* . . . Kalisz, 1681.

Ukraïna pered vyzvol'noiu viinoiu, 1648–1654 r.r., Zbirka dokumentiv (1639–1648 rr.), ed. M. N. Petrovs'kyi and K. H. Huslystyi. Kiev, 1946.

Urkunden und Aktenstücke zur Geschichte des Kurfürsten Friedrich Wilhelm von Brandenburg, 23 vols. Berlin-Leipzig, 1864–1930.

Vimina, Alberto. *Historia delle guerre civili di Polonia divisa in cinque libri progressi dell'armi Moscovite contro Polacchi relatione della Moscovia, Svetia . . .* Venice, 1671.

[*Volumina legum*]. *Prawa, konstytucye y przywileie Królewstwa Polskiego, y Wielkiego Xięstwa Litewskiego, y wszytkich prowincyi należących: Na walnych seymiech koronnych od Seymu Wiślickiego roku Pańskiego 1347 aż do ostatniego seymu uchwalone,* comp. Stanisław Konarski, 8 vols. Warsaw, 1732–1782.

Vossoedinenie Ukrainy s Rossiei. Dokumenty i materialy 1620–1654, comp. P. P. Gudzenko *et al.,* pub. by Akademiia Nauk SSSR, Institut istorii and Akademiia Nauk USSR, Institut istorii, 3 vols. Moscow, 1953–1954.

Vyzvol'na viina ukraïns'koho narodu v 1648–1654 rr. Vozz"ednannia Ukraïny z Rosieiu. Anotovanyi pokazhchyk rukopysnykh materialiv biblioteky, pub. Lvivs'ka biblioteka Akademiï Nauk URSR, Viddil rukopysiv. Lviv, 1954.

Wassenberg, Everhard. *Gestorum gloriosissimi ac invitissimi Vladislai IV Poloniae et Sueciae Regis.* Gdańsk, 1649.

Wójcik, Zbigniew, ed. *Eryka Lassoty i Wilhelma Beauplana opisy Ukrainy,* trans. Sofia Stasiewska and Stefan Meller. Warsaw, 1972.

Wolff, Józef. *Kniaziowie litewsko-ruscy od końca czternastego wieku.* Warsaw, 1895.

Zherela do istorii Ukraïny-Rusy, pub. by Naukove tovarystvo imeni Shevchenka, 16 vols. Lviv, 1895–1924.

Zhizn' kniazia Andreia Mikhailovicha Kurbskogo v Litve i na Volyni. Akty, izdannye Vremennoi komissiei, vysochaishe uchrezhdennoi pri kievskom voennom, podol'skom i volynskom general-gubernatore, ed. N. D. Ivanishev, 2 vols. Kiev, 1849.

Zhukovich, P. *Materialy dlia istorii kievskogo i l'vovskogo soborov 1629 goda.* St. Petersburg, 1911 (= Zapiski Imperatorskoi Akademii Nauk, VIII, no. 15).

Źródła dziejowe, pub. Towarzystwo Naukowe Warszawskie, Wydział II: Nauk antropologicznych, społecznych, historyi i filozofii. Komisya historyczna, 24 vols. Warsaw, 1876–1915.

Secondary Works

Abraham, W. *Powstanie organizacyi Kościoła Łacińskiego na Rusi.* Lviv, 1904.

Amman, A. M. *Abriss der Ostslavischen Kirchengeschichte.* Vienna, 1950.

Andrusiak, Mikołaj. "Sprawa patriarchatu kijowskiego za Władysława IV," *Prace historyczne w 30-lecie działalności profesorskiej Stanisława Zakrzewskiego.* Lviv, 1934, pp. 269–285.

Anichenka, Uladzimir. *Belaruska-ukrainskiia pis'movamoŭnyia suviazi.* Minsk, 1969.

Antonovych, Mykhailo. "Pereiaslavs'ka kampaniia 1630 r.," *Pratsi Ukraïns'koho istorychno-filolohichnoho tovarystva v Prazi,* V (1943): 5–41.

Antonovych (Antonovich), V. "Pol'sko-russkie sootnosheniia XVII v. v sovremennoi pol'skoi prizme, po povodu povesti G. Sen'kevicha *Ogniem i mieczem*," *Kievskaia starina*, XI, 1885, no. 5, pp. 44–78.

———. *Korotka istoriia kozachchyny*. Kolomyia, 1912.

Anushkin, N. *Na zare knigopechataniia v Litve*. Vilnius, 1970.

———. *Vo slavnom meste Vilenskom. Ocherki iz istorii knigopechataniia*. Moscow, 1962.

Apanovych, O. M. *Zaporiz'ka Sich u borotbi proty turets'ko-tatars'koï ahresii. 50–70-i roky XVII st.* Kiev, 1961.

Bahalii (Bagalei), D[mitrii]. "Kisel' (Adam)," *Entsiklopedicheskii slovar'* XV. St. Petersburg, 1895, pp. 155–156.

Bantysh-Kamenskii, Dmitrii. *Istoriia Maloi Rossii ot vodvoreniia Slavian v sei strane do unichtozheniia Getmanstva*. 4th ed. Kiev, 1903.

Baranovskii (Baranovs'kyi), S. "Pravoslavnyi volynskii pomeshchik A. Kisel' kak pol'skii diplomat v epokhu B. Khmel'nitskogo," *Volynskie eparkhial'nye vedomosti* 1874, *Neofitsial'naia chast'*, pp. 747–766.

Baranowski, Bohdan. "Geneza sojuszu kozacko-tatarskiego z 1648 r.," *Przegląd Historyczny* XXXVII (1948): 276–287.

———. *Organizacja wojska polskiego w latach trzydziestych i czterdziestych XVII wieku*, Prace Komisji Wojskowo-Historycznej Ministerstwa Obrony Narodowej, ser. A. X. Warsaw, 1957.

———. *Polska a Tatarszczyzna w latach 1624–1629*. Łódź, 1948.

———. *Stosunki polsko-tatarskie w latach 1632–1648*. Łódź, 1949. (= *Prace Instytutu Historycznego Uniwersytetu Łódzkiego*, no. I.)

———, and Zofia Libiszowska. "Problem narodowo-wyzwoleńczej walki ludu ukraińskiego w XVII w. w historiografii polskiej," *Kwartalnik Historyczny*, LXI, no. 2 (1954), 197–217.

———. "Problematyka stosunków polsko-rosyjskich XVII wieku," *Zeszyty Naukowe Uniwersytetu Łódzkiego*, ser. I, Nauki humanistyczno-społeczne, XVI (1958): 41–58.

Bardach, Juliusz. *Historia państwa i prawa Polski do połowy XV wieku*. Warsaw, 1957. (= *Historia państwa i prawa Polski do roku 1795*, ed. Juliusz Bardach, vol. I.)

Baron, Salo Wittmayer. *A Social and Religious History of the Jews*, 2nd ed. XVI: *Poland-Lithuania 1500–1650*. New York-London, 1976.

Baranovych, Oleksander (Baranovich, A. I.). "Naselenie predstepnoi Ukrainy v XVI v.," *Istoricheskie zapiski AN SSR*, XXXII (1959), 198–232.

———. *Ukraina nakanune osvoboditel'noi voiny serediny XVIIv*. Moscow, 1959.

———. *Zaliudnennia volyns'koho voievodstva v pershii polovyne XVIIst*. Kiev, 1930.

Barsov, T. *Konstantinopol'ski patriarkh i ego vlast' nad Russkoiu Tserkov'iu*. St. Petersburg, 1878.

Barsukov, Aleksandr. *Rod Sheremetevykh*, 8 vols. St. Petersburg, 1881–1914.

Bartoszewicz, Julian. "Adam Kisiel, Wojewoda Kijowski," *Tygodnik Ilustrowany*, II (1860): 413–414, 429, 438.

————. *Szkic dziejów Kościoła Ruskiego w Polsce.* Cracow, 1880.

Bartoszewicz, Kazimierz. *Radziwiłłowie.* Warsaw, 1928.

Batiushkov, P. N. *Volyn'; istoricheskie sud'by iugo-zapadnogo kraia.* St. Petersburg, 1888.

Bednov (Bidnov), V. *Pravoslavnaia tserkov' v Pol'she i Litve po "Volumina Legum."* Katerynoslav, 1908.

Belokurov, S. A. *O posol'skom prikaze.* Moscow, 1906 (= *Chteniia,* Moscow, 1906, no. 3.)

Bennigsen, Alexandre et al, *Le Khanat de Crimée dans les Archives du Musée du Palais de Topkapi.* Paris-The Hague, 1978.

Bevzo, O. A. *L'vivs'kyi litopys i Ostrozhs'kyi litopysets: Dzhereloznavche doslidzhennia.* Kiev, 1970.

Bieńkowski, Ludomir. "Organizacja Kościoła Wschodniego w Polsce," in *Kościół w Polsce,* 2 vols. to date. n.p. [1966–1969]. II, *Wieki XVI–XVIII,* pp. 733–1050.

Bilets'kyi, O., ed. *Khrestomatiia davn'oï ukraïns'koï literatury (do kintsia XVIII st.).* Kiev, 1967.

Bilets'kyi, Platon. *Ukraïns'kyi portretnyi zhyvopys XVII–XVIII st.: Problemy stanovlennia i rozvytku.* Kiev, 1969.

Bogucka, Maria. "Gdańsk—polski czy międzynarodowy ośrodek gospodarczy," in *Polska w epoce Odrodzenia,* pp. 100–125.

————. "Zboże rosyjskie na rynku amsterdamskim w pierwszej połowie XVII wieku." *Przegląd Historyczny,* LIII, no. 4 (1962): 612–628.

Boiko, Ivan Davydovych. *Selianstvo Ukraïny v druhii polovyni XVI-pershii polovyni XVII st.* Kiev, 1963.

Boniecki, Adam. *Herbarz Polski.* 10 vols. Warsaw, 1901–1910.

Borucki, Marek. *Sejmy i sejmiki szlacheckie.* Warsaw, 1972.

Boyko, Max. *Bibliography of Church Life in Volhynia.* Bloomington, Indiana, 1974. (= Publications of the Volhynian Bibliographic Center, IX.)

Brückner, Aleksander. *Dzieje języka polskiego,* 4th ed. Wrocław, 1960.

————. "Spory o unię w dawnej literaturze," *Kwartalnik Historyczny,* X (1896): 578–644.

Budilovich, V. *Russkaia pravoslavnaia starina v Zamost'e.* Warsaw, 1886.

Bugoslovskii, Grigorii. "Kievskii voevoda Adam Kisel' i vystroennaia im v s. Nizkenichakh, Vladimir-Volynskago uezda, tserkov'," *Sbornik statei v chest' grafini Praskovii Sergeevny Uvarovoi.* Moscow, 1916, pp. 232–248.

Butsinskii, P. N. *O Bogdane Khmel'nitskom.* Kharkiv, 1882.

Bystroń, Jan Stanisław. *Dzieje obyczajów w dawnej Polsce: Wiek XVI–XVIII,* 2 vols. Warsaw, 1960.

Chistovich, I. *Ocherk istorii Zapadno-russkoi tserkvi,* 2 vols. St. Petersburg, 1882–1884.

Chodynicki, Kazimierz. "Geneza równouprawnienia schyzmatyków w W. Ks. Litewskiem: Stosunek Zygmunta Augusta do wyznania grecko-wschodniego," *Przegląd Historyczny,* XXII (1919–1920): 54–135.

———. *Kościół Prawosławny a Rzeczpospolita Polska 1370–1632.* Warsaw, 1934.

———. "Z dziejów prawosławia na Wołyniu (922–1596)," *Rocznik Wołyński,* V–VI (1937): 52–106.

Chrząszcz, I. E. *Stosunki kozacko-tatarskie z uwzględnieniem stosunków z Turcją, Mołdawią i Siedmiogrodem w I. poł. 1649 r.* Lviv, 1929.

Clark, George. *The Seventeenth Century,* 2nd ed. London, 1947, paperback, 1961.

Cynarski, Stanisław. "Sarmatyzm—ideologia i styl życia," in *Polska XVII wieku,* pp. 220–243.

Čyževs'kyj, Dmytro. *A History of Ukrainian Literature: (From the 11th to the End of the 19th Century),* trans. Dolly Ferguson, Doreen Gorsline and Ulana Petyk, ed. George S. Luckyj. Littleton, Colorado, 1975.

Czapliński, Władysław. *Dawne czasy. Opowiadania i szkice historyczne z XVII wieku.* Wrocław, 1957.

———. *Dwa sejmy w roku 1652.* Wrocław, 1955.

——— and Adam Kersten, ed. *Magnateria polska jako warstwa społeczna.* Toruń, 1974.

———. *Na dworze Władysława IV.* Warsaw, 1959.

———. *O Polsce siedemnastowiecznej. Problemy i sprawy.* Warsaw, 1966.

———. "Parę uwag o tolerancji w Polsce w okresie kontrreformacji," in *O Polsce siedemnastowiecznej.* Warsaw, 1966.

———. "Polityka Rzeczypospolitej Polskiej w latach 1576–1648," *VIII Powszechny Zjazd Historyków Polskich w Krakowie 14–17 września 1958,* III, 95–100.

———. *Polska a Bałtyk w latach 1632–1648.* Wrocław, 1952.

———. "Senat za Władysława IV," in *Studia historyczne ku czci Stanisława Kutrzeby,* I (Cracow, 1938): 81–104.

———. *Władysław IV i jego czasy.* Warsaw, 1972.

———. "Władysław IV—próba charakterystyki," *Roczniki Historyczne,* XVII (1948): 126–142.

———. *Władysław IV wobec Wojny 30-Letniej (1637–1645).* Cracow, 1937.

———. "Z problematyki sejmu polskiego w pierwszej połowie XVII wieku," *Kwartalnik Historyczny,* LXXVII (1970): 31–45.

Czermak, Wiktor. "Kilka słów o pamiętnikach polskich XVII wieku," *Studya historyczne.* Cracow, 1901, pp. 249–276.

———. *Plany wojny tureckiej Władysława IV.* Cracow, 1895.

———. *Z czasów Jana Kazimierza. Studya historyczne.* Lviv, 1893.

Czartoryski, Paweł. "Rodzime źródła kultury umysłowej polskiego Odrodzenia," *Polska w epoce Ordrodzenia*, Warsaw, 1970, pp. 266–283.

Cześcik, Łucja. *Sejm warszawski w 1649/50 roku*. Wrocław, Warsaw, Cracow, Gdańsk, 1978.

Darowski, Adam. "Zatargi o starostów pogranicznych 1618–1654: Szkic historyczny na podstawie rosyjskich źródeł historycznych," *Szkice historyczne*, series III. St. Petersburg, 1897, pp. 185–287.

Davies, Norman. *God's Playground: A History of Poland*, 2 vols. New York, 1982.

Dembińska, Anna. *Wpływy kultury polskiej na Wołyń w XVI wieku (Na łonie warstwy szlacheckiej)*. Poznań, 1930. (= Prace Komisji Historycznej Poznańskiego Towarzystwa Przyjaciół Nauk, XVI.)

Dembiński, Bronisław, Oscar Halecki and Marcel Handelsman. *L'historiographie polonaise du XIX-me et du XX-me siècle: VII-e Congrés International des Sciences Historiques*. Warsaw, 1933.

D-kii, E. "Dopolnenie k biografii Adama Kiselia," *Kievskaia starina*, 1886, no. 4, pp. 826–831.

Długosz, Teofil. "Niedoszły synod unicko-prawosławny we Lwowie 1629 roku," *Collectanea Theologica*, XIX (1938), 479–506.

Dobrianskii, Antonii. *Istoriia episkopov trekh soedinennykh eparkhii, Peremysh'-skoi, Samborskoi i Sanotskoi, od naidavneishikh vremen do 1794 g.*, 3 vols. Lviv, 1893.

Dobrowolska, Wanda. *Młodość Jerzego i Krzysztofa Zbaraskich*, Przemyśl, 1926.

Doroshenko, Dmytro. *Narys istorii Ukraïny*, 2nd ed., 2 vols. Munich, 1966.

————. *A Survey of Ukrainian Historiography*. New York, 1957. (= The Annals of the Ukrainian Academy of Arts and Sciences in the U.S., vol. V–VI.)

Druzhinin, N. M., ed. *Voprosy formirovaniia russkoi narodnosti i natsii: Sbornik statei*. Moscow, 1958.

Druzhytz, V. "Palazhenne Litoŭska-Belaruskai Dziarzhavy paslia Liublinskai Vunii," *Pratsy Belaruskaho Dziarzhavnaho universytetu*, 1925, no. 6–7, pp. 216–251.

Dworzaczek, Włodzimierz. *Genealogia*. Warsaw, 1959.

Dzięgelewski, J. *Polityka wyznaniowa Władysława IV*, Warsaw, 1985 (Read in dissertation form; announced for publication.)

Dzyra, Ia. I. "Samiilo Velychko ta ioho litopys (Do 300-richchia vid dnia narodzhennia litopystsia)," *Istoriohrafichni doslidzhennia v Ukraïns'kii RSR*, no. 4. Kiev, 1971, pp. 198–224.

Eingorn, Vitalii. *Ocherki iz istorii Malorossii v XVII v: O snosheniiakh malorossiiskogo dukhovenstva s Moskovskim pravitel'stvom pri Alekseie Mikhailoviche*. Moscow, 1899.

Engel, Johan Christian. *Geschichte der Ukraine und der Cosaken*. (= Vortsetzung der Algemeinen Welthistorie durch eine Gesellschaft von Gelehrten in Deutschland und England ausgefertigt, no. XLVIII.) Halle, 1796.

"Etudes sur la noblesse," *Acta Poloniae Historica* XXXVI (1977) (special issue).

Filaret, Archbishop [Gumilevskii]. *Istoriko-statisticheskoe opisanie Chernigovskoi eparkhii,* vol. IV. Chernihiv, 1861.

Filipczak-Kocur, Anna. *Sejm zwyczajny z roku 1629.* Warsaw-Wrocław, 1979.

Fisher, Alan W. *The Crimean Tatars.* Stanford, 1978.

Florovsky, Georges (Florovskii, Georgii). "The Problem of Old Russian Culture," *The Development of the USSR,* pp. 125–129.

————. *Puti russkogo bogosloviia.* Paris, 1937.

————. *The Ways of Russian Theology,* ed. Richard S. Haugh, pt. 1 (Belmont. Mass., 1979). The Collected Works of Georges Florovsky, V.

Forsten, G. V. "Snocheniia Shvetsii i Rossii vo vtoroi polovine XVII veka (1648–1700)," *Zhurnal Ministerstva narodnogo prosveshcheniia,* CCCXV (February, 1898): 210–277; CCCXVI (April, 1898): 321–354; CCCXVII (May, 1898): 48–103; CCCXVIII (June, 1898): 311–350.

Franko, Ivan. *Ivan Vyshens'kyi i ioho tvory.* Lviv, 1895.

————. "Khmel'nyshchyna 1648–1649 rokiv v suchasnykh virshakh," *ZNTSh,* XXIII (1898): 1–114.

Frąś, Ks. L. "Bitwa pod Zborowem w r. 1649," *Kwartalnik Historyczny,* XLVI, no. 3–4 (1932): 344–370.

Freylichówna, J. *Ideał wychowawczy szlachty polskiej w XVI i początku XVII wieku.* Warsaw, 1938.

Gajecky, George. *The Cossack Administration of the Hetmanate.* 2 vols. Cambridge, Mass., 1978.

Gierowski, Józef Andrzej, ed. *Dzieje kultury politycznej w Polsce.* Warsaw, 1977.

[Giżycki, Jan Marek]. *Z przeszłości Hoszczy na Wołyniu.* Cracow, n.d.

Godziszewski, Władysław. "Granica polsko-moskiewska wedle pokoju polanowskiego 1634 (wytyczona w latach 1634–1648)," *Prace Komisji Atlasu Historycznego Polski,* III (1935): 1–96.

————. *Polska a Moskwa za Władysława IV.* Cracow, 1930. (=Polska Akademia Umiejętności, Rozprawy Wydziału Historyczno-Filozoficznego, series II, vol. XLII, no. 6.)

Gołębiowski, Seweryn. "Pamiętnik o Tomaszu Zamoyskim, Kanclerzu W. Kor.," *Biblioteka Warszawska* III (1853): 197–229, 397–432.

Golobutskii (Holobuts'kyi), V. A. *Diplomaticheskaia istoriia osvoboditel'noi voiny ukrainskogo naroda 1648–1654 g.g.* Kiev, 1962,

————. *Zaporozhskoe kazachestvo.* Kiev, 1957.

Golubev, S. T. *Istoriia Kievskoi Dukhovnoi akademii; Period do-Mogilianskii.* Kiev, 1888.

————. *Kievskii Mitropolit Petr Mogila i ego spodvizhniki (Opyt tserkovno-istoricheskogo issledovaniia)*, 2 vols. Kiev, 1883–1898.

————. "Neizvestnoe polemicheskoe sochinenie protiv papskikh pritiazanii v Iugo-Zapadnoi Rossii (1633 goda)," *Trudy Kievskoi Dukhovnoi akademii*, 1899, no. 2, pp. 300–341.

————. "Priskorbnye stolknoveniia Petra Mogily s svoim predshestvennikom po mitropolii i kievo-nikol'skimi inokami," *Trudy Kievskoi Dukhovnoi akademii*, 1897, no. 10, pp. 209–226.

————. "Zapadno-russkaia tserkov' pri mitropolite Petre Mogile (1633–1646)," *Kievskaia starina*, 1898, no. 3, pp. 397–420, no. 4, pp. 20–50.

Górka, Olgierd. "Bohdan Chmielnicki, jego historycy, postać i dzieło," *Sesja naukowa w trzechsetną rocznicę zjednoczenia Ukrainy z Rosją, 1654–1954.* Warsaw, 1956, pp. 65–102.

————. *"Ogniem i mieczem" a rzeczywistość historyczna.* Warsaw, 1934.

Górski, Konstantyn. "O działaniach wojska koronnego Rpltej Polskiej w wojnie z Kozakami (okres od dnia 19 lutego do 10 lipca 1651, Bitwa pod Beresteczkiem," *Biblioteka Warszawska*, 1887, no. 2, pp. 215–234; no. 3, pp. 21–41.

Gorzkowski, Maryan. *O rusińskiej i rosyjskiej szlachcie.* Cracow, 1876.

Grabowski, Tadeusz. "Ostatnie lata Melecjusza Smotryckiego," *Księga pamiętnikowa ku czci Bolesława Orzechowskiego*, Lviv, 1916, pp. 297–327.

————. *Z dziejów literatury unicko-prawosławnej w Polsce 1630–1700.* Poznań, 1922.

Grodziski, Stanisław. *Obywatelstwo w Szlacheckiej Rzeczypospolitej.* Cracow, 1963.

Grzybowski, Konstanty. *Teoria reprezentacji w Polsce epoki Odrodzenia.* Warsaw, 1959.

Guldon, Zenon. "Badania nad zaludnieniem Ukrainy w XVII wieku," *Kwartalnik Historii Kultury Materialnej*, XIII (1965), 561–566.

Halecki, Oskar. *Dzieje unii Jagiellońskiej*, 2 vols. Cracow, 1919–1920.

————. *From Florence to Brest, 1439–1596.* New York, 1959.

————. *Ostatnie lata Świdrygiełły i sprawa wołyńska za Kazimierza Jagiellończyka.* Cracow, 1915.

————. *Przyłączenie Podlasia, Wołynia i Kijowszczyzny do Korony w roku 1569.* Cracow, 1915.

————. "Why Was Poland Partitioned," in *The Development of the USSR: An Exchange of Views*, ed. Donald Treadgold. Seattle, 1964, pp. 296–305.

Herasymchuk, Vasyl'. "Vyhovs'kyi i Iurii Khmel'nyts'kyi. Istorychni studiï," *ZNTSh*, LIX (1904): 1–40; LX (1904): 41–70.

————. "Vyhovshchyna i Hadiats'kyi Traktat," *ZNTSh*, LXXXVII (1909): 5–36; LXXXVIII (1909): 23–50; LXXXIX (1909): 46–90.

Herbst, Stanisław. *Zamość.* Warsaw, 1954.

Hering, Günnar. *Okumenisches Patriarchat und Europäische Politik (1620–1638)*. Wiesbaden, 1968.

Hernas, Czesław. *Barok*. Warsaw, 1973.

Holowackyj, R. R. *Seminarium Vilense SS. Trinitatis (1601–1621)*. Rome, 1957.

Horn, Maurycy. "Chronologia i zasięg najazdów tatarskich w latach 1600–1647," *Studia i Materiały do Historii Wojskowości*, vol. VIII, part I (1962): 3–71.

———. *Walka klasowa i konflikty społeczne w miastach Rusi Czerwonej w latach 1600–1647 na tle stosunków gospodarczych*. Wrocław, 1972.

———. *Żydzi na Rusi Czerwonej w XVI i pierwszej połowie XVII w.: Działalność gospodarcza na tle rozwoju demograficznego*. Warsaw, 1975.

Hrabianka, Hryhorii, *Diistviia prezil'noi . . .* (Kiev, 1854).

Hrabovets'kyi, Volodymyr. *Zakhidno-ukraïns'ki zemli v period narodnovyzvol'-noï viiny 1648–1654 rr.* Kiev, 1972.

Hrushevs'kyi, Mykhailo. *Istoriia Ukraïny-Rusy,* new ed. 10 vols. New York, 1954–1958.

———. "Khmel'nyts'kyi-Khmel'nyshchyna. Istorychnyi eskiz," *ZNTSh*, XXIII–XXIV (1898), 1–30.

———. *Kulturno-natsional'nyi rukh na Ukraïni XVI–XVII st,* 2nd ed. n.p., 1919.

Iakovliv, Andrii. *Dohovir Bohdana Khmel'nyts'koho z Moskvoiu, 1654*. New York, 1954.

Ihnatowicz, Ireneusz, Mączak, Antoni, Zientara, Benedykt. *Społeczeństwo polskie od X do XX wieku*. Warsaw, 1979.

Isaievych, Ia. D. *Bratstva ta ïkh rol' v rozvytku ukraïns'koï kul'tury XVI–XVIII st*. Kiev, 1966.

———. *Dzherela z istoriï ukraïns'koï kul'tury doby feodalizmu XVI–XVIII st*. Kiev, 1972.

Istoriia Kyieva, pub. by Instytut Istoriï Akademiï Nauk URSR, 2 vols. Kiev, 1960–1961.

Istoriia Ukrains'koï RSR, editor-in-chief K. K. Dubyna, 2 vols. Kiev, 1967.

Jabłonowski, Aleksander. *Akademia Kijowsko-Mohilańska. Zarys historyczny na tle rozwoju ogólnego cywilizacji zachodniej na Rusi*. Cracow, 1899–1900.

———. *Historya Rusi Południowej do upadku Rzeczypospolitej Polskiej*. Cracow, 1912.

———. *Pisma (Aleksandra Jabłonowskiego)*. 7 vols. Warsaw, 1910–1913.

Jobert, Ambroise. *De Luther à Mohila: La Pologne dans la crise de la chretienté 1517–1648*. Paris, 1974. (= Collection Historique de l'Institut d'Etudes Slaves, XXI, Paris, 1974.)

Kaczmarczyk, Zdisław and Leśnodorski, Bogusław. *Od połowy XV wieku do r. 1795,* vol. II of *Historia państwa i prawa Polski,* 4th ed. Warsaw, 1971.

Kaczmarczyk, Zdzisław. "Oligarchia magnacka w Polsce jako forma państwa,"

VIII Powszechny Zjazd Historyków Polskich w Krakowie 14–17 września 1958, VII, 61–76. Warsaw, 1959.

Kamanin, Iv. "Pokhodzhenne Bohdana Khmel'nyts'koho," *Zapysky Istorychnoï i fil'ol'ohichnoï sektsii Ukraïns'koho naukovoho tovarystva v Kyievi*, XII (1913): 72–77.

Kamiński, Andrzej. "The Cossack Experiment in *Szlachta* Democracy in the Polish-Lithuanian Commonwealth: The Hadiach (*Hadziacz*) Union," *Harvard Ukrainian Studies* I, no. 2 (June 1977): 178–197.

———. "Neo-Serfdom in Poland-Lithuania," *Slavic Review*, XXXIV, no. 2 (June 1975): 253–258.

———. "The Polish-Lithuanian Commonwealth and Its Citizens: Was the Polish-Lithuanian Commonwealth a Stepmother for the Cossacks and Ruthenians?" *Poland and Ukraine: Past and Present*, ed. Peter Potichnyj. Edmonton-Toronto, 1980, pp. 32–57.

———. "The *Szlachta* of the Polish-Lithuanian Commonwealth and Their Government," *The Nobility in Russia and Eastern Europe*, ed. Ivo Banac and Paul Bushkovitch. New Haven, 1983, pp. 17–45.

Karpov, Gennadii. *Nachalo istoricheskoi deiatel'nosti Bogdana Khmel'nits'kogo*. Moscow, 1873.

———. *V zashchitu Bogdana Khmel'nitskogo*. Moscow, 1889.

Kartashev, A. V. *Ocherki po istorii Russkoi tserkvi*, 2 vols. Paris, 1959.

Kasymenko, O. K. *Rosiis'ko-ukraïns'ki vzaemovidnosyny 1648-pochatku 1651 r.* Kiev, 1974.

Keenan, Edward L. *The Kurbskii-Groznyi Apocrypha: The Seventeenth-Century Genesis of the "Correspondence" Attributed to Prince A. M. Kurbskii and Tsar Ivan IV.* Cambridge, Mass., 1971.

Kersten, Adam. *Stefan Czarniecki, 1599–1665*. Warsaw, 1963.

Kharlampovich, K. V. *Malorossiiskoe vliianie na velikorusskuiu tserkovnuiu zhizn'*, I, Kazan', 1914.

———. "Ostrozhskaia pravoslavnaia shkola," *Kievskaia starina*, 1897, no. 5, pp. 117–207; no. 6, pp. 363–388.

———. *Zapadno-russkiie pravoslavnye shkoly XVI i nachala XVII veka, otnoshenie ikh k inoslavnym, religioznoe obuchenie v nikh i zaslugi ikh v dele zashchity pravoslavnoi very i tserkvi*. Kazan', 1898.

Khoma, Ivan. "Ideia spil'noho synodu 1629r," *Bohosloviia*, XXXVII (1973), 21–64.

Khyzhniak, Z. I. *Kyievo-Mohylians'ka akademiia*. Kiev, 1970.

"Kisel', Adam Grigor'evich," *Russkii biograficheskii slovar'*, VIII. St. Petersburg, 1897, pp. 717–719.

Kobierzycki, Józef. *Przyczynki do dziejów ziemi sieradzkiej*, 2 vols. Warsaw, 1915–1916.

Kochanowski, J. K. *Dzieje Akademii Zamojskiej (1594–1784)*. Fontes et Commentationes Historiam Scholarum Superiorum in Polonia Illustrantes, VII. Cracow, 1899–1900.

Koczerska, Maria. *Rodzina szlachecka w Polsce późnego średniowiecza.* Warsaw, 1975.

Kohn, Hans. *The Idea of Nationalism: A Study of Its Origins and Background.* New York, 1958.

Kompan, O. S. "Do pytannia pro zaselenist' Ukraïny v XVII st.," *Ukraïns'kyi istorychnyi zhurnal,* 1960, no. 1, pp. 65–77.

————. *Uchast' mis'koho naseleniia u vyzvol'nii viini ukraïns'koho narodu 1648–1654 rr.* Kiev, 1954.

Konopczyński, Władysław. *Chronologia sejmów polskich 1483–1793.* Cracow, 1948.

————. *Liberum veto.* Cracow, 1918.

————. "Udział Korony i Litwy w tworzeniu wspólnej polityki zagranicznej, 1569–1795," *Pamiętnik VI Powszechnego Zjazdu Historyków Polskich w Wilnie 17–20 września 1935 r.,* I, Lviv, 1935.

Korduba, Myron. "Borot'ba za pols'kyi prestil po smerti Volodyslava IV," *Zherela do istoriï Ukraïny-Rusy,* XII. Lviv, 1911, pp. 1–60.

————. "Der Ukraine Niedergang und Aufschwung," *Zeitschrift für Osteuropäische Geschichte,* VI (1932): 30–60; 192–230; 358–385.

————. "Jeremias Wisniowiecki im Lichte der neuen Forschung," *Zeitschrift für Osteuropäische Geschichte,* VIII (new series IV) (1934), 221–238.

————. *La litterature historique sovietique-ukrainienne. Compterendu 1917–1931,* Reprint of the Warsaw 1938 edition. Munich, 1972 (= Harvard Series in Ukrainian Studies, X.)

————. "Mizh Zamostem ta Zborovom (Storinky znosyn Semyhorodu z Ukraïnoiu i Polshcheiu), *ZNTSh,* CXXXIII (1922): 39–56.

————. "The Reign of John Casimir; Part I, 1648–1654," *The Cambridge History of Poland. From the Origins to Sobieski (to 1696).* Cambridge, 1950, pp. 502–517.

————. "Venets'ke posol'stvo do Khmel'nyts'koho," *ZNTSh,* LXXVII (1907): 51–67.

Korolko, Mirosław. *Klejnot swobodnego sumienia: Polemika wokół konfederacji warszawskiej w latach 1573–1658.* Warsaw, 1974.

Korzon, Tadeusz. "O Chmielnickim: sądy PP. Kulisza i Karpowa," *Kwartalnik Historyczny,* IV (1892): 34–79.

Kościół w Polsce, ed. Jerzy Kłoczowski, vol. I *Średniowiecze,* n.p., [1966] = vol. II *Wieki XVI–XVIII,* n.p., [1969].

Kosman, S. M. *Na tropach bohaterów Trylogii.* 2nd ed. Warsaw, 1973.

Kossowski, Aleksander. *Zarys dziejów protestantyzmu na Wołyniu w XVI i XVII w.* Rivne, 1933.

Kostomarov, N. I. "Bogdan Khmel'nitskii, dannik Ottomanskoi Porty," *Vestnik Evropy*, 1878, no. 12, pp. 806–817.

———. *Bogdan Khmel'nitskii, Istoricheskaia monografiia.* 4th rev. ed., 3 vols. St. Petersburg, 1884. (= Istoricheskie monografii i issledovaniia Nikolaia Kostomarova, IX–XI.)

Kot, Stanisław. *Georges Niemirycz et la lutte contre l'intolerance au 17-e siècle.* The Hague, 1960.

———. *Jerzy Niemirycz w 300-lecie ugody hadziackiej.* Paris, 1960.

———. *La reforme dans le Grand-Duché de Lithuanie: Facteur d'occidentalisation culturelle.* Brussels, 1953.

———. *Socinianism in Poland: The Social and Political Ideas of the Polish Antitrinitarians in the Sixteenth and Seventeenth Centuries,* trans. Earle Morse Wilbur. Boston, 1957.

———. "Świadomość narodowa w Polsce XV–XVII w.," *Kwartalnik Historyczny,* LII (1938): 15–33.

Kotłubaj, Edward. *Życie Janusza Radziwiłła, Ś. Państwa Rzymskiego Xiążęcia na Birżach i Dubinkach, . . . Wojewody Wileńskiego, Hetmana Wielkiego W. X. L. . . .* Vilnius, 1859.

Krajcar, J. "The Ruthenian Patriarchate—Some Remarks on the Project for its Establishment in the 17th Century," *Orientalia Christiana Periodica,* XXX, no. 1–2 (1960): 65–84.

Krauzhar, A. [Aleksander Kraushar]. "Posol'stvo Iakova Smiarkovskogo k Bogdanu Khmel'nitskomu vo vremia osady Zamost'ia v 1648 g. (po rukopisnym istochnikam)," *Kievskaia starina,* 1894, no. 12, pp. 445–460.

Kryp"iakevych, I. P. *Bohdan Khmel'nyts'kyi.* Kiev, 1954.

———. "Sotsial'no-polityczni pohliady Bohdana Khme'nyts'koho," *Ukraïns'kyi istorychnyi zhurnal,* 1957, no. 1, pp. 94–105.

———. "Studiï nad derzhavoiu Bohdana Khmel'nyts'koho," *ZNTSh,* CXXXVIII–CXL (1925): 67–81; CXLIV–CXLV (1926): 109–140; CXLVII (1927): 55–80; CLI (1931): 111–150.

———. "Z pohranychnoï ukraïns'ko-moskovs'koï perepysky," *ZNTSh,* CL (1929): 81–91.

Kubala, Ludwik. *Jerzy Ossoliński,* 2nd rev. ed. Warsaw, Lviv, 1923 (= vol. I, *Dzieła Ludwika Kubali: Wydanie zbiorowe,* 2 vols. Warsaw-Lviv, 1923–1924.)

———. *Szkice historyczne, Seria I i II,* 5th ed. Warsaw-Lviv, 1923 (= vol. II, *Dzieła Ludwika Kubali: Wydanie zbiorowe,* 2 vols. Warsaw, Lviv, 1923–1924.)

Kuchowicz, Zbigniew. *Obyczaje staropolskie XVII–XVIII wieku.* Łódź, 1975.

Kulish, P. A. *Otpadenie Malorossii ot Pol'shi (1340–1654),* 3 vols. Moscow, 1888–1889.

———. "Pol'sko-kazatskaia voina 1638 g.," *Otechestvennye zapiski,* 1864, no. 9, pp. 327–355, no. 10, pp. 514–543.

Kurylas, Bohdan. *Z"edynennia arkhyepyskopa Meletiia Smotryts'koho v istorych-nomu i psykholohichnomu nasvitlenni.* Winnipeg, 1962.

Kutrzeba, Stanisław. *Historia ustroju Polski w zarysie.* vol. I, *Korona,* 5th ed. Lviv, 1920; vol. II, *Litwa,* 2nd ed. Lviv, 1921.

————. *Sejm walny Rzeczypospolitej polskiej.* Warsaw, 1923.

————. *Unia Polski z Litwą: Polska i Litwa w stosunku dziejowym.* Cracow, 1913.

"Kysil', Adam Hryhorovych," *Ukraïns'ka radians'ka entsyklopediia,* VI. Kiev, 1961, p. 379.

Lappo, I. I. *Ideia edinstva russkogo naroda v Iugo-Zapadnoi Rusi v epokhu prisoedineniia Malorossii k Moskovskomu gosudarstvu.* Prague, 1929.

————. *Velikoe Kniazhestvo Litovskoe za vremia ot zaklucheniia Lublinskoi Unii do smerti Stefana Batoriia.* St. Petersburg, 1901.

Latacz, E. "Ugoda zborowska a plany tureckie Jana Kazimierza," *Historia,* III, no. 3 (1933): 1–10.

Leitsch, Walter. *Moskau und die Politik des Kaiserhofes im XVII Jahrhundert,* pt. 1 (1604–1654). Graz-Cologne, 1960. Wiener Archiv für Geschichte des Slaventums und Osteuropa. Veröffentlichungen des Institut für osteuropäische Geschichte und Südostforschung der Universität Wien, IV.

————. "Russo-Polish Confrontation," in Taras Hunczak, ed. *Russian Imperialism from Ivan the Great to the Revolution.* New Brunswick, N.J., 1974, pp. 131–166.

Leliavskii, B. M. "Adam Kisel', russkii posol na seime," *Vremennik Stavropigiiskogo Instituta na 1928 g.* Lviv, 1927, pp. 17–24.

Łempicki, Stanisław. *Działalność Jana Zamoyskiego na polu szkolnictwa, 1573–1605.* Cracow, 1921.

Leontovich, F. I. "Boiare i sluzhilye liudi v Litovsko-russkom gosudarstve," *Zhurnal Ministerstva iustitsii,* 1907, no. 5, pp. 221–292; 1907, no. 6, pp. 193–264.

————. *Soslovnyi tip territorial'no-administrativnogo sostava Litovskogo gosudarstva i ego prichiny.* St. Petersburg, 1895.

Lepszy, Kazimierz, ed. *VIII Powszechny Zjazd Historyków Polskich w Krakowie 14–17 września 1958.* Section III. *Historia Polski od połowy XV do połowy XVIII wieku.* Warsaw, 1960.

Leszczyński, Józef. "Projekty reformy państwa polskiego na sejmie koronacyjnym Jana Kazimierza w 1649 r.," *O naprawę Rzeczypospolitej XVII–XVIII w. Prace ofiarowane Władysławowi Czaplińskiemu w 60 rocznicę urodzin.* Warsaw, 1965, pp. 88–96.

Levitskii (Levyts'kyi), Orest. "Cherty vnutrennogo stroia Zapadno-russkoi tserkvi," *Kievskaia starina,* 1884, no. 8, pp. 627–654.

————. "Iuzhno-russkie arkhierei XVI i XVII st.," *Kievskaia starina,* 1882, no. 1, pp. 49–100.

———. "Sotsinianstvo v Pol'she i iugo-zapadnoi Rusi," *Kievskaia starina*, 1882, no. 4, pp. 25–57; no. 5, pp. 193–225; no. 6, pp. 401–432.

Lewanski, Richard, comp. *Guide to Polish Libraries and Archives*. New York, 1974.

Lewicki, K. *Książę Konstantyn Ostrogski a Unja Brzeska, 1596*. Lviv, 1933.

———. "Sprawa unji Kościoła wschodniego z rzymskim w polityce Rzplitej," *Sprawy narodowościowe*, VII (1933): 491–508, 650–671.

Libiszowska, Zofia. *Żona dwóch Wazów, Maria Ludwika Gonzaga de Nevers*. Warsaw, 1963.

Likhachev, D. S. *Natsional'noe samosoznanie drevnej Rusi: Ocherki iz oblasti russkoi literatury XI–XVII vv.* Moscow-Leningrad, 1945.

Linnichenko, I. A. *Cherty iz istorii soslovii v Iugo-Zapadnoi (Galitskoi) Rusi XIV–XV vv.* Moscow, 1894.

Lipiński, Wacław. "Bój o Żaworonkowe wzgórza i osadzenie Szeina pod Smoleńskiem (16–30 października 1633 r.)," *Przegląd Historyczno-Wojskowy* VII (1934): 217–254.

———. "Działania wojenne polsko-rosyjskie pod Smoleńskiem od października 1632 do września 1633 r.," *Przegląd Historyczno-Wojskowy* V (1932): 165–206.

———. "Organizacja odsieczy i działania wrześniowe pod Smoleńskiem w 1633 r.," *Przegląd Historyczno-Wojskowy*, VI (1933): 173–227.

———. "Początek działań rosyjskich w wojnie smoleńskiej (1632–1634)," *Przegląd Historyczno-Wojskowy*, V (1932): 29–61.

———. "Stosunki polsko-rosyjskie w przededniu wojny smoleńskiej 1632–1634 i obustronne przygotowania wojskowe," *Przegląd Historyczno-Wojskowy*, V (1932): 235–272.

Lipiński, Wacław, see Lypyns'kyi, Viacheslav.

Liubavskii, M. *Litovsko-russkii seim*. Moscow, 1901.

———. *Oblastnoe delenie i mestnoe upravlenie Litovsko-Russkogo gosudarstva*. Moscow, 1892.

———. *Ocherk istorii Litovsko-Russkogo gosudarstva do Liublinskoj Unii vkliuchitel'no*. Moscow, 1910.

Lohvyn, H. N. "Mykhailivs'ka tserkva v Hoshchi," *Ukraïns'ke mystetstvoznavstvo*, no. 4 (Kiev, 1970), pp. 92–93.

Longinov, Ar. *Pamiatnik drevnego pravoslaviia v Liubline: Pravoslavnyi khram i sushchestvovavshee pri nem bratstvo*. Warsaw, 1883.

Łoziński, Władysław. *Prawem i lewem: Obyczaje na Czerwonej Rusi w pierwszej połowie XVII wieku*, 2 vols., 5th ed. Cracow, 1957.

Lubomirski, J. T. *Adam Kisiel, Wojewoda Kijowski*. Warsaw, 1905.

Łukaszewicz, J. "Jerzy Niemierzyc, podkomorzy kijowski, starosta owrucki i krzemieniecki. Przyczynek do historyi panowania Jana Kazimierza," *Biblioteka Warszawska*, X (1860): 355–370.

———. *Zakłady Naukowe w Koronie i Wielkiem Księstwie Litewskiem od najdawniejszych czasów aż do roku 1794*, 2 vols. Poznań, 1851.

Luzhnyts'kyi, Hryhorii. *Ukraïns'ka tserkva mizh Skhodom i Zakhodom.* Philadelphia, 1954.

Łużny, Ryszard. *Pisarze kręgu Akademii Kijowsko-Mohylańskiej a literatura polska.* Cracow, 1966.

Lypyns'kyi, Viacheslav. *Ukraïna na perelomi, 1657–1659. Zamitky do istoriï ukraïns'koho derzhavnoho budivnytstva v XVII-im stolittiu.* Vienna, 1920.

———. [Lipiński, Wacław], ed. *Z dziejów Ukrainy. Księga pamiątkowa ku czci Włodzimierza Antonowicza, Paulina Święcickiego i Tadeusza Rylskiego.* Kiev-Cracow, 1912.

Lyzlov, C. M. "Pol'sko-russkie otnosheniia v nachal'nyi period osvoboditel'noi voiny ukrainskogo naroda 1648–1654 gg. (Do Zborovskogo mira)," *Akademiia Nauk SSSR. Institut slavianovedeniia. Kratkie soobshcheniia*, XXI (1957): 58–82.

———. "Pol'sko-russkie otnosheniia v period ot Zborovskogo mira do Zemskogo sobora 1651 g.," *Akademiia Nauk SSSR. Institut slavianovedeniia. Kratkie soobscheniia*, XXVII (1959): 45–67.

Maciszewski, Jarema. *Polska a Moskwa: 1603–1618: Opinie i stanowiska szlachty polskiej.* Warsaw, 1968.

———. "Społeczeństwo," in *Polska XVII wieku*, pp. 120–150.

———. *Szlachta polska i jej państwo.* Warsaw, 1969.

———. *Wojna domowa w Polsce (1606–1609)*, vol. I. Wrocław, 1960.

Mączak, Antoni. "Problemy gospodarcze," in *Polska XVII wieku*, pp. 324–326.

Majewski, Ryszard. *Cecora: Rok 1620.* Warsaw, 1970.

Majewski, Wiesław. "Krytyczny przegląd źródeł do dziejów powstania Chmielnickiego w okresie początkowym (jesień 1647–maj 1648)," *Studia Źródłoznawcze*, XXVI (1981), 141–164.

———. "Plany wojny tureckiej Władysława IV a rzekome przymierze kozacko-tatarskie z 1645 r.," *Pzegląd Historyczny*, LXIV, no. 2 (1973): 267–282.

Makarii [Bulgakov]. *Istoriia Russkoi tserkvi*, 12 vols. St. Petersburg, 1877–1891.

Makhnovets' L. E., comp. *Ukraïns'ki pys'mennyky: biobibliohrafichnyi slovnyk*, vol. I. Kiev, 1960.

[Maksimovich (Maksymovych), Mikhail Aleksandrovich]. *Sobranie sochinenii M. A. Maksimovicha*, ed. V. B. Antonovich, P. G. Lebedintsev, I. I. Malyshevskii, and S. I. Ponomarev, 3 vols. Kiev, 1876–1900.

Małowist, Marian. "The Economic and Social Development of the Baltic Countries from the Fifteenth to the Seventeenth Centuries," *Economic History Review*, 2nd ser., XII, no. 2 (1959), 177–189.

Mańkowski, Tadeusz. *Genealogia sarmatyzmu.* Warsaw, 1946.

Martel, Antoine. *La langue polonaise dans les pays Ruthenes: Ukraine et Russie Blanche, 1569–1667.* Lille, 1933 (=Travaux et Mémoires de l'Université de Lille, Nouvelle Serie: Droit et Lettres, XX.)

Marusyn, M. "Blick auf die Unionsbestrebungen in der Ukrainischen Kirche der I Halfte des 17 Jhrts.," *Analecta OSBM,* section II, vol. IV (X) (1963): 95–111.

Medlin, William K. "Cultural Crisis in Orthodox Rus' in the Late 16th and Early 17th Centuries as a Problem of Socio-Cultural Change," in Andrew Blane, ed. *The Religious World of Russian Culture,* 2 vols. The Hague, 1975, II, 173–188.

Medynskii, E. N. *Bratskie shkoly Ukrainy i Belorussii XVI–XVII vv.* Kiev, 1954.

Metodicheskie ukazaniia i bibliografiia po izucheniiu spetskursa "Osvoboditel'-naia voina ukrainskogo naroda 1648–1654 gg. i vossoedinenie Ukrainy s Rossiei," pt. 1. Dnipropetrovs'k, 1980.

Mienicki, Ryszard. "Przegląd badań nad dziejami Litwy, 1569–1696," *Pamiętnik VI Powszechnego Zjazdu Historyków,* I, 26–36.

Molchanovskii (Molchanovs'kyi), N. *Ocherk izvestii o Podolskoi zemle do 1434 goda.* Kiev, 1885.

Mykhailyna, P. V. *Mista Ukraïny v period feodalizmu (Do pytannia pro stano-vyshche mist v umovakh inozemnoho ponevolennia v kintsi XVI-pershii polo-vyni XVII st.)* Chernivtsi, 1971.

Myshko, D. I. *Sotsial'no-ekonomichni umovy formuvannia ukraïns'koï narod-nosti.* Kiev, 1963.

Myślinski, Kazimierz, ed. *Zamość i Zamojszczyzna w dziejach i kulturze pol-skiej.* Zamość, 1969.

Nalyvaiko, D. S. "Zakhidnoevropeis'ki istoryko-literaturni dzherela pro vyz-vol'nu viinu ukraïns'koho narodu 1648–1654 rr.," *Ukraïns'kyi istorychnyi zhurnal,* 1969, no. 8, pp. 137–144; no. 9, pp. 137–143; no. 10, pp. 134–145; no. 11, pp. 131–136; no. 12, pp. 128–132.

Nemirovskii, E. L. *Nachalo knigopechataniia na Ukraine: Ivan Fedorov.* Moscow, 1974.

[Niesiecki, Kasper]. *Herbarz Polski Kaspra Niesieckiego S. J. powiększony do-datkami późniejszych autorów, rękopisów, dowodów urzędowych,* ed. Jan Nep. Borowicz, 10 vols. Leipzig, 1839–1846.

Normann, David. *Gustaw Adolfs politik mot Ryssland och Polen under Tyska kriget.* Uppsala, 1943.

Novitskii, Ivan (Novyts'kyi). "Adam Kisel', Voievoda kievskii, 1580(?)–1653g.," *Kievskaia starina,* XII (1884): 51–72, 204–219, 408–430, 612–638.

Novosel'skii, A. A. *Bor'ba Moskovskogo gosudarstva s tatarami v pervoi polovine XVII veka.* Moscow-Leningrad, 1948.

Nowak, Tadeusz Marian. "Polish Warfare Technique in the 17th Century, Theoretical Conceptions and their Practical Applications," in *Military Technique, Policy, and Strategy in History*. Warsaw, 1976, pp. 11–96.

Nowak-Dłużewski, Juliusz. *Okolicznościowa poezja polityczna w Polsce. Dwaj młodsi Wazowie.* [Warsaw], 1972.

Obuchowska-Pysiowa, Honorata. *Handel wiślany w pierwszej połowie XVII wieku.* Wrocław, 1964.

Ohloblyn, Oleksander. *Dumky pro Khmel'nychchynu.* New York, 1957.

Olianchyn [Oljancyn], Domet. "Aus dem Kultur und Geistesleben der Ukraine," *Kyrios*, 1936, no. 3, 264–278 and no. 4, 351–366.

———. "Ukraïns'ko-brandenburs'ki politychni znosyny v 1648–1657 rr. *ZNTSh*, CLI (1931): 151–179.

Olszewski, Henryk. "Nowe materiały do chronologii sejmów polskich," *Czasopismo Prawno-Historyczne*, IX, no. 2 (1957), 229–258.

———. *Sejm Rzeczypospolitej epoki oligarchii: Prawo, praktyka, teoria, programy.* Poznań, 1966.

O naprawę Rzeczypospolitej XVII–XVIII w. Prace ofiarowane Władysławowi Czaplińskiemu w 60 rocznicę urodzin. Józef Gierowski *et al.*, eds. Warsaw, 1965.

Orlovskii, Petr. "Kievskii sobor v 1629 r.," *Kievskaia starina*, 1905, no. 7, pp. 168–173.

Osvoboditel'naia voina 1648–1654 gg. i vossoedinenie Ukrainy s Rossiei, pub. Akademiia Nauk Ukrains'koi RSR. Kiev, 1954.

Ottman, Rudolf. "Adam z Brusiłowa Kisiel, wojewoda kijowski. Kartka z lat 1648–49," *Przegląd Powszechny*, IX (1886): 182–205, 340–360.

Pałucki, Władysław. *Studia nad uposażeniem urzędników ziemskich w Koronie do schyłku XVI wieku.* Warsaw, 1962.

———. *Drogi i bezdroża skarbowości polskiej XVI i pierwszej połowy XVII wieku.* Wrocław, 1974.

Pamiętnik VI Powszechnego Zjazdu Historyków Polskich w Wilnie 17–20 września 1935, I. *Referaty.* Lviv, 1935.

Paszkiewicz, Henryk. *Polityka ruska Kazimierza Wielkiego.* Warsaw, 1925.

Pavlishchev, N. I. *Pol'skaia anarkhiia pri Iane Kazimire i voina za Ukrainu*, 3 vols. St. Petersburg, 1887.

Pelenski, Jarosław. "The Incorporation of the Ukrainian Lands of Old Rus' into Crown Poland (1569): Socio-Material Interest and Ideology—A Reexamination," *American Contributions to the Seventh International Congress of Slavicists (Warsaw, August 21–27, 1973)*, III. The Hague and Paris, 1973, pp. 19–52.

Pelesz, Julian. *Geschichte der Union der ruthenischen Kirche mit Rom von den eltesten Zeit bis auf die Gegenwart*, 2 vols. Vienna-Würzburg, 1878–1881.

Petrov, N. I. *Istoriia Kievskoi Dukhovnoi akademii: Period do-mogilianskii.* Kiev, 1886.

———. *Kievskaia akademiia vo vtoroi polovine XVII v.* Kiev, 1885.

Petrovs'kyi, M. "Do istorïï derzhavnoho ustroiu Ukraîny XVII v.," *Zapysky Nizhens'koho pedagohichnoho instytutu,* XI (1931): 87–97.

———. *Vyzvol'na viina ukraïns'koho narodu proty hnitu shliakhetskoï Pol'shchi i pryednannia Ukraïny do Rossïï, 1648–1654 rr.* Kiev, 1940. (= Narysy z istorïï Ukraïny, IV.)

Picheta, V. I. *Belorussia i Litva XV–XVI vv: Issledovaniia po istorii sotsial'no-ekonomicheskogo, politicheskogo i kul'turnogo razvitiia.* Moscow, 1961.

———. "Pol'sko-litovskie unii i otnoshenie k nim litovskoi shliakhty," *Sbornik statei, posviashchennykh V. O. Kliuchevskomu.* Moscow, 1909, pp. 605–632.

Pietrzak, Jerzy. *Po Cecorze i podczas wojny chocimskiej: Sejmy z lat 1620 i 1621.* Wrocław, 1983.

Pirling, P. "Alberto Vimina. Snosheniia Venetsii s Ukrainoiu i Moskvoiu 1650–1663," *Russkaia starina,* CIX (January, 1902): 57–70.

Plebański, Józef Kazimierz. *Jan Kazimierz Waza. Maria Ludwika Gonzaga. Dwa obrazy historyczne.* Warsaw, 1862.

Podhorodecki, Leszek. *Hetman Jan Zamoyski: 1542–1605.* Warsaw, 1971.

———. *Sicz Zaporoska.* 2nd ed. Warsaw, 1970.

———. *Stanisław Koniecpolski ok. 1592–1646.* Warsaw, 1978.

——— and Noj Raszba. *Wojna chocimska 1621 roku.* Cracow, 1979.

Polska XVII wieku: państwo, społeczeństwo, kultura, ed. Janusz Tazbir. Warsaw, 1969.

Polska służba dyplomatyczna XVI–XVIII w., ed. Z. Wójcik. Warsaw, 1966.

Polska w epoce Odrodzenia: Państwo, społeczeństwo, kultura, ed. Andrzej Wyczański. Warsaw, 1970.

Polska w okresie drugiej wojny północnej, 1655–1660, ed. Kazimierz Lepszy, 3 vols. Warsaw, 1957.

Poppe, Andrzej. "Ze studiów nad najstarszym latopisarstwem ruskim. I. Sweneld ojciec Mściszy, czy Sweneld-ojciec zemsty?" *Studia Źródłoznawcze,* XVI (1971): 85–102.

Porshnev, B. F. "K kharakteristike mezhdunarodnoi obstanovki osvoboditel'noi voiny ukrainskogo naroda 1648–1654 godov," *Voprosy istorii,* 1954, no. 5, pp. 44–58.

———. "Bor'ba vokrug shvedsko-russkogo soiuza v 1631–1632 gg.," *Skandinavskii sbornik,* I (Tallin, 1956): 11–71.

———. "Gustav Adol'f i podgotovska Smolenskoi Voiny," *Voprosy istorii,* 1947, no. 1, pp. 53–82.

———. "Na putiakh k Polianovskomu miru 1634 g.," in *Mezhdunarodnye otnosheniia. Politika. Diplomatika XVI–XX veka. Sbornik statei k 80-letiiu Akademika I. M. Maiskogo,* Moscow, 1964, pp. 512–538.

———. "Sotsial'no-politicheskaia obstanovka vo vremia Smolenskoi Voiny," *Istoriia SSR,* 1957, no. 5, pp. 112–140.

Powidaj, Ludwik. "Adam Swietoldycz Kisiel, wojewoda kijowski, nosowski, bohusławski starosta," *Dziennik Literacki*, 1865, pp. 139–141, 147–149, 157–158, 166–167, 174–175, 181–183, 190–191, 198–199, 213–214, 220–221, 229–230, 237–238, 244–245, 252–254, 260–262, 268–269, 275–276, 283–284.

Prace historyczne w 30-lecie działalności profesorskiej Stanisława Zakrzewskiego. Lviv, 1934.

Pritsak, Omeljan. "Das erste turkisch-ukrainische Bündnis (1648)," *Oriens*, VI (1953): 266–298.

———. "The External History of the Texts of the Hypatian Chronicle," *Minutes of the Seminar in Ukrainian Studies*, III (1972–1973), 19–21.

———, and Reshetar, John S., Jr. "The Ukraine and the Dialectics of Nation-Building," in *The Development of the USSR: An Exchange of Views*, ed. Donald W. Treadgold. Seattle, 1964.

Prochaska, Antoni. "Wyhowski, twórca Unii Hadjackiej i jego rodzina," *Przewodnik Naukowy i Literacki*, XLVI (1920): 18–33, 113–125, 209–221, 305–322, 399–411.

Przyboś, Adam, and Roman Zalewski, eds. *Dyplomaci w dawnych czasach.* Cracow, 1959.

Ptaśnik, Jan. "Walka o demokratyzację Lwowa od XVI w. do XVIII w.," *Kwartalnik Historyczny*, XXXIX, no. 2 (1925): 228–257.

———. *Miasta i mieszczaństwo w dawnej Polsce*, 2nd ed. Warsaw, 1949.

Radzimiński, Zygmunt L., comp. *Monografia XX. Sanguszków oraz innych potomków Lubarta-Fedora Olgerdowicza, X. Ratneńskiego*, I. Lviv, 1906.

———, and W. Rulikowski. *Kniaziowie i szlachta między Sanem, Wieprzem, Bugiem, Prypetią, Dnieprem . . . osiedleni: Opowiadania historyczno-genealogiczne i obyczajowe.* I. Cracow, 1880.

———. *S. P. Kazimierz Puławski (1845–1926). Wspomnienie pośmiertne.* Cracow, 1928.

Ranum, Orest, ed. *National Consciousness, History, and Political Culture in Early-Modern Europe.* Baltimore, 1975.

Rawita-Gawroński, Franciszek. *Bohdan Chmielnicki do elekcyi Jana Kazimierza.* Lviv, 1906.

———. *Bohdan Chmielnicki od elekcyi Jana Kazimierza do śmierci.* Lviv, 1909.

———. "Kisielowie, ich ród-pochodzenie-posiadłości," *Przewodnik Naukowy i Literacki*, XL (1912): 1008–1023, 1116–1124.

Rembowski, A. *Konfederacja i rokosz w dawnym prawie polskim.* Warsaw, 1896.

Rhode, Gotthald. "Staaten-Union und Adelstaat: Zur Entwicklung von Staatsdenken und Staatsgesteltung in Osteuropa, vor allem in Polen/Litauen, im 16. Jahrhundert," *Zeitschrift für Ostforschung*, IX, no. 2/3 (July 1960), 184–213.

Rogger, Hans. *National Consciousness in Eighteenth-Century Russia.* Cambridge, Mass., 1960.

384   **Between Poland and the Ukraine**

Roos, Hans. "Der Adel der Polnischen Republik im vorrevolutionären Europa," in Vierhaus, Rudolf, ed., *Der Adel vor der Revolution. Zur sozialen und politischen Funktion des Adels in vorrevolutionären Europa*. Göttingen, 1971.

Rudnyts'kyi, Stefan. "Kozats'koho-pol'ska viina r. 1652. Istorychna rozvidka," *ZNTSh*, XVII (1897): 1–42.

Samsonowicz, Henryk. *Historia Polski do roku 1795*. Warsaw, 1973.

Savych, A. *Narysy z istoriï kul'turnykh rukhiv na Ukraïni ta Bilorusi v XVI–XVII v.* Kiev, 1929 (= Zbirnyk Istorychno-filolohichnoho viddilu. Vseukraïns'ka Akademiia Nauk XC.)

Semkowicz, W. "Po wcieleniu Wołynia: Nielegalny zjazd w Łucku 1569 i sprawa językowa na Wołyniu," *Ateneum Wileńskie*, V–VI (1924): 183–190.

Serczyk, Władysław. "The Commonwealth and the Cossacks in the First Quarter of the Seventeenth Century," *Harvard Ukrainian Studies*, II, no. 1 (March 1978), 73–93.

Seredyka, Jan. *Rzeczpospolita w ostatnich latach panowania Zygmunta III (1629–1632): Zarys wewnętrznych dziejów politycznych*. Opole, 1978.

———. "Stosunki ukraińsko-rosyjskie w 1648 r.," *Zeszyty Naukowe Uniwersytetu Wrocławskiego. Historia* III, seria A, XXIII (1960): 158–189.

———. "Stosunki ukraińsko-rosyjskie w drugiej połowie 1649 roku," *Zeszyty Naukowe Wyższej Szkoły Pedagogicznej w Opolu: Historia*, III–IV (1963): 233–252.

———. "Stosunki ukraińsko-rosyjskie w I połowie 1649," *Zeszyty Naukowe Wyższej Szkoły Pedagogicznej w Opolu: Historia*, II (1961): 171–194.

Sesja naukowa w trzechsetną rocznicę zjednoczenia Ukrainy z Rosją, 1654–1954. Materiały. Warsaw, 1956.

Ševčenko, Ihor. "Byzantium and the Eastern Slavs after 1453," *Harvard Ukrainian Studies*, II, no. 1 (March 1978), 5–25.

———. *Ljubomudreišij Kyr" Agapit Diakon: On a Kiev Edition of a Byzantine "Mirror of Princes,"* Supplement to *Recenzija*, V, no. 1 (1974): 17–18.

Shamrai, S. "Misto Kobyzhcha u XVIII st.," *Zapysky Istorychno-filolohichnoho viddilu. Vseukraïns'ka Akademiia Nauk*, XXVI (1930): 229–313.

Shevchenko, F. P. "Dyplomatychna sluzhba na Ukraïni pid chas vyzvol'noï viiny 1648–1654 rr.," *Istorychni dzherela ta ïkh vykorystannia*, I (1964): 81–113.

———. "Istorychne mynule v otsintsi B. Khmel'nyts'koho," *Ukraïns'kyi istorychnyi zhurnal*, 1970, no. 12, pp. 126–132.

———. *Politychni ta ekonomichni z"viazky Ukraïny z Rosieiu v seredyni XVII st.* Kiev, 1959.

Sienkiewicz, Henryk. *With Fire and Sword*, trans. Jeremiah Curtin. Boston, 1916.

Slipyi, Iosyf. *Sv. Iosafat Kuntsevych. Materialy i rozvidky z nahody iuvyleiu*. Lviv, 1925.

Smirnov, N. A. "Bor'ba rossiiskogo i ukrainskogo narodov protiv agressii sultanskoi Turtsii v XVII veke," *Voprosy istorii,* 1954, no. 3, pp. 91–105.

———. *Rossiia i Turtsiia v XVI–XVII ss.,* 2 vols. Moscow, 1946. (= Uchenye zapiski: Moskovskii Ordena Lenina gosudarstvennyi universitet, XCIV.)

Smirnov, V. D. *Krymskoe khanstvo pod verkhovenstvom Ottomanskoi Porty.* St. Petersburg, 1887.

Sokolov, I. I. "Pro vidnosyny Ukraïns'koï tserkvy do hrets'koho skhodu na prykintsi XVI ta na pochatku XVII st. za novovydanymy materiialamy: Istorychnyi narys," *Zapysky istorychno-filolohichnoho viddilu, Vseukraïns'ka Akademiia Nauk,* 1919, no. 1, pp. 53–84.

Solov'ev, S. M. *Istoriia Rossii s drevnieishikh vremen,* eds. L. V. Cherepnin *et al.,* 29 vols. in 15 books. Moscow, 1959–1966.

Stadnyk, M. "Hadiats'ka uniia," *Zapysky Ukraïns'koho naukovoho tovarystva v Kyievi,* VII (1910): 65–85; VIII (1911): 5–39.

Stashevskii, E. *Smolenskaia Voina, 1632–1634 gg.: Organizatsiia i sostoianie moskovskoi armii.* Kiev, 1919.

Stecki, Tadeusz Jerzy. "Grobowiec Adama Kisiela," *Tygodnik Illustrowany,* III (1869): 200.

Stökl, G. *Die Entstehung des Kosakentums.* Munich, 1953. (= Veröffentlichungen des Osteuropas-Institutes, III.)

———. *Der russische Staat in Mittelalter und Früher Neuzeit.* Wiesbaden, 1981.

Stsepuro, D. "Vilenskoe Sv. Dukhovskoe bratstvo v XVII i XVIII st.," *Trudy Kievskoi Dukhovnoi akademii,* 1898, no. 7, pp. 75–96; no. 8, pp. 345–373; 1899, no. 3, pp. 546–577; no. 5, pp. 225–262; no. 6, pp. 523–566; no. 7, pp. 30–52.

Sucheni-Grabowska, Anna. "Walka o demokrację szlachecką," in *Polska w epoce Odrodzenia,* pp. 9–67.

Sydorenko, Alexander. *The Kievan Academy in the Seventeenth Century.* Ottawa, 1977.

Symmons-Symonolewicz, Konstantin. "National Consciousness in Medieval Europe: Some Theoretical Problems," *Canadian Review of Studies in Nationalism,* VIII, no. 1 (Spring 1981), 151–166.

Sysyn, Frank. "Adam Kysil and the Synods of 1629: An Attempt at Orthodox-Uniate Accommodation in the Reign of Sigismund III," *Harvard Ukrainian Studies,* III–IV (1979–1980), 826–842.

———. "The Problem of Nobilities in the Ukrainian Past: The Polish Period, 1569–1648," in Ivan L. Rudnytsky, ed. *Rethinking Ukrainian History.* Edmonton, 1981, 29–102.

———. "Regionalism and Political Thought in Seventeenth-Century Ukraine: The Nobility's Grievances at the Diet of 1641," *Harvard Ukrainian Studies,* VI, no. 2 (June 1982), 167–190.

———. "Seventeenth-Century Views on the Causes of the Khmel'nyts'kyi Uprising: An Examination of the 'Discourse on the Present Cossack or Peasant War,'" *Harvard Ukrainian Studies,* V, no. 4 (December 1980), 430–466.

———. "Ukrainian-Polish Relations in the Seventeenth Century," in Peter Potichnyj, ed. *Poland and Ukraine: Past and Present.* Edmonton-Toronto, 1980, 59–82. Revised version in Polish, "Stosunki ukraińsko-polskie w XVII wieku: Rola świadomości narodowej i konfliktu narodowościowego w powstaniu Chmielnickiego." *Odrodzenie i Reformacja w Polsce,* XXVII (1982): 67–92. Warsaw, 1982.

Szajnocha, Karol. *Dwa lata dziejów naszych, 1646, 1648,* 3 vols. Warsaw, 1877. (=Dzieła Karola Szajnochy, VIII–X. Warsaw, 1877).

Szaraniewicz, Isydor. "Patryarchat wschodni wobec kościoła ruskiego w Polsce i Rzeczypospolitej polskiej," *Rozprawy i Sprawozdania z Posiedzeń Wydziału Historyczno-Filozoficznego Akademii Umiejętności,* VIII (1878): 255–344.

Szegda, Mirosław. *Działalność prawno-organizacyjna Metropolity Józefa IV Welamina Rutskiego (1613–1637).* Warsaw, 1967.

Szelągowski, Adam. "Układy Królewicza Władysława i dysydentów z Gustawem Adolfem w r. 1632," *Kwartalnik Historyczny,* XIII (1899): 683–733.

———. *Rozkład Rzeszy i Polska za panowania Władysława IV.* Cracow, 1907.

Tanczuk, D. "Quaestio Patriarchae Kioviensis tempore conaminum Unionis Ruthenorum (1582–1632)," *Analecta OSBM,* series II, 1949, no. 1, pp. 128–144.

Tazbir, Janusz. *Arianie i Katolicy.* Warsaw, 1971.

———. *Historia Kościoła Katolickiego w Polsce, 1460–1795.* Warsaw, 1966.

———. *Kultura szlachecka w Polsce: Rozkwit-upadek-relikty.* Warsaw, 1978.

———. *Państwo bez stosów: Szkice z dziejów tolerancji w Polsce XVII wieku.* Warsaw, 1958.

———. *Piotr Skarga: Szermierz kontrreformacji.* Warsaw, 1978.

———. "The Political Reversals of Jurij Nemyryč," *Harvard Ukrainian Studies,* V, no. 3 (September 1981): 306–319.

———. "Prawdziwe oblicze Jerzego Niemirycza," *Przegląd Historyczny,* LI (1960): 721–726.

———. "Problemy wyznaniowe," in *Polska XVII wieku,* pp. 189–220.

———. *Rzeczpospolita i świat. Studia z dziejów kultury XVII wieku.* Wrocław, 1971.

———. "Społeczeństwo wobec Reformacji," in *Polska w epoce Odrodzodzenia,* pp. 197–224.

———. "Wzorce osobowe szlachty polskiej w XVII wieku," *Kwartalnik Historyczny,* LXXXII (1976): 784–797.

Teksty, no. 4. Warsaw, 1974.

Teodorczyk, Jerzy. "Bitwa pod Gniewem (22. IX—29. IX 1626)," *Studia i Materiały do Historii Wojskowości,* XII, part 2 (1966): 70–172.

T[itov], Khvedir [T. F.]. "Urok s zapada," *Trudy Kievskoi Dukhovnoi akademii*, March, 1902, pp. 450–479.

——— [T. F.]. "K voprosu o znachenii Kievskoi akademii dlia pravoslaviia i russkoi narodnosti v XVII–XVIII vv.," *Trudy Kievskoi Dukhovnoi akademii*, November, 1903, pp. 375–408, and January, 1904, pp. 59–101.

———. *Stara vyshcha osvita v kyïvs'kii Ukraïni XVI–poch. XIX v.* Zbirnik Istorychno-filolohichnoho viddilu Ukraïns'koï Akademiï Nauk XX. Kiev, 1924.

Tkachenko, Mykola. "Narysy z istoriï selian na Livoberezhnii Ukraïni v XVII–XVIII vv.," *Zapysky istorychno-filolohichnoho viddilu Vseukraïns'koï Akademiï Nauk*, XXVI (1931): 31–179.

Tomashivs'kyi, Stepan. "Odyn moment pid Zborovom 1649 r.," *ZNTSh*, CXVII–CXVIII (1913), 115–125.

———. "Samuil Kazymyr Kushevych, l'vivs'kyi raitsia i ioho zapysna knyha," *ZNTSh*, XV (1896): 1–24.

Tomkiewicz, Władysław. "Bitwa pod Kumejkami (16 XII 1637)," *Przegląd Historyczno-Wojskowy*, IX (1937): 239–261.

———. "Cerkiew dyzunicka w dawnej Rzeczypospolitej Polskiej. Okres walki z Unią Kościelną 1596–1635," *Przegląd Powszechny*, CC (1933): 149–178.

———. *Jeremi Wiśniowiecki (1612–1651)*. Warsaw, 1933. (= Rozprawy Historyczne Towarzystwa Naukowego Warszawskiego, XII.)

———. "O składzie społecznym i etnicznym Kozaczyzny ukrainnej na przełomie XVI i XVII wieku," *Przegląd Historyczny*, XXXVII (1948): 248–260.

———. "Ograniczenie swobód kozackich w roku 1638," *Kwartalnik Historyczny*, XLIV (1930): 125–175.

———. "Powstanie kozackie w r. 1630," *Przegląd Powszechny*, CLXXXVII (July-August, 1930): 104–128.

———. "Unia Hadziacka," *Sprawy Narodowościowe*, XI (1937): 1–31.

———. "Wołyń w Koronie (1569–1795)," *Rocznik Wołyński*, II (1931): 26–45.

Treadgold, Donald W. *The Development of the USSR: An Exchange of Views.* Seattle, 1964.

Tretiak, Józef. *Historia wojny chocimskiej.* Cracow, 1921.

———. *Piotr Skarga w dziejach i literaturze Unji brzeskiej.* Cracow, 1912.

Tselevych, Oleh. "Uchast' kozakiv v Smolens'kii Viini 1633–34 rr.," *ZNTSh*, XXVII (1899): 1–71.

Tyszkowski, Kazimierz. *Kozaczyzna w wojnach moskiewskich Zygmunta III (1605–1618).* Warsaw, 1935.

Ulewicz, Tadeusz. *Sarmacja: Studium z problematyki słowiańskiej XV i XVI wieku.* Cracow, 1950.

———. "Zagadnienie sarmatyzmu w kulturze i literaturze polskiej (Problematyka ogólna i zarys historyczny)," *Zeszyty Naukowe Uniwersytetu Jagiellońskiego*, no. 59, *Prace Historycznoliterackie*, no. 5, *Filologia*, no. 9 (1963).

Urbanowicz, Eugenjusz. "Cerkiew w Niskiniczach na Wołyniu," *Ziemia* XVI, no. 5 (1931): 91–95.

Vainshtein, O. L. *Rossiia i Tridtsatiletniaia Voina 1618–1648.* Leningrad, 1947.

Vasylenko, Mykola. "Pravne polozhennia Chernihivshchyny za pol'skoï doby (1618–1648)," *Chernihiv i pivnichne Livoberezhzhia, Zapysky Ukraïns'koho naukovoho tovarystva v Kyïevi,* XXIII. Kiev, 1928, pp. 290–300.

Velykyi, A. H. [Welykyj, A. G.]. "Anonimnyi proekt Petra Mohyly po z"iedynenniu ukraïns'koï tserkvy 1645 r.," *Svitla i tini ukraïns'koï istoriï: Prychynky do istoriï ukraïns'koï tserkovnoï dumky.* Rome, 1969.

———. *Sviatyi Iosafat Kuntsevych: Ioho zhyttia i doba.* Toronto, 1967.

———. *Z litopysu khrystyians'koï Ukraïny.* 5 vols. Rome, 1968–1972.

Vernadsky, George. *Bohdan, Hetman of Ukraine.* New Haven, 1941.

Viktorovskii, P. G. "Zapadnorusskie dvorianskie familii, otpavshie ot pravoslaviia v kontse XVI i XVII vv.," *Trudy Kievskoi Dukhovnoi akademii,* 1908, no. 9, pp. 17–60; no. 10, pp. 189–206; no. 11, pp. 344–360; no. 12, pp. 502–524; 1909, no. 6, pp. 178–214; 1910, no. 3, pp. 339–392; no. 11, pp. 409–420; 1911, no. 2, pp. 259–273; no. 6, pp. 257–272; no. 7–8, pp. 396–424.

Vladimirskii-Budanov, M. F. "Naselenie Iugo-Zapadnoi Rosii ot vtoroi poloviny XV v. do Liublinskoi unii (1596)," *Arkhiv Iugo-Zapadnoi Rossii,* pt. VII, vol. 11. Kiev, 1890.

Vlasovs'kyi, Ivan. *Narys istoriï Ukraïns'koï pravoslavnoï tserkvy,* 4 vols. in five books. New York, 1955–1966.

Volyns'ka oblast': Istoriia mist i sil Ukraïns'koi RSR. Kiev, 1970.

Volyns'kyi, P. K., I. I. Pil'huk, and F. M. Polishchuk. *Istoriia ukraïns'koï literatury: Davnia literatura.* Kiev, 1969.

Vossoedinenie Ukrainy s Rossiei 1654–1954. Sbornik statei, pub. Akademiia Nauk SSSR . . . , Moscow, 1954, ed. A. I. Baranovich, *et al.*

Vozniak Mykhailo. *Istoriia ukraïnskoï literatury,* 3 vols. Lviv, 1920–1924.

Weinryb, Bernard D. "The Hebrew Chronicles on Bohdan Khmel'nyts'kyi and the Cossack-Polish War," *Harvard Ukrainian Studies,* I, no. 2 (June, 1977), 153–177.

———. *The Jews of Poland: A Social and Economic History of the Jewish Community in Poland from 1100 to 1800.* Philadelphia, 1972.

"Wiek XVII" Kontrreformacja. Barok. Prace z historii kultury, ed. Janusz Pelc. Wrocław, 1970.

Winter, Eduard. *Russland und das Papsttum,* 3 parts. Berlin, 1960–1972 (= Quellen und Studien zur Geschichte Osteuropas VI.)

Wimmer, Jan. "Wojsko," in *Polska XVII wieku,* pp. 151–189.

———. "Wojsko i skarb u schyłku XVI i w pierwszej połowie XVII w.," *Studia i Materiały do Historii Wojskowości,* XIV, pt. 1 (1968), 3–91.

———. *Wojsko polskie w drugiej połowie XVII wieku.* Warsaw, 1965.

Wisner, Henryk. *Najjaśniejsza Rzeczpospolita: Szkice z dziejów Polski szlachec-kiej.* Warsaw, 1978.

Witusik, Adam Andrzej. "Elekcja Jana Kazimierza w 1648 roku," *Annales Univ. M. Curie-Skłodowska,* Sec. F. *Nauki filozoficzno-humanistyczne,* XVII, *1962* (1965), pp. 119–153.

————. *Młodość Tomasza Zamoyskiego: O wychowaniu i karierze syna mag-nackiego w Polsce w pierwszej połowie XVII wieku.* Lublin, 1977.

————. *O Zamoyskich, Zamościu i Akademii Zamoyskiej.* Lublin, 1978.

Wójcik, Zbigniew. *Dzieje Rosiji 1533–1801.* Warsaw, [1971].

————. *Dzikie Pola w ogniu. O kozaczyźnie w dawnej Rzeczypospolitej,* 3 rev. ed. Warsaw, 1968.

————. "Feudalna Rzeczpospolita wobec umowy w Perejasławiu," *Kwartalnik Historyczny,* LXI, no. 3 (1954): 76–109.

————. *Historia powszechna XVI–XVII wieku.* Warsaw, 1973.

————. "Kisiel, Adam Swietoldycz," *Polski słownik biograficzny,* XII (1966): 487–491.

————. "Międzynarodowe położenie Rzeczypospolitej," in *Polska XVII wieku,* pp. 13–51.

————. "Niektóre zagadnienia polityki wschodniej Rzeczypospolitej w końcu XVI i w XVII wieku w literaturze zagranicznej lat ostatnich," *Rocznik Lu-belski,* V (1962): 7–43.

————. "Poland and Russia in the 17th Century: Problems of Internal Devel-opment," *Poland at the 14th International Congress of Historical Sciences in San Francisco: Studies in Comparative History,* Wrocław, 1975, pp. 114–133.

————. *Polska służba dyplomatyczna XVI–XVIII wieku.* Warsaw, 1966.

Wojtyła, A. "De Tentaminibus Novae 'Unionis Universalis' in Polonia-Lithuania Anno 1636 Factis," *Orientalia Christiana Periodica* (1952): 158–197.

Wyczański, Andrzej. *Polska—Rzeczą Pospolitą szlachecką: 1454–1795..* Warsaw, 1965.

Zaborovskii, L. V. *Rossiia, Rech' Pospolitaia i Shvetsiia v seredine XVII v.* Mos-cow, 1981.

Zacharias ab Haarlem, *Unio Ruthenorum a morte Sigismundi III usque ad co-ronationem Ladislai 1632–1633.* Tartu, 1936.

Zaikin, V. *Uchastie svetskogo elementa v tserkovnom upravlenii, vybornoe na-chalo i sobornost' v Kievskoi mitropolii v XVI i XVII v.* Warsaw, 1930.

Zajączkowski, Andrzej. *Główne elementy kultury szlacheckiej w Polsce: Ideo-logia a struktury społeczne.* Wrocław, 1961.

Zarys dziejów wojskowości polskiej do roku 1864, 2 vols. Warsaw, 1965–1966.

Zarzycki, Wacław. *Dyplomacja hetmanów w dawnej Polsce.* Warsaw-Poznań, 1967. Bydgoskie Towarzystwo Naukowe. Prace Wydziału Nauk Humanistycz-nych, ser. E. no. 8.

Zhukovich, P. *Seimovaja bor'ba pravoslavnogo zapadnorusskogo dvorianstva s tserkovnoi uniei od 1609*, 6 parts. St. Petersburg, 1901–1911.

Zhukovs'kyi, Arkadii. *Petro Mohyla i pytannia iednosty tserkov.* Paris, 1969.

Zielińska, Teresa. *Magnateria polska epoki saskiej: Funkcje urzędów i królewszczyn w procesie przeobrażeń warstwy społecznej.* Wrocław, 1977.

Ziomek, Jerzy. "Z dziejów myśli i literatury Renesansu," *Polska w epoce Odrodzenia.* Warsaw, 1970, pp. 283–304.

Żurkowski, Stanisław. *Żywot Tomasza Zamoyskiego, Kanclerza Wielkiego Koronnego.* Lviv, 1860.

Unpublished Secondary Works

Bartoszewicz, Julian. "Adam Kisiel, Wojewoda Kijowski," in Wojewodzkie Archiwum Państwowe w Łodzi, Archiwum Bartoszewiczów, MS. 1768, 19th century.

Chynczewska-Hennel, Teresa. "Świadomość narodowa kozaczyzny i szlachty ukraińskiej w XVII wieku." Warsaw, Instytut Historii, PAN, 1981. Ph.D. thesis.

Kartoteka posłów do sejmu. Deposit at Zakład Dokumentacji Instytutu Historii PAN w Krakowie.

Kartoteka Polaków studujących zagranicą. Deposit at Zakład Dokumentacji Instytutu Historii PAN w Krakowie.

P[ułaski], K[azimierz]. "Wiadomość o Życiu i czynach Adama Kisiela, podkomorzego Czernichowskiego, potem Wojewody Kijowskiego w latach 1628–1639." MS. 725, 19th century in Biblioteka PAN w Krakowie (Dawniej PAU).

Świtalski, Zbigniew. "Sojusz polsko-rosyjski z roku 1647." Warsaw, 1970. Ph.D. thesis. Abstract in Instytut Historyczny, Archiwum Uniwersytetu Warszawskiego, Dział VIII-a, Nr. 3630–B.

Velychenko, Stephan. "The Influence of Historical, Political, and Social Ideas on the Politics of Bohdan Khmel'nyts'kyi and the Cossack Officers between 1648 and 1657." London School of Economics, 1980.

Index

Abraham, W., 245, 366
Abrahamowicz, Zygmunt, 321, 365
Adersbach, Andreas, 160, 331
Adrianova-Perets, V. P., 363
Aleksei (Mikhailovich), tsar, 135
Aliab'ev, Grigorii, 74, 76
Alsace, 33
Altmark, truce of, 65
Amman, A. M., 366
Anatolia, 142
Andriewsky, Olga, ix
Andrusiak, Mikołaj (Mykola), 301, 366
Anichenka, Uladzimir, 249, 366
Antitrinitarians, 18, 40, 41, 44, 205, 206, 244, 256
Antonovych, Mykhailo, 267, 366
Antonovych (Antonovich), V. B., 365, 367, 379
Anushkin, N., 288, 367
Apanovich, E. M., 322, 327, 367
Armenians, 32
Articles of Confederation, 18
Asia Minor, 23, 132
Azov, 131, 308

Bahalii (Bagalei), Dmitrii, 367
Baievs'kyi, Teodozii (Baiewski, Theodosius Wasilewicz), 127, 128, 213, 306, 358
Bakovets'kyi, Iosyf, 57, 62
Baliński, Michał, 358, 363
Balkan Christians, 185
Baltic Sea and coast, xv, 6, 14, 16, 18, 19, 40, 79, 105, 130, 138, 242, 341
Banac, Ivo, 241, 374
Bandini, Octavio, 272
Bantysh-Kamenskii, N. N., 226, 308, 311, 312, 358, 367
Baraboi, A. Z., 349, 359
Barącz, Sadok, 236, 287, 319, 364
Baranovskii (Baranovs'kyi), S., 223, 273, 367
Baranowski, Bohdan, 228, 243, 248, 283, 284, 308, 319, 321, 367

Baranovych, Lazar (Baranowicz, Łazarz), 140, 318, 358
Baranovych, Oleksander (Baranovich, A. I.), 231, 245, 247, 254, 256, 257, 260, 261, 300, 358, 388
Bardach, Juliusz, 240, 296, 367
Baron, Salo Wittmayer, 244, 247, 367
Barsov, T., 367
Barsukov, Aleksandr, 312, 313, 368
Baroque, 8
Bartoszewicz, Julian, 222, 363, 368, 390
Bartoszewicz, Kazimierz, 258, 368
Barwiński, Eugeniusz, 359
Basarab, John, 319
Batih, battle of, 199, 200, 346
Batiushkov, P. N., 255, 368
Batory, Stefan, 6, 16, 23, 246, 247, 261
Bednov (Bidnov), V., 244, 368
Behm, Michał, 325
Belokurov, S. A., 307, 368
Belorussia, 24, 41, 55, 89, 90, 104, 107, 119, 250, 251
Belz and Belz palatinate, 21, 38, 54, 106, 161, 171, 217, 220
Bennigsen, Alexandre, 248, 284, 321, 342, 368
Berestechko, battle of, 192, 193, 208, 343, 344
Bevzo, O. A., 254, 255, 358, 368
Bieleiowski, Hieremias, 109, 298, 359
Bieńkowski, Ludomir, 256, 288, 289, 368
Bila Tserkva, 152, 195, 196; agreement of, 180, 193, 194, 196, 197, 198, 199, 205, 344, 345
Bilets'kyi, O., 368
Bilets'kyi, Platon, 254, 296, 368
Bilhorod, 45, 262
Birkowski, Fabian, 275
Birkowski, Szymon, 263
Bisacconi, Maiolino, 236, 320, 359
Black Sea and coast, 25, 72, 75, 78, 79, 81, 105, 136, 143, 145, 146, 149, 163, 174, 189, 280

Blane, Andrew, 250, 379
Bobrykovych, Iosyf, 57, 58, 60, 281
Bohemia, 32, 35
Bohuslav, 345
Bogucka, Maria, 242, 368
Bohun, Ivan, 186
Bohushevych, Filon, 53, 216, 219, 270. *See also* Hulkevych-Hlibovs'kyi, Filon
Bohushivka, 219
Bohuslav starostvo, 155, 170, 191, 219
Boiko, Ivan Davydovich, 247, 368
Bolesław Chrobry, 46, 263
Bolkhovskii (Bolkhovskoi), Semen, 150, 322, 323
Boniecki, Adam, 259, 260, 261, 349, 368
Borets'kyi, Iov, 52, 55, 56, 57, 59, 60, 61, 62, 65, 69, 91, 271, 273
Borovytsia, 86, 87, 88
Borowicz, Jan Nepomucen, 261, 380
Borucki, Marek, 242, 368
Boryskovych, Izaak, 59, 273
Boyko, Max, 255, 256, 257, 368
Brandenburg, 159
Bratslav and Bratslav palatinate, xvi, 21, 22, 25, 26, 35, 40, 47, 67, 78, 91, 114, 116, 119, 131, 133, 134, 152, 173, 174, 175, 178, 184, 186, 194, 197, 199, 203, 219, 246, 338, 339, 343
Brest and Brest palatinate, 200
Brest, Union of, 19, 30, 33, 34, 41, 44, 49, 54, 56, 62, 66, 89, 90, 91, 107, 108, 115, 118, 119, 181, 187, 190, 200, 203, 211, 251, 304
Briansk, 75
Broniewski, Mikołaj, 217
Brückner, Aleksander, 253, 368
Brusyliv, 54, 258, 261, 265, 270
Budilovich, V., 264, 368
Bugoslavski, Grigorii, 225, 295, 368
Buh River, 43, 162, 170
Burchacki (Burkhots'kyi), Adam, 218, 220
Busha (Iaruha), battle of, 51, 265, 266
Bushkovitch, Paul, 241, 374
But, Pavlo, 84. *See also* Pavliuk
Butiatychi, 216
Butovych family, 44, 54, 260, 261; Mykhailo, 54, 270
Butsinskii, P. N., 368
Butych, Ivan, 233, 349, 359
Bystroń, Jan Stanisław, 257, 368

Byzantine rite, 50, 81, 121
Byzantium, 29
Bzhozovs'kyi, Maksymilian, 164, 191, 221, 323, 333, 341, 344

Calvinism, 18, 40, 62, 67, 100, 159, 257
Candia, war of, 141
Capponi, A., 305
Cavazza, Hironimo, 345
Chaplych-Shpanivs'kyi family, 41
Chartorys'kyi (Czartorys'kyi *or* Czartoryski) family, 40, 45; Ivan Fedorovych, 44; Iurii, 257; Maryna Kysilivna, 44, 259; Mykhailo, 261
Chełm and Chełm land, 21, 47, 101, 119, 164, 176
Chełm diocese, 89, 92, 93, 99, 100, 101, 118, 289, 327
Chełmno (Kulm) law, 14
Cherkasy, city and starostvo, 184, 191, 219, 332
Chernihiv, city, palatinate, and lands, xvi, 16, 21, 22, 25, 38, 51, 54, 65, 70, 71, 72, 74, 75, 76, 77, 78, 85, 88, 95, 97, 113, 114, 116, 119, 120, 122, 131, 132, 138, 147, 152, 173, 174, 175, 176, 178, 183, 186, 190, 194, 195, 196, 200, 203, 215, 217, 218, 246, 261, 265, 267, 268, 278, 283, 291, 292, 295, 298, 299, 309, 343, 346
Chetvertyns'kyi family, 42, 44, 45, 95, 258, 269; Chetvertyns'ka, Sviatopolkovna, 258; Hryhorii, 53, 118, 257, 269; Iurii, 257; Stefan, 257; Zakharii, 164
Chevalier, Pierre (P'er Sheval'e), 359
Chistoi, N., 314, 317
Chistovich, I., 369
Chodkiewicz, Anna, 338
Chodkiewicz, Jan Karol, 51, 266
Chodynicki, Kazimierz, 243, 244, 250, 251, 254, 255, 257, 267, 270, 271, 273, 275, 289, 291, 369
Cholkans'kyi, Kamin', 157, 329
Chornobyl', 116, 133, 335
Christina, queen of Sweden, 162
Chruszczewski, Adam, 302
Chrząszcz, Izydor Edmund, 337, 369
Chudynky, 220
Chyhyryn, city and starostvo, 143, 144, 150, 173, 181, 185, 186, 198, 343, 345

Chynczewska-Hennel, Teresa, 254, 390
Cicero, 48
Ciekliński, father, 329, 330
Clark, George, 307, 369
Congregation for the Propagation of the Faith, 62, 94, 118, 119, 124, 125, 271, 272, 273, 274, 290, 296, 301, 302, 303, 304
Constantinople, city, patriarch, patriarchate, 29, 30, 41, 59, 60, 61, 62, 123, 125, 126, 135, 179, 305
Copernicus, Nicholas, 6
Costin, Miron, 306, 359
Cossacks, xvi, 2, 16, 22, 23, 24, 25, 26, 36, 49, 51, 52, 59, 60, 62, 65, 67, 71, 72, 73, 74, 75, 78, 79, 80, 81, 82, 83, 84, 89, 91, 94, 111, 117, 129, 130, 132, 136, 137, 138, 141–213, 228, 246, 278, 279, 280, 281–287, 297, 314, 316, 319
Counter-Reformation, 8, 30, 34, 36, 64, 65, 112, 254
Cracow, city and palatinate, xv, 14, 116, 153, 167, 222, 235, 265, 284, 300, 330, 343; Academy, 53, 236
Crete, 142
Crimea, peninsula and khanate, 6, 25, 79, 80, 84, 88, 128, 130, 134, 136, 139, 145, 184, 204, 248, 307, 344. *See also* Tatars
Cynarski, Stanisław, 241, 369
Čyževs'kyi, Dmytro, 250, 253, 369
Czapliński, Daniel, 144, 168
Czapliński, Władysław, 234, 239, 241, 242, 243, 244, 256, 257, 268, 274, 275, 277, 279, 283, 291, 296, 297, 299, 300, 307, 308, 309, 330, 345, 346, 369
Czarniecki, Stefan, 50, 265
Czartoryski, Paweł, 250, 370
Czermak, Wiktor, 235, 236, 302, 304, 307, 309, 310, 311, 312, 320, 321, 331, 363, 365, 369
Cześcik, Łucja, 339, 370

Daneykowicz, Jan Ostrowski, 359
Daniłowicz family, 256; Stanisław, 80
Danubian principalities, 128, 166, 307
Darowski, Adam, 312, 313, 370
Davies, Norman, 240, 370
Dehtiv, 220
Dembińska, Anna, 255, 256, 370
Dembiński, Bronisław, 370

Demosthenes, 48
Denhoff, Gerhard, 116
Denmark, 248
Derman', monastery, 39
Desna River, 221
Deulino, peace of, 76
Divovych, Onisyfor, 29, 251
Divytsia, 86, 116, 217, 282
Długosz, Jan, 263
Długosz, Józef, 241, 300
Długosz, Teofil, 270, 272, 370
Dnieper River and region, xvii, 20, 22, 23, 24, 25, 55, 61, 68, 79, 82, 84, 86, 144, 146, 163, 178, 197, 199, 204, 247, 317
Dnieper Ukraine, 54, 104, 165, 194
Dobrianskii, Antonii, 289, 294, 370
Dolgorukii, Iurii Alekseevich, 143, 317, 318
Don Cossacks, 131, 138, 143
Don River, 82, 131, 143, 145
Dorohynychi, 43, 44, 45, 218, 258, 259, 260, 261
Doroshenko, Dmytro, 347, 370
Drevyns'kyi family, 42; Lavrentii, 49, 52, 57, 58, 59, 60, 61, 62, 66, 67, 71, 95, 257, 264, 267, 272, 276, 291
Druzhinin, N. M., 249, 370
Druzhytz, V., 240, 370
Dubno, 152
Dubno monastery, 39, 49
Dubrawski, Franciszek, 156
Dubyna, K. K., 373
Dworzaczek, Włodzimierz, 241, 258, 370
Dzisna River, 288
Dzhalalyi, Fylon, 213
Dzvyn, 219
Dzyra, Iaroslav, 361, 370

East Slavs, 29, 244
Eingorn, Vitalii, 251, 370
Engel, Johann Christian von, 226, 370
Ermolenko, A. F., 342
Estreicher, Karol, 306
Euthanasius, Victorinus, 362

Fedorov, Ivan, 251
Fedro, Jakub, 99
Ferguson, Dolly, 250, 369
Filaret, patriarch, 71
Filipczak-Kocur, Anna, 272, 371

394 **Index**

Filipovich, Afanasii, 120
Filonardi, Mario, 118, 301, 302
Fipolo, Antonio Francisco, 304
Firlej family, 256; Andrzej, 161, 171, 172, 335
Fisher, Alan W., 248, 371
Florence, Council of, 30, 124, 125
Florovsky, Georges (Florovskii, Georgii), 250, 253, 302
Forsten, G. V., 341, 371
France, 28, 33, 278
Franko, Ivan, 252, 320, 359, 371
Frąś, Ludwik, 336, 337, 371
Freeze, Gregory, ix
Freylichówna, J., 263, 371
Friedrich Wilhelm of Brandenburg-Prussia, 331, 332
Frycz Modrzewski, Andrzej, 6, 8

Gajecky, George, ix, 371
Galaktionov, I. V., 309, 310, 359, 363
Galicia, 224
Galician-Volhynian principality, 20
Gazotti, Pietro, 359
Gdańsk, xv, 14, 78, 234, 242
Gedimin dynasty, 39, 109
Gębicki, (Gembicki), P., 230, 354
Germany, 19, 29, 65, 284
Gierowski, Józef Andrzej, ix, 241, 371, 381
Gizycki, Jan Maren, 291, 299, 346, 371
Gniew, battle of, 52, 268, 269
Gniezno archdiocese, 147
Godziszewski, Władysław, 248, 282, 307, 308, 309, 310, 311, 316, 371
Goliński, Marcin, 347, 356
Gołębiowski, Seweryn, 268, 269, 371
Golobutskii (Holobuts'kyi), V. A., 246, 248, 284, 318, 320, 340
Golubev, S. T., 218, 231, 232, 252, 255, 264, 271, 273, 274, 276, 277, 278, 279, 280, 281, 287, 288, 289, 291, 292, 293, 294, 295, 297, 302, 304, 340, 359, 371
Gorsline, Doreen, 250, 369
Gorzkowski, Maryan, 372
Górka, Olgierd, 228, 321, 372
Górski, Konstantyn, 372
Grabowski, Ambrozy, 332, 333, 334, 335, 336, 338, 344, 348, 349, 359
Grabowski, Jerzy, 327

Grabowski, Tadeusz, 222, 233, 253, 271, 372
Great Poland, 40, 104, 111, 210, 256, 296
Grigorovich, Ioann, 359
Grochowski, A., 68
Grodziski, Stanisław, 240, 372
Grondski de Grond (Gradzki), Samuel, 338, 360
Grzybowski, Konstanty, 242, 372
Gudzenko, P. P., 350, 366
Guldon, Zenon, 247, 372
Gumilevskii, Filaret, 295, 296, 310, 371
Gustavus Adolphus of Sweden, 64, 71, 79, 274, 275

Hadiach, agreement of, 203, 204, 205, 347
Habsburgs, 13, 16, 18, 64, 248, 274. *See also* Holy Roman Empire
Hajda, Lubomyr, ix
Halecki, Oskar, 240, 245, 246, 251, 254, 255, 370, 372
Haluščynskyj, Theodosius T., 271
Halych, 164, 176
Handelsman, Marcel, 370
Hankiewicz, Stefan, 231, 278
Hannover, Nathan, 320, 360
Hartleb, Kazimierz, 288
Helcel, Antoni Zygmunt, 350, 362
Herasymchuk, Vasyl', 338, 372
Herbst, Stanisław, 263, 372
Herburt, Jan Szczęsny, 250
Hering, Günnar, 373
Hernas, Czesław, 250, 373
Herodotus, 48
Hlebiv, 53
Hlukhiv, 202
Hlyniany, 156, 157
Hniino, 152, 191, 217, 325; St. Nicholas nunnery, 275
Hois'kyi family, 41, 257; Roman, 256
Holobuts'kyi, Vsevolod. *See* Golobutskii
Holowackyj, R. R., 288, 373
Holy Roman Empire, 109. *See also* Habsburgs
Holy See, 94, 99, 118
Horn, Maurycy, 244, 253, 308, 373
Horodlo, 156; Union of, 17, 43
Horyn River, 168, 169, 183

Hoshcha, 145, 152, 156, 168, 169, 172, 188, 190, 218, 291, 325, 335; monastery, 148; school, 116, 292
Hosius, Stanisław, 48
Hoverbeck, Johann von, 332
Hrabianka (Grabianka), Hryhorii, 226, 373
Hrabovets'kyi, Volodymyr, 373
Hrodna, 90, 200
Hromyka, Mykhailo, 195
Hrushevs'kyi, Mykhailo (Hruszewski, Michał), 1, 2, 226, 227, 237, 239, 245, 246, 248, 251, 252, 253, 263, 265, 267, 270, 271, 275, 277, 279, 280, 283, 284, 285, 286, 287, 289, 290, 292, 295, 319, 320, 322, 323, 324, 327, 328, 330, 331, 334, 336, 337, 338, 339, 340, 341, 342, 344, 345, 346, 347, 349, 373
Hubin, 218
Hulevych family, 42, 95; Hulevych-Voiutyns'kyi, Semen (Sylvestr), 92, 93, 97, 98, 99, 101, 102, 257, 289, 293, 295
Hulkevych-Hlibovs'kyi family, 53; Hulkevych-Hlibovs'ka, Anastaziia Bohushevychivna, 53, 54. See also Kysil, Anastaziia; Bohush, 53, 270. See also Bohushevych, Filon
Hunczak, Taras, 377
Humanism, 29, 31
Hungary, 6, 32, 35
Huslystyi, K. H., 365
Hymy, 221

Iakovychi, 219
Iakovyts'kyi, Havrylo, 262
Ialovyts'kyi, Danylo, 218, 220
Iaruha. See Busha
Ielets', Teodor, 218
Ihnatowicz, Ireneusz, 240, 373
Ihor, prince, 262
Ingoli, Francesco, 124, 296, 301, 302, 304, 305, 327
Irkliïv, 185, 342
Irpen' River, 53
Irynach, monk, 311
Isaievych, Ia. D., 229, 251, 252, 289, 373
Isajkowski, Franciszek, 310, 312, 313
Islam Girey, khan, 145, 156, 171, 172, 192
Israel, 175
Istanbul, 172
Italy, 28, 29, 327

Iurii, 217
Iuzefovich, M., 257
Ivanishev, N. D., 350, 363, 366
Ivanyts'kyi family, 41, 44, 45; Ivan, 269; Ivanyts'ka-Kysil Teodora, 44
Iziaslav, 152

Jabłonowski, Aleksander, 245, 247, 252, 253, 255, 259, 299, 347, 373
Jagiellonian dynasty, 13, 64
Jan Kazimierz, xv, 13, 117, 138, 159, 160, 161, 162, 163, 167, 178, 185, 190, 195, 219, 282, 318, 330, 331, 332, 343, 347, 353, 354, 355, 357
Jemiołowski, Mikołaj, 236, 360
Jesuits, 36, 151, 201; schools, 8, 19, 46, 47, 48, 49, 173, 264, 295
Jerlicz, Joachim (Ierlych, Ioakhym), 236, 270, 306, 338, 360
Jerusalem, 164
Jews, 6, 17, 19, 24, 32, 147, 193, 244, 247, 320
Jobert, Ambroise, 256, 373
Józefowicz, Tomasz Jan, 236, 360
Justinian, 48

Kaczmarczyk, Zdzisław, 240, 241, 242, 243, 258, 307, 349, 373
Kalinowski family, 109; Marcin, 77, 146, 150, 190, 191, 192, 194, 195, 196, 199, 208, 298, 343, 345, 346
Kalush, city and starostwo, 77
Kalushovs'kyi, Petro, 218, 269
Kamanin, Iv., 374
Kam"ianets'-Podil's'kyi, 72, 171, 210
Kaminski, Andrzej, 241, 242, 347, 374
Kaniv, 82, 198
Karaimovych, Iliiash, 86
Karol Ferdynand (Vasa), 159, 160, 161, 162, 331, 337
Karpov, Gennadii, 374
Kartashev, A. V., 374
Kashirsk, 317
Kasymenko, Oleksandr, 2, 318, 324, 374
Kawecka-Gryczowa, Alodia, 295
Kazanowski, Adam, 116, 133, 218, 298, 299, 309, 311
Kazanowski, Marcin, 74
Keenan, Edward L., ix, 251, 374

Kersten, Adam, ix, 241, 265, 342, 343, 344, 369, 374
Kharbkiv, 220
Kharlampovich, K. V., 252, 257, 263, 374
Khmel'nyts'kyi, Bohdan, 1, 2, 3, 140, 141–213, 239, 319
Khmel'nyts'kyi, Mykhailo, 144
Khmel'nyts'kyi, Tymish, 186, 199, 339
Kholmogorov, V. I., 311, 360
Khoma, Ivan, 270, 374
Khotmyzh, 150, 318
Khotyn, battle of, 16, 51, 53, 88, 130, 266
Khreniv, 260
Khvorostiv, 219
Khyzhniak, Z. I., 252, 374
Kiev, xv, 23, 25, 28, 31, 41, 45, 46, 54, 55, 57, 58, 59, 72, 73, 74, 86, 91, 118, 152, 157, 163, 164, 165, 177, 180, 182, 183, 200, 201, 202, 210, 211, 215, 231, 239, 262, 263, 271, 273, 281, 284, 287, 289, 317, 335, 338, 340; Brotherhood of the Epiphany, 31, 55; brotherhood school, 49, 55; cathedral of St. Sophia, 53, 72, 263; Caves monastery, 31, 55, 81, 96, 125, 127, 264; collegium, 31, 97, 127, 164, 165, 236, 299; Jesusit school, 173; metropolitanate, 29, 31, 55, 61, 69, 71, 73, 74, 89, 91, 123, 125, 141, 166, 251, 333; monastery of St. Michael, 73, 281; monastery of St. Nicholas, 80; Vydubets' monastery, 89
Kievan palatinate, xvii, 21, 22, 25, 35, 40, 44, 52, 53, 54, 57, 70, 78, 110, 111, 113, 114, 116, 119, 133, 142, 151, 152, 155, 165, 170, 173, 174, 175, 176, 177, 178, 181, 184, 191, 192, 193, 194, 195, 196, 200, 202, 203, 205, 216, 218, 219, 221, 246, 258, 260, 264, 265, 268, 280, 282, 283, 292, 300, 302, 323, 326, 333, 334, 335, 338, 347
Kievan principality, 21
Kievan Rus', 20, 25, 27, 29, 45, 140, 210, 211
Kirchholm, battle of, 16
Kishka, Lev, 273
Kisiel, Adam Franciszek, 273
Kłoczowski, Jerzy, 302, 375
Kobierzycki, Józef, 344, 374
Kobierzycki, Stanisław, 360
Kobryn', 171

Kobyl'skii, I. S., 317
Kobyshche, 116, 138, 217, 299, 305
Kochanowski, Jan, 6, 48
Kochanowski, J. K., 263, 264, 374
Kochowski, Wespazjan, 189, 236, 343, 360
Koczerska, Maria, 257, 375
Kodak (fortress), 79, 87
Kohn, Hans, 375
Kohut, Zenon, ix
Kojałowicz, Wijuk Wojciech (Koialowicz, Albertus Wiiuk), 319, 337, 360
Koil'no, 220
Kolbuszewski, Kazimierz, 288
Komovskii, V., 359
Kompan, O. S., 247, 254, 375
Konarski, Stanisław, 271, 350, 366
Konashevych-Sahaidachnyi, Petro, 49, 51, 265
Koniecpolski, Aleksander, 142, 144, 150, 208
Koniecpolski, Stanisław, 71, 72, 73, 74, 76, 78, 79, 80, 81, 82, 83, 84, 85, 86, 87, 88, 105, 116, 128, 131, 132, 133, 137, 141, 150, 232, 256, 279, 280, 282, 283, 284, 285, 286, 287, 300, 307, 309, 311, 320, 357
Koniskii, Georgii, 360
Kononovych, Sava, 84
Konopczynski, Władysław, 234, 240, 242, 291, 360
Koppi, Carolus, 338
Kopyns'kyi, Isai, 65, 69, 72, 73, 92, 255, 277, 280, 281
Kopystens'kyi, Zakharii, 254
Kopystyns'kyi, Fedir, 102
Korduba, Myron (Miron), 226, 236, 319, 323, 324, 330, 331, 340, 341, 361, 375
Korets'kyi family, 39, 95
Korolko, Mirosław, 244, 375
Korsak, Rafail, 289, 290, 291, 296, 301
Korshumov, Aleksander F., 302, 361
Korsun', 195, 199; battle of, 146, 147, 188, 322, 344
Koryciński, Marcin, 97
Koryciński, Mikołaj, 278
Koryciński, Stefan, 346
Korzon, Tadeusz, 321, 375
Kosiv, Sylvestr (Kossów Silwester), 45, 49, 96, 125, 126, 127, 142, 155, 166, 167, 178, 205, 258, 259, 261, 262, 263, 264,

266, 268, 292, 303, 304, 305, 335, 339, 361

Kosman, Marceli, 228, 375

Kossowski, Aleksander, 256, 288, 375

Kostomarov, Mykola (Nikolai), 223, 226, 321, 342, 376

Kot, Stanisław, 244, 249, 288, 347, 376

Kotłubaj, Edward, 357, 376

Kovel' starostwo, 256

Kowalska, Halina, 320

Kozarhorod, 217

Krajcar, J., 272, 376

Krasnosile,, 220

Krasyliv, 220

Krasnystaw, 100

Krauzhar, A. (Kraushar, Aleksandr), 333, 376

Krem"ianets', 218, 220, 260

Kronenberg, Ludwik, 224, 233

Kropyvnyts'kyi, Mykhailo, 57, 58, 60, 61, 62, 63, 67, 71, 272, 278

Krosnowski, Mikołaj, 330

Krupets'kyi, Atanazii, 90, 91, 92, 93, 97, 99, 101, 289, 294

Krupets'kyi, Fedir, 260

Kryp"iakevych, Ivan, 227, 233, 235, 245, 246, 272, 273, 274, 287, 320, 321, 322, 323, 324, 325, 327, 349, 359, 361, 376

Kryvonis, Maksym, 156, 157

Kubala, Ludwik, 2, 227, 235, 278, 284, 297, 300, 306, 307, 309, 311, 321, 324, 325, 326, 327, 330, 331, 333, 336, 337, 338, 341, 343/344, 344, 346, 376

Kuchowicz, Zbigniew, 376

Kuczwarewicz, Marcin, 361

Kukhary, 219

Kulaha-Petrazhyts'kyi, Ivan, 66

Kulish, Panteleimon, 226, 284, 319, 357, 376

Kuczwarewicz, Marcin, 361

Kumeiky, battle of, 85, 87, 286, 287

Kuntsevych, Iosafat, 52, 55, 90, 271

Kurbskii, Ivan, 251

Kurdiumov, M. F., 361

Kurdydyk, Jarema, x

Kurevychi, 217

Kurkuriv, ordinance of, 325

Kursk, 75

Kurylas, Bohdan, 271, 272, 377

Kutrzeba, Stanisław, 240, 242, 296, 298, 299, 377

Kysil family, 43, 44, 45, 47, 96, 200, 258, 259, 261, 262, 263, 267; Anastazia, 266, 270, 344. *See also* Hulkevych-Hlibovs'ka; Andrii, 259, 260; Halyna, 218, 260; Havrylo, 260; Hnevosh, 44, 260; Hryhorii (Gregor-Hrehory), 44, 45, 49, 53, 216, 260, 261, 262, 269; Illia, 259, Ianush, 44, 262; Iurii (Jerzy Kisiel Dorohinicki), 258, 260; Ivan, 259, 260, 261; Maria, 260; Maria (Tryzna), 259; Maryna (Chortorys'ka), 44, 259; Matvii, 261, 265, 283; Mykola, 44, 52, 152, 162, 164, 191, 217, 219, 260, 267, 283, 311, 331, 332, 333, 336; Mykyta, 258, 259; Olekhno (Oleksander), 258, 259; Oleksander (son of Andrii), 260; Oleksander (son of Ivan), 261, 268, 283; Pavlo, 260; Petro, 259, 260, 261; Teodora (Orans'ka), 45, 49; "Timofei" (Ivan), 260; Tymish, 260; Tymofei or Tykhno, 43, 44, 258, 259; Vasyl', 259

Kysilevychi, 221

Kysil'horod forest, 221

Kysilivka, 202

Kysilivshchyna, 44, 54, 258, 259, 260

Lagoshniak, Orysia, x

Lahoshniak, Wasyl, x

Lanckoroński, Stanisław, 171, 190, 192, 208, 336, 339

Lappo, I. I., 240, 377

Lashch, Petro, 269

Łaski, Jan, 6

Laskiv, 219

Lasko, Petro, 148, 150, 152, 157, 169, 325, 335

Łaszcz, Samuel, 327

Latacz, Eugeniusz, 337

Latin rite, 27, 121, 187, 190, 252

Lavrynenko, 75

Lazarevskii, Aleksandr Matveevich, 361

Lebanon, 135

Lebedintsev, P. G., 379

Left Bank (of Dnieper), 25, 72, 73, 131, 133, 145, 151, 176, 183, 194, 195, 196, 299, 302, 310, 326, 346; monasteries, 65

Leitsch, Walter, 248, 377

Leliavskii, B. M., 225, 377

398

Łempicki, Stanisław, 263, 377
Lenchary, 221
Leningrad, 239
Lenkiewicz family, 258
Leont'ev, Z. S., 317
Leontovich, F. I., 246, 377
Lepszy, Kazimierz, 243, 341, 377, 382
Leszczyński family, 256; Andrzej, 153, 160, 162, 170, 171, 185, 190, 195, 196, 199, 207, 328, 333, 336, 343; Rafał, 65
Leszczyński, Józef, 377
Leśnodorski, Bogusław, 240, 349, 373
Levitskii (Levyts'kyi), Orest, 251, 261, 357, 377
Lewanski, Richard, 378
Lewicki, K., 254, 257, 378
Lewin, Paulina, ix, 295
Libiszowska, Zofia, 228, 248, 319, 367, 378
Likhachev, D. S., 363, 378
Linage de Vauciennes, 361
Linnichenko, I. A., 245, 378
Lipinski, Wacław, 279, 281, 378
Lipinski, Wacław. See Lypyns'kyi, Viacheslav
Lithuania, xvi, 6, 9, 19, 21, 27, 38, 41, 49, 69, 70, 73, 109, 133, 166, 243, 245, 313; Grand Duchy of, xvi, xvii, 16, 17, 19, 20, 21, 22, 27, 28, 32, 33, 38, 39, 43, 44, 66, 67, 89, 90, 91, 92, 99, 104, 105, 110, 111, 113, 132, 133, 134, 135, 137, 138, 155, 170, 171, 193, 210, 246, 255, 256, 259, 288, 289, 291, 296, 309, 311, 312, 315, 327
Lithuanian statute, second, 21
Little Poland, 40, 104, 105, 111, 210, 256, 278, 296
Liubavskii, M., 245, 246, 378
Livonia, 104, 334, 348
Livonian Order, 6
Livy, 48
Lizola, Franz, 331
Lobachivshchyna, 219
Lohvyn, H. N., 378
Longinov, Ar., 294, 378
Łoś, Jakub, 361
Low Countries, 14
Łoziński, Władysław, 245, 289, 294, 296, 378
Lozka family, 44, 54, 259, 260

Łubieński, Maciej, 147, 149, 154, 287, 322, 323, 325, 326, 327, 328, 329, 330
Lublin, Union of, xvii, 9, 16, 17, 20, 21, 22, 28, 33, 35, 38, 39, 41, 42, 44, 46, 109, 112, 203, 204, 240, 246, 247, 254, 255, 256, 260, 298
Lublin, city and palatinate, 99, 101, 172, 329, 336
Lublin brotherhood church, 49, 93, 99, 100, 104, 108, 257, 294
Lublin tribunal, 80, 99, 231, 284, 293, 296
Lubomirski, J. T., 225, 261, 262, 263, 266, 292, 378
Lubomirski, Stanisław, 116, 153, 300, 330
Lubovychi, 218
Luckyj, George S., 250, 369
Łukaszewicz, Józef, 302, 378
Lunig, Johann Christian, 361
Lupu, Roxanda, 186, 199
Lupu, Vasile, 186, 199
Lutheranism, 8
Luts'k, city and county, 67, 116, 151, 152, 218, 244, 269, 276, 324
Luts'k Orthodox diocese, 39, 59, 89, 90, 91, 92, 98, 99, 118, 122, 289, 304
Luts'k Roman Catholic diocese, 68, 256
Luts'k Uniate diocese, 92, 98, 99
Luts'k brotherhood, 42, 71, 257
Luzhnyts'kyi, Hryhorii, 288, 379
Łuzny, Ryszard, 379
Lviv, city and county, xv, 14, 20, 28, 30, 41, 57, 58, 60, 62, 71, 72, 91, 156, 157, 159, 164, 176, 186, 210, 227, 233, 236, 239, 289
Lviv brotherhood, 30, 41, 42, 60, 66, 91, 95, 230, 251, 279, 280
Lviv Orthodox diocese, 20, 42, 59, 60, 72, 89, 91, 92
Lviv Roman Catholic archidiocese, 20, 101, 330
Lviv St. George's Orthodox cathedral, 72
Lynshchyna, 219
Lypyns'kyi, Viacheslav (Lipinski, Wacław), ix, 227, 245, 250, 255, 257, 267, 277, 280, 320, 327, 330, 332, 336, 350, 378, 379
Łysakowski, Alexander, 217
Lyzlov, G. M., 318, 340, 379

Maciszewsky, Jarema, 240, 241, 242, 243, 246, 379

Mączak, Antoni, 240, 242, 373, 379
Magdeburg law, 14, 17, 48
Magno, Valeriano, 303, 305
Mahilioŭ, 288
Majewski, Ryszard, 266, 379
Majewski, Wiesław, 307, 309, 321, 379
Makarevychi, 221
Makarii (Bulgakov), 289, 379
Makhnovets', L. E., 257, 271, 276, 379
Makoshyn, 218
Makoshyn St. Nicholas monastery, 295
Maksakiv monastery, 296
Maksymovych, Iurii, 224
Maksymovich, Mykhailo (Maksimovich, Mikhail Aleksandrovich), 257, 277, 278, 292, 379
Mal, 263
Małowist, Marian, 242, 379
Malyshchyns'kyi, Iliia, 269
Malyshevskii, I. I., 379
Manastyrs'kyi, Fedir, 102
Mańkowski, Tadeusz, 241, 379
Maria Ludwika, 162, 190
Martel, Antoine, 244, 245, 252, 253, 254, 256, 380
Marusyn, M., 380
Masovia, 5, 8, 19, 111, 160
Matuz, Josef, 308
Medlin, William K., 250, 380
Medynskii, E. N., 252, 380
Mehmed IV, sultan, 171
Meller, Stefan, 247, 366
Melzi, Camillus de, 335
Merseburg, 277
Mesch, Abraham J., 320
Miaskowski family, 337; Wojciech, 164, 166, 332
Michałowski, Jakub, 222, 232, 233, 287, 322, 323, 324, 325, 326, 327, 328, 329, 330, 331, 332, 335, 337, 338, 341, 342, 343, 344, 345, 347, 349, 357, 362
Middle East, 166
Mienicki, Ryszard, 240, 380
Mikhail Fedorovich, tsar, 134, 135
Mina forest, 221
Mnishyn, 220
Mohyla (Movila), Peter, 31, 49, 50, 55, 56, 57, 59, 60, 61, 62, 66, 67, 69, 70, 71, 72, 73, 80, 81, 92, 95, 116, 118, 120, 122, 123, 124, 125, 126, 127, 141, 142, 218,
252, 253, 264, 271, 273, 275, 277, 279, 280, 281, 291, 292, 295, 299, 301, 302, 303, 304, 320. *See also* Euzebii Pimin
Mohyl'no, 217
Molchanovskii (Molchanovs'kyi), N., 245, 380
Moldavia, 16, 25, 30, 31, 165, 181, 182, 186, 196, 199, 249, 251
Montague, Henry (Earl of Manchester), 361
Morokhovs'kyi, Iliia, 63, 274
Moscow, xv, 125, 134, 135, 137, 138, 139, 149, 153, 157, 169, 230, 239, 249, 265, 311, 312, 313, 315, 317, 327, 340, 341, 354; patriarchate, 29
Mozyria, Lukia, 195
Mstislaŭ, 288; Orthodox diocese, 89, 289
Mukosilevychi, 221
Muscovites, xvii, 28, 29; army, 70, 73, 74, 75; government and state, 77, 80, 117, 133, 136, 137, 138, 139, 142, 143, 149, 154, 156, 164, 165, 184, 202, 224, 248, 282, 284, 285, 300, 307, 308, 309, 310, 311, 312, 313, 315, 318, 322, 327, 340, 341
Muscovy, xvi, 6, 9, 16, 19, 21, 25, 28, 29, 51, 55, 65, 66, 67, 69, 70, 71, 73, 74, 76, 77, 79, 80, 84, 94, 117, 128, 130, 131, 132, 133, 134, 135, 137, 138, 139, 140, 141, 142, 143, 145, 146, 147, 149, 150, 154, 159, 181, 182, 183, 184, 185, 186, 188, 197, 199, 202, 203, 204, 206, 209, 226, 249, 251, 261, 262, 265, 271, 275, 279, 282, 284, 296, 300, 301, 307, 309, 310, 312, 314, 315, 316, 318, 324, 341
Muslims, 17
Mykhailyna, P. V., 247, 380
Myrhorod, 75
Myshko, D. I., 245, 380
Myśliński, Kazimierz, 263, 380
Mytsyk, Iu. A., 362

Nalyvaiko, D. S., 319, 380
Naruszewicz, Adam, 233
Natoński, Bronisław, 264, 302
Navahrudak, 89
Nedryhailiv, 133, 134, 311
Nemirovskii, E. L., 289, 380

Nemyrych family, 44, 45, 258, 259; Iurii (Jerzy Niemirycz), 203, 205, 206, 212, 347, 348
Niemcewicz, Julian Ursyn, 307, 362
Niesiecki, Kasper, 222, 261, 263, 264, 266, 380
Niezabitowski, 329
Nikifor, Ihumen, 102
Nikolaichik, O., 311, 362
Niskina, 263
Normann, David, 275, 380
Noryns'k, 258
Nosivka, 71, 116
Nosivka starostwo, 217, 265
Novhorod-Sivers'kyi, 76, 282, 302; Jesuit school, 119; Starostwo, 267
Novitskii (Novyts'kyi), Ivan, 223, 224, 226, 380
Novosel'skii, A. A., 248, 308, 312, 314, 315, 316, 380
Novosilky (Nowosiołki), 53, 166, 219, 269, 317
Novyi Brusyliv, 54, 217, 220, 270
Novyi Volodymyr, 221
Nowak, Tadeusz Marian, 308, 341, 380
Nowak-Dłużewski, Juliusz, 344, 381
Nowy Targ starostwo, 180, 220, 340
Nyzkynychi, 43, 44, 47, 53, 116, 201, 216, 217, 258, 260, 261, 263; Orthodox monastery and church, 121, 225, 295, 304

Obuchowicz, Teodor, 156, 335
Obuchowska-Pysiowa, Honorata, 242, 381
Ochakiv, 189
Ohloblyn, Oleksander, 319, 381
Ojców starostwo, 97, 278
Okolski, Szymon, 85, 87, 283, 284, 286, 287, 292, 362
Oljančyn (Oljanchyn), Domet, 265, 381
Olszewski, Henryk, 234, 242, 291, 362, 381
Opaliński family, 256
Orans'kyi family, 45, 262; Ivan, 51; Mykhailo, 270; Pakhomii (Pachomiusz Orański-Wojna), 45, 50, 103, 236, 262, 264, 362
Orany, 219
Ordin-Nashchokin, Afanasii Lavrent'evich, 309, 310, 363
Orlovskii, Petr, 273, 381
Orłowski, Ryszard, 263

Orsha, 288; battle of, 260
Orynin, battle of, 51, 266
Ossoliński, Jerzy, 100, 108, 109, 116, 117, 120, 124, 125, 126, 128, 131, 133, 142, 146, 147, 148, 149, 150, 151, 152, 153, 154, 155, 156, 157, 158, 159, 160, 161, 162, 163, 167, 168, 169, 170, 171, 172, 174, 175, 178, 182, 185, 187, 188, 207, 219, 220, 227, 278, 287, 290, 297, 300, 301, 302, 305, 306, 307, 311, 317, 322, 323, 324, 325, 326, 328, 330, 331, 333, 334, 335, 336, 337, 338, 339, 340, 348
Ostrianyn, Iatsko, 88
Ostrogska-Chodkiewicz, Anna, 254
Ostrogska-Zamoyska, Katarzyna, 267
Ostroh Bible, 41
Ostroh, 157, 254, 328; Orthodox scchool, 41, 42, 47, 256, 257
Ostroróg, Mikołaj, 48, 100, 110, 150, 153, 326
Ostrowski, Donald, x
Ostroz'kyi family, 39, 44, 144, 255/256, 257, 299. See also Ostrogska-Chodkiewicz and Ostrogska-Zamoyska; Ostroz'kyi, Konstantyn Konstantynovych, 41, 42, 90, 95, 212, 225, 257
Oświęcim, Stanisław, 220, 236, 306, 319, 340, 344, 363
Ottman, Rudolf, 224, 317, 381
Ottoman empire and Porte, 2, 16, 25, 29, 30, 33, 51, 71, 76, 82, 84, 88, 128, 129, 130, 131, 132, 134, 136, 138, 139, 142, 143, 145, 147, 151, 165, 169, 181, 185, 186, 187, 197, 202, 204, 206, 248, 302, 307, 308, 318, 337
Ovruch, 44, 259
Ozdiutychy, 220

Pac, Kazimierz, 134, 311, 312, 315, 327
Paisius, patriarch, 164
Pałucki, Władysław, 242, 381
Pamphili, Camilo, 304
Panaitescu, P. P., 306
Panzirolo, Giovanni, 305
Pasicznyk, Uliana, x
Pastorius, Joachim, 236, 319, 363
Pastukhiv Islands, 221
Paszkiewicz, Henryk, 245, 381
Pavlishchev, N. I., 226, 381

Pavliuk, 84, 85, 86, 87, 88, 98, 148, 283, 286, 287, 326. *See also* But, Pavlo

Pawłowski, 72, 73, 280, 281

Pawsze, Szymon, 340

Pechenegs, 45, 262

Pelc, Janusz, 264, 388

Pelenski, Jarosław, 246, 254, 255, 381

Pelesz, Julian, 381

Pereiaslav, 72, 80, 82, 84, 86, 281; agreement of, 202; commission of, 164, 165, 166, 167, 332, 333; council of, 285

Perekop, 135, 216

Pernal, Andrew, 347

Petrov, N. I., 381

Petrovs'kyi, Mykola, 229, 319, 365, 382

Petrushevich, A. S., 236, 363

Petyk, Ulana, 250, 369

Piasecki, Paweł, 363

Piaseczyński, Aleksander, 72, 119, 267, 268, 279, 280

Picheta, V., 245, 246, 382

Pidhaitsi, 216, 217

Pietrzak, Jerzy, 266, 382

Pil'huk, I. I., 388

Pimin Euzebii (pseud), 50. *See* Mohyla, Peter

Pinsk, Uniate diocese, 89, 91

Piotrków tribunal, 293, 296

Pirling, P., 382

Plebański, Józef Kazimierz, 382

Pleshcheev, Nikifor Iurevich, 316, 318

Pochaïv monastery, 39

Pochapivs'kyi, Iov, 90, 98, 289, 294

Podhorodecki, Leszek, 228, 246, 266, 320, 382

Podillia and Podillian palantinate, 21, 25, 26, 38, 71, 72, 78, 106, 111, 157, 167, 199, 224, 245, 264

Podlasie, 246

Polatsk, 90, 288; Orthodox archdiocese, 56; Uniate diocese, 89, 91, 289

Polianovka, treaty of, 75, 76, 130, 134, 282, 308, 311, 318

Polishchuk, F. M., 388

Polissia, 20, 92, 119

Polonne, 152

Polovtsians, 135

Polupanshchyna, 44, 216, 261

Ponomarev, S. I., 379

Popel', Ivan, 295

Poppe, Andrzej, 262, 263, 382

Porshnev, B. F., 275, 279, 282, 308, 318, 320, 382

Potichnyj, Peter J., 239, 374, 386

Potii, Ipatii, 41, 42

Potocki family, 109; Mikołaj, 48, 85, 86, 87, 132, 141, 145, 146, 150, 181, 186, 187, 190, 191, 192, 193, 194, 195, 225, 283, 286, 287, 300, 309, 313, 320, 321, 322, 326, 340, 342, 343, 344, 345; Stanisław, 82, 86, 200, 284, 285, 287; Stefan, 145

Powidaj, Ludwik, 222, 223, 383

Prażmowski, J., 340

Pritsak, Omeljan, ix, 249, 262, 321, 383

Pritsak, Nina, ix

Prochaska, Antoni, 383

Proskura family, 60, 95. *See also* Sushchans'kyi

Protestants and the Reformation, 9, 17, 18, 19, 30, 31, 32, 34, 35, 41, 42, 62, 65, 68, 69, 90, 96, 137, 159, 244, 275, 288, 331

Protestant schools, 46–47

Prussia, 8, 14, 49, 52, 65, 104, 265, 269, 322

Prussian expedition, 268, 269

Przemyśl, xv; Orthodox diocese, 20, 42, 89, 90, 91, 92, 93, 97, 100, 101, 102, 104, 108, 289, 294, 295

Przyboś, Adam, 310, 383

Przyłęcki, Stanisław, 338, 351, 363

Przypkowski, Samuel, 348

Ptaśnik, Jan, 242, 253, 383

Pułaski, Kazimierz, 217, 223, 231, 262, 266, 267, 268, 269, 270, 272, 273, 276, 277, 279, 280, 281, 282, 283, 363, 364, 390

Pułaski, Franciszek, 233, 338, 363

Pushkin, Grigorii Gavrilovich, 76, 136, 182, 282, 316, 317

Putyvl', 25, 72, 74, 75, 138, 139, 143, 280, 281, 316, 317, 318

Puzyna family, 42; Atanazii (Oleksander), 98, 99, 118, 122, 289, 294, 304; Iurii, 67, 257

Pyliavtsi, battle of, 158, 160, 188, 329, 330

Radom, taxation tribunal, 78

Radoszycki, Paweł (Paulus Radoszchicki), 48, 264, 364

Radwański, Zbigniew, 234, 364

Radziejowski, Heronim, 190, 191, 198, 342, 343, 344
Radzimiński, Zygmunt L., 259, 364, 383
Radziwiłł family, 41, 232, 256; Janusz, 192, 195, 200, 232, 331, 340, 342, 343, 344, 345, 351, 355; Krzysztof, 62, 65, 67, 68, 73, 90, 166, 258, 277; Albrycht Stanisław, 58, 70, 103, 117, 171, 172, 220, 234, 234/ 235, 236, 257, 273, 275, 276, 277, 278, 283, 287, 291, 292, 293, 294, 296, 298, 300, 325, 326, 331, 333, 336, 339, 340, 346, 347₂ 350, 364
Raszba, Noj, 266, 382
Rákóczi family, 331, 337; György I, 159, 160, 330, 331; György II, 165, 169, 187
Ranum, Orest, 383
Rawita-Gawroński, Franciszek, 2, 219, 224, 227, 228, 233, 259, 261, 309, 313, 320, 321, 324, 326, 328, 332, 340, 364, 383
Reformation. See Protestants and the Reformation
Rembowski, A., 243, 383
Renaissance, 8, 31, 47, 90
Reshetar, John S. Jr., 249, 383
Rhode, Gotthold, 241, 383
Riccardi, V., 124, 304
Richelieu, Arman Jean, 226
Riedlmayer, András, ix
Right Bank (of Dnieper), 23, 85, 152, 186, 223
Rogger, Hans, 383
Rohoza, Mykhailo, 41
Roman Republic, 111
Romanov dynasty, 51, 75
Rome, 18, 19, 27, 31, 41, 56, 57, 62, 104, 107, 108, 118, 119, 123, 124, 126, 135, 149, 201, 203, 235, 271, 272, 278, 290, 297, 301, 304, 306. See also Holy See
Romny, 310
Roos, Hans, 240, 384
Rudawski, Laurentius, 236, 364
Rudnytsky, Ivan L., 239, 245, 385
Rudnyts'kyi, Stefan, 384
Rulikowski, Edward, 346
Rulikowski, Wacław, 219, 259, 356, 383
Runkevich, S. G., 350, 362
Rurik dynasty, 39, 109, 212
Rusavka, commission of, 285

Russia, 27, 28, 51, 225, 324. See also Muscovy
Ruthenian palatinate, 20, 21, 24, 25, 33, 38, 91, 93, 106, 111, 151, 170, 235
Ruts'kyi, Iosyf, 54/55, 56, 57, 58, 59, 61, 62, 63, 67, 89, 96, 103, 270, 271, 272, 273, 274, 278, 287, 288, 290, 292, 296, 301
Rykaczewski, Ed., 364
Ryznia, 221

St. Petersburg, 284
Sakovych (Sakowicz), Kasian, 49, 50, 118, 120, 121, 122, 127, 236, 249, 254, 255, 264, 302, 303, 364
Samsonowicz, Henryk, 244, 384
San River, 68
Sandomierz palatinate, 326
Sangushko (Sanguszko) family, 40; Aleksander, 117, 118, 153, 301, 326
Santa Croce, Antonio, 58, 63, 235, 272, 273
Sapieha family, 116, 357; Kazimierz Leon, 170, 171, 232, 299, 310, 312, 313, 335, 336, 338, 339, 340, 346, 348, 355; Lew (Leon), 277
Saracino, Pietro, 304, 305, 327
Sarmatians, 10, 314
Sataniv, 220
Savych, A., 253, 384
Savych, Semen, 198, 346
Schletter, Zygmunt, 363
Seliava, Antin, 119, 124, 296, 302
Semkowicz, Władysław, 240, 253, 298, 384
Senai, Hadzy Mehmed, 321, 365
Seniuta family, 41
Seniv forest, 218
Sens, Brenda, x
Serczyk, Władysław, 247, 384
Seredyka, Jan, 324, 384
Ševčenko, Ihor, x, 252, 384
Ševčenko, Margaret, x
Sevsk, 25, 75, 81, 202, 317, 318
Shagin Aga, 283
Shamrai, S., 217, 299, 384
Shaw, Peter, ix
Shein, Boris, 75
Sheptyts'kyi, Andrei, 304, 362
Sheremetev, Fedor Ivanovich, 309, 310
Shevchenko, F. P., 229, 251, 318, 320, 322, 341, 384

Shuiskii, Ivan, 137, 138, 138/139, 315, 317
Shields-Kollman, Nancy, ix
Sielski, Aleksander, 156
Sienkiewicz, Henryk, 228, 384
Siveria, 72, 202, 268, 279, 327
Skarga, Piotr, 34, 251
Skupiński, K., 276
Skydan, Pavlo, 85, 86, 89, 287
Slavonic Rite, 27
Slavs, 135
Ślesiński, Stanisław, 344
Sliozka, Mykhailo (Mikhail), 96, 266, 292, 295, 365
Slipyi, Iosyf, 384
Sloboda, 216
Sluch River, 168, 177, 183, 189
Sługocki, Dziersław, 329
Śmiarkowski, Jakób, 167, 169, 333, 335
Smilianka, 217
Smirnov, N. A., 308, 318, 385
Smirnov, V. D., 248, 385
Smolensk, 65, 182, 184, 280, 281, 293, 327; Uniate diocese, 89, 91
Smolensk land, 25, 51, 97, 138, 183, 293
Smolensk palatinate, 78, 97, 98, 283
Smolensk war, 16, 52, 71–77, 78, 96, 130, 131, 230
Smolnytsia, 102
Smotryts'kyi, Meletii, 56, 57, 59, 271, 272, 273, 365
Šmurlo, E., 235, 271, 273, 274, 276, 278, 290, 293, 299, 301, 302, 303, 304, 305, 306, 327, 350, 365
Sobieski family, 256; Jakub, 48, 356
Socinians. See Anti-trinitarians
Sokolov, I. I., 251, 385
Solomorits'ka, Regina, 116, 218, 220, 291
Solov'ev, S. M., 140, 282, 312, 313, 314, 315, 385
Solovii, M., 271
Soltan, Mykola, 217, 282
Soltyk, Bazilii, 98, 293
Soltyk, Pavel Ivanovich, 315
Sornell, Jerzy, 327
Sosnyts'kyi, Ivan, 176, 338
Sovianka, Maryna, 259
Soviet Union, xv, 4, 227, 239
Spain, 46
Stadnyk, M., 385
Stanisław, August, 354

Stashevskii, E., 279, 385
Stasiewska, Zofia, 247, 366
Stecki, Tadeusz Jerzy, 225, 385
Stempkowski, Daniel, 218
Stempkowski, Gabriel, 133, 134, 311
Stökl, Günter, 246, 249, 385
Struminsky, Bodan, ix
Strypa River, 172
Stsepuro, D., 288, 385
Subotiv, 144
Sucheni-Grabowska, Anna, 241, 385
Sukhodol'ska (Petro Kalushovs'kyi's wife), 218
Sukhodol'ski, Andrii, 218
Sukhodoly, 219
Sula River, 133, 134, 311
Sulyma, Ivan, 79, 83
Sushchans'kyi-Proskura, Fedir, 57. See also Proskura family
Svenald, 262, 263
Sviatold(ych), Sventold(ych), 45, 96, 210, 226, 263, 269, 292
"Sviatopolk," 269
Sviatoslav, 262
Svishchivs'kyi family, 45; Anna, 260
Švitrigaila, 38, 255, 258
Svoichiv, 218
Sweden, 6, 64, 65, 71, 79, 138, 162, 170, 181, 182, 183, 184, 202, 203, 248, 268, 274, 283, 316, 331, 341
Swedish War, 1626–1629, 52
Świtalski, Zbigniew, 308, 390
Sydorenko, Alexander, 252, 385
Symmons-Symonolewicz, Konstantin, 249, 385
Sysyn, Frank E., 232, 245, 254, 296, 297, 298, 320, 365, 385
Szajnocha, Karol, 226, 233, 287, 320, 322, 323, 324, 325, 328, 330, 365, 386
Szaraniewicz, Izydor, 251, 386
Szegda, Mirosław, 252, 270, 271, 273, 386
Szelągowski, Adam, 274, 275, 386
Szilágyi, Sándor, 365
Szornel, Georges, 353
Szymonowicz, Szymon, 50

Tanczuk, D., 271, 386
Tatars, 16, 22, 23, 25, 51, 81, 111, 117, 120, 128, 129, 130, 131, 132, 133, 134, 135, 136, 138, 139, 141, 142, 146, 148, 150,

154, 156, 158, 165, 168, 169, 172, 181, 183, 186, 187, 188, 189, 192, 193, 195, 196, 197, 203, 209, 248, 285, 297, 307, 308, 312, 313, 314, 315, 316, 318, 321, 323, 328, 329. *See also* Crimean Khanate

Tatar incursions, 38; raids, 51, 74, 78, 79, 111, 308

Tarnawsky, Maxim, x

Tazbir, Janusz, 240, 241, 243, 244, 248, 249, 251, 296, 347, 382, 386

Temberski, Stanisław, 236, 319, 329, 365

Teodor, monk, 59, 60

Teodorczyk, Jerzy, 269, 386

Terentyiv, 218

Teutonic Knights, 6

Terlets'kyi, Kyrylo, 41

Terlets'kyi, Metodii, 93, 99, 118, 119, 124, 289, 291, 302, 304

Theiner, Augustinus, 287, 290, 300, 301, 302, 365

Thirty Years' War, 16, 18, 130

Time of Troubles, 16, 75, 131, 137, 265

Thucydides, 48

Titov, Khvedir (T. F.), 236, 252, 253, 264, 365, 387

Tiepalo, Giovanni, 307, 309

Tkachenko, Mykola, 247, 299, 387

Tomashivs'kyi, Stepan, 323, 387

Tomkiewicz, Władysław, 228, 246, 255, 256, 267, 282, 285/286, 287, 288, 289, 297, 298, 299, 300, 302, 309, 310, 311, 320, 323, 324, 326, 327, 328, 330, 335, 387

Tomylenko, hetman, 84

Torres, Juan de (Giovanni), 124, 126, 127, 185, 190, 197, 302, 304, 305, 306, 323, 327, 335, 338, 343, 346

Tovmach starostwo, 220

Transylvania, 159, 164, 165, 181, 182, 184, 187, 203, 330

Treadgold, Donald W., 240, 249, 372, 383, 387

Trekhtymiriv, 86, 198

Trent, Council of, 18, 19

Tretiak, Józef, 248, 251, 252, 254, 387

Trofimovych-Kozlovs'kyi, Isai, 49, 264

Trubchevsk, 128, 131, 133, 134, 296, 310

Trubetskoi, Aleksei Nikitich, 136, 316, 317

Tryzna family, 45; Iosyf, 125, 292, 305; Mykola, 90; Maria, 260

Tselevych, Oleh, 279, 387

Tsetsova, battle of, 16, 51, 143, 266

Tuchap, 269

Tumin, 218

Turiia, 217

Turgenev, A. I., 301, 358

Turkey, 25, 51, 78, 79, 117, 120, 123, 141, 154, 189, 197, 254, 297, 302. *See also* Ottoman empire

Turkish War of 1621, 16

Turowski, Kazimierz Józef, 266, 284, 362, 387

Twardowski, Samuel, 228, 236, 365

Tysarivs'kyi, Iarema, 59, 91

Tyshkovychi, 44, 45, 216, 261

Tyszkiewicz, Janusz, 119, 151, 153, 167, 168, 324, 329, 334

Tyszkowski, Kazimierz, 387

Udai River, 133, 134, 311

Ulewicz, Tadeusz, 239, 241, 314, 387

Uman', 152

Umanets', Pylyp, 202

Urban, Wacław, 323

Urban VIII, pope, 94, 118, 122, 278, 290, 301, 303

Urbanowicz, Eugenjusz, 225, 295, 388

Vadkiv, 221

Vainshtein, O. L., 279, 388

Vasa dynasty, 16, 64, 129, 161, 307, 354

Vasylenko, Mykola, 246, 270, 388

Velychenko, Stephan, 390

Velykyi, A. H. (Welykyj, A. G.), 270, 271, 276, 278, 289, 290, 301, 302, 303, 304, 349, 358, 359, 361, 388

Venice, 128, 130, 132, 134, 142, 143, 181, 197, 206, 307, 345

Vepryn, 219

Vernadsky, George, 321, 388

Veryna, 218

Viazma, 265

Vidoni, Pietro, 201, 347

Vienna, 185, 335

Vierhaus, Rudolf, 240

Viktorovskii, P. G., 256, 388

Vil'ky, 220

Vilnius, city and palatinate, 28, 30, 39, 47, 89, 90, 91, 99, 100, 126, 127, 210, 277, 306; Orthodox brotherhood, 30, 41, 60,

66, 67, 91, 96, 276, 281, 288; Uniate brotherhood and seminary, 67, 91, 276, 288
Vil'shanka, 134
Vimina, Alberto, 185, 236, 341, 365
Vinnytsia, 152, 191; Orthodox school, 97, 292
Visconti, Honoratio, 94, 290
Vistula, 15, 24, 242
Vitsebsk, 55, 90, 210, 259, 260
Vladimirskii-Budanov, M. F., 247, 388
Vlasovs'kyi, Ivan, 289, 388
Voiskovychi, 219
Volhynia and Volhynian palatinate, xvi, 8, 21, 22, 24, 35, 38, 39, 40, 41, 42, 44, 52, 57, 66, 67, 71, 75, 90, 91, 95, 99, 106, 110, 111, 114, 116, 119, 151, 152, 153, 156, 157, 167, 170, 171, 172, 173, 176, 177, 189, 192, 200, 215, 216, 217, 218, 219, 220, 223, 224, 231, 235, 245, 255, 256, 257, 258, 260, 268, 269, 272, 276, 283, 288, 289, 291, 295, 296, 297, 298, 300, 309, 326, 328, 329, 346
Volhynian principality, 21, 38
Vol'ka, 218
Volodimer the Great (Saint), 45, 96, 121, 135, 179, 262
Volodymyr-Volyns'kyi, 58, 138, 154, 169; Orthodox church of St. Illiia, 47; county, 43, 44, 53, 216, 217, 218, 261, 262, 268, 269, 277; Orthodox diocese, 39, 44; Uniate diocese, 63, 89, 91, 92; Uniate school, 63; starostvo, 218, 256
Volodymyrivka, 220
Volyns'kyi, P. K., 388
Voronych family, 258
Vozniak, Mykhailo, 263, 388
Vyhovs'kyi, Ivan, 176, 203, 205, 212, 338, 345
Vynnyts'kyi, Fedir, 102, 295
Vyrva, 221
Vyshens'kyi, Ivan, 252
Vyshnevets'kyi family, 40, 55, 95. *See also* Wiśniowiecki
Vysochans'kyi, Marko, 102, 295
Vytkiv, 54, 217, 267

Wallachia, 165, 182
Walmirski, Sebastian, 329

Warsaw, xv, 11, 14, 56, 68, 115, 116, 137, 138, 149, 152, 153, 156, 159, 160, 162, 284, 325, 329, 336, 345, 346; confederation of, 17, 65, 244; government, 2, 118, 129, 130, 141, 147, 164, 175, 181, 182, 184, 185, 186, 187, 188, 190, 203, 211, 301, 328
Weinryb, Bernard D., 244, 320, 388
Wassenberg, Everhard, 366
Weiher, Ludwik, 327
Weintraub, Wiktor, ix
Welykyj, Athanasius G. *See* Velykyj, A. H.
West Prussia, 232, 234
Wetryha, Stefan, 216
White Mountain, battle of, 33
Wiczki, 332
Wilbur, Earle Morse, 244
Wimmer, Jan, 243, 248, 257, 265, 298, 388
Winter, Eduard, 232, 388
Wisner, Henryk, 240, 389
Wiśniowiecki, Dymitr, 199, 219
Wiśniowiecki, Jeremi, xv, 74, 75, 76, 77, 109, 110, 116, 117, 131, 133, 134, 137, 142, 151, 152, 153, 155, 156, 157, 158, 160, 161, 162, 167, 168, 170, 171, 172, 192, 193, 207, 208, 225, 228, 254, 255, 298, 300, 302, 309, 310, 311, 317, 320, 324, 326, 327, 328, 329, 334
Wiśniowiecki, Konstanty, 220
Witowski, Łukasz, 76, 219
Witusik, Adam Andrzej, 263, 264, 330, 331, 389
Wizeły, Szczęsny, 76
Władysław-Jogaila, 38, 258
Władysław IV, xv, 2, 13, 16, 51, 52, 54, 64, 66, 67, 68, 69, 70, 72, 74, 75, 76, 79, 88, 94, 95, 96, 97, 99, 108, 112, 113, 115, 116, 117, 118, 120, 125, 126, 127, 128, 130, 131, 132, 134, 138, 141, 142, 143, 146, 149, 151, 154, 159, 162, 163, 174, 197, 213, 217, 218, 219, 234, 243, 252, 263, 265, 266, 267, 268, 270, 275, 277, 280, 281, 282, 283, 285, 288, 289, 290, 291, 292, 293, 299, 300, 301, 307, 308, 309, 310, 312, 313, 314, 316, 317, 325, 352, 353, 354, 355
Wójcik, Zbigniew, ix, 225, 228, 243, 246, 247, 248, 307, 308, 318, 366, 382, 389
Wojakowski, Jan, 325, 326

Wojcicki, K. Wł., 270, 306, 360, 363
Wojtyła, A., 301, 389
Wolff, Józef, 259, 366
Worcław, 234; diocese, 159
Wyczański, Andrzej, 239, 240, 248, 296, 382, 389
Wysłouch, Bolesław, 356
Wysłouch, Maria, 356

Zaborovskii, L. V., 308, 389
Zabus'kyi, Semen, 172
Zacharias ab Haarlem, 277, 389
Zadorski, Stanisław, 330
Zahorovs'kyi, Vasyl', 47, 49, 261, 262
Zaikin, V., 251, 389
Zajączkowski, Andrzej, 241, 389
Zalewski, Roman, 383
Zamość, 152, 159; Academy, 47, 48, 49, 50, 53, 230, 262, 264
Zamostychky, 219
Zamoyski family, 144; Jan, 47, 48, 50, 263; Tomasz, 49, 50, 52, 54, 76, 264, 267, 268, 269, 279, 356
Zamoyska, Katarzyna, 268. See also Ostrogska-Zamoyska, Katarzyna
Zaporizhzhia, 79, 85, 143, 145, 146, 181
Zaporozhian army, host, 23, 51, 52, 60, 61, 65, 66, 72, 73, 81, 84, 89, 100, 103, 141–213. See also Cossacks
Zaremba, Andrzej, 190
Zarzycki, Wacław, 248, 389
Zasławski (Zaslavs'kyi) family, 40, 144, 257; Aleksander, 273; Dominik, 116, 150, 153, 299, 326, 327; Jerzy, 51, 266, 268

Zbarazh, siege of, 157, 172, 175, 336, 338
Zbaraz'kyi (Zbarazki) family, 39, 40, 256, 269
Zboriv, agreement and articles, 164, 173–183, 187–189, 203, 205, 207, 208, 337–340, 343; battle, 172, 336
Zebrzydowski, Mikołaj, 13, 243
Zebrzydowski revolt, 1606–1609, 13
Żegota, Pauli, 361
Żelewski, Roman, 310
Zhovti Vody, battle of, 145, 322
Zhukovich, P., 251, 267, 270, 271, 272, 273, 274, 366, 390
Zhukovs'kyi, Arkadii, 252, 299, 304, 390
Zhydychyn, monastery of, 39, 57
Zhytomyr, 177, 181, 268, 340, 343
Ziatkivtsi, 177
Zielinska, Teresa, 241, 390
Zientara, Benedykt, 240, 373
Ziomek, Jerzy, 250, 390
Zmijowskie family, 221
Żółkiewski, Jan, 48
Żółkiewski, Łukasz, 75, 76/77, 79, 80, 82, 83, 84
Żółkiewski, Stanisław, 51, 143, 283, 284, 285
Zolochiv, 336
Zorenychi, 53, 216, 270
Żurkowski, Stanisław, 264, 390
Zygmunt, August, 5
Zygmunt I, 260
Zygmunt II, xv, 13, 14, 18–19, 33, 42, 51, 52, 54, 56, 58, 59, 62, 63, 64, 65, 66, 67, 120, 124, 216, 217, 242, 243, 265, 266, 268, 269, 272, 275, 290, 353, 355